Testimonials for *A Son's Promise*

The story that lies herein, is the epitome of what can be achieved if you permit God to lead your life. As you will see, Dr. Flumo's unwavering faith led him through times others would say are best forgotten.

> —Carl H. Cannon
> Lieutenant Colonel, United States Army Retired

Perseverance is the story of Marsilius Flumo whose life journey took him from Liberia to my hometown Spokane, Washington. Readers will be captivated by Marsilius' vivid descriptions of his idyllic childhood in a remote village, the challenges and privations he experienced as a student in Sanniquellie, Monrovia and Korea, and his struggles to establish himself and his family in the US after being forced to flee Liberia in 1990. Some of the key themes in the book are the value placed on education, the importance of family and community support and sacrifice, and above all the power of a mother's love. No matter who you are, whether a scholar of Liberia, a friend or family member of Marsilius, a fellow Liberian, or someone who has never been to Africa, this book will open your eyes and your heart.

> —John C. Yoder
> Emeritus Professor of African history and politics
> Whitworth University

A SON'S PROMISE

A Memoir of Perseverance
from Liberia to America

J. Marsilius Flumo

In honor of my Mom, Yah Flumo

Acknowledgements

All glory to Wlah who "tempest tossed" me out of the hellfire of the Liberian Civil War and planted my feet upon the shores of America. Without His guidance, love, and protection, this book would not have come to fruition.

To my Dad in heaven, thank you for telling me to take care of my Mom. To my sisters, Sennie Dingamonlay (in heaven) and Esther, thank you for sacrificing to support me while at St. Mary's School in Sanniquellie, Liberia. My children, Lila, Wonkermie, Oretha, Marsetta, Blodah, and Jo-Weh, encouraged me in their own ways to complete this project and I am grateful for their support and proud of them as ever.

To LTC Carl H Cannon, USA (Ret), one of my biggest cheerleaders, who read the manuscript inside-out and provided valuable feedbacks, I am eternally grateful. I am also thankful for the love and support of my John R Rogers High School family in Spokane, Washington, especially the Science Department. I would also like to thank my friend and colleague, Michael Dewey of Spokane, Washington, also a member of the John R Rogers High School family. He read the manuscript and provided valuable feedbacks. Moreover, we had several fulfilling conversations about my experience over beer and delicious Liberian dishes. Although the manuscript was a fodder for our conversations, only disrupted by the covid-19 pandemic, he thought that the time had come to let it go.

To my many students who, even after they graduated, kept asking me when the book will be finished so that they can get a signed copy, I am grateful. To my friends, Patricia Ford of Washington, D.C., Yah Zowa Boyah of Philadelphia, Pennsylvania, and John Guewell of Stockton, California, thank you from the bottom of my heart for taking interest in my work, reading the manuscript, and giving me invaluable feedbacks.

Anna Goodwin, a board member and treasurer of Bitterroot Mountain Publishing, is the incredible mentor who opened the door and guided me into the publishing world. Thank you, Glen Scott, for introducing Anna to me.

CONTENTS

Introduction

THIS BOOK IS NOT MERELY about what happened in my life, but what led me to tell my story. It is not only about the obstacles I encountered or how I overcame them, but also about how the God of Abraham and Jacob, whom my people call "Wlah," guided me through it all.[1] This is not a religious book, yet Wlah looms prominently. I am grateful to Him for bringing me into this world through Yah Flumo's womb, the woman who nurtured and shaped me.[2] I owe Wlah for giving me the gift of being Yah Flumo's son and everything good I have become.

This book is a tribute to my mom, Yah Flumo, an exemplary mom, a woman of tremendous strength, perseverance, and an undying faith in Wlah. Through her prayers in search of me before I was conceived, she wove our stories intricately into an inseparable tapestry. She wanted the story told but she could not read or write. Therefore, her main reason for sending me to school was to fulfill her long-held dream, which I knew of since childhood. She wanted me to tell the story. Finishing this book is a fulfillment of that dream.

This book is an opportunity to honor my dad, Blodah Yarkpa Flumo, too. He was an early evidence of Wlah's handiwork in my family. His mom and dad died before he took his first steps. His three elder brothers, Saye Guanue, Miatee Garteh and Mahnwon Mantor, reared him. Dad's dream for sending me to school was to finish eighth grade and return to Yehyeelakpoa.[3] He wanted me to read and interpret his government-issued tax receipts.

1

Even though I did not stop in eighth grade, I read and interpreted Dad's government-issued tax receipts on many occasions while I was at St. Mary's School in Sanniquellie, Liberia. Dad's dream, like those of other indigenous Liberian parents, was bigger than reading and interpreting his tax receipts to ensure that no one cheated him. He wanted dignity and a better life for himself and his family. Dad did not realize all his dreams because he did not see me for the last ten years of his life; he did not enjoy the material benefits of his dreams. Due to the Liberian Civil War, Dad missed out on almost my entire adult life, which I have been living in the United States.

In addition, this book is a tribute to exemplary individuals whom I met along this incredible journey. I crossed paths with good and caring people from the village to Sanniquellie, from Monrovia to Seoul, Korea and from New York City to Greensboro, North Carolina, as well as during my return to Liberia in May 1987. In June 1990, while escaping the Liberian Civil War to the United States, the story of meeting ordinary people with extraordinary hearts was no different. Each step I took into the unknown in New York City, Washington, D.C., and Greensboro, North Carolina, a path appeared. Each door I knocked at in Fayetteville, Wadesboro and Laurinburg, North Carolina, opened. Each ear I sought in Spokane, Washington, listened.

In retrospect, I am convinced that meeting all the incredibly wonderful people was no accident. I believe Wlah placed them along my journey for a purpose. He took me out of the village and, through the love, kind deeds and guidance of the wonderful people I met along the journey, made somebody out of a wretched person like me. Indeed, through caring, good advice, prayers, and kindly spoken words, the good people I met along my journey have had a hand in shaping the man that I have become. It is now my turn to lift them up to show my appreciation.

In a measure, this book is an account of the time and struggles it takes to become a man, especially an African man. It is a story about a sense of responsibility; a story about trials and their character-fashioning and creativity-releasing effects; a story about the life-giving and life-sustaining effects of a mother's prayers. In a larger context, it is an appreciation of my Mahn culture, its emphasis on self-discipline, patience and individual as well as collective responsibility.

CHAPTER 1

My Parents

A S I GREW UP FROM a child to an adolescent and then to a young adult, I thought I had my own mind entirely. I thought I had total freedom to create my own path and to do and be whatever I wanted; I thought I had the freedom to live my life. However, the older I became, especially during my formal education, I soon realized that freedom for me would be something other than what I originally had in mind. The freedom I discovered was not about choosing any random path to do and be whatever I wanted. Freedom for me was choosing my own path to explore, discover and act upon a charge Mom and Dad gave me during childhood. I had been superficially aware of the charge since childhood. However, it was not until I became older and a little wiser that I perceived that charge was directing and assigning purpose and meaning to my life. In plain language, in a large measure, the course for my life had already been set. My parents' experiences—their sufferings—had been written into my DNA, into my consciousness and imprinted upon my heart. As a result, my life had to be a measure of relief for them.

BLODAH YARKPA FLUMO

Dad, BlodahYarkpa Flumo, was the last of four children. His parents named him after his maternal grandfather, Blodah Yarkpa, a warrior. Besides him, each of his siblings, Saye Guanue, Miatee Garteh, and Mantor Mahnwon, had a name with a meaning associated with circumstances of their birth.[4] I do not know Dad's exact date of birth, but based on historical evidence

3

and my own observations, I believe he was born either a few years before or after 1910.

L–R, Esther, Mom, & Dad, with nephew, Anderson Glay, kneeling

At the time of Dad's birth, the Mahn people were isolated in rural Liberia. Formal schools for their children were nonexistent, with interests in them limited to their exploitation. Zoes (experienced midwives) who performed deliveries were illiterate, and as celebrating birthdays was not a tradition, there were no incentives for finding efficient ways of recording births. The advent of modern medicine, however, saw recorded births with deliveries at hospitals or health centers, although records of birth, to this day, are still not systematic in Liberia. Rural people in the culture still rely on counting old farms, beginning with the farm at the time of a child's birth to the present farm. This simple method of telling a child's age depended on shifting cultivation because one farming cycle in Liberia is equal to one calendar year.[5] This method only worked for children up to six or seven years of age because, as fallow periods shortened due to population pressures, identifying old farms became difficult.

Dad was a miracle child because the odds were stacked against him after he was born. His Mom and Dad died before he took his first steps. He did not have the luxury of parental care and all that children learn from their parents in preparation for adulthood. His brothers, and later relatives, reared and taught him everything he learned as a child. Even

4

though Dad was not withdrawn, as a child, I perceived him as a loner. He interacted with many people, but he did not have or refer to anyone as his friend. The only friends he had were his three brothers, although he did not refer to them as such. I only understood his demeanor after Mom told me the story of his early life.

Dad stood at about 5'7", with dark complexion, thick black eyebrows, and dark wavy hair. His little toe to big toe arrangement, a trait he shared with his siblings, was like a five-tread stair from the floor to the landing. There were no photographs of my grandparents. So, I was never able to tell from which grandparent Dad and his brothers inherited their characteristic pointed nose. He was a workaholic, an early sleeper, and an early riser. By 7:30 p.m., he had fallen asleep and usually woke up around 5:00 a.m. to prepare to go to the farm, especially during the milking stage of upland rice when birds were a problem. Dad was skilled at every aspect of upland rice farming. After rice harvest, he also scaled tall palm trees to harvest palm nuts for palm oil. His workday usually started on the rice farm but sometimes ended on the coffee farm. His time off work involved traversing the perimeter of the fence around the farm to ensure ground hogs had not breached it. To him, work was therapy.

Afraid that someone might wrongly accuse or misrepresent him, Dad was very cautious, especially wary of watching over or feeding other people's children maybe because of his Dad's ordeal. Perhaps because of the pain, Dad never shared that story with me. The story his siblings shared with Mom is the account I tell, and it came up only after I asked Mom why Uncle Miatee Garteh wanted to know whether I learned about "Nandin Bo" in school.[6]

Granddad's Ordeal

Quizees, according to Mom, took a male conscript from Duo Tiayee, my Dad's actual birthplace, to Monrovia, Liberia's capital.[7] He was one of many rural indigenous people the Liberia Frontier Force (LFF) recruited under duress with the involvement of top government officials and sold to white planters.[8] The recruits were taken to the Fernando Po Islands to work on plantations. The Duo Tiayee male recruit did not go on to the Fernando Po Islands because he died in Monrovia due to unknown causes. Upon news of the death reaching Duo Tiayee, Seh Gbehyee allegedly said, "I am bayeekpa, (cassava stem cutting), and my roots extend to faraway places."

In Liberia, even up to this day, there had to be a reason, especially a sinister one, for any death. If one could not be determined, the default reason was witchcraft. Based on what Seh Gbehyee allegedly said, relatives of the deceased accused him of involvement in witchcraft; they accused him of killing their kin. With his good name scandalized, Seh Gbehyee had two options: accept guilt based solely on what he allegedly said or drink a poison to prove that he had nothing to do with the death of the recruit.[9] He was innocent if he took the poison and vomited it, and guilty if he did not vomit it. Determined to clear his good name, Granddad drank the poison, but he did not vomit it. Thereafter, those who administered the poison concluded that he was guilty of murdering their kin. In exacting their measure of justice, they inserted a long half-inch diameter "Fehyee" stem into his rear end and pulled it out along with his intestines.[10] Granddad died shortly thereafter. Following that, Darwehyee, my grandmother, died, seemingly out of a brokenheart, leaving Dad and his brothers as orphans.

Dad's Experience with *Quizees*

Dad served as a *porter* [italics are mine]. A porter is defined as "One who carries luggage for hire; an employee who sweeps, or cleans in a bank or store."[11] In Liberia, porter, pronounced by the Mahn people as *"Plotor,"* has a meaning that goes beyond Webster's New World Dictionary and Thesaurus' sanitized definition. Porter means forced labor. Dad was a porter before I was born and even after. *"Quizees"* forced him to carry them in hammocks or to carry their messengers' luggage on his head on numerous occasions. Through the *porter* system, *"Quizees"* imposed their will on native Liberians. In an original Liberian context, a *"Quizee"* more likely than not was an Americo-Liberian.[12] A *quizee* possessed power and, either directly or through an emissary such as an armed soldier invariably of native background, imposed his will on indigenous Liberians. The original meaning of *"Quizee"* is no more in full effect today as it once was during the heydays of Americo-Liberian domination and oppression. Nowadays the expression refers to any educated or civilized person.

"Quizees" neither spoke kindly to Dad nor treated him with respect. He was never paid. I witnessed Dad's humiliating experience on more than one occasion when I was an adolescent. Dad and his elder brothers narrated stories of *quizees'* humiliating treatment of them because they

were illiterate. *Quizees* forcibly recruited Mahns and others as porters for the manual construction of the Ganta-Sanniquellie Highway, the artificial Lake Teeleh and the airfield, the latter two in Sanniquellie, Liberia. They told stories of unmerciful beatings and numerous deaths, as a result.

Dad and his brothers told me that, besides the use of illiterate natives as porters, "*Quizees*" also imposed their will on the Mahns and other native Liberians through taxation. Dad often talked about "*Neehinsuhn*" (taxes) when I was a child. He also talked about how "*Quizees*," government tax collectors assisted by a "*Buusoya*" (armed soldier), acting as an emissary for Americo-Liberians or Congo people, tortured villagers to pay their hut taxes. He told stories about "*Yehmgbehkutu*," a device used to torture people.[13] *Yehmgbehkutu* consisted of two sturdy pieces of stick roughly an inch in diameter and a foot and a half long. If an individual did not have money to pay his taxes, government tax collectors and their "*Buusoyas*" used "*Yehmgbehkutu*" to torture him in the public. They placed a victim's leg between the two sticks at right angles and tied both ends tightly. The upper stick pressed against the tibia while the lower stick pressed against the flesh covering the fibula.[14] The tighter the sticks were tied, the more painful the experience was while the upper stick made a groove into the thin flesh covering the tibia.

Yehmgbehkutu always had the desired effect: to make someone other than the victim to find the money to pay the taxes. Tax collectors were often aware that victims did not have the money to pay, yet they carried out the public spectacle anyway. They used unbearable pain to humiliate delinquent taxpayers and to subject their relatives to emotional pain to force them to pay. Hut tax was supposed to be a one-time payment per year, but Dad paid it more than once a year. Unable to read or write, Dad could not tell whether government-issued flag receipts accurately reflected the amounts he paid in taxes and fees.

DAD'S INFLUENCE IN MY LIFE

Dad's presence was his most important contribution in helping shape my early development. He was not as close to me as Mom was. He did not cuddle me as frequently as Mom did, but his presence was unmistakable. He did not have to be three feet away from me to sense his presence. He was present even when he was away temporarily. Whether Dad was physically near, on the farm, or somewhere else, he loomed like a gigantic frame I had to grow up and fit into. I loved him intensely. His love, which he communicated in a variety of ways, including words and deeds, was constant and important in my early development. I felt Dad's love through the music of his cadence in recognizing me or calling out my name. After giving him a tight hug around the waist upon his return to the village from the farm or somewhere else, he showed his love by holding my hand and walking the remaining yards to the house. In gatherings, he often let me lean on him while he was sitting. At other times, he held me between his legs while my left and right arms rested on his left and right thighs, respectively.

I ate either together with Dad or with him and other men by Mahn tradition. Even though food was plentiful in our household, Dad always left more food for me in the bowl whenever we were the only ones eating together. Inasmuch as I hated combing my hair, Dad gave me regular haircuts. A thorough bath with soap, a rough scrubber made of plant fibers and Dad's calloused hands from years of farm work awaited me every evening. Like the pain of having a comb go through my dry hair, I hated the pain of soap in the eyes as well as the feel of Dad's rough hands on my back, but they were unavoidable because my habitual play activities often turned my skin into a badly done graffiti.

Today, my fond memories of Dad include his promises of a young pet squirrel, the "thorough" baths with his calloused hands and the runs around I gave him to avoid taking a bath. I learned every aspect of upland rice farming by working alongside Dad. He taught me how to set different kinds of traps, hunting at night with a headlight or during the day with dogs, using a single barrel shotgun. He did not teach me how to scale tall palm trees because he was afraid I might fall, but I learned the skill on my own. No one would have known what kind of dad he was or what kind of human being I would turn out to be if he had not sent me to St. Mary's School. He gave me only three pieces of advice, "Do not join others to plot against another person," "Take care of your mom" and "Get married."

YAH FLUMO

Mom, according to "*Quizee*", was Mrs. Yourh Kporweh Flumo, but she preferred Yah Flumo. She stood at 5'6" and weighed about 145 pounds, especially in her old age. She was born in Gordin, located in a large area of the Guinean Forest Region the Mahns occupy.[15] The area was formerly a part of Liberia, but French colonial powers arbitrarily imposed the existing boundary, dividing the Mahn people.[16] Similar divisions occurred among the Kpelle, Kissi, and Lorma peoples along the Liberian border with Guinea. With the involvement of the French in the Ivory Coast and the British in Sierra Leone, colonial boundaries between Liberia and those countries resulted in similar divisions.[17]

Mom

"SOMETHING GOOD"

Mom was "something good" that came out of a bad situation, lending credence to the cliché, "Out of every bad situation, something good happens." The bad situation resulted from a confluence of two circumstances in my family and one in Liberian history. While my dad was a baby, still crawling, my paternal grandfather, Seh Gbehyee, was murdered in Duo Tiayee, his hometown. Taken alone, the evil as well as tragedy of that incident was unspeakable. As if to add insult to injury, shortly thereafter, my paternal grandmother, Darwehyee, died. In no time, Dad and his elder brothers were orphans. Dad's elder brothers assumed parenting roles; they had to nurse him. He was not old enough to remember the passing of his parents, not to mention understanding the challenges his brothers faced.

The straw that broke the camel's back was *"Ka kporyee neehinsuhn,"* the hut tax President Arthur Barclay institutionalized in 1910.[18] Unable to pay the hut tax, Dad's brothers fled Duo Tiayee to Sehyeekainpa to be with Tokpah Tee, their maternal aunt, who was known as Nya Quoi Tokpahlay. District Commissioners and *buusoyas'* (armed soldiers') brutality during the hut tax collection was the major reason for their fleeing to Sehyeekainpa.[19] Tokpah Tee cared for Saye Guanue, Miatee Garteh, Mahnwon Mantor and Blodah Yarkpa Flumo for some time and then fled across the St. John River with them for the same reason. They settled in Gosopa, a hamlet on the other side of the St. John River, founded by their maternal uncle, Quoi Gahn, who had fled his ancestral home of Sehyeekainpa, near Sanniquellie, Liberia.

Quoi Gahn would come to play a fateful role in Mom and Dad's rendezvous. The story was a *"Pianyeewon"* ("Once upon a time" as in a fairy tale) not for its suddenness but because it happened as though a higher hand plotted it. The circumstances of their relationship from the outset turned Mom into "something good" that came out of Dad's tragic childhood and the brutality of early twentieth century Liberia. Quoi Gahn, had many wives, perhaps more than normal in a polygamous culture, but he was no outlier. Due to chiefs' status and relative wealth, they often had more wives than ordinary people. Soodah, the eldest, was his head wife. Upon Tokpah Tee's arrival in Gosopa with the boys, Soodah, by virtue of age, assumed a major parental role and the boys saw her as their mother.

In the meantime, a journey for an undetermined purpose surfaced and added another twist to Dad's and his brothers' fate. Along a more than fifty-mile footpath in the jungle, Nyan Mahnmie, Mom's uncle, traveled from Gordin to Gosopa. While there, through happenstance, he met Quoi Gahn and Soodah and stayed with them. In Gosopa, Nyan Mahnmie started an open secret romantic relationship with Soodah. Chiefs not only tolerated this kind of relationship, but also accorded their head or elder wives the respect they deserved according to the culture because they had numerous wives and often paid little or no attention to their elder wives. Eventually, Nyan Mahnmie returned along with Soodah to Gordin, where they settled in a farming village some distance from town. On the other hand, Quoi Gahn, his younger wives, niece, Tokpah Tee, as well as the boys and other *looseekehmia* (refugees) left Gosopa.[20] Tokpah Tee, Dad, Saye Guanue, and Mahnwon Mantor settled in Karnsonon, also known as Kankore. Quoi Gahn established Blehyeesonon, another hamlet, near Karnsonon. Garteh, Dad's elder brother and second in order of age, never settled in one place. He was a trader; he bought goods in faraway places and sold them upon return.[21]

Upon Garteh's return to Gosopa from a trip, he learned that Nyan Mahnmie and Soodah had left for Gordin. He then traveled to Gordin, where he also learned that Nyan Mahnmie and Soodah lived in a farming village some distance away. Upon arrival, Soodah not only greeted him warmly but also asked for his brothers. Moreover, she expressed her pleasant surprise that the boys remembered her. Garteh told Soodah that his brothers had moved to Karnsonon.

Meanwhile, upon hearing about the boys' tragic story from Soodah, Nohn Sennie, Mom's older sister, encouraged Garteh to ask his brothers to move to the farming village to live with Soodah and Nyan Mahnmie. Garteh told Soodah that, on his return from Lorlah for goods, he would tell his brothers to come along to visit with her. His return visit along with his brothers to see Soodah was when Mom saw Dad for the first time. Mom described herself as a thirteen-year-old at the time. As Nohn Sennie had asked, the boys, except Garteh, stayed with Soodah and built their own huts. Mom and Dad married when they reached adulthood. Their first two children did not survive.

COMMITTED

The man Mom met and eventually married had not had a normal life since birth. He had not learned with regularity all that children usually learn in preparation for adulthood. He and his brothers always lived in the same village, town, or community, except when they returned to Yehyeelakpoa. In 1965, they settled on the ancestral land of their paternal uncles rather than returning to Duo Tiayee, where their dad was murdered. Mahnwon Mantor was the only one who left his brothers and settled in Duo Tiayee against their advice. Hence,

Mom entered the marriage, relying on all the social assets she acquired from her Mom and Dad as well as extended family. She became both the caretaker and the pillar. The "something good" that came out of Dad's tragic childhood circumstances was Mom. She was compassionate, loving, independent and a pillar. I came out of her womb and benefited from the "something good" that she was. It is because of her that I call myself a human being.

Sometime after Mom and Dad lost their first two children, Dad and his eldest brother, Saye Guanue, became ill with Hansen's disease (leprosy). The only nearby place a cure for the disease existed at that time was Ganta, back home in Liberia, where Dr. George Way Harley of Asheville, North Carolina had come in 1926 and established a medical mission. The facility later became the Ganta United Methodist Hospital. Mom left the security and comfort of her parents in Gordin and moved to Liberia with Dad and his brother to seek treatment. They settled near Dingamon, Liberia, about four miles away from the Ganta United Methodist Hospital and built a hamlet called Gartehpa, named after Paye Garteh, Dad's mentor, who worked for the Ganta United Methodist Hospital as a laundry man. Dad and his brother completely recovered from the disease without losing any limbs or phalanges. In short, Mom was a definition of commitment.

QUINTESSENTIAL MOTHER

The Mahns say, "We know a mom by what she carries on her back or by what she holds in her bosom."[22] Mom pounded rice in a mortar, fetched water in a metal tub, and traveled to or from the farm while carrying me in a lappa on her back until I was four or perhaps older. She held me in her bosom either to breastfeed or comfort me whenever I cried, a coveted cuddle, unlike Esther, I enjoyed.[23] She cared for my sisters and me. It was not out of the ordinary. Nor was it extraordinary that she cared for and breastfed my cousin, Patrick Mahnwon Mantor.[24] However, my experience with her in sixth grade in 1971 set her apart as a quintessential mom.

My 1970 school year was a fun-filled one. It was also a successful year. I moved on to grade six. Almost two years earlier, Mom traveled to Guinea and she was still there. Dad and I expected her return in early January 1971. For that, I was excited for the upcoming long December-February vacation and a blast during the 1971 school year. Dad and I harvested coffee and felled trees on our new farm in anticipation of Mom's return. That was one of the best vacations I ever spent with Dad in the village.

As expected, Mom returned in January 1971. Soon my vacation was over. I returned to Sanniquellie and school started uneventfully. However, sometime in May, I felt an itch between my left middle finger and the left ring finger. I scratched it, but the itch would not go away. I continued scratching the affected area until it became very tender. Not long after, my left hand started to swell as the affected fingers began to separate farther and farther apart from the top. It seemed someone held the fingers at their tips and pulled them apart, creating the letter "V." As the swelling and pain grew increasingly worse, I left school and traveled to Mom in the village to seek help. It never occurred to me to go to the hospital in Sanniquellie. My first instinct was to go to Mom.

Upon arrival in the village, Mom stopped short of crying, but I sensed her anguish, especially upon the sight of me walking the twenty or more miles from Sanniquellie to the village in severe pain. She sat up and fanned my aching hand with her folded lappa all night, the indestructible imagery of a loving and compassionate mom I see when I think of her. By the end of that first week, my hand had swollen to more than two times its original size. Mom sought the help of a native doctor who not only diagnosed my swollen hand as "Quoigbaan" (branched wood), but also showed her the medicine to cure it. She went into the woods, returned with fresh leaves, and pounded them thoroughly along with clay. She then applied the medicine to my hand and put it in a "Head tie" (Liberian English for head scarf) and tied it around my neck as if it were in a cast. As the moistened clay-leaf mixture dried, it had the effect of squeezing the back and palm of my hand. The medicine pushed the pus from all areas of my hand to that one single location where it was most tender in the beginning.

After a couple of days, the swelling went down, and it seemed someone took a syringe and drew the pus out of my hand. The pain gradually went away and the two middle fingers that formed the "V" started to come back to their original positions. In the next few days, the pain went away completely. The only visible sign that something had happened to my left hand was the old skin that covered the affected area as if I had had a serious burn. The old skin peeled away as the wound below healed gradually and firmed up. As time went on, I gained full use of my left hand, although I was careful not to bruise it. Shortly thereafter, I returned to Sanniquellie to resume school.

"Craftsperson of Functional Life"

In the culture, mat, woven yarn, and kola play important roles, with mat in first place followed by kola. Upon the birth of a child, mat is an appropriate gift because it is the equivalent of a mattress. Rural people still sleep on mats despite the transition from clay beds to mattresses on wooden or metal beds. Mats remain the primary floorings in rural households and are part of a collection of items a groom's parents present to a bride's parents as dowry. A bride's parents, on the other hand, send her away to her husband with rolls of mats and other gifts. Mats are also an equivalent of coffins because the deceased are buried in them. When sympathizers assemble at a burial, for example, they present monies to the bereaved family as "Putting mat under the deceased," regardless of whether the deceased is in a golden casket.

Kola's cultural value is more important than its economic value. The collection of items a groom's parents presented to a bride's parents as dowry contained kola as well. A fixture in the culture, kola can be kola nut or anything of value including money given as a thank you gift, a token of welcome or an apology. Kola tree is equally important in its cultural value. It was a measure of inheritance, passed down from one generation to the next. Through kola trees, families communicated with posterity and connected their children to their parents' stories. Kola trees also told the stories of ancestral lands and delineated where children and later generations could farm.

Woven yarn played important roles too. Zoes, including elders and native doctors, for example, requested woven yarn and other cultural items when they called upon deceased ancestors' intercession with Wlah on behalf of the village during sacrifices of burnt offerings. Woven yarn was a part of dowry while native doctors required it as payment for medicines for illnesses. In addition, chiefs as well as village elders required woven yarns as penalties for violating serious norms.

In weaving, like mat making, Mom found her purpose; she was an earthly "craftsperson of functional life."[25] Like seeping water in dry soil, her life-building and sustaining activities crept into the lives of the family and village. She envisioned situations and prepared for them.[26] Old culture, in her outlook, was not a relic but the equipment for recreating the future. She held onto mat making and weaving as the culture transitioned to modernity. She saw increasing diminishing interests and skills in mat making, weaving, and blacksmithing with the availability of imported floorings, fabrics, and tools. She witnessed the disappearance of indigenous manufacturing and the diminishing availability of mats, traditional woven yarn, and tools.

In the future Mom saw, modernity neither trickled down readily nor radically changed the course of life. Instead, individuals continued wrongdoing, violated norms, married, became sick and died. The need for kola in welcoming, thanking or offering an apology for wrongdoing; kola, woven yarn and mat for dowry; mat for the birth of a baby or burying the deceased; kola, woven yarn, and mat for securing medicines or paying fines remained. She was concerned about the security, health and happiness of her family and village. Mom made mats from "saha" and woven yarn from cotton she cultivated and gave them away for the birth of a baby, securing medicines, marriage, and burial.[27] I wondered what could have been if she had had a formal education.

"Food is Human Being"

Mom grew more food than our family needed because she believed "Food is human being," meaning food is the basis of "Meena" (Relationship). In her vision of the future, she saw someone coming who was hungry. As she put it, "You never know when a stranger will arrive unexpectedly." Therefore, she always kept prepared food around. The hired hands who unanimously decided to work an extra day on gratis for Mom because as they put it, "They had never eaten so well, and no one had ever fed them as Mom did" only validated the selfless and loving Mom I had known all my life.

Wise, Independent and Practical

Mom knew her place and understood her role. Her family was her primary concern and responsibility. She had an abiding faith in Wlah and believed in the goodness of people. Yet, she felt strongly that her family's well-being as well as future was in her hands. She loathed leaving the future of her family to others to determine. As such, she envisioned her family's future and worked diligently to realize it. She was fiercely independent, with an instinct for sensing problems before they arrived.

To augment our family's income and to help pay the cost of my education, Mom and Dad cultivated coffee. In 1970, the status of her ownership in the coffee plantation changed while she was away in Guinea. On one occasion, upon arrival in the village for a weekend with Dad, I discovered a total stranger in our house, a woman I had never seen before. I sensed something was awry, but I did not have the courage to ask Dad because children seldom asked such questions of their parents in the culture. On a different weekend, however, I mustered the courage and asked others who the woman in our household was. I learned she was from Garr Bini, Nimba County.

Luolay Tiakpa was the woman whom I discovered in our house. She stood at 5'2, stoutly built, with a laser stare in eyes that swiveled rapidly in unusually depressed eye sockets. Like roots of an epiphyte around a palm tree, in no time, she took hold of Dad's heart. With his consent, she took over the coffee plantation he and Mom established. Luolay Tiakpa's stare greeted me followed by her extended hand for a handshake whenever I returned to the village. Her rapidly swiveling eyes were more noticeable at the opening of school, especially after Mom returned home. With Dad's invitation, she attended family meetings where Mom and Dad gave me money for tuition and supplies. Uneasiness fell upon the gathering whenever Dad extended his hand to Mom with money from proceeds of coffee sale for my tuition. I sensed anguish in Luolay Tiakpa's swiveling eyes, suggesting she had given a pound of flesh under duress.

During those family meetings, Mom showed no displeasure with Luolay Tiakpa's lording over the coffee plantation she and Dad established. Instead, she always thanked her for whatever amount Dad provided for tuition. "We have blood in our stomachs yet vomit water," was the calm response she always gave me upon asking why Luolay Tiakpa deserved a thank you. "Luolay Tiakpa helped harvest the coffee; prepared meals and hot water to bathe for your Dad; that's why I honor her labor and sweat," she continued.[28] In 1967, Mom planted a separate coffee plantation over which she had exclusive control. Moreover, when Uncle Miatee Garteh became ill, he willed his coffee plantation to her before he passed away in 1982. Mom's coffee acreage increased in size significantly. Initially, I saw the world through a child's eyes but eventually, I came to see the world through Mom's eyes and wished Luolay Tiakpa were alive to receive a portion of my appreciation for her labor. She died long before I first returned to Liberia in October 2011.

MIDWIFE

I was not surprised when the villagers turned to Mom in their search for a knowledgeable and responsible woman to assume the roles of village caretaker and midwife. I knew her all my life as a "craftsperson of functional life." She cared for everyone, particularly women, including pre- and post-natal mothers, and delivered babies. Although Mom became a Zoe without a regimented training expressly in traditional medicine, she had more than a rudimentary knowledge of traditional medicine. She turned to a repertoire of medicines she acquired from her family and native doctors who treated her. She acquired other medicines in her collection through offers of gifts including rolls of mat, money, bottles of cane juice, (a locally made spirit,) and food. Villagers whom Mom treated or whose babies she delivered often offered chickens, kola nuts, rolls of mat, or woven yarn in appreciation. However, she did not engage in midwifery and the practice of traditional medicine as a means of earning a living.

PHILANTHROPIST

Mom did not have the kind of money Warren Buffett and Bill Gates have to help promote causes far and near. However, she was a philanthropist; she met a different need. In Nimba, for example, many rural families often experienced the "hunger season," a time of food scarcity including the months of July, August, September, and sometimes October. For various reasons, they ran out of rice before the next harvest. Cassava, from the previous year's farm, was a backup food source, but availability depended on whether farmers prevented ground hog infestations by fencing their farms properly.

Mom was a lifesaver for those who experienced food scarcity. Her rice harvest was plentiful and accumulated in storage over time, not to mention eddoes (taro roots), yams, and sweet potatoes she cultivated. With a family of only five, hers was a household of abundance. During "hunger season," she gave food away liberally to families who came to the village in search for food. She fed them, let them harvest cassava from her farm and gave them seed rice at the time of sowing. Mom's brand of philanthropy was not limited to feeding people. She encouraged other people's children through their education. Without fanfare, she contributed financially to their education. She did not have a formal education but knew more about education than anyone in the village because she educated a son from kindergarten through college who went on to earn a Ph.D. from Gonzaga University in the United States in 2006. At the time of her burial in January 2014, a young woman whom I did not know wept uncontrollably as she recounted how Mom took care and helped her complete her education.

No Pushover

Mom believed "Food is human being" but, more importantly, she was a human being; someone who loved, felt pain, got angry, cried, and had empathy. She made me to become a human being as well. In 1976, Mom's humanity showed when I provoked her unintentionally. I deeply regretted my action and wished I could undo it. I tell this story because it was one of the important moments in my development as a human being.

On that day, Mom paid what seemed like a surprise visit, but it turned out she stopped by while she was on her way to Dahnlorpa to visit with someone who was sick. Cousin Saye Glee and I were at school. So, she figured she would see us on her way back to the village. When she returned from Dahnlorpa and stopped by to see us, I was excited to see her. As always, she brought me some food and gave me a little pocket change, even though she was not coming directly from the village. She was in a hurry to return to the village the same day. So, I walked with her to the Duo Tiayee parking station, where she would take a minibus, taxi, or passenger pickup truck. While on our way, I noticed Mom was wearing a clean but faded "Lappa," something I would not recommend.[29] I was not ashamed that Mom wore faded clothes, but I wanted her in clothes that stood out. We had about a quarter of a mile to reach the parking station, but it seemed like it took forever to cover the ground because of my preoccupation with Mom's faded lappa. I was having a quiet yet uncomfortable conversation with myself and felt tortured mentally. Mom was proud of me. She always bought nice clothes for me because she wanted me to look presentable. I wanted the same thing for Mom. I loved her dearly and wanted the world to recognize her as my mom.

I was not acting out of low self-esteem or vanity. Instead, I lived in a culture, where, as Herbert Spencer once said, "The ornamental comes before the useful."[30] To this day in Liberia, appearance matters more than substance. I did not know how to communicate to Mom that I would not recommend the faded lappa she wore. Eventually, when I mustered the courage to tell Mom what I was thinking, we were about twenty-five yards from the main street in Sanniquellie. I lifted my head up and muttered something, which Mom did not hear clearly. "What did you say?" she asked in Mahn. My heart fluttered then I dropped my head and asked the unthinkable. "Could you have worn one of your newer lappas rather than the faded one?" Mom's reaction was swift and natural. She turned to me and angrily said, "Your something," and more in Mahn.[31] I was out of touch and insensitive because I did not understand Mom's sacrifice. I did not make the connection that the money she spent on my school and well-being was the same money she could have used to buy new clothes for herself. I wished I could go under the ground to avoid the shame I felt and the hurt I caused. I am sorry, Mom.

Quest for Children

In the culture as well as other African cultures, a husband expects his wife to bear children because they are an insurance. Children are expected to become successful, take care of their parents when they become old and bury them when they die. More importantly, because Liberia is a patriarchal society, where the family line runs through the male, a husband's expectation of a wife to have children is a code for fear of losing the family name or line. Women are doubly whammed. If a woman, for whatever reason, does not bear children, society looks down upon her. She becomes a subject of vicious gossips about involvement in witchcraft. Moreover, if a woman fails to bear children, society sees her as having implicitly given her husband an excuse to find another woman who can bear children to carry on the family name. All these aspects of African culture make the pressure to bear children intense.

Mom was under the same pressure to have children when she married Dad. One after the other, she had children, named them according to the naming order in the culture and exhausted the list.[32] Unfortunately, she came away empty-handed.[33] Although their deaths were apparently due to childhood diseases, they were, instead, attributed to witchcraft, the predominant belief at the time. The culture expected Mom to accept her predicament as "Wlahkerwon".[34] So, at first, she resorted to tears, but she changed course and turned to Wlah for answers. She petitioned incessantly, sacrificing burnt offerings. Occasionally, with a plea for children and Wlah's protection and blessings upon them, she called on deceased parents and relatives for intercession. In the meantime, she traveled anywhere a glimmer of hope flickered to find answers. She consulted with sand cutters on what to do to prevent her children from dying. Only one child, Kou Dingamonlay Sennie, out of her first nine children survived.

Mom did not believe she would have children again, but Gbeakeh Flo, a native doctor, reassured her of having children.[35] He advised her against using the traditional naming order because witchcraft practitioners prowled at night to rob children so named. Flo believed Mom continually lost children because witchcraft practitioners devoured them in their evil spirit world. He told Mom if she had a male child, she would put a hole in its left ear and name it Luogon (slave or slave man) and if the child were a female, she would name it Gboe (dirt). Flo's advice put the onus for losing Mom's children upon her. Essentially, every time she named a child according to the traditional naming order, she advertised it to witchcraft practitioners. Witchcraft practitioners did not bother the slave child with the hole in the left ear or the dirt because they were not interested in anything filthy. Mom did exactly as Flo instructed and my younger sister, Esther, and I survived. In the end, Wlah granted her wish and three out of her thirteen children survived.

Sennie Kou Dingamonlay Flumo, my older sister, (deceased)

Esther Flumo, my younger sister

Gbeakeh Flo's advice left me wondering because his instruction also appears in the Holy Bible in two instances. Exodus 21:6 states, "Then his master shall bring him unto the judges; he shall also bring him to the door, or unto the door post; and his master shall bore his ear through with an aul; and he shall serve him forever." Deuteronomy 15:17 also states, "Then thou shalt take an aul, and thrust it through his ear unto the door, and he shall be thy servant forever. And, unto thy maidservant thou shalt do likewise." As an adult, I have wondered about the origin of the practice in the culture. Although Mom explained the story of the hole in my left ear very early, it was a source of irritation in elementary school because my friends teased me, believing that Mom mistook me for a girl.

Mom's Influence in My Life

Mom was an ordinary kind and practical woman who saw the world as it was. She pushed the boundaries and set examples of how she wanted the world to be, but she also conducted herself in the world as it was. She saw the masks people wore and the people behind them for who they were. She knew children took the mask for the real person behind it and was steeply in tune with the Mahn culture.[36] She did everything she could at the appropriate time to protect her children. For example, at an early age, my extended time in school, except for a few weekends, deprived me of an opportunity to eat significant salt with my extended family in the village. Every vacation Mom not only saw me as the child I was but also my extended family saw me as a stranger and treated me accordingly.

In the culture, a stranger is seen as an evaluator, someone who carries impressions of a community to faraway places. So, villagers greet strangers warmly upon arrival, treat them kindly during their stay and send them off with fine gifts and heartfelt wishes. Such courtesies and treatment blind strangers. Hence, a child and a stranger cannot distinguish the mask from the person behind it. More importantly, Mom saw the treatment strangers receive for its potential goodness and danger. She thought I could not tell that someone quite different in character could be behind a mask. Seeing the world as it was, Mom's recognition that "Other people's children's successes do not make everyone happy" was one way she helped shape my life. Only later, as an adult, did I fully understand that she was trying to protect me from hidden jealousy in others.

Respect for women as well as their dignity is one value Mom taught me to uphold. She did not champion any feminine agenda, yet she did almost anything a man could do in the culture. She probably could have been an ideal poster child for the American feminist movement if she had been born in America. Mom took on roles traditionally considered provinces of men, but she never challenged the role of a man in the culture. Based on her life, I knew since childhood that a woman could do whatever a man could do. However, Mom was a courageous and practical woman for whom nothing stood in the way of her children's safety and wellbeing. No action reflected that disposition more than the moment she looked straight into my eyes upon entering adulthood and said, "Do not tell your heart to a woman."[37]

Mom developed contingencies to outlast her for ensuring my safety. One of such contingencies was a strategy for dealing with an enemy. She put me on a hypothetical journey along a footpath from the village to another town. After covering substantial ground, my enemy would take off from the village in pursuit of me, hoping to catch up and do physical harm to me. He would focus on landing properly because he wanted to avoid stumbling into the stones and roots of large trees that crossed the footpath at various angles. At the same time, he would be planning and revising his plans to harm me. Consequently, he would lose his peripheral vision. Once I saw the enemy closing in on me, I was to genuflect on the shoulder of the footpath, facing the direction of travel with my head bowed over my knee. The mentally occupied pursuer would pass without noticing me on the shoulder of the footpath. Once I lost sight of him, I was to return to the village. The enemy would continue until he destroyed himself. I live by that advice to this day.

Mom's life was the script for how to care for each other to sustain community cohesion in the village. She made that script the tradition in the village before the civil war. Everyone treated Mom with deference, and it seemed the tradition she helped establish would endure. However, when the winds of the civil war swept through the village, not to mention Liberia, the casualties included the values, norms, and tradition that Mom helped establish. After I fled Liberia following the onset of the civil war, that tradition in the village changed. Individuals forgot Mom's positive roles in their lives while the deference she once enjoyed dissipated. People took off their masks while lids on potential conflicts in the extended family came off. Still further, family relationships took on a new nature: you do for me;

I do for you. In light of the change, Mom, again, showed her practicality by defining family as those who "look out for and care about each other" and as "more than blood." She adjusted, and taught me the importance of adjusting when conditions change.

Although I live in the United States, my deep affection for the soil and motivation for working it at this moment in the village come from Mom. The soil was her means of maintaining the dignity of the family. Through working the soil, she kept food abundantly and readily available for the family and ensured the success of the project she and Dad undertook.[38] Mom cultivated rice, going beyond farming activities for women and performing those considered men's domain.[39] She planted rice with seeds such as sesame, okra, and corn and also cultivated coffee and bananas interspersed with pineapple and sugar cane. At harvest, she carried large tubs of produce on her head to sell in Kpaye Lehpula, Duo Tiayee or Sanniquellie; an hour, an hour and a half or over three hours away, respectively. I often accompanied her, carrying a portion of the produce on my head. She not only saved proceeds from the sale for my education but also hewed out of the soil the life she gave me.

CHAPTER 2

School

MAHN PEOPLE'S EXPERIENCES WITH "*QUIZEES*" greatly influenced my parents' decision to send me to school.[40] In general, Mahn parents developed a clear idea of their children's education. They regarded it as a protector—an enterprise to protect themselves and their children from the whims of *quizees*. Mom and Dad believed in education as a "Protector." They had very clear ideas about what education could do for one's life. It occurred to Dad that going to school and learning how to read and write were an important part of being a *quizee*. He wanted my education to protect me from *quizees* and to help me escape the scourge of being a *porter*. Dad did not want me to carry someone in a hammock or his luggage on my head. He did not want me to be a victim of extortion at the hands of *quizees*. However, Dad also had a short-term goal for wanting me to get an education. He wanted to protect himself from tax collectors' extortion. He wanted me to learn how to read and write; to finish the eighth grade and return to the village to help examine his government-issued flag receipts to tell whether he had been cheated or not. Mom and Dad both believed in the same goals for sending me to school. However, unlike Dad, Mom's short-term goal did not become apparent until later when I made significant progress in grade school.

An Unusual Preschool

I was a typical indigenous Liberian child of my generation, especially having come from rural Liberia. Without the luxury of parents who could read or write, there was no such thing as learning how to read or write at home. Papers in the household included hospital cards, government-issued flag receipts for taxes Dad paid, large photographs of President William V.S. Tubman, the 18th President of Liberia and the flag of Liberia.

English is Liberia's official language. There were no formal preschools. Our preschool settings were outdoors or open spaces where children gathered to play. I learned such expressions as "Hey you," "You boy," "You girl," "Come here," and "My friend" from older boys, passersby, people in the streets or in other public places. In addition, we often met in open spaces to play soccer, the only sport we knew how to play. We used tennis balls or anything round such as green oranges or grapefruits as soccer balls. Moreover, we communicated the language of the sport in English. "Hey man, here, here … pass it to me;" "Kick the ball;" "Penalty;" and "Corner kick." Of course, we were not always pleasant in communicating the language of the sport, at least, among ourselves. In an event of a foul play, profane languages such as "den fool," meaning "damned fool," among others often resulted in fistfights.

Older boys already in school taught us at playgrounds. They showed us how to write our letters in the sand and say them. The learning experience was not always out of kindness to help a friend or a younger kid. In most instances, it was a challenge intended to humiliate those of us who had not enrolled yet or who did not know how to write or say the alphabet. That kind of learning experience, as important as it may have been, did not last long enough and did not occur with regularity to make a big difference. In other words, I learned how to read and write when I started school in March of 1966. Moreover, at that time, no one in my family or even in the village was in school. No one had ever started or completed elementary school, let alone high school or college. I had no role models to give me the faintest idea about what it meant to go to school. I had no idea of what an education could do for one's life.

Falapa

Dad had his eyes set on Falapa, the St. Mary's Catholic Mission School in Sanniquellie, Liberia.[41] He remembered French Catholic priests and the work they did in the Guinean Forest Region as part of the French colonial educational system before the struggle for independence drove them out. Only later I figured that his impression of French Catholic priests' work influenced his decision to send me to St. Mary's School. Although my parents identified an ideal school for me, they, like other Mahn parents, faced the same problem: when it came to the education of their children, the available and good schools were not in their villages or towns, but located in larger towns or cities faraway. There were no motorcar roads from many of the villages or towns to the larger towns or cities, let alone any thought of bus transportation for students. As a result, Mom and Dad turned to the only alternative other parents facing similar situation had. They considered sending me to live with a relative or someone of means in Sanniquellie to go to school. Hence, the conversation with the Guah family of Sanniquellie.

St. Mary's Catholic Church, Sanniquellie, Liberia; the Brothers' Residence in the background right (Courtesy Brother David)

The conversation about taking me to live with the Guahs in Sanniquellie occurred between Kou Lehyeay and her husband, David Guah (formerly David Watson), and my parents. Kou Lehyeay (deceased) was a member of Dad's extended family. The Guahs were not ordinary Mahns. They were at another social level, a higher one, among the Mahns in Sanniquellie. Officials of the Liberian government through their emissaries, including District Commissioners (DCs) or *Buusoyas*, apparently recruited David Guah (deceased) to work at the Firestone Rubber Plantation in Liberia.[42] According to his son, Joseph Saye Guah, who lives in Atlanta Georgia, it is not clear how David Guah acquired the "Watson" surname. However, as he put it, the likelihood is that an Americo-Liberian family took him in and gave him the surname "Watson" because of his good conduct and work habits. This explanation for the origin of Mr. Guah's former surname, "Watson," is more plausible because names Firestone overseers gave to other Mahn recruits at the Plantation at the time were undignified, even though such names suggested excellent work habits. "Fineboy," for example, was a common name Mahn recruits who returned from the Firestone Plantation had. Mr. Guah also received an education, perhaps up to the sixth grade or a little more. He projected fearlessness and had an air of sophistication about him. I often sensed a fascination with the *quizee* mystique in my parents' conversations about him.

Later, the conversation Mom and Dad had with the Guahs and their eventual decision to take me to live with them did not seem out of the ordinary at first glance. However, the more I examined my parents' decision to send me to live with the Guah family to go to school, the more I thought that it was extraordinary, if not risky. I could not understand why a woman who had lost ten out of thirteen children would send her only son such a long way from home to live with other people. In my mind, that extraordinary decision bordered on either the strength or reliability of the extended family system, child neglect, or an act of providence.

My parents did not discuss my going to Sanniquellie for school openly. There was no mention of a date of my leaving for school at any time. I was completely in the dark. I had no time to prepare psychologically for the separation from my family; for the separation from the village, the place I would later call the "Garden of Eden" based on imageries of Old Testament Bible lessons at St. Mary's School. Over time, Mom discreetly prepared for my leaving. She did not want to alarm me because she sensed I might resist leaving her to go to a faraway place. When I saw her climbing up into the rice storage and getting rice for drying and milling, I just assumed she was preparing for some occasion. After all, climbing up into the rice storage for rice to prepare and cook, sell, or take to a relative was routine. I had seen it happen repeatedly.

CHAPTER 3

The Journey Begins

I THOUGHT IT WAS JUST ANOTHER trip when Mom told me we would go to Sanniquellie on "Loryenneh" (Saturday) sometime in February 1966. On numerous occasions, I helped carry Mom or Dad's bag to Sanniquellie. So, when I heard about going to Sanniquellie again, I was excited because I was thinking about "Baylay" (bread of any kind) and "Bonbon."[43] However, this time around, there was something different about the Sanniquellie trip. On the morning of that Loryenneh, we did not leave the village as early as everyone else did. I awoke, looked around and could not find Mom. I ran outside and realized that the sun was up. Right away, I started to cry because I thought my parents had left me. Moments later, I was relieved when I found out that Mom was in the kitchen preparing "tea", which consisted of rice with okra. She doused the rice with roasted and ground sesame seed and ground "dry bony".[44] Mom also added the usual condiments, including salt, pepper, and bouillon cube. As the late rapper Heavy D once put it, "You can't have ice cream without whipped cream."[45] That meant, in Mahn country, you cannot cook new rice with okra, add the usual condiments and forget palm oil! Mom "wasted" freshly made palm oil on that rice and made it irresistible. The sight and smell of the food had me thinking and murmuring, "Yes! That's why I love this place."[46]

Despite my excitement at the sight and smell of the food, I was puzzled. We were supposed to be on our way. The sun was up in the clear blue dry season sky, others going to Sanniquellie had left and I did not understand why we were not on our way. When I asked Mom, she said that we were not carrying anything to sell or coming back the same day. "Why are we carrying all these things Mom packed if we are not going to sell anything?" I wondered.

After we had tea, Mom, Dad, and I set out on the journey to Sanniquellie. The load Mom had to carry on her head included dry meat, dry freshwater fish and sesame seed. Other food items included ground pepper, palm oil, plantains, and rice. She spread a lappa on a mat, placed the base of a large white metal tub over it and meticulously packed the provisions, rising a few inches above the rim of the tub. She then tied the ends of the lappa over the provisions to prevent the food items from falling off. Dad, on the other hand, packed a jute sack with more rice, plantain, eddoes, and sweet potatoes. I looked up into the mid-morning clear blue sky again and saw a passenger jet flying over thirty thousand feet overhead. Because I could not wait any longer for baylay and bonbon, I made a frivolous request to the jet airliner as if it were a person, "Lehyee killen (airplane), stop and take my parents and me to Sanniquellie."

Aside from baylay and bonbon, I was thrilled over the load I had to carry. A rooster was one of the items Mom and Dad were taking along, although it did not occur to me that my parents were taking it for the Guahs. The rooster did not raise any suspicion about my parents' motive because taking livestock to Sanniquellie on Loryenneh was not out of the ordinary. Rural marketers carried their produce as well as their livestock to Sanniquellie for sale. Carrying that rooster was my responsibility. Considering the loads Mom and Dad had to carry, I thought I was the luckiest one. I had the lightest load to carry, so I thought. The prospect of carrying a live rooster was exhilarating. I even put some rice in my pocket to feed the rooster along the way.

To make carrying the rooster easier for me, Dad made a cage out of two palm branches. Each palm branch with the leaves intact was about a foot and a half long. The base of the cage was rectangular; the front and back ends were triangular; and the sides were trapezoidal. Once inside the cage, the rooster rested with its feet on the base and head pointed toward the front end. It could stand on its feet, but not turn around. Its beak and

30

head could go through the spaces between the palm leaves to eat and drink. Its claws also came out through the holes in the base since it was also made of palm leaves, while the feces fell through the holes as well. Dad wanted to fix a "mini" for me, but when I lifted the cage with the rooster, walked around and felt nothing considerably heavy, I told him I did not need the mini.[47] Upon leaving the village, I lifted the cage and carried it in my right hand. I walked as if I were the strongest kid around.

The road was a footpath and we walked in a single file. Mom was ahead, Dad was behind, and I was in the middle. Mom was ahead and Dad was behind for good reasons. Mom protected me from real harm such as scorpions, snakes, particularly the green mambas, and "Yeanayzu" (a poisonous spider) because children normally are not attentive to such dangers on the road. Places along footpaths where the sun's rays go through canopies and hit the ground are ideal warming spots for green mambas. Dad, on the other hand, was behind to protect me from imagined danger, ghosts, or spirits. The Mahns believe that, when someone dies, the ghost, a real being that ordinary people cannot see, lurks in the grave until after three days for a woman and four days for a man. They also believe that children and certain people endowed at birth can see ghosts.

My first test came on "Glehtohwn" (rockhill), less than half a mile from the village. As we climbed up hill, Dad saw me switch the cage from the right hand to the left hand and asked if everything was okay. "Yes," I replied. As I struggled with the cage on the hill, he again offered to fix a mini. Reluctantly, I agreed. He knew what he was talking about when he first suggested fixing the mini. After a bit of reality check, I concluded that carrying the cage on the head would be easier. At that point, I still could not imagine what carrying the cage on my head over a mini would be like. Dad made the mini once we reached the summit of the hill. I realized that the rooster would not sit still even with the cage rested on the mini. Since the rooster could not turn around in the cage, it moved forward and backward, shifting the center of gravity from the front to the middle and then to the back, repeatedly.

It was irritating to say the least. I complained bitterly due to the rooster's constant back and forth agitation. "Hold onto it tightly," Dad said. However, that did not solve the problem. To add insult to injury, the rooster started to drop its feces. At first, I felt something cold and wet over my right shoulder. Soon, I realized that the rooster had done its "stinking thing" on my shoulder. I almost threw the entire cage over the side of the road. Right away, I started doing what I knew how to do best when I was in trouble. I cried and told my parents that I could not carry the caged rooster anymore. Dad took the cage and carried it until we reached "Deemeeyee" (the creek where the cattle drank). I washed off the rooster's feces and we continued the journey. It was a classic "Do not judge a book by its cover" experience. What a stinking lesson!

After we crossed Deemeeyee, we walked for about fifteen minutes and arrived at Burglehyee, a pristine creek that flowed through layers and crevices of rocks under canopies of large trees and made soothing sounds that summoned travelers to take a breather to recharge. But Burglehyee was not exactly what it seemed. It personified "All that glitters is not gold." Upstream, beyond the virgin forest that covered the crossing point, a large sugar cane plantation existed, along with a distillery for Cane juice, a favorite local spirit. The creek was a cesspool of every imaginable refuse.

Our next stretch of distance was on relatively level sandy ground interspersed with patches of fine gravel. We walked past coffee plantations that belonged to residents of Bursonnon new town on both sides of the footpath. The next body of water we crossed, Burkarmehin, a stream on the outskirt of Bursonnon old town, was unlike Burglehyee in every way.[48] Vast swamps lay on both sides of the crossing point. For about one and a half minutes, we walked through water knee-high.

The road from the village to Bursonnon new town passed through the center of Bursonnon old town. Coffee and cocoa plantations completely took up both sides of the footpath towards the west end of the old town. Mom and Dad showed me a gigantic cotton tree, initially planted as part of a fort to protect the town from attacks during the *quizees'* war against the Mahns in the early 1900s.[49] Graves and grave markers in the old town scared the heck out of me. I wondered whose remains were in those graves and what caused their deaths.

I recall three observations as we walked past the coffee and cocoa plantations on both sides of the road, heading towards Bursonnon new town. First, secondary footpaths branched off the main footpath we were on at approximately thirty degrees and headed into the coffee and cocoa plantations. Depending on which direction one was traveling, the branching footpaths were like merging roads or exits along a highway. Inquisitively, I wanted to know where those branching footpaths headed to and remember Mom saying that they were roads to farms belonging to residents of Bursonnon new town.

Second, I saw sheep and goats along the footpath heading towards us. In addition, other sheep and goats were grazing in the coffee plantations on both sides of the footpath. This time, without my asking, Dad told me that the presence of livestock on the road was an indication that the next town was near. Next, I saw several newly covered graves on both sides of the footpath. I could visibly see mounds of red dirt over the precise places of burial. Strewn over the graves were red and green empty shells of single-barrel shotgun casings. I got scared because the scenes reminded me of dreadful ghost imageries every Mahn child does not want to imagine. It did not seem that Mom being ahead and Dad being behind provided much security against ghosts. I felt like I needed two more people, one on my right and the other on my left, to protect me. I did not ask questions about the graves because it was obvious that Bursonnon residents had buried people there. Moreover, I did not want any prolonged answers about graves, which only heightened my anxieties.

As soon as we passed the first set of graves, we climbed down a hill over which a large "Poho" tree stood.[50] The tree's ripened fruits fell and rolled downhill towards a swamp. Poho fruits are not edible, but because of their sweet and irresistible aroma, I always wished I could eat them. In fact, the only way Mom was able to get me off her back with my nagging question "What would happen if I ate the fruit," was to put it bluntly to me: "It will kill you!" Poho, which the Mahns treat with reverence, has a fruit slightly larger than an apple or an orange. Poho fruits contain latex. To harvest it, one must remove the skin of a ripened fruit to obtain the fleshy portion like that of an apple. Poho trees usually grow in the jungle far away from the towns or villages, but people who do not know the importance of the species have destroyed them during farming activities.

After we descended the hill over which the Poho tree stood, we were about a quarter of a mile from reaching present-day Bursonnon. Once our climb downhill past the Poho tree ended, the ground leveled off with white sand into an ankle-deep stream. The stream, also called Burkarmehin, flowed north-south in an area with almost the exact same elevation as Burkarmehin near Bursonnon old town. As soon as we crossed the stream, I looked to the right and saw a cleared area with a pit almost at the boundary of the dry land and the swamp. I quickly turned toward our direction of travel as my heart pounded, although my mind was fixated on the image of the pit I saw. I thought residents dug the pit for an imminent burial. Instantly, the dread of ghosts consumed me. Fearful, yet outwardly subdued, I asked my parents "What is that pit for?" and expected them to tell me that it was intended for a grave. I was pleasantly disappointed when Dad said the pit was a "Bayhee" "gulu" (pit).[51] With Dad's response, which temporarily relieved my fear of dead people and their lurking ghosts, we were just 500 yards away from Bursonnon new town. "No more graves and grave markers to remind me of dreaded ghosts!" I gleefully murmured to myself.

In less than a minute, that glee turned into disappointment and heightened fear. I was mistaken to think that the sights of graves were over. As I looked on the left and right of the footpath, cleared paths about three to four feet in width led directly to graves one could see from the road. Again, strewn over mounds of red dirt on graves were shotgun shell casings, pans, and buckets. Upon seeing those artifacts, I cringed. Earnestly, my educational career had begun, but it was not the education Mom and Dad had in mind. Instead, I was learning about the culture. "Why are buckets and pans over those graves?" I asked. "They are grave markers, so people do not forget where the graves are," Dad said. "The buckets and pans are also meant for the departed ones to take along on their journeys," he went on. Mom, too, added that "If the items on the graves are such things as spears, broken bottles, or any material that could cause bodily harm, then the family members believe that the departed died as a result of witchcraft." Moreover, Mom went on, "Weapon-like grave artifacts show that the deceased is being armed to avenge against the person responsible for his death." "What about the shotgun shell casings?" I asked. "Oh, they came from shotgun blasts, a send-off, a salute to the dead upon burial," Dad replied.

In the next few minutes, we arrived in Bursonnon new town, walking through the approximately 30-foot wide east-west alley dividing the town into two. The townspeople created the alley upon founding new Bursonnon with the hope that a motorcar road would come through someday. They wanted to avoid future demolition and damage to properties. As we proceeded through the town, people whom Mom described as distant relatives converged and greeted us with the distinctive Liberian handshake, where the fingers make an audible snap. I heard some say "Ko weakeh ay yeaka" (Let us do the handshake better), suggesting a feeling comparable to receiving a cup of tea without sugar. The greetings and accompanying questions about the well-being of other family members in the village slowed us down considerably.

The human traffic along the path from Bursonnon to Sanniquellie was much heavier than what we encountered on our way from the village to Bursonnon. In addition, travelers along a different footpath from Gbein Yohnyee as well as Duo Tiayee and beyond joined us in Bursonnon. The heavy human traffic in both directions resulted from regular villagers and Guineans who worked in the diamond mines along nearby Yar River. Beyond Bursonnon, I saw diamond miners and others who left early morning and traveled to Sanniquellie on their way back carrying all kinds of cargo, including plastic five-gallon containers with gasoline, on their heads. The miners used the gasoline to run their water pumps at the diamond mines. On-coming human traffic along the road to Sanniquellie slowed us down considerably because every time we met on-coming human traffic, someone had to step aside to let the other people pass.

As we did between the village and Bursonnon, we trekked level sandy grounds as well as stretches covered by gravel until we arrived at a notable stream, "Kiapee Meeyee" (the stream where the captain drank). Kiapee Meeyee, as my parents later explained, was a reminder of *quizees*. The Mahns carried *Buusoyas* in hammocks. The *Buusoyas* were the emissaries. *Quizees* sent them to enforce their ordinances and to collect hut taxes. According to Dad, a captain of the Liberian Frontier Force (LFF) stopped at that stream and had a drink of cold water because it was pristine. Since then, the stream assumed the name "Kiapee Meeyee." Beyond Kiapee Meeyee, the footpath looked like a roller coaster. We climbed up and down hills, crossed creek after creek, stream after stream, and stepped on and, at other times, jumped over large roots, which crossed the footpath at varying angles. At different points along the way, the footpath meandered through cool virgin forests. In other places, I saw "Suoos" (old upland rice farms) on both sides of the footpath through strips of virgin forest. Farmers purposely left strips of virgin forest along both sides of the footpath to keep it shaded and cool to protect travelers from the scorching tropical sun.

We also stopped at several rest areas near a creek, under a large tree or over a crop of rock along the way to get a drink of water or to let someone attend to nature (to use the restroom). Even up to that point, I was not listening to glean anything from my parents' conversation. They were not talking about why we were going to Sanniquellie and I was not thinking about the purpose of the trip. The only matter that concerned me was how much distance we still had to cover to arrive in Sanniquellie because I was daydreaming about baylay and bonbon. In addition, I was imagining the different cars I would see in Sanniquellie. Every time Dad sent me to call a relative over to our house in the village for dinner, I ran, sounding an engine with my mouth "Kpun yon dee umh dee umh deeeeee…" as if I were driving. On that day, I was daydreaming about real cars and looking forward to seeing real drivers. As I was daydreaming and thinking about stories I would tell upon my return to the village, something consequential about my life and future had already happened without my knowledge. Mom, Dad, and the Guahs had already closed a deal about me. I was going to Sanniquellie to stay. Mom and Dad knew that I would not want to stay in Sanniquellie; that I would cry bitterly, but they were determined to take me away for school.

After more than two and a half hours, we arrived in Soopeay, a town located about two miles from two mountains of solid rock called Soo. The mountains are next to each other and look like a pair of U-shaped bowls placed upside down. Legend has it that the one closer to the footpath is the "female" and the one in the back is the "male." From Soopeay, we continued the journey for about thirty minutes and arrived at a creek called Whenehyee. A motorcar road existed from that creek to Sanniquellie. Minibuses, taxis, or trucks traveled to the creek to pick up marketers who came from Soopeay, Bursonnon, Gbein Yohnyee, the village, Kpaye Lehpula, and Duo Tiayee. Marketers who did not have money as well as others who felt it did not make sense to travel such long distances and then take a taxi or a minibus for the remaining three to four miles just continued their walk to Sanniquellie. I was overly excited, thinking that my parents would let us take a taxi or minibus to complete the trip, but Mom and Dad felt it did not make sense to take a taxi for the remaining distance. So, we walked the remaining three miles and arrived in Sanniquellie in the afternoon almost four hours after we left the village. It took us a little longer than usual because unlike others who were going to sell produce to return the same day, we were not in a hurry. We did not have anything to sell, and we did not have to return the same day.

CHAPTER 4

Take Care of Our Child

UPON ARRIVAL AT THE HOME of the Guahs in Sanniquellie, they greeted us with the usual "Haa oos," greetings said while hugging someone at the same time, followed by the distinctive Liberian handshake. As most children new to an area do, I was quiet, but observant. The kids around were lively. They ran in and out of the house. Unlike the village, where I could stand at the front of our house and count all the houses on my fingers, there did not seem to be an end to the city when I stepped outside no more than ten feet away. The Guahs' house was less than a quarter mile from the magnificent marble public market building. I could hear indistinguishable noises from the market. I could also hear the honking of different vehicles on the main street, the Monrovia-Yekepa highway.

A little while after our arrival, Kou Lehyeay, Mr. Guah's "Karlaylay," instructed Zehyee Mahnmein (Mr. Guah's second and younger wife) to get some of the rice we brought to prepare dinner.[52] "What if we had not brought the rice?" I wondered. Kou Lehyeay's instruction was a sign of what was to come—a household where we did not have enough to eat due to the sheer number of people, a household of hunger. However, I did not take note of it as such. Gung-ho about the possibility of their son attending Falapa, Mom and Dad did not seem to have focused on the meaning of that instruction either. Dad was obsessed with Falapa. Nothing, not even the possibility that I would be hungry in that household was going to change his mind about leaving me in Sanniquellie with the Guahs to go to school at Falapa.

After dinner, Mom and Dad asked Mr. Guah, his two wives, Kou Lehyeay and Zehyee Mahnmein, and Saye Moore (Mr. Guah's eldest son, also known as Joseph Saye Guah) to assemble in the piazza. Their reason for calling the meeting was to inform the Guahs why they had come. Saye Moore did not appear to be interested in the meeting, perhaps because he had something important to do. However, his parents made him to sit in the meeting because as they put it "You are the eldest son whom all the children that will be coming to live here and go to school would be looking up to for guidance about school." At that moment, it dawned on me that the meeting must be about me.

I did not follow everything said in the meeting closely, but I noticed the kola nuts and rooster that my parents handed over to Kou Lehyeay. Essentially, the message was they had brought their son to her so that she and her husband can look after and educate him. The rooster and kola nuts signified that they were giving Kou Lehyeay the authority to watch over me as she would watch over her own children. She, in turn, took the rooster and kola nuts and gave them over to her husband with word that her people had come with their son to live with them to be educated. Mr. Guah took the items and not only thanked my parents, but also spoke about the importance of education. He went on to reassure my parents that all would be well because his children were in school and that all of us would be together happily.

Dad picked up after Mr. Guah with a typical advice as if he had forgotten to say something. His advice was one that almost any child brought by his parents to live with other people in similar circumstances to go to school could have heard. "Do not walk about," Dad said. In the culture, few things worry parents as much as a child who "walks about," a child who goes out to places where he has no reason to be without adult supervision. For this reason, Mahns have a parable for sending the message of the dangers of "walking about" to children: "Gbayinpeay keh nehfu leh bur ay lay beelee lah."[53] The parable uses mothers because, generally, they are the mainstay of their families; the glue that holds their families together; the ones without whom children's well-being and future successes are at risk. For that reason, in defense of their mothers' physical safety or reputation, it is common for people to fight or attempt to lay down their lives.

The message in "Gbayinpeay keh nehfu leh bor ay lay beelee lah" frightens children who roam without supervision by laying the responsibility for the deaths of their mothers at their feet. As most children seldom understand parables, unfortunately, that dreaded one often falls upon deaf ears. To my amazement, Dad went on saying, "Do whatever you are asked to do and read the books you came to learn; do the work you came to do," without making any distinction between good and bad. "Do the work you came to do? What work? I thought I had come along to get my baylay and bonbon?" I wondered.

In the end, Dad made the biggest gamble with what seemed like little thought. He gave the Guahs the authority to use the switch to discipline me if I did not listen or do what they tell me to do. To emphasize the seriousness of that authority, he resorted to his tired story about Mr. Saye Tee and his son, Mr. Moses Saye Tee. Sometime after Mr. Saye Tee enrolled his son, Moses Saye Tee, at Dingamon Public School, it soon became apparent that he was skipping classes to hang out with his friends in Dingamon, a town about six miles north of Ganta, Liberia. Upon hearing the complaints about his son's indiscipline and truancy, Mr. Saye Tee took his son to school and whipped him before the student body. Although the teachers tried to persuade him that he could not whip his son at the school, he would not listen. Instead, Mr. Tee told the teachers that he wanted to show them how to discipline his son. The message to the Guahs about how to deal with my indiscipline was clear: "Do not spare the rod!" For heaven's sake, I was not a problem child!

I heard Saye Tee and his son's story, but it did not sink in. I did not get the point. However, I freaked out when Dad said, "Do not walk about," because it meant they were planning to leave me and return home. Even though I assumed I would go with Mom and Dad when the time came to leave for the village, I did not see it in their faces.

CHAPTER 5

Quest to Return Home

O N SUNDAY THE FOLLOWING DAY, Mom and Dad set out to return to the village. David Guah, his head wife, Kou Lehyeay, and I made up the "Dorhzuu" (escort) party. Upon leaving the Guahs' house, I picked up Dad's bag, which contained several items, including his "Zanakpahtuu."[54] The unmistakable smell of his "Zanakpah" (dried tobacco) was a reminder of something I hated doing. On countless occasions, he sent me to find his zanakpahtuu whenever he forgot it at home or somewhere else on the farm. Other unforgettable items in the bag included a "Made in Liberia" three-red-and-gold-star-labeled carton of matches and "Zartan" (a wire used for traps). Dad used the matches to light his pipe if he were not near a wood-burning fire to do what then seemed to me a wonder. He would take an ember with his bare hand and place it on his pipe. Dad also used the matches to start a fire with pieces of wood to prepare food or let smoke rise as a signal that someone was around whenever he was alone on the farm. As for the zartan, it was a mechanical pest control method, a silent "medicine" or remedy for ground hogs, which devoured rice shortly before their milking stage. A farmer who ignored ground hog infestation did so at the price of an empty harvest. Ground hogs were the equivalent of crawling locusts; they invaded rice fields at night.

Kou Lehyeay, on the other hand, took Mom's large white metal tub and securely positioned it over a "Mini" on her head as almost all rural Liberian women characteristically do. The tub contained a 4" by 4" by 4" blue and white cubical "Firestone" washing soap, "Blehbleh," and a metal gallon of kerosene for the lanterns.[55] Other items in the tub were dry salt-water fish, bouillon cubes (referred to as chicken soup in Liberia), "Koto" (a brownish piercing and burning ointment), and "Lululalah" (a small flat bottle with an alligator image label). The latter two were Chinese-made medicinal ointments widely in use at the time for backache and aching joints.

With Dad's bag in my possession and convinced that I was returning with them, I took the lead on the escort. My parents had no worries of my being at the front. After all, we were in the city. No grasses on the way for snakes or scorpions to hide in and bite a kid. I was not afraid of anything, not even the ghosts! People were all over the place. Mom and Dad were in no hurry to purge my excitement about returning with them. They knew that I would soon be disappointed once asked to return with the Guahs. We went by the south side of the public market, walked past several houses and hit the street on the backside of Chief Bonah Suah's Compound, where the Gbano tree was.[56]

GBANO TREE

Since 1966, I knew the Gbano tree was an important landmark in Sanniquellie. It stood at a strategic location, where the footpath from the elegant marble public market intersected with the street that merged into the road to the village. On Saturdays, marketers from nearby villages and beyond, walked by the tree to the public market, stepping repeatedly over its exposed roots. Under its shady canopy, other marketers sold produce of all kinds. In addition, men of means from Sanniquellie and others from elsewhere talked local politics as well as bread and butter issues over gourds of palm wine. Students from surrounding villages and towns often waited there for their parents, too, to get some food or pocket change. Still further, others met their sweethearts by happenstance while wayward children cracked the tree's seeds for nuts to relieve hunger.

As locations under large trees, by rivers, or at the feet of mountains are often "Sites of offerings" in the culture, perhaps because they are regarded as the earth maker's ears, the Gbano tree was an observer and a witness. Those who walked by, stood, or sat under the tree's extended canopy unwittingly traded carbon dioxide for oxygen. Moreover, through their complaints about raw deals, joys about great sales, gossips, or conversations about their worries, hopes and joys, they unknowingly invited the Gbano tree. Simply put, the Gbano tree recorded a piece of everyone's story. Until a bulldozer mowed it down in preparation for Liberia's 163rd Independence Day celebrations in 2010, the Gbano tree told stories. Today, the Gbano tree does not exist anymore, but I knew its value because it was a witness to an important part of my story. They say old habits die hard. A spot across the street from where the Gbano tree once stood is now where traders sell the best palm wine in Sanniquellie.

The Gbano tree looms large in my memory because of the events of the Sunday Mom and Dad left me in Sanniquellie in 1966. Indeed, the Gbano tree was a witness to an important drama in my life. It was Sunday. No one was sitting under the Gbano tree, waiting, selling, or buying produce, selling or buying palm wine. The tree could not have missed the drama unfolding merely fifteen yards away when Mom said to the Guahs, "You have come far enough; stop here and return home." The Guahs stopped and said their goodbyes to my parents. At that moment, I was standing with Dad's bag on my head, oblivious to what was about to happen. Suddenly, all eyes turned to me as if they and I had agreed that I would do something upon reaching that location. "Give me my bag and return with the Guahs," Dad said to me. I refused. Instead, I told Dad the bag was my load and that I was going back with them to the village.

The Guahs tried gently to assure me that all would be well. "There are other children at home to play with you," the Guahs said. But that went into one ear and came out of the other. Instead, I clung onto Dad's bag and insisted that I was not staying. As Dad tried to force the bag out of my hands, I turned around and clung onto Mom in such a way that she was not able to walk. At that point, Kou Lehyeay had already given the tub to her. Mom had to hold the tub with one hand as she tried to get me off with the other hand. Finally, the Guahs helped get me off Mom and held onto me securely to prevent me from running away to join my parents. As they walked away with their backs turned to me, Mom did not look back for a last glance at me. I did not know what was going through her mind as she was leaving behind her only "button on Joe's coat." Exhausted from my struggle to release myself to follow my parents, I gave up and followed the Guahs reluctantly. I wept until we reached the home of the Guahs.

Later, I stopped crying, but I remained sad during the entire afternoon. The Guahs tried fruitlessly to comfort me. I was completely in another world, imagining myself along the road to the village. I was visualizing where, along the road, Mom and Dad were at on their way back home. I wished I were with them, seeing, smelling, and feeling familiar surroundings. Imagining the smell of new rice; especially new rice cooked with bitter balls (miniature eggplants) and okra with a mixture of ground chicken soup and sesame seed doused with freshly processed palm oil was irresistible. "How dare Mom and Dad!" "Why did they have to rip me away from the 'Garden of Eden' to bring me to a place where I was not sure about having enough to eat?" I muttered to myself.

I wondered about hunger. I wondered whether Sanniquellie would be like my older sister, Kou Sennie (deceased), described it. Whenever I refused to go on an errand for her, she frightened me with horror stories about hunger in Sanniquellie. "Okay, you do not want to go where I sent you, just wait until you go to Sanniquellie where you will be sent to go to school. "Lorh lehlo ee zokoboho" (hunger will scrape your stomach). As my mind rattled with thoughts of things, real or imagined, I could not help but wish I were in the village, where hunger did not have power.

Besides fear of not having enough food to eat in Sanniquellie, I wanted to return to the village because it seemed the vegetation, waters and air reflected Mom's personality—her loving heart, compassion and calming voice. The village had an indescribable and idyllic ambiance. The perpetually lush green landscape at the outskirt was breathtaking. A walk in the surrounding woods begged for standing still, closing the eyes and taking deep breaths because the air was filled with sweet scents of various blooming wildflowers. In addition, soothing murmurings of meandering streams flowing along changing gradients calmed the nerves. At night, choruses of night creatures added to comfort and reassurance. With Mom's presence, the village was like a giant magnet.

The village was a place of abundance. I could stand in the open village center and see grapefruits, mango, and orange trees at the perimeter. Other fruit trees merely a stone throw away included guava, tangerine and paw-paw (papaya). As mangoes of different varieties weighed on their branches to breaking points, oranges interspersed lush green leaves like ornaments on Christmas trees. I could see towering plantain and banana trees in the groves behind the houses too. Their broad green leaves swayed peacefully in the breeze, apparently signaling the stress-free life in the village. Crops included rice, cassava, and eddoes (taro roots). Other crops consisted of sweet potatoes, corn and so on. With that kind of environment, when Mom and Dad were talking about staying in Sanniquellie with the Guahs to go to school, my reaction was "School? What school?" I was not ready for school. I was not ready to separate from the village—the "Garden of Eden."

CHAPTER 6

St. Mary's School

DAYS AFTER MY PARENTS RETURNED to the village, Mr. David Guah took me to St. Mary's Catholic School to register. The registration fee in 1966 was fifty cents while the yearly tuition was three United States dollars. My parents gave the money, which covered registration, uniforms and first semester tuition, to Mr. Guah before they returned home. Following registration, we walked over to the uniform store, where I tried on shirts and shorts to select the right sizes for me. The uniform consisted of a pair of pine green shorts and a white short-sleeved shirt. The shorts had two rear pockets, two side pockets and belt straps. On the other hand, the shirt had a left breasted pocket, horizontally laced with pine green. In addition, the shirt had a pine green collar while the sleeves were laced at the edges with pine green as well. The uniform became an important part of my identity.

Taken by the campus, I looked around, beginning with the east-west oriented humongous red brick structure, which housed the church and the kindergarten. The building, a gable roof design with corrugated zinc roof, sat at the peak of the hill, overlooking St. Mary's Elementary, Lake Teeleh and a partial view of Sanniquellie. The Monrovia-Yekepa highway, only a few yards away to the east, separated the building and the nuns' residence. Across the highway, large orange and grapefruit trees, which partially surrounded a soccer field at the front of the nun's residence, reminded me of the village. Farther downhill towards the city, a few large mango trees and other native tree species lined the highway on one side, next to the large elementary school courtyard. Still further, sandwiched between the highway and the Buchanan-Yekepa railroad were the nuns' residence, boys' dormitory and the clinic. A forested area behind the boys' dormitory prevented a clear view of the railroad as well as the airstrip. The Gbemies, with several children, including John and Catherine, lived behind the elementary school. They were important because Mr. Michael Gbemie was one of the kindergarten teachers. Mrs. Gbemie, a tall, stout and imposing woman, on the other hand, was the cook. She prepared Care Food for the students.

CHAPTER 7

Challenges

ONCE SCHOOL STARTED, THE DREAD of not having enough food to eat became a reality. The reason was pure and simple: the Guah household consisted of a multitude. The Guah family alone, including the adults and children numbered ten. That number rose to eleven when I joined. Not too long after I arrived, two of my cousins, Patrick Mantor Mahnwon and Joseph Mark Tokpah (deceased) joined and increased the number to thirteen. Finally, three other children from other relatives of the Guahs joined and the number of people in that single household rose to sixteen.

During my first few days with the Guahs, there was enough food in the house because my parents and other children's parents brought food along when they came to turn us over to the Guahs. Despite all that food in the beginning, I was jittery because I had to eat with the older boys. Every time Mahnmein placed a pan of rice before us, jungle law ensued; everyone fought for himself. Some of the older boys were adept at eating hot foods while others swallowed food without much chewing. Spoons were available, but we always ate with our hands, which we seldom washed. For obvious reasons, everyone preferred going "Natural," using the hand, the spoon Wlah provided. It could amass more rice in one handful than a spoon could. I learned to eat fast and to grab as much as I could whenever a fight over food arose. In a very short time, actual as well as imagined fights over food caused me to develop a unique mindset. No matter how much rice was in a pan for us, I always knew there would not be enough food to eat. I always walked away from eating with a level of hunger. After the first few weeks, it became clear to me that hunger would be a defining feature of this journey.

ZEHYEE MAHNMEIN

Zehyee Mahnmein was Mr. David Guah's younger wife. She had big bright eyes that blinked rapidly. The fair-skinned woman had a high-pitched voice, stuttered slightly, and radiated with love and compassion. She was intense and beautiful. Mahnmein was a difference maker. She understood my plight and those of other children in a household where a three-score meal was unheard of. On numerous nights, Mahnmein was the reason why I did not go to bed hungry.

We ate "Konoh" once a day with no regularity, although the Mahns typically eat at least twice a day, one during midday and the other in the evening.[57] We ate what was available whenever it was available. Sometimes we ate late mornings and, at other times, late afternoons, but mostly late evenings. Mahnmein was no Jesus to feed the multitude with five loaves of bread and two fish, but in the Guah household, she fed the multitude with two and sometimes three "Kainkains" of rice.[58] She did the impossible and, on numerous occasions, I detected the weight of that expectation in her face. Her big bright eyes seemed awash with tears, presumably from the pain of watching over hungry children; they rolled from left to right interrupted by her rapidly blinking eyelids.

Zehyee Mahnmein often sent me to the public market to buy two and sometimes three kainkains of rice depending on how much money Mr. Guah gave her. Depending on whether it was rainy season or harvest time, the cost of a kainkain of rice ranged from twenty-five cents to fifty cents. Along with rice, I often bought other ingredients such as bouillon cube, okra and palm oil. Other ingredients included bony fish and bitter balls. I also bought either charcoal or wood for making fire to cook.

Mahnmein often started cooking by splitting larger pieces of wood into smaller ones to get the fire started as quickly as possible. Sometimes the wood burned out completely before she finished cooking, prompting her to use pieces of cardboard boxes from a nearby landfill to make fire. Because Mahnmein cared deeply and watched over other people's children with compassion, I hung around the kitchen and helped cook. She had a presence, and it was satisfying. I was always willing to fly like a bullet to go on an errand for her. Sometimes I cleaned fish, removed their gills and threw them to stray cats. I cut off tail sections, doused them with salt and pepper and roasted them.

Mahnmein had a policy, which was whoever washed the dishes got the rice crust. In a household of sixteen people, having the crust to oneself was like winning the gold medal. When Mahnmein finished cooking, she often put the boys' food together in a large pan. In no time, they finished their food. On days Mahnmein gave me the crust, the other boys asked for some of it because they did not have enough food to eat. I shared a little bit of my crust with them, but I made sure I had enough to eat. On occasions I did not win the "gold," I thought about the dearth of food and how it would not fill my stomach. Mahnmein knew that the food would not be enough for all of us, but I do not know the thought that went through her mind as day-in-and-day-out there was never enough food for us.

Thoughts of Mahnmein, not to mention my experience in the Guah household, are always with me. Since the early 1990s, retuning to Liberia and seeing her alive was a dream. I sent her a message along with a gift by Mr. Patrick Mantor in the early 1990s, but that was not enough. I looked forward to seeing her face-to-face because I wanted to show my appreciation for her role in my development. Upon his return to the United States, Patrick told me Mahnmein shed tears of joy when she received my message and gift. I wanted to make reaching out to Mahnmein at least a once-a-year habit. Sadly, Mr. Garrison Kerwillain, a high school classmate, who promised to be our link turned out to be a bearer of bad news. Both Garrison and Mahnmein were from Sehyeekainpa, Nimba County. Not long after Garrison assured me during a telephone conversation that he would take messages to Mahnmein for me, he emailed me that she had passed away. He said she had traveled to visit with a relative in the Yekepa area, where she contracted cholera and died. I was shocked and speechless. I did not get a chance to see Zehyee Mahnmein again. In 2006, I paid tribute to her in the acknowledgement of my Ph.D. dissertation.

MANDINGOES IN SANNIQUELLIE

Here is a context for my experience with Mandingoes in Sanniquellie. I provide this background for two reasons. The first is for the purpose of this book, to lift those who lifted me. In each of us, there is more than a consciousness of the other. In me, there is more Mandingo than my awareness that Mandingoes are human beings. In Sanniquellie, Mandingoes contributed to my need for food and thus to the man that I have become. Second, prior to the Liberian civil war, other ethnic groups in Liberia perceived Mandingoes' place in Liberia as questionable. They referred to Mandingoes as foreigners. Consequently, Mandingoes were discriminated against. The perception that Mandingoes are foreigners continues even to this day, contrary to the Liberian law that identified Mandingoes in specific geographic areas and recognized them as one of the tribes of Liberia. Unfortunately, following the civil war, conflicts related to Mandingoes' place occurring in certain parts of Liberia remain intractable.

In paying tribute to Mandingoes who helped me in Sanniquellie, I tell a story of lived experience but with utmost sensitivity. My story is not a justification of the discrimination Mandingoes faced in Liberia prior to the civil war or any intent to discriminate against them in the future. Moreover, the story I tell happened in the context of a larger Liberian society on a continuum, ranging from utopia on the one end to dystopia at the other. In my mind, tone deafness, paucity of wise leadership and a few ethnocentric demagogues facilitated Liberia's precipitous movement toward dystopia on that continuum. In quietude from afar, I see and feel a hurting country and hope that all Liberians can affix their hands on the deck and engage in genuine dialogues for healing.

Mandingoes are one of the ethnic groups of Liberia. Mandingoes in Liberia fall into two categories. The first category of Mandingoes includes those who have ancestral lands in Liberia that have been passed down from one generation to another. In addition, their villages, towns and landmarks such as rivers and mountains have given names in their language that carry meanings in their culture. The second category of Mandingoes includes those who came mostly from Guinea but also from the Ivory Coast and other places. They came mainly for economic reasons and settled in counties in Liberia including Nimba County and made them their homes.

Unlike the United States where being an American is not fundamentally tied to tribe, religion, or blood, but to one's belief in an idea, Liberia is different. Being a citizen of Liberia is more than birth or naturalizing and acquiring a legal status. So, when a Liberian meets another Liberian, the question, "Where are you from?" a code for the "tribal language you speak," is implicit and expected. Based on the response to that question, someone can tell one's tribal language and ancestral land. Cultural attachment to the land, one's ancestral land, although not a legal requirement, is an added dimension of citizenship in Liberia.

The distinction between these two categories of Mandingoes does not justify those who blanket all Mandingoes as Guineans. Instead, it sheds light on longstanding prejudice and discrimination against Mandingoes in Liberia. In my story, I reflect on three interconnected possible sources of discrimination against Mandingoes in Liberia including social, economic, and political. In Sanniquellie, socially, Mandingoes were a part of an organized religion almost as a group. Most Mandingoes in Sanniquellie were Muslims. Unlike Mandingoes, Mahns in Sanniquellie or elsewhere did not belong to an organized religion as a group. Instead, they belonged to various Christian church denominations such as Catholic, Methodist, Baptist, Seventh Day Adventist, Pentecostal, and Inland.

Mahns in Sanniquellie perceived "Kafir" as directed at them and other non-Muslims, even though, in exchanges during conflicts, Mandingoes often used the term to refer to other Mandingoes.[59] Mandingo parents saw their daughters' involvement with non-Muslims, Mahn boys or men, as defilement. Therefore, they forbade their daughters from engaging in such relationships. Daughters who disobeyed their parents were ostracized. Similar rules about whom to date or not to date, however, did not exist among Mahns or Dans (the other major ethnic group in Sanniquellie). Mandingo boys or men dated Mahn or Dan girls or women. Moreover, adult married Mandingo men often used their economic prowess to woo young Mahn or Dan women. A low-level undercurrent existed, which was a kernel of tinder for future conflict, but no organized campaign of hatred or violence against one group by another existed to my knowledge. Mahns and Mandingoes lived together in Sanniquellie in relative peace.

Economically, Mandingoes in Sanniquellie, from the time I started school in 1966 until I graduated in 1977, were major players in the local Sanniquellie economy, second only to the Lebanese. Based on personal observations, I was aware that Mahns in Sanniquellie regarded Mandingoes in Sanniquellie as incomers, mainly from Guinea. Thus, they viewed

Mandingoes' domination of the local Sanniquellie economy with some trepidation, if not outright petty jealousy. Mandingoes' social isolation due to religion, as well as parents forbidding their daughters from dating Mahn boys or men, or Kafirs, did not help that sentiment.

Mandingo men owned and operated diamond mines in villages and towns away from Sanniquellie. Others were brokers, who bought and sold diamonds. Mandingo men also owned and operated taxis, trucks, and convenience stores. They owned and operated other businesses such as tailor shops, automotive repair shops, gas stations, and blacksmith facilities. Mandingo women, on the other hand, were not outdone by their men. At the time, both men and women were mostly unlettered people, but they understood the laws of supply and demand. Mandingo women possessed the most business acumen. In addition, they looked long-term; they engaged Mahns in Sanniquellie and surrounding villages and developed long-term relationships. Some learned the Mahn language. The expression "Zahnmie," a Mahn expression, means a person from Zahn, a Mahn town in Nimba County, Liberia. However, over time, the expression has come to mean a businessperson's trusted and long-term customer. The exact origin of the expression is not clear, but it is widely believed in Nimba County that it originated out of the interactions of Mahn and Mandingo peoples.

Based on the "Zahnmie" relationship, Mandingo women traded with Mahns who brought their produce to the market in Sanniquellie on Saturdays. They bought vegetables of all kinds wholesale and sold them retail at the public market during weekdays. Moreover, during and after harvest in November and December, Mandingo women bought rice and palm oil and stockpiled them to be resold during the rainy season when food was scarce. Mandingo women also traveled to faraway places such as Ganta and Monrovia, where they bought clothes, cooking utensils, and other household items wholesale and sold them retail in Sanniquellie. Mandingo women not only owned and operated restaurants, but they were also as industrious as their men. They used some of the palm oil to manufacture soap.

Politically, long before the civil war, it seemed Mandingoes' industrious-ness as well as business acumen was a blessing and a curse simultaneously, as long as the perception that they were foreigners lived on. The erstwhile America-Liberian oligarchy, forever wary of internal threat to its existence, on the one hand, perhaps recognized Mandingoes' critical role in the vibrancy of the national economy. On the other hand, however, because economic wherewithal also has power implications, the oligarchy ignored Mandingoes' legal status; it let the perception that Mandingoes were foreigners hang over their heads. As long as Mandingoes' role in the economy helped strengthen the oligarchy, it favored their active participation, although they were next to the Lebanese in that preferment.[60]

Mandingoes had more leverage participating in the national economy than other Liberians had. Like the Lebanese, they were reaping economic benefits for being the "other," that is, "non-citizens." Their economic successes were circumscribed, meaning, like the Lebanese, they could amass any level of wealth as long as they did not venture into politics, or use their economic power to threaten the status quo. Like the Lebanese, Mandingoes risked expulsion and property forfeiture if they dabbled into Liberian politics. In that way, the oligarchy maintained its stranglehold on political power because Mandingoes and Lebanese posed no existential threat.

Before President Samuel K. Doe publicly declared Mandingoes as citizens of Liberia at the Monrovia City Hall in 1990, the silence of national leadership during previous administrations on the status of Mandingoes in Liberia raises a question: could successful Mandingo merchants have unknowingly helped keep alive the perception that Mandingoes were foreigners?

The scheme, meaning favoring a group considered to be the "other" with economic benefits while threatening expulsion and forfeiture of properties if that group crosses a certain line, remains a staple of successive Liberian administrations. It explains one reason why Liberia's economic development proceeds at a snail's pace. Before the civil war, however, because this political scheme operated behind the scenes at the upper echelon of power that ordinary Liberians were not privy to, it probably indirectly and partially had a sway on other ethnic groups in creating the widespread perception that Mandingoes were foreigners.

Mandingoes are the only ethnic group in Liberia that the rest of the population regarded as the "other," especially before the civil war.[61] In the past, it did not matter whether a Mandingo had an ancestral land in Liberia, came from Guinea or the Ivory Coast, he was regarded as a Guinean. A Mahn from Guinea could cross the St. John River, Liberia's border with Guinea in Nimba County, and settle in Sanniquellie without fear of harassment from immigration. He could travel to Monrovia and back without facing questions from immigration officers at checkpoints along the way. Similarly, a Krahn from the Ivory Coast could cross into Liberia and settle in Zwedru, Grand Gedeh County, without fear of immigration.[62] He could travel to Monrovia and back without questioning by immigration officers. However, if a Mandingo crossed the St. John River and settled in Sanniquellie, he would face questions from immigration. If he traveled to Monrovia and back, nine chances out of ten, he would be singled out and questioned for immigration papers.

MANDINGO LEFTOVERS

Many Mandingo families lived in our section of Sanniquellie. These Mandingo families were of varied means. Some were wealthy while others were of modest means by Liberian standards. As their involvement in the local Sanniquellie economy demonstrated, they were hardworking people. Foday Toure, the patriarch of the Foday Toure clan, for example, was a very wealthy diamond broker. Most Mandingo families in our area of the city rented from Mahn property owners including Mr. David Guah. Depending on the size of their family, they rented one, two, three rooms or even a whole house. It was common to have more than one family in the same house. They lived modestly. Some saved their incomes to start businesses or to carry on other projects in Guinea.

Mahns and Mandingoes had a common staple, which was rice, although Mandingoes prepared theirs in a different way. Mandingo "kini" (cooked rice) was very soft. Mandingoes ate "soleegbeh," a breakfast made of softly cooked rice with added sugar and milk. Mandingoes savored "morneen," a breakfast prepared from rice pellets with added sugar and lime. In addition, they ate "locoo" (plantain) and "namusan" (banana), which they purchased from Mahns from surrounding villages and towns on Saturdays. Mandingoes seemed to enjoy peanut butter stew and dry okra powder soup prepared along with rice.

Mandingoes in our community in Sanniquellie usually prepared more food than they needed, resulting in leftovers. Like Mahns, Mandingoes ate in groups and with their hands. Men ate together while women ate together. Sometimes they ate only a quarter, half, or three quarters of their food, often served in large bowls. Their leftovers often had visible finger marks made with drenching stew all over in the bowls. At other times, there were no signs that someone touched the food. Mandingoes did not need rocket science to figure out that the sixteen mouths to feed in the Guah household almost never had enough to eat. Instead of throwing their leftovers away, Mandingoes often gave them to the Guah household. Often some of the leftovers were not fit to eat, but the only option was to go to bed hungry. Sometimes the leftovers were the only meals we had.

Foday Toure was a tall, handsome, and imposing man. I always found him quiet and pensive. He leased one of Mr. Guah's three houses for his large family. He and his family were aware of the size of our household. They gave us their leftovers and treated us kindly. They never looked down upon us because we ate their leftovers. Afterwards, Mr. Toure acquired an old store near the main parking station in Sanniquellie, renovated it for residential purposes and relocated his family. At his new residence, we used to peep through glass windows for a glimpse of his black-and-white television in the living room. He had a taste for American luxury items. He owned different brands of vehicles, one of which was a Chevrolet Caprice Classic.

Unlike the Foday Toure family, not all Mandingoes who lived in our community and gave us their leftovers were always kind. Sometimes it seemed they gave us their leftovers only to use the good will to humiliate us at another time. Because we ate their leftovers, some Mandingoes did not think highly of us, not to mention the usual reference to us as "Kafir" whenever there was a fuss over anything else. They never hesitated to humiliate us by pointing to the fact that we ate their leftovers. Despite trivial teenage conflicts, Mandingo leftovers were a lifesaver. They made a difference. Now, looking back, I remember the Mandingoes whose hands contributed to my becoming a man with fond memories. I hope to see some of them alive to show the work of their hands and tell them about Wlah's grace.

BAH PLEASE GIVE ME

Not knowing where my next meal would come from was a constant and nagging burden, particularly while I was in elementary school. Other children in the Guah household and I as well as friends in school who faced similar circumstances survived in imaginative ways. At school, we looked forward to recess with much anticipation. Our six-period school day consisted of periods one, two and three, recess and periods four, five and six. Each period lasted 45 minutes except for recess, which lasted 30 minutes. School started at 7:30 a.m. and ended at 1:20 p.m. Recess was more than a time to run around and play. It was a time to come out and find something to eat.

Shortly before recess, petty traders from Sanniquellie sat side-by-side on the eastside of the elementary school courtyard, next to the highway with various food items to sell to students. Donuts, shaped like figure eight, cost two cents, rice bread was five cents while "kala," a Liberian hush puppy, was one cent. Rectangular box-shaped iced Kool Aid cost two cents while roasted peanuts, sold in bottle lids, cost one or two cents, depending on the size of the lid. Corn bread cost five cents while the cost of oranges and bananas ranged from two cents to five cents. Students whose parents were relatively well-off brought money to school almost every day and bought donuts, peanuts, Kool Aid, or anything they wanted to eat during recess. However, those of us who did not have the means to buy these food items during recess everyday turned to begging our friends for food. Sometimes friends were kind, but, at other times, they looked us right in the eyes and said no.

With the right hand stretched to those who had, the language of begging was "Bah give me." "Bah" was neither Mahn nor anything I knew, but we understood it to mean "my friend." When I carried money to school, which happened following weekends with my parents in the village, I had to repay friends who gave me food. When they stretched their hands and asked, "Bah give me," I had no choice but to share. Those who said no to me in the past when I asked also got a no answer, with a reminder of what they did.

Care Food

Care Food also helped me survive Sanniquellie hunger. I ate Care Food at St. Mary's School beginning grade one during second semester 1966 until the first day of school in grade seven in March 1972. I distinctly remember a handshake logo along with United States of America in bold letters printed in red and blue on bags containing the supplies. The logo suggested the Care Food Program originated in the United States.

Mrs. Gbemie, who lived about two hundred yards away from the elementary school, was the cook. The Care Food menu consisted of cornmeal with added milk obtained from dissolving KLIM, a brand of powder milk, in water; oatmeal with the same kind of milk; buckwheat prepared with cassava leaves, vegetable oil and stock fish; beans; and bread, basically a monster hush puppy about four to five inches in diameter. Each day of the school week had a specific menu item.

We were not even age in elementary school. Ages ranged from actual elementary school age to students who were supposed to be in or out of high school. Mr. Patrick Bamakpa, our elementary school principal, always had extra non-academic assignments for older and stronger male students. Transferring cooked Care Food from the Gbemies' residence to the elementary school was one of such assignments. Shortly before recess, selected older and stronger male students carried the food in large pots, pans, or buckets from the Gbemies' residence to the elementary school, where teachers supervised the distribution.

Each student was responsible for bringing his own bowl or plate along with a spoon from home for the food. Bowls or plates were not necessary on days bread was served. We formed queues towards the distribution point, but the queues moved haphazardly because some bigger and stronger male students often tried to cut the line. Fights were a commonplace because of repeated attempts to cut the line. Sometimes pushing and shoving continued until students overpowered distributers, as supervising teachers stood helpless. In those situations, bigger and stronger boys always got the most food. I often came away with absolutely nothing except with my shirt and pants looking as if I emerged from a pot of oil. After fights for food on days cornmeal was on the menu, I often looked like someone with a badly done make-up job with a mixture of cornmeal and milk.

I did not always come away from the fights for food empty-handed. There were days that smaller and faster kids got the upper hand. On one such occasion, I recall the principal forgot to assign older students to carry the food from the Gbemies' residence to the elementary school. "Bread" was the menu for that day. As soon as the recess bell rang, a few of us ran outside to the distribution point, hoping to be the first in line, but there was no food available. Instinctively, we ran straight to the Gbemies' residence, thinking that Mrs. Gbemie was still cooking due to some delay. Upon arrival, we saw buckets of "bread" lined up with no explanation why they had not been delivered to the elementary school.

The sight of those buckets of "bread" felt like winning the lottery. A friend and I took a bucket away and ran towards the kindergarten building. As we turned around to assess the situation, we felt like thieves running away from the law. In no time, a multitude of students descended upon us.

One person could only get away with so much of the bread. Each bread was like a big ball with a diameter of four to five inches, if not more. It was too large to force more than two or three into one's pocket. So, we took as many as we could and ran. I recall having about six of those suckers in my arms as I ran. We ate and then hid the remaining ones in the grass to get them later to take them home after school.

Care Food was a big blessing. We ate it at school. After school and sometimes over the weekend, we went to Father Michael Francis to ask for cornmeal, beans, buckwheat and cooking oil to take home to prepare food for ourselves.[63] On some days he gave us liberally. At other times, he drove us away when we became a pest. I was one of those students who looked forward to Care Food at school every day. Sadly, St. Mary's School discontinued the program not because of lack of need but because of peer pressure.

As a seventh grader in 1972, I looked forward with excitement to the start of school. Part of my excitement pertained to my expectation that the Care Food program, which supplemented my protein and other nutritional intake, would continue. On that first day of school, I looked forward to eating Care Food during recess. Shortly before the recess bell rang, Brother Joseph Kavaliers, the acting principal, came to our classroom and announced that Mrs. Gbemie had prepared Care Food and delivered it in large containers. He pointed towards the direction of the library, where the food had been placed, no more than ten yards from our classroom doorway.

I was ecstatic when Brother Joseph made the announcement. I could not wait for the recess bell to dash out to eat. As soon as Brother Joseph walked away, something happened that I have never forgotten since 1972. Magdalene Brewer, one of the prettiest girls in the class as well as in the school, made a face, describing the food as awful and unfit for her consumption.[64] Because none of the other girls spoke up with a contrary opinion of the food or showed interest in eating the food, it was as if she spoke for all of them. Magdalene, at that moment, drew an imaginary line in the sand that determined who was worthy and who was not. Following Ms. Brewer's disapproving face and comments about the food, a deafening silence fell upon the class, suggesting everyone understood that crossing that line meant that one would be looked down upon as undignified. No one crossed the line. No one had the courage to step out to eat the food. The peer pressure was not only from Magdalene Brewer and the other girls who agreed with her opinion of the food with their silence but also from all the boys in the class. Everyone in the class recognized the imaginary line and understood what it signified.

I was hungry. Moreover, I did not have any money to buy something to eat at school. In Sanniquellie, Care Food was a lifeline for me. However, for fear of ridicule, no one went out to eat the food on that first day of school. Consequently, Brother Joseph decided to discontinue preparing the food for the entire student body, after he found out that no one ate the food on that day. He did not ask anyone what happened, and it never occurred to me to tell him what happened in class immediately when he left. That was the end of Care Food, as I knew it at St. Mary's School. Peer pressure is real, and it is powerful.

Today, Atlanta-based CARE International runs the Care Food Program. Those who worked for CARE International in the 1960s and in the early 1970s need to take comfort in knowing that they made a difference. Similarly, those who supported the organization's programs in Liberia need to know that they made the world a better place. I was one of those young people who left their parents to go to faraway places like Sanniquellie to get an education. I am not only immensely grateful for the Care Food Program, but also, I am a living witness that school feeding programs work.

GRAPEFRUITS

St. Mary's founders planted fruit trees, including grapefruits and oranges, partially covering the perimeter of the soccer field at the front of the nun's residence. At some point, someone, perhaps a worker, may have harvested the fruit trees for the nuns' consumption. Nevertheless, throughout my time at the school, I do not remember seeing any nuns harvesting the fruit trees. The nuns' seeming lack of enthusiasm for harvesting the fruit trees over the years led me to wonder why the fruit trees were planted.

There were no posted "Off-limits" signs, but by word of mouth, nearly every student knew that the nuns forbade harvesting those fruit trees by any means. Minimizing littering may well have been a reason the nuns forbade harvesting the fruit trees. No matter why the fruit trees were planted; no matter why the nuns forbade harvesting them, the fruit trees were a "problem." Their presence set a stage for an imminent and unavoidable collision between doctrine and reality. The fruit trees were on the premises of a

Catholic institution, where in my catechism classes, "Thou shalt not steal," was an edict. The fruit trees were a temptation.

That showdown occurred one morning in 1967 when Cousin Patrick Mantor Mahnwon and I were on our way to the Guahs' farm, something we did every morning during the week. Essentially, Patrick and I succumbed to temptation, but he escaped, and I was caught in the dragnet. At the time of the incident, both of us attended afternoon school. Every weekday, we left Sanniquellie in the morning, walked the nearly three-mile distance to help on the farm and returned by midday. Afternoon school started at 1:30 p.m.

On our way back to Sanniquellie, we often carried bunches of wood on our heads. We sold the wood to buy soap to wash our clothes. At other times, we sold the wood to buy kerosene for the lantern to study. Sanniquellie had electricity, but Mr. Guah's house number three, a humongous ten-bed room structure, across the swamp from the Bailey Family residence, did not have electricity. On days we did not want to stay indoors to study on lanterns or candles, we walked several yards away to study under extremely bright streetlamps at an AGIP gas station across the street from the public market. Bugs of all kinds, including giant beetles flew right into the bright streetlamps and fell right below. They were a major inconvenience while studying under the streetlamps. At other times, we used proceeds from the sale of the wood to buy palm oil, fish, or bouillon cubes to cook dry rice.

On the day of the grapefruit incident, we walked past the elementary school on our way to the farm when morning classes had already begun. The upper classes at the time, grades seven and eight, used the elementary school in the morning because the current high school had not been constructed. As we went by the elementary school, the seventh-grade classroom windows were wide open. Anyone sitting in that classroom could turn around and see passing traffic on the Sanniquellie-Yekepa highway and pedestrians go right by. Moreover, one could see any activity going on further up the hill around the fruit trees.

As we walked past the elementary school, Father Michael Francis was teaching the seventh-grade class. Apparently, he had a gut feeling that we would find it difficult to resist those bright yellow grapefruits uphill. He suspected we might stop and pick some grapefruits on our way. To Father Francis, we perfectly fitted profiles of kids who devoured the fruit trees and littered the campus as well. He was dead right. As soon as we reached up the hill, Cousin Patrick asked me to do what I was already thinking.

Due to food insufficiency in the Guah household, I always looked for an opportunity to put something into my stomach. I was excited to eat some of those grapefruits on my way to the farm. Besides filling my stomach, I was also excited about showing Patrick my climbing prowess.

I knew the nuns forbade harvesting the fruit trees. However, Patrick assured me he would be on the lookout for anyone coming after us. Moreover, I felt invincible and confident that I could hit the ground and run if the nuns sent someone to apprehend me. Nevertheless, I was not fully aware of the forces at play that led me into the trap. I was in an internal crossfire, caught in the middle, so to speak. "Ringing" in my ears, on the one hand, was the commandment, "Thou shalt not steal." On the other hand, my stomach, desirous of something, urged me to act. Moreover, the irresistible bright yellow grapefruits that sprinkled the lush green canopies of those fruit trees beaconed me to feast.

In no time, I was up in one of the grapefruit trees. As I picked the fruits and threw them down to Patrick, he stacked them together. During that time, Father Francis was watching and timing us. He wanted to make sure that either one or both of us were up in the fruit trees. As soon as he realized that someone was up in one of the fruit trees, he sent some students to apprehend us. I did not check with Patrick to find out whether someone was coming to get us because I was too busy picking the grapefruits and worrying about not slipping and falling. I relied completely on Patrick to be on the lookout, but by the time he realized that people were coming for us, it was too late. He left me up in the tree and fled on the way to the farm.

Unfortunately, as I climbed down, there was no way to escape. The students who were in pursuit of us were waiting for me to touch the ground. As soon as that happened, they held me by both arms and took me to Father Michael Francis. I was certain of what would happen to me. I knew Father Francis would give me a whipping. Upon arrival in the seventh-grade classroom, there was no surprise. He held me with one hand and used a rattan switch to whip me right before the class for stealing grapefruits. He was so fast and brutal that I could not keep a count of the number of lashes he gave me. I cried loudly.

At the time of that incident, Father Francis was doing an activity with his class that involved tape recording. As the students brought me in, he apparently forgot to stop the tape. The tape rolled on and recorded everything including my loud wailing. The students too did not know that the tape continued to record my ordeal. When Father Francis played the tape, on the following day, everyone heard me crying and the entire class had a good laugh. Incidentally, Joseph Saye Guah, Mr. David Guah's first son, was a student in that seventh-grade class. I did not want anyone in the Guah household to know about what happened, but Saye Guah told the story about the whipping Father Francis gave me. My misfortune did not end with Saye Guah's revelation. I received a serious verbal reprimand from Mr. David Guah as well. Thereafter, the boys at home, including Patrick, who should have been ashamed of leaving me in trouble and running away, had a field day ridiculing me.

In addition to serving as parish priest, Father Francis taught classes including catechism at the school. He had a reputation of an old fashion and stern disciplinarian. He did not spare the rod! I did not hold any ill feeling against Father Francis for the whipping I received for stealing grapefruits. I had a real and immediate need to put food into my stomach because of the uncertainty of my next meal. However, I also knew that I was violating one of the Ten Commandments Father Francis taught me. Years later, I came to understand Father Francis did not intend the "rattan switch message" for me alone. Perhaps he wanted the seventh graders to know that "Thou shalt not steal" had a penalty associated with it. He could not teach a lesson on "Thou shalt not steal" and look the other way as I brazenly violated the commandment in the presence of young people.

I accepted the consequence of my action. I did not try to lay the blame on anybody else. However, years later in the United States when racial profiling became a hot-button issue, the irony of the grapefruit incident could not escape me. I framed the incident as the profiling of students from villages and towns up to or more than seventy-five miles away in search of an education. In other words, the profiling of hunger-affected students in Sanniquellie, a hard place dubbed "students' backbreaker" because of the scarcity of food. I wanted to add a lighter note to an otherwise grave matter by letting victims of racial profiling know that a Catholic priest, not a police officer, profiled a hunger-affected kid in Sanniquellie in 1967. The only probable cause was that the kid was walking along the Sanniquellie-Yekepa highway, looking up into fruit trees draped with bright yellow grapefruits. Racial profiling is a serious matter, and it is wrong. It has serious consequences for the affected people and our sense of ourselves as, "One Nation under God, indivisible, with liberty and justice for all."

WEEKENDS IN THE VILLAGE

I returned to the village occasionally for weekends on Fridays because I missed my parents, relatives, and the food. During my early years at St. Mary's, I could not travel to the village alone for fear of ghosts. Patrick Mantor Mahnwon always accompanied me. As I became older, I either made the trip alone or traveled along with other students who went to see their parents in towns beyond the village.

Upon arrival in the village, I often lost my appetite and was unable to eat anything. My big plans to grab and eat voraciously fell through. It felt like my body magically purged the hunger. Later, I came to understand what was happening to me as the effect of being with Mom and in the village. My appetite gradually returned, and, by the evening of the following day, I was fully into my old eating habits.

On Sundays, we needed to leave early to arrive in Sanniquellie before nightfall, but it was always hard to leave because of the village's strong attractions. We often ended up leaving the village at about 4:00 p.m. Prior to leaving, I ate heavily, thinking that my stomach could store food to last for about a week. Moreover, I wrapped additional food in heated banana leaf to eat before arriving in Sanniquellie. We carried an assortment of food items on our heads, endured the rough and tumble of the footpath and took our final break at Whenehyee, where the vehicle-accessible road ended. We loosened the banana leaf, ate the food and threw the leftover into the creek.

CHAPTER 8

Adaptation

BEFORE I STARTED SCHOOL, MOM and Dad told me to be strong, to stand up for myself. At school during recess, teachers were not required to supervise the students. After eating Care Food, we usually played out in the open courtyard, where fights were common. I had to learn to fight. If a fight took place at school between another child and me, I would not tell. No one would tell. What happened at school stayed at school. I quickly learned how to survive in my new environment. I fought back when someone picked on me.

Sanniquellie was a predominantly Mahn city, yet in our section of the city, I grew up with Mandingo children. We played soccer on makeshift playgrounds, where fistfights were common. Sometimes the fights were one-on-one between a Mandingo boy and me and, at other times, they were between Mahns and Mandingoes. I recall the unmerciful whipping Lyee gave me. That Mandingo boy was like a giant. He towered into the air, perhaps 6'5," and probably weighed over 250 pounds. I was a sixth grader. Lyee seemed to relish his size and height. Occasionally, he was on the lookout for Mahn boys he regarded as pompous. He wanted to show that he was tough. He beat me just for the sheer fun of it. There was no apparent reason. Overtime, I became better and better at those fights. I recall scaring other kids into running away to avoid fights. With that, I started to develop the mind of a tough guy too. I was confident that I could beat other kids in fights, and, on occasions, I became the instigator of fights as well.

Long before Lyee beat me, my confidence in winning fights motivated me to start trouble at school with a tall kid whose nose ran all the time. After a few days, the kid mustered the courage to push back. During recess on the day of the fight, I followed him in the open courtyard at the elementary school. Aside from fighting over Care Food, we had no swings or seesaws at school to keep us busy during recess. The occasional fights were our source of entertainment. Fight participants were gladiators in the arena, the human circles that quickly formed around them. In no time, a fight started between the boy and me. I distinctly recall the big circle of children around us. "Do it, do it, do it" they shouted and cheered on. We swung at each other, but my blows did not seem to reach the kid. Soon, I felt a slap across my face and a flash of light in my eyes. The kid struck me numerous times without any significant response. We grabbed onto each other and wrestled to the ground, where he sat over me and punched repeatedly. I fought back and turned him over to the ground. However, as soon as I started punching him back, Teacher Ken, a white Peace Corps Volunteer, grabbed my right hand from the back and prevented me from hitting the kid while he was on the ground.

I was pissed off. In my rage over someone stopping me from hitting back in kind for the merciless blows I received, I shouted in Mahn asking who stopped me from hitting the boy whom I had knocked to the ground. Everyone around who was Mahn heard my words distinctly, which later became a source of constant jokes about me. I badly hated the jokes. Those words in Mahn were "Gbolor kpeh leh aye own koon gbolor beh lah bay?"[65] I did not intentionally direct my rage at Teacher Ken as we fondly called him. I did not know that he was the one who held me from hitting back. The nature of my language and because Teacher Ken was a white man made the entire incident hilarious. All the Mahn children understood how offensive the language was. They all knew that one sure way to start a fight was to refer to someone as gbolor, the opposite of which is "Quiah" (a circumcised person).

EVIL

In elementary school, spelling was a separate subject and a favorite of mine. Teacher Obongorloe, a Sierra Leonean and my first-grade teacher, taught morning as well as evening classes at St. Mary's School. I attended the evening session. Teacher Obongorloe assigned a list of spelling words that we had to study and know how to say and spell correctly. This was easy like eating cake because spelling was one of my favorite subjects. However, other students struggled with pronunciations and spellings. On the next day of class, we lined up and took turns to say and spell the words correctly. At other times, he gave spelling tests, where he said the words and we wrote them down in our copybooks. One day, Teacher Obongorloe asked us to line up. We lined up in front of the blackboard and faced the empty desks as instructed. Starting with the first student from one end of the line, he asked us to spell a given word. He continued one after the other. If one failed to spell a word correctly, it was the next person's turn. Whoever spelled the word correctly got out of the line, moved to the beginning, and gave everyone who failed to spell the word correctly five lashes each in the hand with a strong switch.

As a kid then, I saw Teacher Obongorloe's assignments as responsibilities we had to carry out. I did not think about parents who could not read or write and, therefore, could not help their children with spelling homework. If one did not do his assignment, Teacher Obongorloe interpreted it as laziness. Moreover, one had to turn around and show the buttocks or stretch the hand and open the palm for some lashes. There was no room for excuses! That was in 1966. Today, I am a teacher. I do not believe in or subscribe to that teaching strategy.

In 1966, I spent the first half of the year in kindergarten and moved on to grade one midyear. At the end of 1966, after one semester, I moved on to grade two with most of my classmates. Mr. Henry Gleekia was my second-grade teacher. He took up assignment at St. Mary's Elementary right after graduating from the Kakata Rural Teacher Training Institute (KRTTI). He arrived at St. Mary's School with fanfare. In those days, there was a buzz about having come into the classroom as a graduate of KRTTI. Mr. Gleekia was very fond of me because I did very well in his class. On one occasion after he gave us a spelling test, he asked us to exchange our papers to correct them. Unfortunately, the person who corrected my paper apparently had a vendetta against me. I personally whipped other students in first grade for failing to spell their words correctly. Perhaps the person who marked my paper was one of those I whipped. In any case, the person inserted extra letters between letters of words I spelled correctly and, as a result, caused me to fail the spelling test. The insertions were clearly visible. One could tell them from my handwriting. We were never able to find out who corrected my paper. That experience still did not help me to understand one of the things my Mom often said, "Not everyone is happy about other people's success," until I became an adult.

CHAPTER 9

Respite

A S A CHILD IN THE culture, I thought my family, including my parents, two sisters and I, was an aberration. Polygamy, a practice whose potential for spawning jealousies and lingering conflicts was greater than any perceived advantages, was the norm. Men in the culture did not see anything wrong with it; they took a second, third, or fourth wife when they felt that the time had come. But, as Mom began walking a fine line telling her story gradually, the full impact of polygamy on my family started to appear like a slow-motion movie.

In the culture, an aggrieved wife almost always first sought relief from her husband's family. No matter what believable evidence husbands presented to the contrary, they stood no chance in "courts" where their family presided. On the other hand, wives looked forward to rulings in their favor because such rulings were an indication that their husbands' families had heard their complaints. In addition, a favorable ruling was an incentive to stay in the marriage. "Konu koa keh aye toh paay peay" was the rationale for favorable rulings for wives despite evidence against their complaints.[66]

A favorable ruling for an aggrieved wife in a "court" of her husband's family did not always resolve underlying problems. If a wife's marital problems persisted, even after winning with the husband's family, her next logical step was to return to her parents. The husband often followed not to win a case but to convince his in-laws that the conditions which forced his wife to return home have changed. The redundancy ensured that divorce would be the last option.

Before school opened in March 1969, Mom took a "break." She traveled to Gordin in Guinea to spend time with her parents. She took Esther, my younger sister, along. Following Mom's departure, Dad traveled to Guinea twice. His first trip was a formality, merely to tell Mom's parents that he had come to take his wife back to Liberia. He knew he would not return with Mom on his first trip, but he had to make that request to show he cared. His in-laws never raised any issues that caused Mom to return home. Instead, they treated Dad with courtesy and gave him an extended time to return for his wife.

Dad made his second trip to Guinea sometime in November 1970. Mom confirmed her parents raised issues about her marriage during Dad's second visit. His in-laws reminded him that Mom's well-being was his responsibility. Mom also told me she did not tie her return to the resolution of her marital problems because she could not think of any condition that would make her abandon her children. She and Esther did not return with Dad, but they returned to the village in late January 1971.

Upon Dad's return to the village after his second trip to Guinea, he started making plans to make good on commitments he made to Mom and her parents. I was with him when he took the first step. Using a sharp machete (cutlass), he delineated a large forest for Mom's farm. He surveyed the forest and partly removed tree barks to mark out the perimeter.

Dad contacted Cousin Flumo Tokpah (deceased), then living in Plehdehyee, Guinea, for help in finding a hired hand to cut the bush. Flumo Tokpah already had Mr. Molee Gehyeegbay in mind. Molee, a Mandingo originally from Kouroussa, a town in northeastern Guinea, had been living with Mahns in Plehdehyee for a long time. He spoke the language fluently and was well versed in the culture. Flumo Tokpah and Molee came to the village in Liberia.

Upon Molee's arrival, Dad took him to see the area he had marked for the farm. They walked the perimeter and crisscrossed the length and breadth of the forest. After that, they negotiated Molee's pay to cut the forest and agreed on forty United States dollars ($40). The minimum wage for working on somebody's farm for an entire day at that time was fifty cents. Because Dad and I walked the perimeter as well as the length and breadth of the area of the proposed farm, I thought Molee got a raw deal. However, Molee did not see his $40 pay through my eyes. Instead, he had his eyes set on the future. Later, he told me he accepted the $40 payment because he was going to be in the village for a long time. He considered his first job as an opportunity for building a relationship with my family.

The $40 payment, which I thought was a travesty, made more sense to me when Dad explained factors I did not consider in the beginning. For example, Molee had three meals a day. We provided breakfast, took a heavy lunch to him at work and prepared dinner for him in the evening. Every evening, we gave him a large bucket of hot water to bathe and soothe his muscles after a hard day's work. In addition, Molee did not pay rent for his room. It took him a little over thirty days to complete the work.

Molee (deceased) was originally a Muslim, but he eventually abandoned the practice after he lived with Mahns for a long time. He ate everything we ate and did everything we did according to Mahn tradition. However, he did not drink any alcoholic beverages. More importantly, Molee informally became a member of our family. He helped Mom with her farm work and, at the same time, continued to work for hire for a long time. Molee harvested oil palm and made palm oil for sale. He used Dad's shotgun to hunt. He also set traps that caught different animals for food.

Soon after Molee finished cutting the bush, Dad and I began felling the trees. During the process, Dad taught me many tree names in Mahn. I learned about trees I had never seen before because the area was virgin forest with rare species. Two memorable ones were "yayinyelee," a species that no other tree stood in its proximate radius and "goo," the hardest known tree species according to Dad.

In no time, late January 1971 was upon us. I remember Mom and Esther's return like it happened yesterday. My limbs fluttered and the rhythm of my heartbeat increased as I ran to hug my mom. When I landed into her arms, I held tightly onto her and danced with my feet at the same time. When she let go of me, I felt as if I were walking on air. The joy I felt was indescribable. But at that moment, Mom was merely minutes away from seeing the end of the slow-motion movie. She was about to realize our household would never be the same. Indeed, she was about to encounter Luolay Tiakpa, the strange woman in our house whom I described earlier, for the first time ever.

I do not know the pain Mom felt upon seeing that woman in her house; living in proximity with Luolay Tiakpa; losing control over the coffee plantation; hearing Luolay Tiakpa inject herself as a stakeholder into the affairs of our household. But, with grace and dignity, Mom accepted the curveball life had dealt her; she swallowed the bitter pill. Mom's decision to stay the course meant she had to farm alone. Even though Molee helped, Mom performed all the farm activities on her own. The forest Dad delineated in 1971 was his last farm for Mom. After he and I felled the trees, he was not involved in any significant way to complete that farm. After 1971, Dad only made farm for Luolay Tiakpa.

Mom conducted her life with grace and class. She had no animus against anyone. She never told me to settle scores against those who wronged her. But she wanted me to begin writing her story as early as elementary school, thinking that I might forget. As a member of her "two-being" audience, I often heard Mom tell her story in a soliloquy on journeys when I accompanied her.[67] A dilemma or what Mahns call "Tohn zuhn weeah zeh" (a mixture of crushed meat and palm nut), was her lot from the get-go. In Mahn country, if one ate the mixture and swallowed the meat along with the wiry palm fibers, one is considered a greedy person. On the other hand, if one siphoned the "butter" from the palm nut along with the tasty juice from the meat and spewed away the wiry palm fibers and the meat, the derisions for the despicable act of wastage in times of food scarcity would be swift.

Mom loved Dad. The story of his tragic childhood helped firm her love and devotion throughout their lives together.[68] I never heard them quarrel; use unkind words at each other; or saw them hit each other. Early in their marriage, Mom stayed with Dad throughout his illness until he fully recovered. She endured repeated traumas of bearing and losing children, not to mention countless sacrifices she made to keep and sustain the family. But Mom and Dad were like everyone else, in that their marriage life had its ups and downs. Moreover, her commitment did not shield her from marital transgressions.

In telling her story, Mom was not looking for a win against Dad, the man she loved with the fiber of her being. Instead, she wanted me, the earthly member of her audience, to see and hear her; to know the life she was laboring to help me have had a huge hidden cost attached; I could not be a goofball; I could not squander my life. But I was a child. A full unadulterated story entailed her joys and disappointments, wrongs she suffered and sacrifices she made. She recognized such a story had a potential of destroying the image I had of my dad. Indeed, Mom was between a rock and a hard place from the beginning.

Mom opted for a veiled story, where she remained tight-lipped about certain matters to protect two people she loved dearly. As a child, I listened, sensed pain in Mom's voice, but never fully understood the nature of her soliloquies. As I became older, it occurred to me that I was the other member of Mom's audience. I filled in the blanks for things she left unsaid. More importantly, I figured out Mom's goals in telling a veiled story: to preserve the image and love I had for Dad and to lead a meaningful life in honor of her love and labor.

CHAPTER 10

Survival

LOVE AS A SURVIVAL MECHANISM

BY 1970, AS A FIFTH grader still living with the Guahs, St. Mary's School had virtually become a niche, making the school year a fun-filled and memorable one. I wore the green and white uniform with deep pride and bubbled with joy each time people talked about me with a mention of St. Mary's. Love of St. Mary's took hold of my being and the school became an important part of my identity. In addition, St. Mary's turned into an antidote to Sanniquellie hunger, which "broke students' backs" and caused them to quit. I survived Sanniquellie hunger and continued my education, in part, because of love of St. Mary's. Towards the close of 1970, I was looking forward to 1971 while some of my peers were looking forward to the long December-February vacation or dropping out of school. I was not the only one "in love" with St. Mary's. The people of Sanniquellie loved the school too. On Flag Day, August 24th of each year, and other parade days, they came out in droves, lined the main streets and cheered us on. We felt and acted like the "chosen ones" because everything about our school was unique. We bragged and shouted *"God made St. Mary's Number one"* during parades. Our conceit invited scorn and jealousies from students of other schools, perhaps rightly so. But our brazen self-adulation reflected the quality of work the nuns and teachers were doing to prepare us for the future.

Matthew Nimley

Matthew Nimley was Kru, one of Liberia's ethnic groups, but I never heard him speak the language to others who understood it. He only spoke English, as it was characteristic of others from uppity Liberian families, where speaking tribal languages at home or elsewhere was looked down upon. Matthew lived with his dad and stepmother about a quarter of a mile from the Guahs' house. To reach them from the Guah's house, one had to cross a creek with a makeshift plank bridge that floods resulting from Sanniquellie's torrential rains repeatedly washed away. By Liberian standards, Matthew's family was wealthy. His dad worked for the Ministry of Lands, Mines and Energy as a diamond agent. Matthew had his own bedrood and other material things I could only dream of. In their household, breakfast, lunch and dinner were not words like ice cream, apple or stories about Halloween that we only read about in our American textbooks. They ate breakfast, lunch and dinner.

Matthew's dad was tall, light-skinned, and handsome, with receding hair that looked like Kwame Nkrumah, the late and former President of Ghana. Mr. Nimley was a quiet man. I never heard him say anything to his son. He saw me with Matthew, but never asked, at least in my presence, what I was doing at their house. Matthew's stepmother was also light-skinned, beautiful and younger than his dad was. She had an unmistakable uppity aura and seemed unapproachable. In addition, she was quarrelsome. Her relationship with Matthew seemed uneasy.

Matthew and I attended St. Mary's Elementary School. We often played soccer during recess in the elementary school courtyard. At other times, we played soccer on makeshift playgrounds or on the field at their house. Matthew Nimley was physically strong. Occasionally he had an uppity attitude, but he was not mean-spirited. However, he had a laser eye for something about others to laugh at. He habitually reveled in teasing others and making fun of them nonstop. He regarded teasing others as a fun sport and had a kick out of doing it. On occasions, Matthew intimidated others and was a classic bully. I hated his habitual teasing, but he knew that, with his iron man physique, he could get away with it because nobody messed with him. Matthew and I did not get into any physical fights, but our friendship was neither always buddy-buddy.

On one occasion, I came into the crosshairs of Matthew's bullying radar. He made my life miserable for some time. The teasing started with a pair of turquoise rain boots I found at the landfill between the Guahs' property and the Baileys' residence across the swamp. One foot of the boots had a tear near the rim. Using a razor blade, I cut both feet right above the ankle and made them look like regular shoes. Before I found the rain boots, I proudly wore my uniform and walked barefooted or wore a pair of rubber slippers to school. I always kept my sneakers for special occasions such as Flag Day or Gala Day (homecoming day). Walking barefooted to school was nothing out of the ordinary, some of us went to school barefooted.

On the day I wore the pair of turquoise rain boots to school, Matthew Nimley could not miss an opportunity to make fun of me. The unmistakable turquoise made the boots stand out among barefooted kids frolicking the playground. Matthew instinctively figured turquoise indicated girls' shoes and that I found it at a landfill. He called everyone's attention to my boots and then called me "Dump Pile Hero." "Dump pile" is a Liberian expression for a landfill or dumpsite. Even though I stopped wearing the rain boots to school, Matthew would not quit calling me "Dump Pile Hero."

Beneath the tough guy and bully persona Matthew Nimley projected, I found a different young man; a young man who was sensitive and compassionate with a big heart. He would not stand by and let someone take undue advantage of another person. Occasionally after we played soccer, Matthew invited me for dinner. Soon after, the occasional invitations turned into an effort to persuade me to move in with him. Even though I never had enough food to eat at the Guahs' house, I never complained about being hungry; I never told Matthew anything about my living condition.

Matthew told me his dad's job often took him out of town. Perhaps he wanted someone to be with him while his dad was away. I do not even know whether he sought his dad's permission before asking me to move in with him. I never figured out why Matthew wanted me to move in with him. The occasional visits to play soccer led to my spending nights with Matthew. Eventually, sometime after my return from the village following the recovery from my ailing left hand, I left the Guahs abruptly and moved in with Matthew until the mid-year July vacation. I did not plan to leave the Guahs and nothing from the Guahs triggered the move. It just happened.

Strangely, however, the Guahs never made any efforts to find out where I was or to inform my parents that I had left them.

Matthew's invitation to move in with him sounded to me like a joke. I never took it seriously. Even as young as I was, I was fully aware that my parents entrusted me to the Guahs to go to school; they were responsible for whatever happened to me. In the village, my parents had no questions in their minds about where I was. All they knew was that I was with the Guahs. However, in Sanniquellie, the Guahs had no clue whatsoever where I was. I never told them that I was moving out. Any parent who ever asked a child why you did this or that and heard the child say, "I don't know," would understand my state of mind at the time. I just did not think of it.

At the Nimleys' house, I was under no one's care or guidance. I was with Matthew, but I was on my own. I never talked to Matthew's dad for the entire time I was at their house. Not even a "Hello, Sir." Oddly, Matthew's dad saw me with his son on numerous occasions, but he never said hello or asked what I was doing in his yard with his son. He never asked whose child I was. Similarly, I never talked to Matthew's stepmother for the entire time I was at their house. Not even a "Hello, ma'am," as well. She saw me in the yard but never spoke or asked what I was doing with her stepson. Like her husband, she never asked whose child I was.

Matthew did not try to parent or tell me what to do because I moved in with him. He was a casual friend, one of the kids at school. He was about the same age as I was. We had no shared values or experiences other than playing soccer together and attending the same elementary school. No one told me to get up in the morning to go to school. No one told me to avoid going to places without supervision so as not to get into trouble. I could have lost interest in school and returned to the village, where abundant food beaconed me. I could have gotten sick. "Monsee mia" could have abducted me without a trace.[69] Without guidance, there were a thousand reasons to drop out or take a wrong path. Despite the absence of complete parental or custodial guidance, I woke up every morning and went to school. I never missed a day of school. Some people call it staying focused, but I call it the work of Wlah's Hands. It was my experience during my move to live with Matthew Nimley that led me to look upon my parents' decision to take me to live with the Guahs to go to school as an act of providence. Only Wlah could have guided and protected me for the weeks I spent with Matthew Nimley between May and July 1971.

It was not until during the mid-year July vacation that I informed my parents that I had left the Guahs. I was grateful for the care that the Guahs provided for me and never made a case against them to justify why I left. I only told my parents that I would not return to the Guahs. Because Mom and Dad knew the Guah household size and the perennial food challenges, they made no fuss about my decision and no effort to force me to return to them. However, I went further and told my parents that, for several weeks, I had been staying with a friend and that my living arrangements were not definitive. At that juncture, Mom and Dad scrambled and found someone with whom I could live temporarily and go to school for the remainder of the year. The person was Mr. Saye Dada, another one of Dad's relatives. At Mr. Saye Dada's house, I shared a room with two of his wife's relatives who were much older than I was. One of them was Mr. Philip Gonleseh. I do not remember the name of the other person, but until I met him, I had never seen anybody as tall as he was.

THE NATIONAL EXAMINATIONS

A big event in 1971 was the national examinations. Up to 1971, students in grades six, nine and twelve took the national examinations in Liberia. My sixth-grade class was the last cohort that took the sixth-grade examination. After 1971, only students in grades nine and twelve took the examinations.[70] The examinations attracted a lot of attention; they were a big deal, at least in Sanniquellie. The buzz about the national examinations made them high-stake tests; they determined who was serious; who went beyond elementary school to high school or beyond high school to college. Some students who did not pass the examinations dropped out for fear of becoming objects of scorn.

On the day of the examinations in November 1971, I showed up early morning at Sanniquellie Central High School, the test center, with other classmates. After several hours of the examinations, we came out for a break. I was pleasantly surprised to see Mr. Patrick Bamakpa (deceased), our principal, on the soccer field by the campus. Even though test takers are not like sports players to be cheered on, I felt that Mr. Bamakpa came to cheer us on. He opened a box of buns which contained butter and gave one to each of us. I did not have money for snacks. So, I was happy; I was fired up when I returned for the second half of the examinations. Students

77

from other schools who were taking the examinations never got similar treat from their principal. I could tell from the looks in their faces that they wished Mr. Bamakpa were their principal. I knew how privileged I was. After the examinations, I went to the village. When I returned to Sanniquellie in December for the closing of school, I found out that I passed the examinations and moved on to grade seven. I survived the high-stake examinations.

WILLIAM V. S. TUBMAN

William V. S. Tubman was Liberia's 18th president. He succeeded President Edwin Barclay. Tubman assumed the presidency in 1944, fourteen years before I was born. He served as president until his death on July 23, 1971. President Tubman was an important part of my early life because I started school during his presidency. The one opportunity I had to see him was during his birthday celebrations in Sanniquellie in 1966, but I never saw the president because I could not distinguish him from throngs of government officials in dark suits who accompanied him.

The other reason I was unable to see President Tubman in Sanniquellie in 1966 was the infamous United Brothers Fraternity (UBF). The UBF was a secret society and an instrument of social control in the hands of the ruling America-Liberian minority. Along with its counterpart, the Freemason, the UBF was virtually an underground government, where the upper echelons of Liberian society decided important matters. Membership in the UBF bestowed legitimacy because the organization was a major "artery" of America-Liberian hegemony. Through the UBF, the ruling class exercised control over its members, including educated as well as uneducated indigenous Liberians. In addition, the UBF nurtured a culture of impunity. Many educated indigenous people who wanted to achieve a measure of social mobility had to join the UBF. In Nimba County, for example, indigenous leaders including but not limited to paramount chiefs, justices of the peace, district commissioners, superintendents, and county attorneys joined the UBF because they perceived membership as a protection against arbitrary dismissal.

The UBF's infamy went beyond the tendency of local indigenous officials to join the fraternity for job security. In Nimba County, citizens believed that UBF members participated in ritualistic killings to put fear in potential rivals or anyone who considered complaining them to higher authorities in Monrovia. During UBF conventions in Sanniquellie, members paraded the principal streets in dark suits, black shoes, white gloves and gold-laced sashes. Their commanders often led the parades with swords and specially decorated staffs. "Tan leh gbeeni" (the ground is heavy) or "Tan leh tee" (the ground is dark) was the warning parents gave their children during those conventions. In addition, parents told their children to stay inside and avoid going anywhere alone because of tales of abductions involving long black cars. "Tan leh gbeeni" or "Tan leh tee" in Mahn also meant that "Monsee mia" (the UBF people) were in town. Any child sent by its parents to live with relatives in Sanniquellie to go to school understood "Tan leh gbeeni" or "Tan leh tee" as a survival warning.

I never saw President Tubman, but it was hard not to know that he was president of Liberia. Like others in rural households in Nimba County, Dad posted Tubman's old calendar picture on the piazza wall in our house. Moreover, Liberians felt Tubman's persona in tangible ways. His hairstyle, the "Tubman Style," was the trending hairstyle most adult males wore. I hated getting a haircut because of the pain of combing through my hair, but because Tubman Style was the only hairstyle Dad knew how to cut, I ended up hating Tubman Style with a passion. The arrival of Afro hairdo, the bushy hairstyle most young people wore in the seventies, was my "saving grace" from Tubman Style.

President Tubman loomed large in other ways too. He ruled with an iron fist. At the time, I was concerned about food to eat, going to school and things that mattered to children. I never knew anything about local or national politics other than the obvious: Tubman was the President of Liberia. Politics never made sense to me. All I knew was Dad never liked porterage; he never liked carrying government officials' cargo on his head. On top of that, he was sick of paying arbitrary taxes, sometimes more than once a year. He never complained. No one dared at that time to organize rallies against taxes or porterage. Tubman dealt ruthlessly with any sign of opposition, real or perceived. I do not recall any protests or demonstrations against President Tubman.

My parents thought life was good so long they could go to the market, sell their produce and buy whatever they needed. The economy was vibrant, and, in the eyes of ordinary people, Tubman's presidency was a time of stability. Everyone looked up to Tubman, the "Old Man." He was the answer to many problems arising from local disputes. The entire nation went into shock and stood still when the government of Liberia announced Tubman had died in England on July 23, 1971. I was in Sanniquellie with my parents on the day of Tubman's death announcement. It seemed as if everyone had lost a family member. On our way back to the village, the wind stopped blowing, the leaves stopped moving and an eerie atmosphere descended upon the mid-afternoon.

President Tubman's death brought an end to an era; the old passed and a new arose. Indeed, spring sprung with the ascendancy of William R. Tolbert, Jr., to the presidency. Shortly thereafter, the gloom of Tubman's death dissipated, and it was morning again in Liberia. With a clear vision of a new Liberia, a self-reliant Liberia, Tolbert was a breath of fresh air. With a soaring and inspirational voice, he declared war on "ignorance, disease and poverty" and emphasized education, agriculture and rural transportation. Tolbert made a critical connection between the people's knowledge, skills and mindset and their development. He referred to young people as his "precious jewels" and made their development a priority. I survived the Tubman era with more than mere hope. Tolbert made me his "precious jewel"!

KOUKOU

Koukou, my cousin, was Uncle Gonotee Saye Guanue's first daughter. Uncle Gonotee was Dad's eldest brother. Koukou was born in an area of Liberia that ended up becoming a part of present-day Guinea. Her birth followed Uncle Gonotee and his brothers' move to that area after the deaths of their parents. She neither went to school in Guinea nor in Liberia after her parents returned to Liberia. Nevertheless, she was immeasurably brilliant. In Guinea, Koukou learned three languages, Mandingo, Kpelle and Sousou, and spoke them fluently. In Liberia, Koukou learned some colloquial English from ordinary people who never went to school, but she was not fluent in English as she was in speaking Mahn and the other languages she learned in Guinea. Koukou was hard-working, lively and funny. She had a distinctive and unmistakable laugh. She often laughed as if she were in a spell. She was fond of my older sister, Sennie. They fondly called each other "Pehlay ah keh" (What the mouth says or does) and "Kor lah keh" (The hand cannot do). If Koukou called "Pehlay ah keh," Sennie responded "Kor lah keh" and vice versa. I loved Koukou dearly.

During the December-February vacation that followed the national examinations, I found myself between a rock and a hard place. I realized the household size and challenging food situation at the Guahs' house had persuaded my parents not to force me to return to the Guahs. But, because my parents were not a part of my decision to leave the Guahs, we never had a thorough discussion about my living arrangement upon the opening of school in March 1972. Because my stay at Mr. Saye Dada's house was temporary, I never had a place to stay at upon the opening of school. Although living with Matthew Nimley for several weeks had been a smooth transition, returning to live with him for academic 1972 was not an option because we never had that conversation. Essentially, unless my parents and I came up with a plan about where to stay at upon the opening of school, my decision not to return to the Guahs was a bluff. Looking back, I ran the risk of disrupting my education because the long December-February vacation not only made the opening of school seem far away but also minimized the gravity of not having a place to stay at. Luckily, the love of St. Mary's School kept me on course, from drifting mentally to consider dropping out of school until we had a solution. I preferred being homeless in Sanniquellie than dropping out of school and becoming separated from St. Mary's School. I never fully understood my confidence in declaring that I would not return to the Guahs, but I had a suspicion it came from the benefits of Mom's unrelenting prayers.

During that same December-February vacation, Koukou (deceased) was in the village. She immediately recognized the implication of my decision not to return to the Guahs. She knew I would not have a place to stay at in Sanniquellie upon the opening of school in 1972. Driven by familial instinct, she suggested she would talk to her husband, Mr. Peter Dahn, about my predicament. Mr. Dahn had a house in New Sanniquellie prior to marrying Koukou. He had planned to put his house up for rent before the conversation about where I would stay in 1972 came up. Koukou said that she would try to persuade Mr. Dahn to let Cousin Joe Mark Tokpah and I stay at his house rent-free. She followed through and Mr. Dahn agreed.

Upon the opening of school in March 1972, Joe Mark Tokpah and I moved into Mr. Peter Dahn's house in New Sanniquellie, about three miles from St. Mary's School. We were lucky to have a place to stay at to go to school. Like me, Joe Mark's parents took him to live with the Guahs in 1966, but shortly after school started, he left the Guahs because of the household size and food situation I described. His parents did not live far away from Sanniquellie as my parents did. Even though we had been in school together at St. Mary's throughout, the move to Mr. Dahn's house was our first opportunity to live together since 1966.

JOE MARK TOKPAH

Cousin Joe Mark's parents, Nyanquoi Tokpah and Kou Flomo, lived in Gborpa, approximately four miles from New Sanniquellie, where Joe, along with his siblings, were born. Nyanquoi Tokpah had three wives, Ma Mesahn, the headwife, Kou Flomo, the second wife (Joe Mark's mom) and Koo Teekleh, the third wife. Ma Mesahn helped pay the dowries for Kou Flomo and Koo Teekleh.

Joe Mark was a fascinating human being. He was handsome, brilliant and had a magnificent handwriting. Moreover, living with him was an unforgettable experience. It seemed there was no limit to what was funny to him. He laughed loudly about almost everything. In light-hearted ways, he got me into troubles on numerous occasions. He always found something about someone to laugh about. If he did not find anything funny, he made one up and caused me to laugh. A perfect example occurred when Uncle Miatee Garteh (deceased) visited with us in New Sanniquellie over a weekend in 1972. As with everyone else in the culture, Uncle Garteh arrived unannounced because there were no telephone services. At the time of Garteh's arrival, Joe and I were preparing food only for the two of us. As both of us were big eaters, the sudden increase in our number from two to three had an implication for how much food each of us would have. Joe did not say much but I could sense from his body language that he had an outrageous and funny plan.

In no time, the food was ready. Joe dished all the rice in a large pan and poured the "soup" on it. He then took a teaspoon and gave it to Uncle Garteh. At first, I did not notice the spoon Joe gave to the "old man".[71] Both Joe and I sat on the floor closer to the pan containing the food while Garteh sat in a chair and stooped over each time to dip his spoon into the food. After about three dips of the teaspoon into the rice, the old man decided that he would not use the spoon anymore. He asked for water to wash his hands. At that moment, Joe realized instantly that the old man had caught on to his shenanigan. However, the main reason why Joe laughed to the point of almost peeing in his pants had to do with the comments the old man made. In Mahn, Uncle Garteh said, "Kbu ah mee kor pahnon keh ah mee gig dor."[72] Uncle Garteh joined us in the laughter that ensued. Upon his return to the village, he never forgot to tell and retell that story until his death in 1982.

CHANGE IN FORTUNE

Unfortunately, our memorable stay at Peter Dahn and Koukou's house in New Sanniquellie did not last forever. The goodwill that enabled us to live in that house rent-free ended at the close of academic 1972. Ironically, Koukou, the harbinger of the good news of that goodwill, who relieved us at the beginning of academic 1972, turned into the bearer of the bad news that the party was over at the beginning of academic 1973. She informed us that we would not be allowed to go back to live in their house in New Sanniquellie again. She told us that Mr. Dahn wanted to follow through with his original plan for the house prior to the beginning of 1972. He wanted to put up his house for rent.

The house belonged to Mr. Peter Dahn and Koukou. As such, they had every right to do whatever they wanted to do with their property. In that light, their decision to withdraw the housing assistance did not concern me. However, because the laws in Liberia are not clear on properties secured before marriage, there is a tendency to shut out wives in matters involving such properties. It seemed there was more to Mr. Dahn and Koukou's decision not to allow us to live in their house rent-free. Mr. Dahn may have made the decision to withdraw the housing assistance unilaterally; he may have coerced Koukou into communicating that decision to us. Such a scenario was not far-fetched because there was a huge power difference between husbands and wives, at least in the culture.

Notwithstanding Mr. Dahn's suspected unilateral decision to withdraw the housing assistance, Koukou was quite aware of the housing situation in Sanniquellie, particularly at the time of opening school. She knew that students came from all over Nimba County and elsewhere in Liberia to attend schools in Sanniquellie. The demand for rooms at the opening of school in Sanniquellie was so high that having money for rent was no guarantee for finding a room. It certainly would have been helpful if Mr. Dahn and Koukou had informed us at the close of academic 1972 so that we could explore possible places we could stay at for the following year. Instead, they waited and communicated their decision at the opening of school in 1973. Mr. Dahn and Koukou were very kind to let us live in their house during academic 1972. However, their decision at the opening of school in 1973 to withdraw the housing assistance seemed like a calculated attempt to neutralize the effect of their original kindness. Indeed, their seemingly mean-spirited decision left us scrambling and wondering where we would live.

Mr. Peter Dahn and Koukou's shocking decision to withdraw their housing assistance resulted in speculations about their motives. Mr. Dahn had no blood relations to either Joe Mark or me. Looking at Mr. Dahn's decision through the lens of blood relations alone, he did not owe us an explanation. But Mr. Dahn and I had a connection; he was married to my cousin, Koukou. In the culture, a husband treated his wife's family with deference. That treatment was an indication of how much he valued his wife. However, in my search for motives for Mr. Dahn and Koukou's decision, I did not go down the culture road alone, where husbands were expected to treat their in-laws gingerly and with deference. I also looked critically at Koukou's role because she was the one who empathized with me; she was the one who voluntarily persuaded her husband to let us live in their house rent-free. In the course of one year, I wondered, "What happened to the goodwill prompted by familial instinct?" In other words, what led to the change of heart?

Unable to figure out the real motive why Mr. Dahn and Koukou withdrew their housing assistance, I resorted to a familiar approach in similar situations in the culture. It was a path of least resistance taken in search of a motive or cause, especially when there was a search for a reason why someone passed away. There had to be an ominous reason whenever someone passed away. In the culture, let alone in Liberia, the default reason for dying was witchcraft or poisoning. Therefore, when I failed to come up with the reason why Mr. Dahn and Koukou asked us to leave their property, I concluded that there must have been something sinister going on. I felt that putting up the house for rent was a pretext.

My thought about a sinister plot behind the sudden withdrawal of the housing assistance did not fall from out of nowhere. Again, in the culture, pointing to witchcraft as a cause of death did not end the matter. A specific person had to have been involved in the witchcraft. Usually, the culprits were mean old women or barrens.[73] It just happened Koukou did not have any children who could benefit in some way from Mr. Dahn and Koukou's investment in Joe Mark and me. Mr. Dahn did not have any children prior to his marriage to Koukou. I wondered, "What did Koukou actually think of us?" "Did she and Peter Dahn consider us as investments?" "Did they think of our future successes as theirs?" "Could their lack of children have been a consideration?"

Year-after-year, our educational successes became routine. At the end of each school year, our parents heard Joe Mark and I say we moved on to the next grade. Moving on to the next grade at the end of each year became an expectation in our extended family. The warm receptions that greeted me for my educational successes upon returning to the village may have rubbed others in a different way. As such, Mom, who had a better grasp of real life than I had, was always watchful. She often warned, "Not everyone is truly happy about the successes of other people's children." Simply put, jealousy may have been at the heart of Peter Dahn and Koukou's sudden change of mind and withdrawal of their housing assistance.

Despite Koukou and Peter Dahn's decision to ask us to leave their property, I remained grateful to her and Mr. Dahn for the opportunity to live rent-free in their house in 1972. Koukou was one of the people for whom I carried a self-imposed burden. It was more than just wanting to make her proud. I loved her and wanted to show my gratitude for the time we spent living in her and Peter Dahn's house. Out of love and not out of spite, I wanted her to know that the change of mind that led her and Mr. Dahn to ask us not to return to their house in New Sanniquellie was an error in judgment. Unfortunately, I did not have an opportunity to say all that I wanted to say, including how much I loved Koukou. She died in 1986 while I was studying in the United States.

The Family House

Mr. Peter Dahn and Koukou's withdrawal of their housing assistance forced Joe Mark and me to consider the family house, an option we did not have on the radar. Built expressly for us, the house was a product of our parents' foresight. Mom told me that she and Dad discussed the plan for the house with Joe Mark's parents and agreed to contribute funds to build it before we reached school age. Besides the financial contribution my parents made,

Dad also participated in the actual construction of the six-bedroom house. Located along an alley in a very congested area of Sanniquellie, the house was no more than one hundred yards from the Guah family property, where Joe and I lived at during the start of our schooling in 1966. Like other Mahn property owners in the area, Joe Mark's parents, custodians of the family house, rented three rooms to members of the Mandingo ethnic group. The family stayed in the remaining three rooms whenever they came to Sanniquellie on a Friday evening to sell their produce the following day.

One would ask why Joe Mark and I did not move into the family house after completion. Well, Joe and I were too young to live on our own. In addition, our parents did not live in Sanniquellie. My parents lived in the village while Joe's parents lived in Gborpa, about six miles away from the city center, where the house was located. Due to distance, our parents could not live with us to parent and, at the same time, farm to provide food and earn money to pay tuition and taxes. That predicament led to our parents' decisions in 1966 to take us to the Guahs to go to school. Subsequently, the family rented some of the rooms in the completed family house.

Due to our housing crisis, Joe Mark's parents asked one of the tenants to give up his room so that we could have a place to stay. As a result, Joe Mark and I used the family house for its intended purpose for the first time in March 1973. Moving into the family house was, nevertheless, a mixed blessing. On the positive side, unlike Mr. Dahn and Koukou's house, which was about three miles away from campus, the family house was about a mile away from school. On the downside, whereas Mr. Dahn and Koukou did not expect us to go to their farm to work for staying in their house, Ma Mesahn expected us to go to her farm to work for staying in the family house.[74]

MA MESAHN

As indicated, Ma Mesahn was Nyanquoi Tokpah's headwife. She was responsible for bringing Kou Flomo, Joe Mark Tokpah's mom, into the Nyanquoi Tokpah household. She also brought Koo Teekleh, Nyanquoi Tokpah's third wife, into the household. Ordinarily in the culture, head wives occupied positions of power, but as a headwife, Ma Mesahn was in a class by herself. Ma Mesahn could not read or write, but she was steeply educated culturally and inordinately self-conscious. She was exquisitely beautiful; dressed elegantly in the finest African ladies' garments and carried an air of nobility. Ma Mesahn was naturally loquacious, but she talked with a purpose and had very high expectations of how things should be done. She wielded power in the Nyanquoi Tokpah household while her husband, a quiet man, seemed more like a yeoman.

Esther Luolay Dokie, Ma Mesahn's only child, was another factor that enhanced her power in the Nyanquoi Tokpah household. Esther, whom we fondly called Sister or Sister Esther, was the first educated person in our extended family. Esther and I had one thing in common. She was a Luolay (slave or slave woman) and I am a Luogon (slave or slave man), names that suggested our moms not only searched for a long time, but also had troubles having us. For that reason, Ma Mesahn made it seem Esther was the only one that mattered to her. She engaged in very few conversations that did not feature Luolay and bragged incessantly about Luolay and her accomplishments.

Ma Mesahn was not only a strong and independent woman, but also an embodiment of strength. It seemed her life was built around her only child, Esther. However, Esther's passing on October 4, 1982 as a result of complications during childbirth, proved otherwise. Ma Mesahn turned to the Inland Church in Sanniquellie, where she was a devoted member. Moreover, after losing her only child, she became a mother anew, a mother of many children. Her grandchildren, Bindu Sackor and Tarplah Anderson, Jr., as well as the children of Nyanquoi Tokpah's second wife, Kou Flomo, and third wife, Koo Teekleh, became her new focus. She endured the pain of losing Esther and survived the carnage of the civil war. On March 12, 2001, she moved to the United States, along with Bindu Sackor, where she settled in Baltimore, Maryland. Ma Mesahn lived a long and full life until her passing on January 26, 2019.

Ma Mesahn saw Joe Mark Tokpah and me as her children and we looked to her as a mother. She never hesitated to tell us what to do because, culturally, we were answerable to her. Moreover, we lived in the family house she controlled. She expected us to go to her farm to work and then carry sacks of rice and other farm produce from the "bini" on our heads to Sanniquellie.[75] The provisions we carried to Sanniquellie were intended for Esther who lived in Lamco, Yekepa. The "bini" was far away and the farm work was hard, but Joe Mark and I never aired any complaints publicly because Esther, whom we both adored, was the beneficiary of the provisions.

FATHER PAUL VOISARD

Paul Voisard was born in October 1914 in Miecourt, Switzerland. He had an unhappy childhood and eventually became estranged from his family.[76] However, his local parish cared for and educated him. He sought admission into the *"Society of Missionaries of Africa"* also known as *"White Fathers,"* perhaps through the caring impact of his parish. The *"White Fathers"* are a "Roman Catholic international missionary society of priests and brothers whose sole field of activity is Africa." The organization was "founded in North Africa in 1868 by the archbishop of Algiers, Charles-Martial-Allemand Lavigerie." "In 1895 the society extended its work to West Africa."[77]

In preparation for the priesthood, first, Paul Voisard studied philosophy in Kerlois, an area in France that was once "a training camp for young soldiers and then an internment camp for 1,350 men, women and children of Austro-Hungarian origin" during the 1918 war. In the 1920s, the *"White Fathers"* acquired the property for a boarding school for "young people aged 18 to 20" to "stay there for two years and study scholastic philosophy."[78] Next, in 1937, Paul Voisard was admitted to the Novitiate at the Maison-Carree ("Square house"), "an ancient Roman temple located in Nîmes, southern France."[79] A Novitiate is a place where someone desirous of becoming a priest goes "into the desert with Christ in order to prepare for the mission." A place where, "Each day, the novices have Mass, one hour of meditation, one half-hour of adoration, spiritual reading, examination of conscience, Rosary, and Night Prayers with benediction." Indeed, a place where those who want to become priests "receive spiritual direction on a regular basis."[80] Thereafter, he completed four years of theological studies in North Africa (Thibar and Carthage in Tunisia), took an oath in 1941 and was ordained priest in 1942.

Father Paul Voisard's journey in Africa began with his appointment in 1942 to serve in Guinea, West Africa, then a French colony. Although the onset of the second World War delayed his departure for Guinea until 1946, he wasted no time upon arrival in Guinea. He swung into action and immersed himself into the Mahn culture at the newly established Yalenzou mission, where he learned the language and spoke it fluently, although with a deep accent. Subsequently, he moved to Nzerekore, where he occupied himself with the welfare of the youths and their development[81]. During his time in Guinea, Father Voisard not only learned the Mahn language but also developed a script for it. With that, he translated the catechism into

Mahn and spread the gospel to ordinary Mahns in Guinea who did not understand French, the official language. Father Voisard also wrote hymns in Mahn as well as translated Catholic hymns into Mahn.

Father Voisard served in the country now known as the Republic of Guinea when it was a French colony. At the time, like other colonies in Africa, the people of Guinea were clamoring for independence. Seemingly in an attempt to cow French territories to remain in the French community, French President Charles de Gaulle tendered a proposal in September 1958 in which "Each member could accept the Constitution and consequent membership in the community or reject it and immediately sever all ties with France."[82] In urging the people of Guinea to turn down the de Gaulle proposal, Sekou Touré, in a fervor of nationalism, threw down the gauntlet when he declared, "We prefer poverty in liberty to riches in slavery."[83] De Gaulle's reaction was, "Then all you have to do is to vote 'no.' I pledge myself that nobody will stand in the way of your independence."[84] Apparently De Gaulle underestimated the capacity of the people in the French colonies to see the "colonial bed" he made to share with them for what it was.[85]

Subsequently, the people of Guinea "overwhelmingly rejected de Gaulle's offer and instead chose complete independence." With that, Guinea became "the only French colony in Africa that did not accept the proposal." "The French reacted by recalling all their professional people and civil servants and by removing all transportable equipment."[86] Indeed, "As a warning to other French-speaking territories, the French pulled out of Guinea over a two-month period, taking everything they could with them. They unscrewed lightbulbs, removed plans for sewage pipelines in Conakry, the capital, and even burned medicines rather than leave them for the Guineans."[87]

The result of the referendum and the manner in which the French left Guinea created a difficult situation for Father Voisard and other European missionaries. In 1962, Father Voisard spent two months in prison apparently for making some politically incorrect remark against the newly independent government of Guinea amidst the acrimonious tit-for-tat between France and Guinea following the latter's rejection of De Gaulle's proposal.[88] That was not out of character for Father Voisard because I knew him quite well. He spoke his mind. Eventually, European missionaries were expelled from Guinea in 1967.[89] Along with others, Father Voisard left Guinea and went to Liberia, where he continued his missionary activities in Sanniquellie, a parish relatively near the Liberian border with Guinea.

Upon Father Voisard's arrival at the St. Mary's Catholic Mission in Sanniquellie, he recruited and trained two older high school students, Adrian Sandi and Paul Konan, in the Mahn script to become trainers of other recruits. Father Voisard needed additional young people to learn the catechism in Mahn to read it at church on Sundays to the ordinary Mahn people who could not read. Both Adrian and Paul were Mahn. Adrian came from Yalenzou, a large Guinean town close to the Liberian border, where Father Voisard learned the Mahn, while Paul came from Zeinpa, Nimba County, Liberia. Adrian and Paul became adept at reading the Mahn script and singing hymns in Mahn.

It was 1973. Word about the arrival of Father Voisard, the new parish priest and gray-haired white man who was in his seventies or beyond, spread quickly. Moreover, his reputation as a generous priest spread among the hunger-battered student population of Sanniquellie like wildfire. Right then Joe Mark and I, eighth graders at the time, knew we had found a solution to our hunger problem. Once we showed up and got recruited, Father Voisard taught us the Mahn script in the beginning. Later, Adrian and Paul assumed teaching roles.

Learning the Mahn script from Adrian and Paul brought us closer together. Because they were older than Joe Mark and me, we did not see Adrian and Paul as friends. Instead, we saw them like big brothers; we looked to them for guidance. At the end of every evening session of learning the script, Father Voisard gave money to Joe and me to buy something to eat. Moreover, whenever we needed something to buy food or wood to cook, we went to Father Voisard on campus to ask for help. He knew exactly what we wanted whenever he saw us on his porch. Depending on his mood, he could come out, talk to us nicely and give us twenty-five cents each or fifty cents each and sometimes a dollar. At other times, especially when other students had been repeatedly asking for help, he would come out swinging at us with curses directed at our moms to the effect that he did not father us. Sometimes he chased us away by throwing stones at us. We had been around him for so long that we knew who he was. We never took any of his cranky attitudes personally.

Sometime in 1980, a few years after I graduated from St. Mary's High School, Father Voisard returned home to Switzerland for a sabbatical for a few months. For the love of the Mahn people, he returned to Liberia against the advice of his superiors who were wary about his health and safety. Upon his return to Liberia, he founded the Immaculate Heart of Mary Parish in Ganta, Liberia, where, as in Sanniquellie, he worked with the Mahn people, traveling the villages surrounding Ganta, building relationships and evangelizing. Even though his health was failing at the time and could not read or celebrate mass anymore, Father Voisard refused to return home to Switzerland.[90] Instead, he remained and continued to work with the Mahn people in Ganta and its environs. Upon my return from studying in Seoul, Korea and the United States in mid-1987, I lost track of Father Voisard because he was no longer serving as priest at the St. Mary's Parish in Sanniquellie. A different group of European missionaries had taken charge of the parish.

Moreover, I did not see Father Voisard again until he left Liberia during the onset of the civil war in Liberia in 1989. Although the mission that Father Voisard founded in Ganta met the spiritual needs of the community while he was planning to establish a school to meet the educational needs of the youths, it did not escape the brutality of the rebels and government soldiers during the civil war in Liberia.[91] The soldiers and rebels' brutality forced him to escapeto Abidjan, the Ivory Coast from where, eventually, he returned to Fribourg in Switzerland in August 1990.

After Father Voisard regained strength, the organization assigned him to a home for elderly priests in Tassy, France in November 1992. There, he not only told the story of his ordeal in Ganta, Liberia during the civil war but also withdrew, prayed and spent his last but happy years. "I am at home here and the atmosphere of the house is excellent. Besides, I came to Tassy to prepare for death and to be buried by the White Fathers and among the White Pearls," he wrote in 1994. On February 22, 1999, his appointed time arrived, and the Lord called him home. He was buried at a Tassy cemetery in France.[92]

Father Voisard was a compassionate man who devoted his life to the improvement of young people in West Africa. I am a living witness that he acted upon Jesus's charge in Matthew 19:21 "Jesus said unto him, If thou wilt be perfect, go and sell that thou hast, and give to the poor, and thou shalt have treasure in heaven: and come and follow me."[93] Father Voisard wanted to be buried in black Africa, but his wish did not happen. Now, with the completion of this book, let the world know that his wish has been fulfilled. Indeed, in these pages, that is, in the hearts of the young Africans he helped and posterity, he rests perpetually, free from the claws of the grave and the scourge of worms and termites. The Africans to whom he dedicated his life and their descendants will remember him in perpetuity.

PAUL KONAN AND ADRIAN SANDI

Besides the help Father Voisard provided, Joe Mark and I sought food wherever we could find it. Our next strategy for finding food was not for someone who was shy. It was humiliating because Joe Mark and I remembered the song we used to sing as kids whenever we wanted to make an uninvited dinner guest feel unwelcomed. In the village or elsewhere in the culture, someone who did not farm and therefore had no food routinely visited other people at dinnertime. Such a dinnertime visitor always had an interesting story or stories to tell. On the one hand, if the visitor arrived before dinnertime, he told a story to kill time until dinner was ready. On the other hand, if the visitor arrived at dinnertime, he told a story to entertain and establish his relevance. The story was always a diversion; it made people not to think of the visitor as a parasite. Even though such a visitor was regarded as lazy, Joe Mark and I were no lazy duo!

Adrian Sandi and Paul Konan rented a one-bedroom apartment across the main highway from the Sanniquellie public market. Joe Mark and I paid regular visits to Adrian and Paul's apartment because they always had food at their house. The smell of fried fish and onions in their peanut butter stew was a powerful lure. It drew us like a bright streetlamp attracts flying bugs. Adrian and Paul were no kids, but Joe Mark and I imagined them singing to us the same song we sang to uninvited dinner guests when we were little kids. We could hear "Yehlehkeh borbainbo kobennh ko gibain dor" in our heads because we knew exactly what we were doing. If we were in their shoes, we would do the same thing.[94]

As with uninvited dinner guests, we either had to have a story to tell or a good reason for going to Adrian and Paul's apartment. We did not have stories to tell, but we had justifiable reasons to stop to see Adrian and Paul. They were our Mahn catechism tutors! Moreover, Paul and Adrian's apartment was on our way to St. Mary's campus. We also looked to Adrian and Paul like brothers. As greeting people in the culture is a serious matter, stopping to say hello to Adrian and Paul on our way to St. Mary's campus for Mahn catechism lessons in the afternoon was a convenient excuse. But Joe Mark and I did not stop at Adrian and Paul's apartment to greet them.

Our main reason for stopping by their apartment was to eat their food. It seemed as if we had their cooking schedule programmed because we always arrived when they had finished cooking.

Joe Mark and I knew that we were uninvited. Our frequent visits caused Adrian and Paul serious concerns. Every time we arrived at Paul and Adrian's apartment, their body languages spoke volumes. We repeatedly put them in uncomfortable situations. They did not appear to know what to do because, in the culture, one cannot ask an uninvited visitor to leave because the family is about to have dinner.[95] It was the reluctance to ask uninvited dinner guests to leave that resulted in kids taking matters into their own hands with "Yehlehkeh yehlehkeh borbainbo kobennh ko gibain dor." Children sang the song because they saw the world through a fairness lens. They did not understand that aspect of the culture. Mahns prepared food for fewer people and then allowed additional people to join in to eat. As a result, children always felt short-changed; they always had less food.

On one occasion, Joe Mark and I arrived at Paul and Adrian's apartment when they had finished cooking rice with peanut butter stew. The peanut butter stew contained fried fish, "chicken" cubes, and onions. As soon as Adrian and Paul recognized us about fifty yards away, they took the pots of rice and peanut butter stew and pushed them under their beds. They had just one bedroom, which had two single beds, one for Paul and the other for Adrian. Peanut butter stew containing onions has a distinctive smell. Paul and Adrian's task was similar to attempting to hide smoke.

Upon arrival at Adrian and Paul's apartment, we could tell they had not eaten yet. We could also tell they had cooked rice and peanut butter stew. The smells were everywhere. Once we sat down and started a conversation, Adrian and Paul reminded us that they had somewhere to go. It was clear that they had caught on to our scheme. They did not need to ask us to leave. Their body languages and long faces said it all. Joe Mark and I looked at each other and left. Without saying much at that moment, we knew Adrian and Paul were singing "Yehlehkeh yehlehkeh borbainbo kobennh ko gibain dor" in their hearts.

As we continued to St. Mary's campus that afternoon, we talked about what happened at Adrian and Paul's apartment. Joe Mark laughed it out loudly and thought it was funny. He masterfully took the focus from us and put it on Paul and Adrian. If we had been the ones who hid our food under the bed, he would have made me laugh to the point of almost wetting my pants for having crafted an ingenious plan to torpedo the visitors' plan to eat our food. As many Liberians are accustomed to doing, Joe Mark forgot the good, albeit unwillingly and light-heartedly, that Adrian and Paul did for us. We were devouring pests who caused them considerable grief. Instead of being grateful, Joe Mark said "Guanbeh o gay leh yorh o."[96] In Mahn, that sounded funny. I played along with Joe Mark and laughed, but deep down I knew we were being unfair to Paul and Adrian.

Writing about our experience with Paul Konan and Adrian Sandi and their rice and peanut butter stew tells part of the story of how I survived hunger in Sanniquellie. But our experience with Paul and Adrian does more. It reminds me; it refreshes the memory I carry each day of Joe Mark Tokpah, my cousin, who always laughed loudly; who always laughed about anything. I still hear his funny jokes and his loud laughs. He did not live long to reap some benefits of our long struggle with hunger in Sanniquellie. He did not live long to hear our story being told. He passed away in April 2006. Today, the tears for having lost my cousin and the memories of hunger in Sanniquellie are indistinguishable.

CHAPTER 11

Other Early Influences

INFLUENCE IS ANYTHING I PERCEIVED and accepted as worthy and incorporated into my life, believing that it would make me a better person. However, because I agree with Barnard's definition of an individual, "A single, unique, independent, isolated, whole thing, embodying innumerable forces and materials past and present which are physical, biological, and social factors," "Other Early Influences" are only a partial definition of me.[97]

A Weekend with Flumo Tokpah

Mom's stories about Flumo Tokpah made him a legend before we met. He was my cousin, but my first encounter with him felt like one with a lost brother.[98] Since that day he became the brother I never had. I wished he came to the village to stay but his visit was too short. He left me longing for his presence and returned to Plehdehyee, Guinea where he lived at the time.

Flumo Tokpah knew I lived with the Guahs in Sanniquellie and attended St. Mary's School. In November 1970, while on his way from Plehdehyee to Sehyeekainpa to visit with Gonotee Charlie, an ailing relative, he stopped in Sanniquellie to greet me. He traveled along with his wife, Kou Lehyeay, and their eight-month-old baby, Nyanquoi Anthony. I thought they stopped by merely to greet me, but I could not contain my excitement when Flumo Tokpah asked the Guahs to let me go with them for that weekend. My excitement was mainly about the opportunity to eat new rice with palm oil, okra and other ingredients.

The Guahs agreed and, in no time, we were on our way to Sehyeekainpa. In the next few minutes, we passed the artificial Lake Teeleh and set our eyes on St. Mary's campus up the hill on the four-mile trek. As we passed St. Mary's campus, I conveniently avoided the story about the whipping Father Francis gave me for stealing grapefruits in 1967. Instead, I queried Flumo Tokpah about when he would return to settle in the village. Passing vehicles continually interrupted my queries as speeding ones forced us into the gutter repeatedly for our protection. Often, we waited in the gutter for a while to regain visibility after vehicles threw plumes of red dust at us.

A quarter mile from Sehyeekainpa, grave markers on both sides of the road rekindled my fear of ghosts. So, to conceal my fear, I turned everyone's attention to the fork in the road ahead of us, where vehicles either went one way, to Yekepa, or the other, to Karnplay.[99] We took the road to Karnplay at the fork because our hosts lived about twenty-five yards off the highway that went through the town. As we approached our destination, an elderly woman looked our way, with the right hand over her eyebrows, suggest-ing she was having trouble seeing. Moments later, she called out "Flumo Tokpah!" Then, instantly, everyone ran out in excitement and greeted us with hugs and "Ka seneh o, ka seneh o" (a greeting said before shaking people's hands) while others were shaking hands and snapping fingers.

Once the pleasantries subsided, our hosts hurriedly started preparing food. I had a flashback to the village, where Mom always had prepared food waiting for strangers. I was hungry and could not wait any longer. As if she deliberately wanted to distract me from my immediate concern, Lehyeay told frightful tales about the humongous tree in the center of town. The tree's branches extended over a radius of thirty feet or more, covering several roofs, not to mention the Karnplay highway that went right under. According to Lehyeay, "people" in another "world" congregated in the bulging girth of the tree's trunk. Moreover, the town's secret society prohibited cutting any part of the tree. With heightened curiosity, I stepped outside, stood a few feet away and gazed in awe at its sheer size.

"Luogon," someone called out my name as I circled the tree. "Oh gay ee nu" (you are being called). Like scanning antennae, my ears were up for that call; I could not miss it and could not contain my excitement because it suggested that the food was ready. I then dashed to our hosts' house only several yards away. There, on a mat in the piazza, a large pan of rice and a deep bowl of okra soup were placed side by side. Per tradition, Lehyeay ate with the women while Flumo Tokpah and I ate together. I washed my hands, squatted and faced the food as he sat on a stool across from me. Flumo Tokpah used a spoon but I could not use one because, in the culture, a child who ate with adults while using a spoon was considered disrespectful.

Once we started eating, I held the pan in place with the left index finger and thumb, preventing it from sliding back and forth. Then, to show "respect" for rice (a reference to the labor that went into rice farming), I put the left palm under the right palm to prevent wastage each time I took a handful of rice from the pan to my mouth. My left hand alternated between holding the pan and the bottom of my right palm. The large pan of rice was one reason I was elated about the trip to Sehyeekainpa; it felt like a bonanza. I feasted that evening as if I had not had food in a long time.

"Luogon, go to bed. We are leaving early tomorrow morning for the farm," Flumo Tokpah urged me shortly after dinner. "How far is the farm?" I asked. Once he said, "Not far," I knew it was déjà vu all over again because the culture is notorious for downplaying the severity of anything. I knew I was in for a rude awakening the next morning because a stone-throw away often meant a mile or more. Indeed, "Not far" turned out to be more than a two-hour walk. The farm was on perhaps a forty-five-degree slope of Mount Williton, seen from far away as Sanniquellie.

Upon arrival at the farming village, we climbed Mount Williton to harvest rice but there were problems. The intensity of the tropical sun felt like a furnace while tiny mind-bogglingly annoying bugs encircled my head, invaded the nostrils, ears and eyes. I turned to Flumo Tokpah for help, but his strategy for solving my bug problem did not make sense. "Pretend you are lifeless," he told me. "The bugs are looking for materials to make honey," he said. "If you stopped moving, they would stop because a lifeless person does not produce mucus in the nostrils, sweat or earwax," he told me.

As the sun baked me, the bugs would not let up. "What happened to all the fun I thought I would have?" I wondered quietly to myself. I looked for every excuse to climb down to the farming village at the base of the mountain, however, I was afraid to ask because Flumo Tokpah might let me go. I was not prepared to climb down alone because the footpaths and forests were eerily quiet. Ghosts of the recently buried, especially those who had scores to settle, prowled at that time of the day. I put up with the irritating bugs and scorching tropical sun because of fear of ghosts.

Eventually, we climbed down to the farming village. Each of the three cone-shape roof huts contained an upper-level storage space for harvested rice. Moreover, several 10-foot medium sized 12-inch diameter tree trunk pillars supported each hut. The huts had no walls of any kind while the fireplace was in the center of the floor. Everyone lay on mats around the fireplace. Upon nightfall, the perimeter of the village was pitch dark. I could hardly see anything other than innumerable fireflies, which looked like a lit mega city seen from a jet airliner thousands of feet above at night. The fireflies terrified me because they were associated with ghosts and witchcraft. Sounds of different critters which appeared to be in a choral competition only intensified my anxiety. I stayed close to Flumo Tokpah for protection.

As my heart raced due to fear, Lehyeay's eight- to ten-month old baby, Nyanquoi Anthony, would not stop crying. No one knew what the child's problem was except the obvious puffing blisters all over its skin, which were a symptom of an undetermined illness. It seemed it had had burns at intervals all over its body. Once I was in a spot where I felt shielded and protected from prowling ghosts because Flumo Tokpah was lying behind me, he told a frightful story to allay my fears. Aware that I was terribly afraid of ghosts, Flumo Tokpah told a story in which one of the main characters, a monster, was more frightful than ghosts. The monster disguised itself as a man, visited with a young man and his family, and abducted his older sister. He cast me as the young man, the hero, who pursued the monster into the jungle and rescued his sister. Flumo Tokpah believed that casting me as the hero to confront a more frightful creature would give me the courage to overcome my fear of ghosts.

Flumo Tokpah believed in me. Around him, I felt comfortable, complete and dignified. He used to hunt at night with a headlight so that I can have a dish of meat for dinner whenever I was in the village from school. Often, he walked with me from the village to Sanniquellie to ensure that I was safe.

Mrs. Flomo

Mrs. Flomo (no relations), a medium height, dark and imposing woman who wore a hairdo of incomprehensible style and beauty like a palm tree seen from afar, was my kindergarten teacher.[100] She always came to school immaculately and professionally attired. I only remember her switch and not her smiles; she was stern. Given the power she wielded, let alone the rattan switch she carried, she did not need to conceal her smiles. Teachers commanded great respect at the time Mrs. Flomo (same pronunciation as my last name) was a teacher. She demanded respect without uttering a word. She managed a large group of "ABC" students (Kindergarteners) without any difficulty. She never whipped me, but I saw her whip many students who did not know how to say their ABC or SO GO and LO. Teachers at that time considered a child who did not know how to say its alphabet as "dull" (not intelligent). Thus, the "Teeseh" (teacher) used the switch to put "Sensee" (sense) into the child's head.

Mrs. Flomo was a member of the Sanniquellie middle class. Her husband, Mr. Alfred Flomo, was an attorney. She had a textbook family. Her son, Sammy, and daughter, Yvonne, who attended kindergarten with me always came to school smartly dressed and looking almost perfect. Her family's powerful image of a nuclear family in a predominantly polygamous culture helped firm my conception of a family. Mrs. Flomo was a role model in that I looked forward to having a family like hers in the future.

WILLIAM WALKER

Mr. William Walker (deceased), my fourth-grade teacher, also taught me in grade six. He was a household name and a member of the Sanniquellie middle class. Mr. Walker dressed professionally and always spoke Standard English. He was a lay leader in the Catholic Church and attended mass regularly with his family. At school, Mr. Walker carried a switch; he was also a stern and old-fashioned disciplinarian.

Besides Mr. Walker's school and church roles, he was a commander in the Nimba County militia, an auxiliary of the Armed Forces of Liberia (AFL). The militia, a big deal in Liberia prior to the April 12, 1980 Revolution, did not bear arms; it consisted of all able-bodied men eighteen years or older not enrolled in school.[101] The militia regularly assembled for inspection at the Sanniquellie airfield, at which time members wore complete military regalia, including khaki pants and shirts with all their attachments, helmets, and black military boots. Members paraded on the airfield and through the principal streets of the city. I always came out to catch a glimpse of Mr. Walker, dressed splendidly, leading the parade.

Of all my teachers at the elementary school level, Mr. Walker was the only one whom I visited at home and observed up close, although the visit lasted only one day. I went to his house and helped with yard work in 1971 when I was a sixth grader. His family was at home and the environment was peaceful. I felt the same respectability that he had at school. In the community, Mr. Walker also stood out in a positive way. Although no one or no family is perfect, Mr. Walker's family seemed like a TV family. His children were clean-cut while his wife was a consummate professional. The image Mr. Walker and his family projected influenced me to want to have a family like his family.

Two incidents sealed Mr. Walker into my memory. The first incident occurred at the end of the first marking period in fourth grade in 1969. Teachers at St. Mary's School, at that time, marked failing grades (0 to 69%) and passing grades (70 to 100%) in report cards with red ink pen and either blue or black ink pen, respectively. Teachers and students never discussed grading, not to mention parents who had little or no clue what went on at school. Parents saw teachers as all powerful and not only trusted them but also respected them highly. I never questioned my teachers about my grades. Moreover, the subject did not even cross my mind. My responsibility was to go to school every day and do my work. At the end of the first marking period, I was not worried that I was in danger of failing and never expected one red mark, let alone four red marks. However, I received four red marks in my report card and had no clue how that happened.[102]

My fourth-grade class in 1969 was a morning session. On the day of the incident, Father Michael Francis came to the elementary school to hand out report cards. He separated them into three piles. Category one had students who did exceptionally well, category two consisted of students at grade level and category three contained students who were not performing at grade level. Father Francis called out the names of students who did exceptionally well and told them to take their books and move on to grade five. There were two students in category one. Next, he turned to category three, students who had four or more red marks in their report cards. One after the other, he called the students and told them to get their books and go to grade three. Failure had never crossed my mind. Therefore, I was completely at ease as Father Francis called out the names. Then, all of a sudden, I heard my name. My heart pounded as if it were about to fall into my stomach. I was shocked. Father Francis asked me to take my books and go to grade three but, at that very moment, I heard Mr. Walker say,

"No, Father, let him stay." I remained in fourth grade and was promoted to grade five at the end of the year.

I had done very well in third grade. I did not understand why Father Francis asked me to go to repeat the third grade. More importantly, I do not know why Mr. Walker told Father Francis to let me stay in fourth grade. It could not have been my visit to his house to help with yard work because that occurred in 1971 when I was in the sixth grade. Although Mr. Walker may have had a sense of my potential, I believe Wlah's hand was in my remaining in fourth grade to finish the year.

The second incident occurred when I was in the sixth grade in 1971. Students sang the Liberian national anthem every school day upon raising the flag, but they did not know the words very well, not to mention their meanings. On a Friday, Mr. Walker assigned both stanzas of the Liberian National Anthem for homework. Our task was to memorize both stanzas and recite them individually before the class on the following Monday. Almost everyone in the class forgot the homework. No one in the entire class could recite both stanzas of the national anthem. The punishment for failing to do our homework was three-pronged. First, Mr. Walker denied us recess, which meant we could not hang out with our friends or eat Care Food. For those of us who depended on Care Food as a major part of our daily intake, this was no small matter. Second, we stayed in the classroom for the entire thirty minutes and "pumped tire."[103] Third, as if denying us recess and pumping tire were not enough punishments, Mr. Walker walked around the classroom to make sure that no one stopped to take a breather. He whipped me with a switch on my back so hard that I almost urinated in my pants when I slowed down because my knees were about to give up. Other students received similar whipping for slowing down. At the end of the thirty minutes, nearly everyone fell to the floor unable to stand and walk. Although that was the worst punishment I ever endured in school, it did not change my mind about who Mr. Walker was.

ROSE VOKER

Mrs. Rose Voker, a medium height stoutly built fair-skinned woman with a presence, was my fifth-grade teacher. She dressed elegantly, wore large glasses and carried herself with an enviable poise and dignity. Mrs. Voker, also a stern disciplinarian, was my second female teacher. She carried a switch, even though she seldom used it. Fifth grade was one of my best years in elementary school, considering the terrible beginning of fourth grade. The fifth-grade classroom was situated between grades four and six classrooms, with all three classrooms housed in the relatively newer elementary school building.

By 1970, Mom's mind and work habits had solidified my belief in women's ability to do anything men could do. So, having Rose Voker as my fifth-grade teacher further strengthened that belief. She was a member of the Sanniquellie middle class. Her daughter, Roseline, who attended St. Mary's School always looked well-dressed and pretty. The dignity, image, and respectability that Mrs. Voker projected helped me develop habits and attitudes I still have to this day.

Even though Mrs. Rose Voker was a woman, the image she projected influenced the self-image I started forming when I was a fifth grader. She was a fitting role model for fifth and sixth grade girls in 1970 because they were very particular about their appearance. Every day they wore beautiful hairdos and came to school dressed elegantly in their green jumpers and white blouses. The girls added their own unwritten, yet socially enforced standards to the culture of appropriate appearance and cleanliness, which Mrs. Voker epitomized. They started and perpetuated the "White brief" and "Cleanliness" phenomenon, meaning if one wore a white brief, then one was a clean person.

Clothes Dad bought for me were often imported shorts and shirts or t-shirts. Shorts were often rubberized at the waist to prevent sagging. My denim shorts often had permanently attached suspenders, which crossed diagonally at the back. At other times, Dad took me to a Lebanese store in Sanniquellie, bought yards of khaki and then proceeded to a local tailor to take measurements for a new pair of shorts with belt stripes.

Fifth and sixth grade girls in elementary school appeared older and mature. Their chitchats and gossips about white versus colored briefs were an impetus for my interest in wearing briefs, which was a novelty for me. I started wearing briefs in fifth grade in 1970. The girls' preference for white briefs over colored briefs filtered down to others and me. "If that is what the girls like, right on!" I said to myself. Elementary school girls' gossip was the origin of the white brief bandwagon that I am on. I bought my first set of white briefs, at the time twenty-five cents each, after a weekend trip to the village. Fruit of the Loom men's brief manufacturer owes St. Mary's Elementary School fifth and sixth grade girls at the time a debt of gratitude.

Owning and wearing a white brief were not the most important thing. Playground friends had to know that one had white brief on because it was a mark of being "cool." We often took off our shirts to play soccer at the playground at school or in the neighborhood. To show the briefs, we often pulled their white rubberized waist bands up higher than the shorts. If that did not happen, one bent over, pretending to pick up something from the ground, in which case the shorts and brief's waistband separated, exposing the brief.

SAYE GUAH

Joseph Saye Guah, known simply as Saye Guah, the Guahs' eldest child, was the unmistakable role model in the Guah household. The roughly 5'7" fair-skinned dark curly-haired young man was suave with an air of sophistication but approachable. I admired Saye because he was immeasurably articulate. He spoke English as if it were his native tongue. Saye was also the furthest in education. Therefore, everyone looked up to him. When he graduated from St. Mary's School in 1972 and left for Monrovia, no one in the household was able to replace him. In Monrovia, he worked for the Liberia Electricity Corporation and then eventually traveled to the United States, where he lives in Atlanta, Georgia.

In 1987, almost fifteen years after Saye left Sanniquellie, the urge to see and talk to him had not died because he was a larger-than-life figure during my formative years. I had wonderful role models including my parents, but no one made role models more meaningful to me like Saye did. Now, I know role models are like beacons; they guide ships approaching shores, but they do not choose which ships they guide. Moreover, ships furthest at sea are at peril when beacons lose their glows. Saye's departure left captains of ships in Sanniquellie wondering where or how far away the shore was.

I reconnected with Saye while in Greensboro, North Carolina in 1987. Then, in the early 1990s, we communicated occasionally and remained in touch until I moved to Spokane, Washington, in June 1997. In December 2015, forty-three years after Saye left me in Sanniquellie, I met him during Wonkermie Flumo's wedding in Marietta, Georgia. Memories of our lives together in Sanniquellie are the foundation of our relationship.

DAVID GUAH

David Sehlehkpo Guah, simply known as "Deabay" (David), was fair-skinned, stout and no more than 5'6". I did not know his age, but he led a very active lifestyle. Deabay was petit and muscular and aged very slowly; his features never seemed to change at all. He spoke good English, had a magnificent handwriting and, by Liberian standards, was educated. Moreover, Deabay saw the old Underwood typewriter he owned as a mark of an educated man. On countless occasions, I watched him type with the two index fingers, replace the ribbon, or repair it whenever it broke down.

Deabay stressed the importance of education, citing the material benefits as well as his refrain "No one fools or takes advantage of an educated person." Mom and Dad saw Deabay as a *quizee* and took his message seriously. His message resonated particularly with Dad because tax collectors repeatedly took advantage of him. Hence, his motivation for taking me to live with Deabay to go to school.

Reading to one's child was not a part of the culture during my early years because our parents did not read or write. Even though Deabay knew how to read and write, he never read to me. However, he met Mom and Dad's expectations. He put fear in me to avoid "walking about" to stay safe and to keep my head in the books. Everything that pertained to the acquisition of knowledge and skills, including reading and writing, was bundled together as "Sensee" (sense), which the "Teeseh" (teacher) put into my head at school. Deabay expected his children, Joseph Saye Guah, Mary Kou Tailor Guah (deceased), Paul Nyan Guah (deceased), and me to study and achieve. He paid attention to my progress in school by looking at my report card. Deabay, who was trigger-happy with the rod, did not conceal the consequences for failure.

Deabay was short-tempered, impatient, and feisty. He did not appear to be afraid of anybody. His harshness terrified everyone and caused great fear in his household. If Deabay came home unhappy about something, a minor mishap was a cause for whipping. No one including his wives escaped his wrath. He was unnecessarily rough with everyone, including his wives and children. Sometimes, he whipped us for little or nothing. If he did not whip us, he made us "pump tires, although he never made his wives pump tires. However, Deabay was neither hateful nor cold.

Besides impatience and hotheadedness, Deabay's appetite for the acquisition of property was insatiable. Even as a young kid, I could not ignore that aspect of his drive. Ambition was not a part of my vocabulary at the time but the Mahns described someone like Deabay as having a "Zogbuo" (a big heart, a heart that wants a big part of everything, a heart that cannot be easily satisfied). Three houses in Sanniquellie and several hundred acres of land along the railway, three miles to the north of Sanniquellie, not to mention two huge tracts of lands consisting of virgin forest beyond his ancestral home of Sehyeekainpa, did not satisfy him.

Deabay's hunger for more possessions also made him wary. He perceived no immediate enemies but future challenges to his ownership of the massive tracts of lands. Therefore, to establish legitimate ownership beyond the deed that he possessed, he took me along on more than one occasion to plant coffee in selected areas of the virgin forest. I knew instantly Deabay did not intend to raise cash crop. Instead, he was preparing for court battles over land issues he saw coming.

Later, I figured Deabay's taste for property was a foreign idea in the culture because Mahns farmed communal lands with defined boundaries, that passed down from one generation to the next. Purchase as well as deeding of any communal lands as personal property was forbidden. Deabay's taste for acquiring real estate came from somewhere else. Incidentally, *quizee* (Americo-Liberian) culture was the only one where ownership of property was a hallmark of prestige. Deabay not only lived with *quizees* but also adopted a *quizee* surname, Watson; they educated him. *Quizees* owned the best real estate in Monrovia. Although their population remained predominantly along the coast, that did not prevent them from "acquiring" huge tracts of lands from the natives in rural Liberia for their farms.[104] Many used their power and influence to take communal lands from indigenous people.

Deabay reached out to grab onto a world and lifestyle he wanted for himself, a world influenced and shaped by a culture other than his own. *Quizees* shaped that world and had the means to satisfy their "Zogbuo" as well as their desire for real estate. Since the founding of Liberia in the 1820s, *quizees*, took the land and its people like oak mistletoe (Phoradendron leucarpum). Through subjugation and oppression, they bestowed upon themselves and posterity first class citizenship. A hallmark of the culture they created was wealth/property as well as political and economic power. They not only made their acquisition at the expense of the natives but also passed it down from one generation to the next.

Deabay adopted a *quizee* surname, but he did not have a *quizee* pedigree as a means of satisfying his "Zogbuo" and appetite for real estate.

Unfortunately, while he toiled honorably, the desires that stirred his appetite for real estate and other possessions diffused his focus. He sewed clothes for sale on a Singer sewing machine he owned, cultivated rice, and sold "Cane Juice," a locally distilled spirit, in a liquor shop he owned. Other sources of his income included a yearly lease of one of his three houses by the Foday Toure family, monthly rents for individual rooms in one of his three houses and membership in a "Guan".[105] In a guan, each member contributed a certain amount of money and a member received the total amount of money collected each Sunday. Members took turns and received the total sum of money collected each Sunday until the list of members was exhausted.

Deabay's sources of income did not provide a steady reliable cash flow. Tailoring, farming and shop keeping as well as the other sources of income fell short of helping Deabay meet his obligations. Other financial problems as well as ensuring and sending his guan contributions on time often put him under intense pressure. On such occasions, he often turned to Wlah for relief. Like Mom, Deabay asked his deceased parents to intercede with Wlah on his behalf. He prayed for financial blessing, interchangeably using two words, "Sanamah" (luck) and "Lorkee" (Mahn pronunciation for the English word 'luck'). I often wondered whether his habitual request for relief praying for "Lorkee" had any connection to the brand of cigarettes he smoked. Deabay only smoked "Lucky Strike," which he often sent me to buy. He led me to think perhaps smoking "Lucky Strike" had a role in securing an impending blessing or relief from Wlah.

Deabay often prayed at night while traveling from Sanniquellie to Sehyeekainpa perhaps because of the quietude and solitude nighttime provided or perhaps because his deceased parents were listening. I often accompanied him. His prayers were often long soliloquies and he often talked as if he were engaged in an exchange with someone. On occasions Deabay traveled alone, he returned with a message that he had been told to offer a sacrifice of white chicken. The family slaughtered a white chicken and prepared a dinner. Everyone gathered for a libation to climax the "Salah" after the dinner.[106] I always wondered who told Deabay to offer a sacrifice of white chicken. It could be a fortuneteller, native doctor, or a sand cutter, all of whom were influential in the culture. It could also be a relative who had a dream in which the request for a sacrifice was revealed. Despite Deabay's toils and prayers, the world he reached for was always like a mirage in a desert; the harder he struggled and the closer he got to it, the farther it moved away.

Esther Dokie

Outside the village, I had Esther Luolay Dokie to look up to as a role model for my education. Sister Esther, as we fondly called her, was the first person who finished high school in our extended family. She was exquisitely beautiful and sophisticated. I not only regarded her as the de facto "Queen" of our extended family but also adored her. Esther was a cousin but there is no such thing as a cousin in the culture because it puts distance between family members. I took pride in being her family. More importantly, knowing my name and being a model of achievement and success were her biggest influence on me.

Esther attended school in Sanniquellie and later enrolled at the Booker Washington Institute (BWI) in Kakata, Liberia, where she studied secretarial science. After graduation from BWI, she worked in Monrovia with the Mesurado Group of Companies. Esther's career at the Mesurado Group of Companies was an added and important impetus for my education. As it happened, the rumor was that she earned U.S. $100 per month. During the 1960s and early 1970s in Liberia, $100 was a ton of money. Upon hearing about Esther's salary, I was very proud of her. More importantly, the good news about sister Esther's salary spurred my own dream about the future if I pursued my education beyond the eighth-grade goal my parents set. I wanted to be like sister Esther; I wanted to become successful in my educational career to reach if not surpass the status that she attained.

Later, sister Esther moved to Yekepa, Nimba County, to work for the Lamco Joint Venture Operating Company as a senior staff in the Data Processing Department.[107] She remained with Lamco until she passed away on October 4, 1982. Sister Esther perhaps never realized that, by getting an education and having a professional career with the Mesurado Group of Companies and Lamco, she was giving oxygen. More importantly, maybe she never knew that her admirer and grateful cousin was breathing that oxygen.

The Catholic Missionaries

Catholic missionaries, including school leaders, teachers, and other professionals, accepted a call to serve humanity. They left the comforts and safety of their homes and loved ones in the Americas, Europe, and Africa, went to Sanniquellie and built upon Father Michael Francis's legacy of successful stewardship at St. Mary's School. They continued the professionalism and high standard of educational excellence Father Francis established. Moreover, they expanded, improved upon, and maintained St. Mary's physical facilities. Indeed, they sacrificed to educate the young people of Sanniquellie.

Eventually, the missionaries retired and returned to their respective countries, but it was not a normal retirement.[108] There were no retirement dinners, farewell speeches, hugs, or messages of appreciation for their services. With their departure, St. Mary's ceased to be a beachhead in standards and quality education. Due to a dearth of qualified school leaders, teachers and appropriate support, the school still struggles to regain its prewar status. The upheavals of the civil war hollowed the missionaries' lifetime of work and shortchanged Sanniquellie's young people's education.

Now, the onus of the work at St. Mary's School is upon me, and that recognition alone is a tribute to the missionaries who educated me. I beseech Wlah for a measure of strength for the work at St. Mary's School in hopes that current and future students may have the quality of education I received. Therefore, in paraphrasing John Donne's "For whom the bell tolls," "Do not ask me for whom does the St. Mary's bell toll," for I know that it tolls for me.[109]

CLARENCE DOLO

Mr. Clarence Dolo (deceased), formerly Charles Dolo, was Mahn, 5'10" and stoutly built. He hailed from Gotonwin, a town about ten miles past the village, along the Sanniquellie-Bahn road via the village. He was highly knowledgeable about the Boys Scouts and was an effective scout leader. He dressed exquisitely in his Boys Scouts regalia and projected a strong and distinctive self-image. Mr. Dolo was disciplined and had a quiet demeanor.

Ma Ollie, an Americo-Liberian elderly woman, reared Mr. Dolo. She referred to him only by Guankarnue, his Mahn name.[110] Apparently, his parents took him to live with Ma Ollie to go to school in the same way as my parents took me to live with the Guahs to go to school. I did not know Mr. Dolo before his parents took him to live with Ma Ollie in Sanniquellie. I knew him only in Sanniquellie because the house he lived in was merely a stone throw from the Guahs' residence. I often fetched water in buckets from Ma Ollie's well in her yard.

Mr. Dolo and I came from similar indigenous background. After living with Ma Ollie for a long time, his mannerisms and values changed. He had a panache, an air of sophistication about him. He smiled broadly, but said very little, at times suggesting that he knew better than others did. Mr. Dolo did not tell anyone, especially indigenous people that he was civilized. However, by his mannerisms, it was clear that he had adopted the uppity attitudes of some Americo-Liberians. His mannerisms were typical of other indigenous people who grew up under the guidance of Americo-Liberians. I did not adopt his mannerisms, but I admired the way he carried himself. I liked how he dressed and the image of himself he projected. He was always clean cut.

D. K. WONSEHLEAY

Mr. Wonsehleay (deceased) did not know me. I knew him from a distance because he lived perhaps three blocks from where Joe Mark Tokpah and I lived in New Sanniquellie in 1972. He attended Sanniquellie Central High School and walked past where we lived on his way to school. The fair-skinned, popped eye medium height man was a Scout Master. I admired him for his immeasurable eloquence. He personified brilliance, radiance, and self-confidence.

In 1983, Mr. Wonsehleay, also known as D.K., dazzled me with his intelligence and oratorical gifts. The government of Liberia, at the time, arrested him, along with others, for allegedly participating in the Nimba Raid, an alleged attempt to overthrow President Samuel Doe. Although death hung over his head, not to mention the intense pressure he was under, D.K. remained at ease throughout a nationally televised interrogation before a military tribunal. Eventually, President Samuel Doe pardoned him and others after the spectacle.

Unfortunately, following General Thomas G. Qwiwonkpa's abortive attempt to overthrow President Samuel Doe on November 12, 1985, something ugly happened. Soldiers loyal to the president rounded up eminent Nimba citizens, including D.K. and took them to an undisclosed location in Yekepa, Nimba County. Sometime later, they were allegedly tortured and executed. During that tragic incident, Nimba County and Liberia lost an eminent son and a brilliant mind.

SANNIQUELLIE

Sanniquellie, the capital of Nimba County, is located in northeastern Liberia, two hundred and seven miles away from Monrovia. It is the birthplace of the Organization of African Unity (OAU), now the African Union (AU). Eleven years of immersion during my formative years in Sanniquellie shaped me profoundly. Sanniquellie prepared, inspired, and sent me into the world. With hunger, it indelibly inscribed upon my heart an inescapable reminder to return and give back. The city had a unique culture of diverse ethnic groups and a tiered local economy.[111]

Sanniquellie was a center of learning. High schools in the city included Sanniquellie Central High, St. Mary's High, Bishop Thomas High and Dolo Memorial High School. Other schools included Seventh Day Adventist and Baptist School, now Levi A. Martin Memorial High School. The potential education had for broad economic improvement benefits was enormous. In addition, education had an immediate and rollercoaster impact on the city's population because the schools attracted students from Nimba County and throughout Liberia. At the opening of schools each year, new and returning students increased the city's population dramatically. Moreover, their purchasing power supported businesses, although the opposite effect occurred at the close of schools. Unfortunately, due to the secondary school curriculum's almost exclusive focus on academic preparation with little or no instruction in vocational skills, the local economy did not reap the potential benefits of education.

The tiered local economy at the time presented a different hurdle. Although the schools neither taught entrepreneurial skills nor were there banks to lend, involvement in the local economy depended on participants' entrepreneurial skills and financial wherewithal. In the surrounding villages and towns, Mahns cultivated tree crops, root crops, rice, oil palm, and vegetables. They carried their produce mostly on their heads to the market on Saturdays and bought essential household or other supplies. They were major producers as well as consumers, yet they participated at the bottom level of the local economy.

Unlike Mahns, Mandingoes had tremendous entrepreneurial skills acquired through apprenticeships as well as financial wherewithal. In addition, they occupied the next level of the local economy almost exclusively except in the areas of education, agriculture, and local government. The men owned shops on the main streets alongside Lebanese stores; operated taxis, minibuses, pickups, and cargo trucks. They virtually monopolized the commercial transportation industry while others traded diamonds or operated diamond mines in towns and villages along the Yar River. The men also operated tailor shops, bakeries and manufactured farm tools and aluminum pots from scraps. Mandingo women, on the other hand, sold everything including apparel, jewelries, rice, fish, oil, sesame, salt, bouillon cubes, and hair products. They also bought produce from Mahn farmers wholesale and, in turn, sold it retail at the Sanniquellie market during weekdays. Furthermore, they operated restaurants, manufactured soap and processed and sold tobacco products.

Lebanese occupied the top echelon of the local economy, operating stores lining the streets of Sanniquellie. They sold consumer goods including apparels, footwears, household appliances, furniture, electronics, and building materials. As Sanniquellie was a seed that fell on fertile ground, grew into a plant, survived and thrived, things happened, and no one asked. Lebanese traders and others, for example, siphoned the city's vitality as well as their profits from the local economy, giving nothing back. Similarly, those who got their starts in the city, students, traders or others, left and never looked back, leaving Sanniquellie "dry" and notorious for "breaking the backs" of students because there were no jobs for students to help sustain themselves.[112] In addition, the iron ore mining industry next door, in Yekepa, had little or no impact on the local Sanniquellie economy. It too left Yekepa a ghost city. Today, however, the situation is the complete reverse. Local people are in complete control of the economy.

CHAPTER 12

Lessons

THE WRONG PLACE

IN 1973, WHILE JOE MARK and I were living in the family house, I took a weekend trip to Gartehpa, a hamlet located one quarter of a mile off the Ganta-Sanniquellie Highway, about four miles north of Ganta. My parents lived in Gartehpa for a long time. In 1965, they moved and settled in the village. My sisters were born in Gartehpa, although Mom delivered me at the nearby Ganta United Methodist Hospital. In Gartehpa, my parents owned a house and farmlands, including coffee plantations. Mr. Paye Garteh, whom the hamlet was named after, was Dad's mentor. As a result, we considered him and his family as our own and called him "Dad" as well. I created some of my vivid childhood memories in Gartehpa and surrounding villages and towns, including Deegbopa and Dingamon.

Even though at the time I started school at St. Mary's in 1966 my parents had already moved from Gartehpa and settled in village, my emotional attachment to Gartehpa, including its people and ambiance remained strong. I took that weekend trip because I wanted to see the Garteh family and others whom I considered family. Moreover, as I relished St. Mary's

School and wore it as a badge of honor, I was excited to flaunt my school and educational progress to my extended family in Gartehpa.

Before the trip, I informed my parents, while in the village, that I would go to see my other family in Gartehpa. They were perfectly fine with my trip because they knew that the Garteh family would take care of me. As for the Garteh family, my trip to see them was going to be a surprise as it was in the culture. Extended family members and others always arrived for visits unannounced not because surprises had any benefit but because the technology for prior notification did not exist at that time. There was no telephone service in the villages and towns. The landline telephone system in Sanniquellie at the time did not extend to the villages and towns, not to mention cellular phones, which were unheard of during those days.

On a Friday, at the main parking station in Sanniquellie, I took a taxi headed to the commercial city of Ganta. In no time, the driver whisked through the city past the executive grounds and stopped at the checkpoint then located at the old barracks.[113] After the usual feigned checks, literally a scan of passengers' faces and a few questions about hometowns, to identify "aliens" or "foreigners," the driver resumed the trip.[114] Taking off from the checkpoint, he climbed the hill towards Ganta and continued a paved and level section of the road. In a little while, we arrived at the Welcome Gate, where we ended our smooth ride on the paved road. On both sides of the road from that point on, red dust from the laterite road covered tree leaves and shrubberies and made them appear as though they were red-haired people summoned to line the highway to cheer us on along the ride. One after the other, we passed through the familiar towns of Kitoma, Camp 3 and Gbedin. Next, we drove through Zuluyee, Tundin and upon entering Dingamon, I sat straight up and alert because I did not want the driver to forget where to drop me off. In Dingamon, we were less than a mile away from the Gartehpa junction, where the driver needed to drop me off. Upon arrival at the junction, I paid the driver fifty cents, the usual cost for the approximately twenty-mile distance from Sanniquellie to Gartehpa. During the three- to five-minute walk from the junction to Gartehpa, I frolicked with excitement. As expected, the Garteh family was happy as ever to receive me upon arrival.

On the evening of my arrival in Gartehpa, Nyan Farmer, Mr. Paye Garteh's son, also known as Whyan Nyan, asked me to accompany him to "Town," meaning Dingamon, to check out what was going on. Dingamon, a town on the main Ganta-Sanniquellie Highway, is about a mile from Gartehpa. At the time, the town had a reputation for actions—soccer games, bars and good times, often slipping into rowdy behaviors. Unfortunately, the evening of my arrival was one of such unruly days in Dingamon. At that time, I had not come of age. I had not developed interests in girls beyond mere teenage curiosities. As such, I was not particularly keen about going to bars. However, I was excited about going along with Nyan Farmer for the mile walk to Dingamon because I wanted to see the Peters. My parents had left me with the Peters at the end of 1965 briefly to go to school, but the arrangement did not work out well and they had to come back to get me. Even though we did not have any blood relations, the brief time I spent with the Peters also made them my family.

Upon arrival in Dingamon with Nyan Farmer that evening, I did not accomplish my goal of going along. I did not get to see the Peters. The reason was that a crowd of boys, gathered on both sides of the Ganta-Sanniquellie Highway in the middle of the town, distracted us. The north-south highway cut through the town and created east-west sections with the larger section to the west and the smaller one to the east. Out of curiosity, Nyan Farmer and I walked toward the crowd to find out the cause of the commotion. We soon realized that the large crowd of boys, high school age and above, gathered to do things boys from Dingamon had developed a reputation for doing. Dingamon boys had a Wild West tough guys' reputation. It was well established that nobody messed with them. Often when boys who hailed from Dingamon took a passenger vehicle from Sanniquellie to Dingamon, they refused to pay the driver. Instead, they would take off and run away. For that reason, Mandingo drivers who plied that route quickly learned not to pick up passengers headed to Dingamon who appeared to be students.

At about 8:00 p.m. local time that Friday night, the crowd of boys by the road numbered between twenty and thirty people. The boys had gathered to begin pulling off the same old tricks for which they had developed a reputation. Every time a vehicle arrived with passengers, the crowd surged and surrounded it, giving passengers opportunities to get away without paying their fares. It seemed like sports for them. Standing on the west side of the road, Nyan Farmer and I were dumbfounded as the boys made what Liberians call "for nothing" trouble. After a little while, I saw a passenger pickup truck come through from Sanniquellie attempting to pass without stopping, but the crowd surged and charged toward the roadway and made it difficult for the vehicle to pass. The determined driver, however, forced his way and went on without stopping. Having realized that the pickup truck driver was playing hardball because he would not stop, the crowd got angrier and stepped up the trouble with stones and other missiles. The driver then drove on, slowed down and eventually came to a stop. Along with his assistants, the driver charged angrily toward the crowd. Apparently, he wanted to find out what the heck the boys were doing stoning the vehicle. Suddenly, the seemingly invincible crowd dispersed and ran away. Even Nyan Farmer, who was a mere bystander like me, took off and abandoned me. As for me, I just stood there and froze. I reckoned I was not involved in the trouble. I did not stone the vehicle, so I had no reason to run away.

I was wrong in my calculation. The driver and his assistants did not think that I was innocent. In no time, they reached me, forcibly took me away and threw me into the vehicle. Believing that they had apprehended one of their prime suspects, the driver and his assistants would not have any of my complaints that I was not a part of the commotion. Luckily, the angry driver and his assistants did not do any harm to me on the way from Dingamon to Ganta. Considering endemic prejudices against Mandingoes in Liberia, the Mandingo driver and his assistants could have beaten, killed and thrown me into the bush, and no one would have found out, but Wlah protected me.

Upon arrival in Ganta, the driver turned me over to the police. Although he may have said something, I did not hear him say anything to the police officer who was on duty about what I had done. Subsequently, without any questioning by the police officer, I was thrown into a stinking cell. No one asked me about my name, let alone what I had done. I did not see anyone make a note of the time I had been brought in, let alone a full-blown report that any relieving officer could act upon. I was informed of no rights, including the right to remain silent, and the right to counsel, let alone someone having offered food or water. I was the only one in that dilapidated cell. I do not know how I fell asleep, but I slept on the bare floor. By that time, the closest thing to Miranda Rights in the United States, which exists in the 1984 Constitution of Liberia, had not come into existence because the country was still operating under the 1847 Constitution of Liberia.[115] Moreover, as the situation in today's Liberia shows, having a Miranda Rights like provision in the Constitution of Liberia at that time would not have made any difference anyway. Few people involved in law enforcement,

115

particularly in the rural areas, know the laws governing the performance of their duties. Having no doubt about my innocence, I was certain that Wlah would, again, watch over me because I believed then that bad things happen only to those who do wrong.

On the following morning, nobody cared to find out whether I was in that cell or why the driver took me to the Police Station in the first place. I do not even know whether anybody remembered that I was in there at all. I was convinced all along that Wlah was with me from that frightening moment that the driver and his assistants apprehended and threw me into their vehicle. But it was that Saturday, the following morning that it became clear to me that He was working His miracle to save me from the mix-up I had been thrown into by being in the wrong place at the wrong time.

Indeed, I was certain that Wlah was watching over me. I also felt strongly that He was working out a plan to save me from the unfortunate predicament that the trouble Dingamon boys caused that night in Dingamon put me into. My unwavering faith in Wlah at that time was not only on account of my innocence, but also based on Mom's experience. Her story was to some extent akin to Abraham's wife, Sarah's story, although Mom was no Sarah. Mom had not had only one child, a son, in old age when it was biologically impossible. However, she, perhaps, had more unbearable distress than Sarah had. She had lost ten out of eleven children mostly due to childhood diseases before I was born. For years and years, as I have already recounted, she wept and prayed to Wlah. He listened and eventually answered her prayers. He wiped her tears with me, her only son. I was not old enough to know what Mom was going through at the time. However, I imagine Mom may have said "Wlah ah yai ee da ouwn lay; mia oo lo ah laouwn ma ah, ko een ko lo yai ee yeay see ah," something to the effect of what Sarah said when Isaac was born "God has brought me laughter, and everyone who hears about this will laugh with me" (Genesis 21:6)."

Certainty of Wlah's protection and my innocence did not blind me to the awfulness of the brouhaha unruly Dingamon boys caused by stoning the pickup truck that night. I was fully aware that someone in that vehicle could have been injured. Even though no one was injured, I do not believe that it would have been unreasonable if the driver and his assistants had taken their anger out on me. The driver and his assistants apprehended me from where the boys were gathered while causing the trouble. Any reasonable person could have concluded that I was a part of the crowd stoning the vehicle. A beating to the extent of death would have probably been described in Liberian parlance as, "He looked for it."

On that Saturday morning, the police officer in charge was standing at the front of the building and having a conversation with someone. His back was toward me. I could see him because I put my head through a big hole in the wall at the bottom left of the door to the cell. The hole in the wall was big enough for me to pass through it. Almost one-half of my body was in the hallway. I could see the entire hallway and the front of the building through the front door. I do not remember the prayer I said in that cell, but I know that I called on Wlah's name. Right after that, I had the gumption to get through that hole in the wall at the bottom. I got out as if someone inside the cell were pushing me out. The building was oriented north-south with the front where the police officer was standing on the south side. The hallway divided the building into east-west sections. It was not a particularly large building by rural Liberian standards. It apparently had four or five rooms and the veranda also appeared to be a processing center, although, as I already indicated, I was never processed at all when the driver took me to the police.

As soon as I got through the hole and entered the hallway, I crawled toward the front door, but I could not continue all the way to the front door because the police officer was standing out there. I could only see the back of the officer from my vantage point, but I did not fully see the person to whom he was talking. Had I continued to the front door; the officer could have spotted me. Instead, I turned left and crawled into the veranda, which had two window frames neither of which had a pane. Had I lifted my head as I crawled, I would have seen the back of the officer through the window to the south and the person to whom he was talking may have seen me and raised alarm. Instead, I quickly crawled toward the window to the east, where the officer could not have seen me had he turned around. I climbed the window frame, jumped down and landed like a perching bird. I landed on bare ground, but it felt as if I landed on a cushion.

Upon hitting the bare ground, I ran toward the back of the Police Station and found a way to a street that went straight to the Ganta market ground. As I ran by the crowded marketplace, I never looked back. I assumed the police officer was pursuing me. I did not sprint, but my speed was more than that of a jogger. In Ganta, I do not know whether anyone in the marketplace recognized me as someone under distress, but I passed the noisy marketplace like "June passing by July".[116] As I passed the Ganta public market and reached the Ganta-Sanniquellie Highway, I turned north toward the Ganta United Methodist Mission and headed for Gartehpa about two miles away nonstop. Every step I took as I jogged steadily toward the Methodist Mission felt as if each leg weighed one half of its normal weight. Again, each time I landed a foot on the ground, it felt as if I were landing it on a cushion. It felt like my only task was to lean forward. Lifting my legs alternately and pounding the road felt like I was jogging on air. I slowed down where there were on-coming vehicles to protect myself. On the other hand, I got off the road completely and found safe places in the bush to hide whenever vehicles came from the direction of Ganta. Anytime that happened, I assumed that the police officer was pursuing me.

At the Ganta United Methodist Mission, I passed the elegant Methodist Church on the right, the hospital complex on the left and the beautifully manicured grounds I had always admired when I was a child. In less than ten minutes, I passed the African wooden sculpture stand next to Wuopa. Beyond Wuopa, I had a long stretch beginning at the Gbehyeesehyeelah intersection and ending at Mr. Henry Quiqui's farm, with large swamps on both sides of the highway. Soon, I had my sight on Mr. Charles King's farm, then Deegbopa and Bowman's farm. After Deegbopa, I descended into a low-lying area of the road, with swamps on both sides of the highway. In a matter of minutes, I reached the Gartehpa junction. I slowed down to a walking pace and turned left towards Gartehpa. At that moment, I was sweating as if someone drenched me with a bucket of water. I was not tired. Even though I had not eaten anything other than the food I ate upon my arrival in Gartehpa on Friday afternoon, I was not hungry. I was just numb.

It was approaching late morning on that Saturday by the time I made the turn into Gartehpa road. Someone from Gartehpa who was coming toward the main road recognized me and said, "It's Luogon Kporwehgbay" (It's Luogon, Kporweh's son). The person then told me that everybody in Gartehpa had been concerned and assumed the worst. He said Nyan Farmer narrated how a driver and his assistants apprehended and took me to Ganta due to a commotion by a group of Dingamon boys. I heard that, early Saturday morning, Mr. Paye Garteh sent someone to Ganta to find me. Finally, when I reached Gartehpa and told the story of all that happened, everyone thanked Wlah for watching over and protecting me.

Sunday, the following day, it was time to return to Sanniquellie. Mr. Paye Garteh and his wife, Blehlenyee, packed a lot of food for me to take back to Sanniquellie. They treated me in the same way as they treated their own children. The provisions they gave me included rice, eddoes, yams, palm oil and a lot of fruits including grapefruits, avocado pears, and mangoes. My parents planted some of the fruit trees in Gartehpa. Because a variety of fruit trees with low-hanging fruits surrounded the hamlet, Gartehpa, in many ways, was like the village, the "Garden of Eden." Upon my return to Sanniquellie on that Sunday afternoon, I did not tell Joe Mark or anyone the story about the driver and his assistants apprehending and throwing me into jail. The reason was that Joe Mark would have had a field day mocking and laughing at me. Everything was funny to Joe Mark while he was alive.

BETRAYAL

Prior to 1975, a friend to me was someone with whom I played, grew up with, or anyone in my class. In 1975, at the beginning of the new school year, I still held onto that meaning of friendship until the elections for student government leaders at the end of 1976. St. Mary's accepted new students up to tenth grade. Beyond that, the school accepted no new students. In 1975, Mr. Blemie Baikiayee was one of few students the school accepted in tenth grade. Mr. Baikiayee (deceased) attended elementary and junior high school in Camp Four, a once bustling commercial town near Yekepa, Nimba County. Upon meeting Blemie at the beginning of the school year in tenth grade, I took him as another friend. Unlike Blemie, I had the privilege of knowing almost all the students at St. Mary's because I had been at the school since March 1966. In the culture, I was Blemie's "stranger father" (Blemie's host). He had come to a strange place to go to school, and I voluntarily assumed that role. I did what I saw my parents do upon seeing a stranger. I made Blemie to feel at home and assured him that all would be well at St. Mary's.

Before I broke bread with Mr. Baikiayee, he seemed to be a nice person. We hung out at school at the beginning of the school year and eventually became close friends. I liked him not only as a friend, but he was also like a real brother. Others even thought we were actual brothers because, as they put it then, "You guys resemble." Even though Blemie attended school in Camp Four, his hometown was Baynaykplalah, a town southeast of the

119

commercial city of Ganta, quite a distance from Sanniquellie. He could not go home as often as he wanted to because the cost of transportation was a bottleneck. Instead, he often visited with his relatives in Camp Four for help. However, on weekends he did not go to Camp Four, he sometimes did not have enough to eat for the following week. On those occasions, he and I shared whatever foods I had after I had returned from the village.

Until 1975, the only incident of betrayal I knew was the one I read in the Bible in eighth grade, involving Absalom's rise against his father, King David. To be clear, Blemie's betrayal of me did not compare with Absalom's betrayal of his father, King David. However, as the story of Absalom's betrayal of his father was during Biblical times, far removed in time from me, I never had the slightest notion that such a thing could happen in my time. No one in my own life to my knowledge had done anything substantial to me personally to even pale in comparison with Absalom and David's story. Someone may have done something like that to one of my family or extended family members, but I was not aware of it.

As Shakespeare's Duncan put it in Macbeth, "There's no art to find the mind's construction in the face. He was a gentleman on whom I built an absolute trust." Indeed, Blemie had been a gentleman. We spent a lot of time together at school. After school, we sometimes hung out. Sometimes I visited with him at the Lao Clan House, where he stayed at the Chief Compound. He came to see me occasionally at the place where Joe Mark and I stayed. I had no reason to suspect that my friend had a different reason for our friendship, perhaps one of convenience. I had no doubt about him. I had no reason to do what boys do not do about their friends. I did not ask him what he thought about our friendship. There was no reason to even let that kind of thought cross my mind. The reason was that, from my vantage point, our friendship was all about camaraderie. We were partners in the struggle (a reference to hunger) to acquire an education in Sanniquellie, where food scarcity was a routine occurrence. We were far away not only from our parents but also from our villages. It was under those circumstances that we shared whatever I had. Indeed, it was under such conditions that I trusted him blindly, like a child. Even though I never expected anything in return for my kindness to others, as a naïve teenager, I was wrong to think that the generosity I had learned from home only begot generosity.

For the most part, 1975 was an uneventful year. Nothing gave me reasons to suspect that Blemie was not a true friend. At the end of the year, we moved on to the eleventh grade. Following the close of school, we departed for the long vacation during the dry season. He went to Camp Four and I went to the village. As 1975 ended smoothly, so was the beginning of 1976 when we returned to school for our junior year. Everything went well until almost the end of 1976, but something happened shockingly shortly before school closed that put our friendship on the rock. According to a practice the Principal, Brother Sebastian (deceased), introduced, the school held elections for the Student Council at the end of the junior year. The goal was to have the new officers in place upon the opening of school during the following academic year.

In anticipation of the elections at the end of the junior year, student politics dominated the conversations during the last weeks of 1976. I had been in the school long enough, served as President of Young Christian Students (YCS) and felt the time had come to run for the presidency. Because Blemie was also interested in running for the Presidency, it became evident that we were going to compete against each other. At that juncture, he asked me to step aside to let him run. In return, he offered to support my candidacy for first Vice Presidency. Because I felt that running against him would amount to competing against my brother, I accepted his proposal.

Soon, campaigns for the presidency and the first vice presidency began. Along with our supporters, I made posters with Blemie and me, and plac-arded them around the campus. I also talked to students to support us. Nevertheless, as the campaigns heated up, it became evident that Blemie had a hidden plan. He was not campaigning for me as he promised. Instead, he was campaigning for Miss Ophelia Dolo, a tenth grader at the time. I did not find out until friends and supporters of mine discovered the chicanery and notified me. I was flabbergasted and never thought a friend would do such a thing to another friend.

Armed with evidence of the shenanigan, I confronted Blemie. I was disappointed not because he supported Miss Ophelia Dolo. Blemie let me down not because he thought I was unqualified for the first vice presidency. Instead, Blemie's behavior disillusioned me because I realized that he was wearing a mask. The persona he masqueraded was a façade. He led me to believe that nothing existed at his core. He did not need to ask me to step aside for him to run for the presidency if he truly believed that I was unqualified for the lower position of first vice president. He could have crushed me at the polls for the presidency and avoided the spectacle of facing me to answer for his deceit.

I do not know how Blemie concluded that I was unqualified for the first vice presidency. Even though the elections were not about popularity, name as well as facial recognition was an important asset. I began my schooling at St. Mary's School in 1966 and, by the time of the elections, I had been at the school for ten years. That longevity meant I had lived in Sanniquellie for the same length of time. In addition, I knew almost all the students at the school. The president of the student council did not have the latitude to make any significant improvements in the living conditions of the students because the brothers and nuns set the parameters of operations of the student council. Nevertheless, my knowledge of the students' struggles was an asset in communicating with them. Furthermore, the hospitality I learned in the village was an asset. I showed Blemie compassion when he arrived at St. Mary's School knowing no one. I befriended and made him feel at home in a new school. Moreover, with respect to organizational leadership, I had served as President of Young Christian Students (YCS) during the previous year. I was confident and had no doubts about my qualification.

As Blemie demonstrated, the campaigns for the student council elections involved vicious innuendos and "cutthroat" maneuvers. Mr. Baikiayee defeated his rival, Mr. Alphonso Kolliesuah, for the presidency but the elections were contentious. Three rounds of voting occurred for the first vice presidency, with each round resulting in a tie. I was not present at the counting of the ballots but those who participated in counting the ballots told me that when the second round of voting ended up in another tie, Brother Sebastian asked the nuns to vote. Thereafter, a nun broke the tie in favor of Miss Ophelia Dolo. I took the results as announced. I did not have any reason to doubt the results of the elections. I lost the election for the first vice presidency. It was over.

On the contrary, Mr. Alphonso Kolliesuah and his supporters had reasons to believe that something went awry during the elections. At the beginning of academic 1977, the relationship between Mr. Baikiayee and his opponent, Mr. Kolliesuah, was not cordial. Mr. Kolliesuah's supporters in the senior class used different tactics to taunt Mr. Baikiayee. They let him know he had not won the presidency. They believed Brother Sebastian gave him the presidency. Consequently, they had very little regard for him. During that time, allegations of favoritism on the part of Brother Sebastian surfaced and gained momentum. Mr. Kolliesuah and his supporters believed the principal was the invisible hand in the elections. They believed he predetermined the winners and then participated in fixing the results. He reportedly preferred Mr. Baikiayee to his rival, Mr. Kolliesuah, for the presidency while, for the first vice presidency, he preferred Miss Ophelia Dolo to me. I did not have any hard evidence to determine the veracity of the claims. On the other hand, I was completely naïve at that time. I had known Brother Sebastian since 1972. It never crossed my mind that he would do anything contrary to his public persona of a life of chastity and purity to serve Christ. I could not imagine that he would wear a mask and show bias for candidates in mere high school elections.

I was bitter, but, unlike Mr. Kolliesuah and his supporters, I directed my consternation at Mr. Baikiayee, my "friend." He and I did not speak after the elections until 1977, during our senior year. Our mutual friend, Dr. Kou Nehway Gbokolo, intervened and tried to bring us back together as friends. Mr. Baikiayee refused to apologize or ask for forgiveness. I forgave him anyway. In the end, my classmates elected me unanimously as the president of the senior class (a position then called senior prefect) when school started in March 1977.

CHAPTER 13

Reaching Out for the World

MY PARENTS WANTED ME TO escape the yoke of the porter system and extortion, not to mention the abuse by *quizees*. The desire to protect was mutual. As they embarked on a project to help me escape their fate, I also wanted to protect them. Dad's humiliation at the hands of *quizees* was one motivation to reach out for the world through getting an education to escape Dad's plight. Once my parents determined that getting an education would be an antidote to the humiliation Dad endured, they kindled a fire in my belly that no one, not even Sanniquellie's hunger could put out.

The fire in my belly was important in setting me along a course, but it was not enough. I needed to sustain its ferocity along a purposeful journey. Esther Dokie's role in providing a tangible goal to sustain my focus on was almost like a *"Pianyeewon"* (happening in no time like in a fairy tale). Her achievement was the oxygen that sustained the intensity of the fire Mom and Dad's life circumstances kindled in my belly. Esther inspired me to open my eyes and ears for opportunities; to dream for an even bigger success. She was my window to the world, a world that opened in a rather unusual way.

My parents and Esther Dokie set me along a journey because Esther's success helped formulate my goal and was the oxygen that fueled the fire in my belly. However, when I opened my eyes and listened to see and hear about what mattered, I did not see the dominant Liberian culture, the *quizee* culture (Americo-Liberian culture), hovering overhead, permeating, directing and controlling many aspects of Liberian life, including mobility into the *quizee* class. Before I entered school, for example, a sixth-grade education was the gold standard for indigenous Liberians. It seemed someone told indigenous Liberians, "If you want to become *quizees* like us, you must have a sixth-grade education." My parents were farsighted. They looked beyond sixth grade; they wanted me to reach and complete the eighth grade. But when I accomplished Mom and Dad's goal of eighth grade, the goal post to becoming a *quizee* moved further back from a sixth-grade education to a twelfth-grade education. Before I received my high school diploma in December 1977, the goal post had already moved further back to a college education.

JAPANESE COASTER BUSES

In 1976, on the day the window to the world opened for me, two Japanese Coaster buses arrived on St. Mary's High School campus. The buses were emblazoned on the sides with "The College of Agriculture & Forestry, University of Liberia" in bold blue letters against white backgrounds. Those who got off the buses, mostly men, looked older than high school students, distinctly different and sophisticated in mannerisms. It was not clear to me or to any of my friends why the visitors were on campus. They did not arrive early morning to speak to the student body during the morning devotion. Instead, they arrived shortly before recess. The emblazoned letters on the sides of the buses were the only indication about who the visitors were.

The more I inquired about the visitors, the more I became enamored with them. I heard that they were students of the University of Liberia, the next level of education beyond high school. Moreover, others described the visitors as very knowledgeable in their respective disciplines. Someone even told me that the university students were in line for the leadership of the country. Right away, I decided that I wanted to go to the University of Liberia. The imageries of the buses and the University of Liberia in bold blue letters stuck with me. In the evening, Sanniquellie was abuzz with news about the university students. They became instant celebrities. The high school girls' excitement was especially palpable when it turned out that the visitors would be at a dance another high school had scheduled for that evening. It became apparent that the girls were more interested in the university students than in the high school boys in Sanniquellie. Once I figured that the girls were more excited about the men from the University of Liberia than about high school boys in Sanniquellie, I found an added reason to go to the University of Liberia after high school.

The visitors came to St. Mary's School to encourage us to enroll at the University of Liberia. Since they did not have an audience with the student body, they met with the Principal, Brother Sebastian, instead. Thereafter, Brother Sebastian encouraged us to register for the entrance examinations scheduled for October 1977. Brother Sebastian did not need to prod me to register for the University of Liberia entrance examinations. I had a ton of reasons for wanting to go to the University of Liberia, including escaping my parents' fate, protecting them and becoming a center of attention for the girls too. I was one of twenty-six students out of a senior class of thirty-one students who registered and took the entrance examinations in Sanniquellie in October 1977.

Prior to taking the University of Liberia entrance examinations, I told Dad that I wanted to enroll at the University of Liberia. The reason I gave him was that I did not feel a high school education was enough. He did not oppose my plan to go to college but suggested I find a teaching job and work for a few years and save money to finance my education. I did not jump on Dad's suggestion because I felt that once I started down the road he suggested, marriage, settling down and having a family would automatically follow. I was not ready for all of that yet.

I was not completely surprised at Dad's response because I did not think he was prepared to finance my college education. By that time, to his credit, he and Mom had paid tuition and fees at St. Mary's School for eleven years. I thought his suggestion was an attempt to relieve himself from the burden of paying another round of tuition. I imagined he was saying "This kid is about to graduate from high school and all I expected was an eighth-grade education. So, what is he talking about again?" Dad seemed dumbfounded by my comment that a high school education was not enough, especially after he used his phalanges on the hands and feet to count the grades I had completed. He did not understand why I needed a college education, especially when it required a significant financial commitment. However, when I turned to Mom and told her what Dad had said, her response was different and reassuring. Based on pure faith that

126

Wlah would make a way, she encouraged me to go on to college. She told me that she would do whatever she could to support me.

THE PURSUIT OF EDUCATION

As Dad and Mom's experiences were central to shaping my basic outlook on life, I reckoned overcoming the indignities they endured would require more than an eighth grade or a high school education. My idea of what an education could do for me was a little more than what my peers thought about what an education could do for them because my parents' experiences were not the same as their parents' experiences. Redeeming my parents' dignity and securing it for myself was my idea of becoming educated. Earning a living was secondary and only a by-product. I never liked waiting around for motivation to do what was necessary because I hated putting myself in a situation where someone would put me down. That was one reason Brother Sebastian did not need to prod me to register for the University of Liberia entrance examinations. The mere appearance of the University of Liberia students who arrived on St. Mary's campus on the Japanese Coaster buses was enough motivation for me.

Even though my motivation for further education was strong, my desire for going to the University of Liberia was merely a dream. Unlike Sanniquellie, I had no relatives in Monrovia to stay with and go to school. Moreover, my parents did not have the resources to support me in college. The assets I had were determination, ability to survive and a dream. Living in Sanniquellie helped me develop those skills. I dreamed big dreams. I cast a wide net, covering the University of Nebraska at Lincoln and Florida State University in Tallahassee because it did not cost me anything to dream.

The University of Nebraska was my favorite school because of Nebraska's central location on the map of the United States. As for Florida State University, I liked Tallahassee, the name of the state capital. However, the University of Nebraska and Florida State University did not appear out of nowhere. Someone, Brother Andrews, a Dutch Catholic missionary who taught geography at St. Mary's School during my senior year, "Put them into my head." He hung a large United States map above the blackboard at the front of the class. At the time, we were studying North America in depth. I looked at that map every day I went to school. On prom night in 1977, when asked to foretell where I would be in ten years, I drew inspiration from that map and said, "In ten years I would be studying for my masters' degree in geology at the University of Nebraska at Lincoln or at Florida State University in Tallahassee." Geology did not pop out of the thin air either. Mr. Alfred Johnson, my uncle who operated a wheeled dozer at the Nimba iron ore mines, and another relative, who operated a 120-ton Euclid at the mines, took me along on third shift on separate occasions. I spent nights with them and saw the scale and wonders of mine operations first-hand.

University of Liberia Entrance Results

In January 1978, the University of Liberia announced the release of the October 1977 entrance examinations results and posted them on bulletin boards on the Capitol Hill campus. In addition, the Daily Observer (now the Liberian Observer) and other newspapers in Monrovia published the entrance results. Unfortunately, the newspapers were in circulation only in a few places outside Monrovia. Moreover, advances in modern communication today, including the internet, had not occurred. In the absence of remote access, entrance examinations takers in rural areas could not readily obtain their results. Therefore, one way entrance examinations takers in rural areas found out their results was to travel to Monrovia to check the bulletin boards on the campus of the University of Liberia.

Upon hearing the announcement about the entrance examinations results, I decided to travel to Monrovia to find out my results. However, I did not know anyone in Monrovia with whom I could spend a few days while there checking on my entrance results. Moreover, I was afraid to go alone. Even though I had been to Monrovia once, the reason I was afraid to go alone was that I still did not know my way around the city. Several Duo Tiayee citizens lived in Monrovia, mostly personnel of the Armed Forces of Liberia (AFL). I asked people in Duo Tiayee, trying to identify someone in Monrovia with whom I could spend a few days. Someone suggested Francis Karkeh (deceased), one of Cousin Patrick's friends, as a possible host. I settled on Francis Karkeh, even though I knew him only casually. I still had not solved my traveling to Monrovia problem completely because I did not know where Francis lived in Monrovia, let alone how to get to his residence. I then set out to find someone in Duo Tiayee with whom I could travel, someone who knew Francis and where he lived in Monrovia. The person had to have plans to travel to Monrovia at about the same time

I was thinking about traveling to Monrovia. I had little difficulty finding someone because, on the one hand, citizens of Duo Tiayee and the vicinity readily traveled to Monrovia to visit with their relatives while, on the other hand, people from the area living in Monrovia often traveled back home to visit with their families. I found someone who fitted the profile, but the individual's plans dictated the January date on which we agreed to travel.

In the meantime, Mom had been preparing for my trip. She packed provisions including rice, palm oil, plantain, and sesame seeds along with a rooster for my host. Taking live poultry or livestock, particularly chickens or goats, to one's hosts as gifts was customary. The hosts either slaughtered the animals for meat or raised them, depending on where they lived. On a Friday afternoon, Mom, Esther, my younger sister, and I carried the provisions from the village to Duo Tiayee, roughly four miles away, where we spent the night with Sennie, my older sister, and her family.

Sennie, one of the best cooks in the family at the time, woke up early Saturday morning and prepared "Lahapeay" (breakfast). She cooked new rice with okra, bitter balls (miniature eggplants) and added a mixture of ground sesame seeds, dry meat and a collection of condiments. Sennie cooked "dry rice" for lahapeay because Mom wanted me to hurry and leave Duo Tiayee early to arrive in Monrovia before sunset. She saw a Liberian "Elephant" that others including me could not see.[117] Monrovia was the headquarters of "Monsee mia," the ill-reputed United Brothers Fraternity (UBF). In her mind, letting her only son arrive in Monrovia at night amounted to walking into a den of hungry lions. Sennie cooked dry rice for lahapeay because it did not take much time to prepare it. She, in Liberian parlance, "Wasted" palm oil on the dry rice, made the appearance, smell, and taste irresistible and memorable.

After lahapeay, Mom, Sennie and Esther helped carry the provisions to the parking station, about five hundred yards from where Sennie lived. Mary Yeeleeway Zeekeh joined me at the parking station.[118] She was the person who volunteered to be my guide to show me where Francis Karkeh lived in Monrovia. Mary told me she had been planning to travel to Monrovia to visit with her relative, Sergeant Alfred Saye (deceased), a member of the Armed Forces of Liberia (AFL). Sometime before mid-morning, carboys (driver's assistants) of a Toyota minibus we found began preparations for departure. They put the provisions along with other passengers' belongings over the top and tied them securely with rubber from a tire inner tube as

Mom, Sennie and Esther looked on. Thereafter, as each of them gave me a hug and said, "Eelooah ba taha aye lee" (Have a successful trip), I had a sudden flashback to the time Mom and Dad took me to the Guahs in Sanniquellie, but the circumstances on that day were different. I was going to Monrovia voluntarily to find out whether I passed the University of Liberia entrance examinations. Nevertheless, Mom's somber face told the same story of pain and agony. Her son was going away to a far place again.

On that cold memorable January morning, Mary and I boarded the minibus and sat next to each other.[119] After all the passengers took their seats, the carboys climbed down, took their seats by the door and, almost in unison, said, "Let's go boss man!" As the minibus pulled away, I looked back and saw Mom, Sennie and Esther wave goodbye. Moments later, I lost track of them as the minibus descended into a valley near the town and climbed a gentle hill on the other side. Nearing the peak of that hill, I looked out the window at trees lining both sides of the road and reminisced. The vegetation appeared to be moving in the opposite direction faster than the minibus was traveling. The scene was even more exhilarating as we passed Samuel Gaye's large rubber plantation.[120] With their lush green canopies, the rubber trees (Havea brasiliensis), planted in straight lines at equal distance, seemed to move as if they were soldiers marching orderly under the command of a general. Further along, the beauty and harmony of unimaginable diversity of plant species were interrupted only by fields of golden rice straws on newly harvested farms.

On the narrow and treacherous road, the first leg of the trip had me holding my breath at one moment and then breathing a sigh of relief at another, repeatedly. Perhaps because of wisdom and experience, the elderly Mandingo driver kept us safe not only by yielding to in-coming vehicles but also by slowing down in curves, where visibility was less than a hundred yards. Foot traffic along the narrow road increased as we neared Sanniquellie. We passed people, mostly women, from nearby villages and towns carrying sacks and large pans of produce of all kinds to the market.

Eventually, we reached the airfield at the outskirt of Sanniquellie. Soon, we crossed the Buchanan-Yekepa railroad, drove by the artificial Lake Teeleh and arrived at the main parking station in the heart of the city. It was Saturday, Sanniquellie's market day. The city was fully alive. Pedestrian as well as vehicular traffic was heavy. Commercial activities were everywhere. Vendors of consumer goods ranging from apparels, utensils, meats of all sorts, tools, and salts came from cities far away as Monrovia and Gbarnga as well as from countries like Guinea and the Ivory Coast. As traders headed toward the public market by the lake, customer traffic in and out of overstocked Lebanese stores was incessant. The "Yana boys" (street vendors) and "shoeshine boys" were in the midst too trading their goods and services, respectively.

An unmistakable and memorable chorus of beaconing voices at the central parking station was a key feature of the city's liveliness. The voices were those of drivers of minibuses, taxis or pick-up trucks and their assistants. Monrovia, Monrovia, Ganta, Ganta, Lamco Yekepa, Lamco Yekepa, Karnplay, Karnplay, Gbainlah, Gbainlah, Zorgowee, Zorgowee, and Tiayee, Tiayee were the sounds of competing voices. Pee pee, pahn pahn, and pohn, pohn were honking tunes of different vehicles as they interspersed the voices of drivers and their assistants calling on travelers to go with them.

After a brief negotiation with the driver of another minibus, we agreed to ride along with him on the Sanniquellie-Monrovia leg of the trip. Passengers knew the cost per person to travel from Sanniquellie to Monrovia. Therefore, we only negotiated the cost of carrying the sacks of provisions. Nevertheless, everything in Liberia was subject to negotiation. Thereafter, the new driver and his assistants transferred our bags and sacks to the new minibus. Because the driver had to have passengers in all the seats to avoid a loss, we departed Sanniquellie shortly before noon, later than we expected.

Once we got on our way, we had to stop for various reasons including refueling, prayer and immigration inspections. In addition, we stopped for passengers to eat or use the restroom. Traffic violations were another reason for involuntary stops. Like the minibus driver who brought us from Duo Tiayee to Sanniquellie, the driver who took us from Sanniquellie to Monrovia was a Mandingo (a member of the Mandingo ethnic group, one of Liberia's sixteen ethnic groups). At the time, most people in Liberia who owned or operated commercial or passenger vehicles were Mandingoes. Moreover, Mandingoes in Liberia were overwhelmingly Muslims. The driver stopped several times to pray. Others who were Muslims joined in the prayer while the non-Muslims waited in the vehicle.

Immigration officers stopped us at all the checkpoints to determine who was an alien. Again, as before, those stops most often turned out to be ploys by some immigration officers to extort money from commercial drivers. The stops at immigration checkpoints were evidence of discrimination against

Mandingoes in Liberia. At nearly all the checkpoints, some immigration officers carried out the odious practice in the name of official duties. Mandingoes were singled out for questioning because of their dress or appearance as well as names. There are Liberian Mandingoes and Mandingoes from other countries in West Africa, particularly Guinea. Nevertheless, there was a widespread perception in Liberia that Mandingoes were foreigners.[121] Based on that perception, the general population held prejudices against Mandingoes while some people in official circles, particularly in the immigration service, discriminated against them for a long time.

Most Liberians knew that singling out and questioning Mandingoes at immigration checkpoints was wrong. However, very few courageous people stood up or spoke up for Mandingoes. One reason for fear of speaking up was that security officers in Liberia at the time, including police officers, immigration officers and soldiers, carried arms. Historically, they wielded tremendous power, virtually serving as arresting officers, jury and judges at the same time. Nevertheless, the main reason why there were no significant outcries against the treatment of Mandingoes was that almost all the other ethnic groups held prejudices against the Mandingoes. Furthermore, under the entrenched system of divide and rule at the time, one ethnic group seldom saw harm to another ethnic group as harm to itself. In any case, the time we spent at each immigration checkpoint depended on the driver's willingness to pay "Cold Water" (bribe) for the release of those whom immigration officers singled out and took in for questioning. Commercial drivers considered those payments not only as the cost of doing business but also as the norm. As a result, they avoided losses by factoring such payments into the cost of the trip for everyone.

In addition to immigration officers, traffic police in the cities and towns along the highway from Sanniquellie to Monrovia made frequent stops and charged drivers with various traffic offenses. Some traffic charges involved legitimate violations because commercial drivers in Liberia paid little attention to traffic safety. Nevertheless, the police trumped up other charges to extort money from commercial drivers. Feigned traffic violations were the most irritating reasons for which we stopped along the way. Every passenger grudgingly put up with those fabricated charges because arguing with police officers only delayed the trip and made matters worse. We also stopped along the way to eat because, as Liberians often say, "Empty bag cannot stand." The popular dishes included fufu and soup, palm butter and rice and potato greens and rice. Other food items included roasted cassava and corn, boiled corn on the cob, oranges, mangoes, and avocado pears.

Eventually, we arrived in Monrovia shortly before sunset. Normally, the trip took four to five hours, but it took us more than five hours because of the stops for various reasons. The minibus driver dropped us off at the Buzzi Quarter Gas Station, about a stone throw from the perimeter fence of the Executive Mansion, home of Liberia's president. Buzzi Quarter was located near the Barclay Training Center, the headquarters of the Liberian army. In the early days of the Liberian armed forces, many members were from the Lorma people from Lofa County. Because Lorma people were also called Buzzi, after the name of a powerful Lorma chief, the place where many Lorma soldiers and their families lived became known as Buzzi Quarter. By the 1970s many of the inhabitants were Dan and Mahn.

After we paid the driver, I hired a wheelbarrow boy for fifty cents to carry the provisions to Mr. Karkeh's residence. The sacks were too heavy for two people to carry. Because of repeated warnings about Monrovia's "Gronna boys," I was mindful.[122] I did not trust the wheelbarrow boy to carry the provisions unattended. Mary took her bag, led the way to Francis's residence while the wheelbarrow boy followed. I carried my bag over my shoulder and walked behind him for obvious reasons. I had to keep an eye on him for fear that he might get away with the provisions.

Concrete as well as makeshift houses along our way to Francis's residence looked contiguous. It seemed as if we were burrowing as we made our way between the houses. On the other hand, the stench of Soniwhein, a stagnant, meandering open channel drainage that took anything imaginable that residents threw into it, almost gassed us. Soniwhein was not only the name of the water channel or ditch, but also became the name of one part of Buzzi Quarter. As we neared our destination, I saw the humongous building that Francis lived in, standing about two hundred yards away from a dilapidated section of the Atlantic Ocean beach. The government-owned asbestos-roofed building seemed more than fifty years old with very little maintenance. It housed mainly military personnel and their families at the time of my visit. Strangely, however, the occupants of the building were mostly military personnel of the Mahn and Dan ethnic groups of Nimba County and their families.

As Mary Zeekeh and I approached, Francis, who was standing outside, recognized Mary right away and, in excitement, called out her Mahn name.

"Yeeleeway!" "Komah" (What news)? "Meh aye keh" (What happened)? Mr. Karkeh's second question was out of concern because such a surprise visit was often about delivering news of the passing of a relative or family member. Next, Francis gave me a big hug, after which Mary told him that she volunteered to show me the way to his house. Afterwards, Francis helped carry the provisions into a wide dark hallway in the building. Before we reached his room near the middle of the hallway, a child had run and announced that strangers from the "Interior" (from up country or Nimba County) had come. Dee Gorlon, Francis Karkeh's wife, who appeared to have awakened from a nap, opened the door, and asked "Oo gay daiyin aye nu" (They say who came)? "Yeeleeway Zeekeh lu wah James" (Yeeleeway Zeekeh's daughter and James), Francis responded. Gorlon could not see me clearly because I was standing behind Francis. For that reason, she asked again, "James kpeh" (which James)? "Patrick Mahnwon lakay James Flumo" (Patrick Mahnwon's little brother James Flumo), Francis added. With that, Gorlon ran outside and gave me a big hug. Thereafter, we made our way into their room. After the greetings, Mary went to Sargent Alfred Saye, whom she traveled to visit with.

Even though Francis and Gorlon were citizens of Duo Tiayee, Dad's birthplace, they were not my kin. Nevertheless, they treated me with great kindness. Gorlon heated a bucket of water with an electric water heater and took it to the bathroom along with soap and bath towel because it was customary for the host's wife to prepare hot water for a stranger. Dinner was ready when I finished bathing because Gorlon, like other Liberian women, was masterful at multitasking. As soon as we arrived that evening, she swung into action, doing everything including cooking and preparing hot water to make me comfortable. One after the other, Francis and Gorlon asked about family members and others in Duo Tiayee as we had dinner. Since I had not been in Duo Tiayee on a consistent basis, I did not have much to say. I only answered them in general terms.

After dinner, Gorlon asked, "Komah" (What news or why did you come)? I knew then that the time for a conversation about the purpose of my trip had come. I began the conversation with a reassuring note that all was well upcountry and then talked about the University of Liberia entrance examinations I took in October 1977. Francis quickly jumped in with excitement, thinking I had come to enroll at the University of Liberia. Francis's eagerness was justified because of the university's prestige.

In addition, aside from two people, George A. Bolo and James F. Kaye, who graduated from the University of Liberia in 1975, no one else from our home area of more than ten thousand inhabitants was enrolled at the University of Liberia at that time. I understood the sentiment, "Yes! We finally got someone representing us at the University of Liberia," but I had to tell Francis to moderate his enthusiasm because I had come only to find out the entrance results. More importantly, I said I might spend three days to a week with them because I did not know how long it would take to find out the results. In agreeing, they stressed that such a request was not necessary because their home was also my home. After the conversation, I felt reassured as if I had known Francis and Gorlon for a long time.

On Sunday, the following day, Francis, Gorlon and I spent the entire day together. In Monrovia, both were popular among the community of citizens from Duo Tiayee and surrounding towns. Because many people did not work on Sundays, visitors streamed in to see Francis and Gorlon. I met familiar people I had not seen in a long time while I came face-to-face with others for the first time, although I had heard about them long before. Everything including the atmosphere was different as I watched the visitors come, stay for a little while and leave. Swaying coconut branches and leaves from the incessant sea breeze was a distinctive reminder that I was in Monrovia and not in the village. The Atlantic Ocean was merely three hundred yards away! The soil around the building was almost one hundred percent sand. I walked in it gingerly to avoid twisting an ankle and falling. The sandy soil, deposited by nonstop crashing waves eons ago, reminded me that, directly or indirectly, a rendezvous with the mighty Atlantic Ocean was unavoidable.

On that Sunday, either a subtle competition or collusion seemed to be underway between man and nature to intimidate me. On the one hand, the nonstop waves of the ocean increasingly perfected my imagination of a high wave crashing overland and sweeping me away. On the other hand, some visitors projected an aura of sophistication, especially after they realized I had just come from the "Interior." They flaunted their knowledge of the city by calling out names of places such as "Across the Bridge," "Mamba Point," "Waterside," and "Sinkor Old Road" to show their sophistication. Their conversations, which suggested they knew every corner of Monrovia, made me to feel out of place, stupid and "green" or as having actually come from the "country." During my first visit to Monrovia in 1975, I only stayed briefly. For that reason, the city still looked too big and intimidating. I wondered when I would get to know the city the way others knew it.

On Monday, Francis took me to the main campus of the University of Liberia to check on my results. We took the same route Mary Zeekeh and I used on Saturday to get to Francis's house. Upon arrival at Buzzi Quarter, Francis told me we did not need a taxi because he wanted me to see places of interest including the Executive Mansion, home of Liberia's president, the Temple of Justice, the building that houses the Supreme Court of Liberia, and the Capitol Building, seat of the Liberian Legislature. Indeed, we did not need a taxi because the distance from Buzzi Quarter to the campus of the University of Liberia was no more than 15 minutes' walk. The Executive Mansion's well-manicured grounds and the sheer beauty of the architecture of the building awe-struck me. The Temple of Justice and the Capitol Building were also magnificent and impressive, although they paled in comparison to the elegance of the Executive Mansion.

We walked on the concrete sidewalk by the ornate black paint-coated Executive Mansion steel fence, crossed the road midway the length of the fence and headed toward the Capitol Building. In no more than three minutes, we passed by the Capitol Building and stopped at the Capitol Bypass, a thoroughfare in front of the university, for a break in the traffic to cross over. Upon crossing over and entering the main gate of the university, I felt as if I were in the United States.[123] The people on campus, particularly the women, looked elegant. They looked immaculately dressed and beautiful. As a "country" boy from rural Liberia, I saw things differently on campus that day. The people I saw on campus had a distinctive swagger, different from what I knew. The evenly trimmed shrubberies along the concrete fence around the campus were an object of fascination. I wondered whether the carpet grass that covered the grounds around the Louis Arthur Grimes Law School Building and Roberts' Hall was real. I pretended I was picking up something I had dropped just to feel the carpet grass and found out that it was real. The visitors at Francis's house the day before made me to feel that I was a boy from the bush. I had to be careful because I was afraid of that perception of me. I did not want the people on campus to see me in similar light.

Large mango trees, different species of decorative palms and other tree species provided shaded areas all around the campus, where groups of students gathered for conversations. Moreover, it was also hard to miss the noises from running air conditioners attached to buildings and offices all around the campus. Train of cars continuously streamed in through one gate and left through another. Everything on campus looked different, beautiful, and intimidating.

The sheer beauty of the campus captivated and overwhelmed me. It never even occurred to me that most of the people on campus were there for the same reason I had come on campus. Indeed, they had come to find out their entrance examinations results. Francis mustered the courage and asked a passerby to show us where we could find the results of the entrance examinations. Before that, the drama of the looks of elegantly dressed women, luxury cars streaming in and out of the campus gate and the gorgeous landscape completely sidetracked me. The man he asked pointed toward a sizable crowd gathered about 50 yards away in front of a building on campus and said, "Look over there at the front of 'RH.'"[124] With his gap in the upper frontal teeth and distinctive smile, Francis, walking and slightly limping forward and leftward said, "Let's go over there to find out what's going on. The people there might be checking their results, too."

I was at Francis's right and walked just slightly behind him. We did not walk side-by-side. Neither did I walk directly behind Francis. That was my way of showing respect and acknowledging not only that he was my elder, but also, he knew the city and what questions to ask. As we approached RH, I saw people jumping and shouting with joy while others seemed gloomy as they walked away. As it turned out, those who jumped and shouted with joy, smiled and either gave or received "high fives" passed the examinations while the gloomy ones never made it. Francis and I moved closer to the bulletin board on which the university authorities posted the exam results as people who had seen their results stepped away.

Standing less than two feet away from the bulletin board, I did not know where to start looking because the list was long. I thought about going from the beginning to the end, but I quickly realized that the authorities compiled the list by schools. At that moment, my heart was pounding as if I had been running a race. I put my right index finger on the bulletin board and moved it from top to bottom and so on as fast as my eyes could follow. When I discovered St. Mary's High School, my index finger went over the list of students who passed like a flash of lightning. At first glance, I saw J. Marsilius Flumo, but I did not want to believe it because I thought my eyes were playing a trick on me. It was not that I did not believe I could perform and pass the exams. Instead, the thought that, out of the thousands of students across the length and breadth of Liberia who took the exams, I was one of the fortunate ones who passed was thrilling yet overwhelming.

Some people had taken the exams more than three times and failed. Moreover, the entrance examinations had taken a life of their own and become larger than life. Because there was only one state-sponsored university at that time, the examinations became the filter that determined who would become successful. The competition to enter the University of Liberia at the time was intense because the University of Liberia was the only state-sponsored institution of higher learning in Liberia. Cuttington College (now Cuttington University College), the other institution of higher learning at the time, operated under the auspices of the Episcopal Church, and it was more expensive. The second time I went over the list, my index finger moved slowly. Again, I saw J. Marsilius Flumo. However, I saw a note after my name that said, "Passed mathematics and English." I did not see that note the first time I went through the list. I then turned to Francis with widely opened eyes and a big smile and said, "Ouwn deay a sayin yee" (I passed all, meaning both mathematics and English). Francis, the five-ten, dark hair and fair-skinned soldier, shook my hand and said, "Ba yeay lorh" (Congratulations!).

With the good news, we wasted no time on campus. Passing the University of Liberia entrance examinations was a big news. I felt like a little kid who found a treasure. I could not wait to get back to Soniwhein to share the good news with others there from my home area. Francis and I took the same route we used earlier to go to the university campus. However, because I was fixated on my success with the entrance examinations, I did not even notice the humongous domed and double-winged Capitol Building. I was imagining what life would be like once school started. I was buried into thinking about how soon I would be one of the most talked about and coveted students—LU students. The 15-minute walk from the university to Soniwhein seemed like eternity. Upon arrival, we shared the good news with Gorlon and others who were around. I heard congratulatory messages in Mahn and Dan from the Nimba people in the community. I absorbed everything without giving much thought to what my success really meant to those who congratulated me.

In the evening, I informed Francis and Gorlon that I would return home to Nimba on the following day to prepare for registration. I told them the time I expected to return to Monrovia because it was not clear to me where I would stay and go to school. I did not ask Francis and Gorlon that, upon my return, I would like them to host me until I found a place to stay. It happened the way many things happened in the culture. It was obvious that I would need a place to stay and go to school, but they never asked, and I never volunteered information or requested help. We all just assumed that, upon my return, I would be with them or someone else until something worked out. Neither they nor I was sure of what that something would be.

The Good News

On Tuesday, I left Monrovia mid-morning in a Peugeot 504 station wagon along with nine people, including the driver, a Mandingo man. On my return trip to Sanniquellie and to the village, there were no surprises along the highway. We stopped for the same rigmaroles, including prayer, immigration inspections, "traffic offenses," and bathroom as if someone scripted the trip for a terrible movie. Unlike the trip heading to Monrovia, we arrived in Sanniquellie after dusk.

The trip to Monrovia and back to the village was like "pianyeewon," meaning it happened in no time and perfectly. As soon as I got out of the Peugeot 504 station wagon at the main parking station in Sanniquellie, I heard a pick-up truck driver loudly calling out "Tiayee, Tiayee, Tiayee..." for passengers to Duo Tiayee. He was the only driver at the parking station calling for passengers traveling to Duo Tiayee. I was in a hurry to reach my parents to share the good news of the entrance examinations results. So, the pick-up truck driver was a God-sent blessing.

We left Sanniquellie shortly thereafter and arrived in Duo Tiayee sometime after 8:00pm. Still afraid to travel alone especially at night for fear of ghosts, I spent the night in Duo Tiayee with my sister, Sennie, and her family. Upon daybreak, I ate breakfast Sennie prepared, started the nearly four-mile trek to the village and arrived mid-morning. To my pleasant surprise, Mom was at home, but Dad was away on the farm. Mom greeted me warmly. She hurriedly tried to cook for me, but when I assured her that I was not hungry, she wanted to know what I ate. She settled down once I told her that I spent the night in Duo Tiayee with sister Sennie who prepared a heavy breakfast for me before leaving for the village. Turning to the conversation I badly wanted to begin, she asked, "Komah" (What news)? "Taa ohn looah aye lee. Ohn deay" (The trip I made was successful. I passed). I responded. Mom stood up, hugged me and said, "Koo yeaye lorh, koo yeaye lorh" (Congratulation, Congratulations)! Dancing around and hovering over me, she held my arms, one after the other, repeatedly calling me, "Kou leehee, Kou leehee" (Kou's older brother, Kou's older brother) with a broad smile. Kou, meaning Kou Sennie, was my older sister. Calling me "Kou leehee" figuratively made me older and greater than Kou Sennie. In the culture, that kind of compliment was one-way parents thanked and inspired their children at the same time for doing something worthy.

Upon Dad's return from the farm, he greeted me and asked, "Komah" (What news)? "Taa ouwn looah aye lee. Ohn deay" (The trip I made was successful. I passed), I answered. "Ahnnnnn kaa zuoyee" (Okay, thank you people there), he said as if he were referring to a group of people including me. I expected Dad to say, "Ee zuoo" (Thank you) or "Koo yeahe lorh" (Congratulations)! I did not know what to make of his reaction to the good news. I do not know whether he was showing modesty in the wake of my success or whether he was concerned about financial resources to support me at the University of Liberia. As far as Dad was concerned, he had achieved his educational goal for me. We had no one in the village or anywhere near, someone who had finished college, who could help Dad understand what an education beyond high school would do for me. All I wanted to do was to go to college. I was not able to articulate and communicate to Dad why I wanted to go to college. As a result, he could not imagine any use for an education beyond high school.

Mom and I continued the conversation about going to college that same evening. We covered my return to Monrovia, registration and a place to stay as well as feeding. She quickly turned the conversation into another soliloquy, another prayer to Wlah, and continued it the following day on our way to the farm. As always, she asked her deceased parents to add their voices to her petition. Following the petition, she searched places in her bedroom she saved money for eventualities. These places included different locations under the mat and mattress. She also searched a double-stringed zippered pouch she carried around her waist. Moreover, Mom thought aloud about crops to cultivate to sell to earn money to pay for my college education.

Preparations for registration began earnestly when Mom, Esther and I went to the farm. Mom obtained a large quantity of unmilled rice from the storage and spread it on several large mats out in the open sun. Drying unmilled rice eliminated moisture it accumulated in storage and prevented excessive grain breakage during manual milling with mortar and pestles. Holding a long bamboo stick, I watched the rice, driving away chickens from devouring it as Mom gathered additional foodstuffs in the fields. She returned with plantains and root tubers of sweet potatoes and eddoes. Using mortar and pestles, we milled the rice and got almost a hundred-pound bag of rice. Mom climbed up into the storage again and obtained a gallon of palm oil along with some of my favorites, including sesame seeds and peanuts in the shell.

Mom stepped outside the hut, walked around for a few minutes and then called Molee and me, while pointing to a large rooster. She instructed us to catch it for a send-off dinner. Upon our return to the village in the evening, she reminded Dad about my trip to Monrovia to register at the University of Liberia. She asked him to come home early the next day because she wanted to prepare a send-off dinner. In the culture, preparing a send-off dinner was a reference to a feast or sacrifice of thanksgiving. Mom expected all family members including extended ones to gather and eat together.

Like Pianyeewon" (in a fairy tale), Thursday arrived in no time. The entire family gathered in the piazza and ate the send-off dinner. After the meal, nearly everyone took turns and gave me essentially the same advice "Do not walk about; stay focused on the book you are going to learn." On Dad's turn, he said, "Gon Luogon yehboe eeloah peay ah ee nyeehn kea-mon."[125] Moreover, he asked me to sit before him and put my right palm over the left palm face-up. Everyone else was sitting on the mat with his or her back against the wall and watching. He took less than a mouthful of cold water from a calabash, swished and swallowed it. He took a similar mouthful of cold water and splashed it into my palm with considerable force "four times" with words of prayers and blessings after each splash, expressly for love and acceptance, good luck, and safety.[126]

Late afternoon the following day, Mom, Esther and Molee carried the provisions and escorted me to Duo Tiayee. As we did during my previous trip to Monrovia for entrance examinations results, we spent the night with Sennie in Duo Tiayee. This time, I was traveling to Monrovia alone. Mom wanted an early breakfast the next morning so that I could leave early and arrive in Monrovia before sunset for my safety. We all woke up early Saturday morning. Mom looked subdued, did not say much and indicated she did not have a very good sleep. Molee and Esther sensed her anxiety and assured her that Wlah would watch over me. Now, as a parent, I understand and appreciate the depth of Mom's concern at the time.

The "breakfast" Sennie prepared was "zohor" (swamp rice), which was a unique rice in Mahn country. Often, it was the last variety of rice to harvest in Nimba County. "Zohor" is non-sticky, tasty and the grains naturally look like parboiled rice. Moreover, cooked "zohor" slides down the throat as if lubricated, not to mention its ease of digestion. Along with "zohor," Sennie cooked okra soup containing fish, dry groundhog meat and other ingredients. Preparing such a soup with "zohor" amounted to applying a lubricant to a 60-degree slope for someone to slide downhill. Sennie took the food to the piazza, where, by custom, Molee and I ate together while Mom, Sennie and Esther did likewise. As we ate, we all looked at each other and smiled. Everyone knew the reason for the smiles but no one talked about it.[127]

After breakfast, each of us took a sack of foodstuffs and walked to the parking station, where a Toyota pick-up truck driver's assistant was calling for two more passengers to leave for Sanniquellie. That seemed almost like a perfect opportunity but there was a catch. The road from Duo Tiayee to Sanniquellie was in a terrible condition and the pick-up truck was not an ideal vehicle to travel in. In addition to glaring safety concerns, the pick-up truck was a wreck and an eyesore. Wear-and-tear from repeated driving on bad roads was visible on the vehicle everywhere. Torn and ripped leather-sealed sponges on benches exposed the buttocks to hard bench surfaces. Stacked up and secured loads on the top seemed to weigh more than the combined weight of passengers below. Worst of all, the pick-up truck leaned on the left side. I was concerned that we would face trouble ahead along the way to Sanniquellie.

Before I climbed on board and took a seat, Mom, Sennie, Esther and Molee each took turn and gave me a hug. In my seat one person away from the tailgate, I stretched my hand out to Mom, Sennie, Esther and Molee to shake their hands one more time as if the hugs were not enough. Moments later, I heard one of the driver's assistants say, "Let's go boss man." We pulled away slowly as I watched my family waving continuously until I could not see them anymore. After we covered some distance, trains of vehicles of all kinds passed us and headed towards Duo Tiayee to pick up passengers.

Inside the pick-up truck, we sat on two long benches on opposite sides facing each other. We could not turn around to see in the back because the driver's assistants hung tarpaulins to prevent plumes of dust from coming into the vehicle. They also placed additional cargo between the rows of passengers and limited legroom. Showing little concern about their safety, the two driver's assistants stood on the tailgate and held onto the top as we wound our way along the narrow road to Sanniquellie. The pick-up truck's condition worried me each time the driver slowed down in a narrow and bad section of the road. As the vehicle swayed from one side to the other due to potholes, I held my breath. In two instances while driving up steep hills, I thought the vehicle would flip over due to the weight on the top. The center of gravity seemed to have moved directly over the two rear tires. It seemed miraculous to me that the two front tires did not lift as we climbed further and further up those hills.

Eventually, we arrived in Sanniquellie. The main parking station was bustling with choruses of calls for passengers and honks of different tunes from different vehicles. In no time, a young man who looked like a driver's assistant asked where I was going but I was in no hurry to answer because I did not want to ride in another treacherous vehicle. Instead of answering him, I turned the table and asked, "Where are you going?" "Monrovia," he answered. "What type of vehicle do you have?" I followed up. "Peugeot 504," he replied, apparently not knowing the difference between a sedan and a station wagon. After that back-and-forth exchange, I followed the young man to see the vehicle. It was a station wagon. It also turned out he was not a driver's assistant but a hired hand to help find passengers. I agreed to travel in that vehicle because it carried only ten passengers including the driver. Considering the stops at immigration checkpoints for inspections, for example, traveling with fewer passengers was less time-consuming.

Overall, the trip was uneventful because everyone was accustomed to the usual hassles at the immigration checkpoints, which had become an unfortunate norm. Providing "Cold Water" to immigration officers at checkpoints was improper but no one did anything about it other than the hush-hush conversations over irritations for the inconvenience. Upon arrival in Monrovia at about 4:00 p.m., the driver dropped me off at the Buzzi Quarter Gas Station, where the minibus driver dropped us off during the previous trip. As before, I hired a young man with a wheelbarrow to carry the provisions to Mr. Francis Karkeh's house. He charged me two dollars, but we bargained, and I paid him seventy-five cents. I took the lead while the young man followed with the sacks of provisions in his wheelbarrow because I knew the way to the place. I was not afraid that he would get away with the provisions because they were much heavier than the ones Mary Zeekeh and I took with us during the last trip.

Upon arrival, Francis had gone to work at the Executive Mansion. Another child at the house who recognized me from the previous visit ran to Gorlon and told her that I had come again. She ran out in excitement, greeted me warmly and helped carry the provisions inside. Francis was expected home late night. Instead of waiting for his return, I delivered Mom's message to Gorlon. I told her that Mom sent her greetings and wanted them to know she was thankful for their hospitality during my last visit. I also presented the provisions Mom sent to Gorlon. Thereafter, she stacked them in one corner as she awaited her husband's return. Gorlon was nostalgic as we waited. She had not been to Duo Tiayee for quite some time. She asked about a few people including her father, Duo Deesee. I had not been in Duo Tiayee all the time. Therefore, I did not have much to say.

"Komah?" Francis asked upon his return home, shouting out my name in excitement, even though I had not been away for long. "Everything is fine in Nimba. I came to register at the University of Liberia," I responded. At the time, there was something magical about the University of Liberia. Merely uttering the words "University of Liberia" gave me goose bumps. A short while following my response to Francis, I was pleasantly stunned when, out of the blue sky, he told me to stay with them until my accommodation issue was resolved. I did not know whether he discussed his kind offer with Gorlon or whether it was a spur-of-the-moment generosity. In any case, my heart leaped with joy because Francis's offer arrested my anxiety over where to stay to go to school. Even though Francis relieved me with his generosity, the offer he made was almost an impossibility, considering their living situation. They had only one large room. Therefore, having a stranger, whether male or female, in the same room was an inconvenience. Most people would not endure such a sacrifice even for one night, not to mention a week. I was with them for several months. Even more stunning was Gorlon's response to her husband's offer. "Ba ka leh beh orh" (You ought to know that this is your house), she said in support of her husband's proposal. Perhaps Francis and Gorlon also believed that, "An educated child does not belong to one person." Although I never figured out the depth of their compassion, I had a sense that the Wlah Mom petitioned was continuing His work.

On Sunday the following day, there were no activities at the University of Liberia. Moreover, Francis did not go to work. We stayed at home and relaxed the entire day. As I had observed during my previous stay, visitors, mainly Mahns from Duo Tiayee and surrounding towns in our home area, streamed in and out. Some visitors stayed for hours, playing checker, ludo, or cards. They drank Club beer, Guiness Stout, Cane juice, other locally manufactured spirits, or soft drinks, including Orange Fanta, Coca Cola, and Ginger Ale.

I could not help but marvel at the incessant sea breeze and the stupendously elegant Executive Mansion, just a stone-throw from our location. The Mansion, as Liberians called it, was where President William R. Tolbert, Jr. resided.[128] By the time I arrived in Monrovia to enroll at the University of Liberia, I, and perhaps other young people, had assumed the consciousness of the larger-than-life President Tolbert in ways that older people who despised him could not comprehend. I could not believe the president lived that close to where I was staying.

FRESHMAN ORIENTATION

On Sunday night, I slept lightly. I woke up perhaps two or three times, thinking it was already early Monday morning. I was anxious all night about the new world into which I was about to enter. "What would tomorrow be like?" I wondered during that night. I did not expect Francis to take me to the campus like before. He had to go to work on Monday morning. I woke up very early because I was going alone. I knew my way, even though I was nervous. When I got out of the room into the long eerily dim hallway, I was scared. I thought someone might take me for a prowling thief. I looked behind and around me as I approached the front door. In Monrovia, there was no such thing as a suspected thief. Vigilante justice reigned. Mobs meted out that kind of justice mercilessly, sometimes resulting in deaths to thieves or people mistaken for thieves.

Once I got out of the building, I made my way toward the water faucet, where the residents got their water in the open sandy yard. The Water & Sewer Corporation attached a faucet to a pipe that vertically rose a little over two feet above ground. Again, I scanned the surrounding area because I was afraid someone might take me for a thief. To minimize the impact of the water out of the faucet in the empty bucket and avoid raising an alarm, I placed the bucket under the faucet and opened the spigot slowly.

Surprisingly, the very thing I was afraid of happened. The water gushed out and made a loud noise upon impact, although the loudness increasingly decreased as the water level rose in the bucket. The gushing water surprised me because I was used to low water pressure in the yard during the day. I did not consider that water pressure in the pipe depended on water use in the surrounding area. It was early morning and most people in the congested neighborhood were still asleep. On that Monday morning, culture showed its resilience. When the water gushed out of the faucet that morning, I forgot the little science I learned in high school and, instead, relied upon my Mahn cultural schema to interpret the gushing water from the faucet. I took the gushing water as a sign of good luck.

I took the bucket of water inside and heated it, using an electric water heater, the kind that looks like a perforated bagel. I tried to avoid waking Francis and Gorlon up, but I ran into things and woke Francis up. "James, it jeh after 5 in the morning, weh you doing up time like this?" Francis asked in Liberian English. "I fixing hot water to take bath so I can be on campus soon in the morning before everybody," I responded in Liberian English as well. He tried to get me to go back to bed because it was too early, but I told him that my hot water was almost ready. Moreover, because Francis knew that the bathroom was a general one, he got the point right away. I had a pressing issue to attend to, a world awaiting me. I could not wait any longer. Had I slept until daybreak, I would have waited for a long time to use the bathroom.

After my water heated to an ideal temperature, I took it along with a soap dish and towel to the outside bathroom. Everyone used the outside bathroom because all the amenities including indoor plumbing and bathrooms with flush toilets were no longer in working condition. The outside bathroom was located between the building Francis lived in and an incomplete and dilapidated concrete building about 200 yards from the Atlantic Ocean. In constructing the makeshift bathroom, residents drove six-foot long, five-inch diameter sticks into the sandy and moist soil to a depth of about a foot and a half. They positioned the sticks in a circle with a diameter of about six feet. Next, they nailed corrugated zinc sheets, obtained from demolished buildings, to the sticks all around and up to the top to prevent someone standing outside from seeing the person inside the bathroom. The bathroom had no door, but it had an opening comparable to the size of a standard doorframe.

The residents also tied a clothesline from the top end of one to the other of two stick posts that formed the frame of the opening to the bathroom. I hung Gorlon's "lappa" on the clothesline to avoid exposure because anyone could see from the shoulders upward of someone taking a bath, depending on the person's height. The makeshift bathroom was not convenient for several reasons. The "lappa" shield worked only when no wind blew, an unlikely prospect considering the incessant sea breeze from the Atlantic Ocean. The lappa flapped and wiggled as if it were a flag raised on a pole in strong winds, leaving me exposed. Luckily, it was too early for most people to be up and walking around.

The Soniwhein community was in a low-lying area. As a result, drainage was extremely poor. The foul-smelling water in the meandering open channel drainage could not flow into the Atlantic Ocean by gravity because there was no difference in elevation. Soniwhein was a cesspool of unimaginable filth and an ideal breeding ground for mosquitoes. The wastewater from the bathroom was supposed to drain into Soniwhein but it did not flow at all because Soniwhein did not flow. High tide even made the situation worse. Between concrete slabs, wastewater settled and harbored life forms including sand crabs, salamanders and all kinds of weird still water creatures.

With my palms held tightly together into what amounted to a scoop, I stooped over the bucket, scooped hot water and threw it over myself repeatedly. I tried to wash the soap I put into my hair because I did not want it to go into my eyes. However, that was just the beginning of my discomfort. The cool Atlantic Ocean breeze, which supposedly provided relief from Monrovia's sweltering heat, had no shame for exacting a pound of flesh for its service. Indeed, the cool ocean breeze corralled stench from an indescribable place and directed it at me as if I were condemned to die in a gas chamber.

After bathing, I stepped out of the bathroom and encountered another discomfort during the ten- to fifteen-yard walk to the building. I had on a pair of less than half inch-thick rubber slippers (flip-flops) and tiptoed to prevent soiling my soles. I knew I was going over the top by trying to do something stupid and impossible. I tried to walk in sand without sinking to a depth of half inch or a little more. It was like trying to walk on water, something only Jesus had done. Thank God, few people were out at that moment. Otherwise, they would have certainly described me as a "for nothing" human being, someone concerned about insignificant matters.

I finally overcame the hurdle, got through the front door and walked through the long and dim hallway. By that time, several people were up and headed outside. I was not afraid anymore that I would be mistaken for a thief. Once I entered the room, I got dressed, said goodbye to Francis and Gorlon and went to the freshman orientation at the University of Liberia. I wanted to arrive early to sense and absorb the aura of the campus before the mid-morning scheduled orientation. I wanted to stand by the Tubman monument, scan the campus and walk slowly from Roberts' Hall (RH) to Tubman Hall (TH). I wanted to stop for a moment under the giant mango tree. No, I did not want to stop under the giant mango tree because the walk from RH to TH would exhaust me. Instead, I wanted to stop there to close my eyes, inhale deeply and exhale. I was grateful to be one of the chosen ones. More importantly, I wanted to reify and tightly embrace the intangible uniqueness of the university that attracted me. My sense of pride was palpable. I wanted to bask in and savor the liberating yet intimidating aura that permeated the campus.

I took to heart the message I got in high school that students at the University of Liberia were just a step away from national leadership. One of my dreams for wanting to attend the University of Liberia was the prospect of becoming a part of a new breed of national leaders, committed to transforming Liberia to make it work well for all, irrespective of ethnicity, creed or religion. Nevertheless, not all my reasons for wanting to attend the University of Liberia were rooted in high-mindedness. Besides the frivolous reason of securing an advantage in chasing girls, the University of Liberia was the place to want to be because it bestowed prestige. At that time, one had a sense of nothingness if one were not a student of the University of Liberia. There were instances where individuals who had never enrolled at the university carried and used University of Liberia identification cards and extorted benefits in unimaginable ways.

I also wanted to arrive early on campus for the orientation because I was clueless about lots of things. I was familiar with the word "freshman" because upper classmen at St. Mary's School used it to refer to us when I was a ninth grader. Those upper classmen were not kind at all. In fact, they called us "freshmen dogs." With that, I had a sense, as incoming freshmen, we would be objects of ridicule. "Orientation," on the other hand, was a new word. It was not a part of my vocabulary. "What does orientation mean? What will they give us? What are they going to do to us?" I wondered as I made my way from the building through Soniwhein toward the Buzzi Quarter Gas Station.

"What are they going to do to us?" worried me because I heard a rumor that a fraternity of senior students at the University of Liberia would conduct a "debut," an initiation of incoming freshmen. The rumor was that the seniors would blindfold freshmen, parade them on campus and beat them. The rumor also had it that the seniors severely beat and injured some of the students they initiated the previous year. Everyone seemed tight-lipped about the debut, but the rumor would not die. I was frightened at the prospect of the seniors blindfolding and beating me. I was not merely afraid for myself. I felt like a treasure keeper. I was afraid for Mom. As they say in Liberia, I was her only son, her "only button on Joe's coat." Fortunately, the "debut" turned out to be a rumor. It never happened and I was relieved.

As I approached the Buzzi Quarter Gas Station, a familiar scene interrupted my preoccupation with freshman orientation. Taxis were all over the place picking up and dropping off passengers. Unlike the taxi drivers in rural cities like Sanniquellie, taxi drivers in Monrovia did not call out loudly for passengers. Passengers only had to wave to get a cab. If a driver were not already carrying passengers, he would pick up a waving passenger with little or no question. On the other hand, if a driver were carrying passengers, he would stop and ask to find out whether the waving passenger was going in the same direction or nearby. Otherwise, he would continue until he picked up passengers going in the same direction.

Toyota coaster buses and Renault buses tended to carry students and low-income commuters. Unlike cab drivers, their drivers and assistants called out for passengers as they drove through and stopped at every bus stop along the way. Buses came through the Buzzi Quarter Gas Station, made a sharp turn at the confluence of United Nations Drive and Camp Johnson Road and headed toward the Capital Bypass. The scene was reminiscent of the hustle and bustle of Sanniquellie on Saturdays, but on a larger scale. "Old Road, Old Road and Paynesville, Paynesville" the drivers' assistants called out in a chorus of voices.

In no time, I climbed up the gentle hill by the Executive Mansion steel fence. Although Francis and I had walked the same path before, I was still hungry to gaze at the grandeur of the Executive Mansion and the well-manicured executive grounds in admiration. In minutes, I crossed over from the sidewalk by the Executive Mansion steel fence onto the pavement leading to the Capitol Building. I walked by the Capitol Building that seemed to say, "You, village boy, look at me!" Indeed, while I could not ignore the domed- and winged-architecture of the Capitol Building, my eyes were set with a laser focus on the world behind the gate of the University of Liberia. No architectural magnificence, not even Leonardo da Vinci's Mona Lisa could distract me.

Upon entering the campus, I walked toward RH because I still did not know my way around the campus very well. Moreover, the campus was intimidating. I headed toward RH because finding out the entrance examinations results on the bulletin boards at RH earlier that year burnt the place into my memory. I knew we were supposed to attend the orientation in the auditorium, but I did not know where the auditorium was. I had a vague sense of the word "auditorium" and knew we did not have one at my high school in Sanniquellie. Like "orientation," "auditorium" was not a part of my everyday vocabulary. Therefore, I did not know what one looked like. I walked from RH toward TH on a concrete walkway, stopped under a humongous mango tree and turned left because I heard a commotion brewing in the direction of two huts that looked like those in the village. Upon a closer examination, the huts were not the same as the ones in the village. They did not have storage areas, upper chambers where my parents stored harvested rice. These were "palaver huts," places for leisure, where students of the university gathered between their classes to discuss the latest political issues of the day. The palaver huts were a magnet on campus, attracting a wide cross-section of students at any given moment because there was always some hot political topic to discuss. I soon came to learn that politics was the oxygen and pastime at the University of Liberia. There were no such things as NCAA basketball and football. There would have been no life on the campus of the University of Liberia without student politics.

Luckily, I discovered other students at the palaver hut who had already found out where the auditorium was. Together, we walked to the auditorium, which was essentially an extension of Tubman Hall. In no time, students packed to capacity the impressive auditorium, with long and velvet burgundy drapes hanging from its long and ornate windows. The well-decorated stage seated members of the university administration and student leaders who oversaw the program. The orientation was intended to educate incoming freshmen about the registration process and where to find information. However, it turned out to be a spectacle I have not forgotten since 1978. Fiery battle cries from partisans of the Student Unification Party (SUP), one of two or three student political parties on campus, were the most I remember.

A SUP partisan, John Stewart, with a loud and intimidating voice capable of causing a tremor and setting off an explosive device, shouted what sounded like "Zayguay Zayguay, Zayguay, Zanya lacoon Zayguay" and, in unison, the mainly student audience thunderously shouted back "Zayguay." As if the students had not heard enough, the bearded and fiery-looking Stewart suddenly appeared in the aisle and sounded another battle cry sending chills down through my spine. The audience responded to his "Amanga" with "Awaytu" in another thunderous response. For the first time words and phrases such as "Comrade," "Politburo," "Central committee," "The struggle continues," forced their way into my lexicon. It seemed we had come to the university to learn revolutionary politics. After the orientation, I was confused. I did not remember anything important related to the registration.

Following the orientation, I wandered around campus trying to find as much information I could possibly find to help me during the registration on the next day. I got to see the form we would write our courses to be taken on and the computer punched cards we would use the following day. The most important information I found was about scholarships. To my pleasant surprise, I learned that students who passed both subjects on the entrance examinations were entitled to full scholarship, including dormitory accommodations. I was very excited because living in the dormitory meant I would get three meals a day and sleep on a comfortable bed in a decent room with modern amenities.

Later, I returned to Soniwhein and had so much to share with Francis and Gorlon. Mr. Stewart's battle cries at the orientation featured prominently among the activities I witnessed during the day on campus, but the main news I wanted to share with Francis and Gorlon pertained to the scholarship and the possibility of moving into the dormitory. I told them, if all went well, I would be moving into the dormitory in about three weeks. They were excited to hear the news, but also told me, dormitory or no dormitory, their place was my home and that I was welcome at any time. I could not thank them enough for their kindness.

REGISTRATION

Registration was 8:00 a.m. on the next day. Like my preparations for orientation, I woke up early morning, performed all my preparation routines and left the building for the university. I took the same route and arrived on campus before 8:00 a.m. I met other students I had seen the day before and hung around with them, mostly sharing our experience at the orientation. Despite the lack of focus on the registration at the orientation, I had a sense of pride. I had become "the real thing," a bona fide student of the University of Liberia. The awkward sense of being the clueless young man from the village increasingly dissipated, as I got more and more familiar with the campus. I did not need self-convincing anymore to believe that I was legit.

As registration neared, I walked up to and stood before an imposing sculpture of the late President William V.S. Tubman. Engraved below the sculpture were the words *"Lux in Tenebris"* (Latin for light in darkness), as part of the seal of the University of Liberia. I recalled how much I hated Tubman's hairstyle and how many times I tried to run away from a haircut. Suddenly, when I turned right and looked toward the direction of Roberts Hall, I saw a group of people carrying boxes. The group then broke up and headed into different directions as it approached the center of the traffic circle. Some people headed toward the Science Building, others walked toward Tubman Hall and some stopped by the large mango tree near the palaver huts. Each small group set up a large table and sat behind it. Someone told me that the people who carried the boxes were representatives of the various colleges of the university.[129]

I walked up to the table for the College of Agriculture and Forestry, asked questions and obtained a form for listing the courses I needed to take. I recall being told to take a full load of courses, no less than twelve and no more than sixteen and a half credit hours. That advice was the extent of the guidance I received during registration. Still all of that did not make any sense to me. Confident that I had a solid science background in high school, I selected six courses totaling sixteen and a half credit hours. The courses included a four-credit hour algebra and trigonometry course, a four-credit hour introduction to chemistry course, a three-credit hour botany course, a three-credit hour freshman English course, a two-credit hour introduction to agriculture course, and a half-credit hour course in Reserve Officers' Training Corps (R.O.T.C). In addition, I had a three-hour biology lab on Wednesdays and a four-hour chemistry lab on Thursdays.

The next step in the registration process involved the selection of sections for each course in such a way that conflict in the schedule did not occur. I followed others to Tubman Hall, where the courses, sections, times and instructors were on computer printouts and stapled on large bulletin boards.

Without much proper guidance, my main goal in selecting sections for my courses was to avoid conflicts in the schedule. Other freshmen who had friends or other guidance already at the university were making smarter decisions than I was. They had information on the best and worst instructors and did whatever they could to avoid taking classes with the worst ones.

Queuing to register the various courses and sections I selected proved to be my worst experience. I ran from one place to another, pushing and shoving in the queues. On more than three or four different occasions, I fought my way on a queue with sometimes more than one hundred students and reached the registration table only to find out that I was in the wrong line. This went on for hours because there was no guidance. As time went on, sections of courses I selected closed, forcing me to go back to select other sections. It was not until after 3:00 p.m. that I completed registration. Many students also had similar experience.

With dampened spirit due to the chaotic nature of the registration process, I returned to Francis and Gorlon that evening. With such an unpleasant beginning, I wondered what the future would be. I did not tell Francis and Gorlon how I felt about the registration. I only said I registered, and that school would begin early March 1978. I had become a part of the university I dreamed to attend. I could not tell anyone how I really felt, no matter how horrible my experience was. Gradually, I worked through my disappointments and turned my focus on the next important matter, which was lodging. The next day, when I returned to the campus to follow-up on dormitory accommodation, I saw a sign, which suggested that moving into the dormitory might happen in the very near future.

CHAPTER 14

A "Country" Boy's Experience

EARLY MORNING ON FRESHMAN ORIENTATION day, I resorted to my cultural schema, interpreting gushing water out of a faucet as a sign of good luck. Later, on that same day, a new sign, Mr. Harrison Dokie (deceased), reinforced my belief and gave me hope that moving into the dormitory would happen. Mr. Dokie, Dean of men's resident halls at the time, was Mahn. I had not known him prior to enrolling at the University of Liberia but someone showed him to me. He was gracious when I asked to speak with him one-on-one and he listened intently as I explained my dire accommodation need. After speaking with Dean Dokie, I felt more hopeful and, referring to myself, I said, *"Mee lah qui leh keh qui bah qui leh lo mee ka."*[130]

Ethnic connection aside, Dean Dokie was aware of the university's policy of providing accommodations for students who passed both mathematics and English on the entrance examinations, especially with high scores. Mr. Dokie was from Nimba County, where his village was about six miles from Sanniquellie. Thus, he knew Sanniquellie was very far away from Monrovia. I did not have to work hard to convince him that most students from rural areas like Sanniquellie had humble backgrounds and did not have family members or relatives living in Monrovia. I did not make up the story and therefore did not need a fancy argument to convince Dean

Dokie. The circumstances made my case easier to make. With hesitation, he said that there was no vacancy in the dormitories and did not provide any details. However, Mr. Dokie assured me that he would do everything he could to help me get a room.

Before enrolling at the University of Liberia, I already knew that Liberia was a two-tier society, "*Quizees*" or Americo-Liberians and "country people" or indigenous Liberians. I knew that *quizees* did not consider us "country people" as equals but I did not consider myself as a second-class citizen; I did not grow up with my head bowed, harboring any inferiority complex. Nevertheless, my accommodation situation opened my eyes. It made me realize that, in Liberia, unlettered or rural indigenous people were not the only ones who endured oppression and injustices. In my first few weeks at the University of Liberia, I learned about indicators of oppression and injustice other than *quizees* rounding up indigenous people's livestock without paying for it or forcing them to carry cargoes.

Liberian society's *quizee-country* DNA manifested itself in a rather dramatic way after my encounter with Dean Harrison Dokie. Sometime after his assurance that he would find me a room in the dormitory, Dean Dokie followed through by submitting my name to Quilay, Dean of Student Affairs.[131] I found that out during a follow-up visit with him about a week later. Dean Dokie kept his word. Unfortunately, Dean Quilay put his recommendation on the backburner. Days, weeks, and months went by with absolutely no action.

Again, aside from shared ethnicity, I did not know anything else about Dean Dokie before I met him. Later, I discovered that he was well known in Americo-Liberian circles in Monrovia. I learned he had been reared and educated by an Americo-Liberian family. Mr. Dokie did not carry an American or English surname like Richardson or Cooper, but he was Americo-Liberian in mannerisms, especially to Americo-Liberians who did not know his background. Yet, Dean Dokie did not lose touch with his indigenous roots. I picked up on his mannerisms as an Americo-Liberian, but he was a Dokie and remained so at his core. I regarded him as Mahn/indigenous and as one of us.

As time went by without any accommodation relief, Dean Dokie's character showed. He became visibly frustrated over his inability to find accommodations for me and other students in similar situation. I did not have a reliable place to stay to study, but I felt more pain for Dean Dokie than I felt for myself. The reason was that Dean of men's resident halls, the position Mr. Dokie held, was like a shell game. Although Dean of men's resident halls was a big title, it was essentially a façade because the power inherent in the position resided somewhere else. As Dean Quilay dragged her feet in approving the recommendations for accommodations Mr. Dokie made, he apparently felt hollowed and undermined. He was probably afraid that we might know. I felt more pain for him because Dean Quilay's inaction made him appear powerless. He may have been afraid that many needy students, particularly indigenous ones, who looked up to him for similar help might see him as powerless, unreliable, and not worthy of esteem anymore.

The frustrations I saw in Dean Dokie's face were rooted in much deeper societal issues. Through suppression and oppression, Americo-Liberian minority rule shaped indigenous Liberian lives since the founding of Liberia in the 1820s. Despite all the history, I saw the dynamics of the power relations up close at the University of Liberia. For example, even though Dean Dokie had been reared and educated by an Americo-Liberian family, older Americo-Liberians regarded him as an indigenous Liberian. The position of power he had most likely because of his Americo-Liberian connection had to be tethered to the power base; his decisions had to be circumscribed.

On the face, as head of men's resident halls, many indigenous students at the university regarded Dean Dokie as the person in charge; the one who decided matters pertaining to dormitory accommodations. However, behind the scenes, he had to recommend students for accommodation to the Dean of Students for approval. In many instances like mine, his recommendations did not see the light of day. His power with respect to dormitory accommodation was confined. New indigenous students at the university had to learn through situations like mine what was common knowledge to Americo-Liberian students. The power to decide who lived in the dormitories resided with Dean Quilay, an Americo-Liberian woman, and not with Dean Dokie, a "country man."

Aside from who was in control, Americo-Liberian cultural dominance showed in other ways. For example, Americo-Liberians accounted for roughly three percent of the population as opposed to ninety seven percent indigenous Liberians. Yet, the overrepresentation of students of Americo-Liberian background in the men's dormitories was an open secret. Many of these overrepresented students came from wealthy backgrounds. Their parents not only held prominent government positions but also owned properties everywhere in the city of Monrovia and its environs. Unlike students from indigenous backgrounds, especially from the rural areas, who desperately needed accommodations, some Americo-Liberian students did not seem to be in similar dire need.

In other subtle ways, I observed that Americo-Liberian students had easy access to decision makers. For example, they had unfettered access to Dean Quilay. Her interactions with them showed that she knew some of their parents. A kind of family atmosphere existed whenever mostly Americo-Liberian students stopped by Dean Quilay's office to see her. One got the feeling that she was looking out for them. Similar courtesies were not extended to me. It was a perfect example of *"Mee lah qui leh keh qui bah qui leh lo mee ka."*[132]

SONIWHEIN

Meanwhile, Soniwhein, the slum community where Francis and Gorlon lived, was slowly becoming home. The terrible stench I complained about disappeared. Every day I walked by Soniwhein, I did not recognize it as what it was anymore. The serpentine open channel drainage with stinking stagnant effluent became invisible. My morning and evening walk to and from the university lost its drudgery and became a routine task. In a period of about four weeks, I got to know many of the soldiers living in the same building with Francis and Gorlon. Most of them spoke either Dan or Mahn and came from Nimba County.

I forged friendships at makeshift playgrounds while playing soccer with young men of my age living in the same building. John Power Wonlea, the most important friendship I made, was Dan and from Nimba County, but he did not come from my immediate home area. Power was tall, handsome, and soft-spoken. When he heard that I was a student at the University of Liberia, he asked me to confirm. We became instant friends, played soccer and head-butted tennis balls, particularly during weekends since I did not have to go to class.

Power worked as a "houseboy" (domestic worker) for a Lebanese family at Mamba Point, an upscale neighborhood in Monrovia. On one occasion on a weekend, he took me along to see where he worked. We quickly made our way toward the United Nations Drive between congested houses. Power was familiar with the Soniwhein neighborhood and all the shortcuts to getting almost anywhere. In no time, we arrived at the Barclay Training Center (BTC) entrance, where we continued walking along the UN Drive sidewalk until we climbed up the hill in the Mamba Point section of the city.[133] Unlike Soniwhein, the houses and buildings in Mamba Point were fabulous and the neighborhood was clean and very quiet, even though it was during the day. The only noise that caught my attention was that from running air conditioners. I recall having wished I lived there because everything about the place seemed perfect.

Upon arrival at the Lebanese family's property, Power entered the residence, but I remained standing outside, next to a smaller unit about five yards away from the main residence. I did not see any of the Lebanese come out. The family appeared to be away from home. Lebanese were, at the time, the dominant merchant group in Monrovia, let alone across Liberia. The Lebanese family had a stereo system in the smaller unit, including a turntable with several vinyl albums. It was an older version with nothing particularly fancy about it. However, the family's collection of rhythm and blues vinyl records flabbergasted me. "What in the world was a Lebanese family doing with these records?" I wondered. I realized then that Lebanese in Liberia had similarly absorbed the pervasive American influence in the country.

Power and I talked a lot about things young men liked to talk about, including girls. We also enjoyed listening to rhythm and blues on the Liberian Broadcasting Corporation (ELBC). Prior to the April 1980 Revolution, ELBC almost exclusively played American music, particularly rhythm and blues. At the Lebanese family's residence, Power picked out *"Wake up Everybody,"* a Harold Melvin & the Blue Notes album, from a collection of vinyl records and played it for me because he knew Teddy Pendergrass as one of my favorite artists.

More importantly, by the time of the visit to the Lebanese family's residence, I had run out of food that I brought from Nimba. Francis and Gorlon provided food, but they were not people of tremendous means. On the day of the visit, I had not had anything significant to eat since the day before. Power, who instinctively knew my predicament, obtained an entire loaf of French bread from the Lebanese family's residence, cut it open and spread it liberally with mayonnaise. "Here your lunch, my man," he said in Liberian colloquial English.[134] Feverishly, I ripped the aluminum foil off the bread and took a huge bite.

As I savored the French bread with mayonnaise, the sensational voice of Teddy Pendergrass singing, *"Tell the World How I Feel About 'Cha' Baby"* sank into my soul. Momentarily, joy and sadness high-fived each other, followed by a gush of tears. I remember telling myself *"Wlah leh yee zeh"* (God does not sleep). The song, French bread, and mayonnaise, together, encapsulated my experience in Monrovia in 1978. I have a stereo set with a turntable and a collection vinyl records including Harold Melvin & the Blue Notes. I relish French bread with mayonnaise. Each time I hear Teddy Pendergrass's songs, cut open a French bread, or open a jar of mayonnaise, I not only unwrap my struggles in Monrovia in 1978 but also think of my friend, Power, and remind myself of Wlah's grace and Hand in sustaining me.

The loaf of French bread Power gave me at his workplace was not the only time he offered me something to eat. For the couple of months, I spent living in Soniwhein after the visit at his workplace, he occasionally brought me something from work to eat. It was either French bread spread with mayonnaise or sardines. The bread that he occasionally brought me from work reminded me of the *"tuhu"* Mom used to bring me from a *"kuhu"* when I was a child.[135] The *"Tuhu"* often contained meat or fish served on the farm where they worked. Even though Power wrapped the bread he often brought me from work in brown paper or aluminum foil, it qualified as a *"Tuhu."* The intended receiver was the only thing out of place about Power's *"Tuhu."* In the culture, parents who took *"Tuhus"* home from the farm or from a feast almost always did so for their children. Power had brothers, sisters, and other relatives. He could have given his *"Tuhus"* to any one of them, but he kept them for me, someone he had known for no more than three months.

DEAN DOKIE ACTED

Up to that time, Dean Quilay had not acted upon Dean Dokie's recommendation for a space in the dormitory for me. Out of apparent frustration, Dean Dokie then decided to take matters into his own hands. He asked me to pack my belongings in Soniwhein and come over to the dormitory. I asked whether Dean Quilay had approved my moving into the dormitory, he said, "No." "We will figure out something," he went on. At the time of that exchange, he had apparently talked to Messrs. Alfred Gbi Toe and Edwin Rogers. Dean Dokie did not tell me about his communications with the two men. I assumed the conversations were about my moving in with them temporarily as we awaited Dean Quilay's decision. Alfred and Edwin, both students at the University of Liberia, lived in one of the two rooms in the North Annex of the men's dormitory.

Upon Dean Dokie's urging, I packed my personal effects and took them with me to the Simon Greenleaf Hall, the main building of the men's dormitory complex.[136] Dean Dokie also had a suite in the main building. Shortly after I arrived, he took me to the north annex and introduced me to Messrs. Alfred Gbi Toe and Edwin Rogers as their new roommate. I believe Mr. Toe was a junior and Mr. Rogers was a sophomore. Messrs. Toe and Rogers warmly received me and treated me very gentlemanly. Throughout the time I spent with them in the north annex, I found them to be very courteous and accepting.

Messrs. Alfred Gbi Toe and Edwin Rogers's acceptance and treatment of me was a big deal for several reasons. I was obviously a freshman. Neither Mr. Toe nor Mr. Rogers looked down upon me in any condescending manner as a freshman who did not know his way around or anything about university life. I was also a much younger man. Some Liberians, particularly men, tend to elevate themselves with putdowns. They often refer to others as "small boys," suggesting that others do not measure up. Neither Mr. Toe nor Mr. Rogers showed any sign of that snobbish attitude towards me.

Lastly, I was one of those whom Americo-Liberians used to call "country boys."[137] The word "country" suggested that one was of an indigenous or tribal background. However, in Liberian talk, the word meant more than its literal meaning. The expression "country boy," "country man," "country girl," or "country woman" was a caste or ethnic epithet. It did not possess the same potency as the "N-word," the racial epithet often used to disparage blacks in the United States, but it was used with the same connotation. To most Americo-Liberian students at the university, "country boys," particularly from the rural areas were "green," not cultured. Mr. Toe, who hailed from Maryland County in Liberia, like me, had a tribal background. I never figured out whether Mr. Rogers was an Americo-Liberian or someone of a tribal background. In any case, Mr. Rogers did not exhibit any stuck-up attitudes towards me.

I fondly remember Mr. Toe as a popular member of the Student Unification Party (SUP) on campus. He was handsome, eloquent, and seemed to make every dull subject interesting. He spoke distinctively with a fervor that made quite an impression on me. The trending topic, the oxygen on campus, was student politics, which everyone knew was national politics in disguise. I was not steeply involved in student politics as other students seemed to be, but I supported Mr. Toe in a SUP party caucus in his bid to secure the party's nomination for the general election against the candidate of the opposition All Students Allied Party (ASAP). He lost his bid to become the party's nominee to Mr. Dusty Wollokollie, who went on to win the general elections in 1978.

In 1978, SUP and ASAP's memberships reflected the cleavage between Liberians of indigenous backgrounds and those of Americo-Liberian backgrounds in the larger Liberian society. Liberians of tribal backgrounds gravitated to SUP while Liberians of Americo-Liberian backgrounds supported ASAP. The parties had different political philosophies. However, philosophical differences did not divide the student body. Few students knew or understood their party's political philosophy. Political philosophy negligibly influenced party affiliation. Instead, ethnicity or more correctly, indigenousness or being an Americo-Liberian almost single-handedly determined party affiliation. Similar experience, not rationality, determined political behavior on campus. I voted for SUP candidates because I was a "country boy." The unsaid subtext was, "Americo-Liberians and their forefathers had been ruling, oppressing, and suppressing our people since the founding of the nation. On this campus, where we have the freedom and majority, that will not happen."

The division between indigenous and Americo-Liberians on campus showed in many other ways. For example, many indigenous Liberian students resented the opulence many Americo-Liberian students displayed on campus. An Americo-Liberian friend of mine once told me "Man, Marsilius, you can get all the 'A' grades, but you will be walking the streets of Monrovia until the heels of your shoes wear out while I relax in my air-conditioned office." Although my friend meant his statement to be a joke, everyone knew that he was describing what happened to most indigenous students once they graduated from the University of Liberia.

Americo-Liberian students at the University of Liberia did not take the resentment against them supinely. Even though they did not have the numbers to win at the polls against the indigenous-dominated Student Unification Party (SUP) during campus elections, they organized and spoke vehemently against what they considered a communist-inspired SUP, working clandestinely to undermine the national government. The charge by Americo-Liberian students that communist influence had taken hold within the Student Unification Party had some truth to it. It was clear, at least to me, that a miniature political battle was taking place between political opposition in the larger society seemingly allied with SUP and those that SUP partisans called "Reactionary elements." SUP's hierarchy labeled members of the national government, predominantly Americo-Liberians, and their children who were the main supporters of the All Students Allied Party as reactionaries. Opposition voices in the larger society that never spoke up for fear of recrimination were channeled through student politics and let out at the university under the guise of academic freedom. Indeed, it was a fierce battle for the conscience of the nation.

In the meantime, after I moved in with Messrs. Alfred Gbi Toe and Edwin Rogers, Dean Dokie continued to remind Dean Quilay about my situation. He had to keep reminding her because I did not come to live in the dormitory through the proper procedure. Simply put, I was in the dormitory illegally. One privilege of living in the dormitory legally was having a meal ticket to eat in the dining hall. Due to the circumstances under which I moved into the dormitory, I did not have a meal ticket. Dean Dokie temporarily solved my accommodation problem, but my hunger problem persisted.

On one occasion, Dean Dokie gave me a meal ticket with Dean Quilay's signature, indicating that it came from Student Affairs. I asked him how that happened without the approval of my accommodation. He told me that the Student Affairs Office occasionally gave meal tickets to some needy students who did not live in the dormitory. In making up the list of those students, he added my name, otherwise the cafeteria workers would not let me eat in the dining hall. One meal ticket lasted one month. For each day of the week except Sunday, the meal ticket specified B, L, D for breakfast, lunch, and dinner, respectively. On Sundays, only breakfast and lunch were served. For the entire time I spent in the dormitory on the main campus of the university, this was the only time I had a meal ticket.

The dining hall was located on the first floor of Charlotte Tolbert Hall, the women's dormitory. Breakfast consisted of short bread along with butter or cheese, oatmeal, or cream of wheat, and tea or cocoa. The lunch menu included potato greens along with rice; cassava leaf along with rice; and palm butter along with rice. Split peas along with rice was another menu item, depending on the day of the week. Dinner consisted of a variety of foods. Sometimes we had short bread or corn bread, and, at other times, we had rice along with gravy. Because I came from the "Garden of Eden," the lunches we had at the dining hall were about a half or a quarter of what I really needed. However, I did not complain. As it was often said in Liberia, ten is better than zero. I had to adjust my eating habits.

The "Tenth Day Syndrome"

As if trying to survive on half or a quarter of the amount of food I needed was not a struggle, I had to contend against another problem. I had friends on campus who came from Nimba and faced similar circumstances with respect to accommodation and food. These friends were some of the ones who endured and survived Sanniquellie hunger together with me. Culture and my protracted rendezvous with hunger in Sanniquellie made me acutely aware of the problem. Culture conditioned me not to ignore a friend or an acquaintance who was hungry.

Students who did not live in the dormitories came to the dining hall during lunchtime to find friends with whom they could share lunch or dinner. On several occasions, friends joined me and shared the portion of food I described as half or a quarter of what I needed alone. I did not have the stomach to tell anyone you cannot eat my food. Dying would have been easier than saying something like that to anyone. I had to bear the anguish of friends eating my food. I could have used the meal ticket to look after myself. I could have refused to let friends join me to eat the little food I received, preferring such friends to label me as "mean." But I chose to let friends eat my food; I chose to endure what seemed like torture because I would not sleep well had I prevented them from eating with me. I did not act out of the kindness of my heart, but I believed my actions had repercussions for the future. I always imagined the future, where next I would see the person who needed my help.

Tyndale Zoe was a friend who also came from Nimba County, although I did not know him during my days in Sanniquellie. The approximately 6'3," handsome and eloquent man, who seemed like someone who was auditioning for an ironman contest, came to the dining hall to eat with me a few times. On one occasion, I went to the dining hall and stood at the tail of the queue, wishing the line would move faster, but the opposite happened because it was lunch time. As the line moved slowly, I was praying quietly to myself, hoping that the cafeteria ladies would be generous to add a little more than the usual portion to my plate. Eventually, I reached the head of the line and the frantically busy cafeteria ladies put my portion on my plate, but my wish did not happen. With a dampened spirit, I took my food and looked around for a table with no one or one with a few people sitting on. As soon as I found one and sat down, Tyndale appeared from nowhere, pulled an empty chair and sat on the opposite end of the table. Aware that there would be no answer other than a yes, Tyndale asked to eat with me, but he also recognized that my yes was not a normal yes because it was in sharp contrast to my body language, particularly the frown in my face. He obtained a spoon and we ate the lunch.

The moment Tyndale Zoe asked to eat with me, three characters jostled for positions in me simultaneously. The person who battled hunger in Sanniquellie was fully awake and attentive to the request. He was sensitive to the plight of his kind, a Nimbaian who was facing a similar situation. His sensitivity was an outcome of experience and culture, a culture in which strangers were not denied food or accommodation. Thus, his answer to Tyndale's request to share his food was a definitive yes. The second person who captured the essence of my dilemma involving Tyndale's request was my empty and churning stomach, the one who had never been satisfied with the portion of food the cafeteria ladies had put on the plate. To that person, the answer to Tyndale's request to share his food was a resounding no. The reason was that the request essentially amounted to an invitation to have a drink with the ex of one's wife who has not gotten over her.

The frown in my face was the third person, the tortured and angry one. Conflicted, he tried to understand why any reasonable person would put another individual in such a situation; why ask to share a plate of rice that was not enough for one person. He muzzled himself in frustration to resolve the quandary and eventually figured that Tyndale knew what he had done, the consequences of sharing food that was not enough for one person. When the reality hit Tyndale, when he discovered why the frown in my face appeared, he initiated a conversation expressly to appease me. Even though the third person's contribution to the conversation was brief, indicating that he was not interested, he made sense out of Tyndale's action. The sense making was that hunger can be devastating and overwhelming; that it can cause one to do certain things that one would not do under normal circumstances. The sense making on the part of the third person was not an act of kindness toward Tyndale. It was based on recollections of the first person's experience in Sanniquellie. The first person along with his cousin had done almost the same thing to Adrien Sandi and Paul Konan in Sanniquellie.

Tyndale Zoe did not recognize all three of the characters who jostled for positions in me simultaneously. He did not know my background, my experience with hunger in Sanniquellie. As a result, Tyndale could not fathom that such a person saw his plight as his own plight and therefore had compassion upon him. Tyndale could not see the size of my stomach. He did not know the history of my stomach, how much food it could hold in the "Garden of Eden." The third person, the frown in my face, was the only person Tyndale could see. As a result, when he and I parted company, he did not go with gratitude, but with spite. He told more than one person about our dining hall encounter. He told others that I did not want him to eat with me and went on to describe me as a "mean person." Alas, he never told the story about how, on more than one occasion, he ate in the dining hall with me. He did not describe how much food he and I ate. Instead, he badmouthed me, and it did not take long for the word to get to me. His behavior pained me deeply. After that experience, I came up with the "Tenth Day Syndrome," where the help that one provides for someone on nine separate occasions does not matter, but the one on the tenth occasion. In that instance, if one is unable to provide help on the tenth day, one is reviled because it seems the nine previous occasions of help do not matter.

GARPALAH

Meanwhile, to work through my accommodation problem, I turned to the culture for coping strategies. "Zoyagay" (patience) was not a property of any one culture but Mahns invoked it readily in handling difficult situations. Mom developed the habit and used it in dealing with almost every problematic situation. Because getting a college education was not a task I could achieve overnight, I needed "Zoyagay." More importantly, I needed "Zoyagay" to think differently about my accommodation problem to make it less burdensome. "Zoyagay" opened my eyes. It enabled me to see myself in a new light and to laugh at myself. Indeed, "Zoyagay" gave me the inner strength to invite others to join in the laughter. The joy of overcoming difficulty through "Zoyagay" felt more than a hard-fought win because it added to my inner strength and character.

"Zoyagay" enabled me to see my accommodation challenge as "Garpalah" (Garpa safety or cure). Garpa (Ganta), a major commercial center in Nimba County, is a Mahn city. In 1925, Asheville, North Carolina native and Yale University trained physician, Dr. George Way Harley, and his wife, Winifred Frances Jewell Harley, traveled to Liberia. They founded the Ganta Mission (also known as Garpa Mission). Dr. Harley also built the Ganta United Methodist Hospital, a dispensary, and a church. In addition, he built a school, a leper village and two "Sick villages."[138] The leper village and "Sick villages" assumed "Colonies" designation. These facilities remain operational to this day.

As a child, I remember leprosy-afflicted people going to Garpa Mission for treatment. After extended periods, they returned and told their families that their treatment cured them. Unfortunately, the cured returned home with some or all their phalanges missing due to the disease. Their claim that their treatment cured them from leprosy was valid because sores on their skins caused by the disease were absent. In Mahn country, however, where one's livelihood depended on the use of the hands for farming, returning home without some or all the phalanges and claiming to be cured was a dubious victory. Thus, "Garpalah" was claiming freedom from leprosy only to return home to die from hunger. Some of the returnees died from hunger because they could not farm; the disease severed their phalanges they needed to hold cutlasses (machetes).

By this time, I had left the Soniwhein community upon the urging of Dean Dokie. I was living in the dormitory illegally. Soniwhein's swarm of mosquitoes no longer devoured me. Their blood meal field days were over. I had said good-bye to Soniwhein. I was no longer a captive of the unbearable stench. I was now in the opposite world, the "America" I had never been to but had only seen in magazines. Indeed, the America I dreamed of existed in the men's residence halls at the University of Liberia. I had all the amenities of modernity including a shower with hot and cold water, flush toilet and a soft and comfortable bed to sleep on. In addition, I had closet spaces for my belongings, fluorescent lights to study on and a lounge with a television set to watch. Moreover, Simon Greenleaf Hall was located on a gorgeous hilltop enclave with an exquisite scenic view of the city of Monrovia.

My friends, especially the ones who were facing similar dire circumstances like me, recognized my new world; the hilltop Simon Greenleaf

Hall "Small America." Unfortunately, they did not know I was living under a cloud of fear. They did not know I was in the dormitory illegally. They did not know I was terribly afraid Dean Quilay would throw me out if she found out that I was living in the dormitory. My friends did not know I had no meal ticket; that I could not eat in the dining hall. At that point, I did not look forward to Dean Quilay to approve my stay.

Seemingly, I secured my freedom from the harsh living conditions we endured together but my friends did not know that I was in limbo; that my liberation was a hollow one. My friends assumed my worries over hardships were over, but they did not understand the implications of my apparent freedom. They failed to see me as Mahn villagers saw returnees from Garpa Mission. Villagers who understood what it took to live in Mahn country, rightly called the returnees' claim to be cured as "Garpalah." As for my friends, they said, "Man, Marsilius, you got it made." Because they could not see beyond the splendid Simon Greenleaf Hall, I had to expose myself for laughter. I told them, even though I am in the Simon Greenleaf Hall, which looked to them like "Small America," my stay there was essentially "Garpalah." I was like the returnees from Garpa Mission who claimed that their treatment cured them but had no fingers left to hold a machete to farm.

Frustrated over Dean Quilay's foot-dragging, Dean Dokie met with her to discuss my housing situation, but he did not say much to me after their meeting. Instead, he urged me to stop by Student Affairs to remind Dean Quilay about their discussion pertaining to me. I went to Student Affairs a few times to remind Dean Quilay as Mr. Dokie advised. However, each time I reached Student Affairs Office, I did not see Dean Quilay. I had to muster a lot of courage to go to Student Affairs because I did not want Dean Dokie to think that I was not serious about finding a solution to my accommodation problem. Dean Quilay was tall, imposing and intimidating. Her frowns and stares made me tremble; she scared me. Inasmuch as I wanted her to approve my dormitory accommodation, I prayed not to meet her each time I went to Student Affairs. Each time she was absent, I was relieved.

Upon Dean Dokie's prodding to see Dean Quilay at another time, I said, "*Meh leh keh do*" (What has not happened before, meaning what am I afraid of)? Upon reaching her office, I was afraid to knock at the door because I did not have an appointment. Instead, I took a seat in the lounge, waited and hoped that she would step out and ask why I was there. After I waited for over an hour, someone opened her office door and failed to close it. She looked out straight into the lounge where I was sitting directly across from her. With her eyes opened widely and appearing visibly angry, I froze in my seat. "What are you doing here?" she screamed to my utter surprise and chagrin. Moreover, she did not wait for my response. "Get out of here!" she drove me away. Dean Quilay's reaction shocked and surprised me because she and I had not met one-on-one before. I assumed Dean Quilay did not know who I was. Although I felt that her reaction was inappropriate, I did not make a mountain out of that molehill. Instead, I took her reaction as a test. She saw students like me daily, claiming to be needy. I thought that reaction was her way of determining who badly needed help. I desperately needed a place to stay and regular monthly meal tickets to eat at the dining hall. Despite her brash reaction that day, I was not ready to give up.

I told Dean Dokie what happened to me at Dean Quilay's office. "I am sorry. Don't worry, something will work out; be patient," he said while shaking his head. After that apology and reassurance, I waited for a long time without any resolution to my accommodation problem. In the end, Dean Quilay turned down Dean Dokie's recommendation. Shortly after that decision, Dean Dokie asked me to leave Messrs. Alfred Gbi Toe and Edwin Rogers in the north annex and move into another room on the first floor of the south annex. The move puzzled me, but Dean Dokie did not provide any reasons. Based on my cordial relationships with Messrs. Toe and Rogers, I did not believe they had anything to do with my move.

Even though I downplayed Dean Quilay's reaction to me at her office and took it as a test to determine my seriousness about needing dormitory accommodation, *"Ah leh keh yee."*[139] Dean Quilay's harshness including her tone of voice, language as well as body language was bizarre. I thought she did not like me, but she never knew who I was. Therefore, I had no basis for thinking that way. But I later found out the stimulus for her reaction. An informant told her I was in the dormitory illegally upon Dean Dokie's advice. Later, after my encounter with Dean Quilay at her office, she reportedly chastised Dean Dokie verbally for insubordination. Nevertheless, insubordination was not a feature of Dean Dokie's character. In my judgment, a bigger societal issue was at play than insubordination. The dormitory matter, for which Dean Dokie took a "Bullet" for me, was one evidence of cultural dominance and power relations between Americo-Liberians and indigenous Liberians. Had my last name been a Cooper or a Richards, perhaps the outcome of the matter would have been different.

I soon learned that my illegal stay in the dormitory triggered Dean Quilay's reaction at her office, which led to my move from the north annex to the first floor of the south annex. "Did my stay in the north annex interfere with someone's interest?" I wondered. Al and Edwin were kind and courteous to me during my stay in the north annex. They seemed to understand why I moved in with them under those unusual circumstances. As a result, I refused to entertain the thought that either Al or Edwin could have told on me. Moreover, Dean Dokie's reticence in saying why he asked me to move into the south annex resulted in the informant remaining a mystery.

The move into the south annex, next to the general laundry for the men's dormitories, was uneventful. I stayed there for less than two weeks. Beyond mere acquaintance, there was no time to get to know the students who shared the room with me. It seemed that they were in there temporarily, although legally unlike me. Mr. Mousa Dassama, an upperclassman, was the only person in a nearby room whom I recall vividly. Like me, he was a student of the College of Agriculture and Forestry.

About two weeks following my move into the south annex, Dean Dokie, again, asked me to move into another room. In hindsight, it seemed he was playing chess with an invisible hand. In the process, I essentially became a nomad but that did not bother me at all. I would have moved into a storeroom and slept on bare floor if he had asked because getting an education was my focus. I knew why I took the risk and went to Monrovia. I was on a mission for which Sanniquellie had prepared me quite well. Quitting did not cross my mind. Escaping my parents' fate aside, the Liberian society was not kind to flunkies. The stake was too high to quit because I did not have a stable and comfortable lodging like other students.

This time around, I moved into the main building on the second floor. The rooms in the main building, which consisted of a first, second and third floor, took two single beds, two occupants, built-in study tables and closet spaces. After one of the occupants of a second-floor room moved out for an undisclosed reason, a vacancy occurred. Incidentally, the remaining occupant of that room was a relative of Dean Dokie's. Dark polished skin, silver gray Gabriel Dokie (deceased) was approximately 5'10" and about 180 pounds. Considering the role of informants in the chess game that Dean Dokie was playing with an invisible hand, I do not believe moving in with Gabriel Dokie happened merely because a space became available.

Gabriel Dokie was lively, personable, and courteous. I learned valuable lessons from his examples, including his study habits. Until that time, I had not seen anyone who stayed so much in the books. He was an employee of the Lamco Joint Venture Operating Company (LAMCO). LAMCO was the Liberian American-Swedish Mining Company that mined the iron ore deposits in the Nimba Mountains in Yekepa, Nimba County. He was pursuing a degree in management at the University of Liberia. I learned that he was a Lamco scholarship student. Gabriel was a chain smoker as well.

Inasmuch as I liked Al, Edwin, and Gabriel, I was tired of hopping from one room to another. I wished I had a room where I could stay permanently and where my roommates were of similar age, but I had no choice. My longing for roommates of similar age was for my own comfort and out of reverence for Gabriel Dokie. Gabriel was like a father figure. As such, he and I could not have certain kinds of conversations. For example, we could not talk about girls. However, while I was looking for a place to lay my head for the night, any place was fine. Again, I never complained about not having a room where I had roommates who were of similar age.

After about three weeks of stay with Gabriel Dokie, Dean Dokie stopped by one evening and told me he had found another room for me, although under the same cloud. "This time, once you settle in, you will not be moving anytime soon," he said. "Soon" reminded me that there was no guarantee and the worrisome cloud of illegality continued to hang over my head. Aside from my thirst for an education, language helped me cope with the constant distress of trying to make something out of nothing. "Struggle," with a different connotation, was in common usage when I enrolled at the University of Liberia. Partisans of the Student Unification Party (SUP) popularized "Struggle." They habitually invoked Nelson Mandela and the South African people's struggle against Apartheid and other southern African liberation struggles. In taking on the "Decadent" oppressive True Whig Party-led government of Liberia, SUP partisans and their mentors drew inspiration from the southern African struggles because they saw themselves as representatives of the oppressed masses of Liberia. Therefore, a struggle against Americo-Liberian domination or the True Whig Party "Struggle" was the original and widely understood meaning of "Struggle." The goal of the struggle was to get the True Whig Party off the backs of indigenous Liberians, to change the status quo.

However, many of us newcomers who attended high schools far away in the rural areas were not steep into student politics at the University of Liberia. The influence of university professors who discovered truth under the spell of communist as well as socialist ideologies seemed to have diffused from the university outward into the high schools in the city of Monrovia and its environs. We, who were far away in rural high schools, were somewhat shielded from such influence. I did not subscribe to some of the rhetoric of the Student Unification Party because the leadership romanticized communist and socialist ideologies. Anyone who did not agree with their perspective was either a bourgeoisie or a reactionary element. I had friends from the same humble background and the same county who called me a bourgeoisie because I liked nice clothes and shoes. Indeed, on many occasions, the name-calling was a joke. Nevertheless, anyone who attended the University of Liberia with me at that time knew the absurdity of referring to someone like me as a bourgeoisie. "Which bourgeoisie would choose to live in Soniwhein for mosquitoes to feast on him or choose to live illegally in the dormitory under a cloud of constant fear?" I wondered.

My friends and I, particularly many of us from Nimba County who enrolled at the University of Liberia at the same time, wrestled "Struggle" away from the larger student population that supported SUP and redefined it. We were neither callous nor indifferent to the conditions of the Liberian masses. Indeed, we were not oblivious to the oppressive True Whig Party. The "Struggle" for us was not romantic. It was not about a pie in the sky or about changing the oppressive True Whig Party government of Liberia. Instead, the "Struggle" for us was real and immediate. The "Struggle" concerned our immediate conditions. Whenever we talked about the "Struggle," we meant we were hungry, or we did not know from where our next meal would come. The "Struggle" also meant that a property owner was threatening eviction because someone's rent was due and did not have the money to pay.

Johnson Sendolo, a friend at the University of Liberia at the time, was an expert demonstrator and narrator of our redefinition of "Struggle." He often stretched a hand and pointed to it as if we could not see to show how eating dry rice was affecting him. It was not merely showing his hand that captured our new definition of "Struggle," but the way he said it. Johnson wore glasses and had a high pitched yet calming voice. Moreover, making his point in Mahn made his demonstration of the real impact of the

"Struggle" poignant, memorable, yet funny. He would say *"Gon buhu kpon hmm baylay ah ka hmm kohor ghen."*[140] Together, all of us would laugh hard about what Johnson said and, for that moment, forget the hunger or worries about pending evictions. Aside from Wlah's grace, that laughter and the feeling that we were not alone enabled us to overcome. Johnson Sendolo now lives in the state of Minnesota.

ROOM 327

In the meantime, my new room was on the third floor of the south annex. Room 327 was originally a large general men's bathroom, but the university converted it into a bedroom because of the need for more space. Room 327 stood out for several reasons. First, because the annex itself stood on a hill. Seen from afar, Room 327 looked like it was in a four- or five-story building. Second, the view from the window overlooking the city of Monrovia was spectacular. The multipurpose court below, the Capitol Building, the John F. Kennedy Maternity Center, the old facility, and buildings as far away as E.J. Roye on Ashmun Street and the Ducor Intercontinental Palace Hotel on the top of Cape Mesurado were in clear view. Third, Room 327 was immeasurably large. Sky blue bathroom tiles covered the walls from the floor up to a height of four or five feet while marble tiles covered the floor. Finally, Room 327 stood out because of the people who shared it with me.

Room 327 had six occupants including Saa Philip Joe, Sydney King, Emmanuel Freeman, Patrick Forfor (deceased), Caleb Domah and me. Of the six occupants, one, Sydney King, was Americo-Liberian while the remaining five of us were of indigenous backgrounds. Despite the ethnic make-up of its occupants, Room 327 was, at least from my own sense, superficially immune from the perennial national divide, the deep-seated Indigenous vs. Americo-Liberian mindset that permeated student life, student politics and even personal relations.

Despite the intense rhetoric on campus, the raw statistics of Room 327 occupants did not tell the whole story. It was not black or white or a strictly clean-cut divide between Americo-Liberians and native people as many students were inclined to believe about the student population or the greater Liberian society. The indigenous occupants of Room 327 consisted of shades of gray. Saa Philip Joe, who hailed from Lofa County, was Kissi;

Patrick Forfor, Caleb Domah and I, who hailed from Nimba County, were Mahns; and Emmanuel Freeman, who was apparently born or raised in Ganta, Nimba County, was Vai.

The ethnic dynamics in Room 327 was the elephant in the room or, in Mahn talk, the "spider soup."[141] Indigenous Liberians seldom talked about that aspect of intra-indigenous Liberian social relations. Rather than a clean-cut black or white Americo-Liberian-Native divide, Room 327 was more of a continuum. For example, on the bases of speech patterns and mannerism, it was not hard for anyone visiting with us to figure out that Sydney King was an Americo-Liberian. Similarly, from our mannerisms and speech patterns, someone could easily tell that Saa Philip Joe and I were native Liberians, even though we came from different counties. As for Patrick Forfor, Caleb Domah and Emmanuel Freeman, if one did not know them before; one could not easily tell their backgrounds. Based on speech patterns, mannerisms, and associations, they carried themselves as if they were Americo-Liberians. In addition, they had an air of "Americo-Liberianness" about them.

SAA PHILIP JOE

Saa Philip Joe, from all indications, was the eldest of the occupants of Room 327. At the time, he was a junior student enrolled in the William V.S. Tubman Teachers College. The approximately 5'9" freckled face and somewhat soft-spoken Saa Joe, who leaned forward and walked as if he were going against a strong wind, did not spend much time with us in Room 327. He always went somewhere across the "Bridge" (that connects Bushrod Island to Monrovia), sometimes during the week but mostly over the weekends. He was always gentle and collegial on the days that he was with us.

Saa Joe was a skilled organizer. He was a founding leader of the Liberian National Teachers Association (NTAL). He not only led the NTAL with distinction, making it a household phenomenon, but also made it a significant voice in civil society. Saa Joe always referred to me as "Lila's Pa" because he was in on how I came to select that name for our first daughter, who was born on July 13, 1978, at the George Way Harley Hospital in Sanniquellie, Liberia. Throughout the years, he remembered Lila and always asked about her. He currently lives in Liberia.

Sydney King

Sydney King was an Americo-Liberian. I never asked which settlement near the city of Monrovia in Montserrado County he hailed from. By settlement, I mean one of the colonies where the freed U.S. slaves who founded Liberia in the 1820s settled. Sydney appeared to be in the same age group as the rest of us. He was a Civil Engineering major in the College of Science and Technology. It was through Sydney King that I came to know Lila Sunwabe, whom I named our daughter, Lila Kou Wonmein Flumo, after.[142] Lila Sunwabe was from Nimba County. She was Mahn. Not only did she have an imposing presence but also, she was dark and beautiful. Her hair was unmistakably long, dark, and silky.

After Sydney introduced Lila Sunwabe and me, a conversation ensued. Perhaps to spice the conversation, one of my roommates told Lila Sunwabe that I was a proud father. She then turned to me and asked, "What did you have?" as if I had been carrying the baby myself. Hurled into the light-hearted conversation, I responded by saying I had just received word from Sanniquellie that my fiancée, Yei Tokpah, had given birth to a baby girl. Incidentally, Yei Tokpah lived next door to where I rented a room in Sanniquellie. I met her nearing the end of 1976, my junior year. She is the daughter of Mr. William Tokpah (deceased), a long-serving member of the Liberia National Police in Sanniquellie. Seemingly caught up in her own importance, Ms. Sunwabe, with little expectation that I would consent, asked right away "Would you name her Lila?" Until that moment, I had not really given much thought to what name I would give our daughter. However, for some unexplainable reason, the name Lila jumped at me. For the same unexplainable reason, a part of me said, "Yes, that's the name." As a result, in response to Ms. Sunwabe's impromptu request, I responded, "Yes, I would," without hesitation.

Looking back at suddenly agreeing with Lila Sunwabe to name our daughter after her, I recognize how arrogant I was. However, as Father Tikpor once put it, it was arrogance "With a difference." Yei Tokpah carried the fetus for nine months, yet my spur-of-the moment decision did not consider whether the name would be agreeable to her. I never considered whether she was thinking about another name for the baby. Indeed, it was all about me. I went on as if the woman did not have a part to play or an opinion to share. Nevertheless, that instant decision to name our daughter after Lila Sunwabe was arrogance "with a difference" because it was not rooted in any form of disrespect or malice. Rather it was one sign of cultural conditioning about which I was very unaware at the time. I had not become wise enough to understand that, in the culture, there were two personas to a man, a public and a private one.

A man taking charge was an element of the culture children could see and quickly adopt. Taking charge meant he decided matters, provided for the family, and protected his family. Even though men consulted their wives or significant others in making family decisions, the cultural expectation of taking charge came without a caveat. Children never "read" the subtext of taking charge. The unspoken cultural expectation that accompanied taking charge was that a man had to seek advice or consult with his wife or significant other before speaking for his family. For that reason, at the time of the birth of our daughter at age nineteen, all I knew was that a man was supposed to beat his chest and take charge.

Ironically, the trouble I got into upon making the sudden decision to name our daughter after Lila Sunwabe did not concern my seeming arrogance and male chauvinism. I expected Yei Tokpah to make a case for the prerogative to name the child because she carried the fetus for nine months. In addition, I expected her to challenge me for behaving as if I were the only one responsible for the birth of the child. Instead, I got into trouble with Yei for a story someone concocted and told her. The story was that the name I selected for the baby was that of my "girlfriend." A few days later, I traveled to Sanniquellie to see the infant and its mother. Yei was suspicious. Later, she disclosed what someone had told her. "Whoever told you that lie would die for nothing," I remember looking straight into her eyes and telling her in Liberian English. Lila Sunwabe lives in the United States. I hope one day both Lilas and Yei will meet and hear Lila Sunwabe's account of how I came to name the child Lila.

EMMANUEL FREEMAN

Emmanuel Freeman was a fair-skinned 5'10" handsome chap. He leaned forward and walked in short, but quick steps as if the campus outlawed long paces. Freeman had great taste for clothes. He always dressed smartly. In my eyes, Freeman was Mr. Commitment. He adored Rose (a pseudonym), his high school sweetheart, immensely. Freeman hardly talked about anything without mentioning what Rose might think or say. He was friendly and authentic. I was not surprised when I discovered a few years ago that he was a minister of the gospel. He was the only occupant of Room 327 who fiddled with the Bible like a favorite toy. He read the Bible on a regular basis and I watched him pray often. He was also the only occupant of Room 327 for whom sleep seemed to be a pastime. He never seemed to have enough. He would fall asleep early evening and be the last person to wake up the next morning.

Emmanuel Freeman was Vai, one of Liberia's sixteen tribes. Recently I discovered that my birthplace, Ganta, Nimba County, is also his hometown, although the Vais are not one of the principal ethnic groups in Nimba County. Like many members of other ethnic groups, his parents may have settled there. Throughout the time Freeman and I spent together in Room 327, I never heard him speak his native tongue, Vai. At least from my own sense, part of the façade that some young indigenous men and women displayed was an outcome of their socialization in high school. Freeman, for example, attended Carroll High School, where many of the students were children of Americo-Liberians of means from Monrovia. Although Americo-Liberians were only a small minority in Liberia, their culture was the dominant culture. Those who willingly or unwillingly adopted the dominant culture, meaning those who wanted to fit in, or wanted to avoid the "country" boy or girl label, tended to minimize, if not rid themselves of their own tribal identities. Simply put, wearing a badge of indigenousness wherever Americo-Liberians dominated was not a "cool" thing to do.

Freeman was a student in the College of Business and Public Administration. Prior to enrolling at the University of Liberia, he attended the all-boys Catholic boarding school, Carroll High, in Grassfield, Nimba County along with two of the six occupants of Room 327, Patrick Forfor and Caleb Domah. Carroll High School was St. Mary's High School's archrival in sports. The rivalry was intense while I was still a student at St. Mary's. Carroll High School dominated both soccer and basketball. Even though I did not have a girlfriend at St. Mary's, I was not immune to the displeasure that St. Mary's boys felt whenever there was a sport meet between Carroll High School and St. Mary's on our campus in Sanniquellie. Carroll High School boys not only dominated soccer and basketball but also added insult to injury by "taking over" our girls. A sport meet with Carroll High School always felt like an invasion, a spectacle for heartaches because, to our utter chagrin, our girls were fascinated with Carroll High School boys for reasons we did not understand. After the games, I saw Carroll High School boys all over the campus not only walking and talking with our girls but also kissing them as well. We hated Carroll High boys! Of course, it was not a personal hatred.

PATRICK FORFOR

Patrick Forfor was an approximately 6'4" 250-lb fair-skinned person. His eyes were flashy to an extent that hardly anyone could accuse him of inattentiveness. At least in Room 327, I do not remember if Forfor ever offended anyone. Only a boatload of complaints couched in unrequited anger could counter the disarming charm of Forfor's smile. His flashy eyes and disarming smile rendered his pimples a mirage. At one moment, one could see his pimples, but, moments later, those pimples would vanish due to the sheer radiance of his eyes and smile. Patrick walked occasionally with his head down, but he stepped with his full weight as if he were saying, "I am the man," to the ground that he was walking on. He was imposing, yet he was gentle.

Patrick Forfor was Mahn inside out. I knew a little more about him than all my other roommates. By American standards, Forfor came from a middle-class family, but by Liberian and Mahn standards, he was from an upper-class family. His family had a farm and a large house near Dingamon on the highway from Ganta to Sanniquellie. Even though I never stopped at the Forfor family house to take a closer look, it looked impressive and was always a fascination of mine. It was one of those houses that everyone wished it were theirs. Every time the vehicle I was traveling in drove by on the highway, I turned to get a glimpse of that house. I was pleased to share the same room with a young man who came from the family that owned that house. I told Patrick that I knew where their house was and that I had always admired their property. In a small way, it felt like an encounter with one's favorite celebrity.

Despite all of Patrick Forfor's "Mahnness," I never heard him speak Mahn. He always seemed to avoid anything Mahn. He always chuckled whenever I spoke Mahn to him. Like Freeman, Forfor seemed to struggle with the same effect of socialization with uppity Americo-Liberian friends in high school. One could never tell whether Forfor was Mahn. Aside from having hardly spoken Mahn, he seldom closely associated with other Mahns on campus. Part of the shying away from speaking one's native language was self-censorship. Some students of indigenous backgrounds believed that it was impolite to speak their native languages around others who did not understand. On the other hand, others stayed away from their native languages and cultures because they wanted to fit into Americo-Liberian circles or did not want the "country boy" or "country girl" label. Americo-Liberians were not the only ones who referred to indigenous Liberians as "country." Indigenous Liberians who wanted to put others down widely used the epithet. It was common to hear an indigenous girl refer to an indigenous boy she did not like as "country" and vice versa.

Patrick Forfor was perhaps the most fascinating person among the six occupants of Room 327. He towered over everyone in the room, yet he was quiet, gentle and private. He would not hurt a fly. Forfor laughed at jokes, especially if they pertained to Freeman's sleeping habits. However, whenever the jokes were about him, particularly jokes about girls, he would smile and blush. Like all of us, Forfor liked girls, but they did not take much of his time. His favorite sport was basketball. He had the perfect height, size and loved playing the sport. However, like girls, basketball did not take much of Forfor's time. He stayed in the books more than anybody in Room 327 did. A civil engineering major, Forfor studied relentlessly. Freeman once said, "Forfor frustrates me," suggesting that Forfor's study habits made him to feel like an idler who was not accountable for his parents' resources. Our parents were not in Monrovia to yell at us to get up, go to class on time and study our lessons. However, Forfor's study habits loomed like our parents' watchful eyes. It was hard to hang around Monrovia to have a good time while Forfor was in the books, without feeling guilty for wasting one's parents' resources.

Patrick Forfor graduated from the University of Liberia with a bachelor's degree in civil engineering and went on to work for the Ministry of Public Works as a Civil Engineer. Unfortunately, during the early stages of the Liberian Civil War, the future, Forfor slept very little and worked hard in college to secure, vanished. Liberian government soldiers senselessly and violently took his life. Upon hearing the sad and shocking news of my roommate's untimely demise, a part of me died and left a gaping hole.

No mother, father or country should have to lose a son like Patrick Forfor. Therefore, because *It's My Turn*, I can no longer hold back the "boiling blood" in my stomach. Instead, I issue a challenge to Liberia and to the world: unless there is full accountability for the deaths of sons and daughters like Patrick Forfor, Voker Joe-Kolo, Famatta Sherman, and the nameless multitude, what the world sees of Liberia will continue to be a façade.[143] Moreover, because the earth beneath in Liberia unwillingly absorbed immeasurable innocent blood, it will continue to rumble in protest until justice is done. Until the time of justice and accountability arrives, I *lift* Patrick Forfor, Voker Joe-Kolo, Famatta Sherman and the nameless multitude in these pages lest Liberia and the world forget that they were here on this earth.

CALEB DOMAH

Caleb Domah was about 5'6" and weighed no more than 150 lbs. He was swift in everything he did. He walked fast and talked similarly, let alone his speed and ability to dribble with a basketball. Playing basketball was Caleb's passion. Although he was not a tall person, he loved the game and was an excellent player. I watched him play at the multipurpose court at the University of Liberia campus on a few occasions. I did not get to know much about Caleb's background because he was also private. Even though Caleb said very little about anything, he was relentless at teasing others, especially Freeman. His jokes were often also about Freeman's sleeping habits or something about their days at Carroll High School. By all accounts, Caleb was a nice person. However, his pensive and sometimes melancholic demeanor often suggested that he wanted others to stay out of his space. He seemed to be a loner, at least for the time we spent together in Room 327. Parties did not seem to interest him. He was very comfortable talking to girls, but I do not recall seeing a girl come to visit with him in Room 327.

Like Forfor, Caleb Domah was a Civil Engineering major, but he was quite the opposite of Forfor when it came to "staying in the books." He showed some interest in religion, but it was hard to figure Caleb out. He was also Mahn, but, like Forfor, I never heard him speak the language. At least from my vantage point, Caleb was the one who seemed most uncomfortable when someone spoke Mahn around him. He, Forfor and Freeman attended Carroll High School and had the same socialization experience with uppity Americo-Liberian friends. One could never tell whether Caleb was Mahn because he rarely closely associated with other Mahns on campus.

My roommates in Room 327 were unique in their own ways. We came from different parts of Liberia with different ethnic backgrounds. Due to socialization and different life experiences, one needed more time to recognize deeper layers of differences that existed even among those of us who were Mahns. Some of us attended Catholic schools prior to enrolling at the university while others went to public schools or schools operated by other religious denominations. Some of us grew up in rural Liberia with limited exposure to modernity while others came up in and around Monrovia and other urban centers. With respect to student politics, some of us were SUP sympathizers while others supported ASAP. The University of Liberia made a difference because it brought us together and enabled us to forge lasting friendships to live in harmony despite our differences. Moreover, it gave me a great education. Life with my roommates in Room 327 was unforgettable.

CHAPTER 15

Humility

M Y DORMITORY TRIBULATION AT THE University of Liberia caused a change in me. Even though my parents taught me the difference between right and wrong and instilled strong values in me, I had innumerable youthful indiscretions. But I tried to live a life that reflected the character they demonstrated because character mattered to me; having character kept me at peace internally. In rearing me, however, my parents took for granted that all things were equal. But my experience at the University of Liberia showed that all things were not equal. Dean Quilay, for example, presided over an unjust system, one that put the needs of one group of students over those of others.[144]

A change occurred in me when, out of desperation, I agreed and moved into the dormitory illegally upon Dean Dokie's advice. Until that time, I prided myself as someone who did not cut corners. The system I contended against was unjust, but the change that occurred in me was not my agreeing to move into the dormitory illegally. I did not wholly adopt cutting corners as a part of my value system. The change in me was in the way I regarded others who cut corners. Before my experience at the University of Liberia, I was inordinately critical of those who cut corners without knowing their personal circumstances. My dormitory experience taught me to be less critical of others because we all come from different backgrounds and take different paths in life.

The change caused me to see myself during my dormitory experience differently. While Dean Quilay and her informants saw me as an outlaw, someone living in the dormitory illegally, I saw my illegal stay in the dormitory as the case of a man drowning in a deep and swift river. I needed something to hold onto to stay alive. At that time, it did not matter to me whether that something was a long stick with razor-sharp spikes or a long sword. At the time of change during my illegal stay in the dormitory, I stopped feeling guilty that I had cut corners.

COLD BOWL

After I moved into Room 327, I was on my own with respect to food. I did not have the audacity to face Dean Quilay to beg for a meal ticket when the only meal ticket I had expired. She became an obstacle due to her hostility against me. I did not turn to Dean Dokie either, to ask him to beg Dean Quilay for another meal ticket for me. She had humiliated him for my sake, and I did not want that to happen again. Without a meal ticket, I turned to a combination of options to survive. On occasions, for example, I drank a lot of water after friends shared donuts with me. At other times, I bought "farina" (dry fermented cassava, also known as gari) with money Mr. Soni gave me or visited with friends who shared some with me.[145] Farina, sold in measuring cups of various sizes, ranged in cost from five cents to twenty-five cents. It was relatively inexpensive and required little effort to prepare. Once water and sugar were added, it rose like a dough including yeast, but with a different consistency. One hundred percent carbohydrates, farina provided an instant source of energy.

"Cold Bowl" was another option.[146] I do not know the full history of "Cold Bowl" in Liberia. "Cold Bowl" was a food service and a part of Liberian talk. "Cold Bowl" met a need that university policymakers knew about but failed to address adequately. Struggling students turned to "Cold Bowl" at least when I was a student at the University of Liberia. By struggling students, I mean those who were having a hard time meeting their basic needs, such as food and shelter and not students who were having a difficult time with their academic work.

The women who prepared and sold "Cold Bowl" were overwhelmingly indigenous Liberian women. They woke up early morning, cooked the food and, depending on how far they lived from the university or construction sites where they sold the food, they hired taxis or walked. Cold Bowl sold for 50 cents to $1.50, depending on the size of the measuring bowl. "Cold Bowl" got its name from early morning preparation because by noon it had become cold as if it were still food. I bought "Cold Bowl" a few times and friends bought some and shared it with me. Due to lack of funds, I could not buy "Cold Bowl" on a regular basis.

My sustenance at the University of Liberia came not only from the food I acquired and ate, but also from the joy I reaped from collective creativity that hardships engendered. We, meaning my contemporaries and I from Nimba County at the university, adopted English words and assigned to them our own meanings. For example, we assigned our own meaning to "hustle" so that whenever someone said, "I got to hustle to get so and so," the person meant going out to ask friends, distant relatives, or an acquaintance for help. "Hustle" in our language did not mean the dictionary definition of "hustle," which is to obtain something in an aggressive or dishonest way. Nearly every struggling student understood our definition of "hustle."

"I Hold Your Foot"

In the absence of a meal ticket, my other sources of pocket change, or food were not reliable. No friend could share a donut throughout the week. I could not go around into friends' homes expressly to eat whatever they could offer. Mr. Soni gave me pocket change occasionally in appreciation for the help that I provided him, but he was not my piggy bank. Without money, "Cold Bowl" was not in my reach. Dean Quilay's office was a no go because she had humiliated me. I had to figure out a way to eat because an empty and churning stomach did not give me a break. I had to hustle. I asked people here and there and heard about someone in the dining hall to whom I could make a case for help. The person was Mrs. Gore (or Goll), the cafeteria manager. She was light-skinned and "fluffy" with big flashy eyes.[147] Mrs. Gore was intimidating, but behind the façade was a heart of gold, a woman of great compassion. She lived on Lynch Street, less than a block from the Southwest fence of the Antoinette Tubman Soccer Stadium.

One evening, shortly after Mrs. Gore left the dining hall on her way home, I mustered the courage and followed her. I caught up with Mrs. Gore at the front of the Science Building, explained my situation and asked for help. It took a lot of courage to explain my problem. After that, my heart raced because I did not know what she would say in response. Upon agree-ing to help me eat at the dining hall, I almost jumped in excitement, but I caught myself. She never asked me for anything in return for the help but in my excitement to show appreciation, I told her that I would find "Little thing" for her.[148] In Liberia, "Little thing" meant money. I gave her twenty United States dollars on one occasion. Except the one time I gave her the twenty United States dollars, I could not live up to my own commitment to give her the "Little thing" at the end or at the beginning of each month because I did not have the money to do so.

In the first two months, Mrs. Gore allowed me to eat at the dining hall. A cafeteria worker was always present to mark off the meal tickets so that students do not pass them to their friends to eat after they had had their food. I always had to ensure that Mrs. Gore was at the head of the line because I did not have a meal ticket. My roommates were not aware that I never had a meal ticket. I employed other tactics to conceal my lack of meal ticket. For example, as a disguise, I carried the old and only meal ticket I ever had to the dining hall every day to make it appear as though I had a meal ticket. I did not expose it because the color was different from everyone else's meal ticket. It was an embarrassing thing to do but I had to do it to survive.

Without the "Little thing" I committed to give Mrs. Gore at the begin-ning or end of each month, it was difficult to avoid the embarrassment. Overtime, perhaps she took me as a liar. Instead, the reality was that I did not have the means to fulfill my promise. On one occasion while I was in line to get food, she stopped me from taking the food. This happened while many students, including girls were looking. I cringed not only because I had to leave the line and return to the dormitory with hunger but also because I felt humiliated and sick to my stomach. I vividly remember the incident to this day. As I passed the student center and made my way at the back of Tubman Hall toward the boys' dormitory, I had my head bowed throughout.

I felt embarrassed but I did not blame Mrs. Gore. She allowed me to eat for a long time even though I did not give her the "Little thing" I promised. After a couple of weeks, I switched back into survival mode and mustered the courage to go back to Mrs. Gore. She was on her way home after an exhausting day the evening I met with her. Again, I caught up with her at the front entrance of the Firestone Quadrangle (the science building). I called out "Mrs. Gore." She turned around with those big flashy eyes and smiled broadly as soon as she recognized me. She already knew why I needed her attention. "I hold your foot," I went down to her feet with both hands, begging dramatically.[149] She told me not to worry and to come back to the dining hall to eat. She told me she thought about the day she stopped me from getting food and felt terrible. I continued to eat at the dining hall for the rest of the year.

A few days after commencement on February 16, 1983, I went to see Mrs. Gore at her house on Lynch Street. I told her, "I came to say thank you for the help you gave me at the university when I did not have anything to eat." I do not know whether Mrs. Gore is still alive. In any case, I want the world to know that without someone like her whom Wlah used to accomplish His goal, I would not be where I am today. I hope that her children or relatives will have an opportunity to read this book and know how she, in doing what to her might have been an ordinary thing to do, impacted my life in a profound way.

PAYLAH

My will to survive took a beating when Mrs. Gore stopped me from getting food while in line at the University of Liberia dining hall. The humiliation affected me deeply. It took a while to overcome it. During the time I stopped going to the dining hall, I turned to Augustus Flomo.[150] Augustus, also known as "Saye Payleh" (Saye number two), is about 6'and stoutly built. The characteristic gap in his upper front teeth and his distinctive laughter are unmistakable. His hometown is Gbein Yohnyee, about ten miles from the village. He currently lives in Monrovia in the Caldwell community. Apparently, his parents had him after they had had Saye, Nyan, Paye, Wuo, Zarwolo, Fohn and Laywehyee; after they had exhausted the naming order for boys in the culture and had to start all over, hence "Saye Payleh."

In many ways, Augustus Flomo was like Francis Karkeh. Both men had a gap in their upper frontal teeth, stuttered and were exceptionally warm. Like Francis, Augustus was married. I remember Augustus's wife, Paylah, vividly. She was kind to me, but she was also a no-nonsense and feisty woman. She never let Augustus get away with anything. Paylah fascinated me not because she was a feisty woman or kind to me. There was something captivating about her name. It told a story about her parents that one could imagine. In addition, her name told a story about Mahn people's considerations in choosing baby names.

The name Paylah was a classic example of how Mahns communicated their thoughts, feelings, and expectations. Even though Paylah sounded like a Mahn name, it was not a Mahn name. Paylah was a Mahn pronunciation of the English word "Pillow".[151] Whenever Mahns named a child "Paylah," they were telling an implicit story. Such a story often pertained to the joy the child brought into the parents' lives; Paylah reflected happiness for having someone to depend on. Paylah, then, was suggestive of a missing thing, abstract or material, that having the child restored.

Augustus and Paylah lived on Perry Street, a short street that connected Capitol By-Pass to Camp Johnson Road.[152] Augustus was self-employed as a shoe repairer. His shoe shop was a "Zinc Round," a makeshift structure of wood and corrugated zinc sheets. Perry Street was a walking distance from the University of Liberia. As a result, I was a regular visitor to Augustus's shoe shop. My primary reason for going to see Augustus was to find food to eat while my secondary goal was psychological. We came from the same area in Nimba County and spoke the same language. We were like family because we were far away from home. He was someone to whom I could relate. He told stories that made me laugh; I felt at home with him. Augustus always woke up early to begin work on repairing shoes. By 11 a.m., he had made enough money to send Paylah to the market to buy food to prepare. He made sure I had enough food to eat before returning to campus. Whenever he did not see me for some time, he always wanted to know why I did not come over to see them.

Augustus repaired shoes, earned money and gave it to his wife, Paylah, to buy food. In turn, Paylah took the money her husband gave her, went to the market and decided what food items to buy to prepare. Upon her return home, she cut the greens, fish, or meat into smaller parts. In the process, she sometimes cut herself mistakenly. She then made charcoal fire and cooked the food. Again, in the process, hot cooking oil sometimes splashed and burned her, if not burning charcoal. After she prepared the food, she served Augustus and me as if we were royals. She fed me when I was hungry. Moreover, she treated me with great respect. I lift Augustus and Paylah in these pages for the part they played to get me to where I am today. This Paylah was more than Mahn people's hope for what the birth of a child would bring them in the future. She truly demonstrated to me what her name symbolized—a support, someone that one could depend on.

JOSEPH MEATAY

"I always imagined the future, where next I would see the person who needed my help."

Those were my words. I said that when I described my mindset as not having the stomach to tell anyone "You cannot eat my food." That encounter was with Mr. Tyndale Zoe and it occurred during lunch at the University of Liberia dining hall in 1978. That preface is not necessary for what I am about to say about Mr. Joseph Meatay because he asked to eat with me as Tyndale did. Instead, the situation with Mr. Meatay was different because, on one occasion, he offered me food at his home in Monrovia while I was a student at the University of Liberia. I lift him in these pages not only for the food he shared with me, but also for the value of the relationship he and I forged at the time.

Mr. Joseph Meatay was older than I was. I did not regard him as a friend. Instead, he was someone I looked up to, even before I had an opportunity to meet him. He is from my home area, specifically Duo Boe, quite a distance from the village. He went to Monrovia sometime in 1971, when I was only a sixth grader. Over the years, I heard about Mr. Meatay, but I did not know him until I went to Monrovia to attend the University of Liberia. However, his name and reputation were miles ahead of him. I heard he was an employee of the Chase Manhattan Bank. I had heard about the Chase Manhattan Bank in Monrovia prior to 1975. But it was only during my first visit to Monrovia in 1975 that someone showed me the splendid building at the corner of Randall and Ashmun Streets.[153] The sheer beauty and sophistication of the building reinforced the image I had created of Mr. Meatay.

Before I met Mr. Meatay, his image in my mind had become a role model. I wanted to be someone like Joseph Meatay. I wanted to be a no-nonsense uppity necktie-wearing, briefcase-carrying urbanite I had made him to be in my mind. Like the Mr. Meatay in my mind, I wanted my name to conjure "*Quiness*" and sophistication. I wanted to be larger than life. Upon meeting Mr. Meatay, however, he was nothing close to the person I had created in my mind. Instead, he was pleasant and reserved.

Unlike Augustus Flomo, I did not frequent Mr. Meatay's house because I did not know him very well. I recall visiting his home only two times. During my first visit, I did not see him. On the one occasion I met him at home, we ate dinner together. Based on the relationship we forged, Mr.

Meatay became the link between Mom and me during the twenty-one consecutive years I spent in the United States between June 1990 and October 2011 without seeing Liberia. He hosted Mom when she came to Monrovia to communicate with me on a landline telephone in his office.

Mr. Meatay visited with Mom and Dad in the village. He made cassette tape recordings of Mom, Dad and the rest of the family, and sent them to me in the United States. He wrote Mom's will and sent it to me in the United States as well. During my visit to Liberia in October 2011, Mr. Meatay was with me throughout the time I spent in Liberia. Thereafter, he was with me every year I visited Liberia. Mr. Meatay is a prolific written communicator. He stayed in touch with almost all members of my family, relatives and friends, communicating their messages to me through long letters. For my family, he became the de facto go-to person for reaching me in the United States.

Mr. Meatay holds a special place in my heart because he kept me informed about developments with my family and friends in Liberia. He was helpful to my mom in my absence. In July 2013, he was present with me when my mom said her final goodbye to me in Sanniquellie. I am remembering him for the good that he did for my family and me. Due to our long-standing relationship, I regard Mr. Meatay as a family. Moreover, I lift him in these pages because he helped give Mom hope; he helped me stay connected to my family, especially during the civil war years.

CHAPTER 16

Uncertainty and Fear

"There is just so much hurt, disappointment, and oppression one can take...The line between reason and madness grows thinner."[154]

ORIGIN AND ANATOMY OF TROUBLE TO COME

EXISTENTIAL THREAT CAN BE A "Birther" of seemingly justified evil. In the United States, the enslavement of Africans was an economic enterprise that sustained the livelihoods, lifestyles and survival of slaveholders. Slaveholders and, ultimately, slaveholding states regarded any attempts to interfere with the institution of slavery as an existential threat. Therefore, slaveholders as well as slaveholding states put measures, including laws, into place to protect the institution of slavery; to protect themselves or to ensure their survival. For example, slaveholders as well as slaveholding states passed laws that declared slaves three-fifths of a human being. Thus, slaves became commodities, subject to ownership or trade. Slaves could neither claim personhood nor exercise control over their lives; they had no freedom. Owners considered their slaves as workhorses, which they subjected to harsh and inhumane conditions. Slave masters severely punished slaves who disobeyed. It was against the law to teach slaves how to read. Slave masters as well as slaveholding states took these measures expressly to forestall any revolt against the institution of slavery or any threat against their survival. The American Civil War was the South's attempt to prevent an existential threat.[155]

Liberia came into being because of one of the strategies slaveholders as well as slaveholding states adopted to prevent an existential threat. That strategy was the removal of "undesirable black people" (free blacks) from the United States. Slaveholders as well as slaveholding states saw a growing number of freed blacks who bought their freedoms as an existential threat. Leaders including Abraham Lincoln and Thomas Jefferson considered getting rid of black people and taking them somewhere outside the United States. As president, Lincoln considered establishing a colony for freed black slaves in Central America, but he did not pursue it. Before that, Jefferson called for the freedom, removal, and colonization of black slaves, "To such place as the circumstances of the time should render most proper," and their replacement by importing whites from other parts of the world. His justification included "Deep rooted prejudices" whites entertained, "Ten thousand recollections" by blacks of injuries sustained, and the distinction of skin color.[156] Jefferson said that these situations would divide blacks and whites and "Produce convulsions which will probably never end but in the extermination of the one or the other race."[157] Jefferson's proposal was an outcome of perceived existential threat.

The American Colonization Society (ACS) advocated and supported the emigration of freed blacks from the United States to the West Coast of Africa. It nurtured the colonies and helped create conditions that led the settlers to declare themselves as an independent nation in July 1847. The ACS was itself an outcome of a meeting of three "Birthers" including those who saw freed blacks as an existential threat, often labeled as having "racist motives," freed blacks who wanted to escape degradations in the United States and those who saw slavery as morally wrong.

Freed blacks who left the United States, settled the West Coast of Africa and founded Liberia faced a much greater existential threat than that which slaveholders as well as slaveholding states faced in the United States. Natives with different cultures overwhelmingly outnumbered and surrounded the settlers. Socialized in the United States, especially in the South, the settlers arrived at the West Coast of Africa "armed" with a "script" that they learned but had never acted upon. The "script" consisted of the meaning, images, and trappings of civilization.

In the United States, the settlers learned that a civilized man was a Christian and an educated person; someone who attended church on Sundays and read the Bible. They also learned that a civilized man was a master who owned slaves, the labor of which he profited. Indeed, the settlers learned that a civilized man was someone who lived a life of leisure and luxury; someone who enjoyed life abundantly without toils. Moreover, they learned that the civilized were those who recognized existential threat and took every necessary measure to purge it without guilt. For example, before leaving the United States for the West coast of Africa, the settlers witnessed slaveholders as well as slaveholding states pass laws to reduce slaves to commodities, govern the trade of slaves, exclude slaves from citizenship, segregate slaves, and to forbid teaching slaves to read as ways to purge an existential threat.

In the colonies as well as after independence, the settlers acted upon the "script" that they brought with them to the West coast of Africa. They declared themselves the civilized, the "*Quizees*," and looked down upon the natives whom they considered "Heathens" and "Primitive". Moreover, the settlers and their descendants established themselves masters over the natives.[158] They established plantations, owned native slaves who worked on the plantations as well as in their homes as "Domestic servants" or "Houseboys".[159] In addition, even though the natives had no representations in the government, the settlers levied taxes upon them to support their aristocratic lifestyle of antebellum southern United States.[160] The settlers established churches, read the Bible, and went to church on Sundays. They educated their children but put little or no emphasis on the education of the natives. To forestall an existential threat (or a take over and domination by the natives), the settlers supplied rival tribes with weapons and fueled their differences.[161] Furthermore, they used arbitrary boundaries to divide tribes with similar cultures. It was not until the beginning of the twentieth century, almost sixty years after independence, that the settlers granted Liberian citizenship to the natives. The gesture, essentially a shell game, did not make any significant change in the status of the natives.

The natives, on the other hand, did not fold at the arrival of the settlers. They resisted abuses during the expansion of settler control into the hinterland. In reaction to the Frontier Force's abuse of Indirect Rule, the natives, for example, during the Grebo, Kru, Gola, and Joquelle Kpelle Wars in 1910, 1915, 1918 and 1920, respectively, fought back and resisted

Americo-Liberian domination over their lives. The existence of old towns
in many areas of rural Liberia is also a testament to the natives' resistance
against the settlers and their descendants. Eventually the natives acquiesced because the Americo-Liberians were backed up by the "Power of the
United States." [162]

In his memoir, former Liberian Vice President Clarence L. Simpson,
Sr. captured the essence of the script that the settlers acted upon at the
founding of Liberia, the script that birthed the uncertainties, fear or trouble
that was to come.

> Two courses were open to us: one was to merge at the outset
> the comparatively small advanced elements of the population
> into the mass of those who, for various reasons, were at a more
> primitive stage of development and to hope that in due course all
> would progress homogeneously and simultaneously. The other
> was to preserve the ideal of western democracy on however
> small and imperfect a scale and to direct our efforts at gradually
> improving the system and extending it to a broader section of
> the population. We adopted the latter course.[163]

Americo-Liberians maintained power and controlled almost all
aspects of national life since the founding of Liberia. Power, leadership,
and Americo-Liberian/Congo literally meant the same thing. Leadership
reflected the *quizees* or the Americo-Liberians. "To preserve the ideal of
western democracy on however small and imperfect a scale and to direct our
efforts at gradually improving the system and extending it to a broader section
of the population," were code words for outright suppression, oppression,
and humiliations. More importantly, Liberia's founders midwifed a new
Apartheid in the glare of daylight, but the world did not take notice because
there was no distinguishable color line. Historians including Hayman
(1943)[164] and Buell (1947)[165] chronicled the discrimination, oppression,
and humiliations Americo-Liberians meted out to the majority native
population. Buell (1947) predicted that, "As the Liberian tribes become
educated, they will protest more and more against abuse."[166]

Liberian natives were under no illusion that the settlers whom they
resisted would willingly open their arms to accept or to share political power
with them. In other words, acquiescence did not provide relief from the

indignities that natives suffered. The few natives who, by cooptation or force, entered Americo-Liberian circles and became educated, however, escaped public indignities. Thus, getting an education and becoming a *quizee* soon became a passport for escaping the indignities and degradations natives suffered. Therefore, for native Liberians with a grasp of Liberian history, an education has always been something more than a tool for enlightenment and self-actualization. It is also a "savior" and a "protection" against indignities.

On the one hand, to Americo-Liberians, acquiescence did not remove the natives as an existential threat. On the other hand, the "script" that the natives acquiesced and accepted did not guarantee that they would become principal actors.[167] Instead, the settlers and their descendants added a new requirement to protect against what they saw as an existential threat. It was not enough to become educated to join the ranks of the *quizees*. One also had to give up one's name and culture, a sacrifice that still did not guarantee becoming a *quizee* of substance. With that, it soon became apparent that the strategy of "If you can't beat them, join them" was a shell game. As more and more natives became educated, disillusionment led to discontent and the protest that Buell predicted in 1947 earnestly began.

THE APRIL 14, 1979 RICE RIOT

Nineteen seventy-eight, my first year at the University of Liberia (UL), was a rough one because of food and accommodation issues. Nevertheless, I looked forward to 1979 with hope and remained determined to achieve my educational goal. Despite my determination, increasing political agitations against the government of Liberia at the time was not a good omen. Beginning in the 1970s and rising to a crescendo in 1979, the activism demanded reforms for the indigenous people to have greater participation in the national government. Even though Americo-Liberians had never ceased to regard the natives as an existential threat, the agitations mimicked the Israelites' march around the walls of Jericho, except that Monrovia did not have walls. Most Liberians including the natives did not believe that agitations and fiery rhetoric alone would shake the foundation of a ruling class that had been in power for more than a century.

In 1979, the Progressive Alliance of Liberia (PAL), along with its rival, the Movement for Justice in Africa (MOJA), had its eyes set on a showdown with the government of Liberia. In the 1970s, PAL and MOJA were perhaps the two most prominent opposition political movements in Liberia. Even though PAL and MOJA did not seem to have compatible ideologies and approaches, they, however, had the same strategic goal, which was reforms for the indigenous population to have greater participation in governance and the affairs of the country. Moreover, PAL's followers consisted mainly of low-income residents of the boroughs and slums of Monrovia as well as rural indigenous Liberians and operated mainly at the grassroots level. In its political activities, PAL infiltrated trade and workers' unions across Liberia and adopted a tactic of direct confrontation. Over time, the movement chipped away at the legitimacy of the Liberian government.

MOJA, on the other hand, consisted of seemingly left-leaning professors who propagated Marxist-socialist propaganda and captivated many indigenous students. Even though the movement's headquarters were located elsewhere in Monrovia, nearly everyone took the University of Liberia as its operational base. MOJA's followers consisted mainly of supposedly left-leaning students at the University of Liberia. The university students virtually served as con-duits for disseminating an indistinguishable Marxist-socialist ideology to students of the public high schools of Monrovia. MOJA's influence as well as stranglehold on the minds of high school students in Monrovia was palpable in the late 1970s. In its political activities, MOJA also engaged in a direct challenge of the government of Liberia, but at a different level. Although MOJA paled in comparison to the Liberian government in power, resources and reach, its deleterious effect on the government's legitimacy was notable and substantial. MOJA continually exposed the weaknesses of the Liberian government and its leaders at every opportunity, especially at intellectual fora at the University of Liberia.

Although no one openly advocated the overthrow of the Liberian govern-ment, the tenor of the rhetoric by rank-and-file members of PAL and MOJA as well as leaders provided an impetus for others to pursue such a strategy. MOJA and PAL's activities and challenge of the Liberian government set the stage for what was to come. At the University of Liberia, public high schools around Monrovia and in communities around the country, those activities successfully portrayed the government of Liberia as Goliath and cast the downtrodden indigenous masses whom the advocates represented as David.

Upon entering the University of Liberia in 1978, I took the strident campus rhetoric as mere theatrics or pure entertainment. However, PAL and MOJA's challenges and agitations were shaking the knees of the government of Liberia slowly, quietly and dangerously. I was completely blind to what was happening because, like many Liberians, I had come to believe that the government of Liberia, with its vast network of security, was invincible. The seismic April 14, 1979 episode, the "Rice Riot," which changed the country's future trajectory forever, was a prime example of PAL and MOJA's impact. The "Rice Riot" was a PAL-sponsored demonstration, which resulted in the loss of hundreds of lives and untold destruction of property. President William R. Tolbert, Jr. called in the Guinean military to help restore order in Monrovia. The government of Liberia closed the University of Liberia because of the riot. Through Wlah's grace, I was in Sanniquellie during the day of the riot.

ORETHA NYAH

After several months, the government of Liberia reopened the University of Liberia. My "Garpalah" predicament in the dormitory, which provided a "Ten-better-than-zero" accommodation relief, did not continue after school reopened. So, the struggle for stable accommodation and food earnestly continued upon my return to school. However, as church folks often say, "God may not be there when you want Him, but He is always on time," an unlikely and ironic encounter with Oretha Nyah let my studies continue uninterrupted.[168] I met Oretha through Blemie Lewis Baikiayee, my friend who betrayed me during a student government election campaign at St. Mary's School in Sanniquellie. Blemie and I reconnected at the University of Liberia almost three years after the high school rift occurred between us. When Blemie refused to apologize at the time of the rift between us, I let the matter go, instead of paying back, because I did not know what the future would bring. That attitude opened a whole new world to me, a world where I came to know Oretha.

Mr. Baikiayee enrolled at the University of Liberia when school reopened following the April 14, 1979 Rice Riot. Even though the high school betrayal incident did not come up in our interactions, the university provided an ideal setting as well as opportunity to mend the rift. Camaraderie that develops between mere acquaintances when they find themselves in a foreign or far away land helped solidify our renewed friendship. Without much talk, we realized that our survival in Monrovia and ability to achieve our educational goals, in part, depended on working things out.

Not too long after we reconnected, Mr. Baikiayee invited me to see where he was staying. The place, located behind the Liberia Telecommunications complex on Lynch Street, turned out to be Oretha Nyah's home. Blemie was staying with his girlfriend, Loretta, who was staying with her sister, Oretha Nyah. As Blemie and I trekked to Lynch Street, I thought about not having a place to stay and not knowing where to find food to eat. The closure of the university due to the riot amounted to shuffling a deck of cards. It exacerbated the future of my illegal stay in Room 327, which had been uncertain. I had to decide whether to go back to Dean Harrison Dokie to pursue the dormitory accommodation I had been pursuing for more than a year or be upfront with Blemie that I would be delighted were he to let me hang on his coattail.

The dilemma I faced was quitting school and returning to Nimba under the weight of accommodation and food problems or making a request of Blemie to let me hang on his coattail. On the one hand, if I quit, I would not achieve my educational dream. On the other hand, I would be exhibiting insensitivity and further burdening Oretha Nyah if I asked Blemie to let me hang on his coattail. Moreover, asking Blemie in the face of his refusal to apologize for betraying me would make him indispensable.

However, because education was extremely important to me, I could not quit school. Instead, I had to get over Blemie's refusal to apologize for betraying me. I had to be deliberately insensitive to prevent reality from forcing me to quit school. I had to ignore the number of people in Oretha's apartment. I had to "eat my crab without shame."[169] Eating "my crab without shame" meant I would not let Blemie's refusal to apologize for betraying me in high school stand in the way of achieving an education. In addition, eating "my crab without shame" meant knowing the circumstances at Oretha's small apartment, yet asking Blemie to let me hang on his coattail.

The sheer number of people at Oretha's apartment did not leave enough space for someone to stand. Besides her four children, two of her sisters, Loretta, and Kou Martha, also lived with her, not to mention many relatives who streamed in day-in-day-out to eat and ask Oretha for help. Blemie was not working. So, he could not provide any financial assistance to his girlfriend, Loretta. That clearly made him an additional burden on Oretha. I was not working, and I could not provide any financial contribution for the upkeep of Oretha's household. Under those conditions, anyone with a measure of common sense would not ask Oretha to stretch her kindness further.

My situation had two "crabs," getting over Blemie's refusal to apologize and the reality at Oretha's apartment. The latter "crab" was more difficult to "Eat without shame" than the former. Despite my hesitance, I had to eat those "crabs" before asking Blemie to let me hang on his coattail. After I told him what was on my mind, Blemie said something to the effect that whatever the situation was, we would face it together. Shortly thereafter, he talked with Loretta about my accommodation and food problems behind my back. Before Blemie could find words to tell Oretha about my situation, she got a wind of what I was up against at the University of Liberia. Following our arrival from the library at the Cassell Building on the main campus of the University of Liberia one late evening, Oretha preempted what he had been trying to say. In a clear and emphatic language, she said, "Blemie, bring Marsilius's belongings to this house. Whatever the situation is, Marsilius is not going anywhere. He will stay here and go to that school," meaning the University of Liberia.

Oretha Nyah doggedly carved a space for me in her already overcrowded small apartment. The apartment had one bedroom, where she, her sisters and her very young children stayed. The only other space available was the piazza, a passage to her bedroom and the only way in and out. Her bedroom had one window at the back. There was no backdoor. Oretha stored dishes and other household items in the piazza. Blemie and I spread a foam mattress on the bare cement floor passage and slept on it. We were the last to go to bed and the first to wake up in the morning. If we did not wake up before everyone, especially those in Oretha's bedroom, we risked someone not only stepping on us, but also falling. With those searing words instructing Blemie to bring my belongings to her home, Oretha Nyah made me her family and treated me accordingly. She had a special bowl for my food. As any loving and concerned parent would do, Oretha worried on days I never returned home on time to eat.

THE ASSASSINATION OF WILLIAM R. TOLBERT, JR.

PAL and MOJA's overt agitations against the Liberian government were a sign of increasing awareness of systemic inequalities and the discontent it fostered, especially in Monrovia. In the months and weeks leading up to April 14, 1980, the one-year anniversary of the violent eruption of that discontent, PAL and MOJA's stated goal was prime fodder for intense intellectual exchanges among students at the University of Liberia, where politics was the oxygen.[170]

In the late 1970s, PAL and MOJA reframed the debate about how to achieve their stated goal. They superbly crafted a five-second sound bite, "Monkey works, baboon draws," that grotesquely caricatured Americo-Liberians and the government of Liberia. That five-second sound bite distilled indigenous people's political-economic struggle into a stark good vs. evil and a zero-sum game. It not only portrayed indigenous people as "Good" and Americo-Liberians as "Evil," but also painted a picture that empowered "Good" to overcome "Evil." The characterization of Americo-Liberians as "Baboons" who reaped the rewards of "Monkeys'" or indigenous people's labor depicted them as "Super rogues" or "Monsters" who stole everything from indigenous people for over a century. In other words, indigenous people died uneducated and poor because of Americo-Liberian oppression and exploitation. Moreover, the sound bite implied that it was okay to strip the "Baboons" or "Monsters" of whatever they took away from the monkeys.

"Monkey works, baboon draws" was not merely a reflection of history but also of the current reality at the time. Americo-Liberians were the "*Quizees*" as they had been since the founding of Liberia. They held tenaciously to a pervasive ideology that "Country man cannot govern." My dormitory accommodation saga led me to believe that the suppression and oppression of indigenous Liberians were a systematic project. Before 1980, for example, Americo-Liberians, barely three percent of the population, dominated the affairs of government. One did not need a scientific study to know that opportunities for social mobility were not equitably available to Americo-Liberians and indigenous Liberians alike. On a personal level, I received grades in certain courses at the University of Liberia that did not fairly and accurately represent the work I did. On the other hand, some students who did not do half as much work as I did, received grades far higher than what I received because of their Americo-Liberian connections to the instructors. I felt helpless because there was no recourse.

"Monkey works, baboon draws" was PAL and MOJA's attempt to facilitate breaking loose from Americo-Liberians' firm grip and virtual strangle-hold on the prospects of better lives for the majority indigenous population. The economic as well as socio-psychological gulf between Americo-Liberians and indigenous people made it easier for the latter to accept the potentially volatile sound bite as well as its "Good" vs. "Evil" rendition as a least common denominator. In no time, that sound bite not only became a potent feature of Liberian political consciousness, but also began to influence the erosion of the government's legitimacy.

The idea that a handful of noncommissioned soldiers of the AFL could dislodge the entrenched government of Liberia was unthinkable, even amid PAL and MOJA's political agitations. Similarly, the thought that an indigenous Liberian could be at the helm of political power in Liberia was nothing short of heresy. Even though "Monkey works, baboon draws" did not explicitly call for an outright overthrow of the True Whig Party regime, its corrosive impact on the legitimacy of the government provided an opportunity. Inspired and emboldened Master Sergeant Samuel K. Doe and a band of noncommissioned officers of the AFL not only took advantage of that opportunity, but also took matters into their own hands. On the morning of April 12, 1980, the noise and commotion that woke me up turned out to be public reactions to news that Sergeant Doe and his colleagues had stormed the Executive Mansion, assassinated President William R. Tolbert, Jr. and shattered the notion of Americo-Liberian invincibility.

As my heart throbbed beyond its normal rhythm amid confusion, "How could this be?" "Who will now be in charge?" "What will happen?" were few of the questions I asked myself. It is only now that I understand why I was afraid; why I felt as if I had lost a close family member on the morning of April 12, 1980. I did not realize that I had assumed the consciousness of President Tolbert and made it an inseparable part of the "Essential me."[171] Tolbert had been the blood of the "Liberian body," delivering oxygen, nutrients and other essential substances to its cells to do their work. He crisscrossed the length and breadth of Liberia, visited remote hamlets, and communicated his vision of a "Wholesome functioning society" in simple, yet captivating and memorable phrases. "Self-reliance," "From mat to mattresses," and "Total involvement for higher heights" were some of the catch phrases he used in communicating his vision of a new Liberia that implicitly put work over pedigree as a path of social mobility. I considered myself as one of President Tolbert's "precious jewels." I believed in his vision of working to make Liberia a "Wholesome functioning society." Even though at the time I still did not understand my parents' idea of *actual* work as something more than a matter of pride and dignity, meaning that work was also therapy, I took to heart President Tolbert's wisdom in putting work front and center in building the "Wholesome functioning society" that he envisioned.

William R. Tolbert, Jr., the man and the president, set himself apart from everyone, particularly the America-Liberians, as a true unifier. For that reason, despite my parents' experiences with the *quizees*, the history of America-Liberian oppression of indigenous people and my own experience at the University of Liberia, I felt a deep sense of loss over the assassination of President William R. Tolbert, Jr. When the soldiers' bayonets mowed President Tolbert on the early morning of April 12, 1980, they also mowed an important part of the "Essential me."

Political activists' transformation of indigenous people's struggle into a five-second sound bite and the subsequent caricature of America-Liberians came directly out of Liberia's founding fathers' dehumanization playbook. The founding fathers and their descendants dehumanized the natives to ready them for oppression, exploitation and untold abuses and atrocities. They did that by setting themselves apart and above the natives based on cultural superiority. The settlers and, subsequently, their descendants became the *quizees*, the civilized, the people of the superior culture while the natives became the heathens or barbarians, primitive or the "Country people."

Dehumanization was a mind-numbing process, a process of creating an alternative reality. The problem was that the alternative reality not only became the reality but also prevented a return to the original reality. Once settlers and their descendants put the natives at a level comparable to animals, they made exploiting and inflicting harm upon them guilt-free. Similarly, once "Monkey works baboon draws" became a part of indigenous Liberian consciousness, ordinary native people translated the sound bite into what it implied. For example, the chant "Native woman born soldier, Congo woman born rogue" on April 12, 1980 was an explicit rendition of "Monkey works baboon draws."

To this day, the most powerful dehumanizing word in Liberia, particularly in Monrovia, is "Rogue." Once someone shouts "Rogue," a multitude pursues the accused and exacts vigilante justice, invariably resulting in the death of the accused. On April 12, 1980, and the days following the Revolution, "Monkey works, baboon draws" and "Native woman born soldier, Congo woman born rogue" dehumanized America-Liberians, desensitized native people about the humanities of America-Liberians and set them along a course for the kill.[172] For example, native people cheered as soldiers put thirteen Americo-Liberian former government officials on firing squad and shot them point blank. In addition, all around Monrovia, soldiers paraded Americo-Liberians naked in the streets while they confiscated the properties of others.

There was no outcry against the harm directed against Americo-Liberians because "Monkey works, baboon draws" dehumanized them as baboons who committed horrific and inhumane acts against their brethren, literally monsters who feasted on the labors of hard-working monkeys.[173] By that means, the natives not only regarded the harm against Americo-Liberians as something directed at animals but also became numb to the pains of Americo-Liberians. Alas! In less than ten years, President William R. Tolbert, Jr., an Americo-Liberian, perhaps, did more to improve the lot of indigenous people than all the other presidents combined did. Yet political activists pilloried and made him the poster child of Americo-Liberian evil.

In Liberian parlance, a "for nothing" debate about President Tolbert ensued and continued for a long time. The issue of contention was whether soldiers of the Armed Forces of Liberia (AFL) who assassinated him acted alone. Some Liberians speculated the involvement of an "Invisible hand." I thought the debate was a "for nothing" endeavor because it did not matter whether the soldiers acted alone or with the help of an "Invisible hand." At the time of reckoning, when the dust of the Revolution settled, Liberians woke up and realized that they had lost a leader. Neither the soldiers' sword nor the "Invisible hand's" bayonet had the power to resurrect the martyred president.

During the heat of the Revolution, resisting the temptation to think that indigenous people's turn, not to mention their turn to eliminate the "Baboons," had come was a tall order. For example, during the early morning of April 12, 1980, the Liberian Broadcasting Corporation (ELBC) played music I had never heard on the radio before. The songs captured the eeriness of that early morning and foreshadowed the dawn of a new era, albeit uncertain and ominous. I heard Nigeria's Sonny Okosun's revolutionary song, "Papa's Land." I also heard Mahn and Dan songs on the radio. I had an inkling the songs were not randomly chosen. The announcer, Mr. James Karsoryan, did not appear to have either a Mahn or Dan background.[174] In addition, he appeared to have come from nowhere and taken control of the broadcast during that morning of the "Revolution." I had not heard him on the radio prior to April 12, 1980 and did not know who he was or what he did before April 12, 1980. The Mahn and Dan songs Mr. Karsoryan played on ELBC during the early morning of April 12, 1980 were the first signs that the country had changed. Prior to April 12, 1980, I did not hear Mahn and Dan songs on ELBC. The Mahn and Dan songs struck a chord; they evoked an emotion I had never felt before. I felt a visceral connection to Liberia—the land and the people—that had been subdued.

Americo-Liberians never shunned sitting in the same classroom or riding on the same bus with indigenous Liberians. Overt discrimination did not exist in Liberia as the histories of other countries have shown. However, prior to April 12, 1980, it was an open secret that indigenous Liberians were second class citizens as had been throughout the history of the nation. Oppression in Liberia was indirect; it was hidden within the system. In general, for example, Americo-Liberians had more opportunities for social mobility and advancement than indigenous Liberians had. For indigenous Liberians, pursuing similar dreams as Americo-Liberians meant giving up something, their dignity, names, or cultures. That is why, even with the shock and confusion about the assassination of President Tolbert whom I admired, I felt that something taken away or denied me had been restored. Moreover, upon hearing Sonny Okosun's "Papa's Land," I felt that I could lay claim to Liberia and call it my own.

As the sun rose on April 12, 1980, jubilations and chants of "Country woman born soldier, Congo woman born rogue" in the city of Monrovia grew louder and louder. I took hold of Liberia like a personal property, but without the fanfare. I did not join the jubilations in the streets because the assassination of President Tolbert also took away a vision of Liberia in which I could see myself. Nevertheless, at that time, I was not far away in my thinking from the people who celebrated the dawn of a new day. I did not choose a side. Instead, circumstances and history had already cast me on one side of the Liberian divide.

TOWN TRAP

"Monkey works, baboon draws," the five-second sound bite that political agitators constructed, served as a significant piece of the springboard for the April 12, 1980 Revolution. It provided an impetus for Sergeant Doe and his colleagues to assassinate President Tolbert and take over the government.

At the time of the Revolution, Doe declared that he and his colleagues had acted in the interest of the people of Liberia. In addition, he accused the minority Americo-Liberian-led and dominated government of "rampant corruption and abuse of power." Doe's charge against the minority Americo-Liberian government was essentially the same as the agitators' charge contained in "Monkey works, baboon draws."

Unfortunately, neither the leaders of the agitation nor Doe made any appreciable effort to distinguish between individual Americo-Liberians and the government of Liberia and its leaders. No one pointed out that many Liberians including Americo-Liberians became successful through their own ingenuities and "sweat." In addition, being a part of the government or stealing public resources was made to seem the only way to doing well. Absent that distinction, the agitators as well as Doe missed a critical piece in the public discourse, perhaps unintentionally. As a result, most ordinary Liberians, particularly indigenous Liberians, presumed that anyone who "looked nice" was either an Americo-Liberian or someone who worked for the minority Americo-Liberian government and, therefore, stole money, abused power and lived in opulence.[175] Failure to distinguish between public officials and private individuals in constructing the five-second sound bite turned it into what Liberians call a "town trap." A town trap not only ensnares chickens, goats, or sheep but also the town's residents. It was a trap set for every Liberian, Americo-Liberian or not.

During the Revolution, "Monkey works baboon draws" clearly harmed Americo-Liberians. It put the lives of individual Americo-Liberians at risk and made their properties subject to confiscation by the military government. Being an Americo-Liberian with a nice home and a lot of properties became evidence of "rampant corruption and abuse of power" and, therefore, made the properties subject to confiscation. It did not matter whether one was a government employee or not. During the days following the Revolution, I saw people believed to be Americo-Liberians in the Cheeseman Avenue-Fourteenth Street vicinity taken out of their homes and paraded on Cheeseman Avenue with little or no clothes on. The military government, with some members acting on their own, confiscated the properties of many other Americo-Liberians, although some of the properties were later returned to their rightful owners.

"Monkey works, baboon draws" also harmed ordinary Liberians who were not associated with the government of Liberia, individuals who believed in working hard to get ahead and struggled on their own to achieve a semblance of middle-class lifestyle. That harm, however, did not manifest itself immediately after the Revolution. Instead, over the period of the military government as well as during Doe's reign as a civilian president, something apparently changed. The unsuspecting population that did not distinguish ordinary Americo-Liberians and Americo-Liberian government leaders seemingly recognized that the April 1980 Revolution was a musical chair. The population realized that "rampant corruption and abuse of power" were not only features of Americo-Liberian DNA but also of indigenous Liberian DNA. Based on that awakening, looks or lifestyle emerged as a new way of identifying the "Baboon" in addition to one's last name.

Indeed, many innocent Liberians died at the beginning of the civil war and during its entire course due to tribal animus. However, the rebels killed many other innocent Liberians simply because they "looked nice." The rebels presumed "looking nice" as evidence that one worked for the Doe government. The same mentality that fueled the insanity during the days after the Revolution resurfaced at the beginning of the civil war, only with one enhancement.[176] During the Revolution, if an Americo-Liberian looked nice and owned a lot of properties, he or she was presumed an employee or official of the minority Americo-Liberian government of Liberia. Hence, he or she must have engaged in "rampant corruption and abuse of power." He or she was a "Baboon" and must have stolen money from the people.

At the beginning of the civil war, on the other hand, the stakes were even higher because anyone could be a "Baboon!" One did not have to be an Americo-Liberian to become a "Baboon." If one looked nice, the rebels regarded one as a "Baboon" because of the presumption of being a government employee or an official of government. Again, with that presumption, it followed that one must have abused power and stolen money from the people. The rebels and their sympathizers harmed and even killed many innocent Liberians they perceived as doing well. Some Liberians lost their lives while others had near-death experiences during the civil war as they encountered rebels who regarded them as employees of the government of Liberia only because they looked nice.

In that sense, "Monkey works, baboon draws" was a transferrable identifier. It was about economics, what people owned that the rebels and their sympathizers presumed was either taken from the masses through exploitation or theft of public resources. In 1980, the soldiers determined

Americo-Liberians rich or wealthy by their possessions and looks and presumed they were government officials or employees of the government who abused power and stole money from the masses. Americo-Liberians were taken out of mansions and paraded in the streets of Monrovia and not taken out of zinc shacks. "Monkey works, baboon draws" remains intact perhaps because the fundamentals of societal inequalities that birthed and nurtured the mindset remain in place. Unless the mindset changes, unless the inequalities are addressed, "Monkey works, baboon draws" will remain a potent and dangerous opiate in Liberian political discourse.

CHAPTER 17

Omen

SINKOR FOURTEENTH STREET

By July 1980, almost three months had passed since the disemboweled corpse of martyred President Tolbert was hurled, lumped with other victims, and irreverently disposed of in a mass grave at the Center Street Cemetery in Monrovia. While the euphoria over the overthrow of the True Whig Party minority government remained amplified, the shock wave of the president's assassination continued to reverberate, albeit beneath the surface. In the meantime, Sergeant Samuel K. Doe, the new sheriff in town, drove around the city of Monrovia in an open top Honda with much hoopla.

At that time of great change and excitement, there were signs of the perils at the horizon. Rumors of coups abounded; some members of the military government were executed for their alleged involvement in plots to overthrow Sergeant Samuel K. Doe. Yet the mood of the country was with Sergeant Doe; nothing substantial could change it. Mr. Blemie Baikiayee and I were optimistic too. Partly out of that optimism, we discussed moving closer to the University of Liberia. Our search for a one-bed room apartment began shortly thereafter.

Our conversation about moving was not prompted by opportunities for employments to enable us pay rent; we did not win the lottery either.

Moreover, our hostess, Oretha Nyah, did not tell us to leave. She did not hint it in any way whatsoever or complain to anyone that we were a burden on her. Despite the enormous stress Oretha Nyah endured as she juggled her personal life while simultaneously caring for a multitude, she never said anything ugly to anyone including me. However, Blemie and I knew the time had come to move out because of the obvious. Oretha sheltered and fed us at great cost to her personal life. The help that she was giving us was taking a toll on her relationship with her husband.

Our audacity to venture out on our own also stemmed from having another friend, Philip Joe-Kolo, who agreed to join us to make the prospect of paying the rent less burdensome. The search for a one-bedroom place took us to all the communities surrounding the university, including Jallah's Town, Saye's Town, Buzzi Quarter, Perry Street, Sinkor Ninth, Tenth, Eleventh, and Twelfth Streets. It was impossible to find a reasonable one-room apartment, one that we could afford, near the University of Liberia. Property owners in Monrovia at the time were notorious. They demanded at least three months' payment in advance. In areas where we were able to find a reasonable apartment, the landlords gave us terms that were so unreasonable that we could not accept them. Finally, we found a spacious one-bedroom on the second floor of a massive two-story unfinished concrete structure almost at the intersection of Sinkor Fourteenth Street and Cheeseman Avenue. The property belonged to Mr. Zelee, an elderly Krahn man, whom everyone affectionately called Oldman Zelee. Mr. Zelee and his children told us that the room would cost us U.S. fifty dollars per month, but we negotiated with the Zelees and settled on U.S. forty dollars per month.

Incidentally, Blemie did not have a job, but Mr. Peter Willor (deceased), who worked as an insurance agent, often sought his help to write his report. In exchange, Mr. Willor occasionally helped Blemie financially. Mr. Willor was Oretha Nyah's husband at the time. Philip Joe-Kolo was the only one who had a parttime job. He was a cadet at the Ministry of Planning and Economic Affairs. I did not have a job. I never worked for money while I was at St. Mary's School in Sanniquellie. I did not make a choice between working and not working. Opportunities for odd jobs students could do to help themselves were almost nonexistent. My parents supported me, and I devoted my time in Sanniquellie almost exclusively to school. During the long December-February vacation, I traveled to the village to help my parents with rice and coffee harvests.

In Monrovia, I did not return to the village as often as I did when I was at St. Mary's School. My parents remained my support in Monrovia with one difference. My Dad was not invested in my college education as my Mom was. With that, three things sustained me in Monrovia. First, Wlah's grace. I never prayed to Wlah as I do today or put effort into asking Him for His intervention. I just knew that He was there with me. Second, hope. Obstacles to getting ahead as well as ten thousand reasons for quitting abounded, but I knew that I would succeed. And third, Mom's prayers.

I visited with my parents about three times a year including vacations because it was expensive to travel from Monrovia to the village. I never returned to the village and found my Mom unprepared to deal with any financial problem related to my education. On a few occasions, Mom sent Esther, my younger sister, with food and money. Upon my return to Monrovia from a trip to the village, I brought food along and then used a part of the money she gave me to pay my share of our forty-dollar monthly rent. In Monrovia, other people gave me a few dollars in exchange for help I provided with their schoolwork. On one occasion, I received a cash award of $175 from the University of Liberia for getting good grades. Still further, adults like Mr. James Mehn (deceased) and others who took interest in my education occasionally gave me five dollars and sometimes a little more for my pocket change. A pep talk about the importance of an education always followed their financial gifts.

Luckily, I had just returned from the village a few weeks earlier. I had money to pay the two months' advance rent that the Zelees requested. Blemie and Philip promised to reimburse me. Beyond that, we did not know how we would pay our rent regularly and on time. Like all other risks in pursuit of education my friends and I took, we only hoped that the future would deliver; that, as we often say in Liberia, "God will provide." Besides our unwavering faith that God would not leave us in the cold, something else was unique not only about our negotiations with Oldman Zelee and his children but also about Liberia. The Zelees did not ask whether any of us worked or had a steady income. They did not ask for references, let alone someone to cosign for us. Oldman Zelee and his children trusted that we would pay our rent on time without any hassle. They may have assumed that, as students from faraway Nimba County attending the University of Liberia, our parents were our financial backers. Moreover, because opportunities for social mobility, particularly for indigenous Liberians, were rare and like a lottery, an unspoken rule existed that helping students was one way of investing in their futures and a way to have a stake in their future successes, although such a stake could not be reclaimed in a court of law. Still further, we believed that, by renting their property, we and the Zelees would come to know each other and eventually become a family in the Liberian sense.

Even though Oldman Zelee has long since passed away, I still remember my interactions with him and his family. In August 2007 when I traveled from Spokane, Washington to Accra, Ghana to meet with Mom, I saw Mr. George Zelee, one of Oldman Zelee's sons, affectionately called "Big George." I met him at the Budumbura Refugee Camp outside Accra, where Liberian refugees lived. We gave a shout-out and a tight bear hug upon recognizing one another, arousing the attention of the public. It felt as if we were lost brothers who had found each other. That incident proved that the mere act of living together brings people together as a family. After that, I took Big George out and, in a very humble way, showed him what I meant by delivering on their investment in us. My roommate and friend, Blemie passed away during the civil war. I do not know whether he, in any way, delivered any returns on the investment that Oldman Zelee and his children made in us during that unique negotiation for the room in their house on Sinkor Fourteenth Street. Philip Joe-Kolo stayed in Liberia throughout the duration of the Liberian Civil War. He was employed with the Forestry Development Authority (FDA). At one point he was assigned as Regional Forester in Zwedru, Grand Gedeh County, where the Zelees hail. I am not sure whether he, in any way, delivered on the investment that Oldman Zelee and his children made in us.

With only a verbal agreement with Oldman Zelee, we paid eighty United States dollars for the first two months and moved in with the king-size bed that Philip Joe-Kolo had. Oldman Zelee's property was more than two miles from the University of Liberia. Considering our goal of finding a one-bed room apartment near the campus, that may not have been an ideal outcome, but the situation was an improvement over sleeping in Oretha Nyah's piazza, where Blemie and I had no control over when to go to bed or when to wake up in the morning. We walked the approximately two- to three-mile distance from Sinkor Fourteenth Street to the Capitol Hill campus of the University of Liberia for classes or to board the university school bus to the Fendell campus, 17 miles away and returned home in the evening.

With the room in Oldman Zelee's house, our lot improved with respect to accommodation. However, because we moved out of Oretha Nyah's apartment and relocated about six miles away, food availability as a problem resurfaced. We ate only once a day. There was no such thing as breakfast in the morning. We cooked our meals only in the evenings. In that house, only Wlah knows how many cans of mackerel we cooked dry rice with. Due to a lack of steady income to buy food in abundance, our main goal was to fill our stomachs rather than to eat for the nutritional value of the food. As a result, one of our favorite dishes was eddo soup.[177] Eddo has a high nutritional value but, at the time, we did not know the details. We were interested in eddo for a simple reason: rice stirred with eddo soup was heavy; it could take us through the next day until the evening.

Eddo soup was a favorite for another reason besides filling our stomachs. As struggling students, we did not have money to go to the movie or other places of entertainment to enjoy life. We had to figure out other ways of having fun to cope with the stresses of our academic work. Aside from playing scrabble, storytelling was a big and important part of our way of having fun. And no one was better adept at storytelling than Philip Joe-Kolo. I first heard him tell the eddo soup story at Oldman Zelee's house in Sinkor.

During the evening we cooked our first eddo soup at Oldman Zelee's house, we had all returned from classes, wishing that the big bowl of rice with palm oil and every imaginable ingredient that we often heard about in spider stories would be awaiting us. The reality was that no such bowl of rice awaited us. We had no one at home to cook for us. We had to get down to business and find some ingredients to cook. By the time we finished cooking the food, no one could wait any longer. Unfortunately, we had to be patient because eddo soup was not like any other soup. It was gooey and took a long time to cool.

I do not know whether Philip wanted us to "apply our brakes" to avoid burn injury from the hot eddo soup that covered the rice like an advancing molten volcanic lava or whether he simply wanted us to laugh. In any case, he accomplished both goals during that evening. As soon as the pot of hot eddo soup was strewn over the rice, Philip laughed and began the story. All of us held our spoons in our hands and paused to determine where the story was leading to. According to Philip, two friends were traveling in a rural area where there were no cars. They walked the whole day and reached a certain town in the evening where they decided to spend the night because they were tired and hungry. According to Mahn custom, the people of the town welcomed the travelers and gave them a place to stay for the night. The women in the house where the travelers were lodged prepared dinner and, by custom, put the food for all the men in the house together in a large bowl, including the food for the strangers. Eddo soup was cooked that evening. Spoons were given to the strangers. Thereafter, someone took the large bowl of eddo soup and poured it over the rice. Steam from the hot eddo soup billowed as it was poured over the rice. Everyone squatted around the food in a circle while the travelers each sat on a stool because they were strangers.

Tired and very hungry from their long day's walk, the travelers did not understand why the other men were waiting. They did not realize that the others were waiting to allow the food to cool down. The first traveler took a spoonful of the hot eddo soup with some rice and put it in his mouth. The hot food severely burned his mouth, but because he was ashamed to let everyone know that he had burned his mouth, he swallowed the hot food rather than spew it out to make a fool of himself. Suddenly and involuntarily, tears started to roll down his cheek. In the meantime, his friend who was sitting across from him noticed the tears and asked, "What happened?" Ashamed to say what really happened to him, the stranger said, "Every time I see eddo soup, I am reminded of my grandmother; that's why I am crying." Apparently at that time his grandmother had passed away. With that response, the friend who asked also took a deep scoop of the eddo soup and put it in his mouth. He too severely burned his mouth. Like his friend, rather than throw the hot eddo soup out of his mouth, he swallowed it for fear of being made shame. Suddenly, tears started to roll down his cheek. The friend who was the first to be burned asked, "What happened?" He said, "Every time I see you cry about your grandmother, it makes me to cry as well."

Additionally, part of the fun we had while living together on Sinkor Fourteenth Street was the way we made important points of criticism without being hurtful. Philip demonstrated a memorable example. Both he and Blemie appreciated my cooking, a skill I had developed from my years in school in Sanniquellie. Despite all that appreciation, Philip was attentive to everything I did whenever I was cooking. I was notorious for tasting food while I was cooking. As Philip jovially put it one day, "Man, you make me want to cry every time you taste the rice when you are cooking." Philip was right. In cooking rice, it must be stirred to ensure that it does not stick to the bottom of the pot to burn. The cook also must take a bit of the rice in a cook spoon as it is boiling and taste it to make sure that it is cooking just right—not hard or soft. Philip rightly observed that the little amount of rice I needed to take in a cook spoon to taste always looked like half a cook spoon of rice. To Philip, and to anybody for that matter, taking that amount of rice repeatedly to taste meant that by the time the rice was cooked, I had already eaten more than everyone else. In other words, they had been cheated. We laughed hard about the joke, but what an ingenious way to make a point the joke was!

ERIC EASTMAN

Mr. Eric Eastman was a unique human being. He was one of a few Liberians who stupefied other Liberians trapped by the age-old America-Liberian-indigenous divide. He was an Americo-Liberian, but while I was his student in the College of Agriculture and Forestry at the University of Liberia, he never showed any sign of the uppity attitudes associated with some Americo-Liberians. He never talked about being an Americo-Liberian, or about his pedigree; he never put anyone down because of his or her indige-nousness. He was a quiet man with a boxer's physique who seldom smiled. In addition, he was a no-nonsense man who did not take kindly to mediocrity when it came to academics. Regardless of ethnicity, he expected his students to work hard and put forth their best efforts. Yet, some students feared him for his high expectations while others perceived him as unapproachable or mean, a characterization many Liberians quickly attributed to others if their expectations for personal reasons were not satisfied. Nevertheless, behind the veneer of toughness that some students perceived, Mr. Eastman was a deeply caring man who wanted his students to prepare adequately for the challenges of the world.

After Blemie, Philip and I moved into Oldman Zelee's house on Sinkor Fourteenth Street in Monrovia in 1980, Philip and I had some of our classes at Fendell, where the College of Agriculture and Forestry is. In the mornings, we walked to the Capitol Hill campus, boarded the university transport bus to Fendell and returned in the evenings. Our days at Fendell, attending classes and labs, were long and hard. On many occasions, we did not have anything to eat at school. We were often very hungry at school because we cooked only once a day in the evenings.

The rendezvous with Mr. Eastman that brought him into my life story began with a matter of great interest to him—academics. Although he may have been watching my attitude about work, the seminal encounter merely began with a test he gave in agricultural engineering. When Mr. Eastman returned the test papers, he not only indicated that I had the highest score but also that I was the only one who passed the test. The 80% score Mr. Eastman made a big deal about was not particularly high. Neither did I think of myself as better in any way than my classmates. But that did not stop Mr. Eastman from thinking favorably about me. Moreover, he did something out of the ordinary to acknowledge my work. After he returned the corrected test papers, he called me aside and instructed me to go to the cafeteria to see his wife, Mrs. Maria Eastman, the following day. Mrs. Eastman operated the cafeteria on the campus of the College of Agriculture and Forestry. I showed up in the cafeteria as Mr. Eastman instructed during lunch on the following day. Mrs. Eastman greeted me with a big smile and said, "You are here for your food; please have a seat." "What food?" I wondered. Apparently, the Eastmans had had a conversation about why I was going to the cafeteria. I was hungry that day but contending against empty stomach was a routine. After a little while, Mrs. Eastman brought me a large plate of rice along with a dish of cassava leaf. I was pleasantly stunned, and I was the only one who heard the alleluia I quietly mumbled. I did not waste a single grain of that plate of rice. It was delicious. Mrs. Eastman, a Filipino, had become a real pro at preparing Liberian cuisines.

After I finished eating, I thanked Mrs. Eastman and asked her to convey my appreciation to her husband. Thereafter, I walked away with my eyes buoyed in tears of joy. I hung my head as I walked out of the cafeteria because I did not want anyone to see my teary eyes. As I made my way out of the cafeteria, not only did I feel the nearness of Wlah, but also said to myself, "Wow! It feels good to be recognized!" Throughout my educational career, I had never been recognized for anything until that time. The plate of rice along with a dish of cassava leaf recognition Mr. Eastman gave me was not a public event. The rest of my classmates did not know about it, except for a few friends with whom I shared the experience. Yet the recognition meant a lot to me because I did not see it merely as food for nourishing my physical body. Indeed, the plate of rice along with a dish of cassava leaf arrested at least for that day the hunger that violated me. But I saw the recognition also as a statement of belief in me, a statement that I could go on and do something bigger than scoring an 80% on a test.

I also saw the plate of rice along with a dish of cassava leaf recognition as a manifestation of Mom's prayers. At St. Mary's School, from elementary through high school, I had extensive catechism and attended church. Wlah watched over me and provided my needs not because of what I learned in catechism or the prayers I prayed. I attended catechism sessions after school and went to church on Sundays to seek favor with Father Francis to get cups of corn meal or buckwheat to prepare and eat to fight Sanniquellie hunger. If my future depended on attending catechism and attending church in Sanniquellie, I would not be where I am today. A mother's prayers work. Mom's prayers convinced me that I was not alone; that a higher power was watching over me wherever I went. I relished the recognition Mr. Eric Eastman gave me, but I did not use the little work I did to earn an 80% to take credit for it because I could not brush aside the power of Mom's soliloquys and relentless prayers. Repeatedly, she asked Wlah to ensure that those with whom I interact love me and that I encounter sanama (good luck). In my daily fight against hunger at the University of Liberia, no sanama was greater than a plate of rice along with a dish of cassava leaf. That plate of rice along with a dish of cassava leaf marked a turning point on the wild ride Wlah has been guiding me along since I left my beloved village to pursue an education.

ORETHA ELIZABETH FLUMO

Even though Blemie and I moved into our own apartment on Sinkor Fourteenth Street in Monrovia, Oretha Nyah still loomed large in my life. Like Zehyee Mahnmein, she was a larger-than-life figure and another mom away from home. She lived about six miles away from us, but it felt like she was merely a stone throw away, where I could reach her whenever I needed to. I always felt her presence; no matter where I was, I always felt her warmth and compassion.

At the end of academic 1980, I remained in Monrovia to take two vacation courses that ran from January through February 1981. One of the courses was offered only during the vacation at the Fendell campus, seventeen miles outside Monrovia. The other course was one I had previously taken and failed. After classes at Fendell, we returned to the Capitol Hill campus by bus. Thereafter, I walked to Oretha Nyah's apartment to eat. On Sundays, I spent the entire day at Oretha Nyah's apartment.

Even though I was laser-focused on my academic work, I had an active social life. I was a Dad. Our two-year-old daughter, Lila Wonmein, was in Sanniquellie with her mom, Yei B. Tokpah, who was pregnant and nearing labor with our next child. I visited with them occasionally as my studies allowed. Yei's pregnancy with our next child aroused deep concerns, particularly with Mom who lived in the village and visited with her occasionally. Mom worried about Yei as she neared labor due to her health history. Her first pregnancy resulted in stillbirth while she underwent Caesarean section during her subsequent pregnancy. Based on those concerns, Mom sent me an urgent message to return to the village. I wasted no time in traveling to the village because Mom's message was unusual. Upon arrival in the village, Mom shared her concerns about Yei's pregnancy and thought it would be wise to make plans considering her health history and conditions at the G. W. Harley Hospital in Sanniquellie. The quality of care at the hospital had deteriorated considerably and made thoughts about undergoing another Caesarean Section there worrisome. Mom instructed me to take Yei along with me to Monrovia for fear that leaving her in Sanniquellie would endanger her and the unborn child.

Despite Mom's farsighted advice and instructions, taking Yei along with me to Monrovia was almost an impossibility. I was already a burden on Oretha Nyah who was stretched to the limit. She was not only helping me, but also others with similar needs. I did not have the temerity to face her, let alone ask her to take pregnant Yei in. It was patently unreasonable to make such a request of someone who had done more than what any reasonable person could do. Moreover, the only place available to me at Oretha Nyah's home was the piazza, where Blemie and I slept each time we were there. Where else would Oretha Nyah lodge Yei?

I tried fruitlessly to explain my living arrangement in Monrovia to Mom, but she would not listen. She had no clue whatsoever what my struggle to survive to get an education in Monrovia entailed. Mom insisted that Yei's situation was a matter of life or death and that I had no choice, but to take her along with me to Monrovia. Her insistence and stern instruction that I take Yei along to Monrovia placed me again between a rock and a hard place. Yei's condition was dire. She had to have another Caesarean section. Leaving her in Sanniquellie to go to the G. W. Harley Hospital was clearly a risky gamble due to the deplorable condition of the hospital, but I was not my own man. I was not self-sufficient yet.

I returned to Monrovia without Yei, although not out of disobedience to Mom. I needed time to think about the request or, better put, the ultimatum Mom gave me. I could not decide about taking someone, more so a pregnant woman whom I did not have the resources to care for, into someone else's home without having consulted that person. I returned to Monrovia alone and agonized over my options. As friends often do, I shared my predicament with Blemie with the caveat that the conversation stayed where we had it. However, Blemie did not keep his promise. He apparently talked to his girlfriend, Loretta, who, in turn, talked to her sister, Oretha Nyah. Again, when Oretha Nyah heard the story about Yei's situation, she pulled me aside and said that she was not asking me to consider bringing Yei to Monrovia. Instead, she was instructing me to do so without any further delay. She told me that she was going to find a way somehow to accommodate Yei.

Before Oretha Nyah gave me that good-natured ultimatum, she had already contacted two people in preparation for Yei's arrival. A very quiet gentleman whom I remember only by his first name, Ranfell, was her first contact. Ranfell lived in a two-bedroom apartment annexed to Oretha Nyah's apartment. At that time, one of his bedrooms was not occupied. Oretha Nyah had been in the business of helping others so long that it seemed every favor she asked for had already been paid for with her kindness and help in the past. Without any hesitation, Ranfell agreed. Oretha then prepared the bedroom for Yei to stay in while in Monrovia preparing for delivery.

Oretha Nyah was keenly aware that I did not have the resources to pay for Yei's surgery. As a result, she contacted someone she knew who worked at the John F. Kennedy Maternity Center on Capitol bypass in Monrovia. That someone turned out to be the popular Liberian folk singer, Papa Jerome, himself a Mahn from Nimba County. Upon meeting with Papa Jerome, perhaps because of his singing career, he was mightily inviting, warm and cheerful. It was not hard to tell that he was someone with tremendous people skills. The busy hospital staff smiled and greeted Papa Jerome as they moved up and down the hallways and from one unit to another, attending to babies arrayed as if they had come off an assembly line. Papa Jerome seemingly knew and had cordial relationships with the doctors and nurses who worked at the Maternity Center. I do not remember exactly what Papa Jerome's job at the J.F.K Maternity Center was. In any case, Oretha Nyah explained Yei's situation and asked for help. Without hesitation, Papa Jerome agreed to help.

In the Mahn as well as the larger Nimba community in Monrovia, Papa Jerome was a celebrity. In fact, he was a nationally recognized folk singer and celebrity. I was pleasantly surprised and heartened when I realized that he would be our go-to person to have Yei admitted at the Maternity Center. I did not expect the popular singer to also be a healthcare worker at the J.F.K. Maternity Center. After our meeting with Papa Jerome, Oretha Nyah told me that the only thing left to do was to find "Kola" and "Cold Water" for Papa Jerome.

With those arrangements by Oretha Nyah, all was set. I then left Monrovia and traveled to Sanniquellie to bring Yei to Monrovia. The trip to Sanniquellie was uneventful. Yei already knew what the situation was. She had heard Mom make the demand that I take her along to Monrovia. As a result, when I arrived in Sanniquellie and asked her to go along with me to Monrovia, there was no disagreement because she understood that the purpose of the trip was to ensure her safety as well as that of the unborn child. The return trip to Monrovia was also without incident. Bathroom stops and stops at immigration checkpoints were routine; there was nothing out of the ordinary.

Upon arrival in Monrovia, Oretha Nyah greeted Yei as if she were her daughter-in-law. She ushered Yei into the bedroom she had prepared. Oretha Nyah also prepared dinner and kept Yei's company for the evening. She continued to provide home care for Yei throughout while I was taking summer classes. Yei did not waste any time in making herself feel at home. She helped cook the food and helped with Oretha Nyah's children. The neighbors around soon took note of her humility and made complimentary remarks about her. Some suggested that she acted as though she were not a stranger. In the culture, a stranger is supposed to be catered to at least for the first few days after arrival.

During the middle of the third week of January 1981, Yei went into labor. Oretha Nyah and I took her to the J.F.K. Maternity Center as she had arranged. Yei was admitted and, without having told the doctors anything much about her health history, the doctors quickly determined that she would need a Caesarean section to deliver the baby. The surgery was successful. On January 19, 1981, Yei delivered through Caesarean section a 10-pound baby girl. After consultations with her, we named the baby Oretha after Oretha Nyah.

Three days after Yei gave birth to Oretha Elizabeth Flumo, Blemie, Oretha Nyah and I went to see Papa Jerome at his home. We carried the "Kola" and "Cold Water" that Oretha Nyah told me to find for Papa Jerome. The "Kola" and "Cold Water" included a rooster that Yei and I had brought with us from Sanniquellie and thirty-five United States dollars. These items were our appreciation to Papa Jerome for interceding and helping us at the Maternity Center. He gladly accepted the "Kola" and "Cold Water" and wished the baby and its mom well. A rooster and United States $35 for delivering a baby by Caesarean Section? That could only happen in Liberia!

Oretha Nyah was not finished. Without my asking, she went down to the Waterside, a very busy and popular shopping district in Monrovia and shopped for the baby. She returned with everything a baby needed including diapers, baby feeding bottles, towels, lotion, and bathtub. I was stunned. In amazement I only asked, "What manner of woman is this?" when I saw all the things Oretha Nyah bought for the baby. By and large, the mission that Mom thrust upon me was accomplished, albeit with someone else's resources. The time had come for Yei and the baby to return to Sanniquellie. In mid-February a little over three weeks after Yei had the baby, Oretha Nyah's household, Blemie, other friends and I escorted Yei and the baby to the Nimba parking station, where they took a taxi and returned to Sanniquellie. I could not return with them because I was still taking classes during the vacation school.

Voker Joe-Kolo

After Blemie, Philip and I moved into Oldman Zelee's house on Sinkor Fourteenth Street, others joined us one after the other over time in the single room. Voker Joe-Kolo was the first person who joined us. Incidentally, he was Philip's younger brother. Voker was fair-skinned, quiet and soft-spoken. He was very handsome. Voker was 14 years old at the time he joined us and was a math whiz. Upon finishing junior high school, he attended Monrovia Central High School, where he could not wait to graduate to enroll at the University of Liberia. Voker wanted to live with us to achieve his dream, which was to earn a bachelor's degree in mathematics at the University of Liberia.

Our room was large enough to accommodate up to ten people. Blemie, Philip and I were inclined to let any one of our friends who took his education seriously to share the room with us. We felt that way because we had been at the receiving ends of other people's generosities throughout our struggles to achieve our educational goals. As it would probably have happened if it were someone else, we did not need a meeting to discuss Voker's desire to move in to live with us. By golly, it was Voker, Philip's brother! It was fait accompli! Blemie and I told Philip that, as far as we were concerned, our single room was also Voker's home and, therefore, he needed to move in right away to get on with his education. Voker moved in accordingly.

Voker was a very humble young man. He was very respectful to all three of us. Beyond that, among the three of us, Voker looked up to me. I do not know what he saw in me, but he thought that I walked on water. He always referred to me as "Flumo." As evidence of his humility, Voker washed our clothes and made up our bed, even though he slept on a blanket on the floor. He quickly learned how to cook and, no sooner than later, took over the cooking responsibility.

Eventually, Voker graduated from Monrovia Central High School and enrolled at the University of Liberia. He majored in mathematics as he dreamed, and went as far as becoming a junior, but, on December 24, 1989, the unthinkable happened. Carnage, fueled by naked evil and unfettered greed for power, turned into virulent ethnic hatred and descended upon Liberia. Several months after that, the strife engulfed the entire country. The results were horrific and terrifying, far more than the punishments Dante described in the *Inferno*. In the spate of that horror, Voker, the peaceful, soft-spoken, and quiet young man who would not even raise a finger at an ant, was violently erased from the face of the earth because of his ethnicity, as many others were. Voker was Mahn and he was killed in Monrovia allegedly by Krahn soldiers of the Armed Forces of Liberia. I carved out this space for Voker because, without it, as it is with countless other Liberians who lost their lives during the senseless bloodletting, I do not believe that the world will ever know that he walked the face of the earth.

Rev. Gabriel Swope

The second person who joined us in 1981 in the room we rented from Oldman Zelee was Rev. Gabriel Swope. Unlike Voker who was a young man and a student, Rev. Swope was an accomplished man. He was a Methodist minister of the gospel. He had just returned from the State of Tennessee in the United

States, and the United Methodist Church on Ashmun Street in Monrovia appointed him Associate Pastor. He was related to both Philip and Voker.

Rev. Swope did not tell me anything about the arrangements he made with the United Methodist Church on Ashmun Street prior to returning to Liberia. He did not discuss any of that with anyone that I know. However, it was clear upon his return from the United States to Liberia that the church did not readily have a place where he could stay. In the interim, he needed to be somewhere until the church addressed his accommodation. As Rev. Swope was Philip and Voker's kin, we welcomed him with open arms. We had been in similar situation many times during our educational careers, where others were kind to take us in. In addition, I had my own reason why I wanted Rev. Swope to move in with us. I was excited to have him live with us because I wanted to learn about the United States from his personal experience. Indeed, I had some knowledge about the United States from reading books and magazines as well as from watching American movies. However, there was nothing like learning from someone who had lived in the United States. At the time, my dreams to study at the University of Nebraska in Lincoln or at Florida State University in Tallahassee were fully alive.

Rev. Swope moved in with us. Out of respect for him, Philip, Voker, and I slept on the floor while Blemie and Rev. Swope slept on the bed. In addition, Voker and I took turns to press his clothes as well as polish his shoes. Other than Philip's secret joke about Rev. Swope that he was "tight" with money, a joke we often laughed hard about, we had a great time with Rev. Swope on Sinkor Fourteenth Street. Besides my queries about life in the United States, I learned a great deal from Rev. Swope as well.

One important issue Rev. Swope and I discussed was his role as Associate Pastor of the United Methodist Church on Ashmun Street. The settlers founded that church in the 1820s.[178] It has been in existence since the founding of Liberia and remains one of the few institutions at the core of Americo-Liberian identity and culture. Rev. Swope was not an Americo-Liberian, but he had an American and not an African or Mahn surname. Even though he never explained to me exactly how he acquired his Swope surname, he told me about his affiliation with the United Methodist church. Under the auspices of the church, he received his education and traveled to the United States. He studied and earned a master's degree in the United States, where he lived for a long time.

Rev. Swope did not spend all his time within the Mahn culture. Nevertheless, he spoke the language distinctly and correctly. Based on my conversations with him, I knew that he was native or Mahn at the core. Consequently, Rev. Swope's high-profile role as Associate Pastor of the United Methodist Church on Ashmun Street surprised me. Put mildly, his high-ranking leadership role in that church was out of character because, at a deeper level, Americo-Liberian and native cultures were virtually immiscible. Eventually, I mustered the courage and asked him to shed light on how he became Associate Pastor of the United Methodist Church on Ashmun Street.

According to Rev. Swope, when the United Methodist Church on Ashmun Street tapped him to return home to serve as Associate Pastor, church higher-ups did not seem aware of his background. Apparently because he was every bit Americo-Liberian in speech and demeanor, they assumed he was Americo-Liberian. The reality, however, was Rev. Swope knew Liberian history and remained Mahn or native at the core. He told me working in the United Methodist Church on Ashmun Street amounted to reliving his life in the United States, where his public persona as a black man was different from his private persona. Even though he seemed poised on the pulpit, he once said something else was going on within him that left little doubt that he did not belong. He felt an urge for a revolution in that church but had to put the lid on the rage that swirled within him.

In 1990, unfortunately, the civil war that snatched Voker Joe-Kolo's life away forced Rev. Swope to return to the United States. I lost complete contact with him, but memories of our time together on Sinkor Fourteenth Street never faded. Years later, through an internet search in a bid to reestablish contact, I unearthed information about Rev. Swope that I was not looking forward to discovering. It was his obituary, which chronicled his life from Liberia, where he was born, to America, where he received his education at Morristown College, Tennessee Wesleyan College, Gammon Theological Seminary and the University of Tennessee, Knoxville.[179] "He shared his miraculous testimony in many churches" and "returned several times to Liberia to witness for Christ and to build churches."[180] Rev. Swope passed away on Thursday, September 27, 2007, in Atlanta, GA and is "Survived by his wife Carol Ann, Children: Mercy Swope Aquilar, Grace Swope Greene, Joy Swope, Jeff Swope, Hnellesch Payeleh and five grandchildren."[181]

CHAPTER 18

The Hair on My Head

"THE HAIR ON MY HEAD belongs to Oretha Nyah" is a literal translation of "Oretha la wuhn leh uhn ween ah," a tribute for her role in my development.[182] Oretha gave me a chance; she let me sleep on a beat-up foam mattress on bare cement floor in her piazza. Her help opened a whole new world to me; enabled me to travel to faraway places including Seoul, Korea and the United States. But my encounter with Oretha Nyah was no happenstance. She only reinforced my belief that Wlah was watching and looking out for me.

I pay tribute to Oretha Nyah and thank Wlah for the consequential people He brought into my life, especially those who looked out for me while I was in places far away from home in search of opportunities. I lift their names in these pages to appreciate them for their help, guidance, and labor of love, one that involved time and energy. Their labor did not go in vain. Almost forty years have elapsed, not to mention the scourge and trauma of the civil war, yet Oretha Nyah's labor and love as well as those of other kind-hearted people remain indelibly imprinted in my psyche.

Following the outbreak of the civil war in Liberia, particularly during the period 1990-2009, I did not know where Oretha Nyah was. However, thoughts about her well-being and whereabouts lingered in my mind. Even though I tried to locate Oretha prior to 2009 without any success, I did not quit searching for her. In 2009, I resumed my search for Oretha with single-mindedness, but I was apprehensive because a similar attempt to locate Zehyee Mahnmein haunted me. I was afraid that my search for Oretha might end in the same way. Zehyee Mahnmein's fate and conditions in Liberia at the time of her passing in 2005 fueled the urgency of my attempt to locate Oretha Nyah.[183] I wanted simply to tell her that she was my angel before it was too late.

Locating Oretha Nyah involved several people, including Lila Flumo, Andrew Wongeh and Jacqueline Kotee Miatonah. They helped connect me with Eric Willor who, in turn, put me in touch with Peter Willor, his brother and Oretha Nyah's ex-husband. I was overly excited about the possibility of getting a phone number to reach Oretha in Liberia. But I failed to recognize that almost thirty years had passed since I last saw Oretha. I failed to recognize that nothing stays the same; things change. I assumed Oretha Nyah was still married to Peter Willor. As a result, upon reaching Peter Willor in Philadelphia, PA by phone, I asked for his wife, Oretha Willor.[184] In answering me, Peter also made the same mistake. He assumed and answered me in a manner that suggested I had been in communications with him throughout. He thought I was fully aware of every development that had occurred in his life. He told me that his wife was in Monrovia and was doing great. "Thank God!" I said with a deep sigh of relief. I asked for Oretha's phone number in Monrovia, which Peter found and gave me.

I wanted to give Oretha the surprise of a lifetime. I remember her husband treated her with disdain because she went out of her way to take care of other people's children struggling to get an education in Monrovia, including me. I wanted her to know that I had not forgotten her. Moreover, I wanted proof that she was alive. Even though I did not look forward to an ending other than hearing a grateful and happy Oretha, I was aware that, after the civil war, if one did not see someone for a long time, the assumption was that the person had died or been killed.

Surprisingly, when I dialed the phone number Peter gave me, the woman who answered sounded different from the Oretha Willor I knew. Oretha's voice was unmistakable. Like her deeds, it had been burnt into my memory. I was certain that the woman who answered the phone was not the Oretha Willor I knew. "Is this Oretha Willor?" I asked. "Yes," the woman responded, but we were not connecting at all as we talked. I described myself, where Oretha Willor and I lived in Monrovia and named some of her siblings to make sure the woman on the phone knew exactly the person to whom she was talking. However, the woman was completely lost. "Are you not Mrs. Oretha Willor, Peter Willor's wife, who used to live behind the Liberia Telecommunications complex between Ashmun and Broad Streets?" I asked again. At that point, the woman said, "I think you are talking about Peter Willor's former wife, Oretha Willor. They are not together anymore. I am his new wife and my name is also Oretha Willor." The woman was courteous and gracious, considering that I woke her up at about 11:00 p.m. to ask about her husband's ex-wife. Realizing that I had reached the wrong Oretha Willor, it felt like someone moved the goal post back when I was only inches away.

Before we concluded our conversation, I asked the woman about her hometown and languages she spoke other than English. I was trying cleverly to find out which ethnic group she belonged to without asking for her tribe.[185] She was from Nimba County and spoke Mahn like me. In addition, it turned out I knew some members of her family. After the familiarity, she promised to look for Oretha Nyah and get her cellular phone number for me. The following day, I called and received the number for Oretha Nyah. My reunion with Oretha Nyah on the phone occurred on February 12, 2009. That was the first time Oretha and I talked in almost thirty years. Reconnecting with Oretha Nyah was a happy moment. She remains a fixture in my life and a reminder that I did not get to the station I am at in life through my own efforts alone.

CHAPTER 19

Fendell

FENDELL, LOCATED SEVENTEEN MILES AWAY from Monrovia along the Monrovia-Nimba highway, is one of the three campuses of the University of Liberia.[186] Fendell had long been in the plan for the relocation of the University of Liberia, but the massive destruction of buildings and facilities there during the civil war stopped work for a long time. Some progress has been made toward that end in the last few years. Fendell rose to prominence in this story not merely because I took some of my classes at the University of Liberia there. Fendell became a focal point in my story because, less than two weeks before classes started for the second semester of 1981, the University of Liberia administration made a sudden decision pertaining to the opening of the dormitories on the campus of the College of Agriculture and Forestry also located at the Fendell campus. The dormitories had been completed long before their sudden opening announcement.[187] It was not clear why the dormitories remained unoccupied for such a long time, even though there were rumors of concerns that the structures were substandard. Similarly, it was not clear exactly why the university administration suddenly decided to open the dormitories. It seemed obvious that the huge cost of transporting many students six days a week from the main campus in Monrovia to Fendell and back was a factor, but no one communicated that to the students.

A day later, the university administration qualified the dormitory opening announcement, noting that junior and senior students in the colleges of Science & Technology and Agriculture & Forestry would be priority number one in the selection of students to occupy the limited number of rooms in the dormitories. Moreover, the cost of living in the dormitories, including a breakage fee, would be $165 United States dollars. At the time of the announcement, I was a junior student.

Immediately after the dormitory opening announcement, I walked from the Capitol Hill campus to the offices of the National Social Security and Welfare Corporation (NSS&WC) on Benson Street in central Monrovia to see Uncle George A. Bolo (deceased). At the time, he was serving as the Director-General of the corporation. Upon arrival at the NSS&WC, the receptionist told me to wait because someone who had an appointment with the Director-General was meeting with him at that moment. She assured me that, once that meeting was over, she would let him know that I was waiting to see him. The meeting went on for what seemed like perpetuity. As soon as the person who was in the office with Uncle George stepped out, he followed, apparently to find out whether someone else was waiting to see him. "How come you did not let me know that Marsilius was waiting?" he asked the receptionist upon recognizing me.

It was after 5:00 p.m. local time. Uncle George then told me to pick up his briefcase so that he could drop me off on his way home. In a little while, we climbed down the stairs from his office, got out of the building and crossed over to the other side of Benson Street, where his official vehicle, a lime green Chevrolet Caprice Classic was parked.[188] We took off from Benson Street, made a few stops to see some of his friends and then finally headed toward Sinkor to drop me off. While on our way, I explained to Uncle George why I had come to see him. I told him about the opening of the dormitories at Fendell and the preferences that the university administration was giving to juniors and seniors. "I think that moving to Fendell would be helpful for your studies," he interrupted and suggested what I was thinking and getting ready to say. At that moment, I told him about the $165 United States dollar fee that the university was charging. Without hesitation, Uncle George told me to go to his office on the following day to get the money. More importantly, he said, "You study and make the grades; do not worry about the fees. If I do not have it, I will borrow it; if it means I will have to sell my pants, I will do it so that you can continue your studies." His reassuring and comforting words sent a chill over me.

As we neared Cheeseman Avenue and fourteenth Street Sinkor, where I lived, Uncle George drove slowly and came to a full stop right in front of Old man Zelee's house. It was about 7:30 p.m. local time. Some residents of the second floor of Old man Zelee's house were sitting on the front balcony watching vehicular traffic and passersby while others were going in and out of a Ghanaian-owned provision shop below. I could tell all eyes were on the flashy lime green Chevrolet Caprice Classic that came to a stop right before Old man Zelee's house. The curious onlookers wanted to know who would come out of that vehicle. I did not get out of the car right away. Uncle George and I chatted for a few minutes and then he gave me thirty United States dollars in six new five-dollar bills. As I got out of the car, all eyes fell upon me and I could only imagine what the onlookers were thinking. It was about "morale," as Liberians like to say. I was happy, especially with Uncle George's assurance to pay my fees for the dormitory. I felt like a new set of wings had been mounted on me. I could not wait to reach the second floor to share with Philip and Blemie all the good news I had.

Upon reaching our room upstairs, only Voker Joe-Kolo and Philip Joe-Kolo were at home. Blemie was still on campus. I told Philip and Voker what had happened, and they were all happy for me. As Philip too considered moving to the dormitories, he wondered to me how he would get money to pay the fees. Later that evening, Blemie, who had been walking home from the university campus, arrived. With all the excitement, I gave him the good news, expecting to get the same reactions that I received from Voker and Philip. At first there was a dead silence, followed by Blemie's exit. I did not know what to make of his silence and leaving the room, but upon his return, I asked why he had not said anything after I gave him the good news. At that moment, he angrily told me that the friendship that existed between us before the moment I gave him the news would not exist anymore. He said I had had plans all along to move into the dormitories and had hidden them from him. Essentially, his point was that I had betrayed him. I was totally flabbergasted by Blemie's reaction. Even Philip and Voker were both confused, wondering whether we had any recent hidden unresolved issue that flared.

Indeed, Blemie and I had an unresolved issue.[189] As far as I was concerned, at the time of the dormitory incident, that issue had long been resolved. I, the injured party, forgave Blemie and moved on. Philip who got the same information about the opening of the dormitories at the same time was aware that I could not have harbored plans to move into the dormitories if I did not know that the university had plans to open the dormitories. I was angry when my friend Blemie thought that I was evil.

Perhaps Blemie was afraid that Philip and I might leave him alone with the forty-dollar monthly rent. However, that fear absolutely had no basis because we had no intention of leaving the cost of paying the room to him alone. We continued to pay our equal share of the rent because the room on fourteenth Street was our base, the place where we all expected to stay on weekends or during the vacation. After the dormitories opening announcement was made, Philip and I thought it made sense to take advantage of the opportunity to be closer to where our classes were held. There was nothing else to the move to Fendell. It was that simple.

Blemie followed through on his word that our friendship would not be the same. He put it in writing and kept speech from me. Rev. Gabriel Swope who was still with us at the time thought that Blemie's behavior toward me was ridiculous. He intervened and asked Blemie to apologize for what he did to me but Blemie refused and went on to repeat what he said when a friend attempted to mediate the conflict between us in high school: "I will not apologize to anyone even if my mother came and asked me to do so." Again, I forgave him.

It took me a long time to grasp the lesson from my friendship with Blemie. Everyone has a dark side. Naïveté alone did not shield me from that reality. My nearly ideal childhood, adolescent and teenage years of loving kindness also played a part in isolating me from that reality. During my early life, anchored in the village and Sanniquellie, I saw the best in my immediate and extended family. Everyone greeted me with hugs upon arrival in the village at the close of each school year. They received news of my promotion to the next grade with fanfare. Returning to Sanniquellie for school was always a difficult time because I had to leave behind all the people I deeply loved. Their love and tenderness blinded and prevented me from seeing people's dark sides.

In my almost ideal world, the love, kindnesses, and compassion I witnessed were not always directed at me. Mom, the chief dispenser of love, kindness, and compassion, took care of everyone, visited whoever was sick and cheered along with all who had reasons to celebrate. She watched over other people's children as if they were hers. I grew up thinking that taking care of other people when they are in need was just an ordinary way of life. I could not imagine anyone who would have evil in their heart against me. Goodness, I was convinced, begot goodness. As a result, I grew up looking at the world through the prism of pureness of heart and expected the world to see me similarly. I could not fathom why a friend would think evil of me.

The "Catholic" Girl

After Philip and I moved into the dormitories at Fendell, the stars seemed to align for me. I enjoyed my classes and everything that used to worry me, including accommodation and food availability became immaterial. The difference between living illegally in the dormitory at the Capitol Hill campus in 1978 and living legally in the dormitory at Fendell in 1981 was like that between night and day. Like Simon Greenleaf Hall on the Capitol Hill campus in Monrovia, we had all the modern amenities, including showers, flush toilets, and laundry facilities in the dormitories at Fendell. There were two students to a room and each of us had his own bed and lots of closet spaces for personal effects.

Unlike the Capitol Hill campus dormitory, where I stayed illegally, I was a bona fide and legitimate student at the Fendell dormitory. I did not have to find a "Little thing" for one of the cooks or cafeteria workers to allow me to eat. I went to the dining hall as one of the regulars. We had three meals a day, except on Sundays, where only breakfast and lunch were served. As on the Capitol Hill campus, everyone brought a plastic bowl during lunch for extra food for the evening on Sundays. We had so much food to eat that wasting food by some students became a commonplace and problem in the dining hall. On one occasion, Dr. Mary Antoinette Brown-Sherman (deceased), President of the University of Liberia at the time, paid a surprise visit to the dining hall at the Fendell dormitories. She discovered, to her utter displeasure, that some students received their food, left it on the table largely untouched only to be thrown away by the cafeteria staff. Dr. Sherman threatened to cut down on the food if the situation did not change. The students heeded her threat, and, in the end, she did not act on her threat. Under Dr. Sherman's leadership, the university administration fed us properly and adequately. In addition, the environment was pristine and quiet for serious academic work.

Academically, unlike the rough-and-tumble during my freshman year, my junior year was very successful. In fact, first semester of my senior year in 1982 went so well that I traveled to the village during the mid-year break in July to inform my parents that I would graduate at the end of the year. As if I had not had enough fun with my friends as well as with my academic work, second semester of my senior year in 1982 began with a big bang! Indeed, I met charming Luopu, a woman who was determined to rock my world, albeit in intriguing ways. Luopu, a five-six and beautiful Liberian woman, was contemplative and articulate. One unmistakable measure of her sophistication was her magnificent and immaculate penmanship. I had never seen anyone with such artistry in handwriting. She had a very strong personality along with some strong views. Luopu was a healthcare professional prior to enrolling in the College of Science & Technology at the University of Liberia. She was pursuing a degree in biology with the hope of going to medical school at the A.M. Dogliotti College of Medicine. Luopu was Catholic with an air of godliness about her. She seemed to know what she wanted in life. Luopu was a fascinating woman but she was also very critical. Everything had to come under her "microscope."

Incidentally, Luopu was not on my "radar" at all. I was not on the lookout for what, in Liberia, we call a "serious girlfriend." Meeting a woman and dating her with the hope of getting married was not in the cards at that time. I had not thought about it or made any plans about what I would do if I were to run into such a situation. Instead, my focus was on achieving my educational goal. In that light, I heeded Barkpor's advice, even though I was a young man with raging hormones.[190] "A child does not hold onto the tails of two horses." "Chasing girls" was one of the horses while the other horse was my "educational career." I put the tail of "chasing girls" on the backburner and held only onto the tail of my "educational career." I got involved with girls but not to the level of any serious commitment. However, I surprised myself when the artificial wall I built around my heart to avoid serious involvement with any woman until I had completed my educational career crumbled upon meeting Luopu. Luopu's emergence turned out to be a life-changing experience, one that awaited me as if it were a rite of passage to real adulthood.

Proximity and other factors facilitated my meeting Luopu. Even though men and women lived in separate buildings in the dormitories at Fendell, the women's dormitories were less than a stone throw from the men's quarters. A walk from my unit to Luopu's unit took less than two minutes. Our meeting was also possible because the dormitories housed students of the College of Science & Technology as well. In fact, the dormitories were about a mile away from the College of Science & Technology campus. Moreover, students of the colleges of Science & Technology and Agriculture & Forestry also took some of the same required freshman, sophomore, and even junior and senior courses together. Luopu may have been in one of the theater zoology classes that we took at the Science Complex along with biology students. In Liberian talk, "to cut long matter short," Luopu and I met and started a courtship that would later help open my eyes.

Shaped by the experiences I have described, I was naïve; I did not know better. I took the mask for Luopu. I was not sophisticated enough to distinguish the mask from the person wearing it. Moreover, Luopu's beauty, charm, and strong personality along with her elusiveness made her an object of fascination. That fascination, along with Luopu being a "serious Christian woman," swept me off my feet. Upon meeting Luopu, I behaved as if I were in a trance. In Liberia, at that time, age difference was a big hurdle and a relationship destroyer. However, the force of Luopu's personality caused me to overlook the fact that she was a few years older than I was upon meeting.

Luopu seemed to have a handle on everything she wanted to do with her life, but there were exceptions. In the beginning of our courtship, I could not figure out what she really wanted out of the relationship. As time went on, she became fuzzy about her initial goal of going to medical school. Nevertheless, Luopu put the force of her personality to work from the get-go. Without my input, she started setting the rules for our relationship. Rule number one, no sex before marriage, was the one that caught my attention, yet I did not protest or argue against it because my cultural upbringing placed me in the role of the "Pehnamee" in the relationship we had just begun.[191] Essentially, I was luring Luopu into what could be a deeper relationship. I could not nitpick. Harping at that decree could have raised a red flag. Moreover, I did not see any point about arguing the rightness or fairness of Luopu's rules because I was convinced that they were negotiable. Indeed, I had no beef with Luopu over her hubris in handing down rules for our relationship by fiat because she was "playing" the ball in my court. She was a Catholic and I was a Catholic and remain so. I wanted a woman with strong Christian values and clear-cut morals. So Luopu's rule number one was practically a slam dunk. Even though I never claimed to be a devout practitioner, Luopu's rule number one was not a novelty. It happened to be one of the rules I learned during Catechism at St. Mary's prior to baptism.

As 1982, my senior year, neared the end, Luopu and I made verbal plans for my graduation. She agreed to print my graduation invitations while I made plans to travel to the village for money from my parents for other graduation-related expenses. Although agreeing to print someone else's graduation invitations did not mean anything out of the ordinary, at the minimum, I felt the gesture showed that the relationship mattered to Luopu. With those verbal plans in place, I turned my attention to preparing for my final examinations. I had struggled to reach thus far in pursuit of my educational career and could see the light at the end of the tunnel. I made a commitment to myself not to let anything distract me but to finish strong. So, I started preparing very early for the examinations.

Assured that all was well, I took time off to visit with Luopu in her dorm room to chat about classes and other topics that mattered to us, including her parents. Her excitement to introduce me to them was palpable. The relationship seemed to be moving at a lightning speed. Moreover, I could feel myself drawn deeper and deeper into it. Even though the feeling was surreal, I went along for the ride. In addition, I reciprocated Luopu's excitement to show me to her parents. I told her that I could not wait to see the parents of the woman who seemed to incorporate most of the values any man would want in a partner.

"Anything that dances fast does not have fine feet" is a literal translation of "Peh ay tan keh teay teay ah, ah gan wah seh," a warning to watch out for showboaters, especially those who masquerade with evil intent. I was fully aware of the expression and its meaning. I learned it from my parents and other adults at an early age as it was often woven into spider stories. However, that knowledge did not hold up in the face of Luopu's charm, beauty, and force of personality. As if I were blindfolded, I cast every warning aside and charged forward to take hold of Luopu, the object of my fascination.

At last, Luopu took me to her parents in Sinkor Gaye Town, where the family had a nice and modest house. She introduced me to her family, nearly all of whom were educated. My observations at Luopu's home at the time helped me to understand why she unilaterally decreed the rules for our relationship. As Luopu's name suggests, she was an indigenous Liberian. However, the family to whom Luopu introduced me was no ordinary indigenous one. I did not sense anything uppity about members of Luopu's family, but an unmistakable aura of class, dignity and respectability existed about them. I could see an invisible wall that separated them from others in the same neighborhood. Looking back, I can only suspect that Luopu's unilateral decrees for our relationship were an attempt to fashion me to fit into that family. In any case, after the introduction, I made myself comfortable by jumping into work clothes to help paint the interior of the house, a project Luopu's brother had begun.

In the evening, I went back to Cheeseman Avenue and, thereafter, returned to Fendell the following Sunday evening. After Luopu introduced me to her family, I started to take the relationship a little more seriously. However, as the examinations drew nearer, subtle changes in Luopu's behavior began to appear. For example, the frequency of her visits to my dorm room decreased. Moreover, she started to become irritated by the same jokes and conversations that were a source of laughter and joy when we first met. I shared my concerns with my friend, Sophia Richards Nyanue, as Luopu's behavior baffled me. Sophia was not forthcoming about what she really thought, but her warning, "Be careful, Marsilius, because I do not know what Luopu is up to" was enough hint. She was concerned that Luopu's conduct might affect me during the examinations.

As we buckled down in preparations for the examinations, Luopu and I still dropped by each other's room without notice and spent time. On one evening, it was out of character not to see Luopu. So, I went to her dorm room to find out what happened, but she was not there. I checked with other friends she could possibly be with, but I did not find Luopu. I even checked the classrooms where she could have gone to study to avoid distractions, she was not there either. She had not told me that she was going to Monrovia. So, I was at a complete loss. I returned to my dorm room and told my roommate, Philip, I could not find Luopu. I remained unsettled as I tried to do some work.

As I tried to do something to get my mind off Luopu, I heard loud noises and laughter from the dorm room across from ours. I became curious and wanted to find out what fun the men in that room were having. The fellows in that room and I had known each other for a long time. We had fun competing against each other academically whenever we took the same courses. I walked over, knocked at their door and entered. To my utter surprise, I found Luopu in that room. I was stunned and speechless!

"I have been looking for you all over the campus. I did not know that you were sitting right here in my nose" I told Luopu. The fellows knew that she and I had a "thing" going. They did not say anything. Moreover, I was not concerned about them because, as friends whom I had known for a long time, the thought that any one of them could be attempting to start a relationship with Luopu was the furthest thing on my mind.

In the meantime, Luopu was sitting on a table across from me with a cup in her hand containing some food item. I stretched out my hand, took a little bit of the food and expected Luopu to tell me what exactly she was eating. Instead, her reaction was utter irritation and derision as if I were a total stranger to her. With that response, I sensed that there was more to Luopu's being in that room than what I could see. Enraged, I left right away without uttering a word and returned to my dorm room just few yards across from where Luopu was. Shortly after I returned to my room and calmed down, I went to Sophia's dorm and told her about where I had seen Luopu and what happened thereafter concerning the food. This time around, Sophia told me to stay away from Luopu.

I took Sophia's advice because I recognized the trouble that had begun brewing. Preoccupation with Luopu amid preparations for my examinations would be detrimental. The following day, I asked Luopu to come over to my room for a meeting. During that meeting, I proposed that we stop seeing each other until the examinations were over since things did not seem to be going right between us. I already knew what Luopu had up her sleeves, but I did not expect her to put it in my face. I wanted her to agree to my proposal but not in a way that was emotionally injurious. She was neither diplomatic nor nuanced. She jumped at the proposal as if she saw it as a license to cut herself loose from me so that she could pursue other interests. Luopu's resounding "I agree" sent a chill through my spine.

Again, I went back to Sophia and shared what Luopu and I discussed. Even though she did not utter it, I could tell "I told you so" from the expression in Sophia's face. I compartmentalized Luopu, focused on preparing for my examinations and completed them successfully. Following the examinations, revelations of what was to come started to trickle through Luopu's behavior towards me. By that time, the long-awaited end-of-year vacation had arrived. Everyone was in a frenzy packing to leave campus to go to Monrovia or wherever home was. Even though Luopu and I had met and agreed that we would not see each other until after the examinations, suggesting we would pick up from where we left off, I had a sense of the direction our relationship was taking. Nevertheless, I wanted definitive signs that the apparent dead-end to the road we had taken together was not far away. To gather those signs, I went to Luopu's dorm room expressly to remind her of the verbal plans we had made pertaining to my graduation. Upon bringing up the matter, Luopu turned to me with a look of annoyance and asked, "What plans?" "Voila!" I said to myself, quietly. Still playing the fool and pretending as if nothing out of the ordinary had happened between us, I tried to remind her of the promise she made to print my graduation invitations. She found it hard to deny that we had had that conversation. Instead, she cleverly came up with the excuse, "I am traveling to Bong County for the vacation," to avoid doing what she had promised.

Luopu sent me subtle and, at times, blunt messages about the fate of our relationship. However, I had a hard time accepting the reality not because I was hopelessly naïve. I waited patiently to see where my adventure with Luopu would end because I could not fathom how a truly Catholic girl could engage in the unfolding treachery. In the first place, because I did not ask Luopu to take me to her parents, I considered everything that she was doing as a bluff. However, Luopu was not bluffing when she made up her "I am traveling to Bong County for the vacation" excuse. She followed that up with a warning on the following day when I saw her getting on the bus at Fendell to leave for Monrovia. She told me, "Marsilius, please do not come to my house when you go to Monrovia." I had a terrible time figuring out what the heck was going on with the woman because, one moment, she could not wait to take me to her parents, then, in no time, she had a change of heart. On top of that, she became immeasurably shrill.

Later that evening, I packed my belongings, boarded the next school bus and traveled to Monrovia. Convinced that Luopu could not have been serious when she told me not to go to her house, I took a taxi to Sinkor Gaye Town to see Luopu and her parents as soon as I arrived in Monrovia. Upon arrival at Luopu's house, her brother greeted me warmly. He informed Luopu that I had come and then returned to me at the front of the house, where we sat on the concrete foundation for about fifteen minutes before Luopu showed up. She looked like someone who had been deeply asleep and awakened against her wish. She walked past me without a word to her brother's chagrin. "Luopu, did not you see Marsilius?" he called her out. Only at that moment Luopu grudgingly said hello to me. At that very moment, I did not expect Luopu to say anything else because I had seen all the definitive signs, I had been looking forward to seeing. Indeed, her message had finally sunk in! After a little while, perhaps five minutes, I said goodbye to her brother and left. While I was on my way leaving, Luopu followed me and asked, "Marsilius, did not I tell you not to come to my house?" I then turned to Luopu and politely said, "I am sorry. I did not know that you were serious about what you said. If you see me here again, you can chop me with a cutlass (machete)."

The wound Luopu inflicted was ripped open on Sunday, February 13, 1983, on Ashmun Street in Monrovia, immediately after the baccalaureate service for our graduation at the Centennial Memorial Pavilion. As soon as we got out of the hall, Mom, my relatives and friends were standing with me on the sidewalk on Ashmun Street. Suddenly Luopu, walking together with the guy for whom she betrayed me, walked up blindly toward us. As soon as they recognized us, their hands disengaged. They seemed to have literally frozen right in front of us. Had the ground been opened, Luopu and that guy would have probably preferred going into it rather than facing us. She then walked up and greeted me. The sudden and unexpected meeting on the sidewalk finally removed Luopu's veil of secrecy. I finally figured out why she was in the room across from my dorm room on the night I looked for her around campus. Up to that moment, I heard everything, but I had not seen the evidence. Up to that point, the rift between Luopu and me was still hush-hush. However, at the commencement on February 16, 1983, news about Luopu "dumping" me for another guy, circulated like wildfire. The day was supposed to be one of joy, but my smiles were a façade because I was hurting. To add insult to injury, Luopu and her new guy sat at some distance across from my family and me during the graduation reception at Fendell. Everyone was turning and looking at me to gauge my reaction.

It had taken me a long time to dismiss the faith that Luopu claimed. I was vindicated in the end to hope that the Catholic faith she claimed did not die. Years later, while I was in North Carolina, Luopu contacted me through Sophia Richards Nyanue to ask for my forgiveness for what happened in college. At that time, I had already forgiven Luopu. Not too long after Luopu asked and received my forgiveness, she passed away. May her soul rest in perpetual peace.

CHAPTER 20

How the Rubber Met the Road

O N FEBRUARY 16, 1983, AFTER riding on a raft of influences, support and motivations, I paid my dues; I graduated from the University of Liberia. Even though Luopu threw a wrench into my celebration and turned it into a heartache, that curveball did not prevent my name from appearing in the annals of graduates of the University of Liberia. With that accomplished, the time had come to shed a despised cloak, to seek employment to improve my family's lot and to contribute to the development of Liberia.

Immediately after graduation from high school, I basically ignored Dad's advice to take a teaching job to earn money and save for college. Even though I did not have the resources for college, I opted to enroll anyway. I felt a college education was something I had to have because it provided better opportunities to shed a schoolboy image.[192] The image of a schoolboy, at least at the time I was in school in Sanniquellie, Liberia, was not a flattering one. A schoolboy was often regarded as a rogue or a thief and as not responsible. Instead, being employed was a sign of responsibility. For a long time, I was a part of that despised group and, with my graduation from the University of Liberia, the time had come to leave student life to assume full adulthood with its responsibilities and privileges.

On many occasions, I wondered whether one day I would say I am working, going to work, or whether I would take home a paycheck at the

237

end of the month. In addition, the new image I wanted to assume was more than a mere desire to achieve a modicum of economic power. It was also about human dignity. For example, whether one was looking for an apartment to rent, or visiting the parents of a girl whom one was interested in dating, the question, in one way or the other, always came up: "Are you working?" or "Is he working?" if the question were asked in one's absence. Those concerns were a measure of my intense urge to breakaway, to separate myself from that despised group.

Beyond my desire to become one of the respectable ones, I was also afraid. I did not want to be one of the graduates we imagined, talked about and dreaded while we were still in college. That imaginary graduate was the one whose shoe heels wore out from "pounding" the pavements of Monrovia in search of a job. When an acquaintance stole a pair of my shoes, leaving me with only one pair, the prospect of that spectacle became real. I slumped into imagining myself as that imaginary graduate whom nobody wanted to be, even though the graduation dust had not settled. Moreover, that fear loomed stubbornly against the backdrop of a light-hearted, yet poignant joke Abraham Tubman made during our senior year at the University of Liberia. He indicated that it was not about grade point average (GPA) but about who you know. He said that no matter what GPA he earned, he and his likes would get the best jobs and enjoy their air-conditioned offices while we walk the pavements of Monrovia.

Essentially, I had an obligation to deliver, which simply meant I had to find a job. I felt I had an obligation to prove to Dad that I made the right decision. I had to vindicate myself for rejecting his advice. Therefore, I found myself laboring under self-imposed as well as societal-imposed pressure. However, those were not the only pressures on me. I regarded an earned degree or education as a phenomenon with power and luster. I thought the longer I remained unemployed, the more the degree lost its luster and the more its power fizzled. I was also afraid of innocent questions like "Have you found anything yet?" meaning a job or "In what area did you get your degree?" as if I could go back to the University of Liberia and change my degree in a twinkle of an eye if I chose the wrong field of study.

I also felt an obligation to do what others who graduated from the University of Liberia before me did. Former graduates who were in the employ of the government of Liberia, concessions or corporations like Firestone, Forestry Development Authority (FDA), and the Liberia

Produce Marketing Corporation (LPMC) brought their government- or company-assigned vehicles on campus basically to show off. At the time, we called it "gravy" or "enjoying the gravy." I dreamed of landing a job where a car would be assigned to me. I wanted to go back to the university campus and park my government- or company-assigned car to let the students get a sense of what "Gravy" I was enjoying. It was silly but that silliness was a big motivation to achieve, which, to this day, has not lost its power.

As I set my eyes along those "unforgiving and nondiscriminatory" Monrovia pavements to find a job to escape student life and vindicate myself for ignoring Dad's advice, I knew there would be challenges.[193] In the context of a conversation about equal opportunity in the Liberian society at the time, we all knew that the light-hearted joke my Americo-Liberian friend, Abraham Tubman, made in reference to GPA was on the money. So, as I began the journey, I knew that this would be a completely different ball game, one that did not involve reliance on brain power alone.

Based on information I received from the University of Liberia about a job opening at the Central Agricultural Research Institute (CARI), I submitted my application for employment to the Ministry of Agriculture.[194] Luckily, the Ministry of Agriculture was not far away from where I lived. I walked there many times to follow up on my application, but I did not hear anything back from the Ministry of Agriculture. As time went on without any success, Uncle George Bolo sent me with a handwritten note on the backside of his business card to Mrs. Veronica Deagor. Mrs. Deagor was the Deputy Minister of State for Presidential Affairs at the Executive Mansion at the time. She was supposed to ask Dr. Harry Nayou, then the Minister of State for Presidential Affairs, to prepare a letter of recommendation for me to take to the Central Agricultural Research Institute (CARI). I took the note to Mrs. Deagor. Based on the usual Liberian "Go come tomorrow," "Go come next week," "The minister not here ooh," attitude, I do not know how much effort she made to follow up with Dr. Nayou.

Even though Dr. Harry Nayou did not write the letter of recommendation on my behalf to CARI, I know that the request for a letter of recommendation reached his office. On a follow up visit at the Executive Mansion, I met Mr. Dexter Tahyor who, like Dr. Nayou, hailed from Grand Gedeh County.[195] Mr. Tahyor had just come out of a meeting with Dr. Nayou. Even though he did not tell me anything about his meeting, I knew, tangentially, that my job search and request for a letter of recommendation came up. Coincidentally, a vacancy for someone with my academic background existed at the Zwedru Multilateral High School. Apparently at the urging of Dr. Nayou, Mr. Tahyor tried to redirect my job search. He told me to go to his office at the Bureau of Immigration and Naturalization near Broad Street. Obviously, the renewed interest in me appeared to have been motivated by Dr. Nayou and Mr. Tahyor's desire to have me go to teach in their home county. I was willing to go to teach at the Zwedru Multilateral High School. Even with the behind-the-scenes involvement of the Minister of State for Presidential Affairs, the man who had the ears of the President of Liberia, himself a citizen of Grand Gedeh County, my going to Grand Gedeh County did not get off the ground.

As time went on, I started to think about the worn-out shoe heel scenario that Tubman joked about shortly before we graduated from the University of Liberia. I could hear the ringing of his words, "It is not about grade point average, but about who you know."[196] Indeed, as prospects for a job grew dimmer and dimmer, the more I tried to suppress Tubman's shoe heel scenario, but it would not go away. Tubman was not prophetic, but he said something everyone knew to be true. He spoke about a situation that reflected social relations in Liberia and reminded each of us about our pedigrees. I knew mine as an indigenous Liberian and not having descended from a *quizee* stock. At that time, Tubman's pedigree was socially more valuable than mine. As he once put it to me, "I am a Tubman." For me, education, not DNA, was the means to escape the humiliations my parents endured and to claim my place in the Liberian society. I had to work hard. Moreover, in a culture of "Who knows you?" where one needed someone to "pull strings" for one to get a job, I would have been at a complete loss if I had not listened to "Gon Luogon, yehboe ee loa peay ah ee nyeehn keamon."[197] I could have played "the game" as some Liberians played it by seeking a "big shot," taking a goat or cash to him for help to find a job for me, or by giving up my first paycheck in exchange for the help. However, I did not refuse to follow that path to make a point about wanting to "stand on my own." The story I have told thus far is a denunciation of "pulling oneself by the bootstraps." Instead, I rejected that path because "Who knows you?" was not compatible with my thinking and the values I had been taught.

As a culture, Americo-Liberians have a particularly admirable uniqueness that few Liberians have the courage to acknowledge. Such a small minority does not survive and dominate a society for more than a century by accident. Americo-Liberians' uniqueness stems from their pedigree and more. Through cultivated as well as perfected "social literacy", passed down from one generation to another, they have survived and dominated Liberia throughout its history.[198] That social literacy is not only woven into the culture's social DNA but also it is organic and buried deeply within the psyche of Americo-Liberians. Mr. Bolo's attempt to reach Dr. Harry Nayou through Mrs. Veronica Deagor for a letter of recommendation on my behalf was no match but a mimicry of what Americo-Liberians do. That attempt did not spring off a comparable foundation of kinship and sensibilities or sensitivities from which Americo-Liberians launch their efforts to help each other. In that light, nepotism does not capture or fully explain Americo-Liberians' ability to lookout for each other. Their "minority status" as well as their undeniable and unique history in Liberia in part explains why looking out for each other has always been a hallmark of their survival.[199]

In the end, the letter of recommendation Dr. Harry Nayou was supposed to write for the job opening at CARI did not happen. Moreover, the conversation between Dr. Nayou and Mr. Tahyor as well as their interest in sending me to teach at the Zwedru Multilateral High School did not materialize. Another option for employment was Firestone Rubber Company. For graduates of the college of Agriculture & Forestry at the University of Liberia, that company was the equivalent of Wall Street for graduates with degrees in finance in the United States. In addition, Guthrie Rubber Plantations was another such company but to a lesser extent. Working for those companies was a pipedream not only because I did not have anybody to "pull strings" for me, but also because they required traveling long distances.[200] I did not have the money. There was no shortage of advisors who told me what to do or where to look for employment. Some people advised me to consider opportunities in other government ministries where my degree was not necessarily required.

By this time, panic began to set in, especially after those who were watching me going out and coming in realized that I had not found employment. Abraham Tubman's shoe heel scenario was no small part of that panic. In addition, some people began to ask a question I found particularly offensive: "What did you study at the University of Liberia?" In many instances, I did not answer the question, but I changed the subject because I took it to mean that I did not exercise the right judgment in choosing my area of study. I also did not answer the question because I perceived the questioner as implying that my area of study was less important. However, "When one door closes, another opens; but we often look so long and so regretfully upon the closed door that we do not see the one which has opened for us."[201]

While I was focused on the CARI and Zwedru Multilateral High School dead ends as well as fantasizing about Firestone Rubber Company and Guthrie Rubber Plantations, a door was opening for me somewhere else that I did not even know. The College of Agriculture & Forestry at the University of Liberia was seriously recruiting recent graduates as teaching assistants to be sent abroad later for graduate studies as a part of a broader goal of faculty development. A friend who was privy to conversations about the recruitment told me that Mr. Eric Eastman not only recommended me as one of the recruits, but also ensured my employment in mid-1983.[202] My friend told me that the selection was based on grade point average (GPA). My salary per month was US $575.00.[203] Indeed, grade point average (GPA) mattered, but, in the context of the Liberian society, that did not mean Abraham Tubman was wrong. Moreover, I was not conceited to believe that my academic laurel secured the teaching assistant job for me. Instinctively, I took that job as a reflection of Mr. Eastman's commitment to doing the right thing as well as his compassion. More importantly, it was another outcome of Mom's prayers.

CHAPTER 21

Interrupted "Gravy"

W ITH A JOB UNDER MY belt, I was poised to wave goodbye to student life. I moved out of the room Philip, Blemie and I shared on Cheeseman Avenue and rented a one-bedroom from Mrs. Regina Gobewole on Ninth Street Sinkor. Mrs. Gobewole was a student at the University of Liberia as well as an active and passionate supporter of the Student Unification Party (SUP).[204] Finding that one-bedroom in her house was a coincidence, one that turned out to be like an up-close encounter with a celebrity. She was well-known at the University of Liberia because, as Liberians often say, she was involved in student politics "up to her neck."

Shortly after I moved to Ninth Street Sinkor, I heard that plans were in the works at the University of Liberia to send me away to study. Based on dreams I had had since high school to study abroad, particularly in Nebraska or Florida in the United States, one would expect me to be overly excited about that unconfirmed information. But that was not the case because I was having mixed feelings due to another powerful countercurrent working against the desire to study abroad. When I inquired further about what I heard, I was told nothing was definitive about my leaving. With that answer, I thought something might work out in a year's time, if not more. The countercurrent was a desire to "enjoy" the fruits of the sacrifices I had already made. I wanted some time to work for at least three years to acquire

243

some of the material things I wished I had when I was a student. I wanted to furnish my room with every nicety available, including a gigantic stereo system to enjoy my favorite rhythm and blues. Teddy Pendergrass, Barry White, Lionel Richie, Rick James, Stephanie Mills, Gladys Knight, and Prince were some of my favorites. As Liberia was a society in which form mattered more than substance, I also wanted my time of travel to be pushed further back to accumulate material things for others to know that I was "enjoying" the "gravy."

THE BIG SURPRISE

Just when I was steadily achieving my superficial, yet real goal of accumulating material things to "enjoy," I was thrown into a quandary, whose resolution would forever change the trajectory of my life. Unexpectedly, during the last week of February 1984, the University of Liberia informed me that I had less than one week to prepare to leave for Seoul, Korea, to study. I felt as if I had been hit by a boulder. "Damned, why so soon? What about the 'gravy' I had just started to enjoy?" I reacted and wondered. In addition to missing out on the "enjoyment" I had just begun, I could not imagine being away from Mom for an extended time beyond a year. The separation anxiety was as intense as the feeling of missing out on the "enjoyment."

My internal struggle with the opportunity to study abroad did not hinge on "enjoyment" alone. I had a culturally and rightly placed, yet wholly accepted, albatross around my neck that I felt I needed to work to lift off. As children are the equivalent of a life insurance in the culture, I felt I had an obligation to do more than merely show an appreciation for my parents' labor in educating me. I wanted to do something tangible for them so that other parents could see and appreciate the importance of sending their children to school. Moreover, I spent most of my time in school in Sanniquellie and Monrovia and felt I needed to spend some time with them too. Still further, my children, Lila, Wonkermie, and Oretha Elizabeth were young, five, three, and two years old, respectively. I did not want to be away from them for an extended time. My two sisters, Sennie and Esther, not to mention my relatives and friends, were a big part of my life. An extended time from my family was frightening.

The die was cast. There was no time to waste. So, I immediately traveled to the village to inform my parents that I was scheduled to travel to Seoul,

Korea in less than a week. The trip from Monrovia to the village went as usual. The commercial taxi driver stopped at almost all the immigration checkpoints for inspections and paid "Cold Water" to the immigration officers to let us through. At every checkpoint, I wished I had wings to fly. The trip to the village enabled me to work through my initial anxieties and mixed feelings. By the time I arrived in the village, not only was I in a happier mood to deliver the message with the hope of returning to Monrovia on the following day, but also forgot an important aspect of Mahn culture. One does not travel to a faraway place without a sacrifice of burnt offerings, where the family slaughters a white chicken to thank Wlah and ask for His blessings upon the traveler. That sacrifice was scheduled for the evening of the next day to allow time for other summoned extended family members in other villages and towns to arrive.

During the following evening, Dad slaughtered the white chicken and Mom prepared food for everyone who came to wish me well.[205] After dinner, the entire family gathered in our piazza. They thanked Wlah and, as always, called on our deceased ancestors to intercede on my behalf for His protection during my journey to Seoul, Korea. During the libation, Mom and Dad each swished with cold water and drank it. One after the other, each got about a mouthful of cold water and sprayed it into my palms followed by prayers for Wlah's blessings and protection on my trip to Korea.

After the ceremony, I insisted on Mom, Dad and my sisters being at the Roberts International Airport to see me off. I returned to Monrovia thereafter and they joined me three days later. It was my older sister, Sennie, and Dad's first trip to Monrovia. I was thrilled about Dad's traveling to Monrovia to see me off. He finally got out of the village, saw Monrovia and its bright lights as well as the Atlantic Ocean, about which he had heard countless tales. In addition, he must have been gratified at the sight of countless friends and well-wishers who came to bid me farewell on the eve of my departure.

Before my parents arrived in Monrovia, word about my going away to study had spread around Monrovia with lightning speed. As a result, on the eve of my departure, the number of friends who gathered on Ninth Street Sinkor overwhelmed me. My Nimba friends showed up like bugs on bright streetlamps, poured out their hearts and shared their love with memorable speeches. My parents did not understand most of what my friends said because nearly everyone spoke in English. However, they absorbed the messages in other ways. I could tell by looking in Mom and Dad's faces that the outpouring of love heartened them. Wuo Garbie Tappia and George Gonpu's speeches were some of the memorable ones. [206] Wuo Garbie cautioned me to make the best of the opportunity. In addition, he reminded me not to forget those whom I was leaving behind. George, on the other hand, referred to countless Liberians who wished they had the opportunity I had and then told me to remember them. "Do not squander the opportunity," he said. I felt as if I were getting a pep talk to go to battle. My family and friends' expressions of love were unforgettable.

Due to the limited time I had to plan for my departure as well as my level of anxiety, I did not think through all the details. Lodging for my family and feeding as well as entertainment for friends and well-wishers were a preoccupation. An almost flawless plan existed for an early morning departure from Monrovia to the Roberts International Airport because I had a mid-morning Swiss Air flight. That plan included four vehicles, two of which Uncle George Bolo provided along with his drivers, Mehmeh and Jacob. I arranged for two other vehicles to ensure all the family and others who wanted to go to the airport had room.

Nevertheless, an opportunity for a mishap arose when a kind soul lent me a Canon camera to capture ents with family, friends, and well-wishers. I do not remember the person who lent me the camera because, as I recall, it did not involve a face-to-face one-on-one exchange. The camera reached me through another person. The mishap with the camera occurred at the airport. Despite all the pictures we took at the airport, only about half of the film in the camera had been used as boarding time fast approached. Amid the anxiety, I had to hurry to take the film out of the camera to return it to the owner by one of the people who came to see me off. "Houston, we have a problem!"[207] No one knew how to get the film out of the camera. After fiddling with the stuck film for a while, someone pulled it out in such a way that exposed and rendered it useless.[208]

Shortly afterwards, on the morning of February 29, 1984, I hugged Mom and Dad and everyone who came to see me off and boarded a Swiss Air Flight to Geneva, Switzerland on my way to Seoul, Korea. As soon as I put my carry-on away and fastened my seatbelt, I took out the exposed film and tried to push it back into the reel, hoping that a miracle would preserve the pictures. The man sitting next to me turned to me and said what I already knew. "It has been destroyed." No photos of those moments exist. Nevertheless, because they were searing and character-fashioning, I recount them in such details despite the over thirty years that have elapsed.

THE TRIP TO SEOUL, KOREA

I had not been to any other country other than next door Guinea and Ivory Coast prior to my travel to Seoul, Korea. Moreover, I was flying for the first time in my life. Under normal circumstances, institutions provide orientation sessions covering culture and other important information to students traveling abroad for studies. Neither the Korean Embassy in Monrovia nor the University of Liberia provided such an orientation, perhaps because the decision about my travel was made at the eleventh hour. However, I visited the Korean Embassy, at the time, in Sinkor, Monrovia. The embassy official whom I met was more like a salesman. He talked about the greatness of Korea and then gave me a brilliantly colorful Korean tourist magazine that featured many Korean marvels, including the splendid city of Seoul.

The magazine was in both Korean and English, side-by-side. I became concerned when I recognized the Korean script as completely new and different from English. I wanted to know which language I would use in my studies in Korea. The Korean Embassy official assured me that my courses would be in English. Moreover, in Liberia, I never woke up from bed in the morning and listened to the radio to find out what the weather would be. It was either the dry or the rainy season or sunny or rainy and warm throughout the year. Even during the rainy season, I never had an umbrella or a raincoat. If a rainstorm caught me, I took refuge at a storefront or in someone's veranda until it ceased. Going through my daily routine in Liberian weather was as ordinary as breathing. I never questioned the air quality!

So, on weather-related issues, I was completely blind during my conversation with the Korean Embassy official. I did not think about the weather, especially the severity of the winter. The official may also have assumed I had learned about the weather in Korea because I was going there to study. Indeed, I had read about four seasons in other countries, but snow and severe winters including ice-covered roads and frozen lakes were merely imaginary. We talked about ice in Liberia, but only when we needed some of it from a freezer or "icebox" to put it into a glass of water to drink. In short, another mishap was waiting to happen upon my arrival in Seoul,

Korea because I did not prepare properly for the cold winter, especially after I wore an ordinary dress shirt on the morning of my departure. I had no sweater or winter coat of any kind.

Our flight from Liberia made a stopover in Dakar, Senegal. I was not afraid, even though it was my first flight. As we took off from Dakar, I gazed down from my window seat at Wlah's wonders—the seemingly unending Atlantic Ocean. The flight from Dakar to Geneva, Switzerland was smooth and uneventful. There was plenty of food, which I enjoyed. But occasionally, I wondered what lay ahead in Korea. In Geneva, we boarded a jumbo jet. I had not seen anything like it in my life. I wondered how in the world something like that got off the ground, but it happened. We took off smoothly and, after a short flight, landed at the Charles De Gaulle International Airport in Paris, France. In Paris, I took an airport shuttle to the Sofitel Hotel, where I spent the night because my next flight was scheduled for the following day.

At the Sofitel Hotel, a hotel attendant's conduct irked me. I wanted to arrive in Seoul looking presentable because I used to be very formal.[209] For this reason, I asked room service for someone to iron the suit I wanted to wear on the Paris-Seoul leg of my trip. A room attendant picked up the suit and returned it ironed while I was in the shower. When I got out of the bathroom, I was happy to see that the attendant had ironed and hung the suit in the closet. However, upon inspection out of curiosity, I discovered a big hole in my pants that a hot iron clearly made. The hotel attendant cleverly covered the burnt area of the pants with the jacket as if nothing happened. I contacted the hotel front desk about the problem. However, the person who answered the phone said he did not understand English. He gave the phone to someone who spoke English, but that person said that the hotel attendant was not responsible for burning my pants. When I figured that the front desk did not intend to help me, I was furious.

With not enough time to pursue the matter because I had only one night in Paris, I fumed about the situation and resigned to have dinner. While eating, I opened the refrigerator and found different kinds of liquors in little bottles each amounting to a shot or more. "Look at what we have here!" I said to myself. I had had whiskey before in Liberia, but it was a once-in-a-while thing. "They burned my pants and the only answer I got was that they do not understand English. Well, it is time for payback!" as I reached out into the refrigerator. One by one, I took out a bottle and drank it. I do not remember how many of those small bottles I emptied. I know I had a variety and was knocked out that evening. I woke up the next morning, wore an ordinary long-sleeved brown shirt with a pair of brown pants and took the airport shuttle for my flight to Seoul. The hotel attendants must have discovered the one-man ball the African dude had.

I finally arrived in Seoul in the evening on March 2, 1984, where an official of the Korean Ministry of Education was waiting to receive me. Seeing my name on a poster in the hands of a middle age Korean man among a sea of Korean faces heartened me. I walked up to the man, greeted him and introduced myself. "What have I gotten myself into?" I said when I realized that his English was not particularly good. I should have reserved that question for a few minutes later because as we made our way out of the airport building to the car awaiting us outside, I almost ran back inside the airport terminal. It was extremely cold, and I only had on a shirt. The Korean man smiled and winked as he tried to encourage me to muster the courage to reach the car. We then drove off and made our way through a maze of streets interrupted intermittently by throngs of pedestrians in crosswalks. At the time, Seoul was a megacity with an estimated population of 10 million people.

CHAPTER 22

Life in Seoul, Korea

AFTER ABOUT AN HOUR'S DRIVE, we finally reached the International House, a five-story guest house for international students. The Korean Ministry of Education official who took me to my destination ushered me into a nice and comfortable room. On the following day, I went downstairs to the lobby area, hoping to find someone with whom I could have a conversation. Everyone I came across was a Korean and spoke only Korean. The people who were supposed to help me understood some English but spoke very little. I wandered in the lobby and found a large world map hanging on the wall. I walked closer to the map, located Liberia and, suddenly, my heart sunk as I moved my eyes over the map to South Korea's location. In Liberia, a place so far away like that is called "God's back."

Dinner time did not make matters better either. Like Liberians, Koreans eat rice, although for them, breakfast, lunch, and dinner seemed to be all about rice. In addition, the dishes that came along with rice were not anything like potato greens, cassava leaf, or palaver sauce, not to mention Gaygba.[210] I ate spaghetti with a brownish mushroom soup that tasted familiar for the first few days. It took a long time to get used to Korean food. Within the first few weeks, I felt like wanting to go back to Liberia.

All in all, I adjusted quickly, especially after I met other international students at the Korean Language Institute at Seoul National University.

In no time, I started getting out of the guest house, venturing out into the city on my own and immersing myself into the language. I began having fun from that moment, especially with my broken Korean because, for Koreans, watching and listening to a black guy from Africa speaking their language was a novelty. It was like watching a riveting comedy show. Their first reaction was always a surprise, followed by laughter. Everyone wanted to know who the heck I was without realizing that I understood quite a bit of what they were saying. I would let their conversations and sometimes gossips go on for a while and then interrupt by introducing myself. Everyone would raise their eyebrows and cover their mouths in surprise. I had a great time and made many friends with my boldness with the language.

To my pleasant surprise, the South Korea that I saw upon arrival was different from the South Korea that I studied about in high school geography in Liberia. I learned that the country was in desolate ruins with extreme poverty after the Korean War in the early 1950s. However, 30 years after the end of the Korean War, the Republic of Korea (South Korea) had been transformed. To me, as someone from a "third-world" country, South Korea at that time was in every measure a developed country, moving forward with economic and technological development at a lightning speed. In Seoul, the capital city, new constructions were taking place like bubbles over boiling rice. One day I would go to a place and see construction workers excavating and within the next two to three weeks or less, I would return to find people sitting in offices at the very location where I had seen construction workers digging during my previous visit.

After I stayed in Korea for a while, I soon learned that the seemingly miraculous economic and technological change I was witnessing did not come about accidentally. By and large, Koreans seemed to have their priorities in order. At least from my own observations, it was clear that they put "하느님" (God), "우리 나라" (our country), and "가족" (family), first, second, and third, respectively. Besides those three, the emphasis on 교육 (education) to achieve social mobility was extraordinary. At that time, I knew of no other country in the world where the citizens were as proud of their country as Koreans were. Beginning immediately after my arrival in Seoul on March 2, 1984 and continuing until my departure to the United States in early January 1986, nearly every Korean I met asked me the same question "What is your impression of our country?" as if everyone had been programmed. Of course, I would say love of country here is palpable and admirable. Moreover, Koreans are wonderful people with a great country and great culture! Living in Korea was like looking at myself in a mirror. I learned about who I was, what growing up in Liberia did for me and my place in Liberia. More importantly, I asked about my responsibilities; what I owed Liberia. I always loved Liberia but living in Korea bolstered that love and gave me a deeper appreciation of my culture.

Shortly after my arrival in Seoul, I enrolled in a Korean Language Program at the Korean Language Institute at Seoul National University. My language training continued for nine months, from March until December 1984. The thought of learning a new language for nine months and going on to do serious academic work was unsettling. The Korean script was completely new and strange to me. Upon exposure to the Korean alphabet, I not only thought about some of the children who started school with me in Liberia in March 1966 at St. Mary's but also felt like some of them. Unable to say, let alone write, their alphabet, they sang made-up Mahn or Dan alphabet songs. The songs recalled the sweet and stress-free life in their villages where they imagined themselves eating newly harvested corn or leftover GB. At the Korean Language Institute at Seoul National University, I felt like singing "A B C D neay ma loe naown nu peay kpehyee seneh quoi" or "A B C D beykpo yeah tozeh won ka nuahn kabeea" in a different way.[211] I felt like singing "ㄱ ㄴ ㄷ ㄹ" "neay ma loe naown nu peay kpehyee seneh quoi," however, there was no "kpehyee seneh quoi" around.[212] My own village in Liberia was thousands of miles away, now behind "God's back." Wuo Garbie Tappia and George Gonpu's words were still with me. I could not leave school. There was no turning back. I had to learn the language and so I dug in and did.

Indeed, I was far away from home, behind "God's back" and lonely. However, I made new friends, many of whom were Koreans. They invited me to their homes, entertained and helped me cope with loneliness. I have never forgotten their insistence that I sing every time I was invited to a home. Almost in every gathering I socialized, I could not escape singing, a favorite Korean pastime. Once someone said, "Noreh hapshida" (Let's sing a song), I had to figure out a way or make up a song to sing. Whether I could sing or had the voice did not matter. They just wanted to hear me sing. They cheered me on once I started to sing. Even after over thirty years since I was in Seoul, Korea, I still remember how to sing "Sarang hay tangshi nu" (I love you).

Some of my Korean friends advised me to hang out with them to learn the culture and language. They wanted me to go to places where most foreigners did not usually go alone. On one occasion, some Korean friends took me to a 맥주집 (beer house) on Jongro, a major thorough-fare in Seoul. I thought we were in a marketplace when we arrived. It was one of the most popular meeting places for Korean college students who wanted to have a beer and chat. The beer mugs reminded me of an imaginary drinking mug for Goliath. Besides 맥주집, which was almost everywhere one could turn, other places for meeting and socializing included coffee shops as well as "Pulgogi" (roasted beef) stands on streets at night. Coffee was sold in vending machines at nearly every street corner. Coffee shops featured prominently everywhere in Korea not only because of the extremely cold weather in winter but also because people often met there on dates or to strike business deals. In Liberia an offer of "Cold water" in a positive sense could mean sodas or soft drinks, beer, or something stronger. Similarly, in Korea, at least from my experience, "Korpee deleekayo?" (Can I offer you coffee?) could mean a cup of coffee, soft drink, beer, or something stronger, too. At "Pulgogi" stands a mixture of vegetable and beef was stirred and fried in cast iron frying pans and sold along with "Soju."[213] Some of my friends were very eager to take me to places such as 맥주집, coffee shops, and "Pulgogi" stands in the city as well as to other places in the countryside. They wanted me to learn a whole lot about the culture as well as the lives of ordinary Koreans. In their enthusiasm to help me, some either did not know certain boundaries or lost track of them. Some were curious about what lurked in my heart; they wanted to know if I had a girlfriend and, by that, they meant a Korean girlfriend. With little hesitation or difficulty, they always asked, "Do you have a girlfriend?" and a smile without much to say was always my response.

Outside of the Korean Language Institute classroom and aside from the outings that my Korean friends were taking me on, I still had other ways of practicing my Korean and immersing myself further into the culture. One such way was finding out and going to places where ordinary Koreans shopped. Beyond practicing my Korean and learning about the culture, I was also interested in finding these shopping places because of the great bargains. But I was not always successful in getting the bargains for which I was on the lookout.

Perhaps out of solidarity with their citizens or for the sheer joy of sticking it out to foreigners who were often perceived as being of means, Korean vendors had lower prices for Koreans and higher ones for outsiders for the same items. Despite the throngs of ordinary Koreans who often crowded these shopping places and made it difficult to walk, Korean venders did not have to work hard to figure who was and who was not a Korean. It was not difficult to identify a foreigner, especially someone like me who is black. This was not anything unheard of as anyone who has traveled to other countries has probably had a similar experience. Despite being an outsider, I soon figured out how to get around the higher prices for items with which foreigners were being charged. The key was Koreans' fascination with hearing a person who happens to be black speak their language. Upon finding something like a shirt, a pair of pants or shoes that I liked, I pretended to take a closer look. In earnest, however, I was listening intently to the vendor. I wanted to hear what he or she had to say. Nine out of ten chances, someone wanted to know who the heck I was. On many occasions at 동대문 (East Gate), someone, convinced that I would not understand, always whispered the question I expected "이 분 은 누구세요?" I would then turn to the person and say "Flumo rago haminida." "나는 서울대학교 학생 입니다."[214] In response, the flabbergasted vendor, if female, would cover her mouth. The conversation almost always ended with a good dose of laughter and my getting the items on favorable terms. I often felt like a paid performer.

On a different occasion, I went out to look for bargains in Kwee Dong, an area of Seoul where few foreigners frequented. At a busy intersection where several major streets converged, all I could see was a sea of Korean faces. I had no fear because I had quickly determined after a short stay that Seoul was a very safe place to live. In fact, at that time, one could sleep on the bench at a bus stop fearing no harm. As I was looking over the sea of Korean faces and trying to decide which way to go, a young Korean woman ran towards me, held my left hand, and repeatedly rubbed my wrist with her index finger. Perhaps she thought that a black stain would remain on her finger after the rub. As shocking as this may have been to another person, I was not surprised at all. In Liberia, I heard some people in other societies held some wild beliefs about Africans such as having tails and living in trees. In fact, the notion that a black person's skin pigmentation could leave a black stain on another person upon rubbing against it was nothing new. I heard that in Liberia too. So, when the young Korean woman took my left hand and started to rub my wrist, I instinctively knew that she was conducting an experiment. I did not take any offense. Apparently, she had had an argument with someone that something black like a tar remains on the hand after rubbing a black skin. I hope that the evidence from her experiment convinced her that the pigmentation in black people's skin is not a tar.

Learning a new language and culture, particularly as an adult, is a challenge. That is why I agreed with and acted upon my Korean friends' advice to immerse myself into the culture. However, that was not easy to do with every aspect of Korean culture. Mountain climbing, a cherished Korean pastime, was one example. Unless one has had an opportunity to live in Korea, it is hard to understand why mountain climbing is such a favorite activity there. Mountain climbing in Korea is about being physically fit, escaping the busy city life and spending quality time with family. Indeed, mountain climbing is also about savoring the beauty and serenity of nature. South Korea is a mountainous country, with mountains nearly everywhere, including the city of Seoul where marvelous tunnels through them showcase great Korean engineering feats.

During the summer, the weather was warm and beautiful. Families went out to picnic or climb mountains. My Korean friends did not merely invite me to go out to climb mountains. Some engaged in a sales' pitch to get me to go along. Their first and best line had to do with the warm summer weather. Although none of them had been to Liberia, they argued that the weather was like Africa and so I should be excited to get out and enjoy myself. My kind of fun activities included playing soccer, basketball, going to the bar and dancing. Going to school dances was a big part of my teenage and high school years because that was where the girls were in top attire. Rhythm and Blues were a big part of life during my teenage and high school years. The other activity I enjoyed was playing scrabble, but for most of my Korean friends for whom English was a second language, playing a scrabble game would have been a lopsided and boring competition. In that light, being invited to go out to climb mountains made me to feel like I was being asked to go to the opera or a rap concert.[215] I tried to make a case that in Liberia we do not climb mountains for recreation, but that was a nonstarter because the weather was so beautiful that one could not easily find a convincing reason to stay inside. Also, finding an excuse to avoid going to climb mountains was not an easy task because my Korean friends were persistent. I always went along to please them. Once we were there, I could not wait for the day to be over.

The cold winter and snow-covered mountains in Korea created perfect skiing conditions. As they did during the summer, my Korean friends often invited me to ski with them. I had never skied before and did not want to learn how to ski because of the bitter cold weather. Additionally, I thought skiing was too dangerous. These were the few times I was able to make up convincing excuses not to go along to ski. As with their African warm weather counterpoint during the summer, no one could make similar argument for African cold weather.

Other aspects of cultural education about Korea were institutional. For example, the Korean government took other foreign students and me on a tour of the country on a few occasions. I saw places of interest, including the Korean War Cemetery near Pusan and scenic places like a volcanic crater in the Pacific Ocean off the coast of the Korean island of Cheju Do. A cave on land that went underneath the Pacific Ocean, out of which volcanic lava had oozed and hardened, was one place on the island of Cheju Do no one could convince me to go into. I imagined a volcanic eruption occurring in the cave with hot molten lava following and baking me while attempting to escape. Other foreign students on the excursion as well as tourists went into the cave. I told the tour guides that I was the only son Mom had and could not take any risk with my life. I waited outside until they returned.

THE QUINTESSENTIAL MENTOR
It is not out of the ordinary for an ambassador to look out for citizens of his own country resident in the country of his service. Therefore, upon meeting Dr. Cyrenius N. Forh, Liberia's Ambassador to the Republic of Korea, the only extraordinary aspect of the encounter was that he was not who I thought he was ethnically.[216] Prior to our meeting, Dr. Forh sent an emissary to the International House to find out who I was, how I was doing and my living situation. After the embassy staff's visit, I also received a telephone call from Dr. Forh. He invited me to his residence and indicated that I was welcome at any time. He was gracious.

Dr. Cyrenius N. Forh, leaving Seoul on a trip to Liberia

The Liberian Embassy staff's visit and Dr. Forh's call lifted my spirit during the first few weeks when I felt out of place, completely lost, and considered returning to Liberia. I felt like I was not alone. Considering my state of mind, I became excited to see Dr. Forh and his family. However, I was hesitant because I did not know whether they were uppity or ordinary people. The surname Forh sounded to me like Ford. As a result, I took the Forhs to be uppity Liberians, the "*Quizees*," "Civilized," or "Americo-Liberians", as they are known in Liberia. Finally, when someone took me to Dr. Forh's residence, I was pleasantly surprised. I found out that he was an indigenous

Liberian and belonged to the Kru ethnic group. His wife, Mrs. Victoria K. Forh, was as lively and welcoming as her husband. She prepared delicious Liberian foods, which I greatly enjoyed.

Dr. Forh exceeded every expectation I had of an ambassador. He took me under his wings as his son. Even though the Korean government provided my living expenses, Dr. Forh told me to save my allowance and go to his home at any time to eat. Moreover, the entire Forh family treated me as if I were a biological member. After my first year in Korea, Dr. Forh asked me to move into the first floor of the Liberian Embassy Chancery in Hannam Dong. Dr. Forh's hospitality so far was extraordinary because, in general, Liberia was a tribal society, where people tended to look out for members of their own tribe.[217] For example, when someone of a given tribe headed a government ministry or agency, it was common to find a substantial number of the employees belonging to the tribe of that ministry or agency's head.

With that, I did not think of anything unusual when Dr. Forh asked me about my tribe upon meeting for the first time. However, I was surprised to find out that he was thinking about something else when he asked about my tribe. Based on my surname, Flumo, Dr. Forh already knew from the outset that I was not a member of his tribe, Kru. Instead, he wanted to know where I was from because people in three different counties in Liberia, namely, Nimba, Bong, and Lofa widely use my surname. Once I told him that I was Mahn from Nimba County, he started to tell me about his friends from Nimba County, particularly Liberian historian Dr. Joseph Saye Guanue. That was the extent of tribal discussion I had with him. Henceforth, Liberia or Liberia's interests dominated nearly every subject about which we talked. He was a fierce and unapologetic advocate of indigenous Liberians' quest for leadership in Liberia, yet he loved Liberians of every background with the same devotion.

Dr. Forh was a strong man. He was never browbeaten and never sold his soul for a job. His friendships and interactions cut across all social classes. His residence in Seoul, for example, was the place where African American servicemen and women of all ranks congregated regularly to socialize and network.[218] During my time in Korea, he was the unofficial leader of the black community. Through him, I met LTC Carl H Cannon, USA (Ret). I observed Dr. Forh as a devout Christian, a devoted husband and a caring dad. In addition, he was knowledgeable about Liberian history and loved the Kru people with a passion. He reinforced the importance of being patient, having a prayer life and guided me along the path of becoming a responsible and upright man. Our conversations in countless informal sessions about Liberia and its future, a topic that animated both of us, occurred during the periods 1984-1985 and mid-1987-mid-1990 in Seoul, Korea and in Monrovia, Liberia, respectively. Aside from formal classroom lessons and my own readings, I learned most of what I know about political science and Liberian history during my sessions with Dr. Forh. He "walked" his "talk" and demonstrated his love of Liberia through the performance of his duties. Besides telephone conversations, Dr. Forh and I had our last regular informal session and discussed a whole host of issues pertaining to family and Liberia in 1992 when he visited with me in Wadesboro, North Carolina. Thereafter, he passed away in 1993 in Monrovia, Liberia.

Dr. Cyrenius Forh earned a Ph.D. in political science from Indiana University. He lived in the United States for a long time, yet never lost touch with Liberia, not to mention his Kru heritage. He had a special bond with his beloved Kru people. From dawn to dusk nearly every day, people from all walks of life went to see him at his home in Bardnersville, outside Monrovia. They went for comfort in times of sorrow, advice, and letters of recommendation for employment. He was deeply interested in the success of everyone around him. He had an unmistakable inner force as well as presence. Those who went to see him left feeling uplifted.

STUDYING IN KOREA

In December 1984, I completed the beginning, intermediate and advanced Korean Language program and received a certificate for each level. After a long and bitter cold winter, I began studying Agricultural Civil Engineering in Suwon, outside Seoul in March 1985. I took the bus from Hannam Dong, Seoul, to a train station and then caught a train to Suwon for classes on weekdays. Almost always, I was the only black person on the train during the commute to and from Suwon. My presence aroused Korean passengers' curiosity; they wanted to know who I was.

Between those who sat in the few seats on the sides and faced each other, the trains' railcars carried most passengers while standing and holding onto rails or pillars. I often stood and held onto rails or pillars to avoid falling when the train stopped. Without much surprise, Korean passengers reacted to me in the same way as Korean vendors did when I was out shopping for bargains, for example, at Tondemun (East Gate). Initially, they looked askance at me and mumbled words to each other as they wondered. Some passengers thought I was an American GI while others who had seen me on the train more than once were not that sure. Suddenly, I would interrupt the murmurings and introduce myself in Korean after I had had enough of the gossips. "Oh, he understands and speaks Korean!" someone would say while others asked, "What did he say?" Conversations with them that followed often resulted in exchanging phone numbers and forging new friendships. It was a memorable experience.

In the beginning, I wished I were in Liberia with family and friends but, as time went by, I started having fun, especially during my commute to and from Suwon. Engaging Koreans and trying to understand their culture paid off psychologically. The more I learned about Korea and Korean culture, the less I became homesick. Despite my optimism, challenges about the direction of my studies remained. For example, my professors conducted their lectures in Korean, even though nearly all of them studied and obtained their doctorates in the United States. Moreover, they wrote notes on chalkboards using a combination of Korean, English and Chinese.[219] Indeed, most of my textbooks were written in English but some of them were also written in Korean, including scientific terms in Chinese characters. It soon became apparent to me that beyond getting around and engaging in ordinary superficial conversations, my nine-month Korean language training was not enough for the level of academic work I had begun. Language deficit affected my participation in class discussions and other intellectual exchanges, not to mention the use of textbooks other than those written in English.

My education in Korea, formal classroom as well as informal engagement with Koreans and their culture, was useful and fulfilling. Beginning with the Ministry of Education official who picked me up from Kimpo International Airport in March 1984 until my departure for the United States on February 4, 1986, my experience in Korea was positive. I had a nice and comfortable room to stay in at the International House and, more importantly, I was treated with respect and dignity. At school, my professors at the Seoul National University Language Institute at the Kwanak campus and at the College of Agricultural Civil Engineering in Suwon as well as my Korean friends treated me similarly. I did not face any form of discrimination or any kind of unkind treatment in Korea. I left Seoul National University in Korea and transferred to North Carolina A & T State University in the United States because language deficit stood in the way of the intellectual stimulation I desired.

The warm sentiments are evidence of my gratefulness for the opportunity to study in Seoul, Korea. Now that the passage of time has given me a new vantage point to see that opportunity clearly for what it was, I liken it to the culture in the village when I was a child. Upon completing our house in the village, my parents thanked Wlah by offering a sacrifice of burnt offerings. Moreover, they petitioned Him to shepherd strangers from faraway places our way because receiving strangers was a blessing and a mark of being important.

But my parents and others in the village did not expect strangers they received, sheltered, and fed to reciprocate in kind because the strangers were often people from Guinea who came to Liberia to trade or visit with family and relatives. Yet, when the strangers returned home, they generated tremendous goodwill for Liberians. They often spoke glowingly about their experience in Liberia as if every Liberian treated them like my parents and others did. Thereafter, anyone from anywhere in Liberia who visited the strangers' home in Guinea received hospitable treatment. My parents' kindnesses as well as those of others in the village had positive unintended consequences. In addition, I liken the opportunity to study in Korea to the culture in the village when I was a child because living and studying in Korea opened my eyes and reinforced values my parents taught me. Living and studying in Korea bolstered my sense of responsibility for children and caring for one's parents, especially as they become old.

In 1984, the Korean government's scholarship program for international students was like my parents and other people's desires to receive, shelter and feed strangers in the village. The Korean government apparently intended to promote cultural ties between beneficiaries' home countries and Korea. In addition, by inviting students from different countries and diverse cultures, the Korean government probably intended to provide opportunities for Korean students at Korean universities to expand their worldviews.

If the Korean government scholarship program designers believed that it could help project the Republic of Korea in the world in a more meaningful and enduring way, then my story is a vindication. I feel like the archetype they had in mind because I carry my education and experience in Korea like a prized possession and share it with pride. I left Korea early 1986, yet I root for Korea and feel about Korea as if it is my second home. I feel like the participant who was expected to return to his home country and become a virtual, yet ideal ambassador of Korea; someone who would tell the Korean story, a story of a rich culture and marvelous technological advancement, from the perspective of a lived experience.

Every great program deserves a fresh look and some adjustments. Over thirty years have passed, and I believe some adjustments have been made to the Korean government scholarship program for international students. At the time of leaving Korea, I made two observations about the scholarship program. At the Ministry of Education, there may have been a unit staffed with culturally literate and competent individuals, responsible for implementing the Korean government scholarship program for international students. However, while in Korea, I do not remember having any interactions with such staff members. I knew of only one female international student who left Korea disillusioned partly because of a lack of guidance. One incident is not enough for a recommendation for change. However, at the time of leaving Korea, I felt that guidance in the program was wanting.

In my judgment, because language was the gateway to everything I wanted to learn in Korea, the Korean language training program was the most important part of the Korean government scholarship program. As such, the nine-month intensive Korean language training program after which students entered their respective disciplines needed only to be the beginning of the language program. Language training needed to continue formally throughout the duration of participants' respective disciplines until they were finished. Completion of any degree program by international students needed to reflect a mastery of Korean language.

LEAVING KOREA

While language deficit was at the heart of my transfer from Seoul National University to North Carolina A & T State University, the decision to transfer did not occur in a vacuum. Other forces, including my long-held dream to study in Nebraska or in Florida influenced me. In a conversation with Dr. Forh on one occasion, he awakened my latent dream about studying in

Nebraska or in Florida. Perhaps because he studied in the United States, out of the blue, he indicated that he would like me to study in the United States. Dr. Forh's comments opened the window for language deficit, the subject I had up my sleeves but had not found the words to talk about. After describing language deficit and how I felt it stood in my way to learn more, Dr. Forh understood what I meant and was supportive. Moreover, he went from suggesting he would like me to study in the United States to saying, "Marsilius, we need to get you to the United States."

A cultural bias not against Korea but for the United States also influenced my decision to transfer from Seoul National University to North Carolina A & T State University. I believe the only way anyone can understand a Liberian's cultural bias for the United States is to go beyond spending time in Liberia to living in Liberia. In my mind, that is the only way one can see, hear, and feel America's hold on the Liberian psyche; it is deep and pervasive. In today's Liberia in particular, an opportunity to travel to the United States is like being called out of hell to enter the gates of Heaven. That psychological hold on the Liberian psyche is partly a function of the history of Liberia. In addition, American involvement with education in Liberia through the Peace Corps is also partly responsible. For example, most of my teachers from elementary through high school were American Catholic nuns or members of the Peace Corps. It was not by accident that I dreamed about studying in Nebraska or in Florida.

In high school, I thought of Liberia as if it were a cordoned off city, a city with only one gate through which one could look to the outside world, which was the United States. Indeed, through that single gate, our influences, including rhythm and blues, bellbottoms, platform shoes, afro hairdo, and magazines such as Jet came to Liberia. The United States was the place to go outside of Liberia for any reasons, particularly education. More importantly, upon returning to Liberia, one had to be seen coming through that one single gate to the city that showed the United States. Scaling the wall cordoning off the city and entering with any kind of credentials from any other country did not reach the legitimacy threshold. In short, such credentials were not valued as those from the United States. As a Liberian, I was like other Liberians under the same influences with similar biases. More importantly, because my mentor, Dr. Forh, was similarly biased more so by virtue of having acquired his graduate degrees in the United States, I was doubly biased for the United States.

Indicative of his interest in the success of those around him, Dr. Forh immediately contacted one of his closest friends in Korea, LTC Carl H Cannon, USA (Ret) with whom he had a conversation about me.[220] Less than one week after Dr. Forh and I talked, he called me into his office at the Embassy Chancery to discuss my options. It was only a matter of getting ready and going upstairs because I was staying at the first floor of the Embassy Chancery. Upon arrival, surprisingly, I met Col. Cannon along with his friend, Col. Monroe Fuller. Even though Col. Cannon did not know who I was in terms of character, he was gung-ho about the prospects of continuing my studies in the United States. He thought that transferring from Seoul National University to another university in the United States was something doable in that very short time frame. As we brainstormed about a possible university in the United States, Washington State University in Pullman, Washington came up. However, Col. Cannon did not think Washington State University was the right place for me because it was in "the wheat fields in the middle of nowhere."[221] At that point, Col. Monroe Fuller suggested North Carolina A & T State University in Greensboro, North Carolina.[222] "Aha! That's it!" Col. Cannon reacted. While he was aware of Col. Fuller being an alumnus of North Carolina A & T State University, Col. Cannon was excited about the prospect of my going to North Carolina A & T State University for an entirely different and even more important reason. The reason was Mr. Elwood "Rock" Edwards (deceased) who lived in Greensboro, NC. Rock's brother, Sunny, was married to Dr. Mary Cannon's older sister.[223] Col. Cannon was thinking more like a parent. He was interested in my going to a place where someone reliable to watch over me lived.

"God Works in a Mosquito Nest"

"God works in a mosquito nest" is a parody of seemingly unsophisticated Liberians who speak broken or nonstandard English. It is their way of saying "God works in mysterious ways," an expression often used to describe Wlah's grace and wonders. In Liberia, everyone uses "God works in a mosquito nest" because of the power of its vivid imagery. A mosquito is an extremely small creature. Therefore, any being that works within the confines of its nest, if such a thing exists, must be all-powerful and ingenious.

LTC Carl H Cannon, USA (Ret), receiving the U.S. Army Legion of Merit Award in Washington, D.C. as his wife, Dr. Mary L. Cannon, looks on.

A manifestation of "God works in a mosquito nest," in a sense, occurred during the next step in the process of my transfer from Seoul National University to North Carolina A & T State University. This happened when Dr. Forh, Col. Cannon and Col. Fuller wondered about who, at North Carolina A & T State University, would ensure that the admission paperwork got into the right hands. To their pleasant surprise, Dr. McKinley DeShield, Jr. offered to do that as soon as he heard that a Liberian in Seoul, Korea, was trying to transfer to North Carolina A & T State University.[224]

Dr. DeShield served as Dean of the College of Agriculture & Forestry at the University of Liberia before the 1980 "Revolution" in Liberia. Students had a high and positive opinion of his leadership and often described him as an outgoing, approachable, and helpful administrator. He often placed students' registration forms on their backs to sign because his office was wherever they met him. Dr. DeShield was a humble man but, viewed within the context of social relations in Liberia, his willingness to help process my admission to North Carolina A & T State University was no ordinary act. Indeed, based on his work with students in Liberia, Dr. DeShield was an outlier because at a time having a "*Quizee*" stock or being an America-Liberian mattered, he was focusing on helping students and providing opportunities for all Liberians rather than flaunting his pedigree.

Moreover, Dr. DeShield's help for me, Flumo, an indigenous Liberian, was no ordinary act because it came against the backdrop of the 1980 "Revolution" in Liberia that overthrew the ruling America-Liberian minority. I do not know about Dr. DeShield's specific situation immediately after the "Revolution." However, I witnessed some of the harrowing circumstances some America-Liberians endured immediately following the 1980 "Revolution" that forced many to flee to the United States. Against that backdrop, Dr. DeShield, an America-Liberian, was enthusiastic about helping me, a native Liberian, and remained true to the character and reputation he built in Liberia. He was consistent.

Incidentally, a few weeks before I left Seoul for the United States, Dr. Forh traveled to Liberia. He was in Liberia when I received my form I-20 in the mail from North Carolina A & T State University.[225] With excitement, I called and informed his wife, Mrs. Victoria K. Forh. Apparently, Mrs. Forh told her husband that I had received my Form I-20 when he called from Liberia to check on his family. His wife told me that he was overjoyed upon receiving the news about my Form I-20. A few days later, on February 3, 1986, a Liberian Embassy staff returned my passport to me. It had been taken to the U.S. Embassy in Seoul for my visa. Upon receipt of my passport, I opened it and saw North Carolina A & T State University handwritten on the page which the visa had been stamped at the U.S. Embassy Consular Office in Seoul. It was now official that I was going to the United States. My flight from Seoul to Greensboro, North Carolina via Anchorage, Alaska and New York City had already been scheduled. In fact, I was leaving the following day, Tuesday February 4, 1986. Unable to contain my joy, I jumped up and down with excitement, thanked everyone including Col. Cannon and then returned to the first floor of the Liberian Embassy Chancery. I thanked Wlah for all the people with whom He surrounded me.

Beneath my excitement about going to the United States, I was also afraid and sad. Indeed, I had learned a great deal about the United States in Liberia.[226] There was a sense of déjà vu about the United States. It felt as if I had already been there before. Nevertheless, while the United States was not the Republic of Korea where I faced a language barrier, the reality was that, despite all that I had learned about the United States, I had never traveled to or lived in the United States. My fears were about the unknowns rather than about the strangeness of the place.

I was excited about going to the United States to study. However, I was also sad as it dawned on me that I was about to leave behind people who mattered to me. I was mistaken to think that leaving Korea would be easy emotionally because it was not Liberia, where I had to leave Mom, Dad, my sisters, relatives, and friends behind on my way to Seoul, Korea. But my sadness grew deeper as it occurred to me that I might not see for the rest of my life some of the people with whom I forged friendships. Those friends mattered to me because they made life in Korea, behind "God's back," bearable for me. They were men and women from various professional backgrounds from countries all over the world.

My friends in Korea came from Costa Rica, El Salvador, and Columbia. Camilo Riano, who was studying computer science, was from Bogota, Colombia. Others came from the Democratic Republic of Congo (Zaire), Ghana, and Kenya. Kapuco, a congenial man from the Democratic Republic of Congo, always carried an unmistakable smile. However, when the African students tried to establish an African student association in Seoul, Kapuco showed no interest. Upon probing his reticence, I discovered that he had a well-founded fear. His brother had been killed while involved in an association. He vowed never to join an association because a mere conversation about forming an association was a painful reminder.

Martin Zame and Ruben Damptay were both Ghanaians. While Damptay hung out with Martin and me occasionally, Martin was like a big brother. He was also a great company. I had countless conversations and laughter with him over beer. During a Korean government-sponsored excursion on the Korean island of Cheju Do in 1985, Kapuco, Martin, Damptay and I had a hilarious rendezvous at a beer house. The incident involved my relative command of the Korean language and my use of it to shortchange them in the distribution of goodies. Kapuco told me that he will never forget the experience and the cathartic laughter that followed.

Odiambho Odek was a Kenyan friend. Upon meeting, I was keen on letting him know the little knowledge from geography/social studies I had learned about his country, although, on the African continent, Liberia is on the opposite side of Kenya. We talked about the Mau Mau Liberation Movement and former President Jomo Kenyatta's role in African

267

politics.[227] We also discussed Daniel Arap Moi, Kenya's president in 1985, who was a known figure in Liberia. The query I fondly remember from that conversation was, "Are you a Kikuyu or a Luo?"[228] Odiambho beamed with a smile and then told me that he was a Luo. Odiambho and I spent a lot of time together because we studied in the same department at Seoul National University.

Meheret Asrat was a fabulously beautiful Ethiopian woman and the only female African student among my friends. Based on stories she told and family photos she showed me, there was no doubt she came from a privileged family. Apparently, she had come to Korea believing that she would study in English. She was not particularly happy when she realized that she had to learn a completely new language. Eventually, Meheret left Korea for Greece.

In the Asia Pacific region, I made friends from Taiwan, Nepal, and Pakistan. Lieutenant Colonel Ming J. Wang, an officer of the Taiwanese Air Force, was from Taichung, Taiwan while Navadeep Rajbhandary was from Nepal. Abidale Khan, an elderly man from Pakistan, was a silkworm expert doing research in Korea. Of course, I made friends from Korea too. Jong Mun Ja offered me coffee from a vending machine at the Seoul National University Kwanak campus when I newly arrived. A tall and elegant woman, Jong Mun Ja was one of the few Korean students who welcomed and made me to feel at home at the sprawling and marvelously beautiful Kwanak campus of Seoul National University. She eventually left Korea with her fiancé to study at Indiana University in the United States. Indeed, offering a cup of hot coffee and reassuring a stranger who finds himself behind "God's back" that all would be well can secure a place in a memoir. I will always remember Jong Mun Ja's kindness during that supposedly spring, yet cold day in late March 1984.

Kim Bong Seon and her best friend, Boo Hyun Sook, were two fabulously looking young women. I met them in Cheju Do. They were outgoing and quite informed about Africa. They were also engaging and inquisitive. More importantly, I found them friendly and that surprised me. I thought they would be afraid to talk to a foreigner, particularly a black guy from Africa. Kim Bong Seon later moved to Seoul, where we stayed in touch throughout until I left Korea. As for Boo Hyun Sook, her best friend, she moved to Japan.

Mr. Woo was one of the Korean Ministry of Education officials who ran the international student program at the International House, where I stayed for some time.[229] Mr. Woo invited me to his home, where I met his family. I still have a photo of his four-year-old daughter and me that he took. I always turned to Mr. Woo whenever I felt I needed to vent or complain just as a disguise for my loneliness or homesickness. He was very kind and helpful to me. He always found answers when I had a problem.

Youn sonsengyim (Professor/Teacher Youn), one of my Korean language instructors at the Korean Language Institute at Seoul National University, was vivacious and inspirational. Although she was Korean, it seemed she was born or raised in the United States. She spoke perfect English. She made me to believe that I could learn the strange Korean characters. Youn sonsengyim's energy, enthusiasm and encouragement helped me to finish my language program. I owe my ability to find my way and have basic conversations in Korean in part to Youn sonsengyim's encouragement. She took interest in the success of students from different places and backgrounds across the world. She was kind and graceful.

Cho Hey On was another important friend in Seoul. She lived in Song Dong Gu Guee Dong. The gentle spirit, soft-spoken woman was always kind to me. The following three people were not my friends in the truest sense of the word. However, professionally, they took care of me while I was in Seoul. They were Rhee Yong Kuk, MD., my doctor and Jung Zun Suk, RN and Lee Chun Ja, RN, two nurses who worked with Dr. Rhee Yong Kuk. They always treated me with care. Dr. Rhee Yong Kuk's practice was located at 229-136 Noryanjin Dong.

Lynne C. Jeon was a Caucasian woman and not a Korean. However, she married a Korean whom she met in her home state of Ohio in the United States. I met Lynne at the Korean Language Institute at Seoul National University. She was an English instructor in the English Department at Hanyang University in Seoul. Lynne had been in Korea a little longer before I arrived. As a result, she taught me many things about Korean culture that she had learned. She was a great friend.

FAREWELL TO KOREA

Every good thing must come to an end. It was so when the time came to say goodbye to Korea and head on to the United States. On the surface, bidding goodbye to Korea was not supposed to be emotionally difficult as it was upon departing Liberia for Korea. After all, Mom and Dad were not in Korea with me. Neither were my sisters, relatives, and friends. But I suddenly realized that saying goodbye to Korea was not as easy as picking up my luggage, waving goodbye and getting on the plane. Instead, leaving Korea turned out to be perhaps emotionally more difficult than leaving Liberia.

Leaving Korea was more difficult because of those who cared and sought my welfare. Merely knowing them, not to mention their care and interest in my welfare, enabled me to assume their consciousness. Moreover, because I had become more than what I was when I first arrived in Korea in March 1984, bidding goodbye to Korea entailed owning everything I had made of Korea. Friends I made, places I visited, foods I ate, and personal growth I attained were a part of the person I had become at the time of leaving Korea. For example, Koreans' seeming regard of national aspirations as personal aspirations and their habitual use of "Ouree Nara" (Our country) in reference to Korea gave me a renewed sense of obligation to Liberia.

On February 3, 1986, the night before my departure for the United States, Mrs. Victoria Forh hosted a farewell party for me at her and Ambassador Forh's residence. During the party, I felt the full weight of leaving Korea. I was smiling with everyone, but inwardly, I was grieving. The people I was about to leave had become an important part of my life behind "God's back" and given me reasons to laugh and hope. Col. Cannon had wholeheartedly taken ownership of the project.[230] As we savored Scotch, he made funny jokes about me and not only spoke touchingly about his belief in me but also about his hopes in my future. Col. Cannon had become a wind beneath my wings. I bowed my head and teared for his total trust in me and for Wlah's grace.

Before the evening was over, I took time, chatted one-on-one and hugged my friends. When Kim Keong Hee said, "I hate to have known you because I will have to deal with you not being here," it felt as if someone added to the weight I was already bearing. It was an emotional night, but it was also a memorable night. Mrs. Forh prepared potato greens, one of my favorite Liberian dishes. I took the party that she hosted for me as a statement that a place had been carved in the hearts of the Forh family for me. I was leaving Korea, but Korea was never leaving my life because I owned everything I made of Korea.

On the morning of February 4, 1986, Kim Keong Hee, Mrs. Victoria Forh and little Snoti Forh took me to Kimpo International Airport. Others who went along included Mr. Sheikh A. Sheriff, a Liberian student, and Mr. Massaquoi, an official at the Liberian Embassy. After the hugs, I had to do one of the hardest things I have ever done in life—to say goodbye to Kim Keong Hee. With that, I boarded the plane for New York City via Anchorage, Alaska.

CHAPTER 23

The United States

T HE PLANE I WAS TRAVELING on from Seoul to New York
City first touched down on American soil in Anchorage, Alaska.
Upon approaching the airport, I looked through the window and saw a
snow-covered landscape surrounding the airport. At that time snow was no
more a novelty to me, but the breathtakingly peaceful, pristine, and heavenly
scenery spoke to me in the same way as the gushing water from the faucet
did in Monrovia in 1978. I left Korea, fearing the unknowns in America,
but I read the whiteness and serenity of the snow-covered landscape as
Wlah's assurance to me that all would be well in America. Moreover, in my
cultural imagination, I heard a familiar song, "Uhn gay leh pulu leh ziapa
wa uhn gay, ziapa wa uhn gay," often sung in the village upon receipt of a
newborn from "behind the house." [231] I felt like a newborn that America
was about to receive from "behind the house" to shape in some way.

As I basked in that serenity, I also wondered about what time of the
day our flight would arrive in New York City. I could not wait to get on
my next flight to Greensboro, North Carolina. I was not dying to get to
Greensboro for the sake of Greensboro. I had never been to Greensboro
and, therefore, had no attachment whatsoever to the place. But I was dying
to see my friend, Flomo. I wanted to speak Mahn, especially with Flomo
who spoke the language as if he were schooled in it. We were roughly the

272

same age, but he knew parables that elders in the culture did not know. He was a brilliant and hilarious storyteller. His hilarious stories about some of our friends who made fool of themselves were sources of much needed laughter.

Unfortunately, my wish did not happen. We arrived in New York City late in the evening to make my next flight to Greensboro. The airline arranged my stay at the Vista Hotel near the J. F. Kennedy International Airport. Sometime before 11:00 a.m. the following day, February 5, 1986, I took a cab to LaGuardia Airport, where I was supposed to board my connecting flight to Greensboro. At LaGuardia airport, I did not know where my next airline ticket counter was. I became nervous and confused. When I asked for help, someone directed me where to go. I then put the traveling bag over my left shoulder, held it in place with my left hand and carried the heavy suitcase in my right hand for quite a distance. I stopped after every ten to fifteen yards for a breather.

Upon arrival at the right airline counter, blisters were beginning to form in my right palm due to the weight of the suitcase. Even more dispiriting, I found out that my flight plan had changed. Internet, e-mails, or cellular phones were not available at the time to communicate flight schedule changes to passengers. Luckily, the airline agent who informed me of the flight schedule change directed me to the counter where I was supposed to check in, but the new check-in counter was quite a distance away. My right palm had become red and tender from carrying the suitcase to the original airline counter due to the weight of the suitcase. As a result, my first attempt to use the same strategy for carrying the suitcase did not even take me ten yards away.

THE WHITE GIRL

As I struggled to pick up my bag and suitcase after my first attempt, a white young woman about twenty years old walked up to me and said, "I'll help you." Before I looked up, she had my suitcase on her shoulder, heading to the new check-in counter. Indeed, I strongly believe that a woman can do anything a man can do. However, the young woman's boldness in lifting and carrying that heavy suitcase was uncharacteristic; it flabbergasted me. It took us at least three minutes to reach the new ticket counter. The young woman put my suitcase down, wished me well and, before I could gather my thoughts to say thank you, she vanished. I did not get her name and address for a thank you card upon arrival in Greensboro.

Emphasis on the race of the young woman who dumbfounded me at LaGuardia Airport was not an accident. Stereotypes and perceptions about white Americans, I developed particularly in Liberia were intact when I arrived in the United States on February 4, 1986. I had learned that white Americans were mean. With that, one could imagine my reaction when the white young woman picked up my suitcase and carried it for me. "How could this be? How could people who do not let others eat with them help carry someone's suitcase?" I wondered. In writing about the rise of English racism, Peter Fryer fittingly indicated that, "Specific false beliefs about other nations or other human varieties tend to be corrected, sooner or later, by observation and experience."[232] I could not have had a better experience to shake up and wipe my mind clean of my stereotypes than that encounter with the young woman in New York City. That opportunity for personal growth, instead of the Statute of Liberty, greeted me upon arrival in the United States.

In Greensboro, I reflected upon the white young woman who helped carry my luggage at LaGuardia Airport. I blamed myself for not probing quickly to get her name and address and to find out who she was. Eventually, it occurred to me that she could have been an angel. In fact, I interpreted the encounter as Wlah's way of reassuring me once more that He was with me.

GREENSBORO, NORTH CAROLINA

Finally, at about 1:00 p.m., I boarded my flight at LaGuardia Airport in New York City for the last leg of my journey to Greensboro, NC on February 5, 1986. The plane landed in Greensboro in about two hours after take-off. Prior to leaving Seoul, my friend, Flomo, indicated that he would not be available to pick me up from the airport because he would be at work at the time of my arrival.[233] As a result, he informed me that he had asked Dr. McKinley A. DeShield, Jr. to pick me up from the airport. Up until my arrival in Greensboro, everything about my travel had proceeded flawlessly.

Unfortunately, Dr. DeShield's late arrival at the airport to pick me up dampened my excitement. I waited and waited for more than three hours. Eventually, Dr. DeShield arrived. The moment he saw me, his demeanor and mood made up for his inability to be at the airport on time. He was bubbly and warm as I remembered him from Liberia. He greeted me as if he and I knew each other closely while he was in Liberia. He took me to his home on Barksdale Drive, where I waited until Flomo picked me up after work.

At Flomo's apartment on Parker Street off Wendover Avenue, he and I took stock of how much time had passed since I left him in Liberia and traveled to Korea. Indeed, a little over two years had passed. We had so much to catch up on, including what had happened in Liberia and our friends. We had all the excuses to gobble beer, talk and laugh. We caught up on all the Mahn we had not spoken in a long time. Although we were in Greensboro, NC, it felt as if we were back in Liberia. We relived the good times we had in Monrovia and thanked Wlah for being good to us.

Shortly after the joyous reunion, the reality on the ground on Parker Street started to manifest itself. For example, it soon became clear that our living arrangement was not as ideal as I expected. Flomo shared an apartment with Wilmot Gbonah and Stanley Wuo (deceased), both Mahn from Nimba County. Unlike Flomo who had a long history of friendships with Wilmot and Stanley dating to their times in Liberia, I did not know them. Long before I transferred to North Carolina A & T State University, Flomo and I communicated about my thoughts concerning the transfer. Subsequently, he told Wilmot and Stanley that Greensboro was my likely destination to study. More importantly, he asked whether they would be willing to let me share the apartment. In our next communication, Flomo indicated that Wilmot and Stanley were agreeable and did not see any problems with the proposal. Wilmot, a stout and robust man with a distinctive laughter, was the original occupant of the apartment and the one who signed the lease. Stanley and Flomo joined him later in that order. At the time Stanley and Flomo joined, Wilmot imposed a cost-sharing arrangement that, from all indications, was unfair. Apparently, since Stanley and Flomo had plans to move into their own apartments, they did not mind the arrangement Wilmot imposed because it would be temporary.

The Parker Street Greensboro apartment consisted of two bedrooms. As the original occupant, Wilmot lived in the master bedroom. When Stanley joined him, he lived in the smaller bedroom, yet they shared the cost of the apartment equally. The higher the number of occupants rose, the more egregious the arrangement became. When Flomo joined, they shared the cost of the apartment three-way and equally, yet Stanley and Flomo lived in the smaller bedroom while Wilmot was in the master bedroom alone. One can imagine the direction the apartment cost-sharing arrangement would take upon my arrival in Greensboro.

Indeed, when I joined them, we shared the cost of the apartment four-way and equally, yet Stanley, Flomo and I lived in the smaller bedroom while Wilmot stayed in the master bedroom alone. We had one single bed in the smaller room, on which the three of us lay sideways to avoid falling off. I had lived in Sanniquellie and Monrovia, where I overcame numerous obstacles. Moreover, I never let hard times stand in my way to get an education. The living arrangement I discovered in Greensboro was bleak and unfair, but the situation was not insurmountable.

During my first few weeks in the United States, I realized elephants existed in America too because one was right in our Parker Street Greensboro apartment.[234] Surprisingly, the three African men who shared the apartment with me remained silent about the elephant. I did not understand why. According to American popular culture, Africans roamed with wild animals and, as such, they were supposedly experts on wild animals. However, as soon as I recognized the apartment cost-sharing as well as living arrangement as a reflection of a mindset, one that, essentially, was a trap to make achievement of our educational goal impossible, I understood why Flomo did not make a case against the unfair arrangement.

Flomo, the only one among the three men who was in school, at the time of my arrival, attended Guilford College in Greensboro. Wilmot believed school took a long time and, therefore, was a waste of time. He had tried to persuade Flomo to postpone school to work and get a car, parading the impression that he earned more money than some college graduates. It seemed to Wilmot and Stanley like déjà vu all over again when they heard that I had come to study at North Carolina A & T State University. They had seen others come to study for their bachelors or master's degrees, but ended up quitting and doing the same, as they say in Liberia, "who want work" (dirty jobs). They shrugged off what they considered a big bluff and went about their businesses.

In the face of not being taken seriously, I took my cues from Flomo. I did not let the distractions bother me. However, the distractions did not only come from Wilmot and Stanley, the ones who never regarded me seriously, but also from within. I left Liberia with the "gravy" or "enjoyment" mindset, which made me to wish my going to Korea were postponed. Even though I spent two years in Korea, that mindset remained latent, alive, and intact, not to mention powerful. Moreover, in the United States, where I had dreamed to be, triggers to reawake that mindset abounded. For example, while cars were in no measure a novelty in Liberia, they were the magic every college graduate dreamed of getting along with a job. Indeed, there was no bigger "gravy" than a car. One did not need a dime in the pocket, but only a car to get the best-looking girls.

Upon arriving in Greensboro and seeing Wilmot and Stanley with their own cars, I admired them greatly. Wilmot's compact sedan was nice and relatively new. "He had it going" and was "enjoying" as they say in Liberia. Moreover, he had a stereo system in a well-furnished bedroom with the latest things, including a waterbed, the first one I had ever seen. As for Stanley, he had a late 1960s or early 1970s Impala with a tail section that looked as if it had been submerged in a pond for ten years. Even though Stanley's old brown gas-guzzling Impala had an ugly rotten tail section like an alligator's tail, it ran well and took him wherever he wanted to go.

Enamored by their lifestyle and the trappings of a "Good life," Wilmot did not need any effort to persuade me to get a car or seek a life of "Enjoyment." The motivations, including their cars and other niceties were powerful enough by themselves. The urge to get my own car was so strong that I seriously thought about buying a car with the funds I had to sustain me during the first semester. But Barkpor's words, "A child does not roast two rats because his attention will be on one while the other one burns," gave me a pause.[235] A graduate degree was one rat while a "good life" was the other one.[236] I voted to roast the former rat, to pursue a graduate degree. I did not want to return to Liberia without a graduate degree because Liberians were not kind to flunkies.

To their credit, Wilmot and Stanley were nice to me, at least during the first few weeks, considering that I did not know them before coming to the United States. Stanley was particularly gracious whenever I needed a ride to or from school. Moreover, we got along very well. However, as the middle of the semester neared and it became apparent that I was determined to study, things changed. No one was rude to me, but the camaraderie along with the goodwill began to wane. A request for ride often got a flat no. Their message to me, essentially, was "No pain, no gain." They were breaking their backs in doing "who want work" to live a "good life." Since I chose to get an education, I needed to figure it out on my own. In response to the changing attitudes, Flomo said, "This is America," which I took to mean that we were in America, in a different culture.[237] In other words, we were not in Liberia anymore, where the community has a role in contributing to a child's education because an "educated child" does not belong only to its family, but also to the community. In any case, I was grateful to Wilmot and Stanley for their help.

THE GREENSBORO LIBERIAN COMMUNITY

Rumors are oxygen in Liberia. There is nothing out of the ordinary about them when they start in Liberian communities elsewhere. Sometimes they come out of the thin air and, at other times, they have a spark. Moreover, rumors in Liberia have something in common with the belief in witchcraft, which, as indicated elsewhere in this book, is the cause of any unexplainable occurrences. "White man got witch" is what villagers often say upon seeing jet airliners flying at high altitudes because they do not know or understand Bernoulli's principle.[238] There must be a reason, usually a sinister one like witchcraft, if, for example, someone dies of an unexplainable cause.

Rumors about me started when some members of the Greensboro Liberian community wondered about the source of funding for my studies at North Carolina A & T State University. Since no one knew the answer, one had to be fabricated. The rumor was that I was a member of Liberian President Samuel Doe's intelligence service, conducting a clandestine operation for the Doe government. I had been stationed in Greensboro to collect intelligence on the activities of Liberian government opponents in the area. In short, Doe's security was bankrolling my graduate education. Wlah was my vindication because He knew the only employment, I had in Liberia prior to traveling to Korea and then to the United States was my service with the University of Liberia as a teaching assistant.

To the Greensboro Liberian community rumormongers' credit, the rumor about me did not come out of the thin air. Instead, it had a spark, which was, for all intent and purposes, frivolous. In other words, the scandalmongers were looking for a frame to make up a story and I gave them a perfect opportunity. That opportunity arose when Flomo and I were having transportation difficulties getting to and from school and work. Flomo was working at the International House of Pancake (IHOP), saving part of his earnings to buy a car to help alleviate the problem.[239] A few months later, when Flomo bought a used red 1982 four-door Lada sedan, a Russian-made, it only proved how much we knew about cars. He was always under the hood because the car broke down frequently. If it were not the battery, it was something else. It was a disaster, but as Flomo's first car with which he had a first love type of attachment, he would not let it go.

Flomo juggled work, attending classes and picking me up from school, not to mention the stress of dealing with an unpredictable car. To lighten his burden, I decided to buy a set of walkie-talkies he and I saw at RadioShack. The idea was to use the walkie-talkie to call Flomo only when I was ready to leave campus. In that way, he would avoid coming and waiting and have time to rest after a hard day's work. The walkie-talkies had long antennae like kids' toys, but I only cared if they were able to send and receive signals. Flomo had one and I had the other. As it turned out, those suckers did not work as we expected, and we left them at home.

The frivolous aspect of the walkie-talkie incident was my secondary motivation for buying the set. I wanted to fulfill a fantasy. Immediately following the April 12, 1980 "Revolution" in Liberia, walkie-talkies became the principal means of communication among the military elite and government officials. Walkie-talkies were more than a tool for communication. They were a status symbol. In Liberia, status and style matter. In 1980, I was not far removed from high school, where I was like most other young people, wanting to be "cool" and absorbing influences. Style and status "things," which included platform shoes, bell-bottom pants, and Afro hairdos mattered to me too.

In Monrovia, at the time of the 1980 "Revolution," my exposure to the influences of the new era was a given. I was particularly enamored by immaculately dressed military officers, other security officers and the "big shots," especially when they carried their walkie-talkies. It was a fascinating time and I sometimes wished I were one of the officials. More importantly, the soldiers and other officials with the walkie-talkies had no problems getting the best-looking women. Even though I did not buy the set of walkie-talkies to get girls, having the equipment to communicate with Flomo provided an opportunity to fulfill a fantasy. That is how I helped the rumormongers to smear me.

Unfortunately, while I was trying to make it convenient for Flomo to pick me up from school and fulfill a fantasy from the time of the 1980 Liberian "Revolution," some Greensboro Liberian community members were making me into someone I was not. Those who did not know me had their minds made up about how I was financing my studies. The walkie-talkies were evidence that I worked for the Samuel Doe security network in Liberia. Of course, I was not and had never been a member of Doe's security or any other security network in Liberia.

JEFFERSON COUNTRY CLUB

Contrary to rumors in Greensboro that Samuel Doe's security was financing my education, money from my allowance I saved in Korea and funds I received from the University of Liberia and Dr. Cyrenius N. Forh paid for my living expenses and first semester at North Carolina A & T State University.[240] Moreover, two other sources of funds included a graduate assistantship, which applied directly to my tuition and a work-study at the Student Union Building, which covered my contribution to the rent and other costs at the Parker Street apartment. After I depleted the funds from Korea, I had to take an off-campus job. Upon the advice of Forrest, a friend, I applied at Jefferson Country Club and got hired.

On the first day we entered the Jefferson Country Club property and meandered on the winding road to the clubhouse at the back of the magnificent facility for work, I knew I was in for an experience. There were no signs that read "No Colored Allowed," but, after scanning the sea of faces in the clubhouse, no one needed to tell me that the facility was exclusive and for the rich. Except for a few of us who washed the dishes and cleaned the tables, everyone I saw dining at the clubhouse was white. At no time did anyone treat me poorly or discriminate against me. Each day, before we started work, our supervisor fed us with some of the same foods we served at the clubhouse, not to mention the courtesies he accorded us.

On the first day of work, the supervisor assigned me to work along with a Caucasian young woman who was cleaning tables and taking dishes away. Even though I was not ashamed to do that kind of work, I had not worked in a restaurant before, not to mention an exclusive country club. The supervisor took me to my area of assignment and showed me what the young woman was doing. The first thing that caught my attention was the food. Customers ordered large quantities of expensive foods and ate only a fraction. In my mind, that kind of waste was clearly a sin. The scene triggered flashbacks from my hunger days at St. Mary's School in Sanniquellie and at the University of Liberia in Monrovia.

Then, for a moment, when it seemed like all eyes were staring at me, the young woman who had apparently been doing that kind of work for some time, picked up her pace and moved between the tables so fast as if she were on roller blades. Because I had come to help clean tables and take dishes away, I expected the young woman to slow down and greet me, but that did not happen. Instead, she went by swiftly, looking not particularly happy. Forrest later explained to me that the young woman was having an "attitude" to protect her turf. She thought I was eyeing tips customers left her on the tables, but I did not even know about tips. I would not have taken any money had I seen it.

In the meantime, the stares, which made me feel as though someone were saying, "You do not belong here," made me to rethink my assignment. I remember telling myself, "This is not my kind of job. I rather sweep the streets." As a result, after my first day on the job, without giving any reasons, I asked the supervisor to reassign me to the dishwasher and he did. I continued to work at the country club for a few weeks until I ran into transportation problems. Since I did not have a car, I depended on Forrest to get to and from work and when he quit, I had to quit the job as well.

McNair Hall

Not too long after I quit the job at Jefferson Country Club, I found work that involved hauling mixed concrete in a wheelbarrow and performing other unskilled work as assigned. At the time I was doing that menial job, I did not recognize its significance. Looking back, however, a tragic and big historic event, which occurred seven days before I boarded a Korean Airlines flight from Seoul to the United States, gave meaning to that menial job that I did in 1986. That tragic historic event was the explosion of the Space Shuttle Challenger on January 28, 1986, killing all seven crew members. On that day, President Ronald Reagan made a short, yet memorable speech to the nation. "…we will never forget them nor the last time we saw them this morning as they prepared for their journey and waved goodbye and slipped the surly bounds of earth to touch the face of God." As I left Korea on February 4, 1986, and headed for the United States, I had no clue that I was going to play a small, yet meaningful part in remembrance of one of the astronauts who died in the Space Shuttle Challenger disaster.

Upon enrolling at North Carolina A & T State University, I discovered that Dr. Ronald McNair, the African American astronaut who died with six other crews during the Space Shuttle Challenger disaster, was a graduate of the institution. In 1986, when construction work started on the Engineering Building, which was named after Dr. McNair, John Berne of Middlesex, NC, the architect, or construction manager, hired me as a laborer. At the time, doing the job was all about survival. However, upon reflection today, a new meaning has emerged that connected me to the crew of the Space Shuttle Challenger who died on January 28, 1986. That connection was the small, but meaningful role I played in the construction of the Engineering Building at North Carolina A & T, named after Dr. McNair with his statue positioned before it.

ELWOOD 'ROCK' EDWARDS

Meanwhile it did not take too long for evidence of Col. Carl Cannon's decision to sway me toward North Carolina A & T State University to show. Once I arrived in Greensboro in February 1986, I wasted no time in contacting Mr. Edwards. The way he received me spoke volumes about him and what he thought about Col. Cannon. He told me if I were the one Carl spoke to him about, I was good to go. He accepted me as if he knew who I was.

Aside from Rock's employment with North Carolina A & T State University, he was also a prominent and well-connected citizen of Greensboro. Moreover, he ran his own courier business. He helped me get the work-study job in the Student Union Building, working with Clyde in the games room. Rock also visited with me at our Parker Street apartment occasionally and dropped bags of assorted foods for us. On one occasion, Flomo said, "What manner of man is this Mr. Edwards?" He thought it was out of the ordinary for someone to take interest in other people's children who had come from Africa to a foreign land to acquire an education. But that was precisely why Col. Cannon made me to choose North Carolina A & T State University over Washington State University. Every time I had an experience like that, I thought about Mom's incessant prayers to which I have repeatedly alluded.

AVALON ROAD

Flomo and I had conversations about moving out of the Parker Street apartment without hesitation once we had the means to do so. The time to move out came after we found apartment 411-B on Avalon Road at the end of 1986. Despite what we considered an unfair living arrangement at the Parker Street apartment, we never let our relationships with Wilmot and Stanley deteriorate. On many occasions, we invited them to eat with us, especially GB, our favorite dish. Thereafter, we drank beer, told funny stories, and laughed.

FOOD STAMPS

Flomo and I grew up in Nimba County and attended high school in Sanniquellie, Liberia. Even though Flomo attended public school while I attended private school, our experiences were similar, particularly with respect to hunger in Sanniquellie, where we learned how to survive.[241] After high school, we took different paths. He enrolled at the Tubman National Institute of Medical Arts (TNIMA) while I went to the University of Liberia. Our common experience with hunger in Sanniquellie and Monrovia as well as our struggles to get an education played a role in how we related to Dillon, another Liberian we met studying at North Carolina A & T State University.[242] Dillon lived with his family in Wilkesboro, NC, about 83 miles away. He commuted from Wilkesboro to Greensboro for classes and visited with us occasionally at the Parker Street apartment.

Dillon was nice and very funny. During those occasional visits, we shared whatever we had with him without expecting anything in return. After we moved out of the Parker Street apartment, Dillon continued to visit with us at 411-B Avalon Road. On one occasion, he spent the weekend with us because he had a lot of assignments to do and making the 80 plus-mile commute back home would have been a lot of stress. Flomo and I were very happy to accommodate Dillon because, like us, he was struggling to get an education. During the weekend Dillon spent with us, he did something we did not expect or ask. He felt he needed to reciprocate our kindness. Sometime mid-morning on a Saturday, Dillon took us to the Food Lion on Market Street to buy groceries.

After Dillon picked up different food items and filled the cart, we made our way toward the checkout counter. He was ahead, I was next, pushing the cart while Flomo was behind me. It seemed Flomo had a sense of what Dillon had up his sleeves. I was busy pushing the cart and paid little attention to anyone's body language. The cashier, an African American young woman, scanned all the food items and, thereafter, Dillon took a stack of food stamps out of his pocket and handed it to her. In no time, Flomo flew by me toward the cashier while shouting "No, no, no Dillon, please don't do that!" He told the cashier to return the food stamps to Dillon and she did. Flomo then took out forty dollars from his wallet and gave it to the young woman to pay for the groceries.

The Food Lion incident was a matter of pride, but not vain pride. Flomo did not want Dillon to pay for the food with food stamps because we shopped for our groceries at that Food Lion on Market Street. The workers and cashiers there knew us as the African students who shopped there regularly. Flomo thought we might be stigmatized as the strong African students who lived off the system even though they could work and feed themselves.[243] I shared Flomo's view. However, neither he nor I felt so from a place of arrogance. We were not any better than those who were on welfare. We felt welfare was meant for those who could not or were unable to help themselves; people who had fallen through the cracks. We were strong young men who could take odd jobs and, in fact, had odd jobs, which enabled us to earn money to feed ourselves. Personally, I dreaded welfare or food stamps for other reasons beyond stigmatization. I was afraid of food stamps because I felt doing so would extinguish my inner drive. For the same reason, I ended up abandoning follow-up of an unemployment compensation claim a friend persuaded me to submit in Wadesboro, North Carolina in 1991 because I perceived it as a handout.

Our pride did not arise in a vacuum. We were keenly aware of negative sentiments about Africans in the United States. Moreover, we frequently ran into widespread and deeply held perceptions or stereotypes of Africa and Africans. "How is it over there?" "Over there" meaning Africa as if Africa is a country. "Do you all live in houses or trees?" "Do you all wear clothes like these over there?" "Do you all live in a village?" "Are you a member of a tribe?" "Do you all have cars?" and so on. To our dismay, we ran into questions like these from supposedly informed people. It was a reality that we had no control over; a reality that we could not change. However, we were determined not to add to that reality with our conduct; we did not want to prove right anybody who held distorted perceptions of Africa and Africans. For the record, I come from a village in Liberia and belong to a tribe, the Mahn tribe. I learned the value of work early and my bias for work is, in part, cultural because, in Mahn country, an able-bodied man is not highly regarded if he does not work to feed his family.[244] My bias for work was also spiritual because work kept me close to Wlah.

In the United States, the welfare or food stamps program is important and necessary. If I became permanently disabled or fall through the crack, I would take food stamps. That is the purpose for which the program was intended. I remember former U.S. President Ronald Reagan's portrayal of welfare or food stamps recipients in the 1980s. The view I expressed in this publication about the welfare or food stamps program is not a tacit approval of Reagan's portrayal of welfare or food stamps recipients because his life experience was quite different from mine. I came to this view from a different experience, an African experience. The notion of "pulling oneself up by the bootstraps" flies in the face of my own life story. Even though by virtue of culture, Liberia is a welfare society, there is no institutional welfare system as we know it in the United States. Those of us who left our villages and towns and traveled far away to places like Sanniquellie, Gbarnga, Voinjama, Zwedru, and Monrovia to attend schools, for example, survived on help beyond our parents' support. Total strangers helped us, too. We left our homes sometimes depending only on our moms' prayers and believing that Wlah would never let us die from hunger. In pursuing my studies at North Carolina A & T State University in Greensboro, and ten years later at Gonzaga University in Spokane, Washington, total strangers helped me to succeed as well.

CHAPTER 24

The Call of Home

I LOOKED FORWARD TO GRADUATION DAY, May 3, 1987, at North Carolina A & T State University with great excitement. My excitement stemmed not merely from the prospect of graduating and returning home to Liberia, but also from a desire to fulfill an unmet need. On a previous graduation day, December 4, 1977, at St. Mary's School in Sanniquellie, my mom, sisters and extended family came to show their love and to share in the joy of the first fruit of their investment. Bursonnon Tulu, along with friends and well-wishers, came in full support and graced the occasion festively at the William V. S. Tubman Birthday Hall in Sanniquellie.[245] Despite the festive atmosphere on that day, Dad's noticeable absence put an unforgettable damper on the celebrations. I was sad because Dad was not present, but I was not sad for myself. Instead, I was sad for Dad. I loved him dearly and always wanted to prove to him that I was a worthy son, a son to be proud of. I never heard any reasons why he did not attend my graduation. I was disappointed, but I never complained.

Mom and Dad emphasized education to avoid their fate. Indeed, graduation for me was about reaping the rewards of heeding their advice and doing what they expected me to do. I was looking forward to making them proud, as a way of acknowledging their labor, sacrifices and encouragement in achieving my goal. In addition, I looked forward to reaping the joy of

286

accomplishing something. Still further, graduation was also a momentary occasion of freedom to escape, to be a child again, to bask and to share in the love of family and friends. In that respect, my high school graduation did not pass the muster. I did not reap the full inner joy I expected because Dad did not attend. As a result, I always looked forward to another similar opportunity to make up for that unfulfilled moment of joy with him.

A latent motivation for enrolling at the University of Liberia was to have another chance at a graduation, perhaps a grander one, but February 16, 1983, graduation day at the University of Liberia, was far from a make-up. It turned out to be doubly disappointing because Dad did not attend again, thus robbing me of another opportunity to thank and appreciate him publicly.[246] Through it all, Mom, my "Go-to," helped me weather the disappointments. The joy with which she beamed, soothed my aching heart and reassured me. Despite failing to show up for my graduation two times in a row, I loved my Dad with the same intensity as before because throughout my childhood he never showed a streak of meanness.

As May 3, 1987, neared, that botched February 1983 University of Liberia graduation remained etched in my mind. I was not looking forward to any redemption because Mom and Dad were not in Greensboro. I did not expect them to be there. Yet I looked forward to my graduation from North Carolina A & T State University with eagerness. Flomo, Emmanuel Kaye, and his wife, Dainnie Wheeler Kaye, were the three people who attended my graduation at the Greensboro Coliseum on May 3, 1987. I did not hold anything against Dad in 1977 and 1983 and had no intention of doing so for not being in Greensboro, North Carolina, where the probability of his coming was zero. In fact, the Atlantic Ocean, which separated Dad and me because he could not swim that vast ocean was a perfect excuse for my Dad's inability to be at my graduation for the third time.

Mom and Dad were not physically present with me in Greensboro on the day of my graduation, but they were with me in spirit. Upon exiting the Greensboro Coliseum at the end of the ceremony with a Master of Science (MS) degree in Agricultural Education, Emmanuel Kaye and his wife, Dainnie Wheeler Kaye, congratulated me warmly. Moreover, in great excitement and joy, Flomo embraced me tightly and lifted me off the ground. I was afraid I was going to fall. His embrace seemed to have done the trick because I felt the unusual excitement and expression of joy parents usually exhibit at graduations that more than often get their children cringing. Momentarily, I felt like I had been lifted by my dad. I felt like I had made him happy. Flomo's thrilling embrace meant a whole lot to me.

THE PULL FACTORS

Immediately after graduation, returning to Liberia became my focus. I had been away from my family for almost four years, something I never imagined. The imageries of St. Mary's and the Eden-like village etched in my mind took on a new life and made Liberia's pull on me irresistible. I imagined being on a thrilling excursion at St. Mary's School in Sanniquellie. I not only looked at, admired, and talked with beautiful girls at ease, but also displayed a vain impulse that I once was reticent to show. I had returned to claim a reward because an adult once advised me to put chasing girls on the backburner and focus on my education. Upon completion of my education, as he put it, "You will get the best-looking girls." Of course, at the time, I took the advice to be "utter nonsense." Moreover, during that imaginary visit to St. Mary's School, I saw myself as a "chosen one" in the same way as others and I once regarded those who studied in the United States and returned home.

Besides the frivolous as well as sentimental reasons for looking forward to returning to Liberia, I wanted to see my parents badly. In addition, I wanted to return home to find a bride, marry and establish my own family; a family like that of my parents' as well as Mr. William Walker's. I wanted to create wonderful childhood experiences for my children, like those my parents had provided for me. Moreover, I wanted to apply all the great examples I had learned from Dr. Cyrenius Forh and Colonel Carl H. Cannon.

The purpose of setting out on the journey on the winding road that took me to Greensboro, NC was not only a pull factor, but also an obligation. Professor Eric Eastman recommended me to study in Korea. He counted on me to finish my studies and return home to join the faculty of the University of Liberia. I wanted to vindicate him; to show that I was dependable. In short, I felt a sense of duty to return to Liberia to fulfill my obligations to the University of Liberia.

Aside from the reasons I have given for returning to Liberia in May 1987, other factors made that decision easy. The time I spent in Korea as well as the ethos that enabled the country's rise from the ashes of the Korean War to the economic powerhouse it has become today, almost in a twinkle of an eye, was a factor. I do not know what Koreans have in their hearts when they invoke "Haniyim" (God). However, while I was in Seoul, they not only worshipped in splendid churches, but also exercised unusual restraints. I did not understand political issues that prompted daily student demonstrations on the Kwanak campus of Seoul National University and elsewhere in 1984 and 1985. Riot police inundated the campus daily like rising sea, yet, to my knowledge, no incidents of government suppression of student protest came close to "Move or be removed."[247] The place "Kajook" (family) holds in Korean life and their love of country are two influences I absorbed.

My idealism and Dr. Forh's reawakening of my patriotism influenced my return to Liberia in 1987. I did not merely want to return to the University of Liberia to fulfill my obligations, but also wanted to give back what others like Mr. William Walker gave me when I attended school in Sanniquellie. His mere presence was a gift from which I benefited. He was an example to whom I looked up. I believed my turn had come to contribute to the development of Liberia because I took President Tolbert's repeated reference to others and me as his "precious jewels" literally. If I were a "precious jewel," then I had a value that the country would need. I wanted to return to Liberia to show that Tolbert's words meant something.

THE COUNTER-PULL FACTORS

Some equally powerful forces in the United States acted against my desire to return to Liberia. I had always harbored a desire to pursue a terminal degree. So, when I faced a choice between accepting an opportunity to study at Pennsylvania State University and returning to Liberia, I found myself between a rock and a hard place. Aside from the indirect peer pressure to pursue the American dream, meaning to stay in the United States, work and live large as other Liberians were doing, I had not abandoned my own idea of living large. My understanding of the American dream was from a Liberian perspective, which was, enjoying the "gravy" on a grander scale. In Liberia, that was one reason why everyone was dying for an opportunity to go to the United States. Most Liberians who traveled to the United States to study stayed to build their lives. When I talked about returning to Liberia, some Liberians in Greensboro were baffled because they expected me to stay to do what everyone was doing.

Perhaps a serendipitous encounter with Mekaneh, a Liberian woman, in a Washington, D.C. suburb presented the most challenge to my desire to return to Liberia.[248] Prior to meeting, I did not know Mekaneh in Liberia or in the United States. At the time of meeting, the stars had already aligned. A week or two earlier, Uncle George had arranged a one-way ticket for my return to Liberia. I was scheduled to leave New York City on the evening of Saturday May 23, 1987.

Mekaneh was not a part of my agenda as I mapped out my trip from Greensboro to New York City within the days between May 3rd and 23rd, 1987. Visiting with Col. Cannon, on the other hand, was a part of my plans because we had not seen each other for quite some time. I thought the days between May 3rd and 23rd were an excellent opportunity to spend some time together before returning to Liberia. Col. Cannon not only welcomed the idea but was also excited. He picked me up from the Amtrak station near Alexandra, Virginia. Thereafter, I stayed with him and Dr. Cannon in Annandale, Virginia for a little over a week before continuing my journey to New York City.

While at the home of the Cannons in Annandale, I called an old friend in the Washington, D.C.-Maryland area. During our conversation, he told me about a Liberian celebration in Silver Spring, Maryland, that evening. "After all, I have finished my studies. What better time to have fun?" I wondered. Recalling Liberians' adeptness at throwing parties, I could not resist the urge to go to Silver Spring to hang out with my friend. I had my North Carolina driver's license but figuring out my way through the complicated maze of road network in the Washington, D.C., suburb was a challenge. However, I mustered the courage, wrote the directions down on a piece of paper and drove Col. Cannon's big, long and exquisitely comfortable beige 1974 Ford Thunderbird to Silver Spring. I was nervous because I was afraid to lose my way. Luckily, that did not happen.

At the party, my friend took me around to see some of our old friends from Liberia, at which time I saw Mekaneh. I asked her for a dance and, thereafter, had a lengthy conversation. Afterwards, she invited me to see her house. Mekaneh drove what appeared to be a grayish white Toyota sedan while I followed in Col. Cannon's Thunderbird. Upon entering her big immaculately furnished house situated in a plush well-manicured neighborhood, I was stunned. I saw Mekaneh's two children, a little girl about five years old and a little boy about three years old. Instinctively, Mekaneh noticed my uneasiness. Perhaps she figured I was thinking that a woman with two little children living in a fabulous house like that must have a man. Apparently to allay my anxieties, she voluntarily offered information on the children's dad. Mekaneh was exquisitely beautiful, not married and one of the calmest people I have ever known, not to mention her inviting and reassuring voice and smile. She was intelligent, unassuming, yet exuded an indescribable aura of confidence. It was déjà vu even though we were meeting for the first time.

Despite everything Mekaneh did to reassure me, my antennae remained up throughout my time at her house because I had reasons to be in that state of mind. As Mom's only son, as they say in Liberia, the "only egg in her basket," I was seldom reckless. In addition, I recalled Proverbs 6:34, "For jealousy arouses a husband's fury, and he will show no mercy when he takes revenge." Even without the lesson of Proverbs 6:34, in Liberia, I had seen men take revenge based on mere suspicions, let alone upon discovering another man in their homes. I did not want to be in any man's home behind his back.

With Mekaneh's calming and reassuring voice and smile, the moment I did not expect arrived. She put her hands around me while standing, looked straight into my eyes, and asked, "Why do you want to return to Liberia, why don't you stay?" Mekaneh was far more sophisticated than I was. I did not think she would consider me as worthy of her status. So, I was caught off guard. An outright "no" was not a tactful way to respond. I had to figure out a quick, convincing, and tactful response. I tried to talk about my mom, the fact that I had not seen her in almost four years, but she suggested we could work on bringing her to the United States. I was not so stupid as to tell Mekaneh that one of my primary goals for returning to Liberia was to marry. Had I done so, I would have had a difficult time to make up another excuse if she had said, "Well, here I am, marry me." Internally, I was already grappling with that proposition. "Well, Marsilius, here is an educated woman with everything you ever dreamed of; why not stay and figure out what could be worked out in terms of a relationship?" I soliloquized quietly to myself. Mekaneh seemed like a good woman. Under normal circumstances, I would have taken the chance to stay to get to know her. However, I reckoned staying and getting involved with Mekaneh would have meant permanently standing in the shadow of the man who fathered her two young children. Inasmuch as I felt strongly attracted to Mekaneh, I was afraid. I decided to return to Liberia, instead.

Twenty United States Dollars

With the decision to return to Liberia, the only thing that stood between the airline and me was the Annandale, Virginia-Manhattan, New York City leg of my trip. However, because I was leaving Annandale on Friday, May 22, 1987, and my flight to Monrovia was scheduled to leave New York City the next day, I had to find accommodation in New York City. Unfortunately, I did not have enough money to pay for hotel accommodation, but my friend and high school classmate, Saye Lorluo Garmie, lived in Manhattan. I was not disappointed when I called Saye. He agreed to pick me up from the Amtrak Station in New York City, lodge me and then take me to the John F. Kennedy Airport the following day for my flight to Liberia.[249]

During the evening of the day before my departure for New York City, Col. Cannon had some concerns about my returning to Liberia, but I remember not having lost an opportunity to provide all the answers and assurances that all would be well. He realized that nothing he could say would change my mind about returning to Liberia. I assured him that I would stay in touch with him. On May 22, 1987, Col. Cannon dropped me off at the Amtrak Station in Alexandra, Virginia. We hugged and said goodbye.

Upon arrival in New York City, Saye picked me up from the train station. I spent the night with him. May 23, 1987, the day I had been looking forward to all that time finally arrived. The time had come to depart the United States. With me were a little suitcase, a cardboard box containing my books and papers and twenty dollars in my wallet. Saye dropped me off at the John F. Kennedy Airport in the evening. As with Col. Cannon the day before, Saye and I hugged and said goodbye. Thereafter, I checked in, went through security, and left that evening on an Air Afrique Flight directly to Monrovia.

Herbert Tonnel

Upon arrival at the Roberts' International Airport (RIA), my longtime friend, Herbert Tonnel (deceased), was waiting for me. He agreed to pick me up after he and Uncle George had discussed my arrival. Herbert was one of the friends who made returning to Liberia something I had to do. He was exceptionally brilliant. In addition to his heart being in the right place, he saw my success as his success. He was a force in that his smile and laughter alone were enough to fill me. He greeted me with a bear-hug and a broad smile, interrupted only by his characteristic deep and slow voice.

As the Liberian custom officers seemed disappointed that I did not have anything of importance for them to rummage through, Herbert and I quickly made our way out of customs with my suitcase and cardboard box containing my books and papers and headed along the Roberts' Field-Monrovia Highway. As we approached the ELWA area, traffic was extremely congested, and I wondered what had happened. Herbert told me that the Ivory Coast national soccer team was playing the Liberian national soccer team, the Lone Star, on that Sunday. We made our way through the heavy traffic and came to ELWA Junction, where we took the way to the Red Light in Paynesville and then drove to Gardnersville, where Uncle George and his family lived.

Immediately upon arrival in Monrovia, my first order of business was not finding and hugging my parents and children. One would have expected me to do just that because I had indicated that they were a principal reason for my return to Liberia. They mattered so much as I had indicated, but they were not in Monrovia. Instead, the children were 207 miles away in Sanniquellie while Mom and Dad were further beyond in the village. One would have also expected that I might try to find an old girlfriend to reconnect with after spending almost four years away, but that was not the case with me. With my parents and children far away in Nimba County, the only thing that occupied my mind was my friends, mainly Blemie and Philip. As a result, as soon as we arrived at Uncle George's house in Gardnersville, I decided to go to Sinkor 14th Street to find Blemie and Philip. Even though I was hungry, I did not even wait to get something to eat. That was how badly I wanted to see my friends whom I had missed for so long.

I had my North Carolina driver's license and felt an urge to drive, but Herbert persuaded me to let him drive. We took Uncle George's newly assigned 505 Peugeot sedan and headed out along the same route that brought us to Gardnersville. At the Red Light, we turned right and drove towards ELWA Junction. By the time we arrived at the ELWA Junction, the soccer match between Liberia and the Ivory Coast had ended. Moreover, Liberia lost the match. Angry that the referees cheated Liberia, spectators took their frustrations on innocent people and their properties, including vehicles. Unfortunately, Uncle George's vehicle was one of those that the angry spectators wrecked. Out of nowhere, right at the ELWA Junction, a large boulder flew towards us and landed on the windshield. It crushed it completely. Luckily, the boulder did not go through the windshield to hit either one of us. We continued because the angry mob would have beaten and injured us had we stopped. We arrived at Sinkor 14th Street and discovered that only Blemie, along with his fiancée, Sunday Zarwolo, lived at our old place. Philip had long since moved out and was living somewhere else in Monrovia. I remember the reception from Blemie as bland, but he was no stranger to me. Everyone else around the neighborhood who remembered me seemed excited to see me come back home.

At the end of our visit, we returned to Uncle George's house in Gardnersville. I felt terrible on the drive back for an obvious reason. I was responsible for the damage to Uncle George's vehicle. Had I arrested the urge to see my friends and waited until the following day, the vehicle would not have been damaged. Upon reaching home, Uncle George did not say anything verbally about the vehicle. However, his body language showed that he was not particularly happy about my decision to visit with my friends immediately upon arrival. The next day, he sent the vehicle to the garage for windshield replacement. Luckily, it sustained no other damages except the broken windshield. I regretted the pain I caused Uncle George. I do not know whether I would have handled the matter quietly as he did if I were in his shoes.

The other issue that troubled me along the drive back home was the price I continued to pay for maintaining the friendship, particularly with Blemie. I had him and a few other friends high up on the list of friends in my heart. Over the years, from every indication, I realized that I was certainly not high up on the lists of friends in their hearts. Initially, I did not see that problem as mine. Instead, I tried to find faults with those friends, believing that something might have been wrong with them for failing to see my importance in their lives. Eventually, a friend helped me to see what should have been obvious from the get-go. The problem was not my friends' problem. Instead, it was mine. As that friend put it, my attachments to those friends were my creations. They were a sense of my own importance and its relevance in their lives. The truth was that those friends did not see me as I saw myself. I was not relevant in their lives as I perceived myself to be. Accepting that reality along with weaning myself emotionally from those friends was a significant personal growth and an important aspect of becoming a happier person.

Back at the University of Liberia

During the week of Sunday May 24, 1987, I went to the Capitol Hill campus of the University of Liberia and reported that I had returned. At that time the University of Liberia still had its prestige. Its infrastructure, faculty and staff had not been decimated as it happened during the civil war. All was not perfect, but a system was in place for all returnees from study leave to receive what was then called a "resettlement" allowance. The amount was $500 United States dollars. I needed that money badly and appreciated receiving it because I only had $20 United States dollars in my pocket upon my arrival in Liberia. Aside from the resettlement allowance, an office space was given to me in the William V.S. Tubman Teachers' College on the Capitol Hill campus in Monrovia.

While still in Monrovia, I remembered friends and others who had not only been supportive of me, but also celebrated my leaving to study abroad. Thoughts about their words of encouragement, offering me a place to sleep, giving me a plate of cassava leaf and rice to eat, not to mention French bread with mayonnaise to eat, sustained me during my low points while I was away in Seoul, Korea and in the United States. During the weeks before I traveled to the village, I made rounds in Monrovia to check in with those friends and supporters to show my gratitude.

Eventually, the time for returning to Sanniquellie and to the village arrived. Even though no one in Sanniquellie or in the village was definitively sure that I had returned to Liberia, rumor had circulated and reached Sanniquellie and the village that I had come back to Liberia. The restlessness was not only in Sanniquellie and in the village where my children and parents lived, respectively, but also in Monrovia. I could not wait any longer. Each day leading up to the date of my travel to Sanniquellie and to the village seemed longer. I wanted to hug my children and parents. In addition, I wanted to tell them about my experience in Korea and in the United States. In a sense, I was like a child growing up during my early years who would run home with a penny, nickel, or another child's missing toy found on the playground in excitement to show it to Mom and Dad. Leaving home and returning with a master's degree was like finding a penny, nickel, or dime on the playground. I wanted to run back home to show the degree and share the excitement with my family.

On the day I traveled to Sanniquellie, my friend, Herbert Tonnel, went along. We took a taxi from Gardnersville to the Nimba parking station near the intersection of Johnson and Water Streets in Monrovia. Upon arrival at the parking station, without much thought, I did something others had done to me many times before. The taxi we saw at the parking station traveling to Nimba County already had passengers who had taken their seats. However, two seats were still unoccupied. In addition to my fear of reaching Sanniquellie at night, I did not want to be sandwiched by other passengers as four people sat in the back. As a result, I approached the taxi driver and asked how much money he would earn with a full load of passengers. Upon his response, I told him that I would double the amount if he agreed to take only Herbert and me. Blown out of the water with the windfall, the taxi driver looked into my eyes intensely, smiled broadly and then said, "Yes sir, "Boss man." [250] In no time, he turned to the passengers who had already taken their seats and told them that his vehicle had been chartered. With a little better financial situation, I technically strong-armed the passengers who had already taken their seats. Like me, they were trying to reach their families, but capitalism worked against them because they did not have the financial means to compete. Even though I did not set out to disrupt the other passengers' travel plans, my fear as well as impatience to see my family blinded me from seeing anything out of the ordinary about using the few dollars I had to my utmost advantage.

We departed Monrovia with four passengers including the driver. The fourth passenger was an elderly woman, traveling to Ganta, about 30 miles before Sanniquellie. I allowed the elderly woman to travel with us and paid her way because she reminded me of my Mom. Upon arrival in Ganta, I not only felt the liberation of a familiar territory, but also sensed the nearness of Sanniquellie. Still wide and lined on both sides by the same Lebanese stores from the time of my childhood, the Monrovia-Yekepa highway, the principal street of the city, had not changed in any significant way. Motorists plied the street in both directions while scores of pedestrians crossed anywhere along the street once it was safe to do so. We made a brief stop to drop off the elderly woman who was traveling with us. She attempted to pay the driver, but I told her that I had already paid her fare. I remember telling her to use the money she intended to pay the driver for salt and "chicken soup" (bouillon cube). She looked startled and thankful.

After we dropped the elderly woman off, I urged Herbert to move into the front seat while I remained in the backseat. Both of us rode in the backseat from Monrovia to Ganta while the elderly woman was in the front with the driver. We wanted to sit next to one another to talk and laugh. Shortly after we resumed the journey, we drove by the Ganta United Methodist Mission and hospital complex, where, as a kid, I was enamored by the meticulously manicured landscape. Even though Herbert and I continued our conversations and laughter, I was reminiscing about my connections to the places we were driving through. Herbert did not know about those connections until 1999.[251]

As we passed the Methodist Mission, I looked left and right to find important landmarks of my childhood, including the road to the leper colony and the place where lepers made Liberian or African wooden sculptures near Wuopa. Not every thought pertained to memories of my idyllic early childhood in the area. As soon as we passed the African sculpture stand, I recalled my daring escape from jail in Ganta in 1973. I had been wrongly taken there the night before following an incident in Dingamon involving a crowd stoning a pickup truck with passengers.

ARRIVAL IN SANNIQUELLIE

While away in Korea and in the United States, I created images of Lila, Wonkermie and Oretha; images of how big and active they would be upon my return to Liberia. As the driver approached Sanniquellie, I descended into deep thoughts and played a virtual two-player game about the images of the children. The players were an "Optimistic Marsilius" who expected significant growth and a "Skeptical Marsilius" who thought that changes in the children might not be readily noticeable. Upon arrival, those images and the virtual game heightened my anxieties. Over three years had elapsed since I last saw them. It was obvious that there would be significant changes in the children, but I was not definitively sure. I was in a competition with myself and could not wait to compare them with their images in my head. I wanted to beat "Skeptical Marsilius" badly. Amid the anxieties, questions like "Would they remember me? How would they react upon seeing me?" swirled in my head. All my apprehensions quickly dissipated as soon as I saw Lila running with both arms opened to embrace me. Oretha, who did not want to be second in the race to reach and get the big hug, was only a few yards behind her. They were not expecting me. It was a pleasant surprise.

In the excitement upon arrival, I momentarily forgot that I was a dad due to my own need. I had been almost four years away from Mom and Dad. The need to run to them for a hug was intense. As Lila and Oretha raced to reach me for their hugs, I slipped into another virtual world. Even though I could see the children running towards me for their hugs, I pictured myself running towards Mom and Dad in the village to plunge into their arms.

On Saturday morning, the day after our arrival in Sanniquellie, Herbert returned to Monrovia while the kids and I set out on a trek to the village. Lila, Oretha and I walked the streets past the main parking station and continued down the hill to the public market by Lake Teeleh. Marketers from the village and Bursonnon gathered in a designated area of the market. I wanted to go to that area to find, meet and greet relatives and others whom I had not seen for all the time I had been away. Even though I first traveled to Korea before going on to the United States, ordinary people only had one interpretation of going abroad, which meant America. As soon as the word got around in that section of the market that I had returned from America, I became an instant celebrity. I basked in the hugs and warm wishes and felt a deep sense of fulfillment.

Our next task before heading on to the village was to pick Wonkermie up. She was staying with Zaykua, her grandmother, near the Buchanan-Yekepa railway. When we arrived at Zaykua's house, Wonkermie was out playing with other children some distance away. Zaykua stepped out and called Wonkermie, but she was hesitant to come home. She was having fun playing with her friends and apparently thought her grandmother would ask her to run an errand. When Zaykua raised her voice and insisted that she come home, Wonkermie finally showed up with a look of wonderment. We never intended to surprise her, but it was unavoidable because she did not know that I had returned. She did not know what was going on until she caught a glimpse of me standing by the corner of her grandmother's house. At that moment, she yelled, "Papa" and ran to hug me. I picked up her small lanky frame and held her in my arms. She had a big grin of joy in her face.

In a little while after, we took off, crossed the railway, and embarked on our trek to the village. I wished I could shorten the distance to reach the village in less time to see everyone I was dying to see, but that was not possible. However, because accomplishing my goal of traveling to Korea and the United States felt like competing in a race and winning a gold medal, the trek did not seem to be the drudgery it once was when I was in grade school. The excitement I felt in returning to show my degree or trophy to my parents wiped the drudgery away. It felt like I was running to my parents to let them know that I got it or won it; like a child bubbling with excitement after having discovered a treasure.

On our way to the village, we passed all the notable landmarks from the time of my grade school years. I looked upstream and downstream the Whenehyee creek and thought about the Sundays we ate rice wrapped in banana leaves while returning to Sanniquellie. We also passed Mount Soho, Kiapee Meeyee and soon we were in Bursonnon. We attempted to pass through the town unnoticed, but our efforts were fruitless. Relatives and others in the town recognized and greeted me. In the process, they slowed us down significantly. After we resumed the trek, we passed the graveyard I used to be afraid to pass by. My fear of ghosts had not completely gone away, but I could not show any sign of fear because the kids depended on me.

ARRIVAL IN THE VILLAGE

Finally, we reached the village. Mom and Dad and a whole host of relatives greeted us upon arrival. They sang familiar songs, danced, and praised Wlah for my safe return. I heard them sing, "Ah yobay yobay zuuba yobay zualehleh, ah yobay yobay zuuba yobay zualehleh."[252] I also heard them sing, "Tay lah whyne lehpeh leh lon lon lokolokuhn."[253] The songs, along with the clinging and clanging of used pans, empty zinc buckets, and empty one-gallon metal vegetable oil cans were interspersed with "Kwa yeaylor oo, Kwa yeaylor oo" (Congratulations! Congratulations!) by others who returned from their farms and joined in the celebrations. Certainly, my return from America made me like a newborn. Dad led the greeters, singers, and dancers. Moreover, he stole the show. It was the first time in my entire life to see Dad openly express his joy and happiness. It was as if he were making up for his absences at my high school and college graduations. I was very happy because I felt I had accomplished what I always wanted to do to make Dad happy.

Family and relatives celebrated upon my return to
village from the United States mid-June 1987

Gathering for a celebration of my return to the village

Group photo sometime during the celebrations

Later in the evening, the family gathered in our piazza for dinner and exchange of formal greetings. I took time and answered some of the many questions they had about my time away in Korea and in the United States. Sitting four to five feet away in the packed piazza, Kou Lehyeay whispered to someone, wondering whether I still remember how to speak Mahn. I heard her whisper and told her that my Mahn was better than hers. I gave one of the parables I learned from Flomo in Greensboro to prove that my Mahn was better than hers. After that, there was no question about my Mahn. After I answered a slew of questions about my time in Korea and in the United States, someone suggested that I needed time to rest because I had traveled a long distance. However, that concern for me was couched in a stereotype about Americans. To them, since I came from America, I had now become a *quizee*, a civilized person or someone who lives like a white person. To my family, Americans, assumed to be all white, or *quipulu* went to bed early and got up very late in the morning, suggesting that *quizees* were lazy. I tried in vain to convince them that Americans included other races and that they were some of the hardest working people in the world.

Of course, when my family referred to me as a *quizee*, they did not mean anything disparaging. One had to be able to read between the lines to understand what people meant when they referred to someone as a *quizee*.[254] Even though the reference to me as a *quizee* was not intended in any negative sense, I did not want to be a *quizee* while I was with my family. I did everything I could do to be an ordinary person. I ate the same foods, helped fetch water from the well by the creek in buckets and did everything I used to do. I knew who I was at my core; a native young man who was blessed to go to school at St. Mary's School; an indigenous lad who studied at the University of Liberia, Seoul National University and North Carolina A & T State University and returned home. No one could convince me that I was anything other than what I felt deep down at my core.

I too was anxious to know about what had happened in my absence. First, I wanted to know about the kids who were just infants when I left as well as those who were born in my absence. I asked about everybody including those relatives who lived in faraway towns and villages. For me, it seemed the longer I stayed away from my family and relatives the more precious they became in my life. I asked about the farm my parents worked on at the time of my leaving and the places I used to go to hunt with a headlight at night.

On the following day, I informed my parents and relatives that I would be returning to Monrovia on the following Saturday because I was expected to start work right away at the University of Liberia. With that information, the family met in the evening and decided to have a sacrifice to thank Wlah for the many blessings and for taking me abroad and returning me safely to my family.[255] They sent messages to my relatives in faraway towns and villages to be present for the occasion. On the day of the celebration, everyone gathered in the village and offered sacrifice to Wlah and thanked Him for all His blessings.

A Visit at St. Mary's High School

On my way back to Monrovia, I spent time in Sanniquellie. More importantly, I visited with Brothers Sebastian, Joseph, Andrew, and others at their residence at the Catholic Mission. All of them were very happy to see me. They had all heard that I was back in Liberia and were anxious to see me. On the following day, I visited St. Mary's School while school was in session. Brother Sebastian took me to all the classes and introduced me as a 1977 graduate and former Senior Prefect who had just returned from studying in the United States. Everything about my return to Sanniquellie and the village proceeded as I had imagined while I was in the United States. After Brother Sebastian introduced me in the senior class, there was a burst of applause, which sent chills of joy through my body. Momentarily, I did not know whether this was happening in real life or whether I was dreaming because I remember being years ago in the same position in which the students were. I spoke briefly to them, pointed to the very seat that years earlier I was sitting in and encouraged them to study hard. Moreover, I pointed to the map of the United States, still hanging above the blackboard at the front of the class. I told the story about my dreams and fascination with Nebraska; how the state's name sounded cool and inspired me to want to go to the United States to study at University of Nebraska in Lincoln. After the classroom tour, I came out and looked at the campus landscape and felt like taking the entire campus and everything in it and putting it on my back to take it with me. There was so much memory in the place. I spent eleven solid years on that campus; from 1966 to 1977 and, to this day, I remain intensely connected to the school.

AT WORK

After the visit with my family, I returned to Monrovia, where I concentrated my efforts on my responsibilities as an instructor in the William V. S. Tubman Teachers' College. I worked with students in the College of Agriculture & Forestry and Teachers' College, some of whom were already trained teachers from non-degree granting teacher training institutions pursuing a bachelor's degree in education or agriculture education.[256] Others who were not teachers were working towards a similar goal with the hope of becoming teachers after completing their studies.

At twenty-nine, it was not unusual for some of the students to be older than I was, but the respect they accorded me made my work meaningful and fulfilling. I had always taken great pride in the education I received from the University of Liberia. Moreover, when I had that opportunity to work with some of the best students, I was prouder of the university. I was convinced that those students could go anywhere in the world and compete with anybody. William Gizi, Howard Mendoabor and Evangeline Pelham were some of the most outstanding students with whom I worked. Others

303

were Abu Massallay and Samuel Duo. They all have gone on to become successful people in their own careers.[257]

The work at the University of Liberia was exciting and meaningful. I felt vindicated that I made the right decision to return to the University of Liberia. Even though my annual salary at the University of Liberia at the time was a little over $11,000 United States dollars, I felt fulfilled because it was not the love of money that took me back to Liberia. I was driven by boundless idealism. I believed people like myself were ideally suited in whatever roles they assumed to create a Liberia of peace, justice, and opportunities for all, irrespective of background.

One reason I felt so strongly was that I had an asset, my parents' story, which served as a springboard. It reminded and motivated me to press on and to overcome obstacles in pursuit of my education. In addition, my experiences included struggles with hunger in Sanniquellie and Monrovia. I experienced what it meant not to have academic guidance and also felt a sting of discrimination at the University of Liberia. More importantly, from Sanniquellie to Monrovia to Seoul, Korea to Greensboro, NC, I saw Wlah's goodness and grace in Zehyee Mahnmein, Oretha Nyah, Eric Eastman, Dr. Cyrenius Forh, Col. Carl Cannon and many others.

Aside from my parents and others who found me worthy of their love, encouragement and support, someone else found me worthy. That someone was President William R. Tolbert, Jr. who not only referred to Liberia's young people as his "precious jewels," but also made a gamble that if he invested in their futures, they would deliver for Liberia. I was not as wise as I am today when I returned to the University of Liberia in May 1987, but deep down in my heart I knew I had returned to deliver a return on President Tolbert's investment in Liberia's young people in my own small way. For these reasons, I prepared my students beyond what was required. I arranged and taught Saturday tutorial classes and provided snacks out of my own pocket without any expectation of reimbursement. Even though some of my students were older than I was, I regarded their futures as if they were my own children's futures. I expected my students to give their best to Liberia. In the same way as I was President Tolbert's precious jewel, they too were my precious jewels.

CHAPTER 25

Transition

USAID

SOMETIME DURING THE FIRST QUARTER of 1989, I heard that a short-term fellowship was in the works for me. The information I got was that the government of Switzerland was offering the fellowship to the Liberian government through the Ministry of Foreign Affairs (MOA). I was supposed to travel to Switzerland to attend some kind of training program. It was not clear to me what the training program was about. Information about the training program filtered out before any paperwork between the MOA and the University of Liberia was finalized. At the time, I was still an instructor in the William V. S. Tubman Teachers' College at the University of Liberia (UL).

Based on my experience in March 1984, where the University of Liberia informed me about my travel to Korea almost at the eleventh hour, I decided to prepare my travel documents in advance when I got a wind of the short-term training program in Switzerland. Unfortunately, the plan to travel to Switzerland fell through the cracks without any word on what happened. I was not surprised at the turn of events because it often happened to others. Perhaps someone with a connection to the University of Liberia went on that training program. If that were the case, all it may have taken that person was family connection, friendship, or "Cold Water." On the other hand, someone completely unconnected to the University of Liberia may have used "Cold Water" or their connection to someone at the MOA to go on that fellowship. In any case, the plans I made were for naught.

As people in the faith community often say, "As doors shut, windows open." Sometime in August 1989, my friend, John B. Menwon (JB), saw a job advertisement by the United States Agency for International Development (USAID) in a newspaper. [258] He brought a clipping of that newspaper with the ad to me. I was interested in the job because it was the kind of opportunity to which I had been looking forward. A few days later, I stopped by the USAID office at the time in Sinkor, Monrovia and picked up an application packet. The application required filling in all kinds of information, some of which could not fit in the spaces provided. The complexity of the application turned me off and I put it aside. I hated completing complicated paperwork. As a result, I waited until less than one week to the deadline before I mustered the energy to complete the application packet. In addition, I completed the application with some help. It was not that I was incapable of providing the information required. Neither was it that I could not write. I needed help because the boxes and spaces provided on the application were unreasonably too small. Left alone, I could not fit the information in those boxes and spaces as I would have preferred. JB just happened to be the help I badly needed. His handwriting was magnificent, like a type print. With his help, I completed the entire packet and submitted it on the day before the deadline.

JB is a definition of a true friend. He is witty, intellectually sharp like a razor blade and fun to be around. I know of few people who made me laugh as much as he did when we lived next to each other in Bardnersville, Monrovia. We are about the same age. He is Dan and I am Mahn and we both come from Nimba County. [259] He was a student at the University of Liberia pursuing a degree in accounting at the time we were living in Bardnersville. At that time, I already had a graduate degree, yet the issue of education never came up. I held him in high esteem and the feeling was mutual. We always ate together. If he were not at home, I would always wait until he came home so that we could eat together. Food did not mean anything to me if JB were not there to share it with me because whenever we ate together, it was our gentlemen moments. We used all the parables we learned from our parents and laughed at what they meant in our lives at the time. At that time, the parables were making sense to us because as adults we were experiencing the life situations that resulted in the formulation of those parables. We also talked and laughed about other issues of the day including politics, international affairs, our children, or our future plans. My friendship with JB is another indication that, in Liberia or perhaps in most other African cultures, food is not just for filling the belly and nourishing the body. It is a fodder for building relationships.

During the weeks after I submitted my application to USAID, I stopped by the organization's Sinkor, Monrovia, office to check on the status of the application. On one occasion when I stopped by to check again, I was pleasantly surprised to find out that Dainka was a senior USAID Liberian staff.[260] I had never lived anywhere with Dainka, but I had known him for a long time as a Mahn and someone from Nimba County. I was thrilled because, once again, I was reminded of the Mahn saying, "Mee lah *qui* leh keh *qui* bah *qui* leh lo ee ka."[261]

The Americans at USAID had their own system of evaluating and hiring employees. However, I was overly elated about Dainka being a big man at USAID. The reason was that "Who knows you?" was ingrained in Liberia as the primary means of climbing up the ladder of social mobility. At some level in my mind, I thought the Liberian way would trump the American way. I assumed I was in a better situation because Dainka was my *quizee* among the *quizees*. After all, he is a citizen of Nimba County and a Mahn. Moreover, he was on the interview committee. With that kind of mindset, I was certain that Dainka would put the word in or look out for me.

Dainka greeted me warmly on the day I first met him at USAID. There was no point in introducing myself because we knew each other. At that time, I did not know he was monitoring the list of applicants for his own ulterior motive. My excitement about Dainka was not a one-way feeling, at least from everything outwardly I observed about him. He was bubbly and seemed perfectly happy upon telling him that I applied for the opening at USAID. In addition, over the weeks I stopped by USAID office to follow up on the status of the application, Dainka became overly enthusiastic about me. On one occasion, he even suggested that I consider another job with a USAID-sponsored project at Cuttington University in central Liberia. He told me that the Cuttington job was better in terms of pay and benefits than the one for which I applied. As Dainka tried to persuade me to disregard my application in order to apply for the Cuttington job, I became really concerned. In the first place, I did not want to go to work at Cuttington. Neither did I tell him what I really felt about his Cuttington job proposal.

Tribal affinity in Liberia is very strong and pervasive, but it is not always detectable in people's preferences. For their own utility, some people look out for others in search of jobs on the bases of having come from the same home county or being members of the same ethnic group. These reasons, by the way, have nothing to do with qualifications. However, there are others who look out for others out of the goodness of their hearts. Dainka's sudden interest in me shown by his Cuttington job proposal certainly did not present him as an example of either the former or the latter scenario. It was too good to be true.

Once again, I took the mask for the person behind it during my experience with Dainka. Everyone wears a mask, and it does not matter whether someone comes from one's hometown or speaks one's language. Aristotle was on the mark when he said that men cannot talk about knowing each other until they have "eaten salt together." One cannot claim to know someone until one has shared experiences or spent a lot of time with that person. In spite of Dainka being a Nimba citizen and a Mahn, he was merely an acquaintance. I really did not know him. My excitement about him being my *quizee* among the *quizees* and that he would look out for me was misplaced.

As it turned out, Dainka had a friend who worked with the Liberia Produce Marketing Corporation (LPMC) in Grand Gedeh County. Apparently, that friend had a run-in with people in Grand Gedeh County or the Samuel Doe administration. As a result, he was either fired or at the point of being fired from his job. Dainka wanted his friend to get the job for which I applied. He felt that if I were not in the pool of applicants, then his friend would stand a better chance of getting the job. For this reason, each time I stopped by the USAID office to inquire about the status of the application, Dainka tried to get me to apply for the Cuttington University job he recommended.

Dainka's efforts on behalf of his friend stuck with me. Later, someone informed me that 39 people applied for the job and that an initial screening was on-going. After that initial screening, four people were selected, including Dainka's friend, two other candidates and me. After the initial screening, we took a written test. Each candidate had a different schedule for the test and, as a result, we did not see each other. The results of that test eliminated two of the candidates. The remaining two candidates were Dainka's friend and me. After the test, we faced interviews at different schedules. The interview committee consisted of ten people including Dainka. I was later informed that, after the first round of interviews, our scores tied. Dr. Peter Wiesel, who was going to be the immediate boss of the person who would be hired, told me later that a suggestion was made to toss a coin since our scores turned out to be the same. However, Dr. Wiesel said since he would be the boss, he wanted to have a one-on-one interview with each of us. After my one-on-one interview with Dr. Wiesel on the day I was scheduled, he told me "Marsilius, I have never done this after an interview, but I want you to know that you got the job."

Up to the point of my one-on-one interview with Dr. Peter Wiesel, I still did not know what Dainka was up to. As a result, as soon as I left Dr. Wiesel's office, Dainka was the first person I talked to. Again, under the impression that he was rooting for me, I told him, without hesitation, that I got the job. But Dainka's activities leading up to my getting the USAID job were not the end of his chicanery. Blinded by idealism and the Mahn cultural idea, "Wah gay ma ma ma ah, ma ma ma waka leh bay," I was the only one who did not see through Dainka's shenanigans.[262]

Before I officially started work with USAID, I had to come in to negotiate my salary. Dainka went so far as having the audacity to contact some of the Liberian ladies in the office to give him information about my salary. As I was later informed, he wanted to make sure that my salary was not higher than his was. His beef was that he had been working with USAID longer than I had been. Since I did not know that he had different feelings about me, I continued to treat him as if he were my brother or confidant. Again, when I completed negotiations for my salary, I stopped by his office and shared the information with him. He seemed relieved for reasons I did not understand. The same ladies he contacted to gather information about my salary for him went further to inform me that Dainka took exception to the office space given to me. He felt that since he had been there for a longer time, he deserved that particular office space.

As masks are artificial, the one Dainka wore was no different. It finally came tumbling down, leaving the true Dainka exposed. All the deceit and the ugly stuff he harbored about me including disparaging comments he made about my competence came to light. That happened after he refused to attend the opening of my restaurant in Saye Town, Monrovia. As always until up to that point, when I thought about investing in a restaurant, it was Dainka with whom I first discussed the idea. I sincerely took him like a brother and asked his opinion. He discouraged the idea and said everything to persuade me not to do it. I went on and made the investment anyway.

On the opening day of the restaurant, I invited everyone at work including Dainka. Everyone I invited including the Mission Director attended the opening ceremony except Dainka. It was only my shock and surprise at Dainka's absence at the opening of my restaurant that caused someone to rip his mask off. That someone was Ely Gabisi, a workmate of Sierra Leonean background. Mr. Gabisi shared everything Dainka had been up to including his desire for his friend to get the job. Mr. Gabisi also told me the disparaging comments Dainka made about my competence, suggesting that his friend was more qualified than I was. It also became clear that Dainka's suggestion that I apply for the other job with a USAID funded project at Cuttington was an attempt to ensure that his friend got the job for which I applied.

If there was anything Dainka never wanted me to know, it is this story that I am telling about his actions at the time I applied for that job at USAID and the ugly things he said about me. One would ask why I did not confront Dainka at the time. Dainka's actions pained me. The urge to confront him, to be ugly with him was there, but I had been down that road before. I took a different path and forgave the friend who betrayed me during a student government election in 1976 at St. Mary's even though he swore that he would not apologize for his actions if his mom asked him to. The outcome of the choice I made to forgive that friend was that, years later, it was through that same friend that I came to know Oretha Nyah to whom the "hair on my head" belongs, the woman whom my daughter, Oretha Elizabeth, was named after.

I did not confront Dainka at the time he treated me with such contempt because I pick my battles; while climbing up, I choose what hill to die on. As the Mahns put it, "Kwa leh kaha gbo lah kwa seahn zeh."[263] I had a larger goal; I came to USAID to gather edible termites. My focus was to ensure that my lantern or burning flame was bright enough to attract the termites once they started coming out of their mounds. I had no time to take note of the smelling human feces some unscrupulous person had released nearby. I told others to cover the feces with layers of dead leaves so that the task of gathering edible termites could continue.

Mr. William Nyanue, a good and long-time friend, often talks about "doing what is expected," a widespread tendency among Liberians and perhaps other populations elsewhere. For example, if someone undermines one's efforts as Dainka did to me, people expect me to payback in kind. Far be it from me to claim that I have never had that kind of mindset or that I have never felt that way before. However, on the consequential decisions I have made along this journey, I have seldom, if ever, done what was expected.

I vividly recall October 1990 when the then Acting USAID-Liberia Mission Director, Dr. John Roberts, came up to me at the Department of State in Washington, D.C., and said that, with the on-going violence in Liberia, we will have to close down USAID's operations in Liberia. He also said that we needed to maintain a skeletal staff in Monrovia so that if the need arose for restarting operations, we would not have to start from scratch. Next, Dr. Roberts turned to me and asked, "Who do you have in mind that we could keep on the skeletal staff in Monrovia?" I gave him three names. One was Dainka and the other two were Patricia Johnson and Adelaide Supuwood.[264] Patricia and Adelaide were both Liberian staff at the USAID office when I took assignment. They were very kind to me. I gave their names to Dr. Roberts in remembrance of their kindness. I am 100% sure that Dainka was maintained on the USAID skeletal staff in Monrovia. However, I am not so sure about Patricia Johnson and Adelaide Supuwood. The reason is because, at that time, anybody who could get out of Liberia was either out or was trying to get out.

I am not claiming that I employed Dainka or made the decision to put Dainka on the USAID skeletal staff in Monrovia. Dr. Roberts asked me, and I gave those names to him. I am not claiming to be a saint. I am only suggesting that had Dainka been in my shoes, I am not sure whether he would have given my name to Dr. Roberts. That would perhaps have been a perfect situation for me to say, "Heck, why would I want to recommend someone who bad-mouthed and undermined me?" I did not choose that route. Now, it is my turn. It is my turn, in spite of the residual pain from my experience with Dainka at USAID-Liberia, to tell this story. I do so not to shame him but to highlight the power of a mother's prayer. One cannot stop what it has set in motion to do.

The opportunity at USAID was the second step in fulfilling one of the pull factors that brought me back to Liberia after my studies in the United States. The first step was my two-year stint at the University of Liberia.

I wanted to make President Tolbert's words mean something; I wanted his inspiration in the form of a reference to me as his "precious jewel" to mean something in practical terms for Liberians.[265] Without much ado, I got into full swing with my work at USAID and found it to be the kind of opportunity I had been hungering for to make an impact.

As Project Manager of the USAID's 20-million-dollar Agricultural Research & Extension project, I was enthusiastic about the project's ambitious agenda: to modernize the Central Agricultural Research Institute (CARI) to make agricultural research more relevant to ordinary Liberian farmers. My proudest and most memorable experience at USAID was my tour of Bong, Nimba and Grand Gedeh Counties, visiting with ordinary rural farmers involved with USAID-sponsored small-scale agricultural projects. The tour gave me a clear sense of the project's potential impact on improving small-scale agricultural production. As I reeled in the joy of that three-county tour, the rebel storm cloud in 1989 that eventually engulfed and destroyed Liberia was gathering across the Liberian border with the Ivory Coast.

CHAPTER 26

Charles Taylor's War

T HE THREE-COUNTY TOUR OF AGRICULTURAL activities I took occurred shortly before Christmas 1989. The tour itself was like Christmas in terms of the joy I reaped from interacting with ordinary rural farmers. I came face-to-face with rural farm production and life and felt as if I were watching a movie of my childhood years. While I was still reeling in the joy of that experience, Uncle George A. Bolo suggested that we travel home to Nimba to celebrate Christmas with a larger group in one town where everyone from Monrovia and other areas in Nimba would gather. It was not a normal Christmas, the one where children are the focus, even though children are the focus when it comes to Christmas in rural Liberia with the only difference being that ordinary rural Liberians do not put up Christmas trees.

I agreed to go to Nimba along with Uncle Bolo. I was an adult, responsible for myself, but because I had very high regard for him, I do not remember ever saying no to him whenever he asked me to go somewhere with him. If he showed up at my door after midnight and asked me to take him somewhere, I would get ready and go along. Culturally and out of respect for Uncle George, I was his bag carrier. Treating my elders with deference came to me naturally, notwithstanding my educational level. I learned very early that true humility was good for the soul. When Uncle George asked me to go along with him to Nimba, I consented without thinking about my girlfriend and my children. I left the children with my girlfriend in Monrovia and traveled to Nimba with Uncle Bolo and others. We left Monrovia during the evening of Friday December 22, 1989 and arrived in Bursonnon late in the evening. That 1989 Christmas was almost like a showcasing of the "Who's Who" in status and education from our home area, perhaps to inspire the younger people to take their education seriously.

Saturday morning, on the following day, I trekked the hour and twenty-minute distance from Bursonnon to the village to see my parents. I had visited with them about three weeks earlier. As a result, there was a little look of surprise in Dad's face about why I had come. Even though they always wanted me near, neither they nor I felt that I had to spend that particular evening with them. I told Mom and Dad that Uncle Bolo and I had come to Bursonnon to celebrate Christmas with other friends and relatives. I also told them that we would spend the rest of the week-end there and then return to Monrovia. They were perfectly fine with my explanation. There was nothing extraordinary about my leaving. I was not traveling to another country or anything like that. There was no hug from Dad. "Yehboe bah peay ah ee nyeehn kiahmon; ma waay Sia wah nohnbay ah o bah," Dad said, as he headed to the coffee farm with a cutlass under his arm.[266] Mom was doing some little work around our house. She, too, extended her greetings, but without any advice like Dad. "Bah loah ma waay Sia wah ay laaynu wah nohnbay ah nu o bah," Mom said.[267] I left and returned to Bursonnon with Hasting Gbamon, a friend who accompanied me to see them. At that time, I did not know that this would be my last time to see my Dad alive.

Hasting and I returned to Bursonnon, where the celebrations were already in full swing. In different sections of the town, different musical and singing groups were performing as people either stood by and enjoyed the performances or danced along. Small shop owners were happy because business was good. They were selling liquor and other beverages as fast as they could. Liquor and beverages of all kinds available in small town shops particularly during Christmas season included Club Beer, Guinness Stout, Black Deer, a liquor distilled in Monrovia at the time, Cane Juice and all kinds of imported beer and liquor including Heineken and Night Train.

On the morning of Sunday December 24, 1989, the townspeople respon-sible for the logistics of the celebrations erected a large tent made of sticks and palm branches and leaves at the front of the chief's residence. The celebrations attracted people from all the surrounding towns and villages and continued at different levels including a soccer match between the townspeople and those of us who came from Monrovia. We lost the soccer game because the town's team was comprised of young people for whom soccer was every evening affair. They were much more physically fit than the adults who made up our team. In any case, it was just for the fun and not so much about winning.

That Christmas Eve, Sunday, December 24, 1989, was not an ordinary Sunday. Something sinister and alarming was taking place in Buutuo, a town in Liberia next to the border with the Ivory Coast, without our knowing even though Buutuo was no more than seventy miles away. It was the day Mr. Charles Taylor and a group of rebels under his command invaded Liberia from the Ivory Coast. Mr. Taylor and his rebels attacked Buutuo, killing several people and sending shock waves in the border area that took some time to be felt in other areas of Liberia.

Meanwhile, the celebrations in Bursonnon continued as they did in different parts of Nimba. With no other means of instant communication, the only way we could have known that something like that was happening in Buutuo was to hear it on a transistor radio, which nearly every household had. However, BBC's Focus on Africa, which featured events in Africa, aired shortly after 5:00 p.m. on weekdays. And before BBC could pick up the story and air it, someone had to be present to pass on the information or a BBC reporter had to be present. Perhaps Mr. Taylor and his men also calculated that their best strategy was to attack on Christmas Eve because Christmas is a big celebration in Liberia. Until Taylor's invasion, the days leading up to Christmas 1989 were all about joy and celebrations. Everyone was completely absorbed with little time to sit around and even listen to the BBC.[268]

On Christmas Day, the cow intended for the celebrations was slaughtered that morning and divided among selected people, mainly women, to prepare the food. As always, when the Mahn people gather for celebrations, certain rituals including libations are performed and speeches or remarks by elders are made. These celebrations were no exception. Of importance were Elder Karmah Saiyee's remarks. Mr. Karmah Saiyee, an elderly man from Duo Gbeah, a town about 20 miles away, seemed ordinary. There was nothing flamboyant about him, yet the air about him signaled that he had something he had been wishing and waiting for a long time to say, particularly to the younger generation. I do not know whether it was fate that put me in Bursonnon during that bright midmorning sun on December 25, 1989. It was, to me, a kind of blessing to be present to hear Elder Karmah Saiyee. His words were a treasure that needed to be written and passed on. They left a lasting impression on me. Elder Karmah Saiyee's remarks were directed at us, the educated ones, especially those of us who came from Monrovia for the Christmas celebrations. He singled us out and made note of the fancy vehicles we traveled in, including Mitsubishi Pajeros. Elder Karmah Saiyee highlighted the contrast between the fancy vehicles we traveled in and the mud brick and zinc houses which the vehicles were parked next to.

After having captured the full attention of the audience with his imagery, he said "No matter what education you have or what fancy cars you drive, your education means nothing if the thatched, zinc-roofed, or mud brick houses in which you were born remain as they are." Elder Karmah Saiyee's words meant so much to me because they captured the essence of one of the burdens educated and thoughtful Liberians or Africans carry. It was as if he were speaking directly to me. I took his message personally. I was hearing him say that, as a part of my heritage, my grandparents left my parents with a thatched hut. In fulfillment of their duty in taking what was passed on, making it better, and passing it on, my parents transformed the thatched hut into a mud brick and zinc house and passed it on to me. They did so within a culture with little or no formal education but wherein family values, respect for the elderly and social stability mattered. On that Christmas morning, Elder Karmah Saiyee was telling me that with my graduate degree, the time had come for me to take that heritage and make it better than my parents made it. It was time for me to do so and pass it on to my own children. It was a powerful charge, one that still hangs figuratively around my neck.

Again, unaware that something out of the ordinary was happening somewhere in Nimba, we carried on with the celebrations as before. That evening, Uncle George told me that we were going to leave early the next morning for Monrovia. Since it was his assigned government vehicle that we were traveling in, I could not argue with his suggestion. I felt he had some business that needed to be taken care of and so he wanted us to get back to Monrovia as soon as possible. Leaving that early on the day after Christmas was out of the ordinary. Normally, in Liberia, on the day after

Christmas, the celebrations are still in full swing. They even continue until the New Year arrives. But as Uncle George suggested, we left Bursonnon early and got on the highway to Monrovia. We passed through Sanniquellie and Ganta without any sign of anything out of the ordinary. The checkpoints in Sanniquellie and in Ganta as well as others along the way to Monrovia were quiet with little activities because people were very busy with the Christmas celebrations everywhere in the country. The security personnel at the gates all along treated us with courtesy as most of them recognized Uncle George as the Deputy Minister of Finance for Revenues. He and I returned to Monrovia without any incident along the highway even though the civil war that Mr. Charles Taylor and his rebels started two days earlier was raging at the same time without the knowledge of many in the country, including the security people who were guarding the checkpoints along the highway from Sanniquellie to Monrovia.

Immediately upon arrival in Monrovia that afternoon, I learned that Charles Taylor and his rebels had invaded Liberia through the border in Nimba County from where we had just arrived. "Nonsense," I told Prince Gbeinsaye, a friend who gave me the news. "Pure garbage, I just arrived from Nimba, where I neither heard nor saw anything that resembled chaos, let alone armed rebels attacking in a war," I told Prince. "If there were any truths to that news, we would have seen unusual movements on the part of the security at the checkpoints along the highway from Sanniquellie to Monrovia," I argued forcefully. "If you do not believe what I am saying, just turn on your radio this evening and listen to BBC's Focus on Africa," Prince said. Indeed, when I turned on my radio that evening, Prince was right. Liberia had been invaded and not too far from where we had been in Nimba County, celebrating the Christmas. Correspondent Robin White was on the air that evening and went on to have an interview with Charles Taylor. From that point, Robin White and Elizabeth Blount, who had by that time been a fixture in the psyche of Africans as a result of her reporting during conflicts, again became a mainstay over the airwaves.

This was the beginning of the civil war that would come to turn Liberia into complete ashes and kill over an estimated 250,000 people. The next two days after our return from Nimba, the county became a no-go area, a literal war zone. No one who wanted to live could leave Monrovia and travel to Nimba. Similarly, no one still alive in Nimba County who wanted to live could travel to Monrovia on the Sanniquellie-Monrovia highway. In fact, some of the people, like us, who traveled to Nimba for the Christmas, but decided to return during the night of December 26, 1989, or the days immediately following, were slaughtered at the checkpoints by government soldiers. Everyone traveling from Nimba at that point was declared a rebel and either fled or was subsequently killed. When news of the killings along the highway reached other parts of Nimba, those who were planning to return to Monrovia, but had not done so by then decided to flee to neighboring Guinea or Ivory Coast.

I worried about the fate of my parents and relatives in Nimba County. Mom and Dad too thought the worst. They assumed that I had been killed. There was no way to send word to them that I was still alive and that I was in Monrovia. It was a dangerous time to be a citizen of Nimba County because Charles Taylor's war was framed as a war between the Nimba people and the Samuel Doe government—essentially a war between the Nimba people and the Krahn people—since many Liberians perceived the Samuel Doe government as a Krahn government. My life and the lives of other people from Nimba County were in danger. Every morning there were decapitated people assumed to be from Nimba County in gutters around the city of Monrovia and its environs. At that time, most Liberians who were not from Nimba County felt that only Nimba people were in harm's way. Though Nimba people were deemed rebels, harassed, and killed in Monrovia and mass killings in Nimba County at the hands of government soldiers were reported, life was going on for most people in Monrovia as if nothing was happening.

With the imminent danger, I put my concerns about safety in writing and sent the letter to Gontee.[269] I asked whether a training program in the United States could be arranged to keep me away from Liberia until the worsening security crisis could be resolved. I wrote that letter believing the United States government, whose influence in Liberia was pervasive like no other place in the world, would intervene diplomatically and resolve the crisis. Upon receipt of my request, Gontee and I had a conversation during which I provided more details about the danger than I had described in the letter. Aside from being a citizen of Nimba County, educated Nimba people, of whom I was one, faced the greatest risk to their lives. At that time, the notion was that educated Nimba people were aware of plans for the military uprising. Moreover, they were the ones who stood to benefit if the armed invasion succeeded. Also, the rebels were believed to be doing the "Dirty work" for the educated ones. Once the rebels succeeded, they would turn to the educated ones to take over and run the government. These rumors, in part, fueled the retribution against educated Nimba citizens as well as ordinary Nimba people particularly in Monrovia and its environs.

Aside from my own safety, I was also thinking about my parents and even my grand- and great grandparents in another light at the time I was making that request to Gontee. They were not literate; they could not read or write. A few episodes about their lives like Uncle Miatee Garteh's tales about the conduct of the Liberian Frontier Force (LFF), which terrorized the Mahn people, survived through oral history. Uncle Miatee Garteh told me stories of wars the *quizees* fought against the Mahns as they sought to expand their territories into the hinterland of Liberia. Today, unfortunately, the only history "Books" of their lives they left behind are the remnants of scores of deserted towns and villages, graves, grave markers, and other artifacts. Besides those, their accomplishments were never recorded; their stories were never told. I do not know the songs they sang to their children and the medicines they used to cure their sick. At the time, I was making that request to Gontee, I was thinking that my fate would be the same; that, in the future, no one would know anything significant about me, the Nimba people or what we did when we were alive.

The persecution and killings of Nimba people on the bases of ethnicity and other falsehoods reminded me of similar fate that befell the Jews during the Holocaust. I was afraid that no educated Nimba citizens would remain to write stories like Elder Karmah Saiyee's admonishment during the Christmas celebrations of December 1989 in Bursonnon. As an educated Nimbaian, I saw myself as a repository of cultural as well as historical information no matter how scant. As a descendant of people who died without leaving any significant recorded information about their lives and what they did, I wanted to make a difference. I wanted to write something, to record important memories for my children. Had I remained in Liberia and died at the hands of those who championed the slaughter, writing and passing on that information to future generations of Nimbaians or Liberians would not probably happen.

At decision time, Gontee turned down my request with a classic bureaucratic response. He told me that my request could not be granted because the organization could not make similar arrangements for every Liberian staff in a similar situation. No exception could be made. It did not matter that I was the only person from Nimba County who made the request. As a Liberian or an African, Gontee's decision presented me a unique situation because I perceived him as having the power to decide. More importantly, as an African American or a black man, I expected him to be sympathetic to the plight of his kind—black people. Meanwhile, in May 1990, three months after Gontee turned down my request, the entire American staff at the organization, including Gontee, was ordered to evacuate due to the worsening security situation in Liberia.

For many Liberians who were not from Nimba County, however, the situation was like a live frog in a pot of cold water placed on a hot plate. In the beginning, at the point of turning on the hot plate, the water was still cold. The frog jumped and wiggled around in apparent excitement. As the water temperature started to rise, the frog hardly recognized it as the beginning of something bad to come. This was exactly how most people in Monrovia, including some Nimba people, saw the civil war at its onset. First, they took it as a joke. In the wake of President Samuel Doe's increasing unpopularity among the general population, except for his Krahn ethnic group, some Liberians started to "flirt" with Charles Taylor. They could not wait for the rebels to come to town, meaning Monrovia.

BARDNERSVILLE ORDEAL

Shortly after the American staff at USAID-Liberia left, my day of reckoning arrived. This happened towards the middle of June 1990 amid a palpable fear that gripped the City of Monrovia and surrounding areas. More and more bodies of mutilated and decapitated people in gutters and along back roads were discovered. Nimba people who went out at night in Monrovia and its environs were essentially playing Russian roulette with their lives. I thought constantly about the possibility of being the next person whose body would be discovered. I felt completely helpless. I was staying at Dr. Cyrenius N. Forh's house near the Bardnersville Estate to avoid being recognized as a Mahn or someone from Nimba County. Dr. Forh was my mentor. He belonged to the Kru ethnic group. His house seemed a perfect place to disguise myself and hide. We prayed constantly at Dr. Forh's house and often walked to an area behind the Bardnersville Estate to pray at the home of Brother Tarpeh, a "private preacher."[270] Being with my mentor gave me some assurance that all would be well. I felt safe.

With that assurance of safety at my mentor's house, I made a serious and life-changing mistake during the evening of June 10, 1990. I mustered the courage to get out for a while. I walked away for about a quarter of a mile amid an evening breeze that deceptively felt as though all was well. I arrived at the home of two young Mahn men, Joseph and Albert Sonkarlay. I knew them through their sister, Mrs. Margaret Yelekor, whom I met while I was an instructor at the University of Liberia. They and I became friends, but our friendship took on another meaning as we, together, saw ourselves as persecuted people under siege. Joseph greeted me and said that his brother, Albert, was away.

Behind Joseph and Albert Sonkarlay's house stood a hut which served as a kitchen as well as a palaver hut for recreation. Joseph asked me to sit with him under the hut and have a beer. Have a beer? That sounded like a song in my ears! I wanted to have a cold beer and, more importantly, I wanted to have a conversation about nothing else but the imminent danger we were in. I wanted to know what new information Joseph had that I did not know. Even though at that time we knew that other Liberians were pointing out people from Nimba County to the authorities, we had not experienced it yet and therefore assumed it could not happen to us. Moreover, we felt that we were way out on the outskirts of the city of Monrovia and, therefore, did not think that we ran the risk of being exposed as Nimba people. We did not think anyone would see us and call us rebels.

Unfortunately, as Joseph Sonkarlay and I sat under the hut and drank our beer, it seemed that someone had already told "Pordor," an officer of the Armed Forces of Liberia, that we were rebels.[271] In Liberia, the closest provisions in the Constitution like the 1878 Posse Comitatus Act signed by President Rutherford B. Hayes, which prohibited the military from being used as a domestic law enforcement agency, are Article 19 and Article 21, Section (e).[272] In spite of those provisions, it was and still is not uncommon for members of the Armed Forces of Liberia to arrest, detain, judge civil cases, or simply enforce the laws. So, when Pordor, who was armed, came, greeted us, and took a seat, it was not out of the ordinary. Right away I had an eerie sense that he was up to something more than his friendly greeting suggested, but I remained at ease. Joseph offered him some beer, but he did not accept the offer. Later, Pordor started a conversation and went on talking about rebels. When he realized that we were not interested in his conversation and even told him so, he then asked if we were rebels. Joseph told him that we were not rebels, rather, we were just ordinary Liberians having a beer and a conversation. The more Pordor continued with all kinds of questions, the more irritated Joseph became. Eventually, Joseph responded angrily, and an argument started between them, providing the perfect opportunity Pordor needed to carry out an arrest.

As the argument between Joseph and Pordor grew more intense, the word quickly got around the neighborhood that rebels had been identified in the area. In no time, a large crowd started to gather to witness what was unfolding. At that instant, Pordor was more focused on Joseph because it was Joseph who was taking him on. Joseph and Pordor were already on their feet. At the soldier's order, they left me under the hut and went around the house. The moment they left me alone, I was literally trying to figure out what I would do. I am talking about a decision I had to make in a split second because the argument between Joseph and Pordor had grown louder.

As Pordor tried to call for reinforcement because he, not to mention the gathering onlookers, was convinced that we were rebels, I took off and ran toward the other side of the house. At that instant, I saw a middle-aged woman standing in an open area. Her eyes and mine locked on as if we were aiming at each other with a laser. At that moment, she pointed in a direction with her right hand without uttering a word. I was certain that the woman was Wlah's angel whom He positioned in that place for my safety. My feeble mind cannot comprehend my survival and escape from those harrowing circumstances. I can only attribute them, again, to Mom's prayers and petitions to Wlah, to which I have alluded time after time.

After escaping the scene of the argument, I ran toward the area where the woman had pointed. I reached a swamp, plunged into it, and crossed a deep muddy mess. With the adrenalin, I was on the other side of the swamp as if I had wings to fly. It was only after I crossed the swamp that I realized my pants were wet up to and above my knees. As soon as I crossed the swamp, I saw Margaret Kermah, a woman from Nimba whom I knew at the University of Liberia, where she was a student. The condition I saw her in signaled to me that Nimba people were in dire straits. She had her hair shaved and wore clothes that were uncharacteristic of her. She was completely disguised. It was she who recognized me. When I figured out who she was, my heart pounded. I felt the weight of the danger in the air. Ms. Kermah then showed me the path to the main road from the

Gardnerville Highway toward Bardnersville. Years later in the United States, I was amazed to hear that Ms. Kermah went on to become Senator of Nimba County during Charles Taylor's rule. Indeed, she, too, survived the Liberian Civil War.

With the help of Margaret Kermah's directions, I reached the Gardnersville-Bardnersville Road. I then took a cab and went to my apartment, about a mile and a half away. Upon arrival, I put my ordeal in writing and sent it by Ms. Margaret Tumbay to USAID-Liberia head office in Sinkor, Monrovia.[273] While, at the time, Nimba people were the main targets of harassments, decapitations, or secret killings by agents of the regime, the possibility of real danger to Ms. Tumbay due to her association with me existed. I acknowledge the risk she took for my safety and I remain eternally grateful to her.

By the time the letter was delivered to USAID-Liberia head office in Sinkor, the entire American staff had been evacuated with the exception of Mr. Roy Johnson, a white American. At the time Mr. Johnson was serving as the Executive Officer. Upon receipt of my message, he sent a vehicle to my apartment to pick me up for a meeting with him at USAID-Liberia head office. During our meeting, I narrated my entire ordeal. After our meeting, Mr. Johnson sent a facsimile to Washington, D.C., informing Dr. John Roberts that I had had an encounter with death and had miraculously escaped.[274]

After my meeting with Mr. Roy Johnson, I came out of the compound and stood on the sidewalk on Tubman Boulevard. It was an overcast and eerily gloomy day. In a little while, I saw throngs of Liberians in white t-shirts, marching on Tubman Boulevard from the direction of the J. F. Kennedy Memorial Hospital headed toward Capitol Hill. They sang and carried placards calling for peace and the intervention of the United States to save Liberia from a looming bloodbath. My eyes buoyed in tears and chills fell over me at the sight of the marching multitude, placards, and chorus of voices. All along until that moment, I thought that I was the only one who felt that the United States had the influence and power to stop the unfolding tragedy. I did not know other Liberians felt the same way and were organizing to act. I found out later that day that the marchers went to the United States Embassy at Mamba Point and presented a petition to the George H. W. Bush administration, calling for a diplomatic intervention to stop the conflict.

Meanwhile, about two blocks from where I was standing and watching the marchers, hundreds of Nimba people had taken refuge at the Lutheran Church Compound. They had fled their homes all around the city of Monrovia and come to the Lutheran Church Compound with the hope that they would be spared from the wrath of agents of the Samuel Doe government. At that time, those agents were identifying Nimba people, entering their homes at night, and slaughtering them to send a message to their kinsmen who were fighting alongside Charles Taylor in Nimba County.

A friend who happened to be from Nimba County asked me to take a walk to see first-hand the conditions at the Lutheran Church Compound, where Nimba people had been gathering. As we made our way on the sidewalk, the topic of taking refuge at the Lutheran Church compound came up. However, we did not get to the heart of the conversation because it did not take too long to arrive at the compound. Upon arrival, I scanned the church and church yard and saw a sea of people. The compound was overflowing with Nimba people, some of whom I recognized.

Momentarily, I was speechless. I gazed at the multitude and at the same time felt a strong internal pull from them. They were Nimba people, my people, I reckoned. Under the cloud of persecution, I felt a strong bond with them; I wanted to be with them, I wanted the world to see me with them as a part of the persecuted. Young children and babies on their mothers' laps were sitting on overflow sheets spread outside the compound next to the sidewalk of Tubman Boulevard. It was well after 11:00 a.m., but the little children were still eating the corn meal breakfast that had been prepared for them. In spite of the strong urge I felt to be with the people, I ruled out the thought of coming to stay at the Lutheran Church for safety because the place was too overcrowded. Once again, as Wlah had done just days earlier in saving my life during an encounter with a Liberian government soldier who accused a friend and me of being rebels, His guidance steered me away from deciding to take refuge at the Lutheran church compound in Sinkor, Monrovia. As it turned out, the Lutheran church compound was the scene of a horrific massacre of over 600 people including men, women, and children on July 29, 1990, almost exactly one month after I arrived in the United States. The massacre was allegedly carried out by members of the Armed Forces of Liberia loyal to former President Samuel K. Doe.

Meanwhile, upon receipt of the facsimile Mr. Roy Johnson transmitted to Washington, D.C., Dr. John Roberts communicated with the U.S.

Embassy in Monrovia and facilitated the issuance of visa to me to travel to the United States without further delay. I received that visa on Friday, June 18, 1990. After that, another hurdle arose. Unless I was attempting to sneak out of Liberia in disguise, I had to get official permission from the government of Liberia to travel. That permission came in the form of an exit visa. At that time, the war raging in Nimba County was largely seen as one between the Nimba and Grand Gedeh people or between Nimba and Grand Gedeh Counties. Nimba people were under the microscope in Monrovia on suspicions of supporting rebels and, for that matter, being persecuted, if not killed. Under those circumstances, the Bureau of Immigration and Naturalization was the last place someone from Nimba County could think of entering. The reason was that a member of the President's ethnic Krahn headed the Bureau. Moreover, many employees of the Bureau were of the Krahn ethnic group.

In my mind, I had done nothing evil to anybody. I did not expect anybody or Krahns working at the Bureau of Immigration and Naturalization, some of whom I knew on a name basis, to do me any harm. Neither did I expect others at the Bureau who knew me either as a former student or graduate of the University of Liberia, or at that time as an instructor in Teachers College at the University of Liberia, to prevent my travel or to do harm to me. But I was not satisfied with that self-assurance because being nice or blameless is no antidote to collective guilt in Liberia. The saints are not differentiated from the devils when negative tribal sentiments poison social relations in Liberia. All are slaughtered and their corpses thrown into the gutters for the dogs and vultures to feed on, if not thrown into mass graves. I did not rely on my laurel of having had great personal relationships with all peoples; I did not take chances. I figured that going to the Bureau of Immigration and Naturalization would suggest that I was trying to leave because I had knowledge of the on-going invasion. I also reckoned that doing so amounted to willingly giving my head to those who were decapitating people on the basis of rumors or mere ethnicity.

Luckily, I did not go to the Bureau of Immigration and Naturalization. Gipolay, a friend's sister, offered to take my passport to the Bureau of Immigration and Naturalization to obtain my exit visa.[275] I gave Gipolay a long stare and wondered whether she was intoxicated when she made the offer to obtain my exit visa. Gipolay, who is still alive, is from Nimba County and is Mahn. Her predicament with respect to the looming threat to the lives of Nimba people was no different from mine. "Why would she offer to risk her life to obtain my exit visa?" I asked myself. She said that she had "lots of friends" at the Bureau of Immigration and Naturalization when I stared at her further and intently to figure out what the heck she was up to. In response to my suggestion that she sounded as if she were out of her mind, she smiled my comments away and acted as though she had everything under control. Again, with a smile, she went on to suggest that, "After all, I am a woman," which I took to mean she had a charm that I did not have. But whatever it was that Gipolay had, it worked. Sometime later during the afternoon of Friday, June 18, 1990, she returned with my passport with an exit visa stamped in it.

All was set. I had already purchased my air tickets to travel from Monrovia to Abidjan, Ivory Coast and from Abidjan to New York City. Normally it did not make sense to purchase an air ticket prior to obtaining a visa from the U.S. Embassy, but I was given the assurance that I would be granted. I had no reason to hesitate to buy my tickets. I felt some sense of relief that I would escape the wave of violence in Monrovia until the U.S. used its tremendous influence to settle the conflict. I was certain that the United States would not leave Liberia in the "cold" under those circumstances. In my mind, I was going to the United States for a temporary stay, perhaps two to three months, and that I would then be back with the rest of the American staff who had been evacuated a month before.

CHAPTER 27

In Search of Refuge

DEPARTING LIBERIA FOR THE U.S. IN 1990

ON FRIDAY JUNE 18, 1990, all was set for leaving Liberia, but my actual departure date was Monday June 21, 1990. It was not going to be an ordinary departure because my parents were in the village in Nimba County. I would not have taken the risk to travel to the village to say good-bye to them if I had the time for obvious reasons. The fate of everyone I was leaving behind including my parents and children weighed on me.[276]

Meanwhile, in Monrovia, Norah Johnnie, a relative, wanted a quick departure because my encounter with an AFL soldier terrified her. She felt that the longer I waited, the more dangerous the threat to my life grew. Early morning June 21, 1990, Norah sent the taxi driver she hired to Dr. Forh's residence to pick me up. I left the Forhs with a heavy heart and headed to my apartment to pick up Norah, my fiancée, Ms. Margaret Tumbay, and eleven-month-old Marsetta. I looked forward to a cup of tea, if not regular food, but there was absolutely nothing available to eat.

We left my apartment in Bardnersville and headed for Spriggs Payne airport located in Sinkor in an eerily quiet taxi; no conversation whatsoever. I held my tongue. The silence continued upon arrival at the airport. After

I boarded the cargo plane, it occurred to my fiancée that a goodbye was necessary. At that moment, she walked up to the location by the aircraft where the ladder touched the ground and stretched out her hand to shake my hand. Unwillingly, I stretched my hand and shook hers because I did not want to shun her. After the handshake, she turned around and walked away without saying anything. I only watched in disbelief. This is not a tell-all book, but I can say that the events of my departure from Liberia were a sign of what was to come years later in the United States.

In the meantime, the scale of events around me quickly turned my attention away from the personal to a bigger picture, meaning the catastrophe that hung over the country. Spriggs Payne Airport was chaotic and desperate. It seemed everybody was fighting to get out of Liberia. I learned the flight I was about to board was the last one out of Monrovia. More disturbingly, having a ticket did not guarantee a seat on the flight. Samukai, a little boy about eleven or thirteen years old, compounded my problem at the airport. His mom, Esther, asked me to drop him off with her family in New York City. Esther worked at a Travel Agency on Broad Street and sold me the air ticket for my flight from Abidjan to New York City.

Our flight from Abidjan to New York City was supposed to be on Zambian Airways. However, when Samukai and I arrived in Abidjan, we encountered problems with our tickets. Zambian Airways did not fly out of Abidjan on our schedule. Luckily, Esther knew Mr. Wilson Tarpeh who, at the time, was working with the African Development Bank in Abidjan. Prior to leaving Liberia, she gave me his contact information. When the ticket problem arose upon arrival in Abidjan, we immediately contacted Mr. Tarpeh. He met us in downtown Abidjan and helped resolve Samukai's ticket problem. As for me, a very tall, beautiful, and kind Ivorian airline agent whom I remember distinctly helped redirect my ticket for New York City. I asked for her full name to send her a thank you note upon arrival, but she only said that she was Hawa.

Our stay of one week in Abidjan not only seemed like eternity but also the place was extremely expensive. How ordinary people survived living in Abidjan was a wonder to me. Moreover, friends warned me in Liberia to "keep a low profile" in Abidjan. The Ivory Coast fully backed Charles Taylor's invasion of Liberia and Ivoirians regarded him as the de facto leader of Liberia. I heard members of his intelligence service viewed travelers from Monrovia to the Ivory Coast with suspicion, believing that President Doe sent them to spy on the activities of the rebels in the Ivory Coast. I knew that I was not out of the woods by being in the Ivory Coast.

I stayed at Hotel Liberty, a low-cost facility, which was technically a brothel, judging from local customers who filed in and out almost nonstop. Occasionally, I strolled out in the evening to buy roasted fish, served along with a local beer. One week in Abidjan was not enough to assess life in the Ivory Coast but, in terms of freedom, Liberia felt freer even as things were falling apart due to the civil war. I felt a suffocating tension in Abidjan.

Eventually, June 27, 1990, the day of my departure for New York City came. At the airport, when I boarded the New York City-bound Air Afrique flight, I could not dust Liberia off my feet. As death hung over my head, hunger also took its bite out of me upon leaving Liberia, as if my life in Sanniquellie during my grade school years was yesterday. Moreover, I left for the United States as if I were deserted at my deathbed; the people I expected to see while dying never showed up. I felt like I did not matter.

Upon leaving Abidjan, I put on an earphone and heard the unmistakable voice of Madonna, the "Material Girl." Her song, "Live To Tell," was playing on the airline entertainment system.[277] Madonna's words, "I have a tale to tell; sometimes it gets so hard to hide it well; I was not ready for the fall; too blind to see the writing on the wall," struck a chord in me. I did not have to be a woman to speak about a man who "can tell a thousand lies" to experience that reaction to "I've learned my lesson well" and "Hope I live to tell." The song perfectly captured and preserved the external as well as internal circumstances of my departure from Liberia. As a result, the farther June 27, 1990, recedes into the past, the more meaningful "Live To Tell" has become.

I own my experience in Liberia from May 1987 to June 21, 1990, and point a finger at no one. The world I create is inescapable. Words and actions emanating from my thoughts generate disturbances in the universe. Those disturbances may take a few seconds, a day, a month, a year, or even several years, but they eventually return to me. I romanticized Liberia. I could not wait to reunite with Liberia and everything it represented while studying in the United States. I dreamed not only about the landscape, the palm trees, and my childhood but also to find a bride upon my return. A few life curveballs and the tragedy of the Taylor invasion soured my experience in Liberia, but they could not extinguish my love of Liberia.

New York City

On the evening of June 27, 1990, Samukai and I arrived at the John F. Kennedy International Airport in New York City. Once I got off that plane, went through immigration and reached the passenger pick-up area, I breathed a sigh of relief. I was now in America, the land of safety I sought in my request to USAID's Mission Director, Gontee, in Liberia. Even though Gontee denied my request at that time, my safe arrival in New York City achieved what I asked: for fear of my life, I wanted to leave Liberia until the conflict was resolved.

I was no stranger to New York City and was in no awe at its magnificent skyscrapers and bright lights. Yet, in New York City, I felt out of place psychologically. Unknowns I could not think about in the frenzy of my departure from Liberia gushed up and overwhelmed me. I was not worthy of Wlah's grace, yet I could not resist the spiritual implication of my arrival in America. I did not feel like one of the "chosen" ones. I was one of the "chosen" ones. I was supposed to point towards Heaven with my index finger in praise of Wlah. I should have jumped with joy, but I felt like a fish thrown out of a lake upon the shore. I was melancholic. I was removed from the raging carnage in Liberia, but nearly everyone who mattered to me was left behind in Liberia. Instead of greeting the New York City breeze that blew against my forehead with a smile as soon as I got out of the terminal building, I hung my head and looked towards the ground with a heavy heart.

In New York City, Samukai and I spent the night with Ms. Josephine Paye Tozay, a Dan woman from Nimba County who arrived from Liberia not long before our arrival for the same reason. Even though Josephine and I are from Nimba County, I met her through Dr. Forh and Mrs. Victoria Forh. The Forhs hailed from southeastern Liberia and spoke tribal languages different from those spoken in Nimba County. Josephine had never been to America before. I did not know anything about her living arrangement. However, she and the family that accommodated her were gracious. They fed us and gave us a comfortable room to stay in for the night.

I told Josephine the story about Samukai's coming to America along with me. As his mom, Esther, directed, I contacted her relatives to pick Samukai up from me. On the following morning, I was worried about missing my flight to Washington, D.C., because the person who was supposed to pick Samukai up did not show up on time. I loathed the terrible bind this person put me into because I ended up leaving Samukai with Josephine to be picked up. If I had not made that decision, I would have missed my flight to Washington, D.C. I felt horrible leaving Samukai at Josephine's place without meeting the person who was supposed to pick him up, because Samukai was a human being and not a package to leave at a location for someone to fetch. In any case, after I arrived in Washington, D.C., I called Josephine to find out whether Samukai's relative came and picked him up. She told me someone picked Samukai up after I left. I was unable to reach the person who picked Samukai up and no one attempted to reach me. I have never heard from Samukai or about him since June 27, 1990. I am still on the lookout to find out what became of him.

WASHINGTON, D.C.

In Washington, D.C., I joined some of the USAID-Liberia American staff who were evacuated in May 1990. I first stayed at the beautiful, yet eerily quiet and gloomy State Plaza Hotel at 2117 E Street NW, Washington, D.C., right across the street from the Department of State. After about three weeks, I moved out of the State Plaza Hotel to the Ambassador Hotel, less than a mile away, believing that the former's ambiance was affecting my mood. Even though the gloomy dungeon-like interior of State Plaza Hotel did not help, I later realized that it was the situation in Liberia, not the hotel that affected my state of mind.

In the days that followed, I enrolled in a series of short-term USAID-sponsored management training courses as we awaited conditions in Liberia to improve. However, it soon became clear that there was no Liberia as we knew it to return to. As a result, a decision was then made by USAID higher-ups that, other than a skeletal staff in Monrovia, all USAID activities in Liberia had to be phased out. With no purpose for continuing to support my training indefinitely, I was kept on payroll and asked to help with the phase-out activities until October 31, 1990. Doing my job at that time was somewhat comparable to having someone work on his own funeral plans before his death, the difference being that it was not a physical death, but a psychological one.

I saw the pain of abrupt separation from Liberia in the faces of some USAID-Liberia American staff at the Department of State as they grieved the unfolding disintegration of Liberia. At display was shared experience as workmates in Liberia and humanity. Huddling with that group albeit temporarily provided a measure of comfort and healing. Knowing that the ultimate purpose of my work was to dismantle the group that shored me was more than stepping into the unknown.

Beyond concerns about the family I left behind, which consumed me up to that point, I did not give appreciable thought to the loss of country. Therefore, when I realized that a return to Liberia in the near term was a dim prospect, it was a hard and bitter pill to swallow. Even though I had not heard from my parents, I was grateful that any immediate family had not been killed. Instead of spending emotional energy on chasing a country that did not exist anymore, I started weaving efforts to bring my family to relative safety in the United States.

The only family I had in the United States at that time was Col. Carl H. Cannon. I tried to reach him and discovered he was away on assignment in Germany. Until Col. Cannon returned to Annandale, Virginia, I moved into Mrs. Viessa Williams's home in Washington, D.C., and rented a single room. Patricia Ford, a friend who worked at the West Africa Desk at the Department of State, recommended exploring the room Mrs. Williams had. Upon meeting and agreeing to rent the room to me, the elderly African American woman was strictly business. She never asked who I was or what my circumstances were. She indicated she did not work for me and did not expect to see any dirty dishes or trash in the house. I had no problems with the rules because they were very simple, clear, and agreeable. Patricia Ford helped move my belongings to Mrs. Williams' house, where I stayed at for about a week. She did not raise her voice at any time or complain about garbage or dirty dishes because I did not leave any. Upon Col. Carl Cannon's return from Germany, he came to Mrs. Williams' home and took me to Annandale, Virginia.

One of my worst fears became a reality while I was with the Cannons in Annandale. The civil war, which had been raging in rural Liberia at the time of my departure from Liberia, entered Monrovia, the capital. The bombardment of the city knocked out the landline phones. I had no way of contacting anyone in Monrovia, but graphic television images of the violence inundated the airwaves in America. Col. Cannon, who rightly sensed that the situation would drag out for a longtime, advised that I apply for asylum and regularize my status in the United States. Beyond advice, he took me to the Immigration and Naturalization Service (INS)

Office located at 4420 N. Fairfax Dr., Arlington, Virginia, where I picked up the application materials. Without the help of an attorney, I completed the asylum application and submitted it on August 14, 1990. A few days later, I received a notice of receipt of my application for asylum from the U.S. Department of Justice, Immigration and Naturalization Service dated August 17, 1990.[278] I was hopeful.

Meanwhile, Col. Cannon and Dr. Cannon continued what families do when a member is in distress. They provided support and reassured me that all would be well. They took me to the Naval Recreation Station at the Solomons Islands in Maryland, where I stood on a deck and crabbed in the Patuxent River with a crab net on a long pole while others went about crabbing in boats. As always, due to my fear of water and my inability to swim, no one was able to convince me to get on a boat. After the harvest, we had an unforgettable weekend, feasting on buckets of wonderfully seasoned and cooked crabs along with a variety of spirits. On another occasion, Dr. Cannon took me for a tour of the White House, where I saw its grandeur. The carpets were rolled to the side to avoid getting them messy and, of course, tourists were not allowed to enter the family quarters.

At the Cannons' home in Annandale, Col. Cannon and I spent quite a bit of time in his den on numerous occasions. We had conversations, laughed about our time in Seoul, Korea, and gobbled shots of the best spirits one could imagine. Our forays in Col. Cannon's den with strong spirits, reminiscing and laughing about our experience in Seoul helped me cope with the stressful situation I was enduring. However, alcohol is not a route I would recommend to anyone going through a stressful situation. Individuals have different levels of tolerance and, more importantly, refuge in the "bottle" is an illusion.

In the meantime, by October 31, 1990, no movement had occurred on my asylum application other than the notice of receipt I received a few days after I submitted the application. Like Col. Cannon, Dr. John Roberts saw what loomed at the horizon and helped prepare me for what was to come. He wrote a strong letter of recommendation, a memorandum for the record and made a request to the Liberia Task Force at the U.S. Department of State to assist with efforts to reunite my family. Dr. Roberts' request followed information I received that some members of my family had fled Monrovia due to the bombardment and violence. At that time, there were indications that they might cross the Sierra Leonean-Liberian border and go to the

United States Embassy in Freetown, Sierra Leone, without passports or other documentation.[279] Eventually, Dr. Roberts left for a new assignment in Madagascar. One after the other, the other USAID-Liberia American staff who huddled with me and provided a zone of comfort in Washington, D.C., left for reassignments to different countries around the world. As expected, the professional support group fell apart.

GREENSBORO, NC FULL CIRCLE

As it became increasingly clear that I would not be returning to Liberia at least in the near term, I could not sit around and hope hopelessly. My plan B was to get a job and work on bringing my family to the United States. The breakup of my professional support group was painful, but the silver lining was that it created an urgency and impetus for action. Moreover, in formulating plan B, I was in communications with my long-time friend, Flomo, from the get-go. Flomo lived in Greensboro, North Carolina. Our telephone conversations became more frequent as October 1990 neared. We had been friends since our days in Sanniquellie, Liberia, not to mention our time studying in Greensboro, in the mid-1980s.

Fond memories of the people who helped me succeed at North Carolina A & T State University played a role in formulating plan B. I never forgot my former Department Chair, Dr. Arthur Bell, and former professors Dr. Larry Powers, Dr. Francis Walson and Dr. Alton Thompson. Others included, but were not limited to Mrs. Ruth Grandy, Mrs. Sharon Martin and Mrs. Gracie Potts.[280] Flomo had an easy job in persuading me to consider moving to Greensboro, because of the goodwill of those who oversaw my studies at North Carolina A & T State University.

In putting plan B together, I reached out to Dr. Arthur Bell and Dr. Larry Powers for guidance. More than three years after I had graduated from North Carolina A & T State, they cared enough to advise me to take the National Teachers' Exam (NTE). Beyond advice, they also assembled test preparation materials and mailed them to me in Annandale, Virginia. I registered for the NTE, studied the materials diligently and took the test in Alexandra. I passed the NTE and, in a few months, started my public education career in Fayetteville, North Carolina in January 1991. I am eternally grateful to Dr. Arthur Bell and Dr. Larry Powers as well as my other professors and all those who supported me at North Carolina A &

T State University. As the end of October 1990 approached, their support and encouragement, which had already made North Carolina my second home, put it on the top of the list of places I considered moving to.

I needed a place to stay at in Greensboro while I looked for employment. I had saved some money while I was in Washington, D.C. However, getting my own apartment upon arrival in Greensboro before getting a job was putting the cart before the horse. Instead, I asked Flomo if he and his girlfriend, Layea, whom I had met once on a visit before, would be kind to let me stay with them for at least a month before finding my own place.[281] Flomo thought it was an insult to make such a request because he felt his home was my home.

With Flomo's assurance, I flew out of Dulles International Airport near Washington, D.C., on the evening of Friday November 2, 1990, and arrived at Greensboro International Airport in a little over an hour. Based on conversations Flomo and I had had and the excitement that built up to the time I departed for Greensboro, I expected to see him and Layea at the airport waiting to pick me up. However, upon arrival, only Flomo was waiting at the airport. I asked for Layea, but he did not give me a definitive answer. In asking to spend some time with them before finding my own apartment, I impressed upon Flomo to make sure that Layea was aware of my request. He assured me that he would do so. Subsequently, I asked about Layea every time we communicated. Flomo put me under the impression that Layea was agreeable. Against that background, when I arrived in Greensboro and Layea was not with him, I did not make anything out of her absence at the airport.

Upon arrival at Flomo's apartment, I did not notice the cold shoulders Layea gave me because I was blinded by my excitement to see them. She, as we say in Liberia, "kept a low profile" all night. Moreover, I naively assumed that no woman would want to appear unwelcoming to her boyfriend's best friend, especially someone she had not known for a long time. Flomo and I stayed in the living room downstairs all night, talked about our past experiences and laughed while we had gin.

In the next few days after my arrival, I was completely oblivious to the gathering storm of displeasure against me. The first complaint against me was the loudness of my shortwave transistor radio, which I used to monitor worldwide news. When the next complaint turned out to be my failure to stretch out the shower curtain after showering, I eventually caught on to the reality that Layea was not agreeable to my staying with them as Flomo had led me to believe. In other words, I was not welcome.

The mystery about Layea's complaints against me started to unravel on the morning of Saturday, November 10, 1990, when I overheard Flomo and Layea fussing over me in their bedroom. It was then I realized Layea had not agreed to my staying with them. As they quarreled, I packed my belongings and apologized for the problem I had created for them, although at that moment I had not figured out the reason for Layea's hostile attitude. I moved into a motel somewhere across the street from the Greensboro Coliseum and stayed there for one week.

Francis Yarzue

While at that motel, Francis Yarzue, a friend whom Flomo had introduced me to, and his fiancée, Yah Voker, came to persuade me to move in with them until I can find a job and my own apartment. When Francis and Yah Voker came to my motel room, he told me

> Marsilius, as a friend of Flomo's, you are also my friend. Although I know that you were saving some money while you were in Washington, D.C., it does not make sense to let you stay in a motel while we have an empty room that you can stay in as you look for employment. So, we came so that you can go with us to the house.[282]

Francis and Yah persuaded me. So, I packed my belongings and followed them. Following the move, they proved to be more than friends. They were like my own family. Francis would not even take anything from me as a contribution for food and all the expenses in maintaining the apartment. Francis and Yah were very respectful and kind to me. They had three cars, one of which they let me use without taking a penny from me.

Francis was a Nimbaian who, like me, spoke Mahn. However, we did not know each other in Liberia before coming to the United States. I got to know him through Flomo. Francis was adept with Mahn culture and was a masterful storyteller. He was plainly hilarious. We were always in for a good dose of laughter whenever we gathered at his apartment at Overland Heights in Greensboro. There he made our burdens a little lighter.

I lift Francis Yarzue and Yah Voker in these pages because they provided relief along this journey. I have never forgotten the room they gave me to sleep in and the delicious meals Yah Voker prepared for me. Indeed, I have never forgotten the car they let me use to drive to and from Fayetteville along North Carolina Highway 421 when I took a teaching assignment with Cumberland County Schools. Francis and Yah made me feel like somebody and they made me laugh. I remain grateful to them. Sadly, not everyone in Liberia, let alone in the United States and the rest of the world, knows that Francis Yarzue lived and walked the face of this planet. With this story, the world will know that he was here; that he touched me and many others.

After I moved away from Flomo and Layea, the mystery surrounding Layea's attitude bothered me. "If Layea was not agreeable, what exactly made her disagreeable?" And "If there were a reason, what could it be?" I wondered. I had never seen Layea anywhere else and could not fathom any disagreements with her. I was completely baffled. Since I did not know Layea's true motivation for complaining about me, I walked away from that apartment with a very negative impression of her. I put her into the compartment of my heart where my enemies belonged. Elvis Presley said, "Truth is like the sun. You can shut it out for a time, but it ain't goin' away." Indeed, the reason Layea treated me like an enemy in 1990 was that Flomo told her about the negative information I provided him.

The trouble started shortly after I visited with Flomo, not too long after my escape from Liberia to the U.S. During that visit in Greensboro, I met Layea for the first time. She had moved in with Flomo sometime before the visit. More importantly, they were planning to have a life together. Upon my return to Washington, D.C., I made a dumb mistake by providing Flomo an unflattering information someone had given me about Layea. I advised him to proceed cautiously if he were planning to have a life together with Layea. I was fully aware of the implications of my action. However, at thirty-two years old, I saw the world through a different lens than I see it now. Flomo and I were like brothers. I could not resist the urge to protect him and hoped that he would guard against disclosing the information as well as its source. Unfortunately, Flomo confronted Layea, who had a hunch about the source of the information. Layea used her womanly skill in extracting the source of the information and my name surfaced. For a long time, I was completely unaware that he had breached the confidentiality I assumed.

I confronted Flomo when I discovered that he had told Layea the information I provided him. However, by that time, the damage had already been done. Layea's attitude towards me was a reaction to something terrible I had done to her. In my mind, she had a legitimate reason to turn me into a foe. If I were in her shoes, I would probably react in a similar way. Had I known what I now know at the time, I would have gotten on my knees, asked for Layea's forgiveness, and given her a kola nut. It is never too late. The time has come to face the truth. Layea, I am sorry. I was wrong to give that information to Flomo. I hope that you will forgive me. As for Flomo, if he were alive, I would give him the kola nut to pass it on to Layea. His reaction would certainly be to find an appropriate parable to augment the kola nut as well as to make us laugh. On the day that I confronted him about divulging information to Layea, he told me what he wanted everyone who cared about him to know about his significant other. He was quite explicit: "If you see someone on top of my wife 'doing her,' please do not tell me."

Kirby Vacuum Cleaner Salesman

After I moved in with Francis Yarzue and Yah Voker, I applied for a teaching position with several school districts in North Carolina. In the interim, I looked around Greensboro to find any kind of job to maintain myself. A Kirby Vacuum Cleaner distributor hired me as a salesperson in training. The training took about a week and, from the get-go, I had a clear sense of the nature of the job. A vacuum cleaner salesman was a job and it was better than doing nothing. However, inasmuch as I was willing to try new things, I knew my strengths and weaknesses; I knew I was not cut out to be a salesman. If sweeping streets and selling Kirby vacuum cleaners were the only two jobs available in Greensboro, I would choose sweeping streets in a heartbeat, despite a master's degree. That was my mindset upon starting the training.

Rock, who was still alive at the time, gave me an NC A & T State University directory and encouraged me to try the vacuum cleaner sales job.[283] An African American woman answered the first call I made during the evening of the same day Rock gave me the directory. The woman wasted no time in tearing me apart as soon as she realized I was calling to sell something to her. She was patently nasty. "Goodness!" I said upon putting the receiver down. "If only she knew the burdens on my shoulders, perhaps she would not be so nasty," I said, shaking my head in disbelief. On the following morning, I took the vacuum cleaner demonstration set back to the distributor. He shook his head in shock and disbelief as well when I told him that I could not do it. He put his hand in his pocket and gave me fifty dollars.

The silver lining in the Kirby vacuum cleaner story is that it made me a better person. I probably would not be as sensitive as I am if I had not had that experience. Telemarketers are persistent when they call. Moreover, it seems they always call when people return home from work and are exhausted. They are not, for that reason, a beloved class of professionals in the United States. I cannot count how many times I have received those annoying calls over the years. Yet, every time a telemarketer calls me, my experience with that woman in Greensboro in late 1990 forces me to think about the caller. Is the caller a single mom trying to earn something to put food on the table for her family? Is the caller a high school student trying to earn money to pay for his or her first car? Is the caller a college student trying to earn money to pay for his or her tuition? Is the caller a refugee who fled from war and chaos in his or her country trying to begin a new life in a new country? Is the caller a newly arrived immigrant trying to earn money to pay his or her rent or get his or her foothold in the American society? I do not remember buying anything from a telemarketer, but I often wait and listen to the sales pitch and then politely and nicely tell the caller that I am sorry I do not need that product at this time. If I am in a hurry on my way out of the door, I simply tell the caller, "I cannot talk to you now." Being nice to telemarketers is important because the answer one gives can make or break a young person or a vulnerable person on their first job.

CHAPTER 28

Fayetteville, NC

S HORTLY AFTER THE KIRBY VACUUM cleaner episode, Cumberland County Schools invited me for an interview for a teaching position in Fayetteville, NC. I drove the nearly two-hour trip and had the interview at Southview High School on Elk Road in Hope Mills, a suburb of Fayetteville. In January 1991, Cumberland County Schools hired me. I taught at Southview High School and at Pine Forest High School located at opposite limits of Fayetteville. I commuted from Greensboro to Fayetteville for the first three weeks of school, using the car Francis Yarzue and Yah Voker lent me. Shortly thereafter, I moved into a two-bedroom apartment on Dunrobin Drive in Fayetteville.[284]

I took the job with Cumberland County Schools in the middle of the 1990-1991 school year. Later, I found out that the teacher who had the position before me was a member of the North Carolina National Guard. He reportedly resigned to go to war in Iraq during the first Persian Gulf War. With the teaching job as my only source of income, I was living from paycheck to paycheck. My high phone bills, which accounted for the largest percentage of my cost of living, were not only a perennial occurrence but also a symptom of a larger problem simmering under the surface.[285] I was calling Liberia regularly, trying to reach anyone for information about my family, not to mention collect calls which were priced exorbitantly per minute. In the United States, Microwave Communications, Inc., (MCI) made a fortune out of me because I racked up huge phone bills calling friends and acquaintances across the country just to talk.

Under the yoke of separation from home and family, I entered an American public school classroom unprepared for the cultural clash that greeted me. Race and culture confronted me at the entrance, but I was tone deaf. Indeed, a deep divide existed in Liberia between Americo- and indigenous Liberians, but skin color never appreciably crept into the Liberian psyche as a feature of that divide. My early education in Liberia also blindfolded me. Most of my teachers were white American nuns and Peace Corps volunteers as well as nuns from other countries in Europe and Africa. As kids, because some white people talked with little lip movement, we not only thought white people "spoke in their throats," but also imitated them. However, upon entering school, we had no trouble understanding whatever they said in their "throats." Moreover, we did not look down upon our white teachers because they spoke in their throats. I did not hear myself differently, but I soon realized that something was amiss as people I encountered outside of school asked, "I detect an accent, where are you from?" I had an accent and, more importantly, I was living in a culture that was overly obsessed with accent. My education in Liberia also prevented me from recognizing that my "accent" could be an impediment to student learning. Thus, on my first day on the job, I believed my students would see me merely as a teacher and a human being.

I learned to navigate issues beyond race and having an accent. I understood that teaching, particularly in an American public school classroom, was more than delivering content. Staying in tune with as well as recognizing where circles of culture meet was a big part of navigating the classroom and becoming a successful educator. Content knowledge notwithstanding, I soon realized that culture was not the proverbial elephant in the room in the United States. Instead, culture was the lion in the room. More importantly, it did not wait for someone to muster the courage over a long time to talk about it. Culture came out swinging and roaring anyway. I learned that Americans have a disdain for pedigree, and it runs deep. An unapologetic "This is America" greets any sign of contempt if they choose not to use profane languages of their preference.

Becoming a teacher in America helped me begin living anew. I thought and talked differently. I did not change my accent or abandon my culture but expressions like "Old man," "Old lady," or words like "Fat," although endearing in Liberia, were not regarded so in the United States. Such expressions and words became dormant in my usage. Moreover, I saw and heard my students only after I looked into the mirror and saw myself. The person I saw in the mirror witnessed his Dad's humiliation and endured hunger while living with relatives far away from home in pursuit of an education. The person in the mirror was me and that experience motivated me to pursue an education with a passion.

In North Carolina, the proverbial elephant in the room not only revealed itself as it existed in the greater society but also stayed put. Unlike adults for whom the social hierarchy in America was seldom a subject of conversations, my Native American, African American, and Caucasian students saw the elephant not as the scary beast adults saw it as but as a toy to dabble with superficially. In general, based on their ages, my students behaved similarly. They inquired and explored; they wanted to learn something new or confirm a stereotype about Africans. As an African teacher with an accent, I made matters worse by not being forthcoming about whether in Africa I lived in a tree. While my African American students were not the only ones who made derogatory comments about Africans, they were the ones who readily made such comments.

IMAGINATION SAVES LIFE

A combination of inexperience and growing up in a different culture almost resulted in a disaster. One day in my tenth-grade class of nearly all white students at Southview High School, a young man wanted to know whether I had ever shot a gun and, if so, what kills had I had. I told the students I had shot a gun and went on to tell them a story about a shotgun my Dad owned as well as a .22 my uncle also owned. Moreover, I told the students that my kills included ground squirrels, pigeons, hawks, ground hogs, snakes, and porcupines. With that answer, I opened a can of worms. Apparently to bring the story closer to home, another male student wanted to know whether I had ever shot a rabbit. "No, we do not have rabbits in Liberia," I responded. Although the exchanges with the students were spontaneous, unknowingly, they were luring me into a trap. Two things happened that made me suspicious that they had something up their sleeves. First, a dead silence followed when another student asked, "Would you go rabbit hunting with us?" Second, in unison, they said, "Yeah, Flumo, you can't say no!" I raced in my mind for an excuse to escape the trap and thought I had a perfect one when I said, "I do not have a shotgun." However, before I finished my response, another student offered to bring one for me on the day of the hunting trip. Quickly, I overcame my apprehension and saw the students' offer as an opportunity to set aside my educator persona to spend time with them as a normal human being. I agreed to go on the trip on a Saturday sometime in the afternoon.

About six to eight all white male students met with me at Southview High School, where we decided to go along U.S. Highway 301 West (Business I-95 West). We drove for about fifteen minutes, parked on the roadside, and walked into the woods. I had not been to the place before, but the students were quite familiar with the area. Before we started hunting, an important role reversal happened. The students gave me a lecture about how the whole rabbit hunting exercise was going to work. We were to encircle a briar patch about a quarter of a town lot. Everyone was to hold his shotgun with the muzzle pointing downward. We were standing about twenty to thirty feet apart, but as we walked toward the center of the circle we created, the distance between us decreased and made it extremely dangerous to shoot at a rabbit when it came out. I did not take any shot during the entire time we were there because we were too close to each other. However, some of the students shot and got a number of kills. I recall the students killed three to four rabbits.

Right after we walked to another area and encircled a second briar patch, I had already imagined the headline in the Fayetteville Observer: "African Teacher Accidentally Killed during Rabbit Hunting with his Students." That imaginary headline in the Fayetteville Observer and the constant reminder I had always had that I am Mom's only son caused me to stop the rabbit hunting. I managed to convince the students that we were standing at close range and it was too dangerous to continue the rabbit hunting exercise. Instead, I told stories and answered their many questions about Liberia, specifically, and Africa in general to appease them. Even though the rabbit hunting exercise was not terribly successful, the students returned home that evening feeling as though they had had a blast and the best time of their lives merely by hanging out with me in the woods. When I think about that experience, I can only thank Wlah for being good to me over the years. Looking back now, I can clearly see the risk I took while I was hunting with my students in 1991 in Fayetteville.

Miracle Temple

The 1991 academic year ended with excitement but there was a tinge of uncertainty. Before the year ended, I contacted my three older daughters, Lila, Wonkermie and Oretha in the Liberian Civil War. That relief lifted my spirit. Right away, I started work on trying to bring them to the United States. On the other hand, right after six months with Cumberland County Schools, I learned that the school district had extant plans to phase-out my position at the end of the school year. Without a job meant I had no health insurance. I had my rent and other expenses covered for the month of June, but beyond June, everything was uncertain. It was a frightening experience.

The saving grace was my church family in Fayetteville. Morris Cole, through whom I built the social support in Fayetteville, was born in Liberia. I felt a sense of déjà vu upon meeting Mr. Cole. Instantly, I felt like I had someone in my corner; I was ecstatic. Deacon Cole, as he is called, took me to his church and introduced me to the pastor, Bishop Bennie L. Kelly.[286] The pastor and everyone in the church accepted me. Bishop Kelly, who was particularly gung-ho about me, quickly learned about my travails and did everything to help. On one particular Sunday, my rent of $375 was due. I went to church without the slightest idea where I would get the money to pay. Although I did not tell anybody what was on my mind, Bishop Kelly sensed that something was troubling me. I told her everything was okay when she asked me. My reticence to tell Bishop Kelly my rent problem stemmed from pride, but not vain pride. After church, she called me aside and insisted that I talk to her because, as she indicated, she was certain that something was troubling my heart.

Reluctantly, I told Bishop Kelly that my rent was due, and I did not have the money to pay. When she asked me what the rent was, I swallowed that pride and told her that my rent was $375. Subsequently, she wrote a check for $375 and gave it to me. In the next few days, I shared the good news with Bishop Kelly that my daughters were with my Mom safely in the village. Upon fleeing Liberia for fear of my life, I left the children in Monrovia in the custody of Yei B. Tokpah, their biological mother. Their trek from Monrovia to Sanniquellie, two hundred and seven miles away, began when Charles Taylor's rebels entered and overran Monrovia. The children later told me stories about the horror they witnessed on their way to Sanniquellie.[287]

Bishop Kelly had been actively involved in efforts to bring my family to the United States. She led prayers on their behalf and encouraged me.

When she asked what she could do to help upon hearing the good news, I told her that I had funds for their transport from Liberia to Abidjan, capital of the Ivory Coast, and their maintenance while awaiting the processing of their travel documents and visas. Thereafter, I instructed Samuel Duo (now Dr. Samuel Duo) and Yei B. Tokpah to take the children from Liberia to Abidjan for their travel documents and visa processing. As soon as I got word from Abidjan that the children received their visas to travel to the United States, I shared the good news with Deacon Cole who, in turn, informed Bishop Kelly. Without hesitation, she purchased the children's air tickets to travel to the United States. I look forward to finishing this book and delivering a signed copy to Bishop Kelly because I do not have the words to thank her for all that she did for me.

RAEFORD ROAD PLANT NURSERY

Lila, Wonkermie, and Oretha were scheduled to depart Abidjan and arrive in Newark, New Jersey via Lisbon, Portugal on July 21, 1991, but the joy and relief I felt about their coming did not reach the bottom of my soul because I had become unemployed. Although I believed that public assistance was intended for those who had fallen on hard times, turning to public assistance was a no go. Instead, I put my master's degree aside and took an odd job at a plant nursery on Raeford Road along U.S. Highway 401 in Fayetteville. I did not tell the approximately forty-year-old white proprietor anything much about my educational background when he asked. I unloaded delivery trucks with plants as well as loaded potted plants in customers' vehicles, earning $4.25 per hour for which I was grateful. I kept some distance from the other workers who had not only been at the nursery longer but also knew quite a bit about the proprietor because they engaged in inappropriate gossips about him. I had come from far away in the village in Liberia and fallen on hard times. As "a child of an orphan," I could not engage in vain talk.

DOLORES (DEE) ROBINSON

Meanwhile about two weeks prior to my daughters' departure from Abidjan, Mrs. Dolores (Dee) Robinson, another member of my support network, helped prepare for their arrival in the United States. I met Dee, an energetic

African American woman, through Col. Carl Cannon and Dr. Cyrenius and Mrs. Victoria Forh. At the time, Dee and her husband, Frank Robinson, were on active duty with the U.S. military in Seoul, Korea. The Robinsons were regulars at the Forhs' residence during get-togethers the Forhs hosted at their home in Seoul, Korea.

The Robinsons retired, returned from Korea, and settled in Fayetteville. So, the first thing Col. Cannon told me upon informing him that I had taken a job in Fayetteville was to look for them. Frank and Dee's names triggered nostalgia about Seoul. I could not wait to see them. I looked them up in the phone book, called them and there were no surprises on the day I met with Frank and Dee in Fayetteville. Frank, low-key as ever, greeted me quietly while the lively Dee Robinson gave me a bear hug. She heard about the tragic civil war in Liberia and wanted to know whether Cy and Vicky also escaped Liberia and came to the United States.[288]

After the pleasantries, I shared a synopsis of the ordeal that resulted in my escape from Liberia and flight to the United States in June 1990. Thereafter, we talked about Cy and Vicky Forh and reminisced our time in Seoul. Moments later, when I told Dee that my older daughters were on their way to me in Fayetteville via Abidjan, Lisbon, and Newark, New Jersey, she sprang into action. She took me to Sam's club in Fayetteville, where she bought large consignments of everything edible, she felt that the children would need. Her words, "Marsilius, the kids have gone through a lot. So, we have got to fatten them when they arrive," still ring in my ears. Upon my return to my apartment on Dunrobin Drive, my kitchen shelves looked like the ones at the supermarket after I stocked everything Dee purchased.

THE HEAVY LIFTING

I planned to fly Lila, Wonkermie and Oretha from Abidjan to a nearby airport, but such flights were not available.[289] Flying them to Newark International Airport, the best deal available, meant renting a car to pick them up. However, by that time, I had depleted my savings. My only option was to drive my 1978 Dodge Magnum-318 to Newark, New Jersey. Although my car had been reliable along the routes in North Carolina, the driving as well as speeding along Interstate ninety-five (I-95) was mindlessly brutal. I did not believe my car could make the one thousand ninety two-mile roundtrips. In the wake of the heavy lifting others were doing in facilitating the children's travel to the United States, that predicament made me to feel inadequate.

The heavy lifting started with Lila, Wonkermie and Oretha. They walked 207 miles from Monrovia to Sanniquellie, seeing bloated and decaying bodies in gutters and on shoulders of the highway. Although they never suffered any physical harm, according to the culture, children are not supposed to see such things because of the trauma and their lingering psychological impact.[290] Their travel from the village to Abidjan was also risky because a death cloud loomed over the Ivorian territory near the Liberian border.[291] Those who traveled between the two countries in that area did so at their peril.

The heavy lifting continued with Yei B. Tokpah. She put her own life at risk in the hope of securing a better future for her children. She picked up the children from the village, crossed that treacherous Ivorian border and took them to Abidjan to secure visas for their travel to the United States. All of this happened in the hopelessness generated by the civil war in the same time frame and risky environment. She decided to send her children away to the United States without any guarantee that she would see them again. She was more courageous than Mom who sent me to live with relatives in Sanniquellie to get an education.[292]

Others like Samuel N. Duo, who helped Yei B. Tokpah navigate Abidjan, Saye Gonleh and Rev. Herbert Zigbuo contributed to the success of the children's travel to the United States. Rev. Zigbuo's travel to the Ivory Coast at the same time I was planning for the children to travel to the United States was essential.[293] The reason was that sending funds to Yei B. Tokpah and Samuel Duo to facilitate the children's travel arrangements in Abidjan was a big challenge. Sending the money through the bank was an option but that meant unnecessary delays in receiving it. Moreover, Ivorian bank policies required releasing the money in Ivorian currency and taking out an undetermined bank fee. The risk of sending one thousand dollars in cash by anyone was enormous. However, barring an attack on Rev. Zigbuo, I had the utmost confidence that he would deliver the funds safely to Samuel Duo. Rev. Zigbuo vindicated me, and I have never stopped thanking him because, according to David Knapp, "Thank you has a half-life of 15 minutes."[294] Unfortunately, Rev. Herbert Zigbuo died in Durham, North Carolina on May 30, 2012. Today, he cannot read this acknowledgement of his role in facilitating my children's travel to the United States. Therefore, I carved out this space in this book to appreciate him. I want his family and the world to know that I remain eternally grateful to him. Perhaps a thank you on a printed page will have a longer half-life.

RALPH SUTTON

Deacon Morris Cole understood my predicament when I felt inadequate; when I could not afford to rent a car to pick up my daughters at Newark International Airport. Apparently, he talked to someone and, soon, I found out that my church members would not let me play the small role I had in bringing my daughters to the United States. Brother Ralph Sutton, a U.S. veteran and a member of Miracle Temple who bubbled with love and compassion, called me and volunteered to take me to Newark to pick up the girls.[295] At the time, he had just purchased a new van.

Brother Sutton and I departed Fayetteville on Monday, July 22, 1991, and spent the night at the home of Maybe Johnson, a schoolmate, near Newark, New Jersey. At Newark International Airport no more than thirty minutes away the following morning, I was jittery because it took a long time for the children to come out to the arrival and greeting area. They were held at Immigration for more than an hour, supposedly because Wonkermie's temporary travel document had a problem. Eventually the problem was resolved even though it was not clear to me what the problem was. That delay at the airport worried me, but Wlah had brought the children thus far and I did not believe that He would let Wonkermie be sent back to Africa.

Finally, the children came out and jumped into my arms. I literally lifted all three of them at the same time because they were so little. Lila's big bright eyes and smiles lit the surroundings while Wonkermie had a look of wonderment as if she were saying, "Where am I?" As for Oretha, she scanned the surroundings as if she were a detective. I found out later that children learned the skill Oretha exhibited during the civil war and instinctively resorted to it for their safety. After the hugs, we returned to Maybe Johnson, where she exchanged greetings with the girls and then we embarked on our journey back to Fayetteville.

Our first stop on our way back to North Carolina was at the home of my friend, Patricia Ford, in Washington, D.C. The stopover was supposed to be brief, but we ended up spending more than two hours because, as soon as we entered, the girls dropped in the couch and instantly fell asleep. Their flight from Abidjan via Lisbon had been so long that they were immeasurably exhausted from the jetlag. To this day, Wonkermie hates the pictures I took of them while asleep.

After we resumed the journey, we stopped somewhere along I-95 near Richmond, Virginia, to eat. I simply forgot how ingrained diet is and thought the girls were going to be excited to grab a hamburger or cheeseburger. However, when they looked through the menu, they could not find anything familiar to order. I ended up ordering hamburgers since they could relate to the buns and meat. While hamburgers were sold in a few places in Monrovia, they did not taste exactly like hamburgers in the United States. Moreover, hamburger or cheeseburger was never a part of their regular diet in Liberia. They looked at each other and did not say much. When the hamburgers were delivered, no one was in a hurry to eat, leaving me to wonder whether they were shy because of being in a different environment. The holdup was that they did not like the hamburgers because of "something." They were afraid to tell me because they did not want me to feel bad. I only found out the "something" that made the hamburgers undesirable when I visited the restroom and returned. Upon my return, Lila was still doing what Wonkermie and Oretha had already done. She was removing the lettuce, tomatoes, and pickles out of the burger. "Aha, these girls are from Liberia where people generally do not eat uncooked vegetables," I said. Lila told me when I talked about stopping to eat, she thought about rice and perhaps fried potato greens. We had a good laugh about the incident and then took off on the last leg of our journey to Fayetteville.

LEGION ROAD ELEMENTARY SCHOOL

During the remaining weeks of the summer vacation, Lila, Wonkermie and Oretha carried on with their adjustments in the United States. They sampled various canned foods Dee Robinson purchased and watched a variety of television programs. In addition, I occasionally took them to see places around Fayetteville and to visit with Flomo and his family in Greensboro. On weekdays, I left them at home alone and went to work at the plant nursery on Raeford Road. Incidentally, I learned only recently about NCGS 14-318, a state law in North Carolina that vaguely addresses the age at which a child can be left at home alone.[296] Indeed, the age cited in that law is eight years.

However, based on my almost thirty years of parenting experience in the United States, I would not have left the children at home alone while I was at work at the plant nursery. Lila, the oldest, was only thirteen years old. I would have taken them to stay with Deacon Cole and his family.

Upon the opening of school in August 1991, I enrolled the girls at Legion Road Elementary, less than a quarter of a mile from Dunrobin Drive. At the same time, I left the plant nursery job and took a part-time teaching position at the same elementary school. I had never taught at an elementary level before and it seemed the rough rides along this journey had not begun until then. Once school started, students receiving special education services were assigned to me, although I had never had any training in special education. The students were a challenge for any inexperienced teacher, especially one like me who had not had training in special education. Some of the students were on specially prescribed medications to calm them in class. I had a tall elegant African American woman as an instructional assistant (IA). She was familiar with the students and it seemed she had been working with them for a long time. Presumably, she had some level of special education experience based on her time with the students.

The kids saw the IA more as a mother than as my helper. As the effects of students' medications for different disorders wore off, disciplinary issues arose like randomly popping corn. On those occasions, the IA stood by as if she were watching a play. Based on her body language, it seemed she was saying, "I will let this African dude whither on the vine." At other times, she instituted her own disciplinary measures without any consultation with me. Whenever I asked a student to stop doing something inappropriate, the student would run to the IA rather than comply with my request. She seemed to relish the experience once it became clear that the kids had chosen her as their favorite person over me. It did not seem to matter to the IA that student learning was the casualty. The IA was supposed to be a helper, but she turned out to be a foe. I confided in two veteran and experienced African American female teachers, Mrs. Martha Colvin and Ms. Nina Cardwell, and they advised me on how to navigate the challenges that the IA presented in the classroom.

AS A JANITOR

The income from the part-time teaching position at Legion Road Elementary School was not enough to maintain the children and me. Aside from the low pay, I could not go back to the plant nursery job because the hours conflicted with my job at Legion Road Elementary School. I needed a job with better pay that I could do in the evening. The only opening that the principal of Southview High School, Mr. Lawrence Buffaloe, could find for me was in the maintenance department as a janitor. He had written a letter which helped secure U.S. visas in Abidjan for my daughters' coming and seemed truly conflicted by the elimination of the job I had. I took the janitorial position at Southview High School, the same high school I taught at during the previous semester. Without the janitorial job, I ran the risk of eviction at a time my children were already with me.

The janitorial job humbled me, even though I had never been a pretentious hothead. Some of my former students saw me cleaning the bathrooms and halls. They spoke to me and still treated me with dignity, but I could not avoid wondering what they thought of me. Although former Duke Basketball star turned coach, Jeff Capel, III, was never one of my students, he and I met once in the boys' restroom near the basketball gymnasium, where I was cleaning at the time. He had been at a basketball practice and came in to ease himself. He did not speak to me, but gave me a pensive look, which I distinctly remember, as he walked toward the urinal. Perhaps he must have been saying to himself here is another black guy cleaning the restroom. I held onto the janitorial position at Southview High School and the part-time position at Legion Road Elementary School while I looked around other North Carolina counties for a full-time employment.

CHAPTER 29

Wadesboro, NC

AFTER I APPLIED FOR A teaching position with several school districts across North Carolina, I received a call from Anson County Schools for an interview in Wadesboro, NC. Upon arrival in Wadesboro on the day of the interview, I felt as if I were at home. I do not know what it was. It may have been my state of mind, but there was something warm and indescribably inviting about the place. I was irresistibly drawn to Wadesboro. I felt a deep sense of liberation. A few days after the interview in December 1991, I received a letter in the mail inviting me to Wadesboro to begin work. The moment upon receipt of that letter was exhilarating because I badly wanted to work in Wadesboro.

There could not have been a better time to move. Lila, Wonkermie and Oretha were still adjusting to life in the United States. Their experience in Liberia still loomed large in their thinking and conversations. They had not been in Fayetteville long enough; they had not established roots or developed stronger emotional ties to the place and to friends. The move was necessary because neither the part-time teaching position nor the janitorial job provided benefits, not to mention enough income to take care of the children. I could not take the risk of having the children with me without health insurance. Moreover, while I had to take the janitorial position to feed the children, it was not a career, but a steppingstone for bridging the difficult transition.

FRANK RICHARDSON

At the time of the move to Wadesboro, Mr. Frank Richardson, an African American, was the Principal of Anson Senior High School. Prior to the move, I met with him to seek his help in finding a temporary place to stay until I could find permanent housing later. That meeting with Mr. Richardson was necessary because I had been living from paycheck to paycheck and did not have the funds to rent a motel for the kids and me for a week or two before finding permanent housing. Mr. Richardson arranged with his aunt, Marjorie Robinson, a place for us to stay. For the time we were at Ms. Robinson's house in the interim, she did not take any money from me. In fact, the permanent housing that I settled for at 812 West Carolina Avenue belonged to Ms. Robinson.

Mr. Frank and Mrs. Marlene Richardson

Lack of funds was not my only handicap at the time of the move to Wadesboro. "Old Faithful" was under the "weather." I had to leave it behind in Fayetteville with the able "car doctor," Deacon Morris Cole, to receive "treatment." While "Old Faithful" was under the care of the "car doctor" for observation and "treatment," I had no way of getting around or going to work in Wadesboro. Again, Mr. Richardson came to my rescue. He gave me "Betsy," his old Chevrolet, to use until "Old Faithful" was back in operation. For the record, I was not the one who gave the name "Betsy" to that car. It had been given the name by the Richardsons prior to my arrival in Wadesboro.

Once I found housing at 812 West Carolina Avenue, I informed Deacon Morris Cole who, in turn, told another member of Miracle Temple who had a truck. They helped pack and move our belongings from Fayetteville to Wadesboro. Since I moved into the State Plaza Hotel across the street from the Department of State after I arrived in Washington, D.C., the move to Wadesboro was my eighth in a little over a year and the children's first since they arrived in July 1991. Moving is an important aspect of the nature of starting anew, especially in the United States, where opportunities abound, and possibilities seem limitless. In my case, the number of moves reflected the struggles of adjusting in a new country, especially following the upheaval in Liberia. Those moves, especially the ones from Greensboro to Fayetteville and then from Fayetteville to Wadesboro, gave me an opportunity to apply one of the important pieces of advice numerous well-meaning people along my journey had repeatedly given me. "Wherever you go, look around and find a church." For the people who cared about my well-being, that advice literally became a mantra. I listened and not only took to heart what was said, but also what was left unsaid.

In North Carolina, especially in places like Fayetteville, Wadesboro, and Laurinburg where I lived, there were very few meaningfully mixed congregations. As a result, "Find a church" invariably meant a black church. The advice did not mean in any way that people in white churches were not kind and gracious. Instead, I understood it to mean that, at a superficial yet impactful level, one would not at the outset feel out of place in a black church. Those who advised me were speaking from their experience. To them, the church always took care of its flock, no matter whether the flock came from the village or from Timbuktu. In Fayetteville, the church was not merely bricks and mortar. It was people like Bishop Bennie L. Kelly,

Deacon Morris Cole, Brother Ralph Sutton, and all those at Miracle Temple who wrapped their arms around us and made us to feel at home.

EBENEZER BAPTIST CHURCH

In my interactions with Mr. Frank Richardson, I soon realized that the feelings I had upon arrival in Wadesboro for the job interview were not just a figment of my imagination. Instead, I had a sense Wlah had chosen him to play a part in directing and guiding me along my journey. I was aware that, like me, Mr. Richardson was a mortal, subject to the same human frailties. So, I was never on the lookout for anything to determine his sainthood. By the same token, I observed the way he looked, listened, and talked. He carried himself with dignity and exuded compassion. I did not need to be told who he was. Over time, I had a sense that Wlah's hands were upon him. I spent a considerable amount of time with Mr. Richardson, helping with some projects or activities he was involved in. His home was our second home. Moreover, I listened intently as he shared his experience coming up through the ranks to become a school principal. Even though I have not yet become a school principal, Mr. Richardson has inspired me to become a school leader. He was a strong, effective, and compassionate leader. Not only is he a consummate family man, but also, he taught me a lot about being a man. It was a privilege to be his mentee.

In Wadesboro, I did not have to look around for a church. I came to Wadesboro under distress; I was seeking employment to provide for my children. However, that distress was no tragedy. It was not comparable to the encounter between Naomi and her two daughters-in-law, Ruth and Orpah. Naomi lost her husband and then her two sons to whom Ruth and Orpah were married. Nevertheless, in a measure, my loyalty to Mr. Richardson was fashioned after Ruth's loyalty to Naomi. Considering everything Mr. Richardson had done for the children and me, and after sensing Wlah's hands upon him, I said to him within my heart "Where you go, I will go, and where you stay, I will stay. Your people will be my people and your God my God."[297] That is how the children and I came to attend Ebenezer Baptist Church located at 612 Salisbury Street, Wadesboro, North Carolina.

The Richardsons still worship in that church to this day. Ebenezer was less than a quarter of a mile away from 812 West Carolina Avenue, where we lived. It was a memorable place to be for many reasons. For example, age and gender-wise, it was a diverse church. There was an ever-present and constant infusion of new blood into the church from the infants and toddlers to the adolescents and teenagers. From the looks of those young people at Ebenezer, one could only imagine the possibilities of a future Wadesboro, North Carolina and America. The adults or role models who attended Ebenezer were a significant part of Wadesboro's professional class. A keen observer could sense from their faces how seriously they shouldered their responsibilities.

The church elders were profound. Not only were they the live repositories of the struggles of African Americans, especially in the south, but also in their hearts, faces and memories abounded African American history. I counted Rev. Dr. W. W. Williams (deceased), the pastor of Ebenezer, among the elderly. He was not a mere pastor; he was an intellectual. He was not a shouting preacher, but a passionate one. His sermons lingered and penetrated deeply. His words were as soft as his palms, yet they caused the heart to awaken to the world around it. His demeanor, words and handshakes were indelibly imprinted in my memory. The great people of Ebenezer Baptist Church touched and helped fashion my life in ways that they will never know.

MARLENE RICHARDSON

Mrs. Marlene Richardson, wife of Mr. Frank Richardson, is an exquisitely beautiful and seemingly aristocratic African American woman. She is one of the most humbled, caring, and loving people I have ever met. In Wadesboro, she took Lila, Wonkermie and Oretha under her wings; she took care of them as if they were her own children. Often, after they had spent an evening or a Saturday with her, she dropped them home with new clothes, shoes, or with their hair nicely done for church and the rest of the week. To this day, she still has not forgotten Lila, Marlene, and Oretha Elizabeth, whom she affectionately still calls "the girls."[298]

Mrs. Richardson was concerned not only about the children, but also about my well-being. One evidence of that concern was a Mrs. Richardson-orchestrated 1992 incident, which I only discovered years later when I was visiting with the Richardsons in 2005. As the stress of rearing three girls and worries about family members in the war in Liberia became palpable, it occurred to Mrs. Richardson that, perhaps, Flumo needed a companion as he worked through the difficult times. With that, Mrs. Richardson either had someone in mind or went to work in search of that person. She found a woman whom she thought might be a good fit and a companion for me. Mrs. Richardson decided to stage the whole episode because, at the time, it was out of character, particularly in the conservative African American South, for a woman to initiate a conversation about a relationship with a man.

I distinctly remember the incident. However, Mrs. Richardson assumed that, just by creating an opportunity, I would see it and make a move. She did not tell me in advance what she was trying to do. She framed the scheme as one involving a female church member who needed help with mathematics. According to Mrs. Richardson, the woman had enrolled at the Anson Community College and was having difficulty with mathematics. Obviously, I was willing to do anything the Richardsons asked of me. I saw them like my own parents. As a result, I told Mrs. Richardson to tell the woman to go to my house anytime in the evening whenever she had time.

I did not expect Mrs. Richardson to know that the last thing on my mind at that time was to find a companion. However, I expected her to have an inkling that my relationship and reputation with the Richardson family were more important to me than silver. I would not do or say anything to anyone she recommended to me for help that would ruin my reputation with the Richardson family, not to mention that "going off the rails" on a woman recommended to me for academic help would have destroyed the healthy and appropriate teacher-student relationship necessary for any learning environment. The Flumo whom the Richardsons saw upon meeting me was the Flumo I was on the inside. I was not one person in their presence and another person when they were not looking.

During the first evening the woman showed up, I got down to business and went over all the problems. I engaged her in a conversation, about how long she had been out of school and what she was planning to accomplish with her current studies. At the end of our first session, I took her outside and said goodbye as she drove off. The woman returned for our second session, but I noticed that she was not engaged as I went through the problems with her. "I do not know how far this woman is going to go with this math," I wondered to myself. After our second session, she did not show up again. The next time I asked about her, I was told that she was busy with other things. In October 2005, thirteen years later, when Mrs. Richardson revealed what she tried to orchestrate, we laughed so hard.

MICHAEL AND CHERYL MCLEOD

Michael and Cheryl McLeod were good friends and neighbors of the Richardsons. They had been so for a long time before we came to Wadesboro. They all worshipped at Ebenezer Baptist Church. At that time, Michael was an administrator at Wadesboro middle school, where Lila was enrolled. He was very helpful in the children's adjustments in school in Wadesboro. On the other hand, Mrs. McLeod often took the girls to her home and treated them in the same way as Mrs. Marlene Richardson cared for them. Together, the McLeods and the Richardsons formed a protective shield around the girls and me and made us to feel at home. It became clear to me that Wlah's Hand was in my going to Wadesboro because the Richardsons and the McLeods were an enormous positive influence in our lives.

THE SENTERS

Our support network in Wadesboro grew larger with newer members whose entry into the group could have been engineered only by a higher hand. After I started work at Anson Senior High School, the word quickly got around that a Liberian was on the teaching staff. Ms. Helen Faulkner, a white lady who was a staff member at the school, became interested in finding out who I was. She had a good reason for doing so. Not too long after she heard about me, she approached me and asked whether I knew a Rev. George Senter. At that time, Rev. George Senter had accepted a pastoral position with Deep Creek Baptist Church in Wadesboro. Ms. Faulkner knew people who attended the church who may have shared Rev. Senter's story with her. She may have also met Rev. Senter in person. She followed up her query about Rev. Senter with word that he had served as a missionary in Liberia.

Ms. Faulkner's mere mention of Liberia in talking about Rev. Senter caught my attention right away. I became interested in meeting him even though I did not know who he was. I was certain that upon meeting him we would make a connection because Liberia is a small country. As it turned out, Ms. Faulkner had more information that would help me figure out who Rev. Senter was. She told me that Rev. Senter's wife and daughter had been killed in Liberia. The murders, according to Ms. Faulkner, had been committed by someone whom the Senters knew and had taken in as a family member. Suddenly, I recalled the story. I read about the murder of Rev. Senter's wife and daughter in a Greensboro newspaper in late 1986. Upon my return to Liberia in 1987, I also heard about it on ELWA, a missionary radio station. With that information, I could not wait to see Rev. Senter.

Now that Rev. Senter was in Wadesboro along with the fact that we had shared experience in Liberia, the tragedies of losing his wife and daughter in Liberia took on a new meaning. Even though my conversation with Ms. Faulkner happened in early January 1992, about six years after Rev. Senter's wife and daughter were killed in Liberia, the story was no more about the distant person I read about in that Greensboro newspaper in 1986. Indeed, the story was no more about that white man from somewhere I did not really remember; that white man whom I heard about on ELWA in 1987 when news about the case involving the killings of his wife and daughter was reported.

The tragedies of losing Rev. Senter's wife and daughter in Liberia also took on a new meaning because, while serving as missionaries in Liberia, the Senters worked with my people—the Mahn people of Nimba County. It had not mattered before and, at that time, it did not matter that he was a white man originally from Gibson, Tennessee. As long as he was in Liberia and worked with the Mahn people in Yekepa, he and I had something in common. He was like one of us from Nimba County. Without ever having met him, I already felt the bond we shared because he and his family dedicated their lives to my people. Moreover, he had secured his place in the hearts of the Mahn people of Nimba County by burying his wife and daughter in Yekepa, Nimba County.

As soon as I got Rev. Senter's phone number, I called and talked with him for some time and arranged a visit to his house. During the visit to their home, Rev. Senter and his new wife, Margareta Senter, were very happy to see the children and me. Incidentally, Rev. Senter met Margareta, a Swedish woman, in Yekepa, Liberia. My thoughts about Rev. Senter being one of us was vindicated when he and I shook hands and made the distinctive snap that one hears when Liberians shake hands. We shared stories about Liberia and spoke all the Mahns that Rev. Senter could remember. This was the beginning of a relationship with the Senters that continued until we left North Carolina in June 1997 for Spokane, Washington.

359

CHESTER & BETH ROGERS

Through the Senters, I met the Rogers family. Like the Richardsons, the McLeods, and the Senters, they, too, figuratively wrapped their arms of support around the children and me. The Rogers and I had another important connection. Chad Rogers, Chester and Beth's older son was a senior at Anson Senior High School and a student of mine. Chad was a gentle heart and he respected me greatly. He graduated from high school in 1992, the year I worked at Anson Senior High School. To this day, I still have a copy of the 1992 yearbook that Mr. Frank Richardson gave me as a souvenir when I was preparing to leave Wadesboro. In it, Chad Rogers looks innocent and gentle as he was in 1992.

I tend to hold onto important events, things or people who have had positive as well as negative impacts on my life along my journey from which I have learned. On November 11, 2010, in my attempt to reconnect with some of the people I left behind in North Carolina, I got more news than I expected. A distraught Mrs. Beth Rogers told me that she had bad news for me. At first, I thought she was going to tell me that she had lost her husband whose health was not good even when I was in Wadesboro. Instead, she first broke the news of the loss of Chad Rogers, her older son. I was devastated and speechless. Chad was the gentle soul whom I talked about. He was my former student. When I told her that I thought she was going to talk about her husband, she dropped another bombshell as if Chad's loss was not enough of a shock. She went on to say that indeed Chester, too, had died, but later than her son. I did not know what to tell Mrs. Rogers. I only wondered how she had managed all this time with such indescribable losses. After we talked about everything, everybody, and memories of my being in Wadesboro, I assured Mrs. Rogers that Wlah would see her through. He had taken me out of the carnage in Liberia and watched over the children and me in North Carolina, where we did not go hungry. As such, I had no doubt that He would do the same for her.

A SEMBLANCE OF STABILITY

I was not the only one who felt at home in Wadesboro. The children felt the same way and their successes at school demonstrated it. The civil war in Liberia had consumed enormous emotional energy and we sorely needed something positive to celebrate. Moreover, with a full-time job, the flicker at the end of the tunnel started to get more and more visible. With that, I thought it was time to pursue dreams which the war in Liberia had forced me to defer. In Wadesboro, I descended into my teenage fantasy shaped by visits to middleclass homes, opulence in Liberia, and Jet magazine. I wanted to own a big house with every imaginable furnishing and a big, long car. At that time, I was fully aware of the typical Liberian mindset I had. I did not have to enjoy anything. I just wanted to appear to be enjoying life. I always wanted to own a gigantic stereo system upon becoming a successful man. So, I purchased a five-component RCA stereo system from Badcock Home Furniture, which I still have for sentimental reasons and for the story it tells.

THE ALBATROSS

Although the children and I were enjoying relative stability in Wadesboro, the plight of the remaining members of my family was uncertain. On August 14, 1991, Mr. Lawrence Buffaloe wrote to the U.S. Embassy in Liberia on their behalf before I left Fayetteville. Then on January 20, 1992, in Wadesboro, upon the advice of Mr. Frank Richardson, I wrote the former North Carolina 8th District Congressman, Bill Hefner (deceased), whose district included Anson County. Mr. Richardson and Mr. Phil Bazemore, then a member of the Monroe, North Carolina City Council, signed the letter. In Annandale, Virginia, Col. Cannon wrote to Ambassador Arlene Render in Banjul on March 24, 1992, seeking her advice on my family situation.

Congressman Bill Hefner replied on April 1, 1992. In addition, he enclosed a copy of a letter from him and Senator Terry Sanford (deceased) to Beverly Wormley, then Director of the Political Asylum Office at the erstwhile Immigration and Naturalization Service (INS). Congressman Hefner and Senator Sanford encouraged Ms. Wormley to expedite my asylum application, a gesture which showed a sign of movement on my application. However, I did not hear from anyone again. These efforts were an attempt to short-circuit a potential long wait that my asylum process might impose. One idea after another, my hope was raised and dashed thereafter. It was as if I were on a roller coaster. I always hoped that the next idea might do the trick.

My Children's Dignity

In Wadesboro, everything was not perfect. I had a fight about treatment my daughter, Oretha, received from an African American female teacher at Wadesboro Central School. The school's principal's role in that matter was not acceptable either. I was not afraid to take on anybody, even Caligula because the matter involved the dignity of my child.[299]

Oretha reportedly had a minor problem at school, which the school took care of and notified me at work at Anson Senior High School. I investigated the incident upon my return home and determined that there was more to the story than I had been led to believe. I found out that the teacher did something to Oretha completely unbecoming of an educational professional. I resolved that I would not remain silent about the matter and demanded a meeting with the principal, and everyone involved. Although outraged, I went into that meeting as a reasonable parent with an open mind and fully aware that teachers make mistakes. I expected to meet someone with the courage to say, "I was trying to do what I thought was right, but I dropped the ball." Sadly, no one owned up. Instead, the adults involved came into the meeting unremorseful. They diverted attention away from the injury they caused. The principal defended the unprofessional behavior and tried to sugar me into accepting what the teacher did as if I did not have the capacity to tell the difference between humiliation and a worthy deed. The meeting was flatly unproductive.

Oretha did not injure herself during a field trip or at a playground at school. School authorities take appropriate measures to care for children in those circumstances and then notify parents. The Wadesboro Central School incident with Oretha was different. As a parent, I expected Oretha's teacher to greet her pupils upon entering class to set the tone for learning. Knowing that school districts go through a rigorous process including FBI background checks to hire teachers, I expected the teacher to be my child's protector while she was in her care. However, on January 9, 1992, neither of those expectations was upheld. Instead, the teacher entered her second-grade class at Wadesboro Central School and set a tone. As expected, her pupils followed her lead. Unfortunately, it was not what the school district hired her to do or what I expected of her.

Upon entering class on the morning of January 9, 1992, the teacher made an unseemly unprofessional and offensive comment about the condition of the classroom. She wanted to know who the culprit was, and her

362

pupils responded almost naturally; they pointed to Oretha, an easy target. She was the new kid in the class. She came from Liberia—Africa, a place that many American children, not to mention adults, usually associate with nothing positive.[300] Oretha was different; she had an accent. That was the context in which Oretha's classmates pointed to her as the culprit.

Oretha was only a child when the Wadesboro Central School incident happened. Nevertheless, her experience was no different from other African children or even adults. Accent especially and skin color, to a lesser extent, made Oretha different from her classmates. Although Oretha's teacher was an African American, she regarded Oretha just as her classmates saw her, that is, someone from "over there," Africa, the place where the tribes roam with little or no clothes and sleep in trees. The alleged conversation between the two adult women that Oretha reported to me reflected the same attitude that led Oretha's classmates to point at her.

The teacher took Oretha out of class to another woman who was a school district employee. The two adult African American women took unusual measures to correct Oretha's condition, a problem her classmates helped the teacher identify. Their treatment involved physically touching Oretha while making demeaning comments as well. Had the women's daughters come from school and complained that a white female teacher treated them in the same way they treated my daughter, the story would have been in the Anson Record and an outcry would follow. Similarly, had the principal's white daughter come home and reported that a black female teacher treated her in the same way as my daughter was treated, the story would have been in the Anson Record and there would even be a louder outcry. In my meeting with the principal and other school officials and the teacher on January 10, 1992, I requested a written account of the teacher's conduct for the records. Even though the principal went out of his way to defend the teacher, he wrote an account of the teacher's conduct on January 13, 1992, and sent me a copy.

The incident with Oretha at Wadesboro Central School was not like my hunger problem in Sanniquellie that my parents' stay-the-course advice helped me overcome. Oretha Flumo was a child, but the attack on her dignity was invidious. Left unanswered, I saw it as having the potential to do harm with lasting effects. I was no prima donna, bent on creating a public spectacle with racial overtones in Wadesboro, but the matter was one that concerned my child's dignity. I was no match for the school system in Wadesboro, but I was determined to have those who humiliated my daughter at Wadesboro Central School hear me. They were parents or relatives of school age children like mine. I wanted them to understand the nature of the injury they caused. With the facts, I not only made my concerns known in a rebuttal on January 28, 1992, but also requested that the records reflect those concerns and that copies be placed in the files of the adults who dealt with my daughter.

I Dropped the Chalk

Anson Senior High School was my second foray into an American public school classroom. Collegiate level teaching at the University of Liberia and my short stint at Southview High School and Pine Forest High School in Fayetteville were the only experience I had under my belt coming to Wadesboro. The university was located in a different culture; the students were adults. Moreover, because the students chose to be in school, issues of discipline were not a concern. At Anson Senior High School, however, most of my students came to school either through the encouragement of their parents or role models. They learned from their parents and other adults that their future successes depended on education but for a few of my students, compulsory meant compulsory. They were in school apparently because the law required them to be in school. Consequently, some students were a challenge.

In the absence of experience, all I had was the model of a teacher I carried in my head. However, first, I did not believe in that model and, second, it was unworkable in America. The archetypal "Teeseh" I remember at St. Mary's elementary school put "Sensee" in my head. Although hunger was a perennial problem in elementary school, the "Teeseh" never asked whether I had something to eat for breakfast, or whether I lived with my own parents. Not only did he deliver content but also assumed his students were dull if they did not understand something he was teaching. In that case, he turned to the rattan switch strategy to make them learn.

In Wadesboro, I was only beginning to understand the impact of students' life situations on their learning outcomes. Before unlearning the nature of the teacher in my mind, I assumed problems my American students faced were similar to those I encountered as a student at St. Mary's School; that classroom walls were impervious to issues they faced in their lives. In many ways, I was like the teacher in my head who focused only on delivering content, believing that students would leave their personal issues at the classroom door. My Liberian experience stood in my way and made my learning curve steeper than it could have been if I had not come from a different culture. Unlearning the nature of the model teacher was the process of becoming an American teacher. In earnest, that process began in Wadesboro because, there, I recognized I needed to be more than the model teacher in my head. I had to wear many "hats" including being an exemplary role model, counselor, and disciplinarian.

Although my students were generally respectful to me, I had a hard time coming to terms with foul language and refusing to work, believing that some students were behaving that way because I was a black man, especially from Africa, although no student ever said, "What the heck does this African guy have to teach me?" My personal life issues were compartmentalized so that they would not interfere with my work as a teacher, but they were not in a suitcase at home. Instead, they were in my memory. I soon found out that the lock on that compartment was not strong enough to prevent my personal issues from popping up into my consciousness. Students' lack of motivation for educational opportunities and their low opinion of school lunch were like hornets, pestering and awakening issues I had put away into my memory. For example, if a student refused to work, my mind ran to Liberia, where the kids did not have opportunities my American students had because, as the civil war raged, they were more concerned about running from the rebels for their lives than they were about sitting in the classroom to learn. My mind ran to Sanniquellie where I endured hunger and ate buckwheat at St. Mary's School when my American students complained that their lunch was not fit for consumption. On occasions, it seemed as if I were watching a split screen television.

I seldom started something and quit. Amid negativity, unseemly language, and low motivation, I watched my American students throw educational opportunities away, yet I felt like "A tree planted by the water."[301] Ironically, Jeffrey Scott Rivers, a senior who not only had a chip on his shoulder but also looked upon me with disdain, was the straw that broke the camel's back. Mr. Rivers interrupted me and would not accept a request to let me take a few minutes to finish with instructions to address his concern. Instead, he continued the disruption with extremely disrespectful and biting words. As a professional, I could not respond in kind. Therefore, I walked up to the table, put my chalk down and walked out of the classroom to the principal's office. I told Mr. Frank Richardson that I took the abuse because I did not want my children to go hungry, but I could not take the abuse anymore.

CHAPTER 30

Laurinburg, NC

I LOVED WADESBORO, ESPECIALLY FOR THE wonderful support system that the children and I had. However, after the Jeffery Scott Rivers incident, Mr. Richardson and I came to an understanding that perhaps Anson Senior High School was not a good fit for me. Again, it was time to move on. With that, I began the search for employment with other school systems right away while school was still in session at Anson Senior High School.

I applied to several school systems in North Carolina, including Duplin County, Clinton City, Whiteville City, Scotland County, Nash County, and Bertie County. Four of the school systems, including Whiteville City, Clinton City, Bertie County and Scotland County Schools, invited me for an interview. Of those four, Whiteville City Schools was number one on my list for a frivolous reason. I had never been to Whiteville at the time of my application, yet I wanted to work there badly because of WZFX 99.1 Fox, the most popular FM radio station in Fayetteville. Even though the radio station was in Fayetteville, I always heard the DJ say WZFX-Whiteville as if it were located in Whiteville. Moreover, I thought Whiteville was a suburb of Fayetteville, but it turned out to be a community quite a distance away. Later, I found out that the DJ's periodic mention of Whiteville pertained to Whiteville being the city of license for the station. In any case, the DJ's

367

repeated mention of Whiteville on the air made me create an idyllic image of the city in my mind and a desire to live and work there. Whiteville turned out to be exactly what I had imagined, a small and beautiful community with a population of about five thousand people. I had a great interview in Whiteville, but I did not get the job. I was not terribly disappointed.

Communities have personalities and they project them in tangible as well as in intangible ways. Entrance to a community, its general architecture, street layouts, serenity, and physical beauty, not to mention the mannerisms of its people, in some ways reflect upon a community and say something about who the people are. Wadesboro was a perfect example. The city not only provided my own definition of what southern charm is, but also set a standard of what a community should reflect in tangible as well as in intangible ways. Against that background, it was not out of the ordinary that something about Clinton did not sit well with me. The less than tepid reception I had upon arrival at the offices of Clinton City Schools for an interview played no small part. I remember feeling that I was in the wrong place. In spite of my desire for a job, I felt a sense of relief when I got a letter in the mail that turned me down for the job.

Windsor was a completely different story. The town was the farthest place I traveled to for an interview. Wonkermie Marlene went along for that interview. I observed everything with unusual keenness. At first glance, upon arrival at the school district office, the building was low level and looked like a portable. The school district official who interviewed me was a male African American. After I finished the interview, he led Marlene and me to Bertie High School campus to tour the facilities. As soon as he took leave of us, she and I looked at each other and had the same exact "Oh wow!" reaction to the apparent paucity of resources at the school.

Compared to Wadesboro, Windsor was a much smaller community. However, like Wadesboro, it had a hometown feel. The atmosphere was exquisitely inviting. There was something special about the place, a sense of déjà vu, so to speak. I had a sense I was going to get the job, but Windsor was too isolated to take the kids there, too far away from all the support systems we had built. I had a big decision to make, but I did not have to make it at that very moment because I had not received any indication verbally or in writing that I was going to get the job.

After Windsor, the next interview was at Scotland High School in Laurinburg, about forty-five minutes' drive from Wadesboro. Like

Whiteville, I could not wait to go to Laurinburg, located on the highway from Fayetteville to Charlotte. The children and I traveled through
Laurinburg on several occasions to Charlotte to process our immigration
papers. Moreover, we drove through Laurinburg during our move from
Fayetteville to Wadesboro. Each time we came through Laurinburg, we drove
past Scotland High School and a magnificent house on a well-manicured
lawn with sporadic and beautiful flowering shrubberies and trees. The house
captured my imagination and I wished to have a house like that someday
in the future. Therefore, when Scotland High School invited me for an
interview, it was not the job that first came to mind, but that gorgeous
house on that idyllic lawn. I was anxious to go to Laurinburg not only to
interview for the job, but also to see that beautiful house again.

Before the Laurinburg interview, I told Mr. Richardson that I had applied
for a position at Scotland High School. He told me that Mr. Ray Oxendine,
the principal at the time, was his friend and that he would call to let him
know that I was coming. Following the interview, which went very well, Mr.
Oxendine took me on a tour of the school. In terms of resources, there was
no match between Scotland High School and Bertie High School. At that
moment, I knew if I had to choose between Bertie County and Scotland
County, it would be an easy decision. One week after the Laurinburg interview, I received a letter from Bertie County Schools, offering me the position.
I had already weighed the pros and cons and decided in favor of Scotland
County. Therefore, I waited to hear from Scotland County before responding
to Bertie County. It took about two weeks before the offer from Scotland
County arrived in the mail, after which I took a deep breath. In a letter, I
thanked Bertie County Schools for the opportunity and noted that I had
accepted a position with Scotland County Schools.

Preparations to move to Laurinburg started right after the job offer
from Scotland County. The time had come for the kids and me to leave our
beloved Wadesboro, where we had a brief, but impactful stay. In mid-July
1992, I traveled to Laurinburg to find housing and found an apartment
in a quiet and partially secluded area of the city on Blues Farm Road, off
Highway 401 South. I used my 1978 Dodge Magnum-318 and made several trips from Wadesboro to Laurinburg, carrying the smaller household
items we had accumulated in Wadesboro. Friends helped carry the larger
items, including beds and mattresses. On the last leg, the children and I
bade the Richardsons and McLeods farewell and moved to Laurinburg.

Parenting is Difficult

School opening for academic 1992-1993 was just around the corner. Wonkermie and Oretha were in elementary school while Lila was in middle school. Shortly after we settled in, I enrolled Wonkermie and Oretha at Washington Park Elementary School about two miles away and Lila at Sycamore Lane Middle School less than a mile from Blues Farm Road. Once the girls started school, they continued the same level of work they were doing with the same level of academic successes they were having in Wadesboro.[302]

Seemingly, the children adjusted at their new schools seamlessly. However, at that time, I did not appreciate the full scope of their reality. In July 1991, they came from Liberia with the trauma of the civil war. Then, in a relatively short time, we moved twice; from Fayetteville to Wadesboro and then from Wadesboro to Laurinburg. Although children are naturally resilient, mine carried burdens. As children have their own ways of speaking, sometimes through silence, frowns, grins, postures, performances, and refuges they seek, I did not pick up on everything that happened in their social lives at school. I was not in tune with how they felt when I took them away from their comforts with the Richardsons in Wadesboro. I was not aware of their anxieties about who their friends would be in their new schools. I did not readily pick up their concerns about whether kids at their new schools would like them or think of them as being "cool." They were concerned about their friends' perceptions of them because they came from Liberia (Africa). Their concerns were well-founded because some African American girls hurled mean-spirited comments at Lila and Wonkermie at Sycamore Lane Middle School. Lila and Wonkermie's run-ins with those African American girls at school finally woke me up.

Until we moved to Laurinburg, I did not fully appreciate what children go through when they change schools, especially in a new country. Until quite recently, I did not understand the full impact of the struggles Lila, Wonkermie, and Oretha endured, adjusting and making new friends each time we moved from one city to another in the United States. I had not developed the capacity to perceive children's communication at the level I now have. In short, everything was not exactly what it seemed. My own school experience played a big part in my blindness to the children's struggles. During my elementary and secondary education at St. Mary's School from 1966 to 1977 in Sanniquellie, Liberia, I never moved to a new community or changed school. I never worried about who my friends would be because they were there with me. Most of us spoke Mahn in addition to English and moved from one grade to the next together. I never worried about whether someone would like me or not. I had too many friends to worry about one who did not like me.

LAURINBURG, A WELCOMING COMMUNITY

Immediately following the move from Wadesboro to Laurinburg, there was no substitute for Mr. Frank Richardson nor was there one for Mrs. Marlene Richardson. However, it seemed as if the people of Laurinburg, a town three times the population of Wadesboro, resolved that they would not be outdone by the people of Wadesboro. At work, the Principal of Scotland High School at the time, Mr. Ray Oxendine, introduced me enthusiastically. He was very supportive. In my absence, he always told students how proud he was of me. He was happy that I was a part of the teaching staff at Scotland High School. Ms. Sally McLaurin, an African American teacher at Scotland High School, helped us find a church. She even took the girls on occasions and did their hair. At Bright Hopewell Baptist Church, our new Church home, where Reverend Garland Pierce was the pastor, the congregation warmly received us. Using the church as a foundation, the children and I, from that point on, started to build a new support system.

In rural America or at least in rural North Carolina, the hiring of a new teacher at a local high school was a worthy newspaper headline, especially when the new teacher happened to be a Liberian whose coming to the new town was connected to a raging civil war in his homeland. In Wadesboro, *The Anson Record Newspaper* featured me with a photo on the front page and made me a small-town celebrity after the story ran. Similarly, *The Laurinburg Exchange* ran a front-page article on me with a photo on the front page when I took the position at Scotland High School.

The two feature articles on me, one in Wadesboro and the other in Laurinburg, made me to feel as if I were back in Liberia, especially in the village. The articles were a Nimba tradition taken to another level. In Nimba County, for example, the people greet warmly with a handshake and offer kola nuts as a token of welcome when a stranger arrives in a town or village. With that, the word soon spreads that a stranger from so and so town or village is in town. In the evening, the townspeople come again to greet the stranger, some with palm wine and others with kola nuts and even money. In doing so, the people not only welcome, but also acknowledge the stranger. In Wadesboro and Laurinburg, no one brought me palm wine or kola nuts, but with the feature articles on me, my presence was acknowledged. Moreover, my family, my country and I became a part of the consciousness of the people of Wadesboro and Laurinburg. Through those feature articles, my children and I made new friends, and the people in Wadesboro and Laurinburg opened their arms and welcomed us.

MOVING WITH ALL THE FAMILY

At the time of our move to Laurinburg, all members of my immediate family were not with me in the United States. "Moving with all the family" meant keeping members of my family who were not with me in my heart and continuing to work on reuniting them. Mr. Ray Oxendine showed his support in that effort when he raised the plight of my family in a school board meeting. Later, he informed me that school board members had read about me in the *Laurinburg Exchange* and were genuinely concerned. A few days after that school board meeting, Mr. Beacham McDougald, a member of the Scotland County School Board, called me and indicated that he would introduce a resolution on behalf of my family in the next school board meeting. He followed through and the Scotland County School Board adopted his resolution. In addition, Mr. McDougald wrote Senator Terry Sanford (D-NC), Senator Jesse Helms (deceased) (R-NC) and Congressman Bill Hefner (D-NC), pleading for their intervention on behalf of my family. Others who helped in the process of reuniting my family included Rev. George Senter and Dr. David A. Martin.[303]

CHAPTER 31

Internal Struggles

THE 1992 U.S. PRESIDENTIAL ELECTION

MEANWHILE, IN 1992, THE UNITED States presidential campaign was in full swing. In the Democratic primaries, the major candidates were Bob Kerry of Nebraska, Tom Harkin of Iowa, Paul Tsongas of Massachusetts, Jerry Brown of California, and Bill Clinton of Arkansas. On the Republican side, the candidates included the sitting president, George H. W. Bush, and Patrick Buchanan, with billionaire Ross Perot on the outside toying with a run as an independent candidate. Mr. Perot eventually ran as an independent candidate, garnering a sizable percentage of the votes.

By the time of the 1992 U.S. presidential election, I had been in the United States for a little over two years following my 1990 escape from the civil war in Liberia. President George H. W. Bush did not cause the civil war in Liberia. Moreover, he was not directly answerable to the people of Liberia. However, since the founding of Liberia in the 1820s, the United States and Liberia had been engaged in a dubious tango. In addition, President George H. W. Bush was the leader of the free world under whose watch the civil war in Liberia started. In light of that tango as well as

America's role as the leader of the free world, the United States could not absolve itself of the tragedy in Liberia. The United States could not wash its hands of Liberia and say to its people, "Tough luck," and go blameless.

Against that backdrop, a little over two years was not enough time to heal from the Liberian tragedy, not to mention the role that the George H. W. Bush administration played in 1990. I know that the pain that other Liberians and I, as well as people from other parts of the world who sympathized with Liberia, felt could not be wished away. In fact, a mere mention of certain names associated with the 1990 U.S. decision not to help Liberia avert the war raised blood pressure. The cost in human lives of what happened in Liberia was huge. Doing something and failing would have been better than doing nothing.

At the time of the 1992 United States presidential election, I faced a conundrum, one that arose from my own doing. I opened my eyes to heal and to grow. In the process, particularly through my consumption of information from the media, I learned about President George H. W. Bush and his service to the United States. The more I learned about the man, the more I liked him as a human being. For this reason, I did not wish for President Bush's defeat in the 1992 presidential election despite my anguish over his administration's 1990 "You are on your own" stance on Liberia. Instead, I looked forward to turning the page, hoping, and praying that the next U.S. administration would do something different. All I wanted badly was an end to the Liberian crisis. I was still convinced that the United States was the only country with the influence to make that happen. Unfortunately, I had never voted in my life in Liberia, let alone in the United States, where I was not yet a citizen. I could not even join hands with others to turn the new page that I wanted to see.

I was keenly interested in the 1992 United States presidential election not as a mere spectator, but as someone who expected the outcome to bring relief, meaning a final resolution of the Liberian conflict. For Liberians, I believed the outcome of the 1992 United States presidential election was existential. The question on my mind was: if an end of the George H. W. Bush administration were a beginning of some hope for Liberia, who, among the array of candidates for the U.S. presidency in either party, would advocate for Liberia? Beginning with Mr. Patrick Buchanan in the Republican Party, I was not convinced that he actually believed in his own vitriol against immigrants. Many of his targets were not only persecuted people arriving at America's shores, seeking opportunities for a new life but also members of minority communities. Mr. Buchanan's presidential campaign was not successful, but he was so shrill that the waves he made in 1992 still reverberate to this day. As I was a particle in the medium through which his waves traveled, my blood boiled every time I heard him speak. He sounded as if he had no heart or feelings for other human beings. Needless to say, I did not look up to Mr. Buchanan to save Liberia.

On the Democratic side, beyond their appearances and utterances on television, I did not know any of the candidates. The only person who made sense to me was Bill Bradley, then a United States Senator from New Jersey. However, Senator Bradley's campaign floundered. He did not go anywhere. Paul Tsongas, the somewhat soft-spoken former senator of Massachusetts, was fixated on the struggling U.S. economy. He did not spell out any message of hope for someone like me. As it turned out, he had been battling a form of lymphoma (cancer of the lymph). He died on January 18, 1997, two days before President Bill Clinton's second inauguration. Jerry Brown of California also made a lot of sense to me. However, for the vast majority of the American electorate, he seemed too radical. Unfortunately, the venerable Tom Harkin did not catch on. As for Bob Kerry, the former democratic senator of Nebraska, I could not figure him out. Perhaps because of Nebraska politics, I did not know whether he was a Democrat who was trying to be a Republican or a Republican who was trying to be a Democrat.[304]

In the meantime, there was still another candidate lurking out there. He was Bill Clinton. He had served as Governor of Arkansas from 1979 to 1981 and lost re-election. He ran again, won, and governed from 1983 until the outcome of the 1992 U.S. presidential election. Bill Clinton looked youthful, but I did not know who he was. I followed all the details of his campaign, the ups and downs and the twists and turns. He was remarkably intelligent and had a natural gift for communicating. For example, he was masterful at conveying a sense that he felt people's pain. He connected with people and was at ease among any category of Americans—Caucasians, African Americans, Asian Americans, and Native Americans. Even though he did not always help himself among his political foes, out of sheer fascination, I started to admire his resilience for surviving almost every accusation hurled at him on the campaign trail. Moreover, the more I listened to what he said on television, the more I started to like him. I felt that he might just be the next president of the United States.

Again, although I could not vote, I followed the issues in the 1992 election closely because I felt strongly that the answer to the Liberian tragedy, in part, depended on the actions of the next U.S. administration. I had high hopes that Bill Clinton would make a difference in putting an end to the bloodshed in Liberia. As I hoped and predicted, Bill Clinton won the 1992 United States presidential election. Like many Liberians residing in the United States as well as in Liberia, I wanted Bill Clinton to do something substantial about Liberia; I wanted him to help bring peace to Liberia. Indeed, I prayed for the new U.S. administration to adopt an assertive posture in ending the civil war in Liberia.

One would ask why I or anyone had hopes in the next U.S. administration after the 1990 hands-off decision by the previous U.S. administration. My response is simple: that 1990 hands-off approach let Liberia descend into hellfire. Watching television images of heaps of human skulls, bullet-ridden cities, towns, and villages, not to mention hearing and reading about Liberians dying slowly in their places of refuge left me with no choice but to hope. Those conditions led me to hope that Bill Clinton would do the right thing. Bill Clinton was no Jesus. He did not promise Liberians that he would end the civil war upon winning the American presidency. Liberia was not priority number one on his foreign policy agenda. So, I kept hoping that if he did not act upon Liberia during his first term, he would do so during his second term.

Two foreign policy investments Bill Clinton made gave me further hope that Liberia's turn would come. Northern Ireland had been embroiled in an intractable and almost perpetual violent conflict, yet with the help of former Senator George J. Mitchell, Jr. (D-Maine) as his Special Envoy, Bill Clinton spent considerable political capital and resolved that conflict. During the Balkan War, public opinion in the United States was against intervention, yet Bill Clinton intervened militarily anyway. Moreover, with the help of Assistant Secretary of State Richard Holbrooke, he secured the Dayton Peace Accords. As Liberia sank deeper and deeper into the tragedy of the civil war, Bill Clinton became the imaginary sword that drowning Liberians hoped would stretch out to them to hold to end their trauma.

As it turned out, during his two terms as president, Bill Clinton was an effective president who did tremendous good for America and other parts of the world. However, on Africa, his record was not good. Liberians did not expect hand-outs, but they expected Bill Clinton to use the influence

America has in Liberia to free them of the violence so that they could rebuild their lives. The people of Liberia and of other countries in Africa burdened by bad leadership, conflict and war thought that they had a champion in Bill Clinton, but he let Liberia "wither on the vine," not to mention his hands-off approach during the Rwandan genocide.[305] Once again, the hopes of Liberians were dashed.

ORGANIZED ACTION

By the time of the 1992 U.S. presidential elections, I had become convinced that organizing and agitating peacefully for a cause were ways to make policymakers respond to citizens' concerns in the United States. I believed organized action was one way to make US policymakers listen to dying Liberians. Drawing lessons from the Proverbs and the Reverend Jesse L. Jackson, Sr., for that reason, I called on Liberians in the United States to organize and make the Liberian tragedy a part of the American consciousness. On account of leadership or the lack thereof, Proverbs 29:18 states, "Where there is no vision, the people perish: but he that keeps the law, happy is he." That scripture verse was a reminder that the Liberian tragedy was man-made and could have been avoided. Moreover, the keg of abuses and injustices Buell (1947), Anderson (1952) and Marinelli (1964) cited was an indication that the tragedy did not arise overnight. Countless peace talks convened resulted in little or no success, Liberians continued to die while the country stood at a crossroad. "There was no need for analysis during paralysis" or benefit in pointing fingers. The urgency for action could not be overestimated.[306]

The ding of nationalistic fervor in my voice over my concerns about what happened to Liberia was misleading. Instead, that ding was from a deep well of personal pain precipitated by the Liberian tragedy. That well of pain bound me as if I were under a skin. For example, the tragedy delayed, if not eviscerated, Mom's dreams for succor from my success, a success she expended every ounce of energy to secure. Moreover, so much of Liberia had been ingrained in me. Its unique landscape, smell, taste, and sounds, not to mention the characteristic ways of speaking, hugging, and shaking hands were embedded into my consciousness. In 1993, when I made the call for action, I knew I was reaching out for Liberia in a fight, which was largely personal. I was reaching out for Liberia, a consciousness, something

377

that felt like one-half of my instantaneous oxygen intake of which I had been deprived. In doing that, I was under no illusion about who would pay attention to my call to action. Liberian refugees in the United States were burdened; they were busy trying to make ends meet in a new country. I did not worry about my efforts amounting to anything as I was concerned about doing something and relieving the pressure that I was under.

Organized action to call on the United States to adopt an assertive role in bringing the civil war in Liberia to an end made sense, but the strategy was not automatic. Moreover, Liberians were a special case because, while activism had a long history in Liberia, a distinctive attitude, "The people thing; y'all leave the people thing" described the population. The expression was a veiled warning to anyone who wanted to "live to tell the story."[307] In Liberia, powerful people, particularly in government, did whatever they pleased regardless of the constitution or laws. As a result, those who had the courage to criticize them or agitate against their interests did so at their own peril; they either went to jail or met eventual violent death. D. Twe, Tuan Wreh, David Coleman, Gabriel Kpolleh, Ellen Johnson-Sirleaf and Tiawan Saye Gongloe were a few examples of those who suffered the wrath of the powerful because they had the courage to speak truth to power.

Still sold on organized action as well as captivated by Bill Clinton and the prospects of his nascent presidency, I suggested in closing my call to action that, "I can foresee a genuine attempt by the Clinton administration to put an end to the bloodbath in Liberia. Though it may not be at the same scale as the Somali operation and may not necessarily involve the use of force."[308] I not only called for unity and peace, but also reminded fellow Liberians that "Great men and women whose ideas and works we read about today did not fall from the sky. We can also work to leave indelible marks on society. Let us neither waver nor withdraw, but act upon our dreams."[309]

In furtherance of organized action, I reached out through phone calls, letters, or travels to other parts of the United States and had conversations with other Liberians. Amid the frenzy to start their lives anew, "Y'all leave the people thing" still had a hold on the Liberian psyche, although I discovered that other Liberians were making similar efforts. In the absence of tools for organizing such as the internet and teleconferencing that we take for granted today, we were operating in silos. I recall wondering, "You mean a new US administration which appears poised to help take on our cause has taken office and we Liberians do not seem to care?"

I hoped and put great stock in the Clinton administration to stop the war in Liberia. Blinded by euphoria and fantasy about what the Clinton presidency would mean for Liberia, I could not see the flaws in my own judgement. Instead, I turned inward and became frustrated with poor Liberians who were struggling to put their lives back together in the United States. I blamed them for not coming together to form a united front to push for the end of the war. In hindsight, I failed to factor the gravity of the struggles that war-weary Liberians were up against in the United States. Indeed, my call to action may have been the proverbial tree falling in the jungle, but for me, it was a measure of hopefulness, something I could not quit doing in that hour of darkness, an offense for which I plead guilty.

Disillusioned, I teetered on quitting, but I still believed in organized action. Moreover, that deep well of personal pain had not subsided. Next, I turned to the Nimba community in the United States as a vehicle for achieving organized action. In Liberia, the point of entry for the December 24, 1989, invasion of Liberia was Nimba County. Upon President Samuel Doe's ordering of troops to Nimba County in response to that invasion, innocent Nimba citizens were killed indiscriminately. They were the first victims of the civil war and the ones who bore the brunt of the mayhem in the beginning. Some Liberians even went as far as accusing Nimba citizens of complicity in the invasion. Nimba citizens became villains overnight. Moreover, as other Liberians saw Nimba citizens through the "rebel" lens, no one could see or feel their pains and sufferings. At the time I was turning to the Nimba community in the United States, I thought they had compelling reasons to unite and work together to bring the war to an end. Indeed, I thought it would be a piece of cake to organize Nimba citizens in the United States to work for ending the war. Again, my assumptions were wrong. Wrangling in the Nimba community made pursuing that goal tantamount to chasing the winds.

Although I loved my Nimba people, believed in their potential and recognized their capacity to make a difference through organized action, their wrangling made my hope for ending the war start to fizzle. I resigned, believing that I had probably bitten off more than I could swallow. Unfortunately, my dwindling hope did not relieve that deep well of personal pain. Having a sense that perhaps the wrangling in the Nimba community in the U.S. was an outcome of the trauma of war may have been a transient psychological relief but no antidote for my pain. So, I had to find an answer. The village became the next place I turned to, not literally but figuratively.

CONFESS AND SURVIVE YOUR ILLNESS

Amid Liberia's disintegration, besides experiencing a deep well of personal pain, I felt like I was in the village. More importantly, things I used to dismiss when I was much younger started to make a whole lot of sense to me. For example, in the culture, when people become sick, the assumption from the get-go is that their illnesses stem from their involvement in witchcraft. In a situation where there is no health center nearby or an individual does not have resources to seek medical attention, he or she is told "If you did something (witchcraft), confess it so that you can survive your illness." Although the request is usually blunt, it is often made by the silence or inaction of everyone expected to help the sick person. In other words, if someone did something terrible through witchcraft, the time is now to confess it, otherwise death would be that person's fate. In that way, when someone dies of an illness, especially if the person failed to confess, the onus is on that individual for refusing to confess, and not on the family or the community.

The village I was in was figurative. The people of my actual village did not watch me languish in illness and pain and then urged me to "confess" to survive if I had done "something." Instead, when the bigwigs in the international community let Liberia wither on the vine through their inaction and abandonment in 1990, Liberia and its people felt like that sick person in the village told to "confess" to survive if he or she did "something." Indeed, in the throes of national and personal pain, I became that sick person in the village, with no clinics nearby or resources to seek medical care. I heard an imaginary person tell me to "confess" to survive when my hope for organized action in ending the civil war in Liberia was dashed.

There was no bone of "something" or witchcraft in me. I was not in any way involved in anything that remotely led to the conflict in Liberia. Even though I had not done "something," I was forced to respond to that imaginary person who urged me to "confess" to "survive" because the national pain, as well as personal pain, was intense. I had to turn every stone to seek relief. Because those who urged the sick to confess involvement in witchcraft were often motivated by other interests including jealousies, I turned to a

Zoe who did not have an axe to grind. I turned to Mr. Randall Robinson, a neutral Zoe, because I wanted my forced confession to bring relief. [310]

As someone who felt the sting of Liberia's ailment, I had no choice but to confess for different actors who made Liberia "sick," if the country were to get a chance to reclaim its nationhood. [311] In doing so, I recounted my reality without pretending to be an unbiased agent. As Liberia's layered and complex socio-economic and cultural context was intricately woven into my life, the tragedy that resulted from the discord in the country was a part of my story. As a result, I could not pretend to be such an agent without spreading a level of falsehood.

The goal of my "confession" was to seek Mr. Robinson's help in doing what he did for Haitians when their president was overthrown and driven into exile in the United States. I asked him to help bring level-headed Liberians, Liberian leaders and all who cared about Liberia together to work with Washington, D.C. to stop the war. The effort was predicated on a consensus that the U.S. had a role in a true settlement of the crisis. The "confession" began with a letter to Mr. Randall Robinson on November 28, 1994, at which time he had been working relentlessly for the return of Haitian President Jean Bertrand Aristide to his country. [312]

Because I wanted relief from the "confession," I was placatory in tone to show Mr. Robinson that he had not been chosen randomly; I had been following his work. "I write to thank you for Haiti and Africa, particularly South Africa. Your unrelenting commitment to uplift and improve the lot of black people in these two regions is highly commendable. "I draw your attention to the nearly five-year old Liberian Civil War, and seek your guidance, support and leadership in its resolution." His work on behalf of South Africa, which contributed to "one-man, one-vote", South Africa's first elections involving all its citizens and, most of all, Mr. Nelson Mandela's victory over Apartheid," led me to him. His work also contributed to the presidential honors Bill Clinton accorded President Nelson Mandela at the White House, not to mention the return of President Aristide to Haiti. [313]

I sought Mr. Robinson's help because Liberians in the U.S. were not like Haitians in Washington, D.C., New York City, and Miami during the crisis involving their president. While Haitians were united and speaking with one voice about the return of their president to Haiti, Liberians in the U.S. were not united and speaking with one voice on seeking help to end the civil war in Liberia. As Haitians took organized actions to ensure that the plight of their deposed president remained a priority on the Clinton administration's foreign policy agenda, Liberians in the U.S. were making no significant progress in influencing the U.S. to help stop the civil war in Liberia. Sadly, a number of factors worked against Liberians' potential willingness to work together. For example, competing interests and loyalties, not to mention the frustrations and trauma of the war, negatively impacted organizing efforts.

With respect to the struggle to return President Jean Bertrand Aristide to Haiti, Haitians in the U.S. demonstrated the meaning of the cliché "God helps those who help themselves." They were united, spoke with one voice and remained at the forefront of their struggle across the United States. They understood the "language" of Washington, D.C., "You lobby to get what you want." God's help arrived when Mr. Robinson, Rev. Jesse Jackson, Jr., as well as others who worked behind the scenes and eventually the Clinton administration joined to make the return of President Aristide happen.

In 1994, the civil war in Liberia had taken a huge human toll. Courageous Liberians including women groups in Liberia were at the frontline campaigning against Liberian warlords. Yet, in the United States where the power and influence to stop the war resided, competing interests and loyalties among Liberians worked against their ability to organize and influence U.S. policymakers. In other words, if ending the war in Liberia hinged on the ability of Liberians in the U.S. to unite and pressure Washington, D.C. as Haitians did, there would be no end to the war in the near term.

PRESIDENT WILLIAM R. TOLBERT, JR.

The Liberian tragedy was not as simple as Americo-Liberians vs. "country people." Everything that went wrong in Liberia was not Americo-Liberians' fault. Neither was every leader of Americo-Liberian background culpable or equally responsible for the ills of Liberia. President William R. Tolbert, Jr., was a classic example of misplaced blame for Liberia's woes. President Tolbert was not an archetypal Americo-Liberian. He was a good leader with a vision that encompassed all of Liberia and all Liberians, irrespective of ethnicity, station, or creed.

President Tolbert understood the link between changing Liberian attitude, improving knowledge and developing skills, on the one hand, and developing the nation, on the other. He traveled extensively in rural Liberia, particularly in Nimba County, emphasizing self-reliance. He declared war on "ignorance, disease and poverty." In addition, he formulated and pursued policies to lift rural people out of poverty, emphasizing education, agriculture, and rural transportation. Tolbert built schools, "farm-to-market" roads and established agricultural cooperatives. His policy slogans, including but not limited to "Total involvement for higher heights" and "From mats to mattresses" took hold of the Liberian consciousness and started to bear fruits gradually in changing attitudes. President Tolbert regarded young people as critical to the future and vibrancy of Liberia and repeatedly referred to them as his "precious jewels." More importantly, he invested in their futures by making education a priority. Tolbert also broadened opportunities, particularly for the indigenous majority whom past Americo-Liberian leaders largely neglected.

President Tolbert's accomplishments, policies and persona greatly influenced me. He graduated from the University of Liberia and went on to become the nineteenth president of Liberia. That accomplishment was one reason I enrolled at the University of Liberia. However, my experience with discrimination at the University of Liberia made me aware that not all Americo-Liberians in positions of authority saw the future of Liberia through the eyes of President Tolbert. That searing and unforgettable experience occurred at a time when indigenous Liberians were "waking up" and asking questions about their status and place in Liberia. With questions, awareness, and pent-up grievances due to de facto second-class citizenship status, indigenous students, particularly University of Liberia indigenous students, widely blamed Americo-Liberians for nearly everything wrong in Liberia. Therefore, as president of Liberia and symbol of the system that shackled and aggrieved indigenous Liberians, critics caricatured President Tolbert as the embodiment of Americo-Liberian domination and exploitation.

During the Tolbert presidency, particularly in the waning years of the 1970s, the feeling that Americo-Liberians were to blame for the oppression, suffering, and underdevelopment of indigenous Liberians was palpable. Upon entering the University of Liberia as an unsuspecting and unsophisticated young man, I understood the essence of the stewing discontent, but I did not fully grasp the way left-leaning students of the university and their mentors framed the lingering issues between Americo-Liberians and indigenous people. Now, with the passage of time, I can appreciate the full scope of the Shakespearean tragedy that unfolded right before me.

The characters, *quizee* and "country man," represented America-Liberian and indigenous Liberian collectivities, respectively. In that epic drama, left-leaning students used intense rhetoric, rooted at the same time in truth and falsity, to accentuate the divide between America-Liberians and indigenous people.[314] Exploitations which maintained America-Liberian dominance over indigenous people were a theme.

Blaming America-Liberians or Congo people for everything wrong at the time was a fad. Considering the propaganda, not to mention agitations the rhetoric spurred against President Tolbert, I could well have pinned my misfortune at the University of Liberia on him. Others made Tolbert the posterchild of America-Liberian power and exploitation. I did not accept that portrayal of President Tolbert and did not change my perception of him as a good leader. I did not regard Tolbert as an oppressive *quizee* or monkey on the backs of indigenous people. Instead, I held him in high regard. However, when critics reviled and blamed Tolbert for everything wrong with Liberia, I did not lift my voice in his defense. In addition, I did not let anyone at the University of Liberia know that I held Tolbert in high esteem.

My experience as a student at the University of Liberia was a classic case of cognitive dissonance.[315] The students I hung out with were mostly indigenous Liberians. Some did not know where my loyalty lay and were therefore suspicious of me. To some of them, merely wearing fine clothes turned me into a "petit bourgeoisie" and a potential "reactionary." Strangely, my actions did not reflect where my heart was. I held President Tolbert in high regard, yet I voted for SUP candidates, the very students who railed against the President. The justification I had was very simple. I never voted against President Tolbert. Rather, I voted in solidarity with other indigenous Liberians for shared experience under America-Liberian domination.

As a youngster, I had a simplistic view of life. I thought that working hard to get an education and going on to "become somebody" would happen as a river runs its course.[316] I thought of life as a matter of taking one's turn. I entered college with that mindset. I did not understand how Liberia worked. All of that changed after two America-Liberian adults in positions of authority discriminated against me on separate occasions.[317] The experience opened my eyes and led to a full appreciation of the deep impact of America-Liberian hegemony, a reinforced skin that suffocated and kept indigenous people in place as second-class citizens. I "woke" up and realized that "Who knows you?" had created a two-tiered society and that it was not something to say and laugh about. I reckoned that the "passport" Mom and Dad sent me to Falapa to acquire to escape the confines of second-class citizenship would not be enough.[318] Relying solely on Wlah's miraculous intervention, for the first time, I wished the removal of the "monkey" off the backs of indigenous people in Liberia.[319]

My wish for Wlah to get the "monkey" off the backs of indigenous people arose within a unique context. The perennial divide between Americo-Liberians and indigenous Liberians had long been manufacturing conditions for a social upheaval. Nonetheless, Liberia was relatively peaceful and had an innocent outlook from the time of my childhood until the April 1980 Liberian "Revolution." I did not imagine an overthrow of the Liberian government because the word "overthrow" had not significantly become a part of Liberian conversations. The thought was not even a possibility because the Americo-Liberian dominated government of Liberia was perceived as having a massive intelligence apparatus and therefore invincible. In addition, violence had not taken hold of the Liberian consciousness and become a mainstay of the lexicon. I envisioned an indigenous leadership in Liberia in the future because it was inevitable. However, I did not know how that would happen. The *quizees* did not intend to cede power to indigenous people whom they believed were inherently incapable of governing Liberia.

The *quizees'* invincibility I perceived was merely a façade. The unjust social conditions that the "divide" spawned, along with agitations by mostly left-leaning activists in MOJA and PAL, precipitously shook the foundation of the all-powerful Americo-Liberian government. The slow but simmering kettle had reached a point of blowing off its lid. There was no turning back. Even though the rhetoric that student activists espoused at the University of Liberia was laced with utopianism and some falsities, the exploitations of indigenous people and their unmet needs and aspirations were an undeniable kernel of truth. Those conditions formed the winds that propelled Master Sergeant Samuel K. Doe and his colleagues to power in April 1980.

PRESIDENT SAMUEL K. DOE

My "confession" was based on my experience in Liberia and reflections while in the United States, fourteen years after the 1980 Revolution. Following the "Revolution," I expected Samuel K. Doe to provide a political/cultural education for two reasons. First, *quizee's* lifestyle of leisure and luxury depended on the exploitation of indigenous people.[320] In addition, the *quizee* was a menace, keeping the country on life support as, year after year, it depended on international budget support or development assistance. It was not uncommon for budget support or development assistance funds to vanish without a trace. *Quizee* also helped create a work-adverse culture. Despite the country's vast arable lands, Liberians shunned working the land and, instead, imported their food. A typical Liberian's dream of becoming a *quizee*, to sit in a plush air-conditioned office and lord over others, was a dimension of that culture.

Second, *quizee* helped create and propagate the pernicious Americo-Liberian ideology of "'Country man' cannot govern." That ideology along with the subjugation of indigenous Liberians conditioned them to believe that they lacked the capacity to change their social and economic conditions. They looked to the *quizees* in Monrovia for guidance in determining their destiny. As a consequence of subjugation and a work-adverse culture, Liberians in general still look largely to Monrovia and to the United States for help to change their social and economic conditions.

I thought that a political/cultural education would wake up the largely cowed and docile indigenous population to take their improvements into their own hands. However, what happened was the exact opposite of what I expected. Upon seizing power in April 1980, Samuel Doe and his colleagues continued with the definition of *quizee*. They left the very structures that perpetuated injustices and backwardness intact and in place; they simply traded places with the erstwhile Americo-Liberian oligarchy. Despite indigenous rule, "'Country man' cannot govern," the pernicious Americo-Liberian ideology that shackled indigenous minds and development continued uninterrupted. The April 1980 overthrow of the Americo-Liberian oligarchy was a disruption in the colonization of Liberia and not a revolution.[321] In Amed Sekou Toure's words, a true revolution is when "Total liberation from the spirit of the 'colonized,' that is to say, from all the evil consequences, moral, intellectual and cultural, of the colonial system" occurs, or at least begins.[322] I agree with Amed Sekou Touré's idea that a true revolution occurs when there is renaissance, or a shift of mind. No amount of social and economic progress occurs where the people do not believe that the loci of control reside within themselves rather than within external agents.

The political/cultural education I expected was a redefinition of the "Liberian *qui*," the ideal person nearly every Liberian child wanted to grow up to become. The resilient *quizee* Liberians relished to become unquestionably remains intact. He is the shackles on Liberians' ability to seize control of their lives to improve their social and economic conditions. The archetypal *quizee* is a "big shot," an America-Liberian, or a "Congo man." Having protruding pot belly, drinking imported spirits, riding chauffeur-driven luxury cars, and keeping domestic servants are distinctive features of a *quizee*. *Quizee* is a symbol of "good life," a "life of enjoyment," one that does not require toils.

A model of a *quideh* I expected is someone for every child or Liberian to want to strive to become; someone educated, law-abiding, who cares about his family and Liberia; someone who considers improving upon the heritage and passing it on to the next generation an obligation; someone who considers ensuring children having opportunities to live out their dreams an obligation; someone who considers serving fellow citizens with integrity and putting national interest front and center an obligation.[323] Indeed, I expected Samuel K. Doe to make becoming a *quideh* the focus of citizenship, and a wellspring of meaning and fulfillment.

The window of opportunity for a political/cultural education was immediately after the April 1980 "Revolution." The nation, at that time, was on cloud nine; for the majority indigenous people, it was a moment of euphoria, infinite dreams, and possibilities. I wanted a continuation of the policy agenda of the martyred President Tolbert, but couched within the framework of that political/cultural education. President Tolbert advocated self-reliance; he wanted to lift rural indigenous people out of poverty and transform Liberia, almost everything indigenous activists were demanding. More importantly, he understood the need to develop the people's capacity to take the driver's seat in transforming their social and material conditions. For that reason, his policy agenda, contained within a different framework (war on ignorance, disease, and poverty), involved education, agriculture, rural healthcare, electrification, and transportation.

President Tolbert was serious and up to something fundamental, but most indigenous activists failed to grasp it. Conservative old guard members of the True Whig Party/ruling oligarchy, however, caught on to the ultimate goal of Tolbert's policies. They resisted his reforms because they saw them clearly and simply as an existential threat. President Tolbert realized that *quizee* was unsustainable. The policies he pursued were an attempt to formulate a definition of a *quideh*, but, for obvious reasons, he could not follow the path I expected Samuel K. Doe to take. He was an Americo-Liberian, the model of a *quizee*. He could not tear down the model that sustained Americo-Liberian supremacy; he could not dismantle the ideology of "'Country man' cannot govern."

Samuel K. Doe was an eleventh-grade student at a night school in Monrovia at the time of the April 12, 1980 "Revolution." By that time, how much Liberian, African, or world history had he read? If education in the classics were readily available in Liberia at the time, how much of such education had he been exposed to? Prior to the Revolution, where, outside of Liberia, had Samuel K. Doe been to or lived? Perhaps such exposures might have expanded his knowledge about the human experience to appreciate the gravity and responsibility of lifting, inspiring and leading a nation.

The assassination of President William R. Tolbert, Jr., on April 12, 1980, left me in a quandary. Liberians call it "John's palm oil wastes on John's rice."[324] I never wanted any harm to befall any Liberian, not to mention President Tolbert. Upon wishing that Wlah miraculously remove the "monkey" off the backs of the indigenous people, I had a truncated definition of a miracle. I considered only the saving aspect of a miracle and not the destructive aspect. I thought of a miracle as the parting of the Red Sea, only considering the safe crossing of the Israelites while forgetting the drowning of the pursuing Egyptian army. I enjoyed eating the palm oil that "wasted" on my rice, but it was unseemly that a clumsy child kicked it into my pan of rice. I relished the burst of freedom that permeated the air on April 12, 1980, but the sudden and bloody path to that freedom ached my heart deeply.

Leaders do not need to know everything, but they need to recognize their limitations. Leaders who recognize their limitations assemble good people with the requisite knowledge, skills, and judgment as well as mindset to help achieve national goals. I do not believe the advisors President Samuel K. Doe assembled, many of whom were indigenous Liberians, had what it took to do the job. Despite the president's ability to learn on the job and his advisors' seemingly splendid credentials, the requisite team for driving the agenda of the "Revolution" was lacking. In short, I expected more of President Doe and his advisors than they had the capacity to deliver. In hindsight, I was tempted to say that my expectation of Samuel K. Doe and his colleagues was unrealistic and thus give them a pass. However, they were adults, and not minors, when they planned and assassinated President Tolbert. Leaving *quizee* intact was a colossal failure in judgment and a significant indictment against Samuel K. Doe and his colleagues. Their actions could not be excused simply because they were not highly educated.

It was important for indigenous Liberians to participate in the affairs of the nation at all levels to vindicate their humanity. They needed to demonstrate that they could serve their fellow citizens with integrity, hold the nation together as one people and move it forward in terms of social and economic development. Perhaps if that type of leadership existed in Liberia throughout since its founding, there would not have been an Americo-Liberian vs indigenous Liberian divide or a revolution. Those who celebrated the dawn of a new day on April 12, 1980, did not expect a musical chair. Instead, they looked forward to an indigenous leadership that would focus on improving the standard of living for all Liberians. Unfortunately, they got an indigenous leadership, which, in many ways, made their conditions far worse than the status quo before April 12, 1980.

THE ERSTWHILE AMERICO-LIBERIAN OLIGARCHY
The erstwhile oligarchy refers to the Americo-Liberian governing class, which was deposed in the Revolution of April 1980. Through fabrication and propagation of the ideologies of cultural superiority and "'Country people' cannot govern," Americo-Liberians dehumanized, exploited, and abused the majority indigenous population.[325] Moreover, the group dominated social, political, and economic life in Liberia since the founding of Liberia in the 1820s.[326] During its 133-year stranglehold in Liberia, group members and their descendants reaped the benefits of their domination. As racial ideology in the United States justified the dehumanization and exploitation of African Americans, cultural superiority and "Country people cannot govern" justified the dehumanization and exploitation of indigenous Liberians. Group members and their descendants were of superior culture while "country people" were primitive. In April 1980, however, that domination came to an end.

Immediately after the April 1980 "Revolution," the erstwhile oligarchy sprang into action to reclaim lost power, but its strategy was brazen. Although it was common knowledge that numerous Americo-Liberians were targeted and brutalized, if not killed, during the days following the Revolution, some members of the erstwhile America-Liberian oligarchy pledged their loyalties to the Revolution. Moreover, some became "loyal supporters" and "trusted confidants" of the Revolution's leader, Master Sergeant Samuel K. Doe.

In addition, it was common knowledge that America-Liberians and indigenous Liberians did not have equal social status. Some America-Liberian parents frowned on their children marrying someone outside the group, not to mention indigenous members of the military.[327] Before the Revolution, indigenous members of the Armed Forces of Liberia (AFL) were at the lowest rung of the Liberian society. However, immediately after the Revolution, what remained of that long existing socially constructed wall between America-Liberians and indigenous people broke down. This was especially true for powerful indigenous military leaders of the Revolution. They dated young and beautiful America-Liberian women openly, had America-Liberian mistresses while others divorced their native wives and married America-Liberian women.

Amid pledges of suspicious loyalties to the Revolution, perhaps the interest in indigenous men after the Revolution was placatory. Although survival from day-to-day in Monrovia in pursuit of education was a preoccupation at the time, I saw the spectacle as a conspiracy to allay the Revolution leaders' apprehensions. Nevertheless, through pledging loyalty to the Revolution as well as its women's newly discovered interest in indigenous men, the group determined that an overt direct military struggle against an overwhelmingly indigenous population was impossible.

Once the slowly resurgent group successfully infiltrated the ranks of the Revolution's leadership, it covertly inflamed dormant seeds of discord among the largely unsophisticated and uninformed military leadership.[328] In no time, the group's efforts began to bear fruits as seeds of discord started to sprout. Master Sergeant Doe would hear about a plot among his colleagues to overthrow him, a kangaroo military tribunal would hurriedly assemble, and summary executions would follow. Summary executions, one after the other, were the main method by which the "Revolution" devoured its babies.

Meanwhile, with little surprise, tribal members of executed Revolution leaders became unhappy and gradually turned against Master Sergeant Doe. As several executed Revolution leaders came from Nimba County, fissures developed between Master Sergeant Doe and members of the military leadership from the county. Consequently, Nimba County turned into a breeding ground for subversive activities aimed at removing Master Sergeant Doe from power. A case in point was the 1983 "Nimba Raid" staged in Yekepa, Nimba County. The "Nimba Raid" turned out to be the prelude to Liberia's Armageddon.

Incidentally, Master Sergeant Doe killed two birds with one stone immediately following the April 1980 "Revolution." He promised that the military would turn the country over to civilian rule and return to the barracks in 1986 to appease the international community and garner domestic support. Sergeant Doe supposedly gave up his military title and formed the National Democratic Party of Liberia (NDPL) as 1986 neared in an attempt to fulfill that promise. He then contested the presidency during the general elections held on October 15, 1985, as the standard bearer of the new party. When it became clear that Sergeant Doe had lost the election to Mr. Jackson F. Doe of Nimba County (no relations), he reportedly ordered the Election Commission, then headed by a prominent Americo-Liberian, Mr. Emmet Harmon, to destroy the ballots. Subsequently, Mr. Harmon declared Sergeant Doe as the winner of the presidential election with fifty-one percent of the votes.

During Mr. Harmon's announcement of the October 1985 presidential election results, the ingenuity of the resurgent oligarchy became apparent. The significance of that event was the recognition that declaring Mr. Jackson F. Doe president of Liberia was not in the group's interest, although he won the election. Declaring Mr. Jackson F. Doe president of Liberia would have erected a roadblock to the oligarchy's plan. It could not declare the popular Jackson F. Doe president of Liberia and then attempt to overthrow him because it did not have the manpower to wage such a fight. Most Liberians would have considered putting Jackson F. Doe in the "Chair" and attempting to overthrow him barefaced and repugnant. Jackson F. Doe's countrymen and women of Nimba County probably would not have accepted that supinely.

On the other hand, declaring Sergeant Doe president of Liberia was strategic because he was very unpopular. Moreover, Doe's mere act of rigging the election poisoned the national well and gave a carte blanche to those who wanted his head. Once Sergeant Doe was declared president of Liberia, an aggrieved party, Jackson F. Doe, arose. By extension, the people screaming over his shoulders, supporters throughout Liberia as well as his countrymen and women from Nimba County, also became an aggrieved party. No wonder why on November 12, 1985, General Thomas G. Qwiwonkpa, a son of Nimba County, supposedly came to remove Sergeant Doe to install Jackson F. Doe, the actual winner of the October 1985 presidential election.[329]

I admired General Thomas G. Qwiwonkpa. He was a good man who had a good heart for Liberians of every background. Nevertheless, those qualities did not set him apart significantly from other military leaders of the "Revolution" who were patently uninformed and gullible. Apparently, he did not know Liberian history; the significance and implications of toppling an oligarchy that maintained a 133-year stranglehold in Liberia. If he were informed, he would not let the group recruit him to do its bidding in the name of installing "Jackson F. Doe, the actual winner of the October 1985 presidential election."

General Thomas G. Qwiwonkpa was given a mask to wear, but he did not recognize it as a mask. Those who asked him to lead a revolt against Sergeant Doe had connections and influence in the West Africa subregion and in Washington, D.C. Moreover, Mr. Emmett Harmon was one of them. If they saw declaring Mr. Jackson F. Doe president of Liberia in their interest, they could have used their connections and influence to make Mr. Harmon declare him president of Liberia. That course could have prevented scores of Nimba people as well as other Liberians from dying as a result of the attempted overthrow of Sergeant Doe on November 12, 1985. As future events in the plan would show, one reason such a course was not taken was that the group believed in the age-old ideology that "'Country people' cannot govern."

On November 12, 1985, blindly, General Thomas G. Qwiwonkpa, Sergeant Doe's trusted colleague turned arch enemy, let the resurgent oligarchy lead him to the slaughter. Even though I was studying in Seoul, Korea at the time, I followed events in Liberia closely. Upon entering Liberia, General Qwiwonkpa declared that he had taken power to stop the excesses of Sergeant Doe and to prepare the country for civilian rule. Not surprisingly, the population greeted General Qwiwonkpa's announcement with jubilation and excitement. Monrovia's streets were reportedly impassable due to human traffic. But the jubilation was short-lived. Several hours later, Sergeant Doe's elite fighting men from Camp Schefflein, about twenty miles outside Monrovia along the Robertsfield Highway, squashed the attempted overthrow. Subsequently, Sergeant Doe declared that he was in control. His fighting men also went on the rampage in Monrovia and in Nimba County, the home county of General Qwiwonkpa, killing indiscriminately.

The November 12, 1985, attempted overthrow of Sergeant Doe was the climax of the first phase of the resurgent oligarchy's strategy to reclaim power. Apparently, the interim goal was to not only neutralize Sergeant Doe's support in Nimba County but also to turn the people against him. Nimba County was the strongest economically, militarily, and most populous county aside from Montserrado County. The animosity in Nimba County against Sergeant Doe and his countrymen had two sources. First, Nimba people were incensed over the deaths of General Qwiwonkpa and many innocent Nimba people following the November 12, 1985 attempted overthrow of Sergeant Doe. Second, Nimba people despised intimidation by government security and the climate of fear under which they lived.

The Nimba-Grand Gedeh divide that developed slowly and came to the fore with General Qwiwonkpa's ill-advised and abortive overthrow of Sergeant Doe created a unique opportunity for the next phase of the resurgent oligarchy's project.[330] The group's bonanza, which could not have been unexpected, was that the Ivory Coast, a stone throw from Nimba County, turned into a haven for dissident soldiers of the Armed Forces of Liberia (AFL). These soldiers, particularly the ones from Nimba County, cooperated with General Qwiwonkpa during the attempted overthrow but escaped Sergeant Doe's wrath. The oligarchy, through its agent, Mr. Charles Taylor, clandestinely recruited men and women from that "gold mine" of dissident soldiers and sent them to Libya through Burkina Faso for military training for the grand project. Operating from the mindset of "The enemy of my enemy is my friend," most of the largely uninformed Nimba dissident soldiers joined the Taylor-led project.

A section of the Liberian border with the Ivory Coast is in Nimba County. In that area of Nimba, the language and culture of the people on both sides of the border are literally the same. On the Liberian side, the Dans and, on the Ivorian side, the Yacoubas, are the same people with similar language and culture. Ostensibly, one reason dissident Nimba soldiers of the AFL took refuge in the Ivory Coast was proximity, familiarity and the lack of language and cultural barriers. However, the resurgent oligarchy's agent, Mr. Charles Taylor, chose the Ivory Coast as a staging point for the grand project for other reasons beyond proximity, familiarity and the lack of language and cultural barriers for his recruits.

The Ivory Coast became a haven and ideal staging base for the grand project due to a tragedy of the April 1980 Liberian "Revolution." Desiree "Daisy" Delafosse, foster daughter of President Houphouet Boigny of the Ivory Coast, was married to Adolphus Benedict Tolbert, the eldest son of President William R. Tolbert, Jr. Following the overthrow of the True Whig Party-led government and the assassination of President William R. Tolbert, Jr., an important matter to President Boigny went awry. According to John Peter Pham, Sergeant Doe assured President Boigny that Adolphus Benedict Tolbert would be safe.[331] Whether by design or merely due to the confusion shortly after the "Revolution," Sergeant Doe's men allegedly killed Adolphus Benedict Tolbert. The incident understandably infuriated President Boigny who, according to Pham, never forgave "Doe for the killing of President Tolbert's son, Adolphus, which left the Ivorian leader's adopted daughter, Desiree "Daisy" Delafosse, a widow."[332] "The death was not only a personal tragedy for the Houphouet Boigny's family, but a public humiliation that had cost the octogenarian Ivorian leader considerable loss of face that he did not pardon."[333]

Long before General Thomas G. Qwiwonkpa turned into Sergeant Doe's arch enemy, Doe had, with the killing of A. B. Tolbert, already created a powerful enemy across the Liberian border with the Ivory Coast. Perhaps it was no surprise that President Houphouet Boigny provided territory for the incubation, birthing, and implementation of the grand project, not to mention moral as well as material support. Liberians may never know whether, in Houphouet Boigny's payback for Sergeant Doe for the loss of his foster daughter's husband as well as perceived threat to his security and power, he considered the future of Liberia.

The man Pham said was "Known to his counterparts and followers alike," as "Le Vieux" (the elder) as well as the "Grand old man of African politics" had uses for "Mats" beyond sleeping on them. "Le Vieux" spread "Mats" in Africa and elsewhere around the world expressly for self- as well as "national-preservation." Shortly before independence, rightly or wrongly, his country voted "almost unanimously" to remain with the French community, although France crafted the Constitution in its national interest. According to Pike, President Houphouet-Boigny "Reminded fellow Ivoirians that their closest and best friend was France and that France made daily sacrifices

for Cote d'Ivoire by offering protected markets and military assistance."
Moreover, in April 1961, France and Cote D'Ivoire signed a "treaty of coop-
eration (the Franco-Ivoirian Technical Military Assistance Accord—Accord
d'Assistance Militaire Technique)". [334] "*Le Vieux*" spread "Mats" in other
ways including giving foster daughter, Desiree "Daisy" Delafosse-Tolbert,
in marriage to A. B. Tolbert and daughter, Chantal Terrasson de Fougeres,
in marriage to Captain Blaise Campaore. [335] Apparently, his mats helped
determine his friends and foes. A. B. Tolbert's death was not only an outright
destruction of Le Vieux's mat but also put Sergeant Doe into his crosshairs.

"*Le Vieux's*" role in the undoing of Liberia in avenging his foster daughter or forestalling perceived threat, account for a Hollywood Alfred J.
Hitchcock's thriller, albeit horrific. Once President Boigny secured a foothold
in Ouagadougou, Desiree "Daisy" Delafosse-Tolbert went to live there with
her foster sister, Chantal Terrasson de Fougeres. Thus, Blaise Compaore's
enlistment into *Le Vieux's* "Anti-Doe Vendetta" was a fait accompli. [336]
According to Pham, Compaore went beyond linking Charles Taylor up with
Col. Mu'ammar Gadhafi of Libya as Taylor sought support and training
opportunities for his recruits for the grand project. He "Supplied Taylor
with Burkinabe passports and a camp where Taylor and his men made final
preparations for their invasion" of Liberia. "Eventually Compaore became
one of the NPFL's main sources for arms and mercenaries." [337]

The oligarchy's agent, Mr. Charles Taylor, found a receptive ear for his
grand project in Col. Mu'ammar Gadhafi who had long been dreaming
of perhaps leading a United States of Africa. [338] Perhaps hoping to lay the
groundwork for his dream of a United States of Africa, Gadhafi tried to
secure a foothold in Liberia by being the first to recognize the military
government of Master Sergeant Samuel K. Doe immediately after the 1980
Liberian "Revolution." However, owing to American influence in Liberia,
Sergeant Doe shut down the Libyan embassy in Monrovia shortly thereafter and, in effect, shunned Col. Gadhafi's diplomatic foray into Liberia.

The shutdown of the Libyan embassy in Monrovia was probably upon
the urging of the United States or Sergeant Doe's ploy to seek favor with the
Reagan administration. Nevertheless, Doe and Liberia fell into Gadhafi's
crosshairs for other reasons as well. Col. Gadhafi may have seen Sergeant
Doe standing in the way of his dream of a United States of Africa as Kwame
Nkrumah saw President William V.S. Tubman standing in the way of his
proposal for a United Africa. Apparently, to Col. Gadhafi, Sergeant Doe was

not only a dream killer but also an existential threat. Col. Gadhafi's motivation for agreeing to help the resurgent oligarchy's agent, Charles Taylor, train his recruits for the invasion of Liberia to remove Doe from power was strategic because he and the group had parallel short-term interests. The oligarchy regarded Samuel Doe, along with the natives of Liberia, as an existential threat. They wanted the removal of Doe from power by any means necessary. As long as Taylor and Gadhafi eyed the removal of Doe from power, Gadhafi's assistance to Taylor in the form of military training as well as arms and ammunitions flowed uninterrupted.

THE DECEMBER 1989 INVASION

After the 1983 "Nimba Raid" and the 1985 Qwiwonkpa abortive coup, relations between President Doe and Nimba citizens deteriorated. Without a doubt, prominent Nimba citizens were involved in the 1983 "Nimba Raid." In the November 1985 attempted coup to remove President Doe from power, Qwiwonkpa's name alone was enough to establish Nimba citizens' collective guilt. In the Liberian context, the two attempts to topple Doe involving Nimba citizens were more than enough to justify his distrustful disposition. President Doe did not hide his feelings and distrust of Nimba citizens. He spoke at least once of "leveling" Nimba County, as in military bombardment, if any such acts were to occur there again. His deep suspicion of Nimba citizens was understandable.

The distrust between President Doe and Nimba citizens, however, was not a one-way phenomenon. Nimba citizens were distrustful of President Doe too. Again, as anyone who stands in the back and looks over one's shoulders in Liberia is guilty of one's actions by association, Nimba citizens' distrust of President Doe likewise generally extended to his people.[339] A separate volume is required to show the origins of Nimba citizens' distrust of President Doe. These include but are not limited to the legacy of Americo-Liberian divide-and-rule tactic and the military leadership's perceptions of leadership and power, let alone the suddenness of the "Revolution" and their unpreparedness. For the purposes of this book, one only needs to recall the early years of the Liberian "Revolution," at which time it started to devour its own babies.

Mr. Charles Taylor, the resurgent oligarchy's agent, used the gradually souring relations between President Samuel K. Doe and Nimba citizens to the group's strategic advantage. Mr. Taylor sold snake oil, but he was no idiot. He was keenly aware that President Doe and Nimba citizens harbored unhealed wounds in their relationship. Moreover, the president had the military might to respond as he had threatened. Considering President Doe's deep suspicion about Nimba citizens, Mr. Charles Taylor's calculation to invade Liberia through Nimba County was a sure bet. He knew that heavy-handedly "leveling" Nimba County with the firepower President Doe had would result in indiscriminate killings of innocent civilians. Taylor believed that invading Liberia through Nimba County was the prudent thing to do because, to him and the resurgent oligarchy, sacrificing Nimba citizens was a price worth paying for reclaiming lost power. In addition, sacrificing Nimba citizens was, in a measure, a payback for the deaths of thirteen Americo-Liberian government officials whom Sergeant Doe and his cohorts executed on April 21, 1980.

Charles Taylor's invasion of Liberia through Nimba County was a ploy to garner Nimba citizens' support for the grand project. In addition, the strategy widened the target that reprisals against Nimba citizens following Qwiwonkpa's abortive coup mounted on President Samuel Doe's back. Taylor's ploy resulted in exactly what he predicted. President Doe sent troops with massive firepower to Nimba County and indiscriminately slaughtered scores of innocent Nimba citizens. In response, as Taylor intended, many Nimba citizens joined the ranks of his rebels to fight against the Liberian government. As Mr. Taylor and the resurgent oligarchy had hoped, the civil war that ensued was between the natives.

To crown his initial victories and gain legitimacy, Charles Taylor invoked General Qwiwonkpa, a name that meant something special not only in Nimba County but also throughout Liberia. He "wrapped" himself up with Qwiwonkpa's name and claimed he had come to "finish the work that General Qwiwonkpa had begun."[340] Moreover, Taylor led Liberians to believe that Qwiwonkpa wanted to install Mr. Jackson F. Doe, the actual winner of the October 1985 presidential election, as president of Liberia. Yet, Jackson F. Doe did not receive a red-carpet welcome upon taking refuge in Firestone, Margibi County, which was Taylor's/NPFL's territory during the early stages of the civil war. Instead, Taylor reportedly ordered his men to take Jackson F, Doe to Buchanan and put him under house arrest. Subsequently, upon Taylor's orders, Jackson F. Doe was taken to NPFL headquarters in Bong County, where, with the involvement of other members of the NPFL leadership, Taylor ordered Jackson F. Doe's execution. So much with finishing "the work that General Qwiwonkpa had begun."

Conditions that led to the war had been in the making for a long time. On December 24, 1989, however, the resurgent oligarchy and Charles Taylor set into motion a wheel of tragedy that did something fundamental and ugly to the young people of Liberia. When Taylor and his rival warlords recruited, drugged, and indoctrinated Liberian children to fight their war, they robbed them of their innocence, futures and developing capacity for empathy. Countless innocent people died "for nothing" because of Taylor and his rival warlords' actions. Although the guns went silent in 2003, the pain they caused lingers. Everywhere in Liberia and in Liberian communities in the United States and elsewhere, reverberations of the war continue in our thoughts, words, actions, and bodies.

At the time of my "confession," stopping the senseless bloodshed was my number one priority, even if it meant letting perpetrators of barbaric atrocities go with impunity. Amid Charles Taylor and his rival warlords' determination to throw Liberia into hellfire, I believed calling for their arrest and trial amounted to tinder. The guns have been silent for about seventeen years, yet the Liberian landscape, drenched by innocent blood during the war years, continues to rumble for justice with intensity. Now, I join the chorus for the river of justice to flow over the land.

BURDENS OF THE LIBERIAN CIVIL WAR

I left Liberia for the United States via Abidjan, the Ivory Coast in June 1990. So, I was not in Liberia during the height of the violence and bloodshed. I cannot speak of hearing sounds of crackling machine guns and the silencing of little critters by deafening bombardments. I cannot speak of being unable to lift up my head to see the horizon due to flying bullets. I can only imagine when Liberians tell of their harrowing experience in their hiding places. However, a desire for an end to the Liberian nightmare was one that we all had. I did not have to be in Liberia during the peak of the violence and bloodshed to qualify to long for the end of the tragedy.

I was in America, but my mind was wrapped around Liberia. The intense psychological pressure made me feel as if my ankle were in a physical restraint.[341] It did not make any difference where I was. Whether I was in America 5,000 miles away or in the throes of the violence in Liberia, the anguish I felt over the war was the same. It was intense and it almost consumed me. Nonetheless, despite my disappointment with the Bush administration's abandonment of Liberia in June 1990, I remained hopeful that America would help stop the Liberian dread. With that hope, I lifted my head and looked towards the horizon, meaning the end of the Liberian Civil War. Not too long after, the horizon I fixated upon turned out to be a mirage in the desert. The more I learned about America and the forces that influenced its policymakers, the more elusive that horizon became. However, because of the untold sufferings in Liberia, I could not stop praying and hoping.

I coped with the pain of the war by reaching out for help for Liberia on my own. A letter to George Stephanopoulos, my latest effort at that time, was the third of such attempts.[342] Two previous efforts, a letter calling on Liberians in the U.S. to unite to help end the war and another to Randall Robinson, seeking similar help, had failed. The former turned out to be a raindrop on a duck's back while, more discouragingly, the waste bin received the latter. The Stephanopoulos letter was another shot at felling a tree in the jungle, hoping that, at least, jungle critters might flee from its falling sound. My inability to stomach the continuing hypocrisy and utter disregard for Liberia, at that time, was not enough. I felt that I had to do something, no matter whether my action amounted to anything.

As an avid supporter of President Bill Clinton, I was having a serious internal crisis over his apparent as well as virtual silence on the continuing tragedy in Liberia. To resolve that crisis, I resorted to a Mahn adage "We have blood in our stomachs yet vomit water." Despite my cultural conditioning, however, by July 1996, I was teetering on vomiting with "blood" over the treatment Liberia was getting in the Clinton administration. I did everything to hold back that swirling "blood" in my stomach over Liberia's placement on the backburner. However, in my contained rage, I thought about tooth and tongue's proximity because their relationship does not always reflect their closeness. Occasionally, tooth bites the tongue. In other words, being a loyal supporter of President Clinton did not mean that one could not ask him tough questions. I was losing sleep over the unimaginable sufferings in Liberia, and I just could not remain silent.

I employed my own device to cut through the apparent numbness to human suffering in the Clinton administration. In the Stephanopoulos letter, I intentionally said exactly the opposite of what I wanted to say. "I write neither to request action on the part of the administration nor to castigate the U.S. government." It was as if I were drowning and yelling out to a lifeguard, "I am not asking you to jump into the river to save my life, but I want you to think about my Mom's long and painful quest for children." I wanted Mr. Stephanopoulos, or possibly, President Clinton, to think about and act upon what I really wanted to say. "I write to ascertain as to whether President Clinton and his closest advisors are fully aware of the nature and extent of the tragedy in Liberia. If so, could the President fathom the agony of Liberians?"[343]

My approach for making a case for Liberia was rooted in a few things I learned in America, one of which is that there are more elephants in America than in any other country around the world. Unlike the savannah elephants of countries south of the Sahara Desert and those of the dense rainforests of West and Central Africa, American elephants inhabit homes, workplaces, and boardrooms. Another thing I learned in America pertains to what is appropriate and what is not. In America, one does not point to the elephant in the living, conference, or board room.[344] While it is obvious that the elephant cannot be mistaken, the appropriate thing to do is to walk quietly around the elephant. In that way, all those who are watching one's steps or movements can discover the elephant for themselves. The notion that some people see the elephant in the room while others do not see it is a make-believe, yet a necessary and important one in American culture.[345] The make-believe avoids the shame of not acknowledging the elephant in the room; it saves face. The takeaway is that one does not shame someone with whom one intends to do business. Shaming President Clinton and deriding the U.S. government would not have advanced the Liberian cause in any way.

In addition to my own device, I also cited cultural and political ties between Liberia and the U.S. I wanted to give Mr. Stephanopoulos a sense of the "funny tango" Liberia and the United States had had for over a century. As if those were not enough, I provided evidence of Liberians' undaunted love and appreciation for America. Despite the absence of reciprocity in devotion commensurate with theirs, anyone who paid attention to Liberia in the days following June 1990 perhaps noted something out of the ordinary. "Liberians refused to, in Patrick Buchanan's words 'pick up their pitch forks' to drive Americans away from Liberia."[346] No issue underscored the question of commensurate devotion more than the U.S. government's decision to stay out of the Liberian conflict.

Liberia was literally disintegrating, and, in the face of that tragedy, I tried to be as realistic as anyone in similar situation could be. On the one hand, I found myself trying to be rational in a situation in which no one was expected to exercise rationality. It was as if my house were on fire and I was trying to make excuses for why the fire truck had taken a long time to arrive or had not even shown up at all. I did this by calling attention to the Liberian tragedy as a real and burning issue while, on the other hand, acknowledging the "Complexity and political ramifications that come with the decision to intervene in one form or another in international conflicts."[347] I found it difficult to maintain that façade of rationality as I vacillated between wanting to "bite" or to "blow." This became apparent when I could no longer resist pointing to the Somalia debacle shortly after the U.S. administration let Liberia to wither on the vine. Some Liberians took the U.S. intervention in Somalia as adding an insult to injury. Most people familiar with Liberia know that what happened to U.S. troops in Somalia could not have happened to U.S. troops in Liberia. Moreover, Liberia was economically and historically clearly more important to the U.S. than Somalia was.

Since 1990, I have gained some new understanding and a change in terms of outlook has occurred in me. I am not the same person I was in 1990. Before 1999, for example, I saw the "defining moment" of the Liberian tragedy through the eyes of an ordinary citizen.[348] I took the matter to be as simple as counting 1, 2, and 3. I thought that President George H. W. Bush and the key people apparently involved in that decision saw the choices as clearly as I saw them. For example, at the beginning of the crisis, the Liberian security forces initially directed their retaliatory killings against members of the Mahn and Dan ethnic groups in Monrovia.[349] The latter's kinsmen and women were fighting alongside Charles Taylor in Nimba County against the government of President Samuel K. Doe. From my vantage point, the killings were more than a clear sign that Liberia was heading for a showdown of catastrophic proportions.

Besides seeing the decision the U.S. government made about Liberia as a simple matter, I also took President George H.W. Bush as the single "decider," or as Allison and Zelikow put it "A unitary, rational decision maker," someone whose action is "Centrally controlled, completely informed" and highly rooted in the values America professes.[350] In addition, America's influence in forming public opinion in Liberia also shaped my expectation of what the U.S. government would do. I could not imagine any decision that could have been easier for any American president to make than telling Charles Taylor and Samuel Doe to STOP and lay down their arms to save Liberia from unnecessary bloodshed.[351] I considered failure on the part of an American president as nothing short of an indication of no concern for black, African, or Liberian lives.

Later, in the United States, after numerous conversations with other Liberians, I realized that I was not the only one who saw the "defining moment" of the Liberian tragedy the way I did. More importantly, contrary to the common notion I had that President George H.W. Bush was the single "decider," I learned from Allison and Zelikow that "A government is not an individual." Instead, they defined a government as "A vast conglomerate of loosely allied organizations, each with a substantial life of its own." Through the lens of Model II, they described the behavior of a government "Less as deliberate choices and more as outputs of large organizations functioning according to standard patterns of behavior."[352]

Allison and Zelikow did not stop at Model II. Apparently, they set out to help people like me avoid situations such as the *Parable of the three blind men and the elephant* and to promote a better understanding of the often-hidden complexities of governmental behavior.[353] They further employed Model III, the Governmental Politics conceptual model. In Model III, the authors focused on leaders of constituent organizations of a government to explain governmental behavior. Their descriptions of such leaders are quite contrary to my own view of such leaders as minions who operate on behalf of heads of governments. Through the lens of Model III, Allison and Zelikow presented each leader of a constituent organization of a government as a "Player in a central, competitive game." The game, "Politics," involves "Bargaining along regular circuits among players positioned hierarchically within the government."[354]

In hindsight, I now have some understanding that "bargaining games" or "politics" may have played a role in the U.S. administration's decision to stay out of the Liberian crisis. Focusing on the "evacuation of its citizens" and letting "the African leaders and the Liberians sort out things for themselves" may have resulted from "the interaction of competing preferences." "Many actors as players," who did not focus or act "on a single strategic issue" or "a consistent set of strategic objectives" may have been involved in that decision. Rather than a "unitary actor" or a big man sitting at the helm, calling the shots, many players, "pulling and hauling," may have contributed to that decision.[355]

My rudimentary view of government as a grand "arena" for political activities largely controlled by a "unitary rational actor" underwent significant revision due to my exposure to Models II and III. The whole thrust of my idea for "organized action" was engaging the U.S. political process and speaking with one voice to nudge Washington, D.C., to stop the war in Liberia. I had known that the "game" consisted of "central players" as well as peripheral players. In addition, I was aware that "Ongoing struggles in outer circles help shape decision situations."[356] However, I had not closely observed evidence of it until Haitians, Haitian Americans and their supporters succeeded in returning Haitian President Jean Bertrand Aristide from exile in the United States to Haiti.

The central theme of Allison and Zelikow's Model III is engagement with the political process. However, engagement does not mean or guarantee a desired outcome because of the inherent nature of the "game." Having different players and organizations with different "preferences and beliefs" often results in "conflicting recommendations." Often, one player or group advocating one action wins over others calling for other actions. At other times, a compromise, or a result completely different from anything desired by any players or groups emerges. Model III's take away is that "the power and performance of proponents and opponents of the action in question" determine the outcome of the "game." Understanding a governmental decision or a governmental behavior therefore requires identifying the "game and players" and a sense of the "coalitions" that emerge during the game. Equally important to know are the "bargains and compromises" players make and a recognition that the game is messy and laden with "confusion."

In June 1990 and for a long while after that time, I saw the U.S. government's response to the Liberian crisis through the eyes of an ordinary citizen. With time and additional knowledge, I eventually came to see that decision differently. I believe now that the decision in June 1990 may have been an outcome of a synthesis of the outputs of the constituent organizations of the U.S. government. In addition, it is also likely that the decision was an outcome of a "competitive game," with many players as actors, involving the interaction of "competing preferences," let alone inconsistent set of "strategic objectives." However, I do not know whether I would have behaved differently in the face of that tragedy had I known what I now know.

The impact of the U.S. administration's decision in June 1990 to stay out of the Liberian conflict has not lost its magnitude just because I now know things that I did not know at the time.[357] What I now know may have been useful, perhaps by helping me keep an open mind. Had I been exposed to Allison and Zelikow's Models II and III, I do not believe that the burdens of the civil war would have been any less. However, I would have avoided blaming President George H. W. Bush. In addition, I would not have accused any American leader who did not see the clear sign of catastrophe I saw as not caring about black, African, or Liberian lives. In the eyes of ordinary Liberians, the George H. W. Bush administration's role in Liberia in June 1990 remains a sore spot in the effects of American foreign policy in Liberia.

I was still looking through the lens of *Model I* while I was building the conscience-pricking plot of the Stephanopoulos letter. As a result, I was under no illusion that those who ran the government in Washington, D.C., would lose sleep over their decision to stay out of the Liberian conflict. Like the previous administration, four years after the Clinton administration came to power, it did literally nothing significant to help stop the war in Liberia. If anything, I expected Mr. Stephanopoulos to do the easy thing—to ignore my letter or trash it—and he apparently did.

At the time of the Stephanopoulos letter, I vividly recall when the Somali crisis and graphic pictures of gruesome killings and wanton destructions in Bosnia sandwiched the Clinton administration. The American public was appalled by the horror in Bosnia, but it remained reluctant in its support for U.S. intervention. Understandably, memories of the shameful ordeal of U.S. troops in Mogadishu had not faded. My experience in Liberia fitted me in the Bosnian shoes and, as a result, I closely followed the slow-motion horror movie in Bosnia and earnestly hoped that President Clinton would intervene. The long wait was excruciating, and one did not have to be a Bosnian to experience the pain.

My vacillation between "biting" and "blowing" surfaced again when I did the thing that one is not supposed to do if one's goal is to appeal to other people's hearts to support a cause. I dowsed my reason for writing with facts and inconsistencies on how the Bush administration before and the Clinton administration had treated Liberia.[358] At that point, my main goal was to remind the Clinton administration that it had an obligation to the world, particularly to Liberia.

At the time, it seemed as if I were watching three horror movies at the same time—the Mogadishu theater, where the corpses of U.S. Marines had recently been dragged in the streets, the Liberian theater, where the bloodbath unleashed by Charles Taylor and his rival warlords raged unabated and the Bosnian theater, where Armageddon loomed. Fortunately for the people of Bosnia, it was better late than never as it happened in Liberia. Based on 'national security interest of the U.S.,' the Clinton administration crafted the Dayton Peace Accords, intervened with full-force, and eventually brought about the cessation of hostilities in Bosnia.

The Liberian conflict may not have been reported on a sustained basis as conflicts in other countries had been in the past. Events in Iraq (the first Gulf War) also placed Liberia on the backburner. However, major U.S. news organizations including CNN, ABC, and others covered the Liberian story, sometimes with excessive graphic images. Aid workers returning from Liberia appeared on national television and gave accounts of the scale of suffering there. Moreover, they called on the U.S. government to do something to avoid an even greater tragedy. Washington's inertia baffled returning aid workers and others, including thousands of Liberians who watched the news in the U.S. and elsewhere in the world. Perhaps they wondered why the Liberian tragedy did not stir the consciences of people in official circles in Washington to respond.

On that note, I pointed to the Clinton administration's vigorous pursuit of the Dayton Peace Plan. The aspect of the plan that called for the removal from power and trial of Bosnian Serb President Radovan Karadzic and Army General Ratko Mladic for alleged war crimes concerned me. I thought the administration was doing the right thing, going after Radovan Karadzic and General Mladic, but, on the other hand, it did not appear to value lives that the Liberian warlords were destroying in the same way. By that time, the death toll in Liberia had exceeded over one hundred and fifty thousand people, an astronomical figure compared to the casualties in the Bosnian war. Moreover, amid intensifying calls for the arrest and trial of Karadzic and Mladic, I did not hear similar calls with the same zest for the arrest and trial of Charles Taylor and his rival warlords.

At that time, Liberia was bleeding and aching badly, but Liberians were not alone in feeling the pain. Americans and other nationalities were feeling the pain too. Some of these people had served in Liberia in various capacities, including the Peace Corps. Against that backdrop, conservative commentators who argued, "The U.S. cannot become the policeman of the world," were not particularly helpful, but they made sense to ordinary Americans.[359] Intractable problems abounded across the length and breadth of America. It did not make sense to ordinary American taxpayers to support interventions in conflicts around the world they did not understand. "The U.S. cannot become the policeman of the world." was an attempt to deflect attention from the failure of leadership during the George H. W. Bush administration over its decision to stay out of the Liberian conflict.

The conservatives do not have a monopoly on failure of leadership. In 1994, an epic failure of leadership, the Rwandan genocide, happened under President Bill Clinton's watch. Moreover, once "The U.S. cannot become the policeman of the world" took hold in American foreign policy circles, it became a convenient refrain. Whether it was a Democratic or Republican administration, it did not matter. The argument did not bother me, but selective interventions did. The Clinton administration's intervention in Bosnia, for example, made me to feel that the administration considered Bosnian lives to be more important than Liberian lives or that the Liberian warlords' lives were more valuable than those of the over one hundred and fifty thousand Liberians whom they had killed by that time.

America's greatest asset in Liberia, at least at the onset of the Liberian Civil War, was its influence. I still do not know of anywhere else in the world where American influence pervades the fabric of the society as it does in Liberia. The U.S. could have used that asset to prevent the bloodshed and untold suffering. There either did not seem to be a recognition or an appreciation of that asset. Had the U.S. intervened diplomatically in June 1990, perhaps it may not have found itself offering financial assistance and pleading with countries in the West Africa sub-region to accept additional Liberian refugees crowded on unsanitary and unsafe vessels sailing from port-to-port along the West African coast.

Honestly, I could not reconcile "The United States cannot become the policeman of the world" with the tremendous resources the U.S. spent during the six years following the start of the Liberian Civil War. Furthermore, I could not resolve the contradiction between "The United States cannot become the policeman of the world" and keeping the U.S. Embassy in Monrovia open amidst the orgy of violence when all other countries deserted Liberia.

CHAPTER 32

Quest to Move On

GONZAGA UNIVERSITY

I MOVED FROM LAURINBURG, NORTH CAROLINA, to Spokane, Washington, in June 1997 because I saw Gonzaga University as a means of social mobility. I wanted to further my education; to learn to know myself better; to take charge of creating my own path to discover my destiny. Until some of the big episodes that helped shape my life's direction, I believed that the positive correlation between education and wellbeing was automatic. I wanted to get more education to become wealthy and, as we say in Liberia, "enjoy." However, Dr. Cyrenius Forh helped me see education differently; as a tool, beyond lifting myself, for serving my people. When he said, "Mars, go get that degree (Ph.D.)," during a visit with the children and me in Wadesboro in 1992, I felt a gust of wind beneath my wings, although I did not have the first penny to pay for a graduate degree. He gave me the courage to face the challenges pursuing further graduate education would bring.

Moving to Spokane was challenging and personal. I used to think that a silver bullet existed for achieving success. Such a thing does not exist, but the closest thing to it is the power of the three simple words in Nike's logo: "Just Do It." Spokane, after all, was completely foreign, like a black hole in my imagination. Moreover, when I discovered where the city was located on the map of the United States, I had a thousand reasons not to go there. The place was behind "God's back," and, besides distance, I was afraid.[360] However, as my knees started to buckle under the pressure of fear, it occurred to me that I had not come thus far through my own strength and ingenuity. It was through Wlah's grace I made it in Sanniquellie, Monrovia and Greensboro. Indeed, it was Wlah's grace that "tempest-tossed" me to the shores of America at the onset of the Liberian Civil War; the same Wlah who delivered Lila, Wonkermie and Oretha from hellfire in Liberia to me in America. I needed not only to lean on Him, but also to "Just Do It." Once I took that "long step," the fog and darkness eventually disappeared, and a path appeared.[361]

Moving to Spokane did not happen because I planned it. I was not a rich man's son who wanted to go far west to go to college and discover himself in the process. Instead, I had two parallel educational goals, neither of which I had money to pay for the cost. I wanted to pursue a PhD or to go to law school. Without any preparation at all, I took the law school entrance examination (LSAT) in North Carolina, thinking that I would breeze through it, but the stupid test was hard. Moreover, an average score was not good enough for acceptance at most law schools. Thereafter, when I discovered that Fayetteville State University offered a doctoral program in educational leadership, I felt relieved because Fayetteville was less than an hour's drive away. I applied and was accepted into the doctoral program. During a get-acquainted tour of the campus, I asked about financial aid and scholarships. The response I got was at best not definitive.

Meanwhile, a few months before I received an acceptance letter from Fayetteville State University, Dr. James Beebe called me from Spokane. He was my immediate boss and mentor at USAID-Liberia in Monrovia. When I arrived in Washington, D.C., in June 1990, he was on his way to South Africa for reassignment. We stayed in contact throughout his three-year stay in South Africa. Upon his return to the United States, he retired and then took a job as a professor at Oregon State University. Later, he moved to Spokane and took another job as a professor at Gonzaga University, a Jesuit institution.

Dr. Beebe and I had repeated conversations about my plans for further graduate education while at USAID-Liberia in Monrovia before the civil war. The subject came up again while we were together briefly at USAID headquarters at the Department of State in Washington, D.C., but the time was not right for pursuing a degree program. He called to find out whether I was still thinking about pursuing a doctorate. If so, he was at Gonzaga University with the doctoral program in educational leadership and wanted me to check it out. I told him that I would do so and get back to him.

Cost and proximity were factors I took into consideration when I applied to Fayetteville State University. If financial aid and scholarships were available, I could commute from Laurinburg to Fayetteville. However, Dr. Beebe's call amid the uncertainty about financial aid and scholarships at Fayetteville State University gave me a pause. In addition, his call brought up the importance of having a strong support system, a factor I never thought much about in applying to Fayetteville State University. Fayetteville is next door to Laurinburg, where the children and I had a wonderful support system, but Dr. Beebe and I worked together in Liberia; he was my mentor. Despite the love and support the wonderful people of Laurinburg gave the children and me, Dr. Beebe and I related in a different way. We could laugh at the same jokes and stories or shake hands and snap fingers because of our shared experience in Liberia. Although Dr. Beebe is a white man, whenever he said, "The man ate my money," or "Let's hang heads," he triggered nostalgia, highlighting our deeper connections. Dr. Beebe's being in Spokane meant that I had family there. Based on that, I told him that I would like to consider the doctoral program at Gonzaga University. He wrote me on January 30, 1997, thanking me for my interest in the doctoral program. In that communication, he provided an overview of the program, contact information and important dates. He also enclosed the application forms.

Feeling hopeful, I informed Col. Carl Cannon of the looming opportunity. He immediately communicated with his dad, Col. John Cannon, in an attempt to identify someone in Spokane who would be our contact upon arrival in Spokane.[362] In addition, Carl wrote a letter of recommendation on my behalf and faxed it to Gonzaga University. In a letter to me, he wrote, "Congratulations many times over. Perseverance certainly has its place in our lives. I'm very proud of you for continuing the struggle." He went on to say, "This could very well be just like going to Greensboro and having Rock and Ozzie as your support system. You'll be just fine. God is good."[363] Indeed, moving to Spokane did not happen because I planned it. It happened through Wlah's intervention.

Carl certainly knew his dad because, in a little over two weeks after he wrote me, he sent me a hand-written note, letting me know that his dad had already identified a fraternity brother in Spokane to be our contact. As a letter to John indicated, the fraternity brother was enthusiastic about receiving us. "I would, of course, be happy to do anything I can to welcome your son's friend, Marsilius Flumo. He has an open invitation to come to my office and meet with me, and I would be honored to take him to lunch," the letter continued.[364] I wrote back and thanked John's fraternity brother. "Thank you for agreeing to be a contact person and for the kind words expressed in your response to the letter written on my behalf by Mr. John Cannon.... I am beginning to feel the warmth of all of you that I will be meeting."[365] I also told him that the girls and I were preparing for the relocation and before leaving North Carolina, I would let him know.

Shortly thereafter, Carl wrote me another letter. He had not forgotten anything. Instead, he was letting me know that John had forwarded a letter he received from his fraternity brother in Spokane, containing information that was apparently meant only for his consumption. The information was a warning about the wisdom of uprooting my children from North Carolina and moving to Spokane. In his latest letter to me, Carl enclosed the information, which included newspaper clippings. More importantly, he took the warning seriously, although he did not try to persuade me to change my plans about moving to Spokane. Carl said, "I feel it is important to pass on this information to you, only so that you may be prepared for the future." Referring to the contact in Spokane, Carl said, "He has pledged to oversee your visit. Even though I have never met..., my feeling is that he means just what he says. Do not hesitate to contact him."[366]

In the fraternity brother's postscript note to John that Carl, in turn, forwarded to me, he said, "Spokane is not an area and Gonzaga not an institution I would recommend to Mr. Flumo if I had been asked in advance," providing documentary evidence, including newspaper clippings to show why he felt so. "I do not wish to frighten Mr. Flumo or interfere with a decision he has already made, but he should know what he is getting into before he pulls up stakes and moves to this area with his children. Because he is your son's friend, I leave it to you to let him know my observations or not," he continued. He closed his message indicating, "Having said all these things, there is an effort underway to improve the climate. There are people of good will and 100 lakes within 100 miles. His experience does

410

not have to be a bad one. I will, of course, pledge to oversee Mr. Flumo's visit and intervene and assist him as needed."[367]

Although the information was not directly intended for me, Carl sent it to me anyway. He felt that I needed the material to make my own decision. Upon receipt, I read the observations and thought seriously about their implications. There was no doubt in my mind that my contact in Spokane knew what he was talking about. Moreover, I was convinced that he provided the information in good faith, out of concern for the well-being of my children and me. Lastly, I prayed about the situation. I then wrote Carl and expressed my gratefulness for the warning. I told him that, inasmuch as I harbored a level of fear of the unknown, the opportunity to go to Spokane to study was too good to let it slip by. "I am going, not depending on my own strength, but on that which comes from God." Later, I called Carl, but he was away from home that evening. His wife, Dr. Mary Cannon, answered the phone. She and I ended up having a lengthy conversation about my contact's observations. I told Dr. Cannon that I would be naïve not to take the warning seriously.

FAREWELL TO NORTH CAROLINA

Upon receiving assurances from Gonzaga University Graduate School that all was well with my application, I communicated with members of our support system in North Carolina. They included the Richardsons, Senters and the Rogers, all of Wadesboro; and the Robinsons of Fayetteville. The letters, which had the same content, in part, read

... I write to let you know that by God's grace the kids and I will be moving [to Spokane] in late June [1997] to prepare to begin my program in the fall semester. When school closes here in Laurinburg, we will come to see you not only to say goodbye, but also to thank you and Mrs. Richardson for all that you have done for the girls and me over the years.[368]

The section above repeated in the letters to the Senters, the Rogers and the Robinsons. Next, I wrote Mr. Norwood Randolph (deceased), Associate Superintendent for Personnel, Scotland County Schools, and not only resigned but also expressed my appreciation for the opportunity to serve. I also wrote Rev. Garland E. Pierce, the pastor of our home church, Bright Hopewell Baptist Church, to thank him and members of the church for their love and support during our time in Laurinburg. Owing a debt of gratitude to Fayetteville State University Graduate School, I sent a formal notification indicating that I had been accepted at Gonzaga University. I thanked the Graduate School for the opportunity accorded me.

THE ROAD TO SPOKANE, WASHINGTON

Even though I had already made the decision to move to Spokane, the time for action, to take the children and drive across the continental United States had come. The looming adventure of driving across nine states before reaching Spokane was riveting. The imminent move was nostalgic because it reminded me of my daring move from Sanniquellie to Monrovia in 1978 for a similar reason. The Sanniquellie-Monrovia move was fraught with risks, yet it had unforeseen opportunities too; it opened the world to me, sending me to Seoul, Korea, and then to the United States to study.

I was a single dad and, at the time, had three of the four children.[369] Blodah and Jo-Weh, the last two children, were not born yet. Therefore, the risks of the Laurinburg-Spokane move far exceeded those of the Sanniquellie-Monrovia move. Yet I felt strongly that they were worth taking because I could not miss the opportunity for personal and professional growth. I had been looking forward to this opportunity for a long time. I felt strongly about the opportunity because my own future and the futures of my family and village depended on it. I was prepared to sweep the streets to support the children if I did not find any professional job to do in Spokane.

The move was also a potent therapy, albeit temporary. The pain of separation from family in Liberia and the cascading and depressing circumstances of the civil war would not let up. In that situation, the euphoria about the move to Spokane was intoxicating and blinding. It prevented me from seeing the dread and anguish my decision presented for the children. Taking them from a place where they had friends and lived in relative comfort to a place about which they knew absolutely nothing was no small matter. I did not see the impacts of the move from their vantage point. It did not seem to me like the difficult and painful decision it really was for them. Instead, I saw the immediate impacts through my own eyes. I was focused on how the move was going to help further my personal and professional success. I felt that once I was in a better shape, the children too would be fine. At the time, I believed in a familiar American political cliché and related it to the move. I felt that the benefits of my personal and professional success would "trickle down" to the children, my entire family, and the village. Amazingly, unlike the "trickle down" I had been accustomed to hearing about during political campaigns in the United States, mine worked. "Trickle down" works as long as one is conscientious about making it work.

As we inched closer to June 20, 1997, I made extensive inquiries with moving companies. I wanted to get a sense of what it would cost to transport my 1987 Toyota Camry and the personal effects we had accumulated over time. The results were not encouraging. The price quotes were all above $5,000. I needed money to start in Spokane and I was not prepared to spend that kind of money to hire movers to transport the vehicle and our belongings. That kind of expense plus flying four people to Spokane would have wiped out a lion's share of the funds I was taking with me to Spokane. Someone then suggested that I could rent a U-Haul truck, attach the vehicle to it on a tow dolly and drive it myself to Spokane. I had seen U-Haul trucks all around, but it never occurred to me that one could rent one without having to worry about returning it to where it was rented. I immediately called U-Haul in Laurinburg and discovered that the cost was far less than half of what the moving companies had quoted to me. I had never driven a U-Haul truck before, let alone across the country. But with that rental agreement in my hand, I was set to embark on a U-Haul truck driving experiment across the continental United States.

All was set for the Spokane journey except one thing. I was not able to sell "Old Faithful," my 1978 Dodge Magnum-318 before our departure date. One man, a friend of someone I knew, took possession to pay $200 for it later. Unfortunately, the man never paid the money. I did not bother to call him because I felt that "Old Faithful" was worth more than money could buy. I thought I would rather let it go without money ever changing hands than to take a paltry $200. For all purposes, the car had taken on a personality and become an icon in the family.

"Old Faithful" helped me weather the stresses and strains of the civil war in Liberia. Aside from taking me to and from work over the six and a half years I taught schools in North Carolina, the car was a regular on US Highway 421 between Greensboro and Fayetteville, US Highways 74 and 220 between Wadesboro and Greensboro as well as US Highways 501 and 421 between Laurinburg and Greensboro. The girls rode in "Old Faithful" whenever they had after school programs, including band concerts and sports. Indeed, it was a repository of memories.

I was in unchartered territory. Since I had never driven a U-Haul truck before, I did not know how to hook a vehicle on a tow dolly and attach it to a truck. So, I drove to the U-Haul compound in Laurinburg and sought help to ensure that my 1987 Toyota Camry was hooked properly to the tow dolly and attached securely to the U-Haul truck. I then returned with the U-Haul truck to Angela Little's house, where we stayed temporarily as we prepared to move to Spokane.[370]

Taking our belongings from Angela's house and transferring them to the truck seemed like removing a tooth. Even as Lila, Wonkermie and Oretha helped carry our belongings to the truck, they looked resigned. They were not particularly happy about the move because they were about to leave their friends behind. Understandably, they were worried about what teenagers in school worry about in such situations; starting all over, making new friends and not knowing who those new friends would be. But the die was cast. As my dependents, they probably felt helpless. So, the work went on slowly. By the time we finished transferring the things to the truck, it was past midday. It was an emotional day. I tried to avoid rubbing into the pain that they were feeling. So, I intentionally kept my cool.

On June 20, 1997, shortly after 2:00 p.m. on a hot sunny day, we each hugged Angela and said goodbye. The moment of physical separation from idyllic North Carolina and the good people who had become a part of our lives and consciousness had come. Even I, the adult, had to hold my head up because it was a teary departure. Years later, Wonkermie confessed that, as we drove away from Angela's house, making our way to the nearest street upon leaving Laurinburg on June 20, 1997, she and her sisters thought the entire departure episode was a joke. As a result, when the U-Haul truck broke down on US Highway 74 in Matthews, North Carolina, about one and a half hours after we left Laurinburg, they were ecstatic. They thought we would return to Laurinburg and forget about moving to Spokane. Unfortunately, help from the U-Haul truck company arrived and dashed their hope.

By the time repair work on the truck finished, it was past 9:00 p.m. Neither the breakdown nor the late evening departure from Matthews dampened my spirit. I was determined to move on. We left Matthews and, in no time, drove through the heart of Charlotte, North Carolina. We set our eyes on Interstate 77 North as my right foot on the truck's accelerator helped continue the work of our physical separation from the state we had come to know as our home away from home. I had some sense of the importance of the trip we embarked upon. As a result, not only did I scan sceneries and landmarks into my memory, but also kept records of every stop we made for fuel and every hotel we stayed in.

A few minutes after 11 p.m., we made our first stop for fuel in Statesville, North Carolina. This stop was not prompted by a low fuel gauge. We stopped because of mere paranoia. I was fearful of being stranded in the middle of nowhere on the highway. For that reason, I never let the fuel gauge fall below half tank, so I filled the tank with diesel fuel at a price of $1.149 per gallon and then returned to Interstate 77. In a little while in Statesville, we exited Interstate 77 and connected to Interstate 40 West.

As we set our eyes on Ashville, North Carolina, and ascended into the Appalachian Mountains, it seemed as if North Carolina's physical grip upon me was gradually weakening. The long climb into the Appalachians from the North Carolina side, followed by an equally long descend toward the Tennessee side, added another dimension to North Carolina's grip upon me. I could sense myself caught up in a virtual tug-of-war between North Carolina and Washington State, assisted by other states along our route to Spokane. Upon pulling up in a parking lot in Powell, Tennessee, near Knoxville, I took a deep sigh and assured myself that we had gotten over the hump; the physical barrier, the Appalachians. We were truly on our way to Spokane; there was no turning back as the children desired. It was far past midnight. Although eerily quiet, the parking lot, which seemed like a loading zone, was well-lit. I parked the truck, engaged the parking brake, and told the kids to sleep. I tried to do the same, but I found myself awaking after every now and then because I was concerned about our safety.

Shortly before 7 a.m. on June 21st, the kids and I pulled up at a convenience store at a service station in Powell, Tennessee. First, we had breakfast and then I filled the fuel tank. We resumed the journey by setting our eyes along Interstate 75 North. We drove through the Cumberland Mountains of Tennessee and the hilly, rugged, yet scenic terrain of the Cumberland Plateau of Kentucky. After a long drive, we took Interstate 64 West near Lexington, Kentucky, to Louisville, Kentucky, where we refueled again. Upon leaving Louisville, we set our eyes on Interstate 65 North and drove through Indianapolis. Beyond Indianapolis, we encountered unending flat lands covered with endless fields of golden corn and wheat.

A service station in Frankfort, Indiana, was our next stop. We used the restrooms, had something to eat and then refueled. We continued along

Interstate 65 North and then merged into Interstate 90 West in Gary, Indiana. We drove through the city of Chicago and pulled up at Auto Truck Plaza in Hampshire, Illinois, about 7:30 p.m. on June 21st, where, again, we used the restrooms and refueled. Upon leaving Hampshire, we drove for quite a while and then took an exit that led us to Country Inn & Suites at 904 E. Main Street, Waunakee, Wisconsin, about two miles off I-90. We spent our second night on the road to Spokane in room 209 of that beautiful and comfortable facility near Madison, Wisconsin.

I needed a rest from the grueling approximately 12-hour drive from Powell, Tennessee, to Waunakee, Wisconsin. However, of all the places along I-90 in the Madison area, I do not know why I exited I-90 and followed that winding, yet narrow paved road up into the hills to Waunakee. As soon as we arrived at the Country Inn & Suites, I realized that exiting I-90 and driving up the hills to the facility may not have been accidental. Fate may have had its hands in that decision. Everything about the place was inviting. Warmth permeated the ambiance, including the facility we stayed in. It felt as if we had reached our destination. During the next morning, leaving the facility was hard. I had a feeling of wanting to hold onto the place and taking it along with me to Spokane if that were possible. Waunakee left an imprint on me. I wondered what manner and character of people lived there.

If the cliché "All good things must come to an end," ever possessed an ounce of meaning, preparing to leave Waunakee must have been one such occasion. On the morning of June 22nd, first, we had breakfast and then resumed our journey. We made our way down the narrow road from the Country Inn & Suites toward the section of the highway where I-90 and I-94 merged into one highway. We covered a long stretch of the highway and then pulled up at a convenience store along Exit 48 on I-90/94 in Oakdale, Wisconsin, shortly before noon. We stopped only to refuel. The journey continued that stretch of highway for quite a while until I-90 veered off to the left near Tomah, Wisconsin. The stretch of I-94 we covered from that point to Minneapolis seemed like no-man's-land.

Minneapolis was familiar territory. I had visited the city two times in the past. I still had a few friends who lived there. Also, I remembered all the good times we had in the city during UNICCO conferences.[371] So, the thought of stopping and spending the night in Minneapolis crossed my mind. However, I felt strongly that we did not need any distractions along our journey to Spokane. Instead, I kept on driving through the city. About 4 p.m. on June 22nd, I pulled up at a service station in Rogers, Minnesota, a suburb of Minneapolis on the west side of the city.

In Rogers, I refueled the truck and continued the drive until the fuel gauge dropped dangerously low, below any level I had tolerated since the beginning of the journey. From that point on, the U-Haul truck, to me, was no longer an ordinary machine on wheels. Indeed, I was in control of the vehicle's steering wheel. However, the truck was carrying us, four human beings whose future depended on how it performed. Shortly after 7 p.m., when I told the kids that I needed to "feed" the "beast," I exited the highway, turned, and arrived at the General Store on Highways 34 & 9 in Barnesville, Minnesota. Apparently, the kids did not understand what was going through my mind. "Beast" was a reference to the truck as if it had assumed a personality and added up to make us five in number. I "fed" the "beast," took off from Barnesville, and continued nonstop until night fell upon us in Moorhead, at the Stateline between Minnesota and North Dakota. We stayed at Motel 75 on I-94 & Hwy 75 South in Moorhead, on the Minnesota side of the border.

Incidentally, it was surprising that I was not spent after all the driving I had done up to the Minnesota-North Dakota Stateline. Instead, I felt like an Energizer bunny when we awoke early morning June 23rd, had breakfast, and readied ourselves to resume our journey to Spokane. I was fired up to get on with the driving. For one thing, had I needed assistance with the driving, the only person who could have provided that help was Lila. But Lila did not have her driver's license at that time, even though she enrolled in a driver's education class at Scotland High School in Laurinburg and completed it. She did not pursue her driver's license with the same sense of "I got to have it" that American teenagers generally have. Lila was born in Liberia, where driving was not a "must do" activity for teenagers. Most people in Liberia do not own cars and Liberian teenagers generally do not regard being able to drive as a rite of passage as, for example, American teenagers do.

So, as long as Lila had a laissez-faire posture about her driver's license, which included her fear of being in control of a vehicle amidst traffic, that was a perfect situation for me. That was one less worry. I did not have to say, "No," out of concern for her safety if she asked to drive my car to some place. Any tendencies like Lila's blasé attitude about her driver's license got an affirmative as well as a quiet "amen" from me. I never thought about the future; that one day I would need her to relieve me from the kind of driving that I was doing on our way to Spokane.

The future Spokane personified and represented seemed like a gold medal that I was reaching out to grasp. No measure of fatigue could dampen my spirit and will to press on. With that determination, we left Motel 75 in Morehead on the morning of June 23rd, crossed the Red River and, in no time, reached Fargo, North Dakota. Shortly after 11:00 a.m., after having traveled a little over 125 miles, we made our first stop in North Dakota on Hwy 30 South in Medina to "feed" the insatiable "beast."

The U-Haul truck's new name, "Beast," arose not only for the great job it was doing by taking us closer and closer to Spokane, but also because it was guzzling diesel fuel as if it had turned into a monster! One moment the needle on the fuel gauge would be at full and the next moment it would be at some point below half tank! Again, I was particularly mindful. I did not allow the needle on the fuel gauge to go anywhere near the quarter tank mark because I did not want us to be stuck anywhere on the highway.

After we left Medina, we got back on the highway and drove for almost 137 miles. About 1 p.m., we made our second stop in North Dakota in Hebron and refueled. Also, we grabbed something to eat and used the restrooms. Before we took off from Hebron to continue the journey, I looked at the map as well as the printed driving directions I had. The distance to Spokane remaining was not encouraging at all. It was a substantial stretch to cover, the most daunting being driving lengthwise across the state of Montana. As a result, I increased the distance of the stretches we were covering before stopping to refuel. Upon leaving Hebron, we drove almost 175 miles. About 4 p.m., we arrived at Interstate Cenex, our first stop in Montana. The service station was located on I-94 in Terry, Montana. The men I saw around the area while I was refueling were very tall and muscular. I wondered about their professions.

Like the flat lands we saw in Indiana, it seemed as if we were driving on a tabletop from Fargo onward until we started to approach the Rocky Mountains. We could see miles away in almost all directions. After we entered Montana, it not only seemed that going through the state would take forever, but also one could see miles away and from horizon to horizon just by making a 360-degree turn. Almost nothing stood in the way to prevent one from seeing the spectacular scenery. At that moment, I realized Montana's nickname "Big Sky Country" was an appropriate one. Long before we were anywhere close to Billings, I also wondered who lived in all the places we were passing through, that seemed like nowhere.

After we left Terry, we got back on the highway and covered a little over 162 miles. Shortly before 6 p.m., we stopped at a truck stop on Exit 14 & I-94 in Ballantine, Montana. I "fed" the "beast" again and looked at the map, hoping to surprise myself. I was hoping that we traveled farther than we actually did. There was no pleasant surprise. Instead, I noticed that Billings, the next big city, was no small distance away. On a completely different but somewhat amusing note, I instantly recalled Daren Billingsley, a student at Anson Senior High School in Wadesboro, in 1992. I kept confusing Billings with Billingsley and always had to catch myself and say, "Oh, I mean Billings."

Upon departing Ballantine shortly after 6 p.m. on June 23rd, I wanted to reach Billings and go as far as possible, surpassing the previous stretches we had covered. Unfortunately, I did not pay close attention to the terrain on the map. I drove through Billings and started to climb up the Rocky Mountains before I became aware of how far we had traveled beyond Billings. I wanted to stop somewhere and refuel before beginning the climb. But when I unknowingly began the climb, I could not stop anywhere. Although the kids did not know, I panicked because I thought we would run out of fuel in the Rocky Mountains while we were on the climb. That fear materialized when I realized that the truck was slowing down during the climb. Until that time, I had never driven in any high mountains and could not readily connect the cause of the slowdown to low air pressure as well as lower oxygen levels at higher elevations. I automatically assumed that we were running out of fuel. For one thing, we had driven about 200 miles since our last stop to refuel. That assumption did not make any sense because the fuel gauge was still a little above the half tank level. I thought perhaps the fuel gauge was not working properly.

There was nowhere to refuel because we were in the mountains. I stopped for a while and checked on the truck to make sure everything else was okay. When we resumed the climb, the truck continued to go slowly. I prayed quietly, asking Wlah to be with us to make it through the mountains. My first relief came upon observing 18-wheeler trucks go by in the next lane. They were also going slowly in similar manner. At that moment, I relaxed a little bit because we were not the only ones experiencing the slowdown.

We kept climbing slowly until we passed the summit of the mountains. As we began descending on the other side of the mountains, looking forward to reaching Butte, Montana, the truck started to pick up speed. I thanked Wlah for taking us safely past the summit of the mountains.

As we descended towards Butte, I realized we still were not out of the woods. The problem we encountered next was not a slowing truck. Instead, going down the mountains was extremely treacherous. Valleys on the right side of the mountains appeared like bottomless pits. It was summer and nighttime seemed like early morning. I saw the deep cloud-covered valleys but remained focused and calm as the steep roadway meandered toward Butte. Suddenly, I heard "Oh! Oh! Oh!" It was Wonkermie reacting to the deep cloud-covered valleys after she looked out the window on the right side. "Shut up!" I said with a raised voice. Not only was she making me nervous, but also, she was causing the other girls to panic. It was not just the truck's payload, but I had a car on a tow dolly attached to it. It was as if we were being pushed downhill by the vehicle attached to the truck.

Eventually, we climbed down the Rocky Mountains and reached Butte. Shortly before 1 a.m. on June 24th, we pulled up at Town Pump on Harrison Avenue and refueled because the fuel gauge had dropped near the empty tank level. We were lucky to see an operating service station at that hour of the morning. We had driven 248 miles, almost non-stop to Butte and badly needed a place to rest. Then, out of nowhere, a frivolous and hilarious argument arose over the pronunciation for "Butte." I had the wrong pronunciation in my mind, but I did not want to say it, even though the kids knew what I was thinking. Lila had the correct pronunciation. The "u" in "Butte" is pronounced as a long "u." Wonkermie and Oretha were merely spectators; they did not take sides. The argument remained unsettled until we pulled up at Comfort Inn of Butte on Harrison Avenue. Lila was certain that her pronunciation was correct and, therefore, could not wait to bring up the argument to the receptionist who was trying to find and assign our room. When she asked the receptionist, the look in his face indicated that he had settled similar such arguments before. He did not answer Lila's question, but asked me what I thought the pronunciation was. As soon as I said what I really thought, that is, "butt," the receptionist said, "Yeah, that is what many travelers through here think it is, but it is what your daughter said." Lila then leaped in excitement for winning the argument.

Our stay in Butte was not a full night, but we rested enough for what essentially was the last leg of our journey. Later that morning, we ate breakfast at the Comfort Inn and departed for Spokane. Shortly before 3 p.m. on June 24th, we stopped in Haugan, Montana. We refueled, ate late lunch, and continued the journey until we arrived in Spokane at 5:30 p.m. We drove straight to the campus of Gonzaga University and then called Dr. James Beebe on a pay phone. He directed us to his South Hill, Spokane mansion, where we stayed for a couple of nights. Seeing Dr. Beebe felt like being back at home in Liberia. We shook hands the Liberian way, with the distinctive snap and had a good laugh. He was still good at the handshake. As the girls settled in, Dr. Beebe showed us the family's art collections from all the places in Africa and elsewhere around the world he and his wife, Dr. Maria A. Beebe, had traveled. There were several collections from Liberia. He beamed with pride as he showed us his collections from Liberia.

An Epiphany

After a while, we settled down and talked about the days ahead as well as our trip from Laurinburg to Spokane. In the middle of our conversation, I told Dr. Beebe that I had an epiphany on the road from Laurinburg to Spokane that I needed to share. My experience was not a religious one. It was not in any way comparable to Paul's conversion on the road to Damascus, but it was a significant eye opener. Dr. Beebe and I had been in a certain conversation for a long time. So, before I began describing my experience, he knew a few things, including how I felt about former President George H. W. Bush's decision to let Liberians down at the advent of the civil war in Liberia. Dr. Beebe knew that for many Liberians, including me, that decision was incomprehensible. He also knew that the bitterness and burden of that decision had become incorporated into our DNAs. As such, former President George H. W. Bush's decision on Liberia was the furthest thing on Dr. Beebe's mind when I indicated to him that I had something to share. He almost fell out of his chair upon hearing me say, "Now, I understand why George H. W. Bush turned his back on Liberia." He was surprised to see me come full circle with my own feelings about America's role at the beginning of the civil war in Liberia.

I was not trying to downplay the horror, destruction, and loss of over 250,000 lives in Liberia. Neither was I saying that former President George H.

W. Bush did the right thing for not having helped Liberia avoid the senseless bloodshed. I was simply saying that after I drove almost diagonally across the continental United States, I saw the vastness of the country and sensed the enormity of the challenges and needs of the American people. It was an awakening to the classic Mahn adage, "Leh bupeh gbuo ay go ee ah, lor leh yen yee."[372] America is indeed a great power; it is a land of plenty with great military prowess. As it has invariably been expected to intervene militarily to save lives, or at other times provide humanitarian assistance around the world, it, too, has unimaginable needs at home. This is a realization that only people like me who have had the kind of experience I have had can appreciate. My experience helped put Liberia's needs at the start of the war as well as the concerns and needs of ordinary Americans into perspective.

Again, those of us who had some sense of the Liberian psyche, at least prior to the civil war, were of the view that the United States did not need to send troops to Liberia to stop the war at its inception. I was convinced that America's diplomatic intervention could have sufficed to prevent the Liberian tragedy. Assume for a moment that former President George H. W. Bush and his Foreign Service staff at the Department of State, as well as other relevant United States government agencies, understood the Liberian psyche at the start of the civil war in Liberia.[373] How else would Liberians, without the experience I have shared, have interpreted former President George H. W. Bush's decision to "leave Liberia in the cold"? Could ordinary Liberians have been faulted for buying into the idea that African lives are not worth much to spend inordinate amounts of American resources on? Appreciating the vastness of the United States taught me that what is obvious is not always true. My pain and bitterness over the civil war in Liberia was indescribable. I could not see beyond it to consider that American leaders could have had other reasons, no matter how unjustifiable, in deciding not to help stop the war at the beginning.

It has been 30 years since I fled the civil war in Liberia and came to the United States. Nothing, including the scale of the destruction, loss of lives and the depth of the psychological effect on the Liberian people, is lost on me. However, upon arrival in Spokane on June 24, 1997, I could not justify why I expected American leaders to turn their attention away from their people in America to Liberians who were waging a war on themselves. Indeed, I could not explain why I expected Americans to ignore their own needs to attend to the needs of Liberians who were destroying themselves and their country for sport. The civil war in Liberia still hurts like nothing imaginable. I would have been extremely grateful if the United States had intervened in some way and prevented the senseless loss of lives. That did not happen. Former President George H. W. Bush turned his back on Liberia. It hurt then and it still does, but I now have some sense as to why.

FAITH

The faith I alluded to in my letter to Carl when I expressed my determination to move to Spokane was not evident by a display as dramatic as the parting of the Red Sea for the Israelites when Moses stretched out his staff (Exodus 13:17-14:29). But, in the household where I lived while I was in elementary school away from my parents, we numbered sixteen people. Hunger reigned supreme in that household like the unrelenting Monrovia rain or incessant deluge of the mighty Mississippi River. Often, we survived on a meal of two cups of rice. As a child then and as an adult today, Zehyee Mahnmein's ability to ensure that each of us children had a portion to eat before going to bed was an artistry. Her care and compassion affected me deeply. In a child's mind, her seemingly magical touch was almost comparable to Jesus's feeding of the five thousand with five loaves of bread and two fish (Mark 6:30-44).

In moving to Spokane, I was self-assured not only because of my faith, but also by the power of Mom's prayers. Relying on those assurances, I did not put due stock into the warning I received. Aside from faith and Mom's prayers, I moved to Spokane, counting on another asset, namely, my socialization in the Mahn culture. While growing up in Liberia, I developed or, more appropriately, learned a habit of putting up with certain things that some societies, including the United States, perceive as injustice.

Mahn parents love their children, but they have ingrained cultural expectations rooted in paying one's debt to society, even if that society turns out to be one's own village or community. Expectations of children growing up, becoming productive and accountable contributing members of society do not have legal sanctions, but they are enduring and powerful. As Oldman Karmah Saiyee's remarks indicated in Bursonnon, Nimba County, in December 1989, these expectations are the true yardstick for determining who is successful and who is not. In that respect, the culture looks upon life as a tree, which starts from a seed in a particular location. It sprouts into a seedling, grows into a sapling and then over time becomes a gigantic tree. In furtherance of continuing the species, the tree develops and disperses its own seeds. Moreover, by dropping its dead leaves and branches below, it pays its debt to the microecosystem because decomposed branches, leaves and other parts feed newer and other forms of life. Essentially, life in the culture is a journey that begins and ends at home.

It does not matter whether one remains at home or travels to a faraway place to become successful. The important thing is to strive and accomplish "something," which must be brought home in one form or another. A Mahn proverb about a *"Pehnamee,"* anyone who struggles to achieve "something" or to become "someone," expresses how this happens. The proverb, *"Pehnamee leh eh bu sehn en balay"* (A person who is looking for "something" cannot eat finely broken rice), means that success requires developing a thick skin through patience and having a singular focus. Drying rice properly before pounding it in a mortar with pestle to remove the hull results in whole grains. Conversely, hastily drying rice results in finely broken grains. The longer time drying rice properly takes denotes the patience required to accomplish "something" or to become "someone" while whole grain rice signifies the singular focus also required to achieve same. On the other hand, hastily drying rice and finely broken grains are indications of lack of patience and a diffused focus, respectively.

Almost everything in Mahn culture involved taking turns. More importantly, because age reflected knowledge and wisdom, it determined the order of one's turn. I always had to wait until older people had taken their turns. In gatherings, for example, I gave up my seat for an older person, even for a late comer to an occasion. An older person's dignity was more important than that of a younger person's dignity. For example, if an investigation into a conflict between an adult and a youngster found that the adult was wrong, he would not apologize to the youngster. Instead, the youngster would be required to offer a public apology.

Young people, particularly "whippersnappers", could not participate in conversations with adults, even if they had something important to contribute. Grown-ups ate the best parts of every meal. Items such as meat, bread, and pocket money that required division among siblings were seldom portioned evenly. Older siblings always received larger portions. No matter how offensive, adults' behavior could not receive a reaction in kind because they were often given the benefit of the doubt. Such offensive behaviors were assumed to have motivations for the benefit of young people who wanted to amount to "something." I often cringed and asked why, but Mom always said "*Ee zoya ee gay*" (Let your heart sit in your stomach), meaning be patient.

The takeaway was the realization that the many spider stories told to teach lessons were about humans, the Mahn people. They were sometimes blatantly cunning, especially in dealing with their children. For example, one occasion where the Mahns gave children preferential treatment involved taking the lead during early morning walks along footpaths to farms. This happened mostly during the milking stage of rice where early arrival at farms to drive rice birds away was critical.

Different plants including grasses grew along footpaths to farms. Plants grew and crossed or covered footpaths if they were not cleared with machetes and removed. Early morning walks along outgrown footpaths were no fun. The reason was that early morning temperatures in Nimba County were relatively low. Water vapor that plants let out during transpiration condensed and formed relatively cold droplets of water on leaf tips as if someone sprinkled water on them. The vexing inconvenience included the prospect of wetting one's feet as well as pants from the ankle up to the knees, let alone the droplets' coldness. To avoid that inconvenience, Mahn adults cleverly fabricated the story about the mysterious power that "*Feelee*" has.[374] According to Mahns, "*Feelee*" makes children grow in height faster. Any Mahn who experienced a village life as a child most likely heard that he had to take the lead during early morning walks along footpaths to the farm to reap that benefit.

Through patience, a virtue in Mahn culture, I developed a thick skin. In America, especially during my journey to Spokane into the unknown, I believed, perhaps naively, that the thick skin would hold up. Indeed, I thought that my cultural conditioning would be an antidote to dignity-stripping and spirit-crushing tribulations that would arise. Additionally, after all, I came up through the hard times and challenges of Sanniquellie and Monrovia and felt I had been toughened enough for what was to come. At some level, I felt as if I were wearing an invisible armor against which life's challenges would hit and fall by the wayside.

AN "UNUSUAL" WELCOME TO SPOKANE

Two days after the kids and I arrived in Spokane, Dr. Beebe and I visited Gonzaga University campus. The purpose of the visit was to find housing.

We had no difficulty in finding one. I signed a rental agreement with the university's student housing department. The lease was for 811 E. Desmet Avenue, a small red house right in the heart of the campus.[375] The house consisted of a bedroom, living room and a kitchen, all located on the main floor. The bathroom was also on the main floor. The basement room was spacious and nice; however, going down the stairs into the basement room seemed like going through a dungeon and entering another world.

The children and I moved into the property right away and settled in. They carried all their belongings into the basement room, and I remained on the main floor. It was summer, but the night temperature was just fine for a restful night. Before retiring for our first night at the property, I took a deep sigh of relief. "We have reached," I said to myself, crashing into my bed. Even though I spoke English when I said, "We have reached," I was merely making a literal translation of what I was saying in Mahn, "Kwa bor", in my mind. Indeed, we had a peaceful and restful night.

In the first couple of days, I soon realized that Spokane had more to offer me than Gonzaga University. I found myself gazing at and admiring the late June night sky because I was new to Spokane. The sky remained bright all night as if the sun were just setting. I came from Liberia, a country located very close to the equator. There, particularly in the rural areas, night is the opposite of day. Night sky is pitch black, where one could see constellations with the naked eye. No need for "Dark Sky Reserve" designation! Aside from Liberia, I also lived in North Carolina, a state which is much closer to the equator than Washington State is. While I understood the scientific reason for the bright late June night sky in Spokane, it was still a marvel to behold because I had not seen one before. As a result, during our first night at 811 E. Desmet, I recall waking up and looking outside more than once before the next morning.

Col. John Cannon's fraternity brother in Spokane warned me about what to expect in Spokane. Even though I did not put much stock into that warning, I was completely aware. In the back of my mind, I knew that I would run into situations like that the longer I stayed in Spokane. By not putting much stock into the warning, I was, in other words, saying that if I were to face such a situation, I would not spend much energy on it as others with different backgrounds and experiences would do. After all, Mom's prayers were my shield and, I was a *Pehnamee*.

The day of reckoning with the warning that I received from Col. John Cannon's fraternity brother in Spokane came on the morning after our first night at 811 E. Desmet. Upon opening the front door, I discovered a bizarre and what I call a *"Shitty"* welcome to Gonzaga University and Spokane. A large clear Ziploc bag filled with human feces and sealed was leaning against my screen door. "What a gesture of welcome," I said. I was completely surprised, but I was not afraid. I knew exactly what the sealed Ziploc bag of human feces signified; it was a version of a tarred baby. I knew that whoever placed it at my screen door had one thing in mind: to scare me, to signal to me that Gonzaga University was not for me, or perhaps, "Go back to where you came from," that is, as I had often heard, "to Africa." I also knew that I would be a nightmare for the anonymous person who placed the sealed Ziploc bag of human feces at my screen door at 811 E. Desmet. I was determined to remain at Gonzaga University for the long haul until my goal was achieved. Certainly, I came to Gonzaga University with the mind of going back "to Africa," specifically to Liberia. However, I was going to go back to Liberia at a time of my own choosing and not by the dictate of an anonymous scarecrow. I certainly thought about the warning I had been given and could hear Col. John Cannon's fraternity brother in Spokane telling me "I told you so."

My reaction to the "Shitty" welcome incident, which came as if it had been rehearsed, was based on three things. First, Mom's prayers, my shield, which I have cited repeatedly. Second, the Mahn *Pehnamee* philosophy, which I have also explained. Third and finally, the realization that I was not a baby, also an outcome of my socialization in Mahn culture. Upon discovery of the large, sealed Ziploc bag of human feces, I immediately called campus police and reported the incident. Within no time word about the incident reached the highest level of Gonzaga University administration. On the following day, administration officials invited me to a meeting. They seemed noticeably nervous not knowing exactly how I would handle the matter. Father Patrick J. Ford (deceased), Vice President for Academic Affairs and a professor in the doctoral program, was present with Dr. James Beebe and others.

I was keenly aware of the incident's potential to soil Gonzaga University's image. Irrespective of the warning I received prior to coming to Spokane, I made a choice to come to live in Spokane anyway. I knew what happened in Spokane from that point on would have far-reaching consequences for my family and me. Moreover, my acceptance to study at Gonzaga University meant that the institution would become a part of my life story. No one asked me to stay quiet about the incident. I had the power to shape the story at that moment and I exercised it judiciously. I knew that Gonzaga University was not a den of racists. I had no appetite for any story in the press that would cast the university in that light in any way, shape, or form.

I was a *Pehnamee*, shielded by Mom's prayers, but my reaction to the "*Shitty*" welcome incident was also based on the realization that I was not a baby, particularly an African or Liberian baby. Typical Liberian (African) mothers carry their babies on their backs. As a result, African mothers' backs are more than donkeys' backs, places where weights of infants are carried. Since Liberian (African) infants spend a considerable time on their mothers' backs, their second beds or homes, per se, are their mothers' backs. However, infants do not have the capacity to appreciate the importance of their mothers' backs. Often, after they have been sufficiently breastfed, they vomit a slimy chyme that flows down their mothers' backs. When the chyme makes its way between an infant's stomach and its mother's back, especially on a hot day, it makes the infant uneasy and uncomfortable. In short, an infant does not know that it is ruining its bed or home when it pukes on its mother's back.

Everyone in the conference room for the meeting with Gonzaga University administration had had "spider soup and knew what it tasted like."[376] So, when I was asked to share my take on the "*Shitty*" welcome incident, I did not say what some people expected me to say. Instead, starting with one person, I scanned the faces of all the people who were sitting around the large ornate conference room table. I remember the room being quiet and uneasy because no one knew what I was up to as I scanned the anxious faces. In the end, those who expected me to talk about race were terribly disappointed. Spokane had become my mom's back, my bed and second home. Talking about race in that meeting amounted to vomiting chyme on my mom's back. I did not allow the "Shitty" welcome incident to define me. I avoided ruining my bed, my home because I was not a baby.

Instead, I told my audience that there was no need to panic about the incident because whoever did it did not know Marsilius Flumo and could have done it to anybody who was black. Moreover, and perhaps to their surprise, I told them that I was aware of the possibility of such incident occurring. Without mentioning anybody's name, I indicated that I had been warned not to come to Gonzaga University, but I chose to come, and I intended to stay and complete my studies. I even challenged the doer of the act to work harder at it because I was not going anywhere. Indeed, I was staying. I also told them that I will not talk to the press and from that meeting no one would hear about the matter. I kept my word.

I voluntarily gave my word not to talk to the press because I came to Spokane determined to study and achieve a goal. I looked long-term. I imagined the kind of atmosphere I would have created if I had let the incident get out of hand. If I were some prima donna, the press could have gotten wind of the incident and the story may have taken a life of its own. The reputation of a respectable institution and community stood at stake and I felt a deep sense of responsibility to safeguard it against the action of a fringe and anonymous element. So, when I chose to let the matter go, I did not set out to seek favor. Again, no one asked me to do so. There was no quid pro quo. I made a strategic decision, but it was one rooted in the values that my parents instilled in me.

In my meeting with Gonzaga University administration, I did not hold back on the most important matter that concerned me; the welfare of my children. I told the people in the meeting that I took a gamble on Gonzaga University and the Spokane community. I went on to say that when I uprooted my children from Laurinburg and moved to Spokane, I had a sense that leaders existed in Spokane. Moreover, I had an inkling that I would find people in the character likeness of my parents, I mean people who would not let the children of a certified public school teacher, able and willing to work no matter what the job, go hungry. I said that if my children went hungry in Spokane, I would certainly question the kind of leaders and people who live in Spokane.

WALLACE WILLIAMS

During the meeting with Gonzaga University administration about the incident involving the Ziploc bag, I put my children's welfare as my most important concern. I offered to take any job, even a street sweeper's job, to ensure that they did not go hungry. My light-hearted comment about taking a "gamble on Gonzaga University and the Spokane community" was not an indication of self-importance. I had not done anything worthy to benefit Gonzaga University or the Spokane community to expect reciprocity. After all, again, I was a *Pehnamee*. I had come to seek opportunities to improve my lot and that of my family and village.

I sincerely hoped that leaders and ordinary people in the character likeness of my parents existed in Spokane; people who would not ignore someone able and willing to work, no matter what the job was. But I never threw down the gauntlet and sat by idly, expecting a job to fall on my lap or someone to give me bread. I did not "hit the pavement" as we used to say in Monrovia because I had a car. Instead, I took assignments with Spokane Public Schools as a substitute teacher at Ferris High School and at Salk Middle School during the 1997-1998 school year. Although I was looking for a full-time teaching job, I did not let any opportunity for employment pass. I took a part-time employment with Spokane Community College as a computer instructor in its Extended Learning Program for adults and another part-time employment with Itron Corporation as a product quality control specialist. I gained full-time employment with Spokane Public Schools in August 1998, thanks to a confluence of themes woven into this book.[377] My credentials did not secure me a teaching position with Spokane Public Schools in 1998. Instead, Wlah, the ultimate decider whom Mom petitioned long before I set out on this journey, gave me the job. Through His infinite wisdom, He already had someone in place in Spokane to place this comma in this sentence of the story. That someone was Mr. Wallace Williams, to my knowledge at the time, the only African American serving as principal in Spokane Public Schools.[378] I did not know exactly how the hiring process worked. However, after a list of qualified candidates was submitted following screenings and interviews, I learned the principal either had the final or a big say in determining the candidate for the position. Mr. Williams had neither seen nor talked to me before, yet I heard he made it clear that he wanted me for the position. I cannot say definitively that I would not have been selected for the position if Mr. Wallace Williams had not been the principal at John R. Rogers High School. However, I know that my employment with Spokane Public Schools, in a measure, fitted into *"Mee lah qui leh keh qui bah qui leh lo mee ka."*[379]

ROBERTA (BOBBIE) LEAGUE

Indeed, leaders and ordinary people in the character likeness of my parents lived in Spokane. Another one of such people is Mrs. Roberta (Bobbie) League. Bobbie saw a need and not only made her services available, but also assumed the role of an advocate. I was looking for a permanent employment as a teacher, but one hurdle existed. My North Carolina Teaching Certificate needed to be converted to a Washington State Teaching Certificate. Luckily, Bobbie was then serving as Director of Teacher Certification in the School of Education at Gonzaga University. Not only was Bobbie task-oriented, efficient, and full of energy, but also, she knew the nuts and bolts of the certification process. She had an invisible laser for cutting through red tape. Bobbie and I started the certificate conversion, and she went as far as paying for the cost of the process. In no time, I received my Washington State Teaching Certificate in the mail.

Bobbie League is passionately devoted to her family and immeasurably compassionate. Once I felt comfortable talking to her, I shared some of my family's story of struggles and endurance. On one occasion, I spoke with Bobbie about the possibility of meeting with Father Harry Sladich (deceased), then the acting President of Gonzaga University. She asked why and I said that I thought he might help solve a problem. Marsetta Flumo and Margaret Tumbay were stuck in Liberia because I did not yet have an immigration status to send for them. After eight years of waiting to hear from the erstwhile Immigration and Naturalization Service (INS), I could not tell when I would achieve that status. At the time in 1998, I had not even had an interview for the application for asylum I made in August 1990. I was looking forward to asking Father Sladich to grant Margaret Tumbay a scholarship to study at Gonzaga University. I thought a scholarship to study at Gonzaga University would "kill two birds with one stone." An opportunity to study was also an opportunity to reunite the family with a single stroke of a pen.

Bobbie thought the idea was worth trying and accompanied me to the office of the president to arrange an appointment. On the day of the appointment, she also went along. Father Sladich greeted us warmly and asked us to sit down. I sat across the table from him as Bobbie sat to his right and listened. After a brief introduction, Father Sladich asked, "What can I do for you?" I told him the story about my family and the long separation mainly due to the slow immigration process. Again, he asked, "What can I do to help?" "If the university could offer Margaret a scholarship, I believe she would be granted a visa to come to study," I replied. "Is that all?" he asked, and I said yes. He then said, "Consider that done." In roughly three weeks after our meeting with Father Sladich, Margaret Tumbay and Marsetta Flumo arrived in Spokane. Again, Wlah intervened with that miracle. Bobbie played an important role in getting Marsetta Flumo and Margaret Tumbay out of Liberia to Spokane in 1998.

CHAPTER 33

Looking Back

YEARS HAVE PASSED SINCE MY 1990 ordeal in Liberia. The long civil war in Liberia turned the temporary refuge I sought in the United States into a permanent stay. Over the years, I have had a long professional career and absorbed quite a bit about American culture that I did not know in 1990 and before. The first experience I want to revisit involved two Americans with whom I worked in Liberia prior to seeking refuge in America. One was black and the other was white. Gontee, the overall boss, was a highly educated and sophisticated African American. He was tall, intelligent, and articulate. I did not have day-to-day contacts with him. Our interactions occurred during periodic briefings with department heads and project managers. I did not know him as I knew my immediate supervisor.

Early 1990, following Charles Taylor's invasion of Liberia, I, like many Liberians who spoke Mahn or Dan and hailed from Nimba County, particularly professionals, stood in the Liberian government's crosshairs. Our countrymen and women were collaborating with Mr. Taylor to overthrow the government. Moreover, Mr. Taylor, along with his rebels, invaded Liberia from the Ivory Coast through Nimba County. The government of Liberia did not need a smoking gun. The guns were crackling like hellfire in Nimba County. I, as well as other Nimba citizens in Monrovia and elsewhere where the government was in control, was fair game. My life was undeniably in immediate danger.

In view of the looming danger, I made a formal written request to Gontee. I asked for a leave of absence and his assistance in facilitating my travel to the United States. I, as well as most Liberians and non-Liberians, assumed that the military conflict underway in Nimba County would, in no more than months, be resolved diplomatically. In a typical company man's fashion, Gontee turned down my request and justified his decision by indicating he could not make an exception because similar assistance could not be provided for other Liberian professionals working for the organization. I was unhappy. Moreover, I developed an unfavorable view of Gontee not only due to a visceral human reaction, but also because of what I had come to see as a distinctive feature of Liberian culture; an entitlement mindset. "Enemy" is too strong. However, generally, it is the word often used in Liberia to describe someone like Gontee who does not give a positive response to one's request and is seen as working against one's interest.

With the passage of time, lessons learned about American culture and a dose of wisdom, the time has come for some modifications to my view of Gontee. I now recognize that his refusal to help me leave Liberia for my safety had more to it than the policy justification he provided at that time. Gontee's response to my request can be explained by the Liberian saying, "Sheep's luck is not the same as goat's luck." John Roberts, the second in command to Gontee at the organization was white. He was not my immediate supervisor. However, John Roberts was a people person who not only interacted readily with me, but also took great interest in me and my work. Upon his arrival at the organization, he became one of my strongest advocates. He was straightforward and truly a remarkable and compassionate man. It was not difficult to know where he stood on the issues. Had he been in charge at the time of my request, he would have put a plan together and assisted me to travel to the United States.

In the end, John Roberts was able to help me. After he and the rest of the American staff were evacuated out of Liberia to Washington, D.C., due to the worsening crisis, he became Acting Mission Director of USAID-Liberia. Shortly afterwards, John Roberts received news of my ordeal in Monrovia. Wlah laid it upon his heart, and he acted swiftly and facilitated my travel to the United States. Upon arrival in Washington, D.C., I worked closely with him at the Department of State. I also observed John Roberts up close, sometimes with teary eyes, as he agonized over the disintegration of Liberia. I still believe in the John Roberts with whom I worked.

In Liberia sheep and goats occupy different levels of the animal social order. Before the 1980 Revolution that brought President Samuel Doe and members of the People's Redemption Council (PRC) to power, chiefs and job seekers carried livestock to Monrovia for different reasons. Chiefs carried livestock as a form of gratuity to seek favors with "big shots".[380] They were often appointed, and gratuities such as livestock or cash helped maintain their jobs. At other times, gratuities ensured that chiefs' rulings in local matters whether fair or unfair were upheld when grievances were brought to Monrovia against them. As for job seekers, particularly government job seekers, livestock was one sure way to obtain a job. Goats were the principal livestock that changed hands.

Goats were and remain expendable in Liberia. Moreover, during big celebrations, goats are often slaughtered to provide meat. Sheep, on the other hand, are considered sacred animals. They are slaughtered only on special occasions as offerings to honor and thank Wlah for His blessings. On the livestock pecking order, sheep are higher than goats. The Liberian saying that, "sheep's luck is not the same as goat's luck" suggests that goats cannot get away with things sheep can do with impunity. In other words, sheep have certain privileges that goats do not enjoy.

Some readers might misinterpret the "sheep's luck is not the same as goat's luck" metaphor as a tacit acceptance of gradations in human worth. So, let me be clear. I do not believe in gradations in humanity. I recognize social structures exist that originated from racism and that such social structures do harm to humanity. Living with such social structures does not mean that I accept the racist ideologies that underpin them. With that said, I have come to realize that, in general, in the performance of their duties, African Americans as well as other people of color operate under either of two conditions that produce the same outcome. In the first and more familiar circumstance, African Americans and other people of color face more scrutiny or, as it is often said, are "under the microscope" in doing their duties.[381] Scrutiny suggests that they cannot get away with things white people can do with impunity.

In the second and less familiar circumstance, African Americans and other people of color instinctively perceive themselves as being "under the microscope" even if an atmosphere of scrutiny does not exist. That perception of being under a cloud of eyes when one does not exist is like "having a necessary conversation with oneself," like conversations about how to interact with the police, which African American parents have with their children. In either situation, as a result, there are heightened sensibilities about performing one's duties well, especially in a majority white working environment.

The "sheep's luck is not the same as goat's luck" metaphor suggests that white Americans are sheep while African Americans or people of color are goats. Without the benefit of what I now know, when I requested Gontee for help because my life was in immediate danger, I assumed that all things were equal. I thought because Gontee was the overall boss, he had more discretion and thus more power to make exceptions to policy. But at decision time, Gontee, the African American, turned me down while John Roberts, the white man, and the number two in command, decided in my favor and facilitated my travel to the United States.

Time and lessons learned have given me an opportunity to see John Roberts' and Gontee's roles in my leaving Liberia for the United States anew. I now see John Roberts' and Gontee's roles through a new lens, "Sheep's luck is not the same as goat's luck," which is a reference to the latitudes or discretions they had in making decisions. I now realize that because John Roberts was white, he had more discretion and thus more power. He could get away with making exceptions to policy that Gontee could not. Thus, even though Gontee may have wanted to help me, he simply could not take the professional risk to do so.

The sheep's luck-goats' luck metaphor reflects American history. Likewise, the real and perceived scrutiny that African Americans and other people of color face is an inherent feature of American culture. I interpreted my experience with Gontee and John Roberts' actions looking through the lenses of American history and culture. Looking through a different set of lenses, others might come away with a different interpretation of the same circumstances. Today, the important thing for me is that, despite the danger that I was in at the time of that decision, I recognize I did not have an open mind to consider other legitimate reasons for Gontee's action.

Indeed, at the time of Gontee's decision, I had lived and studied in the United States, but the time I spent from 1986 to 1987 studying in Greensboro was not enough. I did not mingle sufficiently with Americans at work for adequate exposure to certain aspects of American life and culture.

As a result, I did not understand why an African American, a black man whom I expected to have compassion for my dire plight gave me a cold shoulder and a bureaucratic response. Based on my limited understanding of American life and culture at the time, I concluded that Gontee did not care. I did not like him from that point and my view about him remained tinted for a long time. Indeed, to understand someone's actions, one must stand in their shoes.

THE GEORGE H. W. BUSH ADMINISTRATION

In 1990, my assumption, that the George H. W. Bush administration would do something to prevent a catastrophe when Liberia was teetering at the brink of national tragedy, was downright wrong. Shortly after I took refuge in the United States, the Bush administration decided against playing a role to avert the tragedy. Consequently, more than fourteen years of civil war ripped apart the country of my birth and memories. The pain lingers to this day.

CRITICS OF LIBERIA

At the early stages of the civil war, critics of Liberia, including some Liberians, believed Liberians have long deluded themselves with the notion that Liberia and the United States have a "special relationship." The Bush administration's non-involvement decision in 1990 was their moment of vindication. Liberia's moment of reckoning; the time to sever the umbilical cord had come. Indeed, the Bush administration's non-involvement decision had handed down the final verdict on the "special relationship" and they gloated.

America's suspicious involvement in the founding of Liberia is axiomatic. Nevertheless, critics' rendering of Liberia as having a dubious identity was incorrect. In the critics' call for Liberia not only to re-examine but also recognize itself as a nation situated in the heart of Africa, however, I heard them say that Liberia needs to tell its true story. Liberia has an African identity, checkered by the advent and story of slavery in America, not a dubious identity. It is an African nation whose DNA contains American nucleotides. So, to my indigenous Liberian brethren and to critics of Liberia, here is how I see the issues from my vantage point. Despite African Americans' overwhelmingly positive contributions to the development of the United States and Americo-Liberians' overwhelmingly negative contributions to the underdevelopment of Liberia, as America reckons with its true story, so must Liberia do. In the same way that there is no America without African Americans, there is no Liberia without Americo-Liberians.

Evacuation of American Citizens

After its decision to stay out of the Liberian conflict, the George H. W. Bush administration sent America's mighty military to Liberia to evacuate American citizens. Helicopters, flying over Monrovia's fear-ridden population to airlift American citizens, took off from warships positioned off the coast in Liberian waters. I watched from afar in total disbelief and got the message that some lives were more important than others.

The First Persian Gulf War

In the months following my arrival in the United States in June 1990, the physical safety I sought and secured felt like an illusion. My family was in Liberia, particularly my parents who were at the epicenter, where the war started and was raging unabated.[382] I had no peace of mind. Still feeling the sting of Liberia being declared a non-entity, the first Persian Gulf War started and made Liberia a forgotten story.

Heritage Foundation's Kim Holmes

Amid the anguish over the tragedy in Liberia, Heritage Foundation's Kim Holmes added insult to injury. Essentially, he rendered Liberia as useless and therefore unworthy of American help in its time of need. At that time, I was in the United States and not in Liberia to experience the physical deaths and destruction many Liberians were suffering. However, the pain, which Mr. Holmes' insensitive and uncaring commentary inflicted, made me wonder whether I had taken refuge.

In an ABC Nightline interview also featuring then former Liberian Finance Minister Ellen Johnson-Sirleaf, at a time when Liberians needed comfort, Mr. Holmes was patently mean-spirited, although it did not cost anything to pretend to utter kind words. In responding to Chris Wallace's questions, "What are the limits of U.S. Foreign policy? What should the U.S. do with a situation like Liberia? Should it step in to stop the carnage or should it stay out of it?" Mr. Holmes said, "I don't think it should have stepped in. In the Cold War era it was very clear that we had to sometimes hold our noses and support dictators who happened to be anti-communist. Now that the Cold War is over, I don't feel that there is such a compelling need to do that." He went on to assert that "The United States can't become the policeman of the world, going around enforcing human rights violations or trying to eliminate all of the dictators that happened to be very brutal murderers." [383]

On Mrs. Ellen Johnson-Sirleaf's turn, she seemed visibly agitated by the tenor of Mr. Holmes' answers as perhaps were Liberians who watched the interview. Apparently, she recognized the "American tree" for what it was, very tall with an overly extended canopy.[384] Mrs. Sirleaf made no attempt to sever the branch that she was sitting upon. Perhaps she needed it for support at that time, not to mention sometime in the future for her political career. Her response, therefore, was measured: "…let me say that I think the Liberian people respect the position of the [Bush] administration." Mrs. Sirleaf indicated she was aware that "The [Bush] administration was in communication with all the parties to the conflict." Moreover, she shared a consensus among Liberians that, "The only one possible country of force that could have made a difference through diplomatic intervention was the United States." "There is a general feeling among Liberians that the failure for them [Bush administration] to intervene diplomatically to try and bring about the resolution of the conflict was quite disappointing."[385]

On the Bush administration's failure to help stop the civil war, Mr. Holmes insinuated military intervention, although Liberians never called for American troops. He noted, "That is something that as a matter of principle we cannot have," as if he were a spokesman for the administration. Doubling down, he said, "It's quite alright to say that as humanitarian concern we are outraged at what's happened inside Liberia or any other country and we'll do whatever is within our powers to try to use our good offices to stop it." On a strident note, Holmes went on, "But we are not going to send in U.S. troops; we are not going to expend a large amount of U.S. resources to stop it [the civil war] in Liberia because I don't know where after that point it will stop."[386] The truth is that Liberians did not ask for American troops to be sent to Liberia. Based on the depth of US influence in Liberia, most Liberians shared the view Mrs. Sirleaf articulated, "The only one possible country of force that could have made a difference through diplomatic intervention was the United States."

Mr. Holmes omitted Africa, let alone Liberia, as he listed areas of the third world that were of strategic importance to the United States. He only mentioned Africa as a place that was once a "playing field" during the great competition with the Soviet Union. When Chris Wallace asked, "And what are our strategic interests in Africa, which I have noticed you haven't mentioned?" Holmes said, "I don't think at this point we have any vital strategic interest in Africa." Quizzed by Mr. Wallace on what should the consequence of that be for U.S. foreign policy, Mr. Holmes provided the "normal diet," the one that gave critics of Liberia their lethal potency: promoting through the United Nations or U.S. Foreign Aid Programs the "development of free market economic development" to "eliminate the poverty in Africa," "not out of a strategic interest" but "out of humanitarian concern." As he put it, such an initiative does not require "U.S. troops; it simply involves trying to give the Africans better advice on how to create economic development."[387]

Mr. Holmes was no professor making an academic presentation on a conflict at a college forum, where no one could easily regard his presentation as the views of his community or country. He was someone of stature with an expertise in American foreign policy. He knew the issues of the interview pertained to a nation that was undergoing a great tragedy. Moreover, the interview was on a network watched nationally and worldwide. Many people outside the United States, not to mention Liberia, perhaps took his mean-spirited commentary as representative of American sentiments. I would not be surprised if they, and even Americans, watching the interview interpreted his commentary as creating a negative impression of America.

THE BULK CHALLENGE

In May 1996, I watched images of Liberian refugees on CNN with utter horror and disbelief. They were on an overcrowded passenger freighter, The Bulk Challenge, believed to be carrying nearly 4000 passengers. The refugees were desperate, leaving the fighting in Monrovia. The ship was reported to have sailed from Monrovia to the Ivory Coast, where it was refused to dock because of concerns that some of the refugees were rebels involved in the fighting in Liberia. The Bulk Challenge then continued its journey to Takoradi, Ghana, where it met similar fate. The ship eventually sailed to Nigeria. The CNN images of the refugees aboard the Bulk Challenge captured the desperations of Liberians, even for those who were not aboard the ship. I was speechless because I could not comprehend the scale of suffering that Liberians were going through. The only sense I could make of the situation was that we (Liberians) must have done something terrible for such a divine punishment to be unleashed upon us.

HERMAN COHEN: A TURN AROUND

In May 1996, seven years after the consequential Bush administration's non-involvement decision, Herman Cohen, former Assistant Secretary of State for African Affairs in the administration, appeared on the NewsHour with Jim Lehrer. Cohen regretted that, "a window of opportunity existed that the U.S. could have used" to stop the Liberian Civil War. The U.S., according to Cohen, "decided to concentrate on the evacuation of its citizens and to let the African leaders and the Liberians sort out things for themselves." Strikingly, Cohen went on to support "a more assertive role of the U.S. and a presence of a stronger military force in Liberia," which he suggested the UN must provide.[388]

Cohen did not stop there. In June 2008, during a Truth & Reconciliation hearing at Hamline University in Minnesota, 18 years after the 1990 non-involvement decision, Cohen made a 180-degree turn. He publicly regretted the United States government's decision not to show up when Liberians called. Cohen reportedly provided more details on the U.S. government's behind-the-scenes contacts with President Doe and Charles Taylor to stop the Liberian Civil War. He said that someone in Monrovia "messed up" the plan to evacuate President Doe and his supporters by blocking the evacuation corridor. According to Cohen, a plan B involving the use of an aircraft for the evacuation was scrapped upon "a directive from Washington to cease all engagements to end the Liberian conflict" with "no further explanations" from his "superiors in Washington on the change in policy."[389]

I take no comfort in the vindication of my belief that the United States had the power and influence and only needed an ounce of energy in 1990 to save Liberia from unimaginable tragedy. On the other hand, Cohen's regrets meant absolutely nothing to me because it could not bring back those who were killed "for nothing" in Liberia due to lack of leadership at every level. I could have swallowed the bitter pill of 1990 perhaps with little difficulty had Liberia been a non-entity. However, Liberia was no desolate land, no place of nothingness or hopelessness. Despite its checkered history, Liberia's citizens went to bed after a hard day's work and looked forward to a better tomorrow. Its children harbored dreams for greatness as do children everywhere. Liberia was something; a nation of people whose spirit, with more than a century of oppression, had never been broken. Under tragic circumstances, beginning December 1989, its proud people wallowed and suffocated in misery as if they were under a skin.

AMERICANS CARE

Due to the depth of the anguish Cohen regretted, the good America had done in Liberia almost faded in my memory. I almost stopped hearing the caring voices in America and perceiving the full extent of sacrifices citizens of other West African countries were making in Liberia. Indeed, I almost concluded that no one in America, in the West Africa sub-region or elsewhere cared about Liberia. Luckily, I did not slip into oblivion. I opened my eyes and ears and found out that the United States still had a substantial reserve from the "credit" it accrued in the "Liberian bank," the Liberian psyche.[390] I was a beneficiary of the "Care Food" program while in grade school in Sanniquellie, Liberia. I had several teachers who were members of the Peace Corps. Moreover, as the civil war raged, U.S. humanitarian aid flowed into Liberia uninterrupted. Countless Americans working for aid organizations put their lives on the line to save Liberian lives. The U.S. not only took in thousands of Liberians fleeing from the war, including me, but also resettled hundreds, if not thousands, of others who languished for a long time in refugee camps in the West Africa sub-region.

In large as well as small cities across America, newspapers carried articles and editorials on the Liberian tragedy. The Plain Dealer of Cleveland, Ohio, for example, could not have made a better case for Liberia. "Blood and bodies line the Liberian landscape these days in testament to the civil war that is brutalizing the West African nation. Tribal fighting rages at its ugliest and most deadly; it has turned into more than a Liberian or African crisis." "The Liberian strife became an international concern this week, when government troops loyal to President Samuel Doe stormed a Lutheran churchyard and slaughtered as many as 600 refugees who were trying to escape the violence," the editorial continued. "Accounts described slain mothers who fell with their babies still strapped to their backs. Some victims were found hanging from window frames; the heads of others were smashed open or shattered by bullets."[391] I had considered taking refuge at that Lutheran Church Compound. The editorial not only reminded me of what my fate would have been had I done so, but also of the work of Wlah's hands.

The Plain Dealer editorial argued, "Such atrocities should touch the minds and loose the outrage of any moral people, be they in the neighboring Ivory Coast or in Cleveland, 4,946 miles away. Such atrocities should sway the United States to use all its considerable influence to persuade Doe to leave." It said, "The United States has been supporting governments in Liberia since the American Colonization Society in the early 1800s shuttled off to Africa the freed slaves who, in turn, founded the nation in 1847." It suggested "President Bush and Secretary of State James A. Baker III should make it clear to Doe that the United States is prepared to recognize and work with a new government, an assertion that would probably convince Doe his reign is over."[392]

Prophetically, the Plain Dealer editorial said, "Before Doe would agree to leave, he would need assurance that members of his Krahn tribe will not fall victims to ethnic revenge from the Gio and Mano tribes, who have been gored by Doe's forces."[393] It recommended that a "peace-keeping force would be essential, for even if Doe leaves, there is likely to be fighting between two rebel factions led by Prince Johnson and Charles Taylor to see who would head the country. The Plain Dealer ended its editorial with words that could not have been chosen any better. "Without international attention, the fighting—among tribes and among factions—will only worsen. If ever Liberians needed help from the United States, it is now."[394] These nuances, views and recommendations about what the United States government could do to stop the suffering in Liberia convinced me that they could not have come out of the hearts and minds of inattentive and uncaring people. America, indeed, cared.

1990 Decision Not a Verdict on the "Special Relationship"

In later years, cease-fire violations and failed peace agreements became the norm as the bloodbath continued. However, during a summer 2003 visit to Africa, President George W. Bush acknowledged the suffering in Liberia when he "faced difficult questions about why the United States was not intervening to end the bloodshed. Bush sent a contingent of about 200 marines to join another 100 U.S. troops already there, enough to convince Taylor to flee." [395] Meanwhile, the late New Jersey Congressman Donald Payne, along with other members of the Congressional Black Caucus, advocated for U.S. help to stop the Liberian war. Moreover, in nudging the Bush administration to assume an assertive role in Liberia, Sir Jeremy Greenstock, the British ambassador to the United Nations, said, "If there were a lead nation that was prepared to take action in Liberia, then I think that would be very broadly welcomed internationally."

During his Africa policy speech at the White House on Wednesday, June 25, 2003, President George W. Bush said, "President Taylor needs to step down so that his country can be spared further bloodshed."[396] Liberia-related events that occurred after President Bush's remarks underscored the power of the American presidency and the depth of U.S. influence in Liberia. Secretary of State Colin Powell worked with U.N. Secretary General Kofi Annan and a contingent of 15,000 U.N. troops was deployed in Liberia. The massive U.N. deployment provided an opportunity for Liberia to start anew.

President George W. Bush took another major action that directly impacted Liberia. As guns claimed attention during the civil war, diseases quietly mowed the population and took their toll. In 2003, he launched the U.S. President's Emergency Plan for AIDS Relief (PEPFAR) to fight global HIV/AIDS. The $15-billion commitment was the largest any country had made to fight one disease. Liberia benefited from PEPFAR immensely. Incidentally, Bush had declared himself as a "compassionate conservative" during the 2000 U.S. presidential campaign. In laying out a governing philosophy as president two years later in April 2002, he said, "I call my philosophy and approach compassionate conservatism. It is compassionate to actively help our fellow citizens in need. It is conservative to insist on responsibility and results. And with this hopeful approach, we will make a real difference in people's lives." President George W. Bush's Liberia-related decisions delivered on "Helping Poor Countries Around the World" and making "a real difference in people's lives."[397]

Upon Liberia reaching another crossroad recently, it was an American president who acted. In 2014, at the peak of the deadly Ebola virus outbreak in Liberia, President Barack Obama ordered 4,000 U.S. troops to Liberia to help stop the spread of the deadly virus. Advocacies by Americans and others in the international community on behalf of Liberia have made a difference. More importantly, Presidents Bush and Obama's critical Liberia-related decisions are a testament that the American people care, and that Liberia and the United States share a "special relationship."

Africans Care

In August 1990, a group of West African countries under the banner of the Economic Community of West African States (ECOWAS) stepped up and sent a peacekeeping force to Liberia to help stop the bloodbath. The Economic Community Cease-Fire Monitoring Group (ECOMOG) was the name of the peacekeeping force. Until that time, that kind of courageous and risky undertaking in Africa was unheard of.

Historically in Liberia, the military was regarded as ill-reputed. Armed soldiers were an instrument of abuse and oppression, plain and simple. I witnessed soldiers in action in rural Liberia. They forced my Dad to carry their cargo on his head from the village to Kpaye Lehpula. In addition, they licentiously rounded up our chickens and carried them away without paying. As a teenager, I was one of the kids who used to refer to soldiers as "Nocos," although I did not use the expression in their presence.[398] Due to soldiers' actions in rural Liberia, I did not fully appreciate the contributions of ECOMOG soldiers who deployed to Liberia to help stop the civil war. However, with the passage of time, I came to see ECOMOG soldiers as people who left their wives, children, parents as well as siblings and relatives behind in their home countries to serve in Liberia. Many of them died while others were injured during the fighting in Liberia. I will never forget the full extent of their sacrifices and those of their families and countries.

A New Perspective

On the road to healing from the wounds of the civil war, the on-the-surface truth of "what you don't know doesn't hurt" may hold for some Liberians but not all.[399] Unfortunately, some Liberians survived the war but did not heal from its wounds. Instead, the unbearable weight of hopelessness took their lives. Then there are those for whom lengths of time to heal may vary. Perhaps because there is no "what was" reference to compare "what is" to, the pace of healing may be faster for Liberians born during or after the war. On the other hand, Liberians born well before the war, in whose memories pre-December 1989 Liberia is buried deeply, may need a longer time to heal. I do not mean to suggest that pre-December 1989 Liberia was perfect and flowed with milk and honey. Indeed, problems abounded, and national institutions woefully performed in harnessing the country's vast human and material resource potentials. Despite those failures and stark inequalities, pre-December 1989 Liberia was a time of relative peace and stability. I had dreams, looked forward to achieving them and contributing to a better Liberia.

Mom and Dad were not rich people, but they labored on the farm, dutifully paid my tuition at St. Mary's, and gave me their unconditional love and support. Moreover, the Liberia of my early years was structured somewhat differently, albeit imperfectly. Other people contributed to my education not by paying money or providing any direct guidance but merely by being there. In the Guah household in Sanniquellie, Zehyee Mahnmein fed others and me; she watched over me with care and compassion. As a seventh grader in 1972, I looked up to D. K. Wonsehleay, my Boys Scout Master. William Walker, my fourth and sixth grades teacher, was a "gold standard," a worthy role model. Even a one-morning appearance by University of Liberia students who showed up at St. Mary's on a university bus in 1976 made a difference. They gave me an added reason to become one of them. In 1978, as a freshman at the University of Liberia, Conmany Wesseh, a mesmerizing orator, inspired me when he spoke at the memorial of Edward Gberi at the University of Liberia multipurpose court.[400] Again, while at the University of Liberia, Oretha Nyah, a total stranger, took me in as her own; she fed me and gave me a place to sleep.

Today, due to the disruptions and dislocations of the war, many young Liberians recognize deficits in support for their education, but they may be suffering from a bigger and more crippling deficit that they may not know because they never saw parents like my mom and dad.[401] Although for young people trying to find their paths, I see myself in similar light as I saw others who were a beacon for me, I regard my absence as a loss of opportunity. So, when I see the plight of today's young Liberians and then look back, I ache over the prospect of increasingly diminishing opportunities for a better life. Perhaps these realizations may slow the healing process of my wounds from the civil war.

I managed my pain because I had a chance to see things from a different vantage point. I never sat in the offices of American decision makers or in the privacy of their homes, but I stepped into their shoes by keeping an open mind and remaining attentive to the issues. Although I am still not convinced that the 1990 American decision to stay out of Liberia was justified, I now have a better sense of that decision. Becoming a little wiser and developing the strength and capacity to forgive has given me a new perspective and helped accelerate the healing process.

Reflection was not the only path to gaining a new perspective. I also arrived at my new outlook through the struggles and obstacles I had to overcome at various levels as an outsider in America. Mundane and simple signals others sent, sometimes consciously or unconsciously, constituted some of my struggles and obstacles. Such signals showed themselves in various ways as tilting of heads, fixating ears at an angle, or making various facial expressions whenever I spoke. From my vantage point, those signals suggested either that I was inaudible or that my English was not clear or good enough. Through these signals, I perceived senders as saying I was not an American or one of them. Moreover, due to listeners' fixation on my accent, my message was often lost.

I understand that people are inherently curious and want to learn more about others, especially when they have an opportunity to meet someone who was born in another country. By the same token, sometimes there does not seem to be an awareness that innocent comments like, "You have an accent, where are you from?" stir up deep and painful memories. I did not see any of the grisly and unimaginable atrocities committed in Liberia prior to my escape. However, I endured deaths in my own family due either directly or indirectly to the war. I harbored great pain during my struggles to adjust to life in the United States while Liberia was falling apart. That pain remained frozen intact into my memory like a woolly mammoth in Siberia.

Certainly, the disruptions of the war did not spare me. Despite being an adult, I have never stopped searching for places to belong to or something meaningful to become a part of. So, if such comments and questions still strike at a sore spot in my heart even after over a quarter century in the United States, I can only imagine what newcomers to America, often from worse circumstances, feel. A seemingly benign comment like, "You have an accent, where are you from?" may actually mean "You are not one of us, where are you from?" It stirs up deep emotions because I perceive it more as a subtle rejection. I cannot prove that having an accent has prevented me from getting a promotion or a job for which I applied. However, I know that having an accent has definitively been an obstacle. Unless one is a celebrity, like Arnold Schwarzenegger, having an accent in America is not a plus.

Those who say, "I detect an accent, where are you from?" often expect me to speak for or confirm some information about Africa. I often felt pressured to speak for or to defend Africa, an entire continent, even though I come from a small village in Liberia and do not pretend to know everything about Liberia. In response to inquiries that are often suggestive of Africa being a place of less value than technologically advanced places, I usually resort to an undeniably true and default response. Where I come from, we bury our dead and cry and celebrate the birth of a child. Moreover, we love and are loved, and we dream and aspire. That high-minded response is often a vain attempt to hide my displeasures over inquiries I perceive as patently irksome. My facial expressions often tell the real story.

THE "ELEPHANT" IN THE AMERICAN ROOM

I grew up under the care of my own parents and the Guahs and matured under the mentorship of Dr. Forh, Col. Cannon and many other influential adults I have chronicled in this book. My immersion into many important life issues including the value of work, education, family, and responsibility was not always through conversations. Sometimes adults in my life "talked" through examples. Race, the proverbial elephant in the room in America, never came up during my time with my own parents. Other than the oppression they endured under the settlers' descendants and their domination, my parents did not have formal schooling, did not travel to faraway places beyond the village, where they had to use their education or skills to seek

447

employment to make a living. They never experienced being an outsider in any significant way; they never confronted life issues such as race.

My times with Dr. Forh and Col. Cannon were different. Dr. Forh studied in the United States and lived there for a long time. He was an outsider, someone who came to the United States from a different culture, and experienced some of the same obstacles I had to overcome. Despite my significant time with him, he never touched the "elephant in the room" in America even though he knew what lay ahead. He did not talk about the obstacles associated with being someone from a different culture, the price one must pay for being an outsider. I do not think Dr. Forh slept at the wheel. Instead, I believe that was his way of grooming and teaching me to be a man.

The "elephant in the room" in America thrust itself upon us while I was under the mentorship of Dr. Forh and Col. Cannon. The first incident involved Dr. Forh and surfaced in 1987, after he returned to Monrovia from the Liberian Foreign Service. About two years after Dr. Forh returned home, the unthinkable happened. Charles Taylor unleashed hellfire on Liberia. The full scope of the danger the country was plunged into was clear. Everyone who had the means and could get out of Monrovia before the carnage descended upon the city, left. However, Dr. Forh refused to leave and remained in Monrovia. He told me, "I am not going to leave my country." As devout a Christian as Dr. Forh was and as incessantly as he prayed, he also had common sense. He understood the gravity of the danger that loomed, yet he stayed in Monrovia.

I never understood why Dr. Forh made the calculation to remain in Monrovia in the face of an existential threat. It was only after my long stay in the United States that I was able to put two and two together. He was educated in the United States. He loved America and held it in high esteem. Despite all that admiration for the United States, obstacles to doing what mattered most to him, giving back to America, troubled him.[402] As a result, in the face of threats to his own existence, he did not want to go back to America. He did not want to go back to start all over again. He did not want to face the same obstacles again. Indeed, he did not want to rewrite the same story.

Col. Cannon, on the other hand, is an African American. He rose through the ranks of the United States Army, reaching the level of Lieutenant Colonel before retiring. Like Dr. Forh, Col. Cannon did not say much to me about his experience in society in general or in the Army. As there are certain things heard loudly and more clearly when left unsaid, I knew perceptively that Col. Cannon's career success was no small feat. I knew he had to go through the figurative fire to rise to the level of Lieutenant Colonel. Unlike Dr. Forh, Col. Cannon did not dodge the race issue when it confronted him, at least in relation to matters concerning me. The issue presented itself as a red flag to consider as the children and I were preparing to move to Spokane, Washington. Instead of attempting to persuade me to change my mind in the face of that warning, Col. Cannon wrote, "Perseverance certainly has its place in our lives. I'm very proud of you for continuing the struggle." "You'll be just fine. God is good."[403]

The issue of race in America is ever-present. In hindsight, I am grateful that Dr. Forh and Col. Cannon did not influence me in a way that could have prevented me from stepping into the unknown to create my own path. They let me pick up my own cues, navigate the issue on my own and finally arrived at where I am: knowing people for who they are—human beings, like me, with fears, frailties, and a capacity for good and evil. Instead, they spent their times setting examples of how real men live their lives. They attended to their spouses and family and showed a great deal of responsibility and compassion.

My own children will have a future different from mine, a more hopeful one. That hopeful future begins with me. As a result, just as Dr. Forh and Col. Cannon did for me, I avoid going into depth about my own experiences unless the need or a teaching moment arises. I talk to my children about my own experiences only when they see, hear or experience something similar and want to understand why. I want them to create their own paths, knowing that they are just as good and worthy as anyone. The only exception I have made pertains to the reality of the relationship between law enforcement and people of color, particularly young people of color. I have had explicit and necessary conversations with my son and daughter on how to conduct themselves with law enforcement. I did so in recognition that living a model life and having no fear of the police are no antidote to being wrongly or mistakenly perceived and harmed for whatever reason. With that exception, Dr. Forh and Col. Cannon's model is my preference for dealing with the issue of race.

CHAPTER 34

Life in Spokane

I DID NOT KNOW SPOKANE, WASHINGTON existed until Dr. James Beebe called me in Laurinburg, North Carolina. I did not do any research about Spokane. I just assumed it was a small rural city comparable to Laurinburg, with a population of about twenty thousand people. Instead of gathering information about Spokane to determine the suitability of the community for the move, I said to myself: "If Spokane is good for James, it is good for the children and me as well, because I trust his judgment."

Upon arrival in Spokane, the sheer size of the city surprised me. Spokane was Washington State's little pleasant secret. Its size and the life it offered existed without much ado. However, in the span of two years after we arrived in Spokane, that quietude about the city changed. With no disrespect to Bing Crosby's fame and ties to the city, the epic rise of the Gonzaga University men's basketball team, the Bulldogs, to the NCAA basketball tournament's Cinderella status in 1999 transformed Spokane from Washington State's pleasant and quiet little secret to visibility on the national map. The Bulldogs reached the tournament's Elite Eight that year. Today, the Spokane metropolitan area has a population of over 500,000 people. It is the host city for Bloomsday and Hoopfest. Aside from NCAA basketball tournaments and other sports events, the city is home to world-class healthcare facilities and universities.[404]

I arrived in Spokane with a loaded knapsack of issues, a few of which I could not shake off easily. For example, in a tape-recorded message Dad sent me in 1994, three years before the move, he repeated his perennial advice, "Pay attention to the work you went to do" and then asked for "strong pills" for joint, back and body pains. I took the message as "Son, I need you." Dad's message was essentially a clock, ticking to a time that, no one far away from home as I was, especially in limbo, wanted to imagine. By June 1997, I had been away from my parents for seven years. As far as I was concerned, sending "strong pills" did not suffice. I wanted to see my parents badly, but my ability to travel depended on having an immigration status. I had been waiting nearly seven years for an interview. The only power I had over the INS to schedule that interview was patience.

In Spokane, I had anxieties. I worried about not finding a job right away. I was afraid of falling through the cracks. My children had been living in relative comfort in North Carolina. I uprooted and brought them to Spokane. Moreover, I withdrew the retirement savings I accrued in North Carolina. Indeed, I second-guessed myself, wondering whether I had made the right decision to move to Spokane.

The other issue I was dealing with in North Carolina was the terrifyingly disorienting loss of country. The civil war in Liberia was still raging and the pain could not be wished away. I had a great opportunity for personal and professional growth, but that opportunity did not stop me from being a human being; it did not neutralize my pain. The only way I could get rid of that pain was to stop living, but I had more reasons to live and would not let pain crush my spirit or body.

Lo and behold, Wlah led me to the place where I belonged. Spokane as well as Gonzaga University turned out to be the right place to be at that time in my life. Friendships I forged were sustaining. Aside from the riveting and stimulating intellectual pursuits in which we were immersed, members of my cohort were like comrades in a battle. Gonzaga University was home not only because I lived on campus but also because besides teaching me, my professors believed in me and encouraged me. They were many and I remain grateful to all of them, but the notables were Dr. James Beebe, Dr. Nancy Isaacson, and Dr. Shann Ferch. Others included Dr. Dennis Arthur Conners, Dr. David Whitfield, Sister Jeanette Abi-Nader, and Sister Joan Dixon. The late Father Patrick J. Ford, former Gonzaga University Vice President for Academic Affairs, was in a class by himself. He was one of the most brilliant minds I had ever met. Father Robert J. Spitzer and Dr. Thayne McCulloh supported me too.[405]

I bubbled with energy at Gonzaga University. Despite all the struggles, I had never been more hopeful about the future.[406] However, some professors who sincerely believed in me cautioned, "Marsilius, you need to tone down your optimism because you are in a different place."[407] I talked to some professors about my plans, yet they occasionally asked about my plans, hoping that I would grasp their message about what lay ahead. They wanted to tell me that I had entered a new culture, where it took more than energy and education to climb the ladder of social mobility. The closest one white male professor, an ardent supporter of mine, came to tell me what he was thinking was, "Marsilius, what you want to do is simply not going to happen around here because people are not ready for it." Another professor, a white female, and a strong supporter of mine as well, indicated to me that she did not see me as someone who would lose his soul for social mobility and, as such, she could not see a path forward for me.

Counting on the Wlah who snatched me out of the Liberian hellfire and planted my feet in the United States, I was thankful for my professors' concerns. However, I was determined to press on, believing that He was involved in charting the course of my life. Not long after, I hit the proverbial brick wall about which my professors warned me. It was a time of uncertainty, especially as others close to me wondered subliminally about the value of my education. Disillusionment swirled around me, but it did not sweep me away. I learned from that experience that my path will be like no one else's path and that I will create it.

A Liberian Community in Spokane

In November 1990, familiarity and nostalgia led me from Washington, D.C., to Greensboro, North Carolina to begin anew. In the mid-1980s, I attended North Carolina A & T State University in Greensboro. Flomo, my late friend, as well as those who encouraged me, including professors and others, made Greensboro a home away from the village.[408] My bike rides from Parker Street, off Wendover Avenue, to and from A & T remained seared in my memory like my kitchen helper job at Jefferson Country Club. Every time I thought about working as a laborer during the construction of the Ronald McNair Memorial Building at A & T, I saw the face of John

Berne, the construction manager who hired me.[409] Greensboro turned into a place of fond memories because of my experience and the people who helped me. In November 1990, moving from Washington, D.C., to Greensboro was a no brainer. The move to Spokane, however, was different because I had no attachment whatsoever to the place. It was a case of taking a step into the unknown, believing that a path would appear, although I depended on Wlah and Mom's prayers.

I moved to Spokane primarily to pursue further education, but I had other dreams that I wanted to accomplish. In my own life, having empathy, inner strength, and a will to overcome was like having a beautifully wrapped package handed to a child, containing its most important wish for Christmas. That was my parents', particularly Mom's, gift to me during my idyllic childhood. I struggled and endured hunger along this journey, but the joy of that gift remains with me. The desire for my own children was an attempt to share that gift, but as I became older, it became clear to me that the gift Mom gave me was too critical for success in life and too good to share it only with my own children. For this reason, my wish for every unborn child is to have parents like mine, particularly my mom.

Based on my childhood experience, I believe that there are two kinds of wealth: psychological wealth and financial wealth. Psychological wealth is that which one acquires through the upbringing that well-regulated, loving, and supportive parents provide their children. It turns a child into a well-regulated empathetic human being. Financial wealth means just that—money. I can be psychologically wealthy and be financially dirt-poor, yet happy and hopeful. I cannot necessarily say the same thing about being financially wealthy.

I believe every child deserves well-regulated, loving, and supportive parents, a responsible community, and a chance to develop its God-given potentials. However, not every child lives in a responsible community or society, not to mention having well-regulated, loving, and supportive parents as well as having a chance to develop its God-given potentials. I used to dream for an opportunity to help build a better Liberia, a place where individuals not only know their obligations, but also assume them without mental reservations. However, after the civil war hastened a breakdown of norms and the fabric of the society, that dream changed from wanting to help build a better Liberia to longing to remake Liberia. So, the ancillary dream I wanted to accomplish upon moving to Spokane was to recreate, to the best of my ability, idyllic conditions similar to those of my childhood for young people.

The dream to recreate my childhood for young people came to the fore during casual conversations with acquaintances about why young Liberians were ending up in the criminal justice system in large American cities on the east coast. Other than conjectures, I did not do any surveys to get to the bottom of the problem. Everyone had their own ideas about the causes of the problem, including absent parents, which manifested as truancy, repeated disciplinary issues at school, and brushes with the law. Others proffered lack of education, meaning formal education as a contributing factor to the problem. However, because I was born in Liberia and grew up there, I had a suspicion that other factors, especially cultural conditioning may have something to do with the problem.

In general, given certain situations, Liberians think and act in ways that are different from how Americans think and act. In a queue for service in Liberia, for example, a "big shot" can cut the line with impunity and receive service. In the United States, it does not matter whether one is the President of the United States, cutting the line does not fly; it is completely unacceptable. The frowns and loud protests are often swift. In Liberia, moreover, young people or adults can engage in fist fights and walk away without having to worry about an assault charge, misdemeanor or felony being placed on their records.

If a newly arrived Liberian teenager in the United States were bullied at school or at a playground, his instinct might be to do what he knows. He would fight back because he may not know that a fight in the United States is not the same as a fight in Liberia. A fight in the United States could go on one's record. A violent record is a blight, which can be a hurdle for future opportunities. Looking through the cultural lens, I realized that the wrong trajectory some young Liberians were on in the United States could be averted with one more tool added to formal education and well-regulated, loving, and supportive parents. I thought cultural literacy was necessary to increase immigrant young people's chances of becoming successful in the United States.

I committed I would do for newly arrived Liberians what my parents did to help me succeed if I lived in a Liberian community in the United States. It was like "Pianyeewon" when my extant dream of recreating my idyllic childhood for young people found cultural literacy as a vehicle for its fulfillment.[410] On my way to Spokane, I imagined the ideas I had would come to fruition there, hence the origin of building a community, like the one in the village during my childhood.[411] However, when my kids and I arrived in Spokane in the summer of 1997, the place was ethnically as white as the snow of its frosty winter. There were no Liberians.

In the same way I stepped into the unknown in Spokane, believing that a path for my education would appear, I came to Spokane with the mind to help Liberians, believing that they will move to Spokane. Eventually, Liberian refugees slowly began to arrive in Spokane. According to the culture, my family received some of the newcomers at the airport and hosted them at our home. We helped other newly arrived families with adjustment issues, such as driving them to their appointments, providing guidance on their children's schools and other matters.

Liberian refugees trickled into Spokane mostly through a World Relief Resettlement Program. The time for a conversation about establishing a community organization for providing cultural literacy arrived once the newcomers reached a critical mass in 2005.[412] Mindful of, "I am here to help you," a criticism Liberians often level against some western experts that go to Liberia to work on development projects, I let newcomers start the conversations and joined only when someone approached me.[413] I had definite ideas about how to proceed with such a community organization, but I was reticent to present myself as someone whose experience in America could be useful. However, my reticence was unnecessary because the newcomers' expectations of a community organization were in many ways the same as mine. For example, some parents wanted their children to learn Liberian history and culture while others wanted their children to behave in school. They thought a community organization could help their children "learn to respect their parents, teachers, themselves and others." Their ideas were music to my ears. Similarly, their idea that a community organization would be an ideal forum for conflict resolution was music to my ears, too, because falling through the cracks in America could result from making the wrong decisions in times of conflict, running afoul with the law and ending up in the criminal justice system.

Unity, education, and support surfaced repeatedly as community goals during the conversations about wanting to establish a community organization. Parents talked about help with their children's education while others suggested establishing a learning center that could also serve as a daycare.

Still further, others talked about a need for recognition of achievements and scholarships to motivate their children about their education. Support as a community goal was expressed with phrases such as, "Support each other," "Provide financial assistance in times of emergency," "Support through encouragement," "Being there for one another," and "Help each other."

Teenagers among the newcomers quickly realized that life in America was different.[414] Unlike life in Liberia or in the refugee camps, where some of them mingled freely with their friends, in America, they had to be in school during school hours. Moreover, any outing far from home had to be with supervision. For these reasons, teenagers showed considerable eagerness for starting a community organization because they wanted opportunities to get together to do activities and make new friends. Some teenagers also wanted adults other than their own parents to look up to for good advice or to "show us the way." Other teenagers were interested in a community organization out of concerns for other children and families in Liberia or in the refugee camps who were not as fortunate as they were in resettling in the United States. They wanted the community organization to start an outreach program for other young people that they left behind in refugee camps.

The effort was based on the belief that young people's success anywhere depended on (1) meeting their basic needs, (2) education and (3) cultural literacy, which involves learning to navigate the system and avoiding running afoul of the law. That meant newly arrived parents needed to strengthen their capacities by getting an education and becoming well-regulated culturally literate parents, attentive to the needs of their children.

On December 3, 2005, Liberian refugees in Spokane met at the home of Mr. George Elliott, one of the newcomers to set up a committee to plan for the election of officers for a community organization. After a brief discussion, those present reached a consensus that there was no point in setting up an organizing committee. Everyone agreed to hold the elections right away. I was elected president unopposed while Mr. Henry Browne was elected vice president, also unopposed. Others elected were Lila W. Flumo, General Secretary; Mr. George Elliott, Treasurer; Ms. Claudia Sawyer, Chaplain (elected in absentia); and three advisors, Mrs. Al-Satta Browne, Ms. Meme Besseh and Mr. Joseph Howe (deceased).

I assumed the leadership of the community with a clear purpose and a desire to lead by example. In December 2008 after I had been reelected unopposed, I reported to the community the critical work we had done, pursuant to our focus on young people. The report covered formal education as well as informal education including topics such as living in the United States—the "dos" and "don'ts;" child discipline; spousal relationship; domestic violence; consequences of drunk-driving and driving without a license; driving a vehicle without insurance; building up a credit history; and buying a home as an investment.[415]

The education on child discipline was an on-going conversation that took place wherever members of the community met. It was one of the areas where we encouraged parents to make conscious adjustments to their practices to avoid being entangled with the child welfare system in the United States. The reason was that what may be discipline in Liberia may be considered child abuse in the United States. On spousal relationship with respect to domestic violence, our informal education emphasized that it did not matter whether it was the man or the woman. Laying hands on someone or being violent in anyway was unacceptable.

On formal education, Itron Corporation donated computers to community members, especially the newcomers, while a World Relief Volunteer arranged computer classes for them at the Spokane Community College.[416] At the time of the report, two newcomers of the community, Ericson Weah and Bill Dorley, had graduated from Central Valley High School and Ferris High School, respectively. My daughter, Marsetta M. Flumo, also graduated from University High School. Each graduate received a purse of a modest amount of money as a graduation gift, a policy of the organization.

We celebrated Liberia's Independence Day, Flag Day, and Christmas. Christmas celebrations included gift exchanges, which focused particularly on children. Other celebrations included showers for expectant mothers. The community celebrated its American friends and supporters, including Mary Lou McDonough, Dr. Glen Cosby, Mrs. Greta Cosby, and Mrs. Glenda Lovchik. The community also participated in the life of the city of Spokane.[417]

THE LIFE AND DEATH OF JOSEPH HOWE

War often begins with a high-minded idea, for example, to exact justice, reclaim lost heritage, or to seek freedom, that festers until an opportunity for action arises. As high-mindedness seldom sees the full scope of humanity, not only does it often corrupt such ideas as freedom and justice with its intoxicating promises, but also weaponizes them. Put another way, righteousness distorts the ability to foresee ramifications of starting a war.

In Liberia, it happened. Seekers of "Justice" fulfilled their wishes. Their AK-47s, Berettas and other machine guns crackled, mowed innocent lives, and littered the landscape with corpses. They set off ordnances and dropped bombs, dislodging shrapnel and plumes of dust and particles. Casualties included women, children, and the elderly. Some of the casualties, the figurative particles in the plumes, dispersed a mile away while others were blown across oceans to new lands. Joseph Howe, an elderly man who landed in Spokane, was one of the particles in the plumes the civil war generated. Unfortunately, his plight in Spokane was an example of the collateral damage that high-minded "Justice" and loose talk did not foresee.

Joseph Howe fled with his family to neighboring Ivory Coast due to the violence of the civil war. He told me stories of fear, suffering and humiliation while in refuge in the Ivory Coast. On one occasion, he paused, and his eyes became teary when he recalled his experience with hunger in the Ivory Coast. Mr. Howe spoke of habitual humiliations of Liberian refugees and performing manual labor for food. He said that humiliations did not bother him as much as delays or nonpayment for his labor or payments that were not commensurate with his labor.

Joseph Howe's American story began with hope. After a long time of suffering in refuge in the Ivory Coast, he looked forward to resettling in the United States; an opportunity of becoming one of the chosen ones, entering the gates of Heaven. A native of Maryland County, southeastern Liberia, Mr. Howe was Grebo, one of Liberia's sixteen tribes. He arrived in Spokane on June 15, 2004, without any family member through a World Relief resettlement program.[418]

The Masons are a couple in Spokane. They received Mr. Howe upon arrival and hosted him for a long time. Mr. Howe eventually moved out on his own into the Park Tower Apartments at 217 W. Spokane Falls Boulevard, Spokane. However, the Masons became his adopted family and remained so until his end. The Masons became Mr. Howe's host family through Mrs. Lisa Mason's connection with World Relief.[419] She was a volunteer with the organization before Mr. Howe's arrival. World Relief sought volunteer help for hosting refugees because refugee processing, which included finding temporary accommodation, employment, and attending English classes took considerable time.[420]

Eventually, word about an elderly Liberian's arrival in Spokane got out. We inquired about his host family, contacted the Masons, and invited Mr. Howe to our home for dinner. On the day of the dinner, Mr. Howe indicated that he was not feeling well. My family and I took the food we prepared for Mr. Howe to the home of the Masons, instead.

Mr. Howe lived alone at his Park Tower Apartment, but the Masons visited with him occasionally and took him to his doctor's appointments. Members of the Liberian community reached out to Mr. Howe too. Mr. George Elliott, a native of Maryland County and a Grebo like Mr. Howe, visited with him occasionally and took him to places such as the bank and food shopping. Mr. Beweh Sartoe gave him rides to other places to do business. Mr. Alvin Barry helped transfer funds to his family in the Ivory Coast. "Mr. Flumo, that Gbarry boy, tell him thank you-ooh," he praised Mr. Alvin Barry profusely in Liberian colloquial English.[421] He also praised Ms. Margaret Tumbay and Ms. Evelyn Gosoe, two women who took turns and cooked for him. In addition, others, including Mrs. Linda Unseth and Mrs. Mary Lou McDonough both of World Relief-Spokane at the time were a part of Mr. Howe's support system.[422] Mr. Howe became a valued and participating member of the Liberian community in Spokane.

In April 2007, the sad ending of Mr. Howe's American story began when doctors diagnosed him with terminal cancer. On the day of the diagnosis, he called me and said Lisa took him to the hospital, where a doctor said he had "some kanna disease."[423] Mr. Howe said he had not been sick before going to the hospital, but a doctor, whom he identified, gave him "some kanna medicine" that made him sick. I contacted the doctor and found out the "some kanna disease" to be cancer. When I asked what the diagnosis meant, meaning how long Mr. Howe had to live, the doctor told me he could not definitively tell. However, he said, considering the stage of Mr. Howe's cancer, he thought he might have about six months to a year to live.

With that understanding, I visited with Mr. Howe for a conversation without sounding the alarm about how long he had to live. The conversation was necessary because he was living alone, without a wife or any relatives. The Liberian community wanted to help Mr. Howe, but we had families and work obligations and could not be with him on a daily basis. On that note along with his declining health, I wondered whether he would consider returning to Liberia, where his family would look after him if his health started to fail. At first, Mr. Howe considered my suggestion and named

Kpamusieh when I asked who would be in Liberia to look after him if he returned. Kpamusieh came up repeatedly in other conversations with him.

Mr. Howe's first concern was where to live upon returning to Liberia. On that note, he thought he might save some money to take home to build a house. However, he quickly figured that, after his living expenses, what remained of his social security benefits was a pittance. He thought it would take him almost forever to save the amount of money he might need to build a house. His second concern was feeding, especially when he thought about his experience with hunger in the Ivory Coast. His quick analysis about money he would need to build a house, and fear of hunger made returning to Liberia a dim prospect. Somberly, he looked down and asked me to give him time to think a little more about returning to Liberia. On my next visit, Mr. Howe had had ample time to think about returning to Liberia. He told me without hesitation that he had changed his mind; he did not want to return to Liberia. When I asked why he changed his mind, he told me the hunger he faced in refuge in the Ivory Coast caused him to change his mind. Tears rolled down his cheek as he talked to me.

Moments later, after Mr. Howe pulled himself back together, I reassured him that he was not about to die. However, I told him that we were having the conversation because we were in America and not in Liberia, where, culturally, families seldom talk about death.[424] In America, family members select their burial plots and pay for their funeral costs through insurance. They do that so that funeral burdens do not fall on their families when they die. Upon hearing about burial plot selection while alive, Mr. Howe sat straight up, and his eyes opened widely in surprise. Then in Liberian English, he said "Yeah-ooh my son, we don't do that kanna thing in Liberia."

Talking about death was not easy for me too. However, the dilemma we were in forced us to confront death with a wry and loud laughter, which provided a window of opportunity for perhaps the most difficult question I had for Mr. Howe: "What would you like me to do if 'something' were to happen to you?" Without asking what "something" meant, he said, "My son, bury me here when I die." His response only opened a can of worms when I told him that burying someone in America meant more than one thing. "A dead person can either be cremated or buried in a casket as in Liberia," I said while he twisted in his chair with a look of fear.[425] "My son, if I die, please bury me like in Liberia," he told me.

460

After that conversation, my family and I visited with Mr. Howe at his Park Tower apartment. At that time, he took an envelope out of a sports bag in the closet and opened it. He counted $1,450 in cash, turned to me, and said, "Take this money and use it in the event of my death for my funeral and burial expenses." I did not have a power of attorney with his signature to give me the authority to accept the money. Besides that, other than my family, no one else was present to witness the transfer of money. Therefore, I told Mr. Howe to keep the money. I referenced the law not only to protect myself, but also to prevent him from thinking that I was not being helpful. I had to figure out a workable solution to do what he wanted me to do, because it was not enough to say no to accepting the money.

The apparent solution was an answer to a question I had since his fate became a concern. He was too old to work and did not have skills to hold down any meaningful job. The social security benefits he received paid for his living expenses, with very little left to cover funeral and burial insurance. So, I wondered whether the government, state or federal, would provide any assistance for his funeral and burial if he passed away. World Relief-Spokane seemed the logical place to seek an answer. So, we scheduled a 3:30 p.m. meeting for April 22, 2008, to find out.

Right after work on April 22nd, I picked Mr. Howe up from his apartment and headed to World Relief-Spokane. Upon arrival, a receptionist ushered us into a conference room, where Mrs. Unseth and Mrs. McDonough joined us. At the time of my conversation with Mr. Howe at his apartment, the likelihood of his passing in the near future was no less than it was at the time of the meeting at World Relief-Spokane. However, because I did not want to alarm him, our conversation at his apartment was in the context of a hypothetical situation. I was mindful not to change the nature of the conversation drastically, but it was obvious to everyone during the World Relief-Spokane conversation that we were dancing around a looming tragedy. Mr. Howe did not fail to grasp the specter. Considering that he did not have family or relatives in Spokane, we needed a good answer badly.

The answer Mr. Howe and I got, however, was not good. Moreover, the manner the bad news was communicated left much to be desired in terms of cultural literacy. Mr. Howe was very old, lonely and had just been diagnosed with terminal cancer, with six months to a year to live. If he were in Liberia, no one would deliver bad news to him by "cutting to the chase." Instead, bearers of bad news would "hang heads" to find an appropriate way to deliver it. The answer would be the same, "No," but a "no" that provides an opportunity to work through a difficult situation gracefully. But the answer we got was bare bones, "The government does not provide any such assistance." The exception was that, if he died without any family to claim his body, the government would cremate him. The pain and tears struck and tortured me when Mr. Howe broke down and cried.

Moments later, I told Mrs. Unseth and Mrs. McDonough about the $1,450 Mr. Howe wanted me to use for his funeral and burial in the event of his death. They recommended enrolling him into a funeral insurance, a final care cost/insurance policy, using that money as a down payment. A monthly payment was determined to be $52. Mrs. McDonough also recommended an advanced healthcare directive, a durable power of attorney and a will to authorize me to make decisions for Mr. Howe if he became incapacitated.[426] Mr. Howe went along with the recommendations. However, in no time after those recommendations, Mr. Howe's health status suddenly changed. The Masons visited with him on Sunday, May 25, 2008, found him in a "medically unstable condition" and called 911. A paramedic team arrived and transported him to Deaconess Medical Center in Spokane. When I reached him at the hospital, he was deteriorating so rapidly that pursuing the legal documents became a moot exercise.

I convened an emergency meeting of the Liberian community about Mr. Howe's condition and contacted Mr. George Elliott in an attempt to reach Mr. Howe's family in Africa. A couple of days after, a nurse at Deaconess notified me that the hospital had contacted Hospice.[427] Eventually, upon my return home after a hectic day, my cellphone rang at exactly 9:00 p.m. on Monday, June 9, 2008. Reluctantly, I answered the phone and the person on the other end of the line asked, "Is this Dr. Flumo?" "Yes, this is he," I replied. It was the head nurse with whom I had been interacting at Deaconess. "I am sorry to inform you that Mr. Joseph Howe passed away," she said. "Oh no, oh no, oh no, that's what I was afraid of, I am on my way," I responded.

At the nurses' station at Deaconess, I shook off the fear of ghosts and corpse I had had since childhood and asked if I could see Mr. Howe's remains.[428] A nurse pointed to the same room, where I left him during my last visit. I walked over and found him lying face up, with his eyes closed as if he were sleeping. Not afraid anymore, I stood over and looked at him for a long time. I then closed my eyes, imagined my dad lying in his place and wept quietly for Mr. Howe and my dad as others behind me attempted to walk into the room. When I stepped away from the room, a Liberian, in reference to funeral and burial arrangements, asked, "So, what next?" "Mr. Flumo will be taking care of him [Mr. Joseph Howe]," said Lisa, who had arrived at the hospital along with her family before me. I asked everyone including Lisa for a brief conference in the lounge, where I recognized the Masons. They had been in Mr. Howe's life and remained his family until he passed away. I invited them to join the Liberian community to give Mr. Howe a fitting burial but they chose to grieve their loss in their own way.

I had never done a funeral before, so I did not know where to begin. I took a day off work to do the planning, but I drove to work early morning to consult with colleagues; unfortunately, everyone I needed to talk to was preparing to start class. So, I returned home. On my way home, I said a short prayer for Wlah's intervention while driving as if I were having a conversation with Him, sitting next to me in the car. The emergency planning by the Liberian community was inadequate. While on Wellesley Avenue heading east, I came to a stop at a traffic light, felt lightheaded momentarily and then a sudden calm fell over me. I continued driving toward home and then got off Sprague Avenue near Costco and parked. I called Mrs. Erin Jones, a colleague, whom I had talked to about Mr. Howe's imminent passing. I had asked whether her church could help were he to pass away. Although she tried to reach her pastor, she never heard back from him.

Next, I called Mr. Chuck Anderton, a family friend.[429] I had talked to him about Mr. Howe as well and wondered whether he knew a pastor who could help. The pastor he contacted was not helpful. So, I hit a brick wall and then held my head in both palms, thinking what to do next. In the passenger seat next to me, I had a brochure with a list of funeral homes, including phone numbers. A nurse at Deaconess had given it to me less than a week earlier in anticipation of Mr. Howe's passing. I skimmed through the list of funeral homes and found Thornhill Valley Chapel Funeral Home, which I passed daily on my way to and from work. Moreover, the funeral home had conducted the funeral of Mrs. Nancy Kelly, wife of Mr. Vance Kelly, about a week earlier. The Kellys and our family attended the same church for a few years. We had attended the public viewing of Mrs. Kelly when she was at the facility. I called Thornhill Valley Chapel Funeral Home and scheduled an appointment for 1:00 p.m. Next, I called Mr. Vance Kelly who had had a recent experience with the funeral home to help prep me on what to expect and questions to ask during my meeting with the funeral home. Mr. Kelly agreed and graciously walked me through the planning he did for Mrs. Kelly. He spoke highly of the professionalism of the employees at Thornhill Valley Chapel Funeral Home.

At the Thornhill Valley Chapel Funeral Home, Mr. Bart Ward ushered me into a comfortable office, where he listened intently as I explained Mr. Howe's ordeal and passing. Considering the financial situation, he recommended "Direct Burial."[430] Besides that recommendation, Mr. Ward taught me something new. In the State of Washington, he said, services at the cemetery along with burial are separate and apart from the funeral home. Moreover, he was kind to connect me with Mr. Dennis Fairbank of Catholic Cemeteries who agreed to meet me at 3:00 p.m. that same afternoon at the St. Joseph Cemetery. Before leaving Mr. Ward, he gave me a $1,077.58 invoice for Direct Burial.

I then drove to St. Joseph Cemetery at 17825 East Trent Avenue, for my meeting with Mr. Fairbank. At exactly 3:00 p.m., he arrived and took me to his office, where I explained Mr. Howe's situation. Next, he took me to the cemetery and showed me possible areas for burial site. I selected **Section F-Lot 607-Space 1** for the burial of Mr. Joseph Howe.[431] We scheduled the burial for 3:00 p.m. on June 17, 2008. Thereafter, Mr. Fairbank gave me a burial expense invoice for $1,934, but he told me that he would appreciate any amount that the Liberian community could afford. "Whether or not the Liberian community can pay, Catholic Cemeteries would bury Mr. Howe," Mr. Fairbank said.

Upon my return home, I provided information, including funeral and burial costs, date and time of burial and directions to the cemetery during an emergency Liberian community meeting. I also answered questions and showed a large color picture of Mr. Howe's coffin. Thereafter, a somber quietude fell upon the gathering. We raised a little over $1200 through contributions. On the following day, two community members, Messrs. Hilary Kweh and Sinneh Ville, and I paid Thornhill Valley Chapel Funeral Home the funeral cost of $1,077.58. On June 12, 2008, another community member, Ms. Margaret Tumbay, and I purchased apparel for the funeral home to ready Mr. Howe for burial.

Meanwhile, efforts to reach Mr. Howe's family in Africa paid off when Mr. Roberto B. Natt and his mom, Ms. Mary Hinneh Vinton, called me from the Ivory Coast and provided an email address for communicating with them. I e-mailed and expressed the Liberian community's sympathy for the loss of Mr. Howe and provided updates on the funeral and burial plans. I promised to send them pictures of the funeral and burial. On Monday, June 16, 2008, the day before Mr. Joseph Howe was interred, Ms. Mary Hinneh Vinton, Mr. Joseph Howe's widow, emailed and expressed her "Thanks and gratitude" to my family and the Liberian community.[432]

On June 17, 2008, members of the Liberian community and others who wanted to attend the burial assembled at our home and drove in a convoy to the St. Joseph Cemetery. Shortly before 3:00 p.m., the funeral home hearse carrying Mr. Joseph Howe's remains arrived at the St. Joseph Cemetery. At exactly 3:00 p.m., Bart Ward of Thornhill Valley Chapel Funeral Home; Lahai Samura, Beweh Sartoe, Emmanuel Taylor, Stephen Teah, all members of the Liberian community, and I carried the light blue coffin bearing the remains of Mr. Howe from the hearse to the gravesite and placed it over the casket-lowering device.

Even though the "Direct Burial" package did not include a regular church funeral service, we held an appropriate gravesite ceremony for Mr. Howe. Everyone including members of the Liberian community, friends of Mr. Howe's, the cemetery and funeral home staff and others gathered around the grave for the gravesite ceremony. Mr. Bart Ward opened Mr. Howe's casket and gave everyone an opportunity to see his remains for the last time before he was interred. We sang the first and last stanzas of the hymn "It Is Well With My Soul." Everyone said farewell to Mr. Howe and then I read the scripture, "A Time for Everything," taken from Ecclesiastes 3:1-8. I also read the following text word-for-word and committed Mr. Howe's body to the ground.[433] As I read, Mr. Howe's coffin was gradually lowered into the grave. I used a trowel, took a scoop of soil that the cemetery staff set aside for this purpose and sprinkled it over the coffin as it slowly descended into the grave. Thereafter, each member of the Liberian community and others took a scoop of soil either with the hand or with the trowel and poured it over the coffin as it was being lowered into the grave.

Those who knew Mr. Joseph Howe and other sympathizers made additional contributions at the gravesite to help pay his funeral cost. Immediately after the burial, I paid Mr. Dennis Fairbank of Catholic Cemeteries $524.28, the remaining amount of total contributions of $1650 received at that point. I used additional contributions totaling $105.00 made at the repast for printing and mailing funeral pictures along with a hardcopy of the original death certificate to Mr. Howe's family in the Ivory Coast.

Mr. Joseph Howe's illness and passing reminded me of Dad's illness and death in my absence in Liberia in 1999. Like Mr. Howe, Dad was buried away from home, although in Liberia. Mr. Howe had no son or relatives in Spokane. So, as others stepped up and answered for me at Dad's burial when mourners asked, "Where is his son?" I had to step up and answer for Mr. Howe's son at his burial in Spokane when the mourners asked, "Where is his son?" Beyond my role as the leader of the Liberian community, that mindset was my motivation in all the work the community and I did to lay Mr. Howe to rest. As a particle in the plume dislodged by the bombardments in Liberia, Mr. Howe landed in Spokane, Washington. His American story came to a sad end when terminal cancer silenced him, but he is not lost. He rests perpetually at *Section F-Lot 607-Space 1* at St. Joseph Cemetery at 17825 East Trent Avenue, Spokane, Washington.

STRIFE IN THE LIBERIAN COMMUNITY IN SPOKANE

Despite the work that we tried to do and all the achievements we made in the Liberian community in Spokane, some of which were immeasurable, it was not all "kumbaya". Indeed, there were stinging criticisms. Someone called me a "country man," an expression that does not have the power to cause the same psychic injury as the "N-word" does in the United States but is used in the same pejorative sense in Liberia. I tried to be a humble, upright and committed leader. I did not misappropriate a single penny of the organization's funds. Neither did I violate any part of the constitution or any of the ethical codes that we adopted. Instead, we intervened in family disputes, visited the sick and attended parent conferences at schools. We also attended graduations, celebrated showers, and births of babies. Indeed, we participated in weddings, showed up at the courthouse to support those who needed us and buried the dead.

I accepted criticisms for leading the organization "by the book" and codes of conduct we adopted because I was accountable to those who elected me. Article XVII, Section 17.1 of the Constitution of the Association of Liberians in the Spokane Area (ALSA) clearly states that "The association shall make no loans to anyone, entities, or its members." However, we convened emergency sessions, made exceptions when some members were in dire straits and provided loans to those who were in need. At no time did my family and I benefit from such loans.

I was no perfect leader. I made mistakes, but my mistakes were not about leading the organization by the constitution and the codes of conduct we debated and adopted. No one even pointed out the mistakes I made, but me. Through personal reflections, I recognized two mistakes I made as ALSA's leader, the first of which pertained to my wiring during early childhood and my insatiable appetite for solving problems and making things better. That is why I came to Spokane literally with a script to solve a problem for people who did not exist in the city. The desire to make a difference was intense and irresistible.

My second mistake as ALSA's leader was taking my privilege for granted. By privilege, I do not mean my graduate education, a job that took care of my family and me or the comforts that we enjoyed in the United States. I am referring to a different kind of privilege. What I call privilege others might consider it something else, perhaps a handicap or its source. However, I call my Dad's humiliation by *quizees* and my mom's losing ten children a privilege, not because they were desirable experiences for anyone to endure. Instead, I refer to them as such because they are some of the wrenching experiences that constitute the essence of "grit," the wherewithal that sustains the journey of becoming "someone" in the face of unimaginable odds.

I do not wish every child or any child to witness the humiliation of its dad. Neither do I wish every child or any child to absorb the pains of its mom losing ten children. Moreover, every child does not have a dad who lost his parents while he was a toddler. Neither does every child have a mom who is loving, attentive, compassionate, and prayerful as my Mom was. My parents' experiences gave me a powerful tool to navigate the contours of my journey. Other people's parents gave them financial inheritance. I did not come out of my mom's womb with wisdom. Mom and Dad's experiences made me aware early in my life that the life Wlah gave me had been paid for with a heavy price. As such, every minute counted, and I could not goof off. Although that awareness, which I often took for granted that everyone had, was not the same as the financial wealth others inherited, it was no less a privilege.

Liberian newcomers who arrived in Spokane not only described the hardships they experienced in refugee camps, but also detailed the kinds of support they needed to improve their lives in their new country. I believed in them. Moreover, I also wanted to ensure that the experiences of their new beginning put them on a path to success. However, during my interactions, both in Liberia and in the United States, with Liberians who experienced the horrors and traumas of the war, I observed that they operate in an almost perpetual survival mode. The most fascinating aspect of that phenomenon involves answers to questions asked. Respondents often answer questions based on what they assume a questioner is thinking rather than on the basis of what the questioner is asking. During the war, that strategy made sense for those who stood at the risk of losing their lives based on their responses. Unfortunately, however, that apparent survival strategy during the war has become a permanent fixture of the national culture.

On that note, I wondered whether newcomers really meant what they told me about the kinds of support they needed to improve their lives in Spokane. I do not know whether they figured I wanted to hear about their intense desires for educational opportunities. I do not know whether they really meant it when they asked for opportunities to learn computers. The reason that I wonder, is that they failed to attend computer classes arranged for them free of charge at the Spokane Community College.

I wondered about the help international aid agencies provided refugees too. I do not know whether the help conditioned them in some way. I had those concerns because I heard refugees had learned that governments of their host countries would provide cash and food assistance. With that, I do not know whether such information had any impacts on newcomers' expectations upon arrival in the United States. Lastly, I was interested in the impacts of newcomers' experience in refugee camps on their mindset. What were their individual stories and how did such stories shape their attitudes about everything in America? Gullibility was my mistake too. Moreover, I assumed stories that motivated me to pursue an education with fierceness affected everyone in similar ways. Indeed, I assumed we had the same privilege.

I believe that a vibrant community or nation, one that President William R. Tolbert, Jr., called, "A wholesome functioning society," is created at a price. Moreover, those who have a clear sense of the value of that kind of community or nation fully appreciate its price. Martin Luther King, Jr., understood the price for that kind of nation or society and committed his life to it. My being called a "country man" was a small price to pay for attempting to secure for Liberian refugees in Spokane the same future that my parents and others paid to secure for me.

I may not come close to doing for others what Mom and Dad as well as other well-meaning adults did for me during the process of my development. Nevertheless, I passed on values my parents, Dr. Forh and Col. Cannon instilled in me to those in the Liberian community in Spokane who had ears to hear, eyes to see and minds to perceive. Unlike President Tolbert who paid the ultimate price for having and embarking on achieving the right vision for Liberia, being called a "country man" was a paltry price to pay for trying to do the right thing for the Liberian community in Spokane. My vindication is the harmony in my heart and mind and the peace in my life.

CHAPTER 35

Internal Peace and Meaning

SOME ANSWERS

"WHY DID YOU COME TO America?" and "Why did it take you twenty-one years to return to Liberia?" are two questions that have dogged me for a very long time. While ordinary people I encounter often ask, "Why did you come to America?", it is students I have taught or encountered during my public school educational career in the states of North Carolina and Washington who have posed that question. In addition to my students' curiosity and concerns about my wellbeing, the privilege of educating so many young people has been immensely fulfilling. The answer to "Why did you come to America?" has always been easy because all I had to say was the civil war in Liberia. But as with all teenagers, an answer to one question only generates another one. Until now, answers to their follow-up questions, including "Why did it take you twenty-one years to return to Liberia?", have not been easy to provide as has been the answer to "Why did you come to America?" I have given clues to why it took me twenty-one years to return to Liberia here and there, but the time has come to bring the pieces of the puzzle together.

I left Liberia in June 1990 after the onset of the Liberian Civil War and came to the United States for fear of my life. I was not involved in any opposition group. I did not do harm to anyone. I did not take anything of value from anyone. I left Liberia and took refuge in America for fear of my life because I am a member of the Mahn ethnic group. Shortly after December 24, 1989, Liberia became a divided country. The rules that governed Mr. Charles Taylor's side and those that prevailed on President Samuel Doe's side were the same.[434] Wanton violence was sport. Moreover, being a member of an ethnic group perceived as an enemy or an employee of an institution perceived to be associated with the government of Liberia was considered justifiable and enough reason to be victimized or killed.

My students were not the only ones who asked, "Why did it take you twenty-one years to return to Liberia?" My family in Liberia also asked the same question but in a different way. On the one hand, my students often posed the question verbally as a follow-up after an extended response to "Why did you come to America?" On the other hand, my family often posed the question through their body languages. Their comments often implied, "Why did it take you twenty-one years to return to Liberia?" In any case, two factors contributed to my inability to return sooner to Liberia. First, I was unable to return to Liberia because of the security situation. Second, my immigration status prevented me from returning to Liberia any sooner.

I focus here on my immigration saga and tell it because the security situation in Liberia during the civil war was self-evident. On August 14, 1990, forty-eight days after I arrived in the United States, I applied for political asylum with the United States Immigration and Naturalization Service (INS) in Arlington, Virginia.[435] When I moved from Annandale, Virginia to North Carolina, Mr. Beacham McDougald, a concerned citizen of Laurinburg, helped seek the intervention of my Congressional delegation including Congressman Bill Hefner (D-NC) and Senators Jesse Helms (R-NC) and Terry Sanford (D-NC). Congressman Bill Hefner and Senators Jesse Helms and Terry Sanford each wrote the Arlington asylum office on my behalf, but their efforts came to naught.

By late 1997, shortly after my children and I moved to Spokane, I had contracted the services of two female lawyers, Attorney Teresa L. Donovan of Alexandria, Virginia and Attorney Debby Kurbitz of Spokane, Washington, respectively. By that time, nine years had gone by without a review of my application for political asylum and a determination of my immigration status. In the meantime, a section on "Travel outside the

United States" in the instructions for completing an application for asylum at the time stated that

> If you leave the United States without first obtaining advance parole from USCIS using Form I-131, Application for a Travel Document, we will presume that you have abandoned your application. If you obtain advance parole and return to the country of claimed persecution, we will presume that you have abandoned your application, unless you can show that there were compelling reasons for your return.[436]

I interpreted the statement to mean that, unless one can provide "compelling reasons" for returning to the country of "claimed persecution," U.S. Immigration Agents may not allow one to reenter the United States. Leaving my children in the United States in someone else's care and traveling to Liberia to check on my parents and other members of my family was too great a risk to take. I came to that conclusion because I knew that U.S. Immigration officers wielded tremendous power and exercised broad discretion in determining which reasons were compelling and which ones were not.

Under normal circumstances, the delay in processing my application for asylum may not have been excruciating as it was. The delay hurt because I was far away from home, longing for my parents while Liberia was falling apart at the same time. Since I started school in 1966, I had never spent a full year with them. I had either been away in school in Sanniquellie and Monrovia, Liberia or abroad, studying in Seoul, Korea, and Greensboro, North Carolina. Although by the time of the civil war in Liberia I was already an adult, I still wished for an opportunity to make up for all the time I missed out being with my parents. Moreover, while my application for asylum was pending, applying for a job, renewing a work permit, or filling out any forms that required background information became a hassle. For more than twelve years, I had to explain myself over and over. A simple matter like indicating nationality on a form took tremendous energy, making me to feel a poke with a needle in a sore that did not exist. In addition, imagining Liberia slipping out of my hands and going out of reach like a child losing its helium-filled balloon on a playground on a windy day became second nature.

While I was in limbo, America's hands were wrapped around me only. They had not been clasped yet in acceptance because my immigration status had not been determined. My tribulations felt like a rendezvous in purgatory. To understand how upsetting the situation was, one had to be a Liberian, or from a country where birthplace as well as place of upbringing is intricately woven into one's life and destiny.

Although America's loosely wrapped hands around me had been in place for more than a decade, the first signs that significant movements in them were about to happen emerged on May 15, 2000. On that day, the stars aligned when Dr. Gary Livingston, then superintendent of Spokane Public Schools, visited John R. Rogers High School, where I still work, for an after-school meeting with the administration and staff. Accompanying Dr. Livingston was Attorney Rocco N. Treppiedi, a Spokane lawyer who was then a member of the Board of Directors for Spokane Public Schools. [437]

Immediately after the meeting, I walked up to Dr. Livingston and reintroduced myself, although we had met before. I asked if I could have a talk with him and he consented. I began explaining my immigration ordeal to Dr. Livingston right away, as Attorney Treppiedi, standing about a yard away from us, looked on and listened attentively. After I finished talking, Dr. Livingston assured me that he would communicate my situation with then Representative George Nethercutt (R-WA). Before Dr. Livingston and Attorney Treppiedi walked away, Attorney Treppiedi gave me his business card and asked me to call him.

A few days later, I wrote Dr. Livingston a three-page letter, providing a synopsis of the story I had told him to facilitate his communication with Congressman George Nethercutt. On July 19, 2000, Dr. Livingston, in turn, wrote Congressman Nethercutt. His letter to Congressman Nethercutt started the ball rolling again on my immigration case. In less than one month, Ms. Shelly Short, Congressman Nethercutt's secretary, sent me a copy of a letter on my behalf which the Congressman had written on August 7, 2000, to the San Francisco Asylum Office.

The bigwigs, like Dr. Gary Livingston, Congressman George Nethercutt, and Attorney Treppiedi, were not the only ones who made things happen on my immigration case. My colleagues at work were concerned too. They prayed for me and, often, they stopped me in the hallway and asked about my family. Some even reached out to influential people in Washington on my behalf. I was pleasantly surprised and humbled upon receiving a letter dated October 25, 2000 from United States Senator Slade Gorton (R-WA), indicating that he had written a letter on my behalf upon the urging of Ms. Nancy Carlson (deceased), a colleague at John R. Rogers High School.[438]

In the meantime, a few days after the May 15, 2000 meeting at John R. Rogers High School, I called Attorney Treppiedi as he had told me to do. By the time I reached him, he had already discussed my immigration case with his law firm, Perkins Coie. When he informed me that his law firm had granted him permission to pursue my immigration case on a pro bono basis, I was elated. Thereafter, Attorney Treppiedi's painstaking and professional work paid off. I received a heartwarming letter from the INS's San Francisco Asylum Office, scheduling me for an interview in August 2002 in Seattle, Washington.

On the eve of my August 2002 asylum interview, my entire family and I drove five hours to Seattle and stayed at a downtown hotel only a walking distance from the INS office. The INS had a reputation for being a stickler about appointment time. I was afraid of leaving Spokane on the morning of the interview, driving to Seattle, and running the risk of getting caught in the Seattle traffic. I had waited twelve years for the interview and did not want to be late for my appointment. We adopted the same approach the year before when another member of my family had an interview, although we did not stay at a hotel. Mr. Saye Kinnay (deceased), a Liberian from Nimba County, and his family graciously hosted us in their home. Attorney Rocky Treppiedi flew into Seattle from Spokane on the morning of the interview and joined us as he did the year before.

On the day of the interview, we checked out of the hotel at 11:00 a.m., had brunch at a local eatery and headed for the INS office. We arrived before schedule and had ample time to relax. As we waited in the lounge for 2:00 p.m., I saw scores of young Asian women in detention, wearing what appeared to be uniforms. I heard they were in holding cells, await-ing deportation because they had apparently violated some aspects of the Immigration and Naturalization laws of the United States. Even though I had come to the United States legally and had no worries about violating any laws, I could not ignore the young Asian women because they and I, at least, had one thing in common, the immigrant experience. For various reasons, we left our countries of birth and came to the United States. I imagined them as babies in their mothers' arms, giggling and smiling as their parents hoped for lives of successes for them in the future. I only imagined what the young women were thinking and feeling, what it felt like to be in a holding cell to be deported.

Soon 2:00 p.m. arrived. Attorney Treppiedi and I entered the room where the interview was scheduled to take place. It was a modest office. The agent who conducted the interview was a woman. She was very professional. She went over the guidelines for Attorney Treppiedi and me. In addition, she assured me that I could take as much time to answer the questions and that I could go back to any question and make corrections or add anything I could recall. The interview started and lasted four hours. As Baptists often say, "This is the day that the Lord has made and so let us rejoice," so was the day of my asylum interview. It was the day that the Lord had made. It was a day of healing, a memorable one.

My August 2002 asylum interview in Seattle, Washington was memorable for several reasons. First, the special INS agent who conducted the interview traveled from San Francisco, to Seattle, expressly for my case. Second, Attorney Rocky Treppiedi was by my side throughout the session. Third, and more importantly, I took refuge in the United States, believing that America would protect me, that I would not languish or get lost. Even though my twelve-year wait in limbo along with a whirlwind of tribulations tested every fiber of my being, my Seattle asylum interview reaffirmed my faith in America.

The special INS Agent asked all the questions I had always longed for someone to ask. They were questions I needed to answer to lift the burden off my shoulders. When I came out of the interview, I felt as if I had had a therapy session, as if a 150-pound sack had been taken off my shoulders. The interview made me hear words the agent did not speak: the America you believed in delivers. After that exhaustive four-hour interview in Seattle, my application for asylum was approved in April 2003, nearly thirteen years after I applied for asylum in Arlington, Virginia.

My asylum approval made my status better than being in limbo, but all was not clear. I had to work towards obtaining a green card to become a permanent resident. That process required a one-year wait time after asylum approval. I qualified to apply for a green card in April 2004 because my asylum was approved in April 2003. Moreover, the cost of applying for a green card was not insurmountable. However, the heavy sack that my asylum interview lifted off my shoulders contained the negative effects of the twelve-year delay, stormy family issues and bottled grief from the loss of my dad in May 1999. The sack came off my shoulders following the asylum interview, but it turned into a psychological landmine. Beginning April 2004 until the last quarter of 2007, I tried to apply for a green card, but I pulled back for fear of aggravating the wound beneath the surface. Every time I tried to apply for a green card, it felt like stepping on an explosive ordnance deliberately.

Eventually, I mustered the courage to take the bull by its horns. I applied for a green card despite the pain the process rekindled. However, that courage was not without an impetus. In August 2007, I traveled to Accra, Ghana to visit with my mom.[439] Upon arrival at the John F. Kennedy International Airport in New York City while on my way back home to Spokane, I had another unforgettable experience. At Customs and Immigration, all arriving passengers were separated into two different queues. United States citizens and green card holders were ushered one way while all other aliens were shown the other way. I was among all other aliens. I was not a United States citizen, neither was I a green card holder. I only had a travel document, which the United States Citizenship and Immigration Service (USCIS) issued me expressly for my trip to Accra, Ghana. It did not matter that, by that time, I had lived in the United States for the past seventeen years.

By separating United States citizens and green card holders from all other aliens at the port of entry, John F. Kennedy International Airport, United States Customs and Immigration Officers were doing their jobs to ensure that everyone entering the United States was doing so legally. However, due to my personal experience navigating the immigration process in the United States, ushering me with all other aliens at the John F. Kennedy International Airport became a charged and painful exercise for me. The experience made me to step on the psychological landmine I had been tiptoeing around for a long time. The seemingly benign discriminatory exercise made me to face a painful reality that I did not belong. The experience cut deeply into my being.

Ironically, the Immigration Officer who inspected my travel document became an unlikely source of consolation. Before he handed my travel document back to me, he looked at me and asked, "Why have you waited so long?" meaning, "Why are you not yet a citizen?" "It is about time," he went on. His innocent and comforting concern awoke emotions from deep within me and summoned a full conversation that we did not have time to have. I smiled, told him that it would happen someday and thanked him while walking away.

Upon my return to Spokane from my trip in Accra, Ghana, I gathered all the required documents and applied for a green card late 2007. I was granted permanent resident status in 2008. I then waited for five years and applied for citizenship. On May 21, 2013, I became a citizen of the United States, twenty-three years after I began the process with an application for political asylum in Arlington, Virginia in August 1990.

From L-R, Attorney Rocky Treppiedi, Blodah, Me, and Jo-Weh
on the day I took an oath as a citizen of the United States

At last, I answered my students who wanted to know why it took me twenty-one years to return to Liberia. Even though my response was better than a depressing recount of my experience, it did not pertain to their question. Instead, I told them about the character of America; stories of individuals whose lives, even during tempestuous times, make and keep America a glowing and unmistakable beacon. Indeed, I narrated stories of Bishop Bennie L. Kelly, Brother Ralph Sutton, and Delores (Dee) Robinson, people who lifted me during fogs of life in Washington, D.C., and North Carolina.[440] I painted an American character embodying literary portraits of Roberta (Bobbie) League and Rocky Treppiedi of Spokane. Moreover, the actions of my almost all white students of John R. Rogers High School were no less a definition of the American character. They not only protected me from their peer who called me the "N-word teacher" and threatened to kill me in 2007, but also considered "beating him up."[441]

477

Even in Liberia, I told others about the reach of Veradale United Church of Christ's life-giving tentacles. At the start of school and winter each year, the congregation donated school supplies and winter coats to children and needy families. Some members traveled to New Orleans, following the devastations of Hurricane Katrina, and helped with the rebuilding while others volunteered their time in the community. A prayer shawl which the church's Prayer Shawl Ministry sent my mom before she passed away in January 2014 is alongside her remains in her resting place in the village in Liberia. At spring planting each year, the congregation assembled in the garden, where the Reverend Linda Crowe prayed, followed by the singing of the garden song.[442] Each year, the harvest, which the church donated to the Spokane Food Bank, was not only an indication of Wlah's present day wonders but also an occasion of the opening of the "flood gates."[443] Veradale United Church of Christ cares deeply about Spokane, America and the rest of the world. Currently, under the stewardship of Reverend Genevieve Haywood, the congregation is not only "Acting justly, loving mercy, and walking humbly with God," but also focusing on witnessing "To the core of Christian faith: that all may be one."[444]

In addition, I told others that President George W. Bush talked, Taylor walked, and the guns went silent, bringing an end to the senseless bloodshed in Liberia. It was Bush's lieutenant, Former Chairman of the Joint Chiefs of Staff and former Secretary of State, General Colin Powell, working along with the late and former United Nations Secretary-General, Dr. Kofi Annan, and others who helped restore peace in Liberia. President Bush understood the power of the presidency. More importantly, he cared enough to use it to end the protracted bloodshed in Liberia. Indeed, I talked about President Barack Obama's courageous decision to send 4,000 US troops to Liberia to help stop the spread of the deadly Ebola virus in 2014. These great leaders and ordinary people constitute the character of America, the country that took me in, educated and gave me opportunities to be who I am; the country that I cling onto with pride.

CHAPTER 36

Another Dream

WITH THE EXPERIENCE OF THIS incredible journey, I am not only inspired by fond memories of "Kou Leehee" and "Ndaha" but also see myself in the village near my parents, cultivating the crops they cultivated and extending the "Mansion" they built.[445] Mom and Dad are no longer alive. Therefore, "to be near my parents" is to be close to their resting places. Their nearness reminds me of their sojourn on earth and their labor to make me somebody. This dream is about keeping faith with the past, my responsibilities to my parents, even in their deaths. In addition, it is about remaining connected to my source of inspiration to sustain the strength to help my children become somebody and to contribute to making the village or the world a better place. It is not an option, but an obligation. I see myself in the village breathing new life into the "Garden of Eden;" using the past to create a future. This "Mansion" was erected from materials hewn out of the rich soil in the village. I see myself cultivating the soil to extend the "Mansion" not in any radically different way but with a radically different purpose. I see myself working the soil for dignity and to help dismantle the false and regressive dichotomy in the village between being educated and tending to the soil. Work is perhaps the only thing that can make a people secure a full sense of their dignity and a sustaining and fulfilling future. I still have not found a substitute.

The Conversation

In January 2014, Layelekpeh, a woman from nearby Bursonnon I had known since childhood, spoke profoundly to me.[446] Her words struck me in the same way as Mr. Karmah's words did in Bursonnon on Christmas day in 1989. "Luogon nakay ka nu ya tan kozee nonu o wohn medan ka keleh weh. Suku kozee nonu o yenkiamon wohn oo neaka koo yee dor orh."[447] Layelekpeh spoke about role models. Her words sank deep into my heart because I know the importance of role models; I looked up to them during my early years; most of all, I am one, albeit far away from the village, where I may be most needed.

With written or printed material, other means of mass communication and today's lightning-speed advances in information technology, closeness to a sphere of influence does not seem to be a necessity anymore. However, being present at home or in one's village is still important because guiding one's children or serving as a beacon for young people in the village to want to aspire cannot be met solely by "video chat" or "face time." Although, in countries like Liberia, the widespread availability of cellphone and information technology is mindboggling, the advantages and potential benefits of cellphone technology are often lost to the avalanche of pleasure-seeking applications and the immediate concerns of surviving from day to day.

The Flumos' Residence in Spokane, WA

Layelekpeh's remarks not only evoked but also affirmed "Another Dream" I already had, arising from Mom's dedication to me and wanting to continue her legacy.[448] Long before Mom died, I knew I would bury her at the location I chose behind our house in the village because, in the event of similar fate, I would like to rest right next to her. That was an indication of my appreciation for her life. I committed to watch over her and never to turn my back on her. I will always remember North Carolina. The people there not only gave me a great education but also loved me more than I deserved. As for our home, Spokane, Washington, it is a place of quietude, serenity and peace, a place that is hard to leave. Notwithstanding my intense love of America, owing to its acceptance of me and giving me an opportunity to make something out of my life, in the event my time arrives, I believe it will forgive me and allow my son to take me to the village to rest near my mom as I have instructed him. It is only befitting for a mother who labored so much for children.

At Mom's death, two generations had intervened since I was a child. A lot had changed. Stories about my childhood, including sacrifices Mom and Dad made to educate me had been told, retold, and modified, if not twisted. Moreover, my extended family's role in my early development and education had been reified and exaggerated.[449] Consequently, I saw myself in the village defining Mom's legacy clearly and tending to the soil as one way to continue it to benefit my family, extended family, and the village.

"Investment" does not fully capture Mom and Dad as well as my extended family's roles during my early development and education, yet the term conjures imageries useful in defining and telling the story of Mom's legacy. Beginning 1966, year after year, Mom and Dad cultivated coffee and upland rice. Their harvests provided income to pay my tuition and their taxes and food for the family, respectively. Due to Mom's hands-on role in my education, she never understood the cost of education as limited to tuition or yearly fees. She never depended on Dad for everything. In addition to the farms she and Dad worked, she cultivated swamp rice, large vegetable gardens as well as bananas and plantains, separately and alone.

Mom carried produce on her head to Kpaye Lehpula, about an hour's walk away, where she sold it mainly to Mandingoes who worked in the diamond mines. Under the mattress in her bedroom, or in the zipper-affixed pouch she carried around her waist was the bank, where she kept the money earned from the sale of produce. She paid intervening school expenses, including uniforms, new clothes, sneakers, copybooks, and pocket change from that account.

Miatee Garteh, one of Dad's elder brothers, did not have any children. Therefore, he saw me as his own child and was involved in my education. At the beginning of almost every school year, he contributed to my tuition. He visited with me whenever he was in Sanniquellie. Sennie and Esther, my sisters, supported me too. On weekends I did not go to the village, they walked the over three-hour distance and carried provisions to Sanniquellie on their heads for me.

Send-offs at the beginning of each academic year and happiness for my promotion to the next grade at the end of each year, not to mention coppers some members of my extended family gave me for kala, copybooks or pencils constituted their support during my early education.[450] As some extended family members encouraged me to "say your book" (read), others like Mantor Mahnwon, another of Dad's elder brothers, gave me two options: get an education or return to the village to go to Gbankan.[451]

As with every investment, Mom and Dad expected returns. Mom wanted her story told while Dad wanted me to get an eighth-grade education to inspect his government tax collectors-issued receipts to ensure he had not been cheated. But Mom and Dad did not necessarily think of returns in monetary terms; neither did they focus only on themselves. Mom envisioned the village and showed, by example, how to care for and educate the children to realize that vision. Through her temperament, compassion, and concern for others, she set the tenor of social relations to accomplish that vision. Over time, Mom expected an educated village, family cohesion and future visitors to discover fruits of her hard work. Indeed, she expected future visitors to discover that she and others lived with a purpose. That was Mom's legacy which I saw myself in the village continuing. My extended family looked forward to returns too. They expected educated and important people to emerge from the village; they wanted their own *quizees* among the *quizees* as a measure of protection against ruthless and disrespectful government authorities.

At least over the last generation, Mom and Dad as well as most elderly members of my extended family passed on. Moreover, changes occurred in family relations, not to mention the disruptions and devastations of the civil war. These changes, in part, distorted perceptions of my parents' sacrifice as well as my extended family's support during my early education. Some members of my extended family believe their grandparents paid for my education with the expectation that I would pay for their children and grandchildren's education upon becoming successful. Consequently, family cohesion not only became a casualty but also hopes for individual progress and social mobility faded.

I became successful and a role model as elderly members of my extended family expected from their investment in me. However, some current members of my extended family do not see me as the beacon their grandparents hoped for; someone whose presence and experience would guide them in creating their own paths. Instead, they want to take away the pedestal upon which the beacon stands. Put simply, some members of my current extended family do not see me as an inspiration, but as something else.[452] As a result, dreams which my struggles and triumph were supposed to inspire have been replaced by contempt or hate. In the village, I do not feel the love I once felt as a child anymore. Only nostalgia sustains me.

Erroneous perceptions also modified the extended family system's role and, at least, negatively affected family cohesion. Extended family system's philosophy is that parents and other adults in a child's life have a collective role in the child's development. All things being equal, a child's parents' role in its development is unquestionable because, they are the closest to the child. Feeding, nurturing, protecting, instilling values, working and earning incomes to educate their children are primarily parents' responsibilities.[453] These are aspects of the "Threefold debt" Rousseau called for in his educational treatise beyond bringing forth children.[454] The extended family system is also an important part of a child's development because it serves as a child's safety net or secondary level of protection.

Although not by decree, the extended family system obligates children who go on to become successful, to turn back and show the path of success to those who are next in line. In that way, the system promotes a sense of belonging by keeping its members connected to each other and to their communities. Like other systems, not only must every part work to achieve desired results but also it is subject to abuse. For example, parents who disregard their responsibilities and depend solely on successful members of their extended family to educate their children are guilty of abuse of the system. On the other hand, extended family members who become successful and disregard their obligations to show the path of success to those who are next in line are also guilty of the same offense. The extended family system has not lost its relevance, but heavy reliance on it along with relegation of parental as well as personal responsibility has largely rendered the system unsustainable.

Unfortunately, a more powerful obstacle than the combined effect of distorted perceptions of my parents' sacrifice and of the role of the extended family system exists in the village. Not only is *quizee* that powerful obstacle but also its definition as well as negative impact is more pronounced at the village level.[455] Originally, *quizee* referred to America-Liberians, settlers who founded Liberia in the 1820s and their descendants. However, indigenous people joined the ranks of *quizees*. They did so not only by aspiring, through formal education, to become *quizees,* but also by wholly accepting the definition of *quizee*.

The lure of *quizee* is its added dignity, albeit artificial. Becoming a *quizee* or being perceived as a *quizee* is a big aspect of a sense of self. *Quizee* is not only an ideology that governs the modus operandi of people in my village but also a bridle on their psyche. They only see two social classes, *quizees,* the desirable upper class, and *kwenen mia,* the undesirable lower class.[456] The people of my village think of *quizee* professions, including lawyers, government leaders and other white-collar careers, as symbols of success. On the other hand, they regard practical hands-on professions, including farming, carpentry, and masonry as symbols of failure.

To the *kwenen mia* of my village, one cannot spend long years in getting an education only to engage in professions that are symbols of failure. More importantly, not only do they want their children to become *quizees* but also have a clear definition and expectations of a *quizee*. *Kwenen mia* in my village regard a *quizee* as someone who has acquired an education and said goodbye to menial jobs or to traditional farming tools such as cutlasses and hoes, a successful person; someone who has power; someone who works in an office and receives a salary. Moreover, they believe a *quizee* cannot eat with ordinary people; goes to bed early in the evening and wakes up late the next morning; speaks through an interpreter, no matter whether he or she speaks the same native language as the audience. These expectations of a *quizee* are rooted in lived experience, observations of the lives of *quizees* and many indigenous people who climbed the narrow ladder of social mobility and became *quizees*.

The *quizee* phenomenon has been in existence since the founding of Liberia. Perhaps, the only relatively new aspect of the phenomenon is *kwenen mia's* ridicule of those who return to their villages to engage in, for example, farming. During my childhood in the village, nightly hooting owls, prowling ghosts and giant bats often associated with witchcraft struck fear in me. In addition, my observations of *quizees* ill-treating my parents also struck fear in me. I wanted to get an education to become a *quizee* to avoid the treatment *quizees* meted out to my parents, but I did not know the depth of the harm *quizees* were doing to society at the time.

Today, *quizees*, nightly hooting owls, ghosts and bats do not strike fear in an up-and-coming youngster as they once did. Instead, failure, along with the ridicule associated with it, is the one thing that probably strikes the most fear. If a young adult from the village completed high school or college and failed to find employment, returning to the village, where everything is in abundance, would likely not be an option.[457] The reason is that *kwenen mia* in the village would not regard that young adult as a *quizee*, but as a failure. Defying that belief in the village results in ridicule, which begins with questions like, "Is returning to pick up the cutlass all that Torwabay can do with all that big book he learned?"[458] "Is Torwabay back because he never made it wherever he went to?" Fear of derision is one reason why young people from the village who do not have substantial benefits to show for their education, do not return.

Kwenen mia's definition of a *quizee* as well as their expectations of a *quizee* is not only the bricks and mortar of cognitive schemata driving daily decisions in the village but also at the heart of the decline of the vibrant village Mom and Dad helped build. Torwabay did not merely want to become a *quizee*. He wanted *kwenen mia* to perceive him as a *quizee*. He wanted to return to the village to prove that he was a *quizee*, but he could not do so without the benefits of his education to prove his legitimacy as a *quizee*. As a result, Torwabay remained wherever he was to avoid *kwenen mia's* ridicule.

Torwabay wanted to claim his society-conferred dignity, a particularly valued social commodity. Therefore, he remained away from the village in a place of limited opportunities he had been to work towards achieving the benefits of his education. However, other Torwabays from other villages seeking ways to achieve the benefits of their education were in the same place. The accompanying lack of opportunities led to discontent that, in part, supplied the fuel for the civil war.

Human dignity, the Catholic Church's "bedrock social teaching," holds that because "Humans were created in the image and likeness of God," "Individuals have an inherent and immeasurable worth and dignity." Thus, "Each human life is considered sacred." In a recent papal message, Pope Francis said

...it is certainly necessary to give bread to the hungry—this is an act of justice. But there is also a deeper hunger, the hunger for a happiness that only God can satisfy, the hunger for dignity. There is neither real promotion of the common good nor real human development when there is ignorance of the fundamental pillars that govern a nation, its non-material goods: life, which is a gift of God, a value always to be protected and promoted; the family, the foundation of coexistence and a remedy against social fragmentation; integral education, which cannot be reduced to the mere transmission of information for purposes of generating profit; health, which must seek the integral well-being of the person, including the spiritual dimension, essential for human balance and healthy coexistence; security, in the conviction that violence can be overcome only by changing human hearts.[459]

Mom and Dad were not Catholic; they never learned Catholic Social Teachings, yet they believed that, "Life is a gift of God, a value always to be protected and promoted." Moreover, they applied foundational and sustaining values such as work in protecting and promoting life. They instilled the value of work in me by cultivating the land and toiling in the fields because they recognized protecting and promoting life as a relay race. In bringing me up, they paid Rousseau's "Threefold debt," even though they were unlettered and had never heard of him.[460] They were poor *kwenen mia* whom *quizees* looked down upon and exploited, but they did not make excuses for paying their threefold debt.

As an ideology, *quizee* classified work by assigning earthly dignity to the professions of the upper class while deriding those of the lower class. In a country where an equitable and meritorious criterion for social mobility had never existed, that classification of professions was a condemnation and relegation of an overwhelming majority of the population to a permanent underclass. Fear of ridicule made escaping that underclass a tall order because, for the educated, doing any kind of dignified work that did not represent success was not an option. When Torwabay could not find employment, fear of ridicule prevented him from returning to the village to cultivate the land to support his family. He remained and, instead, turned to begging for hand-outs, thus losing self-respect as well as the respect of his family and the village. *Quizee* fostered "Ignorance of the fundamental pillars that govern a nation, its non-material goods" by providing Torwabay an excuse to neglect his obligations to himself, his family, and the village. Simply put, *quizee* undermined human dignity by its contribution to the decline in the culture of work.

Unlike Torwabay, I returned to the village repeatedly with tangible benefits of my education; I am free from the concerns that prevented Torwabay's return. More importantly, I returned to the village not as the *quizee* that *kwenen mia* knew; not as the *quizee* who bade cutlasses and hoes goodbye; not as the *quizee* who intimidated *kwenen mia* and refused to eat with them; not as the *quizee* who went to bed early in the evening and woke up late the next morning; not as the one who spoke to his own people through an interpreter. Indeed, I returned to the village not as the *quizee kwenen mia* wanted their children to become.

Instead, I returned to the village as a *quideh* (new qui), someone I am striving to become; someone every child in the village should grow up and strive to become; someone who works hard to get an education, plays by the rules and looks after his family; someone who works with others to improve conditions in the village; someone who represents a new definition of success: education for commitment to family and the village. In other words, a *quideh* is anyone whose education has contributed to the wellbeing of his family and improvements in living conditions in the village.

Quideh is a key to unshackle the stranglehold of *quizee*. The wellbeing of the family and improvements in the village rather than "big shot" and "protruding pot belly" are a measure of success. A "good life" or a "life of enjoyment" is a benefit of a culture of work. *Quideh* replaces *quizee*, which bears the mantle of oppression, suppression as well as social and economic strangulation and corruption.

This conversation occurred in July 2017 in Sanniquellie, Liberia. I had been thinking about the conversation for a long time, but chatters in my own family and elsewhere pushed it to the fore. The chatters pertained to why I did not send a car from the United States to Sanniquellie, Liberia, for my personal use during my October 2011 visit. Not only did the chatters echo the same predicament Torwabay faced but also, I was not immune from that predicament because I was living in the United States. If *kwenen mia* in the village expected Torwabay to show fruits of his education upon his return to the village, perhaps they expected three times more of me returning to the village from the United States.

Sending a car to Liberia for my personal use would have certainly made my life a little easier. However, the expectation of me sending a car had little to do with my convenience and everything to do with status. I was expected to prove that I had become a *quizee*. Excluding the grueling two-day Spokane-Monrovia flight, my October 2011 trip to Liberia lasted a little more than two weeks. If I had the extra money to buy a car to send to Liberia for my personal use, it would have taken more than two weeks to arrive, not to mention attempting to free a vehicle from the spider web-like bureaucracy at the Freeport of Monrovia. Notwithstanding the absurdity of that expectation, the chatters provided a window of opportunity for a larger and more meaningful conversation I could not miss.

The question of why I did not send a car to Liberia for my personal use diverted attention away from the "elephant" in the village square. I understood the drastic increase in number of children per household, but no justification for the alarming birthrate in the village made sense to me.[461] Before the 1960s, observers proffered farm labor supply as an economic justification why rural dwellers had many children. Moreover, because of high infant mortality due, in part, to the dearth of modern medicine, mothers were justified in having many children. Although there is still a need for subsistence farm labor, the availability of relatively cheap imported rice in Liberia has made the need for farm labor less acute. In addition, the availability of modern medicine has lowered infant mortality, thus negating the justification for having many children.

Make no mistake, parents in the village are no different in terms of love for their children, but I was not sure about how much thought they put into feeding and educating their children. However, the expectation that successful extended family members would educate their children was pervasive. Mezee who counted eleven children and faced similar predicament as Torwabay was a perfect posterchild of the problem.[462] Unlike Torwabay, he had a government job, but his salary was so low that he alone could not live on it. Like Torwabay, Mezee avoided returning to the village to cultivate the land to augment his government salary for fear of ridicule. His eleven children were not the exception because some parents had more than eleven children.

Due to goodwill, some children without parental support turn out to be successful human beings, but children should not have to wait for goodwill to have a childhood like the one I had. As an heir of a world I am striving to give to my own children, having large numbers of children per household and large numbers of school-age children out of school did not augur well for their futures. Therefore, when chatters about why I did not send a car to Sanniquellie for my personal use persisted, rather than a focus on the needs of children, I realized that the time for this conversation had come.

I am successful and understand the importance of showing the path of success to those who are next in line. I also believe in, "It takes a village to raise a child," but in that village, the burden of feeding and educating children is principally the parents' burden. Extended family members are only in support roles. The conversation I was inching towards recognized at least two conditions. First, social relations and social and economic structures in the village had crumbled, in part, due to the upheavals of the civil war. Second, parents with little or no capacity were not only having large numbers of children but also depending solely on successful members of their extended family to feed and educate their children. The conversation was necessary to help parents strengthen their capacity to feed, educate and give their children prospects for a better future.

The conversation was about starting anew. As a relatively successful member of the extended family, I decided to make it easier; to encourage everyone to participate in remaking our family and village. During the evening of Sunday July 30, 2017, I assembled the family under a tarpaulin tent at the front of my Mom's house. I started the conversation, talking about the prevailing mindset, which I once had: *quizees* had easy jobs, sitting around in their airconditioned offices, telling others what to do; someone with an assigned government or company vehicle had really made it; expected someone who went to graduate school in America and returned home to speak refined English, if not with an American accent; I asked others about such a person, "Did he bring a car along from America?" Those were some of the indicators of being a *quizee* at the time. I was as frivolous as one could imagine, wishing that I had a sister or brother in America, because merely having someone in America provided enough bragging rights to open doors or to get the nicest looking girls.

Upon adding to that story that I heard all the gossips in 2011 about me not sending a car to Sanniquellie from America, a burst of thunderous laughter ensued. Right then I knew I was up to something with my message. During my travels to Liberia since 2011, I observed that attention span had decreased significantly for both children and adults.[463] Except when I was on the farm, I could not find a quiet place for a conversation or complete a thought without interruptions. Therefore, once that loud laughter indicated I had everyone's attention, it was time for a show-and-tell to keep them with me.

No one saw a car with me during the days leading up to the conversation. So, when I said, "I actually brought a car from America this time," everyone looked confused. I then asked someone to go into my Mom's bedroom and bring me a sizable black hard plastic case I had brought in one of my suitcases. With anxious and attentive eyes at me, I opened the plastic case, pointed to a power saw I bought at a Walmart in Spokane, Washington and said, "This is my car." It was not the car that they were expecting. The reaction was mixed. Some looked at each other and smiled; some dropped their shoulders while others wondered what message I was trying to convey. In any case, they stayed with me.

I singled out a few people in the audience, including my sister's children as if I had not introduced enough attention grabbers. My sisters' children were having children one after the other as if it were a competition. Mezee, the poster child of the problem, was sitting right next to me. I asked him for a count of his children, but he was hesitant to tell me the actual number. Instead, he said six. Unfortunately, one of his daughters, standing barely three feet away, intervened, "Papa, we are eleven."[464] At the child's intervention, there was another round of laughter, which meant the audience was tuned in.

I turned to Mezee and asked, "Can your government salary take care of you alone, not to mention your wife or eleven children?"

"No," Mezee said.

"Do the *kwenen mia* in the village regard you as a *quizee*?" I asked.

"Yes," Mezee responded.

"Do you consider yourself as a *quizee*?" I continued.

"Yes," Mezee answered.

"Could you go to the village now and make farm to produce enough food to feed your family?" I asked. Mezee did not respond with a yes or a no. Instead, he looked at me and others in the audience and smiled. I pressed further, "Aren't you afraid to go to the village to farm because you might become a laughingstock?" "Yes," he answered and went on, "Brother, what you are saying is true."

With that, I went on and told the family gathered that I had come for the *kwenen mia* in the village to laugh at me so that Mezee and other *quizees* in the extended family do not have to be afraid to be laughed at. I meant I had come to farm the places where Mom and Dad farmed, to replant the plantation with cocoa, coffee, oil palm, fruit trees, root crops, vegetables, and the gamut.

If I could return from the United States, where the best of life's comforts exists, with all the education I had attained and subject myself to ridicule by putting my hands into the dirt, what reasons would Mezee and other *quizees* from the village provide for being afraid? The message was that remaking our family and the village had to begin with reviving the culture of work. Instead of ridicule, the thing to fear is the inability to feed one's family; the inability to pay one's children's tuition; asking others for handouts to care for one's family; the inability to pay one's taxes. The answer to all that fear is work, which is a therapy and a source of dignity and happiness. In Bursonnon, Nimba County, during the Christmas celebrations in December 1989, that was essentially the same message Mr. Karmah gave others and me. He defined who a *quideh* is.

CHAPTER 37

Conclusion

THE FLUMO CHILDREN

A S WITH EVERYTHING ELSE IN life, the Flumo children started out as a dream that translated into reality. That dream originated from my own family of five, including Mom, Dad, my two sisters and me. The family my parents built was not only the model of my ideal family, but also abounded with love and support. It gave me self-assurance early in life. The joy of growing up in that family stimulated my desire for a family like it from the get-go.

As my life took shape, the dream of having my own family took a parallel course. As a result, early influences that shaped my life also molded my dream to have my own family. For example, Mom's soliloquies about losing ten children during my formative years were the source of the five to seven children I dreamed about having. Rather than any material or pecuniary benefits, my goal of dreaming to have five to seven children was compensatory. I wanted to comfort my mom and to make up for her losses. However, before they set me along the journey for an education to escape their fate, my parents did not know that I had put something into the knapsack they gave me; they did not know I had a dream to have children to make up for Mom's losses.

Culturally, Mom and Dad knew that the family line and name came through the male child. For that purpose, they expected me to have children, but because the issue was a matter for the future, it was off Dad's radar completely. However, because mothers preoccupied themselves with the onus the culture thrust upon their male children, they never slept on the wheels. Instead, they started observing their male children early to ensure that they had the capacities to fulfill the future that depended on them. They watched out to see if their male children were interested in girls or had girlfriends. Moreover, through clandestine arrangements, mothers encouraged their male children to show proofs that they were up to the job.[465] Unfortunately, proofs mothers needed, at the appropriate age, to ensure that their male children would be ready to deliver when the time came, however, ran afoul with the doctrine of Falapa, the place where my parents took me for an education. The Catholic Church frowned on fornication, Mahn mothers' verification that their male children were up to the job.

The Catholic Church in Sanniquellie provided an important and necessary service for Mahn children and others. It educated us. I embraced St. Mary's School and made it a part of the essential me. Looking back, notwithstanding St. Mary's influence that permeates who I am to this day, I remain in the buffer between the Catholic Church and the Mahn culture, profoundly tethered to the latter more than I ever realized during my early years. It is a privilege to behold the interplay between the church and the culture in my own life and, with the births of my children, to behold the deep influence of the culture.

I wanted the focus of this book to remain on Wlah, who made something out of a wretch like me, and on His people, who helped me become the man that I am. However, because I wrote about the dream that the births of my children accomplished, I opened the door for the obvious. A man cannot bring forth a child into this world, but he can only help a woman to do so. As "we have blood in our stomachs yet vomit water," I write circumspectly in the interest of protecting others and avoiding wrong impressions. Suffice it to say that I became divorced in July of 2016.

With the exception of Miatee, who was born in Monrovia in 1984 in my absence and died as an infant while I was studying in Seoul, Korea, the Flumo children are Lila, Wonkermie, Oretha, Marsetta, Blodah, and Jo-Weh. They are the prize that Mom looked forward to. As their names show, naming a child in the culture is a shorthand method of recording current events, family history, or history in general. Thus, a name is a repository.

LILA WONMEIN FLUMO

Lila was born in Sanniquellie, Liberia. My Mom named her after my maternal aunt, Kou Wonmein, to honor her. The name Wonmein means "the dream of something." Mom was envisioning the endgame of her struggles when she named the infant Wonmein. In other words, Lila's birth was a dream or a sign of "something" to come in terms of grandchildren as consolations for the losses Mom sustained during childbirth. In addition, Mom was imagining "something" that would become of her son. Lila holds a bachelor's degree in psychology from Washington State University and a master's degree in community counseling from Argosy University. She serves as Psychosocial Services Director at Fargo Healthcare and lives with her two children, Heaven and Christian, in Chicago, Illinois.

Lila, upon graduating from Washington State University in Pullman, WA

WONKERMIE MARLENE FLUMO

Wonkermie was born in Sanniquellie, Liberia. My Mom named her too. Because Wonkermie means one who does it, meaning one who does it receives the rewards or consequences, Mom was perhaps sending an indirect message about something that happened to her. Wonkermie assumed her middle name, Marlene, in Wadesboro, North Carolina. I named her Marlene after Mrs. Marlene Richardson, wife of Mr. Frank Richardson of Wadesboro, North Carolina. It was my way of honoring and remembering Mrs. Richardson. In the "Village" of Wadesboro, North Carolina, Marsilius Flumo did not raise Wonkermie alone. Mrs. Marlene Richardson's hands helped raise Lila, Wonkermie, and Oretha. On Saturdays, she took them home and brought them back in the evenings with their hair done for church and the rest of the week. On other occasions, she brought them home with new clothes. Indeed, "it takes a village to raise a child." Currently, Wonkermie works for Cobb County Board of Commissioners. In the meantime, her long-held dream of owning a business is taking off with Spice Pot, which serves Liberian cuisines. Wonkermie has three children, Jeremiah, Joshua, and Josiah, and lives with her husband, Mr. Albert Nah, in Marietta, Georgia.

Wonkermie, on her wedding in 2015 in Marietta, GA

ORETHA ELIZABETH FLUMO

Oretha was born in Monrovia, Liberia. I named Oretha after Oretha Nyah to honor and remember her for the courageous role she played in the circumstances during the child's birth. Oretha Nyah is the woman who helped me while I was at the University of Liberia while struggling with accommodation and food issues. Oretha serves as senior facility technician at McKesson Corporation, a medical supplies company, and lives with her two children, Massillon Boyd, Jr., and Kendall, in Aurora, Illinois.

Oretha Elizabeth Flumo in Aurora, Illinois

MARSETTA MBAMIE FLUMO

Marsetta was born in Monrovia, Liberia. I named Marsetta. Mbamie, her middle name, is Mahn, and it means "for the sake of this person, I have dignity."

**With Marsetta, upon graduating from Eastern
Washington University in Cheney, WA**

BLODAH MARSILIUS FLUMO, JR.

Blodah was born in Spokane, Washington. I named Blodah after my Dad
and me. Blodah literally means Blo's father, where Blo means banana or
plantain. Mahns believe in reincarnation. I believe my Dad, whom I left in
the village in December 1989 and never saw again until his death in May
1999, was the one who came to me as my son. Blodah is currently in college.

Blodah at 18 years old

Jo-Weh Margaret Flumo

Jo-Weh was born in Spokane, Washington. Her mom, Ms. Margaret Tumbay, ostensibly dispensed equal opportunity in naming her. She took sections of two people's names and created Jo-Weh. She took "Jo," the first two letters out of Josephine, her mom, and "Weh," the last three letters of Kporweh, my Mom. She then came up with Jo-Weh by joining the letters with a hyphen. Jo-Weh graduates from high school in June 2021.

Jo-Weh, Bowdish Middle School Cross-Country Team, Spokane, WA

Wonkermie, Lila, Oretha, and me in Laurinburg, NC in 1997

Blodah, Jo-Weh and me, Spokane, WA, 2003

Becoming a Man

I now see the process of becoming a man clearer than before because I can look back at the village, my upbringing and life experience. Reaching a certain, perhaps above average, level of awareness as a self-willing being whose purpose is more than self-fulfilling is becoming a man. Travels, education, and losses, including deaths and divorce have been hallmarks of my journey of becoming a man. Travels from the village to Sanniquellie and Monrovia and then to South Korea and the United States made me see and experience the world through different cultural lenses. While education, in a sense, short-circuits travels, I traveled around the world in pursuit of an education and throughout my life, I have either been a student or an educator.

I fought to keep death out of my mind. I pretended it never existed. However, when its cruel hands struck, it permanently lowered Dad, Mom, and my sister's shoulders into their resting places. Death ripped away irreplaceable protective shields; it destroyed platforms my feet rested upon to reach higher. On the other hand, divorce was a firing squad I did not seek to face. However, I faced it intentionally because anyone who refused to recognize the worth of the life Wlah gave me did not deserve to share it. Deaths and divorce broke the hard scales that covered me and enabled journeying on more aware along the road to becoming a man.

Death of a Father

Dad knew he would grow old. Perhaps he looked forward to an old age of relative leisure and not the hard life he had as a child. Out of tradition, he paid the nonnegotiable "Threefold debt" Rousseau also described to create a better future for me.[466] Perhaps paying that debt to make me a productive member of society was an act of self-interest because it also amounted to paying into his social security, retirement, and Medicare. However, while children were the sources of their parents' old age benefits, such things as social security, retirement or Medicare benefits were nonexistent in the culture. Luckily, the same culture that obligated him to pay that debt also conferred upon him the right to expect to cash in upon getting old. Since there was no certificate of insurance or signed legal document to compel me to pay those benefits to Dad in his old age, my becoming a man was the only assurance Dad had that he would receive his benefits. Hence, recognizing that obligation without a reminder was an essential aspect of becoming a man in the culture. Moreover, fulfilling that obligation was one way everyone in the culture knew that a man's children had become successful.

Since childhood, I had never seen my dad dance. However, when I traveled to the village shortly after my return from the United States in May 1987, I saw him dance in a characteristic style. Wearing a stripy traditional gown stretched to the end of his forearms, Dad raised both hands as if he were attempting to hug someone. He turned left and right, moved forward slowly and repeatedly. His face beamed with joy because I had returned home safely, but Dad's exuberance conveyed more than his joy for my safe return. Perhaps he felt that the time had come to receive his old age benefits and for others in the village to give him the recognition he deserved for his son's success.

Unfortunately, Dad's hopes for his benefits did not materialize. The civil war erupted and permanently separated us. Attempts to fulfill my obligation from afar in the United States while I was in limbo were largely an exercise in futility.[467] Western Union and MoneyGram were not in Liberia at the time. Therefore, sending money by others to my parents amid the deprivation of the civil war was comparable to throwing an unbound stack of dollar bills to someone across a swift river. I ignored the risks and sent money by others to my parents merely for the psychological relief of having done something, but I could not wish away the crushing guilt of failing to appreciably pay Dad's benefits.

Before the civil war, illness seldom claimed much attention in the village. Unless someone was at the verge of dying, there was little or no urgency. An illness was something someone contracted instantly; something an enemy "threw" at someone; something someone acquired through involvement in witchcraft; something that old age generated, in which case the reaction was, "It is his or her time." The civil war did not create indifference to illness in the village, but its mayhem and death toll numbed the senses to external distress. If someone's illness did not show dramatic symptoms such as swelling, neighbors paid little or no attention.

My separation from Dad due to the civil war shut the door to receiving his benefits. Indeed, separation was one of the forces that trapped him. If the culture that waited until someone was at the point of death or had a swollen and aching body part was nonexistent before the civil war, perhaps my Dad would have lived longer than he did. Separation followed that culture. Next, the civil war's unimaginable death toll numbed the villagers' senses and made the prospect of an elderly person's death nothing out of the ordinary. The change in the village whereby the norm of caring for the elderly lost its hold, not to mention the "it is his or her time" reaction to an elderly person in distress did not help. Most of all, Dad was no ordinary elderly man. He had a successful son in America! No one contacted me about Dad's illness, yet everyone assumed help was automatic and on its way.

Eventually, news about my Dad reached me in May 1999 in Spokane, Washington. It was not good; he had passed away. Dad helped create the future and life I live, yet he did not see that future. Sadly, I, his successful son in America, failed to deliver his benefits; his "social security" checks, "retirement" or "health benefits." Despite my commitment to the norm of taking care of my elderly parents, I did not provide relief when he was ill. Moreover, when he died, and the question, "Where is his son?" was raised, I was not present to uphold my obligation; to give him the fitting burial he deserved. Only Wlah's assurances comfort me.

DEATH OF A MOTHER

Death was a taboo in the culture because it is terrifying and unavoidable. The Mahns even call it "ugly thing" or "mysterious thing." However, Mom was an exception to the culture's silence on mortality. With an uncharacteristic ease in talking about her own death, she stripped the phenomenon of its frightening power. In tape-recorded messages she sent me, detailing family tree, inheritance, and where and how she wanted to be laid to rest, Mom prepared for death before it arrived. Moreover, she had a will, an uncommon practice in the culture.[468]

Before traveling to Accra, Ghana, in August 2007 to meet with Mom, almost eighteen years had passed since I left her in the village in December 1989. Marauding rebels with AK-47 machine guns, hunger and diseases turned Liberia into no-man's-land, yet Wlah protected and sustained her. With that miracle, I thought Wlah had looked upon me with more favor than I deserved. Therefore, my prayer all along was that He would grant me one more chance to see Mom before she passed away. Wlah granted me that opportunity to see Mom in Accra, Ghana, in August 2007. I carried notepads, a cassette recorder with accessories and a videotape recorder. I wrote down questions about everything I wanted to know I could think of, including the village, extended family, and matters she raised in her tape-recorded messages. She answered all my questions and re-emphasized pieces of advice she had given before. I went to Ghana believing that our meeting might be my last time with my mom. After all, I had asked Wlah for one more chance to see her.

Four years after Mom returned to Liberia from Ghana, she became ill in October 2011. For that reason, I returned to Liberia, for the first time in twenty-one years, to see her. As with my Ghana trip in 2007, I thought the October 2011 trip might be our last time together. I had not told Mom or anybody that I was returning home to see her. So, I took her by complete surprise at the George Way Harley Hospital in Sanniquellie, where she was receiving treatment. The time Mom and I spent together worked wonders not only for her but also for me. It provided healing and lifted our spirits. With shared hopefulness, when the time to return to the United States arrived, not only was I renewed but also Mom looked better than I had seen her upon my arrival in Sanniquellie, Liberia. Moreover, like a thirsty deer seeking water in a meadow, Mom longed for her grandchildren, particularly the last two, Blodah, her only grandson from me, and Jo-Weh, my last child, both of whom she had never seen. In July 2012, Wlah partially granted her wish when I took Blodah along to Liberia.

MOM'S GOODBYE

During my July 2013 visit with Mom in Sanniquellie, Liberia, she did something different from my last three visits, including the one in Accra, Ghana. I remember vividly what Mom did on Tuesday evening, July 23, 2013, the eve of my return to Monrovia on my way back to the United States, but the significance of it did not dawn on me until she died. On that evening, Mom asked to speak to me along with Mr. Joseph Meatay. We sat on the floor in her bedroom, facing each other. Mom's back was towards her bedroom doorway, Mr. Meatay was in the center of the room while I leaned against Mom's king-sized bed, with my feet stretched on the floor.

First, Mom assured me that she was not about to die. "You need not worry," she said. "Since you live far away [in the United States] and I do not know when death would take me away," she went on, "I want you to hear me." She thanked me profusely for being a good son and noted that I exceeded every expectation of a son she had. Mom then returned to mortality, "Since death is unpredictable, I do not want you to cry and worry if you hear that I have passed away." She encouraged me to take care of my family and sisters.

Next, Mom used a regular enamel-plated metal drinking cup and scooped cold water to perform the same libation Dad performed whenever I was leaving the village to go to college or to travel abroad. She first swished with the water and drank it. The second time around, she swished with about a quarter mouthful of water and sprayed it into my palms. She then petitioned Wlah to strengthen me and to ensure that every endeavor I undertake turns out to be a success. With my partially wet palms, I covered my face and then rubbed my hair and face with both palms. I made occasional eye contact as Mom performed the ritual because I knew that Mom was saying her goodbye as in goodbye when someone is about to die. However, momentarily, because I was afraid, I took refuge in her assurance at the outset and the ordinariness with which she spoke. Instead, I tried to give her something, my July 2014 visit, to look up to.

I was not as cavalier as Mom was towards death. I did not want to entertain the likelihood of her passing before my next visit or any time soon. However, the thought was like a mosquito net over me. I could not get it off without touching it. So, on the morning of July 24, 2013, when Mom and I turned to each other for a hug and goodbye, I looked at her face with a laser focus. I wanted to burn that moment indelibly into my memory. That encounter turned out to be our last time together. Moments after, Mr. Joseph Meatay took two photographs of Mom and me, and I left Sanniquellie thereafter with a heavy heart.

In 2013, Mom scripted her goodbye message magnificently. In addition, she couched it in motherly love and delivered it gracefully and beautifully. However, upon receiving the news in the United States that she had slipped away from the face of the earth on Wednesday, January 8, 2014, it felt like my heart fell into my abdomen. Indeed, it felt like an executioner pulled a lever and let me fall through a trapdoor of a gallows. "That's my Mom, that could not be, she could not leave without at least one word to me," I recall saying to myself. "Without at least one word?" Boy, what "one word"? What about her goodbye on the evening of July 23, 2013? What else could she have said?

The child in me wanted Mom to always be there. I could not imagine her absence because no level of preparation and conditioning could ready anyone for losing such an extraordinary mother. Upon regaining my composure, I not only grasped the profundity of the evening of July 23, 2013, with my mom but also remember asking Wlah for only one more chance to see my mom. However, in His infinite grace, He granted me not one, not two, not three, but four opportunities to see Mom before she passed away!

Mom lived fifteen years after Dad passed away. Unlike Dad, she received a measure of her "benefits."[469] More importantly, when she died and the question, "Where is her son?" was asked, I was there, next to her remains, to answer. Upon receiving the news of Mom's passing, I flew from Spokane, Washington, and arrived in Liberia on January 11, 2014. Six days later, I laid Mom to rest in the village. I brought her passport, family photographs and other important documents with me to the United States because a mom never dies.

Bidding Mom goodbye to return to the U.S. in late January 2014

Mom was sick for a long time, but she lived a full, long, and exemplary life. She said that I was a good son, but I deserve no praise because when she fell on the farm in the village and dislocated her right wrist while I was in college, no one was near to pull and put her wrist back in place. It remained dislocated throughout the remainder of her life. I failed to pay for the care to repair her wrist. So, Mom, if you can hear me in heaven, I am sorry for failing to take care of your wrist. This is your story, the one you wanted me to write as early as elementary school, so I won't forget. I do not know of a better, caring, and loving mother than you. I love you, Mom.

"DEATH" OF A FAMILY

It is often said, "What we know of love comes from home." The same, I think, can be said of compassion. In addition to instilling in me the value of life, Mom and Dad also showed me love and compassion. They helped shape my idea of a family, except I did not appreciate the energy that starting, maintaining, and sustaining a family would require. I romanticized having a family, thinking it would be happily-ever-after marriage.

Having a family remains as herculean a task as ever. Yet, in it I found a purpose that guided Mom and Dad in contributing to the vibrancy of the village. I longed for a family like my parents', but the template they used was situated within and conditioned by a culture wherein maintaining peace and stability superseded individual interest or happiness. I learned that the longer a man's Adam's apple protruded outward, the more peaceful or stable his home was. The extent of a man's Adam's apple reflected his patience and energy in maintaining and sustaining his family. My parents were no angels, but I never heard them fight. Dad never hit or put Mom down and vice versa. Even though it was by the extent of Dad's Adam's apple that peace or stability at home was determined, the culture expected him and Mom to "swallow" their angsts about any issues for the sake of the family.

In America, outside the confines of the culture, I remained dutiful to its precepts. I "swallowed" every putdown and outright abuse intentionally. The Adam's apple extended until further extension was impossible. The curtain was drawn in the face of my call for reconciliation, yet my heart never grew shrilled; I never stopped loving. The moment of reckoning was when I could not entrust the security of my person, dignity, and reputation to the other person. I quit maintaining a façade of peace and stability to satisfy the culture and did something, in less than one year after Mom died, that I would not wish upon anyone. I filed for divorce. In doing that, I drew strength from Mom's courage in facing death. I had no doubts whatsoever that Wlah would be with me every step of the way.

THROUGH IT ALL

I am grateful to Wlah for my parents, who set me along this incredible journey in 1966. His unbelievable people enriched my life in countless and immeasurable ways along the journey. He let me experience disappointments, heartaches, and tears, not to mention struggles and hunger. Every success as well as good thing in my life is because of Wlah's incomprehensible grace. I know He is good because He gave me a loving, praying, and faithful mother. No praise or tear of gratitude can suffice to thank Him.

FAMILY TREE

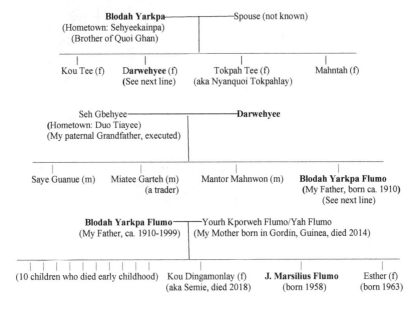

My Parents and Siblings

Blodah Yarkpa————————Spouse (not known)
(Hometown: Sehyeekainpa)
(Brother of Quoi Ghan)

| Kou Tee (f) | **Darwehyee** (f) | Tokpah Tee (f) | Mahntah (f) |
| | **(See next line)** | (aka Nyanquoi Tokpahlay) | |

Seh Gbehyee————————**Darwehyee**
(Hometown: Duo Tiayee)
(My paternal Grandfather, executed)

Saye Guanue (m)	Miatee Garteh (m)	Mantor Mahnwon (m)	**Blodah Yarkpa Flumo**
	(a trader)		**(My Father, born ca. 1910)**
			(See next line)

Blodah Yarkpa Flumo————Yourh Kporweh Flumo/Yah Flumo
(My Father, ca. 1910-1999) (My Mother born in Gordin, Guinea, died 2014)

| (10 children who died early childhood) | Kou Dingamonlay (f) | **J. Marsilius Flumo** | Esther (f) |
| | (aka Semie, died 2018) | **(born 1958)** | (born 1963) |

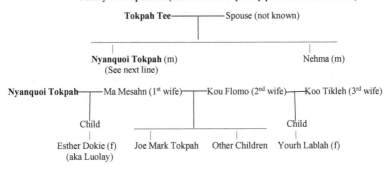

Family of Tokpah Tee (sister of Darwehyee my paternal Grandmother)

Tokpah Tee————————Spouse (not known)

| **Nyanquoi Tokpah** (m) | Nehma (m) |
| (See next line) | |

Nyanquoi Tokpah————Ma Mesahn (1st wife)————Kou Flomo (2nd wife)————Koo Tikleh (3rd wife)

Child   Child

| Esther Dokie (f) | Joe Mark Tokpah | Other Children | Yourh Lablah (f) |
| (aka Luolay) | | | |

509

ENDNOTES

¹ My people refers to the Mahns, the people who speak the Mahn language in Liberia as well as in nearby Guinea. Mano is the other name for Mahn. Mahns are a part of the larger Mande group.

² Mom is Yourh Kporweh Flumo, but she preferred Yah Flumo.

³ Yehyeelakpoa is my home village. Henceforth, I will refer to it as "The Village."

⁴ Blodah literally means Blo's father, where the "Blo" means banana or plantain. Flumo is a given name after initiation in the Mahn Secret Society known as the Poro. Guanue is Mahn for "A man has come," Miatee, "In people's absence," and Mahnwon, "Mahn business."

⁵ Shifting cultivation is a method of farming in which the land is cleared, burnt, cultivated, and then left to fallow for several years. The farmer moves to another area for the next farming season.

⁶ "Nandin Bo" was Uncle Miatee Garteh's pronunciation of Fernando Po (The Fernando Po Islands). He stopped short of telling me why he asked about the Fernando Po Islands. Perhaps he was afraid of telling me a painful story as well.

⁷ "Quizee," meaning "Old qui," is a word I coined out of "Qui." Its opposite is "Quideh," meaning "New qui." Later, I will explain why I coined quizee and quideh. The linguistic origin of "Qui" is unknown. The Mahns, Dans and other ethnic groups of Liberia refer to a "Civilized person" as "Qui." At the outset, the freed slaves from the United States who founded Liberia designated themselves as the "Civilized" and distinguished themselves from the natives whom they designated as "Primitive" or "Heathens." Thus, "Qui" originally referred to the settlers and their descendants known as Americo-Liberians. Over time, anyone associated with Americo-Liberians who exhibited their mannerisms, acted on their behalf, projected, or exercised power was referred to as a "Qui." Although, as cited in *Brothers and Strangers*, "The term was used for black and white,"

511

in Liberia, "*Qui*" is a charged term not only because its meaning includes "A civilized person" and power with its negative connotation but also a reminder of Liberia's painful history.

[8] See Ibrahim Sundiata's treatment of the subject under the heading "Abuse," in *Brothers and Strangers: Black Zion, Black Slavery, 1914–1940*, pp. 79–96.

[9] The poison was made from the bark of a tree the Mahns call "Glee."

[10] "Fehyee" is Mahn for a protrusion-laden rough and spiny vine-type plant.

[11] Webster's New World Dictionary and Thesaurus (2002).

[12] Americo-Liberians are descendants of black settlers from the United States who, in the 1820s, founded what is now known as Liberia. They are also known in Liberia as Congo people.

[13] "Yehmgbehkutu" is a method of torture tax collectors used widely during my father's time.

[14] The tibia, one of the two bones that form the skeleton of the leg, is also called the shinbone. Fibula, the other bone also called calf bone, is smaller, and it is lateral to the tibia.

[15] Gordin is Mahn for "Under the kola tree". It is also known as Toulemou.

[16] Powerful French colonial masters seized the territory with the acquiescence of a weak Liberian government.

[17] There are Dans (Yacoubas), Krahns, and Greboes on both sides of the Liberian-Ivorian border while there are Kissi and Mende peoples on both sides of the Liberian-Sierra Leonean border.

[18] The camel's back is a reference to Dad's three elder brothers' decision to flee Duo Tiayee. "*Ka kporyee neehinsuhn*" was an infamous house/hut tax the Monrovia government imposed and collected even after a hut had been demolished.

[19] Konneh, Augustine. "The Hut Tax in Liberia: The High Costs of Integration." *Journal of the GAH*, XVI, 1996, p. 44., archives.columbusstate.edu/gah1996/50.pdf.

[20] Mahn people inhabited the area across the St. John River the family relocated to. In principle, due to the presence of Mahn people, the area was a part of Liberia, but in reality, French colonial masters exercised influence in the area. For this reason, Mahn people who were further away from the St. John River and closer to French colonial influence referred to Mahns who crossed the St. John River and came to their side as refugees.

[21] I knew about Uncle Miatee Garteh's travels. He took me along on one occasion in 1973. We traveled from the village to Granwie, a small town in the Ivory Coast across the border with Liberia. We carried about a fifty-pound bag of coffee to sell. He had heard that the price of coffee in the Ivory Coast was better than that in Liberia. Cars were plying the Sanniquellie-Karnplay highway, but we walked the entire distance; it did not make any sense. The price of coffee was not better than it was in Liberia. I realized he just enjoyed the adventures of travels.

22 A recognition that motherhood, depicted by a baby on its mother's back and in its mother's bosom when it is being breastfed, is a full-time business, which requires full attention.

23 Mom was sick and unable to produce breastmilk after Esther, my younger sister, was born. She fed the baby with baby formula, which I used to steal until Mom caught on to my shenanigan.

24 Patrick's mother, Kpolo Zohnpu, was sick and unable to breastfeed him.

25 Mom knew how to live; she intentionally taught people how to live.

26 Sometime between July 2013, the last time Mom and I were together, and January 8, 2014, the day she died, Mom gave Esther a roll of woven yarn to give me upon my return to Liberia after her death. The roll of one hundred percent cotton cloth was an inheritance she made from her own yarn. Esther forgot to turn over the woven yarn to me while I was in the village for Mom's burial. I could not remind her because I was not aware of the existence of the woven yarn. While I was in Liberia in July 2017, Esther turned over the woven yarn, indicating that Mom had instructed her to do so upon my return after her death. I was flabbergasted.

27 "Saha" (mat) has the same name as the plant used in making it. The plant grows in virgin forest/jungle.

28 Mom apparently figured that waging and winning such a fight would be a Pyrrhic victory (Victory won at a great cost, named after King Pyrrhus of Epirus); that her son's education might be the principal casualty.

29 Lappa is also known as "Wrapper". It is a wrap-around cloth that Liberian or African women wear and often carry their babies in it on their backs.

30 In this particular instance, I am referring to Liberian culture.

31 "Your something" was a profanity Mom used that is not appropriate to include in a book.

32 The naming order for boys is: Saye, Nyan, Paye, Wuo, Zarwolo, Fohn, Laywehyee and Saye Payleh (Saye two) while the naming order for girls is: Kou, Yah, Yei, Nohn, Koo, Fania and Kou Payleh (Kou two).

33 "Empty-handed" means without a child. She lost a child one after the other.

34 "Wlahkerwon"means something that was done by God.

35 Gbeakeh Flo was from Zoe Luapah, Nimba County, Liberia. He was a tall and fair-skinned old man. He was steep into native medicines. Every time he went into the bush, he came out with a bark, seed, root, leaf, or a different kind of plant part, which he used to cure a certain illness.

36 Henceforth, culture will mean the Mahn culture.

37 I ignored that warning and paid a heavy price, the shadow of which will loom over me for the rest of my life.

38 Project refers to my education.

39 Farming activities such as broadcasting seeds, plowing, weeding, and harvesting were considered women's jobs while cutting the bush, felling trees, and building fences around the farm were considered men's domain.

40 Americo-Liberians or the Americo-Liberian-led government.

[41] "Falapa" is the Catholic Priest's home or where he lives. "Fala" is the Mahn pronunciation for the English word "Father." "Pa" is Mahn for "Home."

[42] The forced recruitment of natives was a fraudulent scheme akin to slavery. The practice eventually led to the resignation of President Charles D. B. King of Liberia.

[43] "Bonbon" was a special kind of candy, at the time imported from the Republic of Guinea.

[44] In Mahn "Tea" may also mean Lipton Tea; but in general, "tea" means breakfast, which can be anything like rice, plantain, eddoes, or yams. "Bony," a type of fish, is widely eaten in Liberia. It is better eaten dried because it is very bony.

[45] Rapper Heavy D was Dwight Arrington Myers. The line is from the album "Heavy D & The Boyz- Peaceful Journey" and the single "Is It Good to You".

[46] Place is a reference to the village.

[47] Mini is Mahn for a circular cushion made of any soft material to lessen the effect of carrying something heavy on the head.

[48] Burkarmehin means Bur (stream) that flows behind the house.

[49] War during Americo-Liberian territorial expansion in the hinterland.

[50] "Poho" is a rare and protected tree species; its fruit contains latex, harvested and used for bird hunting.

[51] "Bayhee" is a white clay that Mahns use for whitewashing their houses or huts.

[52] "Karlaylay" is the woman who owns the house, a title reserved for the head wife.

[53] Mahn for a child who walks about often returns home only to see his mother's corpse.

[54] Tobacco especially made of harvested and dried shoots of tobacco plants wrapped in a brown paper.

[55] "Firestone" washing soap was named this way perhaps because it was the same soap that the Firestone Rubber Company, the world's largest rubber plantation at the time, issued to its workers as part of their benefits. "Blehbleh" was an off-white home-made soap by Mandingo women. It was probably named this way because of its texture or softness.

[56] Gbano tree is a shade tree with edible fruits that look like a miniature Saturn or two saucers bound together.

[57] "Konoh" is food (Mahn dialect spoken in the Sanniquellie area).

[58] A "kainkain" is a flat-bottom aluminum pan with a circular rim. It can hold about one and a half pounds of rice. An undisturbed kainkain of rice looks like an inverted cone above the rim of a seven-inch diameter pan. The name kainkain arose apparently from the sound the pan produces when hit repeatedly with a piece of metal.

[59] "Kafir" is an Arabic term meaning 'infidel,' 'nonbeliever,'or 'pagan' used to put down those who reject Islam.

[60] See Ibrahim Sundiata's discussion of the issue in Chapter 7, "Enterprise in Black and White," in *Brothers and Strangers: Black Zion, Black Slavery, 1914-1940*, pp. 213-214.

[61] The late President Samuel Doe deserves credit for recognizing Mandingoes as citizens of Liberia. In 1990, he publicly declared Mandingoes as citizens of Liberia at the Monrovia City Hall. However, his motive was suspicious. Apparently, he needed their support after Mr. Charles Taylor launched the civil war in Nimba County with the involvement of some Nimba citizens.

[62] Krahn is one of Liberia's ethnic groups. Krahns are from Grand Gedeh and Nimba Counties, but they are also one of the ethnic groups in the Ivory Coast.

[63] Father Michael Francis (later Archbishop Michael Francis) was the founder of St. Mary's School in Sanniquellie, Liberia. Bishop Francis died in Monrovia, Liberia on May 19, 2013.

[64] Magdalene Brewer was one of the "Mission" girls, the ones who lived in the girls' dormitory and had three meals a day.

[65] Which uncircumcised person lifted me off the uncircumcised person I knocked to the ground?

[66] Mahn for "we came to ensure that the woman remains with 'Paay;'" Paay being any man in dispute with his wife.

[67] The two people in Mom's audience as she often talked along journeys to places were Wlah and me. On those journeys, I was the only visible person with her. I knew that she was not directing her talks to me because I often heard her call Wlah's name.

[68] Dad did not know the love of his Mom because he lost her at an early age.

[69] Members of the United Brothers Fraternity (UBF), a feared Liberian secret society.

[70] The national examination does not exist anymore. The West African Examinations replaced it.

[71] In Liberia, to refer to someone as "old man" is a sign of respect.

[72] It is only when one's hand is full of rice that one's stomach can be filled.

[73] This was one reason why Mahn women despised barrenhood. To be a barren meant all eyes would turn one's way for blame if anything bad such as a terrible illness befell someone, or an unexplainable death occurred. A barren was always guilty of evil intent. She was the cause of not having children because she used her womb for witchcraft activities in the spirit world.

[74] Mr. Dahn and Koukou were not being generous for cutting us the slack for working on their farm. Their farm was in the village, far away from Sanniquellie. Ma Mesahn's farm was closer to Sanniquellie and, as the custodian of the family house and Joe Mark Tokpah's Dad's head wife, she made us work on her farm.

[75] "Bini" is jungle, a high forest area between Gborpa, Cousin Joe Mark Tokpah's village, and the Liberian border with Guinea.

[76] Source of information (date of birth, departure from Liberia to Switzerland, date of sunset, and place of burial.): Father Voisard's obituary. Mr. Cooper

Davay obtained it from some French members of his parish in Columbus, Ohio. Mr. Davay worked with Father Voisard at the time of the founding of the Immaculate Heart of Mary Parish in Ganta, Liberia and once served as an altar boy in the church.

77 "White Father." *Encyclopedia Britannica*, Encyclopedia Britannica, Inc., www.britannica.com/topic/White-Fathers. They are called "White Fathers" because of the garments that members wear.

78 "Histoire Kerlois." *Kerlois*, www.kerlois.fr/copie-de-agenda-1.

79 Father Paul Voisard's obituary.

80 "Novitiate [Meaning of]." *Legionaries of Christ, Cheshire*, Legionaries of Christ, lccheshire.org/novitiate.

81 Father Paul Voisard's obituary.

82 Pike, John. "Military." *Ivory Coast - French Relations*, www.globalsecurity.org/military/world/africa/iv-forrel-fr.htm.

83 Dash, Leon. "Guinea's Longtime President, Ahmed Sekou Touré, Dies." *The Washington Post*, WP Company, 28 Mar. 1984, www.washingtonpost.com/archive/local/1984/03/28/guineas-longtime-president-ahmed-sekou-toure-dies/18f31685-878c-4759-8028-3bef7fbc568b/?utm_term=.2035e3d7b762.

84 Pace, Eric. "AHMED SEKOU TOURE, A RADICAL HERO." *The New York Times*, The New York Times, 28 Mar. 1984, www.nytimes.com/1984/03/28/obituaries/ahmed-sekou-toure-a-radical-hero.html.

85 The "Colonial bed" was a shell game or trap to break the backs of the people of the French colonies.

86 "Sékou Touré." *Encyclopedia Britannica*, Encyclopedia Britannica, Inc., www.britannica.com/biography/Sekou-Toure.

87 Dash, Leon. "Guinea's Longtime President, Ahmed Sekou Touré, Dies." *The Washington Post*, WP Company, 28 Mar. 1984, www.washingtonpost.com/archive/local/1984/03/28/guineas-longtime-president-ahmed-sekou-toure-dies/18f31685-878c-4759-8028-3bef7fbc568b/?utm_term=.2035e3d7b762.

88 Father Paul Voisard's obituary.

89 Ibid.

90 Father Paul Voisard's obituary.

91 Conversation with Mr. Cooper Davay, an altar boy who worked with Father Voisard at the founding of the Immaculate Heart of Mary in Ganta, Liberia.

92 Father Paul Voisard's obituary.

93 King James Version.

94 You who camp out for other people's dinner, go away for once so that we too can eat and be filled.

95 A reference to the wild and funny jokes about Americans we heard growing up in Sanniquellie. The story was that if one visited an American home at dinnertime unannounced, one would receive a newspaper to read while the family had dinner.

96 Literal translation is "inside the stomachs of those guys is ugly," meaning those guys are mean.

[97] Definition of an individual by former American business executive and management as well as organizational theorist Chester I. Barnard: Barnard, C. I. (1968). The functions of the executive (30th Ed.). Cambridge: Harvard University Press, p.12.

[98] Flumo Tokpah, also known as Saye Gbehlay, was Uncle Saye Guanue's first son. Saye Guanue was Dad's eldest brother.

[99] Yekepa was a mining city once described as "America" in Liberia because of its bright streetlights, paved streets, and buses; the road to Yekepa was much wider and well-conditioned. Karnplay is a city along the highway to the border with Ivory Coast; the road to Karnplay was much narrower and infrequently conditioned.

[100] Palm tree leaves look like nature's hairdo.

[101] The April 12, 1980 Revolution overthrew the government of Liberia and resulted in the assassination of President William R. Tolbert, Jr.

[102] Mom kept all my report cards from first grade through 12th grade except one that got lost during the war.

[103] Pumping tire involved crossing one's hands, with the right hand holding the left ear and vice versa and squatting and standing repeatedly until one lost the ability to stand.

[104] Before the April 1980 Revolution, some, if not most, of the communal lands deeded to individuals were acquired under dubious circumstances.

[105] "Guan" is Mahn for financial club. It is also known in Liberia as "Susu." Susu remains popular across Liberia and Liberian communities in the United States and elsewhere.

[106] "Salah" is Mahn for sacrifice. It involves slaughtering a chicken or sheep to thank Wlah or ask for His intervention.

[107] Lamco was an iron ore mining joint venture, involving Liberia, Sweden, and the United States.

[108] The rebel invasion of Liberia on December 24, 1989 forced the missionaries to flee Sanniquellie, Liberia.

[109] "No man is an island, entire of itself; every man is a piece of the continent, a part of the main. If a clod be washed away by the sea, Europe is the less, as well as if a promontory were, as well as if a manor of thy friend's or of thine own were: any man's death diminishes me, because I am involved in mankind, and therefore never send to know for whom the bell tolls; it tolls for thee." John Donne, English poet (1572-1631).

[110] Guankarnue is a name given to a Mahn baby after its parents have been longing for a boy for a long time and still want to have more boys. The literal translation is "Men/males should come."

[111] The sectors of Sanniquellie economy included education, commerce, agriculture, transportation, manufacturing, and the local government.

[112] Sanniquellie did not have enough resources to sustain its large student population. Hunger, particularly during the rainy season, forced students

to dropout. Students who came from the far corners of Nimba County and elsewhere in Liberia were particularly at risk of dropping out.

[113] The County Superintendent resides at the Executive Grounds. It is also the place where the President of Liberia resides upon a visit to the city.

[114] The checks for "Aliens" or "Foreigners" were in many instances a pretext for extorting money, doused with prejudices many Liberians shared against Mandingoes. Incidentally, the driver of the taxi was a Mandingo man.

[115] "You have the right to remain silent. Anything you say can and will be used against you in a court of law. You have the right to speak to an attorney and to have an attorney present during any questioning" (Miranda v. Arizona, 1966). A language in the 1984 Constitution of Liberia similar to Miranda Rights states: Every person suspected or accused of committing a crime shall immediately upon arrest be informed in detail of the charges, of the right to remain silent and of the fact that any statement made could be used against him in a court of law. Such person shall be entitled to counsel at every stage of the investigation and shall have the right not to be interrogated except in the presence of counsel. Any admission or other statements made by the accused in the absence of such counsel shall be deemed inadmissible as evidence in a court of law (Article 21, Section (c), 1984 Constitution of Liberia).

[116] "June passing by July"is a saying in Liberia in reference to a person who passes by someone he knows without saying hello. In that personification, which casts June and July as running a race, June must have been running faster than July to arrive before July since June arrives before July on the calendar.

[117] "Elephant" is a reference to a subject that people do not discuss openly.

[118] Yeeleeway is a "voice" of a tree but not a live tree. Instead, the sound of an African drum. The drum is made by hollowing a tree trunk and covering one end with a deer, sheep, or goatskin.

[119] The temperature was about 50 degrees Fahrenheit or a little lower, but the sun shone brightly, and the weather was beautiful. The Mahns called the cold dry season "Gbapehn," meaning the season to begin cutting the bush for farms. The cold dry winds (Harmattan Winds) blew during the day while, at night, they ceased, and tree branches and leaves stood still. My lips dried and split.

[120] Samuel Gaye (deceased) was a tall, soft-spoken, fair-skinned, and handsome man. He once served as Clan Chief of Gbein Clan, which included my home village of Yehyeelakpoa, for a long time prior to the area assuming district status.

[121] I am not sure whether the perception about Mandingoes'place in Liberia among the general population has changed significantly.

[122] The expression "Gronna boys" means grown-up boys, but it has a negative connotation in Liberia. It often means members of street gangs or petty thieves.

[123] United States meaning the image of America I had in my head from reading books and looking at pictures in magazines, including Jet.

[124] "RH" stands for Roberts' Hall, named after Joseph Jenkins Roberts, Liberia's first president. J. J. Roberts founded Liberia College in 1862 and

became its first president. Liberia College became the University of Liberia in 1952.

[125] Luogon, man, you need to stay focused on the work you are going to do.

[126] The splashing of cold water four times showed that a male was the recipient of the blessing. If I had been a female, the splashing of cold water would have happened three times.

[127] The rice was going down the throat faster than normal and no one asked for water to force it down.

[128] President William R. Tolbert, Jr. was the first Liberian president I truly admired and had an opportunity to see.

[129] The colleges of the University of Liberia included the college of Business and Public Administration; Liberia College, the college of Liberal Arts; the college of Science and Technology; the College of Agriculture and Forestry; William V. S. Tubman Teachers' College; and the A. M. Dogliotti College of Medicine.

[130] When one's family member is among those who have power, one cannot be taken away. The statement is in reference to treatments Americo-Liberians meted out against the natives. However, it can be used in any situation where one stands to benefit from having a friend or family among those who are in control.

[131] Quilay (civilized woman) is a pseudonym for confidentiality.

[132] When one has a representative on the negotiating table, one's interest cannot be ignored.

[133] Barclay Training Center is a military base in Monrovia, now the location of the Ministry of Defense.

[134] Steve Burns and Cameron Beemis, this is the story behind my love of mayonnaise. I have never forgotten the loaf of French bread with mayonnaise my friend, Power, gave me at Mamba Point, Monrovia in 1978. I was a freshman at the University of Liberia at that time and hunger was a big problem.

[135] "Tuhu" is Mahn for anything edible or medicinal, wrapped in paper or broadleaf and tied with a string. "Kuhu" or "Guan" is a collective farming activity where all participants work on one member's farm today and then go to another member's farm the next day until all members' farms have been worked on. The member whose farm is being worked on is responsible to feed everyone.

[136] Simon Greenleaf Hall, the men's dormitory at the University of Liberia, was named after Simon Greenleaf, a renowned Harvard Law Professor who drafted Liberia's 1847 Constitution.

[137] Americo-Liberians still refer to indigenous Liberians as "Country men, boys, women, girls, or people".

[138] Peabody Museum Archives, Harvard University.

[139] "Something is there or there is something about it." A broken Mahn as spoken by some Liberian Mandingoes who try to speak the Mahn language.

[140] Man, don't you see what is happening to my hand because of eating dry rice?

[141] "Spider soup" is something that everyone is aware of, yet no one wants to talk about it.

[142] Wonmein means the dream of something to come.

[143] I am expressing outrage at the loss of innocent and precious lives in Liberia. I am saying that the pain wrought by the war is so overwhelming that my culture's ability to contain displeasure cannot suffice. Patrick Forfor was my roommate, Voker Joe-Kolo was my friend's (Philip K. Joe-Kolo's) younger brother, and Famatta Sherman-Nah and I were colleagues in the William V. S. Tubman Teachers College at the University of Liberia. Cowards murdered Famatta along with her husband, Johnny Nah, and stepdaughter, Halaria Nah, in cold blood on July 31, 1990, a little over one month after I escaped Liberia and took refuge in the United States.

[144] The needs of Americo-Liberian students over the needs of indigenous Liberians.

[145] A Vai man, perhaps in his late forties, was a full-time employee of the Ministry of Finance. Occasionally, he gave me a dollar or two or a little more in appreciation for my help with Economics 201. We took the course together at the University of Liberia.

[146] Cold Bowl is rice with either potato greens or cassava leaves, or rice with "bitter balls," "kitily," dried fish, or meat of all sorts and other ingredients such as bouillon cubes, salt, pepper, and cooking oil.

[147] Euphemism for a big person.

[148] Mrs. Gore did not ask me to give her anything. However, if I were going to eat at the dining hall every day, it made sense to give her "Something" or "Little thing" at the end or at the beginning of each month. Had she been a man, "Cold Water" rather than "Something" would have been a more appropriate term.

[149] A Liberian expression, which means to beg someone profusely.

[150] No relations. He now goes by Augustus Yarkpa Garwo.

[151] The Mahns know what a pillow is and what a pillowcase is. However, they have only one name for the two items: "Paylah kade".

[152] Named after Commodore Matthew Calbraith Perry, the U.S. Navy Commander ordered by President James Monroe to escort the first group of ACS emigrants to West Africa. Van Sickle, Eugene S. "Reluctant Imperialists: The U.S. Navy and Liberia, 1819-1845." Questia. Journal of the Early Republic, 01 Apr. 2011. Web. 29 July 2016. <https://www.questia.com/read/1P3-2868615061/reluctant-imperialists-the-u-s-navy-and-liberia>.

[153] Randall Street was named after Richard Randall, the white ACS governor who served from December 22, 1828 to April 19, 1829. Similarly, Ashmun Street was named after Jehudi Ashmun, the white ACS governor who replaced Dr. Eli Ayres, the white ACS governor of the colony. "ON THE GROUND

IN LIBERIA." *-Acs, Settlers, Ashmun, and Leadership.* N.p., n.d. Web. 26 July 2016.

154 Rosa Parks.

155 The dismantling of the institution of slavery.

156 The experiences of African American public-school administrators with the legacy of segregation (Flumo, 2006). Published Dissertation.

157 Ibid.

158 See Ibrahim Sundiata's treatment of the subject under the heading "The Civilizing Mission," in *Brothers and Strangers: Black Zion, Black Slavery, 1914-1940,* pp. 59-64.

159 Keeping "Domestic servants" or "Houseboys" is a practice that continues to this day in Liberia.

160 See Ibrahim Sundiata's treatment of the subject under the heading "The Civilizing Mission," in *Brothers and Strangers: Black Zion, Black Slavery, 1914-1940,* pp. 59-64.

161 Ibid.

162 See Ibrahim Sundiata's treatment of the subject under the heading "The Civilizing Mission," in *Brothers and Strangers: Black Zion, Black Slavery, 1914-1940,* pp. 59-64.

163 Truth and Reconciliation Commission Report, 2009.

164 Hayman, A. I. & Preece, H. (1943). Lighting up Liberia. New York: Creative Age Press, Inc.

165 Buell, R. L. (1947). Liberia: A century of survival 1847-1947 (p. 12), University of Pennsylvania Press.

166 Ibid.

167 By their numbers, native Liberians have done more harm to Liberia with the use of this script than the settlers and their descendants did to Liberia for over a century.

168 Terrell Owens.

169 A decision that is inherently wise, but one on-lookers may consider embarrassing. Crab is a tasty food. However, in the culture, one cannot evade being regarded as greedy while eating crab because of the noise or sounds from breaking the shells.

170 PAL and MOJA's stated goal was reforms for the indigenous people to have greater participation in the national government.

171 The person I was, wanted to become and the world that I envisaged and wanted to help create.

172 The kill was not necessarily a violent physical act. Those who stood idly as soldiers treated innocent Americo-Liberians inhumanely only because they had been declared as "Rogues" also participated in that inhumane treatment, although in a different way.

173 Indigenous people were perceived as the hard-working monkeys.

174 After a few phone calls in the United States to a few people with whom he worked, I found out that, even though Mr. Karsoryan had not been on

the air prior to the April 12, 1980 "Revolution," he was not a stranger to the Liberian Broadcasting Corporation. One source told me that he was a freelance journalist at the Ministry of Information prior to the "Revolution" while another said that he was a long-time employee of the Liberian Broadcasting Corporation, specifically, a librarian. I learned that he was quite familiar with the operation of the broadcast equipment at ELBC.

175 Looking nice is a sign of good life in Liberia.

176 The people had, by that time, figured that the game was a musical chair.

177 In Liberia, soup is an inclusive term used for any dish that goes along with rice.

178 Liberia's founding fathers and mothers, the freed slaves from the United States who founded Liberia.

179 www.legacy.com.

180 Ibid.

181 Ibid.

182 Without Oretha Nyah during that critical time in my educational career, I do not know where I would be today; she provided shelter and food when I was a struggling student in Monrovia.

183 Average life expectancy in Liberia at the time hovered at 39 years.

184 Oretha Nyah's name I knew.

185 A typical Liberian would have asked, "What tribe are you?" As a result of my experience living in the United States for a long time, I know firsthand how unsettling that question is.

186 The other two are the Capitol Hill/main campus in Monrovia, which houses the administrative offices, and the A. M. Dogliotti College of Medicine Campus, located next to the St. Joseph's Catholic Hospital, near the Atlantic Ocean in the Sinkor Old Road area.

187 Construction of the dormitories was a World Bank-sponsored project during the administration of assassinated President William R. Tolbert, Jr.

188 I fell in love with that car on the first day I rode in it because it was my kind of car, big, long, and very comfortable. Riding in that car in Monrovia seemed like the potholes had disappeared. I dreamed of owning one in the future.

189 His betrayal of me during student elections in 1976 at St. Mary's High School.

190 Barkpor (deceased) was a famous Mahn folk singer.

191 Pehnamee is someone who is looking for something.

192 When I was in high school, students who came from faraway places to go to school in Sanniquellie survived in different ways. Some worked on people's farms for food while others raided farms at night and stole cassava and other food items. As a result, all students were referred to as rogues.

193 Personification. Monrovia pavements did not distinguish between the rich and the poor. They wore out shoe heels of the rich and poor with similar vengeance.

194 CARI operated as an autonomous research institute, but it was under the Ministry of Agriculture.

195 Mr. Tahyor (deceased) was a senior official at the Bureau of Immigration and Naturalization (BIN), Republic of Liberia.

196 My friend was referring to the fact that, despite the change in government in Liberia, Americo-Liberians still had the influence; they were still more connected than native Liberians were and, therefore, their children would get the best jobs irrespective of their academic performance.

197 Dad's advice: "Man Luogon, pay attention to the work you went to do". "Work" meaning my studies.

198 Social literacy is survival lessons, outside of classrooms, that members of a particular social group teach their kind. In the case of Americo-Liberians, these lessons include emphasis on kinship, the actual precursor of "Who knows you?" and networking, or "Look-out-for each-other" sensitivities.

199 Americo-Liberians are a minority group in Liberia in terms of their population. However, they still maintain significant social, political, and economic power.

200 At least forty miles outside Monrovia.

201 Alexander Graham Bell.

202 Mr. Eric Eastman was my former professor who recognized me with a plate of rice and cassava leaf.

203 My salary at that time would be US$1,454.75 per month in 2018 or LIB$225,486.25 at the current exchange (July 5, 2018).

204 As if she were not a larger-than-life figure in her own right, Mrs. Gobewole (deceased) introduced me to Frederick Gobewole, Sr., her husband, and a legend of student politics at the University of Liberia. He was a stalwart of the Student Unification Party in earlier years. Mr. Gobewole recounted to me his involvement in SUP and student politics while he was a student at the University of Liberia.

205 The white chicken was often the highlight but not the only source of meat for the sacrifice. Chickens of different feather colors as well as ducks were slaughtered too.

206 Wuo Garbie Tappia (deceased) was allegedly killed by members of the Armed Forces of Liberia shortly after I fled Liberia in June 1990). George P. Gonpu (now Dr. George P. Gonpu) lives in the United States.

207 The 1995 film Apollo 13's version of astronauts John Swigert, Jr. and James Lowell's words on the Apollo 13 moon flight on April 14, 1970.

208 No matter how simple a gadget may be, I learned never to assume that others know how to use it, even if it comes along with a direction for use. It is always useful to walk others through how to use an equipment. If technology makes you feel uncomfortable, you are not alone. It took me over two years to figure out the doggone flashlight on my Samsung Galaxy Grand Prime cellular phone!

[209] But Nancy Scissons, Lori Shauvin, and many of my colleagues and students at John R. Rogers High School in Spokane, Washington have over the years taught me how to be informal. I do not wear a coat and a tie to work every day anymore. I actually have several pairs of jeans!

[210] Gaygba is a Liberian dish that originated from Nimba County.

[211] I thought about kindergarten at St. Mary's School when Mahn and Dan children sang "A B C D, I am gone to my Mom in the corn fields in the village" and " A B C D, bring my cold leftover GB and tell your story."

[212] ㄱ ㄴ ㄷ ㄹ of the Korean alphabet represent the letters G, N, D, and R in the English alphabet. .

[213] Soju is a local Korean spirit.

[214] Tondemun (East Gate) was a popular shopping district. The question I expected was "Who is this person?" and I would say "My name is Flumo. I am a student at Seoul National University."

[215] There is nothing wrong with going to the opera or rap concert. I did not grow up listening to those kinds of music. As a result, I am only beginning to appreciate them now.

[216] Dr. Cyrenius N. Forh (deceased) was no ordinary mortal man. He was an ambassador, a lay preacher, a professor, a mentor, a great dad, and a great leader. Before he became professor of political science at the Ibrahim Babangida School of International Relations at the University of Liberia, we fondly called him professor.

[217] Despite tribal affinity, Liberians were hospitable like everybody else. They welcomed, cared for strangers, and treated others with compassion, especially before the civil war.

[218] There were about 42,000 United States troops stationed in the Republic of Korea at the time.

[219] Some scientific words were written only in Chinese.

[220] Col. Cannon was on active duty as a member of the United States Army Signal Corps at the time in Korea. Even though I had met him before, I did not know him well.

[221] Col. Cannon's comment was not a put down. It had nothing to do with the quality of education at Washington State University. Instead, it was about not having anyone there for me to talk to when the need arose. Ironically, in June 1997, about 12 years later, Lila, Wonkermie, Oretha Elizabeth and I moved to Spokane, Washington, near Washington State University. Lila obtained a BA degree in Psychology from Washington State University in 2009.

[222] This was another classic case of bias. One reason Col. Fuller suggested North Carolina A & T State University was that he attended and finished his ROTC program at that same Institution.

[223] Dr. Mary Cannon is Col. Cannon's wife.

[224] Dr. DeShield (deceased) was a son of McKinley A. DeShield, Sr., former Secretary General of the True Whig Party (TWP) and Postmaster General of

the Republic of Liberia. He studied at North Carolina A & T State University and went on to obtain his doctorate at Cornell University in New York.

[225] Form I-20 is the United States Immigration document that allows a foreign student to enter the United States to study.

[226] In Liberia, English is the official language. Most of my elementary and high school teachers were Peace Corps and Catholic nuns from the United States. Language concern never crossed my mind.

[227] Mau Mau was a militant African nationalist movement that the Kikuyu people of Kenya began. It was an independence movement that resisted British domination in Kenya.

[228] Quite recently, I came to learn that most Kenyans whose last names begin with an "O" are Luos.

[229] The International House was called Guchehwayguan.

[230] Project referred to my transfer to the United States to study and what would become of me from that time on.

[231] Literally, "My stomach is white without a blemish," meaning "My conscience is clear, and I accept you wholeheartedly." "Behind the house" was a secluded place in the woods some distance away from the village, often cordoned off by a fence made of palm branches and leaves, where midwives performed deliveries. Even though midwives perform deliveries in homes as well as in local clinics, "Ka mehin," meaning "Behind the house" is still in use in the culture.

[232] Peter Fryer, Staying Power: The history of black people in Britain (London: Pluto Press, 2018), 135.

[233] My friend, Nya Sua Flomo, went on to acquire the following advanced degrees: RN, MT (ASCP), BS, MSA, Ph.D., MD.

[234] The elephant in our apartment was in reference to the brazenly unfair cost-sharing and living arrangement in our Parker Street Greensboro apartment.

[235] Barkpor was a Mahn folk singer.

[236] A car along with a furnished apartment with the latest trappings of modernity was an example of a good life.

[237] But Flomo was also suggesting that, in America, the mantra is independence.

[238] Work by Daniel Bernoulli, a Swiss mathematician, which explains the operations of airplane wing and carburetor (1738).

[239] Flomo often referred to himself as the "Head dish washer". He was hilarious.

[240] At the urging of Dr. Mary Antoinette Brown-Sherman, President of the University of Liberia at the time, the University of Liberia sent me $3000 in Korea. Dr. Forh also gave me $3000 when I was leaving Korea for school in the United States.

[241] Flomo attended Sanniquellie Central High School while I attended St. Mary's High School.

²⁴² Dillon is a pseudonym for confidentiality.

²⁴³ System was a reference to welfare or food stamps.

²⁴⁴ In "Mahn country," at least at the time I was growing up in Liberia. I cannot say so about the Mahn culture of today because culture does not stand still. Moreover, the civil war in Liberia changed the mindset of the Mahn people as well. While I still believe strongly in the core values I learned growing up, including that of work, not everyone in Mahn country in the Liberia of today does so. Every time I visited Liberia between 2011 and 2014, some Mahn elders spoke about my way of doing things as if I came out of a time capsule.

²⁴⁵ Bursonnon Tulu was the Mahn Band from Bursonnon, the town next door to the village.

²⁴⁶ My broken heart from the "Catholic girl" (Luopu) was the other disappointment. It taught me how fickle human beings can be. Their words can be like falling dead leaves, whose trajectories towards the ground change constantly. Their positions, even on the ground, are uncertain. Summer breeze tosses them from one's yard to a neighbor's yard.

²⁴⁷ President Samuel Doe's order, which resulted in the deaths and rapes of scores of students and the destruction of properties at the University of Liberia in 1984.

²⁴⁸ Mekaneh is a pseudonym for confidentiality.

²⁴⁹ Lorluo is Mahn for market day. Saye Lorluo Garmie was born on a Wednesday, at the time the market day in Ganta. It was later changed to Thursday. Saye and I are both Mahns. Lodging people and taking care of their needs without expecting anything in return was one of the lessons we learned while growing up in Nimba County.

²⁵⁰ Boss man is an expression often used in Liberia to refer to someone of means who can make one's life a little easier. A woman of such means is referred to as "Boss lady."

²⁵¹ I was born at the Ganta United Methodist Hospital. Dad died at the same hospital in May 1999 and was buried in Gartehpa, a hamlet four miles away from Ganta, where my family lived prior to moving to the village in 1965. Herbert broke the news of Dad's passing and helped bury him.

²⁵² A song often sung when a woman delivers a baby.

²⁵³ Another song often sung when a woman delivers a baby.

²⁵⁴ Generally, in a conversation, whenever someone referred to another person as a *qui (quizee)*, it was not positive. More often it meant that the person spoken about was lazy, did not associate with others, put others down, or behaved in an uppity manner.

²⁵⁵ A sacrifice is a celebration where white chickens and other livestock are slaughtered and offered as offerings to thank God.

²⁵⁶ Two non-degree teacher training institutions in Liberia at the time were Kakata Rural Teacher Training Institute (KRTTI) and Zorzor Teacher Training Institute (ZRTTI).

²⁵⁷ Abu went on to earn a PhD from Boston University in Massachusetts, USA while Sam earned a PhD from Penn State University in State College, USA.
²⁵⁸ USAID is the United States Agency for International Development.
²⁵⁹ Dan is the other name for the Gio ethnic group of Nimba County. Similarly, Mano is the other name for the Mahns of Nimba County.
²⁶⁰ Dainka is a pseudonym for confidentiality.
²⁶¹ When a family member or friend is a part of the authorities or those who exercise power, one cannot be taken away to face the law or to jail. The expression does not always refer to a situation where one is perceived to have broken the law. In the United States and perhaps elsewhere, it is this concept that lies to the heart of minority communities' persistent calls for police departments to reflect the communities they serve.
²⁶² When someone goes out and finds a treasure or something valuable, that person runs back to their home or parents to deliver the news; they do not go to someone else's house or parents.
²⁶³ No matter how disconcerting our disagreement is, let us ignore it and focus on the goal that we agree on.
²⁶⁴ When I discovered later that Adelaide moved to the United States and lived in Philadelphia, where she died, it pained me profoundly.
²⁶⁵ President Tolbert promoted policies to lift rural people out of poverty; emphasized education and self-reliance; referred to Liberia's young people as his "Precious jewels;" declared war on "Ignorance, disease and poverty;' his policy slogans included "From mats to mattresses" and "Total involvement for higher heights."
²⁶⁶ Pay attention to the work that you are doing and send my greetings to Sia and the children (At the time Sia was my fiancée; she belongs to the Kissi ethnic group in Liberia).
²⁶⁷ When you go, send my greetings to Sia, her mother, and the children.
²⁶⁸ BBC is the British Broadcasting Corporation.
²⁶⁹ Gontee is a pseudonym, which literally means a black man. He was the Mission Director of USAID-Liberia.
²⁷⁰ Bardnersville is a suburb of Monrovia. In Liberia, a quasi-minister of the gospel who does not have a church or a congregation but to whom people go when they need prayer; people go to private preachers at their homes where they not only pray for those who are in need of prayer but also interpret dreams and visions.
²⁷¹ "Pordor" is a pseudonym for confidentiality.
²⁷² Article 19: No person other than members of the Armed Forces of Liberia or of the militia in active service shall be subject to military law or made to suffer any pains or penalties by virtue of that law or be tried by courts-martial. Article 21, Section (e): No person charged, arrested, restricted, detained or otherwise held in confinement shall be subject to torture or inhumane treatment; nor shall any person except military personnel, be kept or confined in any military facility; nor shall any person be seized and kept among

convicted prisoners or treated as a convict, unless such person first shall have
been convicted of a crime in court of competent jurisdiction. The Legislature
shall make it a criminal offense and provide for appropriate penalties against
any police or security officer, prosecutor, administrator or any other public or
security officer, prosecutor, administrator, or any other public official acting in
contravention of this provision . . .

[273] Margaret S. Tumbay was my fiancée at the time.

[274] Dr. John Roberts was the Acting Mission Director at the time.

[275] Gipolay, "A lady from Gipo," a pseudonym.

[276] Upon meeting in Accra, Ghana 18 years later, Mom told me that, at the
time I was preparing to leave Liberia, she braced for the worst news. Based
on news of the killings of Nimba people along the Sanniquellie-Monrovia
highway at the time of our return to Monrovia immediately after the December
1989 Christmas celebrations in Bursonnon, she assumed I had been killed.
Even though she assumed the worst, she also told me that she did not lose
hope, or give up on Wlah. As she put it, "He knew my struggles and agony in
search of children." "He was aware of the depth of my pain, volume of my tears,
and content of my petitions." Mom told me that she did not believe that Wlah
would allow her only son to be snatched away in the Liberian mayhem.

[277] "Live To Tell" was from Madonna's album, "True Blue," released in 1986.

[278] The notice indicated "RECEIPT NO. WAS-90-238-00086" with the
following messages: "The above receipt number must accompany all inquiries."
"Processing your form will require a minimum of 90 days. If you have not heard
from us within 6 months, then you may contact this office."

[279] Dr. Roberts was the Acting USAID-Liberia Mission Director at the time.
His letter of recommendation, memorandum for the record, and request to the
Liberia Task Force at the U.S. Department of State were dated September 11,
October 1, and October 15, 1990.

[280] Dr. Thompson gave me a bike, which helped my commute from Parker
Street to A & T. Mrs. Grandy, the Administrative Secretary in the Department
of Agricultural Education, called me "Sydney Poitier." Mrs. Martin was
Director of International Students while Mrs. Potts worked in the Office of
International Students.

[281] Layea, which is Mahn for "Beautiful woman," is a pseudonym for
confidentiality.

[282] The house was the apartment that Francis Yarzue and Yah Voker lived in
at Overland Heights in Greensboro, North Carolina. Unfortunately, Francis
passed away in Charlotte, North Carolina in 2009.

[283] Rock was Elwood (Rock) Edwards. He was one of my supporters while I
was a student at North Carolina A & T State University in the mid-1980s.

[284] I was living alone at the time, but I rented a two-bedroom apartment
because I hoped that my family would join me soon.

[285] My continual brooding over separation from family and the destruction of
Liberia. Collect calls were sometimes priced five dollars or more per minute.

286 Deacon Cole's church was Miracle Temple Holy Deliverance Church of God on 1070 Winslow Street, Fayetteville, NC.

287 The horror included flying bullets and corpses left to rot in the gutters along the highway.

288 Cy was Dr. Cyrenius N. Forh while Vicky is his wife, Mrs. Victoria K. Forh.

289 Nearby airports include Fayetteville Regional, Greensboro International, Charlotte-Douglas International, and Raleigh-Durham International.

290 During burials, parents rub charcoal powder in their children's eyebrows and huddle them inside. The charcoal powder is believed to prevent children from seeing ghosts of the deceased. Death is shrouded in secrecy to shield children from the trauma. For this reason, upon death, someone's remains become the remains of a Poro Society mask dancer; only selected people can see the remains.

291 Charles Taylor launched the December 24, 1989 insurgency that left Liberia in ruins from the Ivory Coast.

292 Because of Yei B. Tokpah's sacrifices, I remind Lila and Oretha constantly not to forget about her. Without Wlah and her courage, they would not be in the United States with opportunities to become who they want to become.

293 Mr. Saye Gonleh now lives in Philadelphia, PA. Rev. Herbert Zigbuo was preparing to go to Danane in the Ivory Coast to coordinate relief activities for the United Methodist Church Global Ministry. I met Rev. Herbert and Mrs. Mary Zigbuo through my friend, Flomo. The Zigbuos worked with the United Methodist Church Global Ministry at the Ganta United Methodist Mission in Ganta, Nimba County. Rev. Zigbuo was Mahn and Mrs. Mary Zigbuo is a native of North Carolina.

294 A Veradale United Church of Christ member of mine in Spokane Valley, WA.

295 Ralph Sutton deployed in Iraq during the first Gulf War.

296 "Exposing Children to Fire." *§ 14-318*, North Carolina Legislature, 1994, www.ncleg.net/EnactedLegislation/Statutes/HTML/BySection/Chapter_14/GS_14-318.html.

297 Ruth 1:16, New International Version (NIV).

298 I gave Wonkermie the name Marlene as a tribute to Mrs. Richardson and her role in the lives of the "The girls."

299 Caligula (Gaius Caesar Germanicus) was a cruel Emperor of Rome who ruled from 37 to 41 AD.

300 These perceptions are, in part, due to grotesque television and film images paraded by Hollywood and popular culture.

301 "I Shall Not Be Moved" by John Smith Hurt better known as *Mississippi John Hurt.*

302 There was not enough room on the walls at home for their achievement certificates.

303 McDougald's letter to Senator Terry Sanford, August 18, 1992; McDougald's letter to Senator Jesse Helms, August 26, 1992; and McDougald's letter to Bill McEwen, August 27, 1992. Rev. George Senter wrote the United States Embassy in Abidjan, Cote D'Ivoire (Ivory Coast), on December 21, 1992 while former Scotland County Schools superintendent, Dr. David A Martin, wrote the United States Embassy in Monrovia, Liberia on November 22, 1993.

304 Nebraska is a Republican-leaning state.

305 "Wither on the vine" were Newt Gingrich's words as he spoke about Medicare during a Blue Cross/Blue Shield conference on October 24, 1995 in Washington, DC. (Politics, Gingrich on Medicare, New York Times, July 20, 1996).

306 The words of Reverend Jesse L. Jackson, Sr.

307 President Samuel K. Doe often warned his enemies that if they wanted to "Live to tell the story," they should stop doing what threatened his rule.

308 A solemn call.

309 Ibid.

310 Zoe is a village medicine man or woman with powers to apprehend witchcraft practitioners. The Zoe to whom I turned was Mr. Randall Robinson, founder of TransAfrica. He had been a strong advocate for Africa, particularly South Africa.

311 Disintegration.

312 President Jean Bertrand Aristide had been overthrown and driven into exile in the United States.

313 Letter of November 28, 1994 to Randall Robinson.

314 Left-leaning students who paraded revolutionary bravado within the Student Unification Party (SUP) were mostly of indigenous backgrounds.

315 An emotional state where a conflict exists between belief and overt behavior. The conflict's resolution is the basis for change in attitude, where belief patterns are modified to be consistent with behavior (Reber & Reber, 2001).

316 Becoming somebody means achieving a status that makes one worthy.

317 One incident of discrimination involved an unfair grade I received in Zoology 201 at the University of Liberia. The denial of dormitory accommodation on the main campus of the University of Liberia was another one.

318 My parents believed that education was my passport to escape their fate.

319 "Monkey" is a reference to the *qui* people, Americo-Liberians, or the True Whig Party Led government of Liberia.

320 Quizee is the old Liberian *qui* as defined.

321 See former Liberian Vice President Clarence L. Simpson's statement, Truth & Reconciliation Report, p. 335.

322 "The Political Leader Considered as the Representative of a Culture,"
a speech delivered by President Ahmed Sekou Touré, one year after he
proclaimed Guinea's independence from France on October 2, 1958.
323 Quideh is the new Liberian *qui* as defined. Heritage refers to the villages,
towns, cities, or the country.
324 John habitually eats rice with palm oil. However, he had a different plan for
this bowl of palm oil. Perhaps he wanted to sell it or keep it for expected guests.
Out of nowhere, a clumsy child kicks the bowl of palm oil and it tumbles right
into a big pan of dry rice John was about to eat. The child's clumsiness could
have resulted in a complete waste had the palm oil spilled on the floor. John
did not do what he planned to do with the palm oil, but he relishes rice and
palm oil.
325 "Country people" is a pejorative reference to the indigenous people
accounting for almost ninety seven percent of the population.
326 See p. 2, column 2; Liebenow, J. Gus. "LIBERIA: THE DISSOLUTION
OF PRIVILEGE Part I: Seeds of Discontent." *The Institute of Current World
Affairs (ICWA)*, American University Field Staff, Nov. 2015, www.icwa.org/
wp-content/uploads/2015/11/JGL-2.pdf.
327 See p. 2, column 2; Liebenow, J. Gus. "LIBERIA: THE DISSOLUTION
OF PRIVILEGE Part I: Seeds of Discontent." *The Institute of Current World
Affairs (ICWA)*, American University Field Staff, Nov. 2015, www.icwa.org/
wp-content/uploads/2015/11/JGL-2.pdf.
328 The Americo-Liberian oligarchy maintained a 133-year stranglehold in
Liberia. It fomented tribal differences to divide and rule. The legacy of that
tactic is a feature of Liberia's political DNA.
329 General Thomas G. Qwiwonkpa seemed to have come in his own name, but
that was not exactly the case.
330 Grand Gedeh is Sergeant Doe's home county.
331 See Child Soldiers, Adult Interests: The Global Dimensions of the Sierra
Leonean Tragedy.
332 Ibid.
333 Ibid.
334 President Houphouet Boigny built alliances.
335 A. B. Tolbert was the son of William R. Tolbert, Jr., President of Liberia
from 1971 to 1980. Captain Blaise Campaore became the president of Burkina
Faso after the assassination of President Thomas Sankara in October 1987.
336 Pham, John-Peter (2005). Child Soldiers, Adult Interests: The Global
Dimensions of the Sierra Leonean Tragedy. Hauppauge: Nova Publishers.
pp. 81-82.
337 Ibid.
338 See Reuters, July 27, 2010 "We can build United States of Africa,
Gaddafi says."
339 Sergeant Doe's people is a reference to the citizens of Grand Gedeh County,
particularly the Krahn ethnic group.

[340] "Finish the work" is a reference to General Qwiwonkpa's "objective" of staging the November 12, 1985 attempted overthrow of President Samuel K. Doe: "To prepare the country for civilian rule," which he apparently understood as the removal of Sergeant Doe from power to install Jackson F. Doe, the actual winner of the October 1985 presidential election.

[341] Mahns call such physical restraint "Gbono," which is a wooden device used to keep someone who is mentally ill in one place. The device, often an approximately ten-foot log of about ten-inch diameter, contains a rectangular hole in the middle that allows the ankle to go through but almost impossible to get it out.

[342] George Stephanopoulos was presidential advisor to President William Jefferson Clinton.

[343] Flumo, J. Marsilius, Letter to Presidential Advisor George Stephanopoulos, July 24, 1996.

[344] Elephant is a reference to any subject that arouses anxiety, a difficult subject.

[345] Native-born Americans may not be aware of this aspect of American culture, but it is obvious to discerning outsiders.

[346] Flumo, J. Marsilius, Letter to Presidential Advisor George Stephanopoulos, July 24, 1996.

[347] Flumo, J. Marsilius, Letter to Presidential Advisor George Stephanopoulos, July 24, 1996.

[348] "Defining moment" is a reference to the time in June 1990 that the U.S. government had a window of opportunity to take a stand to avert the Liberian tragedy.

[349] Mahn and Dan, also known as Mano and Gio, respectively, are the two major ethnic groups in Nimba County.

[350] Allison, G. and Zelikow, P. Essence of Decision. New York: Longman, 1999. Print. Second Edition. P. 143.

[351] I still believe wholeheartedly that this could have happened if the American president had made the call.

[352] Allison, G. and Zelikow, P. Essence of Decision. New York: Longman, 1999. Print. Second Edition. P. 143.

[353] The parable of the blind men and the elephant underscores the problem with reliance on one source as the truth.

[354] Allison, G. and Zelikow, P. Essence of Decision. New York: Longman, 1999. Print. Second Edition. P. 255.

[355] Evacuating U.S. citizens and letting the Africans and Liberians sort things out were the words of former Assistant Secretary of State for African Affairs, Herman Cohen, on the NewsHour with Jim Lehrer, May 1, 1996.

[356] Allison & Zelikow.

[357] Over 250,000 Liberians died, Liberia was left in ruins, and, by carrying on as if the world ends tomorrow, I sometimes wonder whether the Liberia that talents and resources exist in Liberia to build will ever become a reality.

358 I pointed out the elephant in the room to the Clinton administration, contrary to what I had learned in America.
359 Kim Holmes of the Heritage Foundation was one such commentators.
360 "God's back" is a reference to a faraway place.
361 "Long step" is a reference to the four days and four nights it took to drive from Laurinburg, NC to Spokane, WA.
362 Col. John Cannon had retired from the military at the time, and he was living in Seattle, Washington.
363 LTC Carl H. Cannon's letter of March 12, 1997 to J. Marsilius Flumo in Laurinburg, North Carolina.
364 Letter of April 3, 1997 to Col. John Cannon from his fraternity brother in Spokane, WA.
365 Marsilius's thank you letter of April 17, 1997 to Col. John Cannon's fraternity brother in Spokane, WA.
366 LTC Carl Cannon's letter of April 20, 1997 to J. Marsilius Flumo.
367 The words of Col. John Cannon's fraternity brother.
368 Marsilius's letters of May 21, 1997 to Mr. Frank & Marlene Richardson, Rev. George & Mrs. Margareta Senter, and Mr. Chester and Beth Rogers in Wadesboro, NC and to Mr. Frank & Dolores Robinson in Fayetteville, NC.
369 The four children included Lila, Wonkermie, Oretha, and Marsetta.
370 Angela Little is a pseudonym for a friend who had been a big part of our support system in Laurinburg, NC.
371 UNICCO is the United Nimba Citizens' Council, an association of Nimba County citizens residing in the United States.
372 A home that provides a big bowl of rice for a stranger has needs for food as well.
373 The Liberian psyche is a reference to the place that the United States holds in the hearts of Liberians, the enormous influence the United States has in Liberia.
374 "Feelee" is cold droplets of water that hang on leaf tips early morning along footpaths.
375 811 E. Desmet was demolished years later. A parking lot first replaced it, and then later the university constructed a huge building at the location. I wanted to include a photo of the property in the book, but the university housing department could not locate one.
376 An obvious matter; a no brainer; everyone in that meeting knew what the incident with the human feces in the sealed Ziploc bag signified.
377 "Confluence of themes" is a reference to Wlah, Mom's prayers, and the incredible people Wlah placed along this journey to accomplish His purpose.
378 Wallace Williams was Principal of John R. Rogers High School from 1987 to 2005.
379 When one's family member is among those who have power, one cannot be taken away. The statement is a reference to treatments Americo-Liberians meted out against the natives in Liberia. However, it is applicable in the

American context and anywhere else. The circumstances of my employment with Spokane Public Schools speak to a hotly contested issue in United States—diversity in workplaces. Perhaps Mr. Williams used a slightly different lens in his selection than a principal of a different race may have used.

[380] "Big shots" are top government officials.

[381] I learned more about the concept of being "under the microscope" during the course of the research for my Ph.D. dissertation on "The experiences of African American public school administrators with the legacy of segregation" (Flumo, 2006).

[382] The epicenter of Charles Taylor's war was Nimba County.

[383] ABC Nightline Interview conducted by Chris Wallace on August 16, 1991.

[384] Mrs. Ellen Johnson-Sirleaf became President of Liberia in 2006 and ruled for 12 years. Her term ended in January 2018 upon the inauguration of Liberian and world soccer legend George Manneh Weah as Liberia's 25th President. The "American tree" is a figurative reference to the power and influence that the United States wields in Liberian affairs.

[385] Wallace interview.

[386] Wallace interview.

[387] Wallace interview.

[388] The NewsHour with Jim Lehrer on May 1, 1996.

[389] Kpargoi, Jr., Mambu James, "Former US Official Provides More on US Role during Liberian War," The Liberian Journal.com, June 12, 2008.

[390] "Credit" is a reference to policies beneficial to Liberians that previous US administrations pursued.

[391] The Plain Dealer, Cleveland, Ohio, August 2, 1990.

[392] Ibid.

[393] On September 9, 1990, even with the presence of the Economic Community of West African States Monitoring Group (ECOMOG) troops, forces loyal to Prince Johnson captured and killed President Samuel K. Doe.

[394] The Plain Dealer of Cleveland, Ohio, August 2, 1990.

[395] Stolberg, Sheryl G. "Bush Ends Tour of Africa with a Visit to Liberia." New York Times [New York City] 21 Feb. 2008: n. page. Print.

[396] Semple, Kirk & Sengupta, Somini. "Pushing Peace in Africa, Bush Tells Liberian President to Quit." N.p. 26 June 2003. Web. 03 Sept. 2016 http://www.nytimes.com/2003/06/26/international/africa/26CND-LIBE.html

[397] Office of the Press Secretary, Fact Sheet: Compassionate Conservatism, April 30, 2002.

[398] "Noco" was our pronunciation of NCO (a non-commissioned officer). Liberians turned being an NCO into something derogatory as, for example, being in the "Poopoo" platoon.

[399] Wounds meaning psychological as well as physical wounds.

[400] Edward Gberi was choked to death by his Lebanese employer at the Center Street Supermarket for allegedly stealing candy in 1978. The Lebanese merchant was acquitted by the Supreme Court of Liberia.

ENDNOTES

401 "Crippling deficit" is a reference to love and support deficit.

402 "Obstacles" meaning barriers rooted in issues of race.

403 Excerpt from LTC Carl H. Cannon's letter of March 12, 1997 to J. Marsilius Flumo in Laurinburg, NC.

404 Providence Sacred Heart Medical Center, Providence Holy Family Hospital, Deaconess Medical Center, Spokane VA Medical Center, Shriners Hospital for Children. Valley Hospital, and St. Luke. Institutions of higher learning in Spokane include Eastern Washington University-Spokane, Gonzaga University, Washington State University-Spokane, Whitworth University, and the Community Colleges of Spokane.

405 Father Robert J. Spitzer was a former President of Gonzaga University. He served from 1998-2009. Upon a written request Margaret and I personally hand delivered, Father Robert J. Spitzer forgave the remaining ten thousand dollars in tuition I owed Gonzaga University. Dr. Thayne McCulloh, the current President of Gonzaga University, served as Vice President for Fiscal Affairs at the time. When Father Spitzer forgave the remaining tuition I owed, he implemented the decision.

406 At the time, I had begun my training to become a school leader.

407 "Different place" meaning a different culture or environment.

408 Those who supported as well as encouraged me included Dr. Arthur Bell, Elwood 'Rock' Edwards, and Mrs. Ruth Grandy.

409 John Berne was from Middlesex, NC.

410 "Pianyeewon" is something happening in no time as in a story or a fairytale.

411 By community, I mean a group of people with a common history, characteristics or interests living in a particular geographic area (Merriam-Webster).

412 Most of the newcomers practically grew up in refugee camps in the West Africa sub-region.

413 Often western experts go to developing countries with ready-made answers to problems. They seldom consult with or seek the advice of local people or experts.

414 With the exception of my own family, almost all the families ALSA served trickled into Spokane through a World Relief Resettlement Program.

415 Mr. Mick Doyle and his wife, Amber Doyle, (now Amber Vietzke and ex-wife) of Spokane provided training on buying a home.

416 Itron Corporation, at the time in Spokane Valley, WA (now in Liberty Lake, WA), donated thirteen computers to the Liberian community in Spokane.

417 Ms. Margaret Tumbay and others volunteered with World Relief and other organizations.

418 World Relief, at the time, was one of about ten such agencies in the U.S. involved with refugee resettlement. It is headquartered in Baltimore, Maryland, USA, with regional offices located throughout the continental U.S. A World Relief official told me, once arrangements with the U.S. government and World

Relief for refugee resettlement are finalized, the Baltimore head office finds out from a regional office whether it could resettle a refugee or a group of refugees. The head office provides notification of arrival if the answer is a yes. Next, the regional office requests volunteer host families for temporary accommodations as refugees are processed. Temporary accommodations can last for one to two weeks and sometimes a little longer.

[419] Mason is a pseudonym for confidentiality. For brevity, henceforth, I will refer to Mrs. Lisa Mason as "Lisa."

[420] Other aspects of refugee processing included learning where to shop for food and essentials, the bus transportation system, locations of health centers for health screening appointments, enrolling children in schools, and so on.

[421] "Gbarry" was Mr. Howe's pronunciation of Barry.

[422] Mrs. Linda Unseth was Director of World Relief-Spokane at the time.

[423] "Some kanna disease" is Liberian colloquial English for "Some kind of disease."

[424] In the past, at least in Mahn culture, particularly before the civil war, when someone passed away, his or her remains belonged to the community. Funeral and burial responsibilities fell largely on the community. However, a shift has occurred in the culture since the civil war. Nowadays, funeral and burial costs are almost solely the responsibility of the family or members of the family who have the wherewithal.

[425] Mr. Howe understood the question to mean what he would like me to do if he were to die. I then explained cremation to him as another way of burying someone that involved burning the body to ashes.

[426] Advanced healthcare directive is a legal document that gives the bearer the power to make critical decisions about a patient's health when the patient is no longer conscious or no longer has the capacity to make such decisions. A durable power of attorney, on the other hand, is a legal document similar to an advanced healthcare directive, but in the state of Washington, it gives the bearer the power to make such decisions in matters relating to both estate (finances) and health of the patient.

[427] Hospice is an organization whose work involves caring for people who are on their death beds. Whether a sick person is at home, at a hospital, or at a rest home, Hospice volunteers go in, read the bible, and do things that make the dying person know that he/she is not alone.

[428] I considered pursuing studies to become a doctor while in high school, but for fear of ghosts I changed my mind. Nothing was more frightening.

[429] Mr. Anderton was also a member of the Board of Directors of the Association of Liberians in the Spokane Area (ALSA).

[430] "Direct burial" involved removing the body from the hospital and transporting it to the funeral home; refrigeration; and preparation for burial. The package also included transporting the body in a hearse but not a funeral service, embalmment, limousine service, or wreaths.

431 Mr. Joseph Howe, a particle in the plume of dust and debris bombs set off during the Liberian civil war landed in Spokane, Washington, USA and is perpetually resting at Section F-Lot 607-Space 1.

432 Mary Hinneh Vinton's message (paraphrased): I am writing to express our thanks to you and the Liberian community in Spokane for what you have done since my late husband, Mr. Joseph Thomas Harmon Howe, died. Mr. Howe and I married in 1973 while he worked at Liberia Sugar Company (LIBSUCO) in Maryland County. Due to the civil war, we fled to the Ivory Coast in 1990, where my late husband and I packed gravel beside the road to sell to earn money to buy food. In 2004, he traveled to the U.S. for resettlement, but I could not go along with him due to an illness I still have. February 2008 was the last time we heard from my late husband. May his soul rest in peace! We do not know you and your family, but may the Almighty God richly bless you for everything you are doing for the burial of my late husband.

433 In sure and certain hope of the resurrection to eternal life through our Lord Jesus Christ, we commit to Almighty God our brother, Mr. Joseph Howe; and we commit his body to the ground; earth to earth; ashes to ashes, dust to dust. The Lord bless him and keep him, the Lord make his face to shine upon him and be gracious unto him and give him peace. Amen.

434 Charles Taylor's side was the rebels' side, the side of those who brought the war while Samuel Doe's side was the government's side.

435 The INS is now the United States Citizenship and Immigration Service (USCIS).

436 Form I-589 Instructions (Rev. 05/25/11) Y Page 14

437 Mr. Treppiedi is also known as Rocky.

438 Rest in Peace, Ms. Carlson.

439 After my Dad died, Mom was denied visa at the U.S. Embassy in Monrovia to visit with me on grounds that she did not have an occupation. My status as an asylee did not permit me to travel to Liberia. So, Mom and I arranged to meet in a third country.

440 Bishop Bennie L. Kelly is still the Pastor of Miracle Temple Holy Deliverance Church in Fayetteville, NC while Mr. Ralph Sutton, an African American Iraq war veteran, is a member of Miracle Temple.

441 The students decided against violence and, instead, reported the incident to the school administration without my knowledge.

442 Reverend Linda Crowe retired in May 2012, but the Garden Ministry continues.

443 Malachi 3:10.

444 Micah 6:8; http://www.firstchurchpittsfield.org/index.php/the-united-church-of-christ/ (retrieved 2/1/2020)

445 "Kou Leehee," meaning Kou's older brother, and "Ndaha," meaning my father, were how my Mom affectionately called me. Crops my parents cultivated included rice, cassava, vegetables, eddoes, plantains, fruit trees, coffee, and

cocoa. "Mansion" is a reference to me, the child that they born and the time, energy, and resources that they put into making me the man that I am.

446 Layelekpeh attended Mom's burial in the village in January 2014.

447 Luogon, my little brother, come and settle down so that our children can learn from you. Since our children graduated from high school, they are just wandering around, and we do not know what they are up to.

448 See Chapter 37 "Another Dream."

449 My extended family's role mainly consisted of providing encouragement and emotional support.

450 Copper is a general name for pennies, nickels, dimes, quarters, or money.

451 "Gbankan" is Mahn for using a machete to cut a thicket (very dense bush) to farm.

452 Perhaps that "something else" is a repository of pecuniary benefits.

453 By work, I mean any dignified activity involving the use of the mind or physical effort such as sweeping the streets, cleaning someone's house, tilling the soil, pushing the wheelbarrow, being an accountant, a lawyer, or a doctor.

454 Rousseau, Jean-Jacques, and Barbara Foxley. 'Emile. Everyman, 1993.

455 Quizee is the old Liberian *qui*.

456 Kwenen mia means the uncivilized; primitive; those who cannot read and write.

457 Abundance means that, in the village, the rain is plentiful, the soil is naturally fertile, and the harvest is plentiful.

458 Torwabay, Mahn for someone who does not have a name, is a pseudonym for confidentiality.

459 www.catholicsocialteaching.org (retrieved 5/12/2019). "Human Dignity." *Catholic Social Teaching*, www.catholicsocialteaching.org.uk/themes/human-dignity/.

460 Rousseau, Jean-Jacques, and Barbara Foxley. 'Emile. Everyman, 1993.

461 My sense of the birthrate was a result of personal observations and not a result of a scientific survey.

462 Mezee, Mahn for someone's own, a pseudonym for confidentiality.

463 The apparent decrease in attention span may be related to the trauma and effects of the civil war.

464 "Papa" was a reference to me. Everyone regards me as the big father.

465 "Proofs" mean Children.

466 Rousseau, Jean-Jacques, and Barbara Foxley. 'Emile. Everyman, 1993.

467 Being in limbo means that, until my pending asylum was heard, and my status determined, I could not return to Liberia, the country I had claimed asylum from, otherwise I would not return to my family in the United States.

468 During the Liberian war years, Mom asked Mr. Joseph Meatay to write what she would like me to do should in case I return to Liberia and she was no more.

469 Dad was not able to see me for most of my adult life due to the separation. When he passed away in May 1999, I could not return to Liberia because of my immigration status (pending asylum)

About the Author

Born to a mother and father of the native Mahn tribe in Nimba County, Liberia, J. Marsilius Flumo learned to grow rice and survive on the land. But his mother wanted much more for him. She sacrificed most of her earnings to send him to St. Mary's Catholic School in Sanniquellie. From there he enrolled at the University of Liberia in Monrovia, where he endured hardships to get his education. After the completion of his bachelor's degree, he received a Korean government scholarship, studied at Seoul National University in Korea, and then finished his master's degree at North Carolina A & T State University in the United States.

In June 1990, Marsilius fled his home country, Liberia, during the civil war, and took refuge in the United States. After a long struggle navigating the immigration system, he became a United States citizen in 2013, twenty-three years after arrival. At present he holds a Ph.D. in Educational Leadership/Leadership Studies from Gonzaga University in Spokane, Washington, and is an educator with twenty-nine years of service in the public schools of America. He is a father of six children and is a recipient of the Spokane Bar Association's Law Day USA Liberty Bell Award for community service.

His wish is that all students will understand that they too can overcome many adversities and be successful. He humbly gives all credit to his mother, his many mentors, and most of all, Wlah (God), for his life and his accomplishments.

CPSIA information can be obtained
at www.ICGtesting.com
Printed in the USA
LVHW010854101022
730337LV00008B/399

9 7816